# BUSINESS MANAGEMENT

# BUSINESS MANAGEMENT

[For BCom (Hons) students of all major Indian universities]

S Talukdar

Formerly of Prafulla Chandra College, Kolkata

J P Bose

Formerly of Umesh Chandra College, Kolkata

To be had of

New Central Book Agency (P) Ltd

DELHI • KOLKATA • PUNE • ERNAKULAM

*Marketed by*

NEW CENTRAL BOOK AGENCY (P) LTD

- 8/1 Chintamoni Das Lane, Kolkata 700 009
- 4262/3 1st Floor, Flat Nos. 105 & 106
  Ansari Road, Daryaganj, New Delhi 110 002
- Shop Nos. 3 & 4, Vinayak Towers
  681/B Budhwar Peth, Appa Balwant Chowk
  Pune 411 002
- GSS Shopping Complex (1st Floor)
  Opposite College Post Office
  Convent Road, Ernakulam 682 035



*Publisher*

CENTRAL EDUCATIONAL ENTERPRISES (P) LTD
54B Patuatola Lane, Kolkata 700 009

*Typesetter*

NEW CENTRAL BOOK AGENCY (P) LTD
8/1 Chintamoni Das Lane, Kolkata 700 009

*Printer*

NEW CENTRAL BOOK AGENCY (P) LTD
Web-Offset Division, Dhulagarh, Sankrail, Howrah

*Cover Designer*

Dulal Haldar

*Cover Printer*

BISWANATH STUDIO
3 Garanhatta Street, Kolkata 700 006

*Diagrams & Charts*

N Radhakrishnan and Narayan Sur

*Project Team*

N Radhakrishnan, Subas Maitra and Ashit Ghosh

**ISBN: 81-7381-345-0**

First Published : 1992
Second Edition : 1993
Third Edition : 1999
**Fourth Edition : 2009**

**Price: Rs 285.00** [Rupees Two Hundred Eighty-five only]

*Dedicated to*
*the sacred memory*
*of my father*
*Late Satish Chandra Talukdar*
*who was an ideal teacher*

# Preface

## to Second Edition

This second edition has been considerably enlarged keeping in view the suggestions received from the teachers of the subject of different colleges.

The present text is designed to be a standard text book for students of different examinations. Authoritative text books on various areas of management have been consulted and the materials needed for undergraduate students have been incorporated. The book summarizes the essential elements of management and as such it will be useful to a wide variety of readers. The 'Glossary' in this edition is a special feature.

I am grateful to the following teachers for their support and encouragement in bringing out this edition of the book. Profs. A. Roy, Dr. S.K. Paul, B. Chatterjee, Dr. S.K. Sengupta, S.K. Nath, P. Paul, D. Mukherjee and D. Poddar (Prafulla Chandra College); Profs. M.M. Ghosh and B. Bhattacharyya (Heramba Chandra College); Profs. C. Chatterjee, P. Roy, M.K. Roy and S. Banerjee (Sivanath Sastri College), Profs. K. Rudra and Sujit Majumdar (U. C. College); Prof. Arun Bhattacharyya (CCCBA); Prof. Jagadindu Bhattacharyya (Jaipuria College); Principal (Dr.) A. Sanyal and Prof (Dr.) Asit Chakravarti (Shyamaprasad College); Profs. S. Kundu, D. Basuthakur and Subir Dutta (Bhowanipur Education Society College); Profs. Amitabha Mukherjee, Sampat Mukherjee and Manab Mukherjee (St. Xaviers' College); Prof. Indrani Basu (Sri Siksayatan) and Prof. G. Khara, my ex-colleague of Prafulla Chandra College.

Sri Amitabha Sen, the publisher and his efficient team deserve sincere appreciation.

I acknowledge the ungrudging cooperation of my family members — my wife Santi, my daughter Sibani and my daughter-in-law Gargi. My son Subrata, a Chartered Accountant and an executive of a big public utility concern helped me much in providing valuable information; particularly on Financial Management. My grand daughter Sayantani also helped her grand father by refraining herself from disturbing him.

I have no words to express my gratitude to Dr. N.G. Choudhury who is well known in the corporate management circle as well as in the academic management world for his valuable guidance in the reproduction of this edition.

Sivanath Bhawan,
Gariahat Road,
Calcutta — 29

**S. TALUKDAR**

April 1993

# Preface
## to First Edition

'BUSINESS MANAGEMENT' as a subject and as an Honours subject for the B.Com.(Hons.) students of Calcutta University is new. The entire syllabus of the subject has been more or less equally divided into four parts excluding an 'Introduction'.

Attempts have been made to discusss every part with equal emphasis without being biased to any particular part or area of management.

The authors are usually inconvenienced to write books on the new syllabi and it becomes all the more difficult for the writers of books on Management — when the term itself could not be defined precisely as yet.

I have made all efforts to confine my discussions within the framework of the syallbus but certain matters relevant to the understanding of the main topics have naturally been discusssed.

The university question papers and suggestions from the teachers of the subject will definitely help us to improve the quality of the book in future. Additions and alterations shall have to be made in the light of the questions to be set at the university examinations.

My thanks are due to Prof. M.M. Ghosh of Heramba Chandra College, Profs. S.Kr. Paul of Prafulla Chandra College and S.K. Nath of Prafulla Chandra College, Prof. P. Roy of Sivanath Sastri College and Prof Arun Bhattacharya of City College of Commerce and Business Administration.

Needless to say that without cooperation from the publishers and proof readers, the book could not have come to light; so to them is my heart-felt gratitude.

Sivanath Bhawan,
Gariahat Road,
Calcutta — 29

1 - 6 - 1992

**S. TALUKDAR**

*Dr. N. G. Choudhury*

M.Com, MBA, FBIM, FCIS, FCS. F.Inst. D, SAT, Ph.D

Chairman, Webel Electro Ceramics Ltd.

Vice President - Institute of Modern Management

Member - Post graduate faculty Council in
Social Welfare, Commerce & Business Management
of Calcutta University.

Ex-Chairman and Managing Director
Tribeni Tissues Ltd., Calcutta.

Ex-Member Company Law Advisory Committee,
Government of India.

Ex-Member Development Council for Pulp, Paper and
Allied Industries, Government of India.

186, Jodhpur Park
Calcutta - 700 068

☎ : 46-0660

# Foreword

In providing a conceptuel framework on the fundamentals of business management covering a wide spectrum, such as, Marketing Management, Financial Management, Personnel Management and Company Management, Prof. S. Talukdar has attempted to make the new edition more useful, purposeful and meaningful. He has recognised that the best underpinning to acquisition of knowledge in business management is a sound theoretical exposition in which such knowledge can be assimilated and stored.

This edition underwent a thorough revision in keeping with the changes introduced in the syllabus for undergraduate studies in commerce. Students will find this book very refreshing, stimulating and interesting and I am convinced that a study of this book will be immensely beneficial to them as this will set them to move to upward journey to higher studies in management.

Prof. Talukdar has added a new dimension to this book by brining into focus new thoughts, new ideas and new techniques so eloquently described and suggested by distinguished management thinkers of the western economic civilisation. Besides B.Com.(Hons.) students, the book will provide an interesting reading to those who recognise management as an important discipline to succeed in life.

N. G. Choudhury

21 March, 1993

# Contents

## INTRODUCTION



## PART I : MARKETING MANAGEMENT

# Contents



(ii) Contents contd......

## Contents

## Contents

## Contents

# INTRODUCTION

# CHAPTER 1

Millions of people throughout the world live in grinding poverty and the situation in countries like ours is worse. Poverty has degrading and demoralising effects. No political slogan can solve this problem and can prevent people from committing crimes. The task of bettering the lot of the semi-starved, ill-clad and ill-sheltered people cannot be accomplished by the politicians, statesmen, authors, poets, actors, composers or soldiers. **Management** can come to the rescue of these people; management can provide material things that a nation needs to improve the lot of its people.

By serving as a pivotal element in the operation of business enterprises, management makes a significiant social contribution. It provides the invigorating force that brings to life what would, otherwise, be only potentialities.

The developing countries need the development of managerial talents to achieve their objective of higher standard of living and social justice.

The achievement of business management, according to Peter Drucker, enables us to promise the abolition of the growing poverty that has been continuing through ages. We need dynamic business institutions that can play a decisive role in the welfare of the society. It is now generally accepted that management is the most vital and strategic factor in the productive process. Management ultimately determines the success of an enterprise. President John F. Kennedy highlighted the importance of management in the followng words : The role of management in our society is critical in human progress. It serves to identify a great need of our time; to improve standards of living of all people through effective utilization of human and material resources. It is a popular belief that bounty of nature makes a country developed and prosperous but natural bountifulness needs proper utilisation where we feel the need for management. The examples of countries like Japan, Switzerland and Denmark demonstrate the truthfulness of such an observation. To add to this, we can mention Iran as a country which being so poor, backward and peasant-based could develop herself because of efficient management. On the contrary, the poverty of some underdeveloped countries can be attributed mainly to poor managerial ability. John F. Mee was much nearer the truth when he remarked that the greatest single factor or key for unlocking the forces of economic growth in any nation had been management.

In developing countries like ours, matters such as — (a) the amount of capital and technical knowledge, (b) export-level, (c) balance of payments, (d) rate of inflation, (e) net work of communications are to be properly looked into for remedy of economic ailments according to economists and politicians. But the role of business and its manager is not mentioned. In India, in spite of increasing savings and investment rates, Indian economy has not yet been able, actually speaking, to reach the take off stage. The fact remains that industrialisation involves not only capital resources, labour and raw materials but also managerial skill. This is the considered opinion of distinguished authorities on management. To quote Peter Drucker, "Management is the crucial factor in economic and social development. It was obvious that the economists' traditional view of development as a function of savings and capital investment was not adequate. Indeed, savings and capital investments do not produce management and economic development. On the contrary, management produces economic and social development and with it savings and capital investment. It became apparent that the developing countries are not underdeveloped, they are under -managed."

Disorganised resources of men, machine and money can only be converted into a purposeful enterprise through efficient management. Newman, Summer and Warren in their considered view opined, "Managers conceive of the service an enterprise can render, mobilise the required means of production, co-ordinate activities both within the enterprise and with the outside world and inspire people associated with the enterprise to work towards common objectives."

It is management that spells the difference between success or failure for any business enterprise. "Inefficient management is a devastating drag on an economy. It wastes important resources in capital and labour and lowers the total capacity of a nation to provide sufficient jobs and adequate income for its people" (Neil H. McElroy). According to R.K. Talwar, good management is a critical input in the success of a business. It is becoming increasingly evident that it is no longer possible to manage a business by hunches or native ability. The days of the "intuitive" managers are numbered, according to Drucker.

In developing countries, accumulation of capital, high rate of investment and technological advancement will have very little impact on the acceleration of the rate of economic growth unless it is matched by managerial skill. We have a very relevant observation by Mr. P.L. Tandon, former Chairman of the Hindustan Lever Ltd. Thus he observed : We have seen that inputs of labour, capital and raw materials do not by themselves ensure growth; they require the catalyst of management to maximise the results. When the management of resources has been good, the results have been better than where management was poor and this is so on the micro level of a firm or the macro level of an economy.

Management has been viewed "as the single most critical social activity in connection with economic progress. Physical, financial and man power resources are by themselves but passive agents; they must be effectively combined and co-ordinated through sound, active management if a country is to experience a substantial level of economic growth and development. A country can have sizeable natural and manpower resources including plentiful skilled labour and substantial capital but still be relatively poor because very few competent managers are available to put these resources efficiently together in the production and distribution of useful goods and services." (*Farmer and Richman*).

The developing countries like ours must develop managerial talents which will form part and parcel of their national policy if they are to achieve their objective of higher standard of living and social justice. "All over the world, regardless of political patterns, growing importance is being attached to managerial training. In a developing society such as ours, management has an even greater contribution to make" (Mrs. Indira Gandhi). Many of the developing countries, even when endowed with adequate capital and surplus labour, have fattered in their quest for rapid economic growth only because they ran short of the essential ability to use those factors in the most efficient manner possible. Managerial revolution is a must for the developing countries to ensure a faster rate of growth.

Managers have a great responsibility in modern India in view of the suspicion about 'big business'. They are a very tempting target for demagogues who are hunting for votes regardless of the economy and social consequences.

Management generates human energies; it is the mover and development is a consequence.

## MEANING OF MANAGEMENT

The term 'Management' defies precise definition. No two definitions are identical. It has not yet been possible to include all the ingredients of management within a single unassailable formula. In spite of the fact that the area of Management is becoming increasingly clear, no universally accepted definition of Management is forthcoming. This is because persons of different professions try to define Management according to their own predisposition or orientation; engineers view Management as a matter of design of product, accountants as a matter of facts and figures, chemists as a matter of formulae and mixtures, so on and so forth.

The different meanings and concepts of Management are due to different points of view of different persons. Some view management 'as a group of managerial personnel', while others define it as a function such as planning, organising, controlling etc.; still others consider Management as an economic resource and there are others to whom Management is a technique of leadership or a means of co-ordination.

Management is so comprehensive in nature covering various facets that it is well-nigh impossible to formulate a definition that will exactly fit in with all the aspects of Management. In fact, the term Management can be interpreted in four different senses : (i) Management as a Team or System of Authority (ii) Management as a Discipline (iii) Management as an Economic Resource and (iv) Management as a Process.

The exact definition of Management poses certain difficulties which stem from the fact that Management is concerned with human beings whose behaviour is unpredictable. Moreover, Management, being a new concept and being in the process of development, naturally cannot be subjected to exact definition. Management experts like George R. Terry observed : "Management is extensive and formulating a comprehensive definition of it poses certain difficulties".

In spite of difficulties, various definitions of management have been offered.

Henri Fayol, the famous French Management expert, defined Management in a manner that gives us a better understanding of the nature of Management. His definition runs as follows :

To manage is to forecast and to plan, to organise, to command, to co-ordinate and to control.

This functional definition of Management gives us an idea as to what a manager has to do.

Dr. F. W. Taylor, the father of scientific Management, defined Management as an art of "knowing what you want to do" and then seeing that it is done "in the best and cheapest way". This definition is productivity-oriented and unlike the one offered by Fayol. The concept of Management divorced from functional aspect was not liked by many including Peter Druker who echoed the definition of Fayol and stated : "Management is an organ; organs can be described and defined only through their functions". Taylor and Fayol defined Management in a way that did not lay much emphasis on the human aspect of Management. This aspect of Management was emphasised later on by a number of experts, one of whom described Management as a personal administration and Management is the development of people and not the direction of things. It was even observed that it is the men whom we build and the men build products. So, Management builds men who, in their turn, produce things. It is no exaggeration to say that in Management, the human aspect is more important; it is the motivational factor on which depends the success of an enterprise.

There have been attempts to define Management from the angle of process approach. Management is a social process. It entails responsibility for effective and economical planning and regulation of the operation of an enterprise of a given purpose on task. E. F. L. Brech stated, "It is the pervasiveness of this human element that gives Management its special character as a social process".

Terry's definition of Management as a distinct process consisting of planning, organising, actuating and controlling, utilizing in each both science and art and followed in order to accomplish predetermined objectives; is very comprehensive with the essential elements that Management is a distinct process and it consists of planning, organising, actuating and controlling. According to him, Management utilizes both science as well as art and it is meant to accomplish predetermined objectives.

Joseph L. Massie, an eminent Management author, defined Management as a process by which a co-operative group directs action towards common goals.

There is no dearth of definitions but to give a long list of definitions will not make things clear; rather it will create confusion. So, a few more definitions, which have been widely accepted, are being given :

Lawrence Appley, once President of the American Management Association, gave a very acceptable definition – Management is the accomplishment of results through the efforts of other people.

Harold Koontz defines Management as the art of following things done through and with informally organized groups.

Sir Charles Reynold, a British Management expert, defined Management as a process of getting things done through the agency of a community.

At present, Management has acquired the nature of trusteeship. A professional manager has to act as a trustee and not as a boss.

The discussion above clearly indicates that too many definitions have been offered for Management but the fact remains that management, in order to be deemed as science, needs to be used in one sense only and this can be secured if the word is not used to mean both status and function.

## Conclusion

To a student of Management, too many definitions of Management make things worse confounded.

There is a perceptible trend towards professional management as we find in case of Tata Iron & Steel Company Ltd. The Tata Management Service and a few others already started in our country, have accelerated the trend towards professionalisation of Management.

The different interpretations of Management are not, as a matter of fact, contradictory views of Management; they are merely different ways of looking at Management from different perspectives. Management definitions, if carefully analysed, will reveal a synthesis of different approaches and viewpoints.

"Many chief executives and educators contend that the most important perspective of top executives should be 'liberally educated on life'. The total concept of Management requires an understanding of the meaning of liberal education and its relationship to Management functions. A liberal point of view is not merely the sum of a finite number of narrow approaches. Its emphasis is on freedom to choose from the widest range of possibilities by discovering new possibilities." (Massie)

## SUMMARY

Management is a term not yet precisely defined. This is because some view it as a group of managerial personnel while others consider it as a function. The term 'Management' is so comprehensive and covers so many aspects that an exact definition touching upon all those aspects cannot be expected. But it can be said that eminent authors like Peter Drucker, Taylor, Koontz & O'donnell, Henri Fayol and others have defined Management in such a manner that all of them taken together give us a fair idea about what is meant by Management.

Management, simply stated, is to get things done through others. It is a functional concept. Various functions such as organising, directing, controlling, co-ordinating are to be performed by a manager. Management is a process. It continues; goes on with the going on of the organisation. Group efforts, that lead to the realisation of the objects of an organisation, need leadership and coordination and the element that acts as the motivating force is the Management. As the organisations are assuming larger size, Management with more human element in it, is coming to play more and more dominant role in directing group efforts of the destination of the organisation in the realisation of its objectives. So, whether it is functional, or personnel or a process, and whether it is a science or art, the fact remains that Management is vital to an organisation.

Modern executives constantly strive towards an ultimate in life. Since Management, today, is 'concerned with ends as well as means', a broad perspective, free from restrictions, must be maintained in achieving the desired goals of Management.

# CHAPTER 2

## SIGNIFICANCE OF MANAGEMENT

Management is an all-pervasive function since group action is essential in every walk of life. Group activity has become a universal phenomenon. Without management, an organisation is merely a collection of men, money and materials. "The Manager is a dynamic life-giving element in every business. Without it, the resources of production remain resources and never become production" *(Drucker)*.

It is beyond controversy that Management is a factor of production today whose contribution is so significant that it does not require too much elucidation. It is self-evident.

To achieve the objectives, to carry on the production process of a big organisation, group efforts are a necessity and indispensable. These group efforts need direction with complete co-ordination which can only be expected from an efficient Management. Management is a group of personnel, Management is a series of functions, Management is a process that is with an organisation from its beginning till its end. Raw materials would have remained as such had there been no Management to direct the group efforts to process the raw materials into finished products.

We cannot conceive of any organisation — be it a club, educational institution, charitable institution or a business organisation – where group activity is not required. It has become, so to say, a universal phenomenon, and Management has become an all-pervasive function. In any organised human activity, Management is a must. The resources of an organisation have to be organised and it is Management that does it. It is no exaggeration to say that with all the resources at our disposal and having no Management to look after, our effort to utilise the resources will be a futile exercise. Collection of men, money and materials without Management is a fruitless effort; Management is the motivating force and it can only direct the whole affair and make the collection of men, money and materials a manifested combination of the desired objectives of an organisation. Peter F. Drucker rightly points out : "The manager is the dynamic life-giving element in every business. Without it, the resources of production remain resources and never become production."

Management plans, organises, directs, co-ordinates, controls and motivates the personnel to achieve the goals of the organisation. It is a catalyst that optimises output and makes development.

With the growth in the size of business units, the significance of Management is increasing. A big organisation needs Management on bigger scale equipped with full-fledged efficiency. The complexities of modern business organisation due to increasing Government interference and the emergence of the concept of social responsibility have necessitated the Management of an organisation to be more efficient, effective and alert. Every decision the Management of an organisation takes has a far-reaching effect, every function that the Management does, goes to add up an element of stability to the entire structure of an organisation.

In the productive process, Management is the

most vital and strategic factor. It is the quality of the Management that ultimately determines the success of an enterprise. " The role of Management is critical in human progress. It serves to identify a great need of our time; to improve standards of living of all people through effective utilisation of human and material resources." (John F. Kennedy)

Of the five Ms of business – Management, Manpower, Money, Machinery and Materials – the most important ingredient is Management because, without it, no other ingredient can contribute to realise the objective of the organisation. It is Management that will direct, organise and co-ordinate; then only the assembling of the factors of production will be effective.

The productivity and profitability of an organisation is very much dependent on its managerial efficiency. Management is one of the most important areas of human activity as it is concerned with getting things done through other people. Management has a significant social contribution; because it is through the Management's endeavour that a business organisation realises its objectives and serves the society. All sections of people of the society – the consumers, the employers, the suppliers of raw materials, the Government – all stand to gain from business activities which, on their part, are a direct contribution of Management. As a driving force, Management inspires people, knits them into one entity and creates conditions for the optimum use of resources.

To quote Drucker, "The emergence of Managment as a distinct and leading institution is a pivotal event in social history. Hardly if ever has a new basic institution, a new leading group emerged as fast as has Management since the turn of the century." President Roosevelt observed that a Government without good Management is like a house built on sand.

Management, meaning thereby the function of a manager, can be well described as very much powerful and purposeful in the creation of utilities that can help people to lead meaningful lives and also can save men and women from the pangs of poverty as observed by an eminent author on Management. Peter Drucker further observed, "Management is the crucial factor in economic and social development. It was obvious that the economist's traditional view of development as a function of savings and capital investment was not adequate. Indeed, savings and capital investment do not produce Management and economic development. On the contrary, Management produces economic and social development and with it savings and capital investment. It became apparent that the developing countries are not under-developed, they are under-managed." Efficient Management is imperative for converting disorganised resources of men, machine and money into a purposeful enterprise. Managers mobilise the required means of production, co-ordinate activities both within the enterprise and with the outside world. They inspire people associated with the enterprise to work towards common objectives.

It is being realized increasingly that neither accumulation of capital, nor high rate of investment nor even the technological advancement can accelerate the rate of economic growth of the developing countries unless it is matched by managerial skills. Management is viewed as "the single most critical social activity in connection with economic progress. Physical, financial and manpower resources are, by themselves, but passive agents; they must be effectively combined and co-ordinated through sound, active management if a country is to experience a substantial level of economic growth and development" – this is the observation of two prominent scholars of Comparative Management. It was the considered opinion of Peter Drucker that wherever rapid economic and social development took place after World War II, it occurred as a result of systematic and purposeful work on developing managers and management.

The significance of management in a country like ours, where a vast number of people are living below poverty line, cannot be over-emphasised. It will not be out of place to mention here that once in a convocation address Mrs. Indira Gandhi, the then Prime Minister, emphasised the need for the trained managerial mind in a developing economy like India. She said, "The old concept of an entrepreneur-owner hiring a few technicians for his plant but running it himself, became obsolete long ago. As technology has grown increasingly complex and as the size of operations has expanded, the manager with leadership qualities has come to the fore." Higher efficiency and higher productivity is the only hope of people; it can be achieved through efficient managerial functions. The poor performance of our public enterprises can mainly be ascribed to the managerial inefficiency. J. L. Lundy, in his Effective Industrial Management, has stated, "The managers of an organisation are concerned with the maximisation of output obtainable from a given amount of input or similarly the minimisation of input for a given level of output. Fulfillment of such a purpose is the only justification for the existence of a managerial function. Management designs job structure and provides opportunities for self-expression and initiative. Management provides human satisfaction and thus acts as an essential instrument of human progress and keystone of modern society.

With the growing complexities in the business world, business executives are called upon to innovate new and newer management techniques to meet the challenge of time. The contribution of Management to the overall performance of an organisation has been universally accepted as of great significance. To develop future managers, management training has been recognised as an essential tool.

## SUMMARY

In today's big business organisations, group efforts are essential and these efforts need to be directed and co-ordinated. The elements of direction and co-ordination are to come from Management. Had there been no Management endeavour, all factors of production would remain unutilized and, even if utilised, the desirable results could never have been achieved. The human element in Management acts as the motivating force to co-ordinate the disorganised parts of production and leads them to achieve the desired goals of the organisation. It animates productive forces, vibrates the organisation with activity, infuses vigour and energy to society by curing various ills in the business organs. Management is getting more and more socially oriented. It is the management that plans, directs and controls the entire sphere of activities of an organisation and ultimately by their overall policy, management renders service to society.

# CHAPTER 3

## SCHOOLS OF MANAGEMENT THOUGHT

Management is as old as civilisation. The co-ordination of human effort can be traced back to the history of mankind. In the ancient civilisations, there are instances of the application of the principles of Management — in Egypt, in Greece, in China and in India also — there are remnants which are testimony to the practical application of the Management principles. "The technique of Management, like the art of administration and the science of organisation, has ancient roots and medieval branches" (Albert Lepawsky).

In spite of its ancient origin, Management as a systematic field of study, developed only in the 19th century. Robert Owen, Charles Babbage, Charles Dupiee and Henry R. Towne laid the foundations for a scientific study of Management and a unified theory of Management was developed. Modern Management emerged through three stages — Classical, Behavioural and Systems.

The growing importance of Management has attracted the attention of scholars from various fields. Psychologists, sociologists, anthropologists, economists, biologists, mathematicians, political scientists and a host of others have given the concept and meaning of Management from their own specialist angles. So, there have developed a number of theories propounded by different categories of scholars and Management thought has, therefore, been divided into a number of schools. A complete view of Management has naturally not come out from any of these theories and actually, as Prof. Koontz has put it, **the development of Management theory represents a jungle with confusion and entanglements of language and findings.**

The various streams of thought flowing from the scholars' depository of specialised knowledge have brought for us quantitative concepts, managerial economics, accounting, universals of Management (principles), scientific Management, human relations and behavioural sciences as described by Haynes and Massie.

Attempts have been made to classify Management thought in different ways by the Management experts. Some have explained Management thought in terms of four basic approaches – behavioural, productivity, rationalistic-model and institutional. Another classification of the schools of Management thought has been offered by John G. Hutchinson of Columbia University. According to him, the classifications are : (a) classical Management theory (2) human behaviour theory (3) social and political systems approaches (4) ecological systems approach and (5) rational decision making concepts. However, we discuss below the seven major schools of Management theory as propounded by Harold Koontz in his article, "The Management Theory Jungle" in the Journal of Academy of Mana-gement.

### 1. Management Process School

According to this school of thought, Management is a process to get things done through and with other people operating in organized groups. The executives perform this process and the process consists of co-ordination, planning, organisation, motivation and controlling. This is a school of thought where we can get a glimpse of the essential function of the manager with their interrelationships having logic behind them to infer how each function may be effectively performed. To this 'Traditional School' or 'Universalist School' belong the eminent Management authors Taylor, Henri Fayol and Urwick. 'Universalist School' as it is called, believes that Management principles are applicable every where and the basic idea is productivity approach. This Classical School of thought believes in the division of labour as expounded by Adam Smith. This Theory of Management is considered as basically static in nature as everything is held constant except the elements involved in the process.

This school claims "the credit of developing the concepts of 'scalar chain', hierarchy of authorities, the idea of 'line and staff' and the structure system and pattern to achieve an objective and the belief in a limited span of control" *(T.T. Patterson)*.

**2. The Empirical School**

As the name suggests, this school considers Management as a study of experiences as a means of teaching with a view to transferring them to the practitioners and students. It is not based on theory. Drucker is the chief exponent of this school along with Dale, Newman, Davis, Sloan and others. The characteristic feature of this theory is that it is closely connected with other schools such as 'Classic' and 'Human relations.' It cannot be argued that by precept and experience, a manager can learn management and many problems can also be solved with the help of these experiences. **The most effective management techniques can be applied by analysing the experience of successful managers.** The 'Operational Approach' followed by the Empirical School is claimed to have established that Management is an art and it can be learnt by practical experience. By studying past operations, facts can be determined and theories can be developed to explain the facts and lastly facts and theories are used to make predictions about future operations. Koontz commented : No one can deny the importance of studying experience through such study, or of analysing the "how it was done" of management. But Management, unlike law, is not a science based on precedent and situations in the future exactly comparable to the past are exceedingly unlikely to occur. Indeed, there is a positive danger of relying too much on past experience and on undistilled history of managerial problem-solving, for the simple reason that a technique or approach found 'right' in the past may not fit a situation of the future. The inherent drawback of this management thought is that very few management situations are identical. Thus relevant experience that can also be repeated is difficult to duplicate. The selection of alternatives poses a problem in this approach to management. When a manager chooses one of several alternatives, he can never compare in future what might have happened had he selected a different alternative.

**3. Human Behaviour School**

This is a people-oriented school of Management thought. It involves application of the knowledge of behavioural sciences like sociology, psychology and anthropology to the understanding of human behavior. The behavioural approach to Management began with the famous Hawthorne Experiments. George Elton Mayo and his team of researchers from the Harvard Business School conducted these experiments at the Hawthorne Works of Western Electric Company in Chicago from 1927 to 1932. This neo-classical theory was propounded to find out the factors having a real impact on labour productivity and performance. The Hawthorne Experiments consisted of three phases – The Test Room Studies, Interviewing Studies and Observational Studies. These studies revealed that physical and environmental factors do not materially influence workers' performance and attitude to work. This school of thought highlights the importance of informal social groups, good human relations, the need for managerial motivation, participation, better communication, good leadership and committee Management. An organisation, according to the school of thought, is a social system and the human factor is the most important element within it.

Here we find a socio-psychological approach to Management problems. Management is viewed as a complex interaction of human beings in groups in a given situation. This school has done a good job by highlighting that top Management must be concerned with the human element in Management. Earnest Dale has, however, pointed out that none of the human relation theories so far has much value in attempting to predict behaviour arising out of highly complex situations or behaviour at the top Management level. Drucker observed : The theory of human relations freed Management from the domination of viciously wrong ideas, but it did not succeed in substituting new concepts. In this school of thought, the empirical work has not been done with a common conceptual framework as a consequence of which generalisations have been difficult (discussed in detail in chapter 5).

**4. Social System School**

That "Management is a social system" is the observation of the propagators of this school of management thought. The school is based on sy-stem analysis and chiefly relies on empirical research. This management thought believes in the cultural relationships of various social groups. It identifies the nature of such relationships and attempts to show them as related and usually as an integrated system. It views an organisation as an open adaptive system that interacts with its environment.

The spiritual father of this school was the late Chester Bernard and it has been developed by researchers who regard Management as a social system. It is based on system analysis and chiefly relies on empirical research. This school regards man in an organization as a socially oriented and directed being. His needs are many and they influence the production environment and, in turn, are subjected to its influence. Man is a being whose reactions are partly foreseeable and partly unpredictable. According to this school of thought, organisations are extremely complex entities and their diverse needs must be met by a balanced, integrated approach to Management. Drucker stated, "The recognition of the organised enterprise as a social organism, subject to all the pressures and conflicts of the cultural environment, has been helpful to both theorist and practising manager. Among other helpful aspects are the awareness of the institutional formulations of organised authority, the influence of informal organisation and such social factors as those called the bonds of organisation." It is said that Social System School has tried to synthesise the classic theory of Management organisation with that of the Human Behaviour School.

Some ideas and studies of the Social System School are of positive significance. Its achievements in applying the systems method in Management and the demand for an overall, comprehensive approach of analysing an organisation cannot be under estimated. D. Gvishiani, even admitting the significance of the school of thought, commented that the theory made the gross sociological mistake of identifying the social relation of production with the organisation of the production process determined by its technical parameters.

We can say that this school of thought, by looking upon Management as a system of cultural inter-relationships, has integrated these relationships into a system. Every system has a number of sub-systems and systems approach emphasises that everything is interrelated and interdependent. A Management Information System (MIS) is the heart of the systems approach. It is a socio-technical system and it emphasises the need to adapt organisation to the changes in society and regard Management as simply a process of decision-making.

This social system approach to management has a significant contribution to the development of management thought. "The recognition of the organised enterprise as a social organism, subject to all the pressures and conflicts of the cultural environment, has been helpful to both theorist and practising manager. Among other helpful aspects are the awareness of the institutional formulations of organised authority, influence of informal organisation and such social factors as those called the bonds of organisation" *(Koontz and O'Donnell)*. The more recent view of the system approach seeks to relate management concepts and techniques. This view is sometimes known as 'The Contingency Approach'. The gap between management theory and management practice, is attempted to be bridged by this approach. The environment is considered as an independent variable and the management concepts and techniques as dependent variables.

Since this school of management thought promotes a view of organisations as extremely complex entities where a balanced and integrated approach to management is necessary to meet the diverse needs of the organisation, it is a most demanding view of management role, for the manager is expected to serve both the owners and the employees and also the customers, government and the public. **This approach to management theory is probably the most comprehensive and also the most realistic.** Representatives of the school rightly point out to the influence of technical and technological factors on the social organisation.

**5. The Decision Theory School**

The basic emphasis of this school is not on people or environmental variables influencing behaviour but on decision itself. "Advocates of this school reason that decision-making is the most critical function of management, thus any study of management should focus directly on decisions themselves" *(Hutchinson).*

Rational approach to decision–making is the basis of this school of Management thought. Management is simply a process of decision-making from several alternatives. Considering decision-making as the most vital function of Management, this theory examines the nature of organisation structure, psychological and social reactions of individuals and groups, development of basic information for decision and the analysis of value considerations with respect to goals, communication networks and incentives.

This theory is the handiwork of economic theorists and, as such, it lays emphasis on model construction and mathematics. Herbert Simon has developed decision-making to a much more sophisticated level so that it now ceases to be an ad hoc affair. **"The principal contribution of this school to the Management process is in those problem areas where parameter relationships are quantifiable and clear and where parameters can be either directly measured or reliably estimated"** (Torgersen and Weinstock).

This school of thought has shortcomings, according to John G. Hutchinson. He says that, for one thing, it has never been proven that either the Management job or the operation or organisation can be explained fully by focussing on the factors usually treated as variables by the decision-making school. Most decision models either cannot or do not include "soft" variables. In its present state, the decision-making school is oriented more towards technique than philosophy. It adds a great deal to the science and art of decision-making, but it has not yet reached full status as a separate school of thinking.

The principal contribution of this school to the management process is, therefore, rightly in those problem areas where parameter relationships are quantifiable and clear and where parameters can be either directly measured or reliably estimated as stated earlier.

### 6. The Mathematical School

This school views Management as a system of mathematical models and process. Management or organisation, planning or decision-making as a logical process, can be expressed in terms of mathematical symbols and relationships. This theory uses the techniques of operational research, linear programming, queueing theory and model building. For improving their decision, the Management executives can make use of many new tools offered to them by this school of thought. The Management can use them by increasing the number of alternatives, by speeding up the decision processes, by providing help in evaluating the relative risks of bold and conservative courses and also by helping to bring into optimum balance the many diverse elements of a modern enterprise.

"The linear programming has solved assignment and transportation problems. Queueing theory has been useful in planning the correct or optimum number of toll booths on turnpikes, the number of tellers' windows in banks, the number of gasoline pumps in filling stations. It is useful in planning the number of loading and unloading docks at transportation terminals and maintenance docks at airports. It is even useful for making up bus schedules." ("Contemporary American Management", Business Perspectives – Robert T. Hof.)

Mathematical techniques in Management are increasingly being used as we find in case of electronic computers. This school of thought has enabled Management personnel to be more statistical minded.

Electronic computers have considerably facilitated the use of mathematical techniques in management. By making management executives statistical minded, it enables an executive to understand business problems in a proper perspective. It ensures a system analysis of problems. To quote Koontz, "They have forced on people in management the means and desirability of seeing many problems more clearly, they have pressed on scholars and practitioners the need for establishing goals and measures of effectiveness, they have been extremely helpful in getting the management area seen as a logical system of relationship and they have caused people in management to review and occasionally recognise information sources and systems so that mathematics can be given sensible quantitative meaning."

### 7. The Comparative Management School

This school of thought seeks to develop generalisations from a study of Management systems in diverse cultures. Management, according to some scholars, is culture-bound. "The applicability of Management principles may be limited to a particular culture or situation and that it may be fruitless to search for a common set of principles of determinate solutions" – (Oberg). "Comparative

Management is a study and analysis of Management as a process and a philosophy in all managerial situations and in all countries where further industrialisation is pursued as an integral part of economic development" (S. Benjamin Prasad). A comparative Management study is likely to provide insight into the problems of large scale enterprises in the public and private sectors, Management comparison also provides maximum effectiveness.

The study on a comparative basis also provides a veritable source of information useful in adapting managerial techniques of one country in another setting and enables the Management to have an insight into the types of problem which may be common to many countries, thus fostering increased internationally pooled efforts to solve these problems. This school of thought also offers opportunity to study the major aspects of the governing forces of economic growth.

The comparative management school seems to be an offshoot of the empirical school. The benefits of the school have been summed up as follows by an eminent authority. It provides :

1. An insight into the problem of the large scale enterprises in different sectors — public, private and labour — when comparisons between sectors are made.

2. A rationale for minimising ineffectuality and maximising effectiveness.

3. A veritable source of information.

4. An insight into the types of problems which may be common to many countries, thus fostering increased internationally pooled efforts to solve these problems.

5. An opportunity to study the major aspects of the governing forces of economic growth.

## Conclusion

The above analysis of management thoughts reveals that modern management is the outcome of diverse contributions of several management thinkers and practitioners. Management, as it has developed today, can not be considered either classical or behavioural. All the schools of thought are complementary developed over centuries.

The different schools of Management thought are simply baffling and confusing. Researchers belonging to different schools have seen Management from their own angles of vision and have tried to prove the vagueness of other schools. Such a large number of theories on Management naturally lead one to ask whether the present development of Management theory represents a jungle or orderly rows of trees ! Professor Koontz actually asked this question. In order to bridge the gap between the variety of approaches, he suggested a pattern of operation on the following lines :

By defining management as the establishment of an environment in which people can effectively perform in a formalized group for the attainment of group goals, it will be the task of the managers to do those things which establish such an environment for performance and develop the conceptual framework by dividing the activities of managers into a number of functions as planning, organising, staffing, direction and control.

While attempts have been made to formulate a unified theory of Management, the main difficulty has been what Richard Neuschel called "shooting at a moving target."

## SUMMARY

Management is as old as civilisation. Different ancient civilisations bear that testimony. A number of scholars contributed to the development of modern Management through different approaches.

Management thought has been classified in different ways. Some have explained in terms of four basic approaches — behavioural, productivity, rationalistic-model and institutional. Other classifications are — classical management theory, human behaviour theory, social and political systems approaches, ecological systems approach and rational decision- making concepts.

Harold Koontz has given seven major schools of management theory : (1) Management Process School (2) The Empirical School (3) Human Behaviour School (4) Social System School (5) The Decision Th.ory School (6) The Mathematical School and (7) The Comparative Management School.

Researchers belonging to different schools have seen Management from their own angles of vision. The large number of theories naturally create confusion. Professor Koontz has tried to bridge the gap between the variety of approaches. He says, Management is an establishment of an environment in which people can effectively perform in a formalized group for the attainment of group goals.

# CHAPTER 4

## SCIENTIFIC MANAGEMENT SCHOOL

In the evolution of Management thought, Scientific Management belongs to the classical period (1900–1930). Frederick Winslow Taylor (1865–1915) is considered to be the 'Father of Scientific Management'. He started his career as an apprentice and rose to the position of Chief Engineer. While working as the Chief Engineer in Midvale Steel Works in Philadelphia, he realised that workers produced only about one-third of what they could. This low production was largely due to the use of 'trial and error approach' by Management, as he understood. He observed that there was no scientific way to determine what constituted a proper day's work and Management had no clear notion of the best way of doing work. It was his realisation that there was lack of efficient work standards, absence of a clear-cut division of responsibility between Management and workers, lack of incentive of workers, unscientific selection and placement of workers.

With a view to improving Management practice, he conducted a series of experiments – time studies, studies of pig-iron handling and shovelling and metal cutting. Through these experiments, he developed the techniques of systematic rest pauses, best shovel load, high speed and precision cutting tools, scientific selection and tracing of works etc. Eventually, Taylor expanded his concepts and techniques into a philosophy which is known as 'Scientific Management'. He wrote a number of books "to point out great loss the country is suffering through inefficiency of production and to convince the readers that the cure lies in systematic Management rather than searching for unusualness". According to Dr. Taylor, to develop each man to his greatest efficiency, to maximise prosperity for both the employer and the employee, should be the objective of Management. By eliminating wastage and inefficiency, production and productivity can be improved and to do that Management should have scientific approach to managerial problems.

Taylor prescribed a manager's functions: A manager will define the task to be performed by workmen. He will select the right men for each job and he will motivate every worker to the highest possible level of efficiency.

Taylor defined Management as "The art of knowing exactly what you want men to do and then seeing that they do it in the best and cheapest way." Management, according to Taylor, is a science based on clearly defined laws and principles which are applicable to all forms of human activity.

Scientific management has for its very foundation the firm conviction that the true interests of the employer and the employee are one and the same; the prosperity for the employer can not exist through a long term of years unless it is accompanied by prosperity for the employee and vice versa; and that it is possible to give the worker what he wants — high wages — and the employee what he wants — a low labour cost — for his manufactures.

### Principles of Scientific Management *

1. Development of a science for each element of

* Principles of Scientific Management — Taylor

a man's work to replace the old rule-of-thumb method.

2. Scientific selection, training and development of workmen.

3. Close co-operation with workmen to ensure that work is done in accordance with the scientific principles which have been developed.

4. An almost equal division of work and responsibility between Management and workers.

The problems of Scientific Management consist of– (i) fixation of working standards (ii) standardisation of jobs through job evaluation (iii) scientific selection of workers and (iv) the mental revolution on the part of Management and workers.

Standards are industrial and commercial in nature. Commercial standards (consumer standards) consist of equipment, tools, materials, planning and control, routing, scheduling, displacing, follow-up, Gantt charts and job standardisation. Job standardisation and selection of workers constitute two important elements of Scientific Management.

Describing the basic philosophy of Scientific Management, Taylor observed that, "Scientific Management is not an efficiency device .... in its essence Scientific Management involves a complete mental revolution on the part of both workmen and Management. And without this mental revolution on both sides Scientific Management does not exist."

## Techniques/Mechanisms of Scientific Management

1. Time study to determine a fair day's work
2. Motion study and micromotion study to eliminate wasteful motions
3. Functional Foremanship consisting of the use of 8 staff specialists – 4 each in the factory office and the shop
4. The Differential Piece Rate Plan of wage payment involving two different rate of wages for efficient and inefficient workers
5. Standardisation of tools, equipment and working conditions
6. Instruction cards, slide rules, graphs, charts, costing systems etc.

Time and Motion studies are described as the "Cornerstone of Scientific Management."

### Time study

Dr. Taylor considered time study as a very important feature of Scientific Management. He carried on detailed study in order to have a standard time load to fix his incentive wage system to carry out a job most efficiently. Time study includes motion study, job standardisation and scientific selection of workers. Time study aims, in the words of Taylor, to find out "the one best way" of doing the work.

The chief advantage of time study is to find out the best possible time in which a job can be efficiently carried out. Thus it helps to keep control on production and other departments of the plant besides finding out the capacity of the plant and installation of the best machinery in the factory. The efficiency of a worker can also be judged by time study. It is also very useful to estimate the cost of production.

### Motion study

It is the analysis of the methods, of the materials and of the tools and equipment used or to be used, in the performance of a piece of work. The analysis is carried on to find out the most economical way of doing this work, to standardise the methods, materials, tools and equipments, to determine accurately the time required by an average worker to do the task and to train the worker in the new method.

Frank B. Gilbreth first developed the method of motion study and he said, "Motion study is the science of eliminating wastefulness resulting from using unnecessary, ill-directed and inefficient motions. The aim of motion study is to find and perpetuate the scheme of least waste methods of labour."

Motion study confers the following advantages: (i) It increases output (ii) It effects a great economy in cost savings (iii) wages are increased; workers are benefitted (iv) production increases and cost decreases, thus the producer stands to profit more (v) It enhances workers' interest and makes them more efficient.

**Disadvantages :** (i) Because of a given pattern of motion, work becomes monotonous (ii) It appears to workers as irksome, restraining their free movements (iii) Individual differences of workers are not taken into consideration and (iv) By Motion study standard of work may not be attained by the workers, according to the industrial psychologists.

One of the cardinal principles of Scientific Management is the mental attitude of the employer and the employees. The need for change of the mental attitude of the employer and the employees cannot be overemphasised; the need is for the interest of both the parties. But, unfortunately, it has not been achieved as yet. The change in the mental attitude of the employer is called for, because today labour cannot be hired and fired according to the whims of Management. Today's militant trade unions are strong enough to safeguard and protect the interests of the workers, if necessary. Henry L. Gantt observed, "The general policy of the past has been to drive, but the era of force must give way to that of knowledge and the policy of the future will be to teach and to lead to the advantage of all concerned."

Management should realise the "human problem" and the workers must fully co-operate with the Management and should not adopt the attitude of a person who works for fixed hours for fixed wages. The spirit of *esprit de corps* must be inculcated into workers.

Others who have contributed significantly to the Scientific Management movement were – Henry L. Gantt, H. Emerson and Frank and Gilbreth. The School of Scientific Management was developed largely by engineers and scientists.

**Taylor's contribution** to Management is **unique** in the sense that he applied scientific methods of observation and experiment to the problems of Management. Though his ideas were not entirely new, it is he who for the first time advocated a mental revolution on the part of both employer and employees. His concepts of functional foremanship, time and motion studies, separation of planning from doing, and revolutionised methods of manufacturing are fundamental.

In spite of the fact that Scientific Management thought contained fundamental ideas that stood the test of time, it could not escape **criticisms.** It has been described by the critics as "a cold philosophy of Management". The essentiality of people in Management was not accepted by Taylor who saw people as inefficient and unpredictable machines rather than as living beings. To him, workers were 'rational economic beings' and inherently lazy, which is not correct. Scientific Management, according to many, is more a theory of industrial engineering than a general theory of Management. The study of Management became in effect the study of shop Management. Taylor has become more dogmatic than practical by theorising complete separation of planning from execution which is neither practicable nor desirable. Last but not the least, a severe criticism is that Taylor, who advocated differential piece rate of wage system for the workers and thought about their welfare and efficiency, led to industrial autocracy and unfair distribution of the fruits of higher efficiency through his Scientific Management principles. Trade unions allege that Scientific Management entails for workers higher workloads, unchallenging jobs and technological unemployment.

It must be admitted that nothing is an unmixed blessing in this world, not to speak of Scientific Management. Scientific Management demands a mental revolution as a precondition for its introduction and some of the criticisms, at least, are due to the absence of the mental revolution. "Scientific Management was an innovation and as such generated opposition" (Massie).

## Opposition to Scientific Management

It must be admitted that Scientific Management has much to say in its favour. Both the employer and the employees are benefitted in a number of ways by the application of the principles of Scientific Management. But the industrial psychologists have taken exception to many facets of Scientific Management. The employer and the employees also oppose certain principles of Scientific Management.

From the employers' point of view, Scientific Management entails **huge expenditure.** Overhauling of the existing plant, making time and motion studies — all these involve too much expenditure. The employers also argue that Scientific Managemnet disorganises the production pattern and the existing plant and machinery become obsolete entailing huge loss. The creation of the planning section under Scientific Management is also criticised by the employers on the ground of expenditure involved in organising such a section.

From the employees' point of view, 'time study is **anti-labour** technique. The employees are very much emphatic on the point that Scientific Management contains in it the element of monotony. Excessive simplification and standardisation destroys initiative, skill and creativeness in the workers; they become completely mechanical. Employees think that Scientific Management is **undemocratic** since it gives enormous powers to functional bosses to exercise control over the workers. Another objection raised by the employees (employee leader) is that **trade unionism suffers** a set-back. Increase in unemployment and less increase in wages and bonus arise out of Scientific Management, as argued by employees.

Industrial psychologists' objection to Scientific Management is in regard to its 'human' element. They point out that workers are human beings and they cannot be standardised in the same way as machines and materials. Psychologists say that there are definite limits to workers' activities, so to fix a set pattern to all the workers is detrimental to human notions. To resist such rigidity is the human nature which is called "freedom reflex". Industrial psychologists also feel that the entire emphasis of Scientific Management is to find out the "one best way" of doing any work without taking into account the individual differences of workers. According to them, there is no 'one best way' of doing work. Dr. Myers, the great industrial psychologist also subscribes to this view.

The opposition to Scientific Management by different interested groups — employers, employees and industrial psychologists are biased and controversial.

As to the objection of employers that Scientific Management is a Management theory that envisages a larger involvement of finance on their part. We consider, this a short term view of the matter. Taking into consideration the long term benefits accruing from Scientific Management, the excess amount that has to be spent to implement the principles of Scientific Management is more than compensated.

Employees' objections centre round some psychological factors and their attitude towards employers. Devices are there to minimise monotony of workers and sufficient measures and methods can be adopted to ensure that workers are not reduced to machines. By making them more efficient through various devices under Scientific Management, they can take more and can give more. That Scientific Management is a clever attempt to weaken trade unions is not tenable. Keeping the workers in difficulty and then to come to their rescue, cannot be the real function of a trade union. No doubt, Scientific Management aims at solving various problems of workers even for the sake of arguement, in the interest of the employers; still there is enough scope for the trade unions to be of help to the workers in different spheres.

Psychologists' opposition is naturally relating to the mind of the workers. Scientific Management calls for mental revolution. A complete change of outlook of both the employer and the employee is a *sine qua non* of Scientific Management. Removal of misunderstanding between capital and labour can be answered to the opposition by psychologists.

**Summary**

Taylor defines Scientific Management as "knowing exactly what you want men to do and seeing that they do it, in the best and cheapest way."

**Principles of Scientific Management are :**
(1) the development of a science for each element,
(2) the selection of workers on the scientific basis,
(3) the co-operation of management with workers,
(4) A more equal division of responsibility between management and workers.

**Problems of Scientific Management are :**

(1) Fixation of standards — equipment, tools, materials, planning and control, routing, scheduling, dispatching, follow up and Gantt Charts, (2) Job standardisation, (3) Selection of workers and (4) New mental attitude.

**'Motion study'** — is the science of eliminating wastefulness that results from indiscriminate uses of motions. The object of motion study under Scientific Management is to find and perpetuate the scheme of least-waste-methods of labour.

Motion study confers benefits such as increase in output, economy in cost saving, increase in labour wages, lowering the price of products and making the workers more efficient.

**Time Study** — A standard time is found out to carry out a job most efficiently. This helps fixation of wages on the basis of standard time ascertained by time study. Production planning schedule can be laid down easily. Efficiency of workers can be measured. Time study has been found to be very useful in cost of production.

As regards motion study, there have been oppositions. A given pattern of motions, according to workers, makes their work monotonous and they are reduced to the status of machines. In motion study, individual differences of workers are not taken into consideration. It tries to synthesise motions by studying the same of different workers and tries to fix a standard one.

## Benefits of Scientific Management

(1) Reduction of cost of production (2) increase in output of individual workers (3) working conditions and environment are improved by standardising plant organisation (4) industrial unrest is

minimised by establishing closer and better relations between labour and capital.

It has to be conceded that Taylor was less than fair to workers. One remarked, "It is doubtful if Taylor saw people as anything other than inefficient and unpredictable machines." However, while assessing Taylor's work it has to be kept in mind that he thought over management over half a century back and naturally, his observations had been influenced by the situation then prevailing in the industrial world.

**Taylor's contributions summed up :**

(a) To the problems of management, it is he who first applied scientific principles.

(b) It is he who first advocated mental revolution on the part of employers and employees both.

(c) He first innovated the concept of the use of "functional foremen."

(d) The separation of the planning of work from its execution was first recognised by Taylor.

(e) According to Haimann, Taylor was the first to state that it was the duty of management to tell the workers what was expected of them and also to specify the way in which the job is to be performed.

(f) The systematic experiments of time and motion study were carried on by Taylor first.

## Criticisms of Scientific Management

Employers, employees and industrial psychologists criticise Scientific Management from their own angles of view.

Employers say that scientific management entails huge expenditure, disorganises the production matters and, with huge expenditure, an organisation has to open a planning section.

Employees argue that Scientific Management makes them work more. It is undemocratic in nature and is not conducive to the growth of trade unionism. Unemployment is likely to occur because of standardisation of job and finally the employees believe that the total benefits that workers get in the form of increased wages and bonus are less than what the employers get as increased profit.

Psychologists, too, criticise Scientific Management on the ground that it attempts to standardise human beings like machines and materials that is unscientific.

It was criticised that Taylor was excessively utilitarian and impersonal and his scientific management was considered to be autocratic or at best paternalistic.

A considerable amount of criticism of Taylor was due to acts of omissions of firms which began to apply the tools and techniques of scientific management without acutually understanding them. "Partial adoption or the use of pseudo-scientific techniques by people who were not prepared or not sufficiently prepared or not sufficiently interested, to take the time and care which Taylor insisted were necessary for the successful introduction of his scheme. Taylor's warning that gradualness was imperative if the workers' confidence was to be fully secured. The effect of ignoring this advice was that in many firms scientific management came to be equated with exploitation and managerial sharp practice in the workers' eyes and this created a resistance to the use of the techniques that Taylor and his followers devised which is still evident today" *(Owen S. Hines)*. Taylor did not develop a science of management, rather he developed a new science for management.

# CHAPTER 5

## BEHAVIOURAL SCHOOL OF MANAGEMENT THOUGHT

Unlike Taylor who spoke about mental revolution or unlike Mayo who emphasised on social solidarity, the essence of behavioural approach is that integration between the needs of employees and the goals of the organisation comes from the use of the behavioural sciences. These sciences help to understand human nature and find out how the individuals and groups can fit into and serve the organisation. Appleby asserts, "management is personnel administration", or, still further, "management is the development of people and not the direction of things."

This school of thought believes in the motivation of the individual and the adherents are heavily oriented towards psychology and sociology. The credit of establishing this school goes to Elton Mayo and his Harvard colleagues. The behavioural approach to Management began with the famous Hawthorne Experiments. The Hawthorne Experiments consisted of three phases :

### 1. The Test Room Studies

These studies were conducted on working hours, lighting, temperature, humidity, rest pauses, piece-work etc. to determine the effect of changes in working conditions. It was found that output increased even in the deteriorating working conditions. It was concluded that the increase was due to the favourable change in the workers' attitude. **So, the attitude of Management and morale of the workers is more important than physical environment.**

### 2. Interviewing Studies

The second phase of study was the undertaking of an interviewing programme. It was aimed at finding out the opinions or attitudes of employees towards their job, working conditions and supervision. The interviews, directly and indirectly taken, **confirmed the overwhelming importance of social factors in the total work environment.**

### 3. Observational Studies

In the last phase of the Hawthorne Experiments, direct observation of operatives known as "The Bank Wiring Observation Group Study" was undertaken. It was revealed that the group was restricting output due to the unofficial standards of performance of the group and various social pressures. This led to the conclusion that informal social groups and psychological factors exercised a much greater influence on workers' productivity and satisfaction than economic and physiological factors.

The Hawthorne Experiments changed the attitude towards the nature of man. It was found that a worker is not merely an economic man motivated solely by money. A sense of security, recognition, freedom of expression — all these matter. An organisation is a social system and the human factor is the most important element within it.

This school of thought is a socio-psychological approach to Management problems. It envisages that social environment shapes employee behaviour. The contributions of behavioural approach to Management cannot be over-emphasised. It brought major changes in teaching and practice of Management leading to constructive leadership with major emphasis on informal group, communication, employee motivation, personal counselling, job satisfaction etc.

Drucker observes : "The theory of human relations freed Management from the domination of viciously wrong ideas, but it did not succeed in substituting new concepts. Human relations put all the stress on inter-personal relations and the 'informal' group. Its starting point was in individual psychology rather than in the analysis of workers and work. As a result, there was a tendency for human relations to degenerate into mere slogans which became an alibi for having no Management policy with respect to the human organisation. Though empirical work has not been done with a common conceptual framework in the Behavioural School of thought, making it difficult for generalisations, it has done a unique job in pointing out that the human element is a very important element in Management.

Earnest Dale has rightly pointed out that none of the human relation theories so far has much value in attempting to predict behaviour arising out of complex situations or behaviour at the top Management level.

In the human relations theory, knowledge of behavioural sciences like sociology, psychology and anthropology is applied; hence this theory is also known as the 'behavioural sciences approach'.

The human relations approach has been criticised on the ground that this is based on a relatively few studies of small samples of human beings. The wider social context has been ignored. Mayo investigated the factory to the almost complete exclusion of its social background. The Hawthorne studies had a pro-management bias. To say that the field of human behaviour is itself the field of Management is not correct.

The criticisms have not undermined the value of Hawthorne studies which are regarded as "a milestone and a turning point" in the history of man at work and in the path of research in industrial psychology and sociology.

It is the human relations movement which has made significant contribution to Management thought since it has focussed attention on the human element in Management. The contribution of human relations lies in new insights than in new theories or new techniques. The approach explains how and why people behave as they do.

This theory brought into limelight human and social factors in organisations. But the concepts were carried too far. It is said that there is no direct and deep connection between morale and productivity. Morale is an elusive quality and it is not a very meaningful concept of Management thought. Till 1960, human relations movement was in full operation and it has been turning away from the extreme human relations ideas, particularly regarding direct relation between morale and productivity.

The neo-classical period (1930-1960) in the evolution of Management thought relates to the study of Management as human relationship in organisations. Neo classical theory is called Human Relation Movement. As contrasted with classical theory, neo-classical theory concentrated on man and not on physical resources. It stressed the importance of individual as well as group relationships in the plant or work-place.

The behavioural science approach to Management is the core of the neo classical theory. Human values in business were recognised as important.

**Areas of Managerial application of behavioural science methods : (According to Elton Mayo)**

(1) The business organisation is basically a social system contrary to the popular belief that it is just a techno-economic system.

(2) Feelings, emotions and attitudes of the employees are no less important than economic incentives; rather they are more significant in determining production efficiency.

(3) An employee has various psychological demands which need democratic leadership for their satiation. Co-operation and not command can go a long way in solving psychological problems of an employee.

(4) Communication is vital for any organisation; there should be an uninterrupted flow of understanding between the employer and the employees which can only be ensured by effective two-way communcation net-work. Hence participation is considered a very powerful tool for human relations movement.

(5) Morale and productivity being closely connected, it is essential that greater interest in employee development and workers' satisfaction is taken.

(6) Group efforts, according to Elton Mayo and his associates, are to be relied upon and, as such,

informal group and informal organisation must be recognised. Group psychology plays a dominant role in any organisation.

(7) Man is a living machine and he is far more important than an inanimate machine. Management should, therefore, develop social skills in addition to technical skills. Employee morale has to be boosted up; with morale of employee going higher, output also gets increased. Man-to-man relationships, team spirit, group harmony are matters that deserve serious consideration of the Management.

The individual, work groups and participative management are **three essential elements of** Human Relations Theory.

This theory emphasises the need for the recognition of individual differences. The feelings, emotions, perceptions and attitudes of an individual must be recognised. Each individual has to be studied separately because each one has his own psychological peculiarities. He comes to his job with some preconceived attitudes and beliefs; he has his own way of life. The management should take all these factors into cognizance to derive the best results. The inner world of the worker is more important than the external reality in the determination of productivity. Human Relations Theory studies these and the classical theories had ignored them. It does not mean that economic considerations are to be ignored. Both physical and nonphysical elements in an individual are to be given due consideration. Human Relations Theory advocates the adoption of multi-dimensional model of motivation.

The 'Workgroups' as an element of Human Relations Theory constitutes the argument that an individual in a group develops social wants. Workers are not isolated, unrelated individuals; they are social beings and deserve to be treated as such by the management. The neo-classical theory (Human Behaviour Theory) emphasises the vital effects of group psychology and behaviour on motivation and productivity. Management must recognise informal organisation which must be integrated with formal organisation. The informal communication works speedily and accurately, so it cannot be eliminated. Each work-group has its own leader, unwritten constitution and its production standard imposed by social sanctions on the group members. This aspect has been given due consideration in Human Relations Theory.

Participative management, an element of Human Relations Theory, is a natural consequence of the emphasis on the importance of individual and work-groups. Workers' participation in management is an outcome of the neo-classical management thought. So, this theory is employee-oriented and group-oriented. The behavioural approach is trying to satisfy personal security and social needs of workers.

"Thus it is eminently clear that social factors have a profound effect on employees' morale and must be considered as an important force in organisations where informal groups are likely to rise and norms of behaviour inevitably develop. Perhaps the most compelling reason for organisation managers to consider the group is that an organisation itself is made up of interlocking groups which must co-operate in the pursuance of organisational goals. As a consequence, the manager must always be aware of the strength of the group and the existence of group norms which may or may not be consonant with orgnisational norms" (Massie).

As we have seen, Elton Mayo and Mary Parker Follett laid the foundation of this theory of management thought, it is interesting to note that Mary P. Follett was not in business but she was interested in the problems of individual organisation and co-ordination. To her, psychology was the foundation of all human activity and, therefore, she applied these to business conditions. She believed that "a human group has a life as a group and is something more than the sum of so many individuals comprising it." According to her, authority should be depersonalised so that the employer-employee relationship rests on functional co-operation rather than status. Conflict should be resolved by the integration of desires of the parties to the dispute — the parties being workers, consumers and investors. Leadership, she believed, is guidance and leading and not dominating.

The behavioural approach is, as a matter of fact, the human relations approach and as such it depends on psychology, sociology and cultural anthropology. "Unlike natural sciences which gravitate towards quantitative thinking, behavioural science 'sifts and weighs' intangibles" *(Shukla)*.

# CHAPTER 6

## PROMINENT PHILOSOPHERS OF MANAGEMENT THOUGHT

### Introduction

A peep into the history of human civilization reveals that human beings have developed out of group life and it would not be incorrect to say that the story of development of management is essentially a story of mankind, co-operative and collective efforts became imperative for human beings to achieve their goals. Religious and military organisations would provide group endeavour in primitive stages. Thes Haimann has stated, "The co-ordination of human effort is as old as mankind and, therefore, it can be said that management has an equally long history."

Principles of management were effectively used by the Roman churches in the early times. A large number of scholars have contributed to the development of modern management thought. The earliest protagonist of scientific management was Walter of Henley of the thirteenth century according to Oliver Sheldon. Schuyler Walace refers Babbage as the predecessor of Taylor. Albert Lapawsky said "If modern management is modern in origin, it is so by definition only. The technique of management, like the art of administration and the science of organisation, has ancient roots and medieval branches".

A brief account of personalities who have large contribution to management literature and thought is given in the following pages :

### Charles Babbage (1792 - 1871)

**Charles Babbage conceived the idea that the methods of science and mathematics could be applied to the operations of factories.**

Born in 1792, he graduated from Cambridge in 1814. He was a professor of mathematics at his own university. He was a prolific writer and wrote quite a large number of books and articles on mathematical, scientific and philosophic subjects.

Babbage's contribution — (i) Benefits of division of labour (ii) Use of science and mathematics (iii) Emphasis on cost reduction (iv) Anticipated modern practices (v) Importance of sevice objective (vi) Invention of a "Difference Engine" and (vii) Varied interests.

In his master-piece — on 'the Economy of Machinery and Manufactures'—Babbage explained what can be obtained from division of labour and intelligent organisation of workers. He stated, ".... that the master manufacturer, by dividing the work to be executed into different processes, each requiring different degree of skill or a face, can purchase exactly that precise quantity of both which is necessary for each process."

Babbage was perhaps the first to perceive that the methods of science and mathematics could well be utilised for formulating management principles in factories.

He advocated that each employer could reduce costs by the discovery of improved methods, by cultivating knowledge of the precise expense of every process and by the knowledge of which processes offer the greatest possibility of cost reduction through study.

The mechanism of time and motion study was also anticipated by Babbage.

He predicted the importance of service objective for all concerned. He advised producers to make articles in perfect form.

His most significant contribution to managerial thought was the building up of "difference machine" which he hoped would make it possible to extend tables of interest or interest premium or tables of tidal ebb and flood, indefinitely and automatically" *(Earnest Dale).*

He had various other interests such as his interest in automatic recording device. He developed a numerical system of occulting light houses, worked on submarine designs, suggested the use of rockets for boosting projectiles and a coloured lighting apparatus for the theatre.

The origins of scientific management have been traced back in his writings. He is one of the foremost early British thinkers on management. McFarland states, "To Babbage goes the credit for advocating in relation to industrial problems the fundamental thinking which preceeded the formulation of a science of management".

Babbage laid considerable emphasis on accurate data collection, specialization, work measurement, wage incentives, cost reduction, better methods of work performance and utilization of machine and tools. To quote Urwick, "Babbage pointed out the possibility of developing general principles based on scientific analysis to govern the conduct of industrial undertakings". It is also claimed that Babbage was a pioneer of operation research. According to Douglas Garbutt, "Babbage is a varitable poet of industrial and commercial processes". It will not be out of place to mention here that American thinkers on management did not give any recognition to the work of Babbage, which is rather unfortunate.

### Frederick Winslow Taylor (1856 - 1915)

Born in 1856, Taylor started his career as an apprentice in a small machinery-making shop in Philadelphia in 1875. In 1878 he joined Midvale Steel Works as a machine shop labour. His was a very good service record; ultimately he became Chief Engineer in 1884. Of course, in 1883, he obtained a degree in Engineering by evening study. As a man he was very dutiful and never failed in his social obligations. Drinking and smoking were unknown to him; he even did not drink tea or coffee. He has been described as possessing 'a whale of a New England conscience'. The varied nature of duties that Taylor performed in his life to use to a high position from a very low position made him to believe that workers produced only one-third of what they could. His observation was that the low production was largely due to the labours practicing traditional methods of production. The exact nature of the work to be done or the best of doing it was nobody's concern — this was his experience.

In the Midvale Steel Company he realized that greater output was possible but most of the workers were engaged in what he called "systematic soldiering". He considered it his first duty to know what constituted a proper day's work. Taylor conducted time studies at Midvale Steel Company which was of immense help to him in founding Scientific management principles.

In the Bethlehem Steel Company he conducted his famous studies of pig iron handling and shovelling and metal cutting experiments. In pig iron handling, Taylor discovered that periodic rests enabled a worker to produce more than by continuous work. In his shovelling experiments, Taylor found that an average load of 21 pounds gave the best results. With the help of new types of shovels, training of the men in better methods and advanced planning of work, he was able to reduce the crew to less than one-third its original size. The average output increased and earnings jumped up.

The metal cutting experiments resulted in the discovery of high speed steel which greatly increased the output of metal cutting machinery. Another result was information about the proper speed and feed for lathes, planers, drill presses, milling machine and related equipment. Albert comments : "The achievements of the metal cutting experiments were in many respects more important than Taylor's other contributions. High-speed and precision cutting tools are an essential ingredient of large scale production".

As to the publications of Taylor, we can say he started publishing articles in the form of papers by submitting them to the American Society of Mechanical Engineers. His major publications are : A Piece Rate System, Shop Management, On the Art of Cutting Metals, The Principles of Scientific Management.

The basic philosophy of Taylors' Scientific Management was that there was a need for a fundamental change of attitude on the part of both managers and men. He spoke of 'mental revolution" of both the employer and the employee without which, he believed, scientific management cannot exist.

Taylor wanted that management should take the responsibility of planning, directing and organizing work. He laid great emphasis on time and motion studies to determine the best way of doing each job or task. He wanted elimination of waste of all types whether of men or material. He summed up his concept of scientific management as under:

*Science, not rule of thumb*
*Harmony, not discord*
*Co-operation, not individualism*
*Maximum output in place of restricted output.*

The development of each man to his greatest efficiency and prosperity.

In 'Shop Management' Taylor stated that the best management rests on a foundation of high wages and low costs. In order to practise management as an art, Taylor advocated the application of the following principles :

(1) A large daily task (2) Standard con-ditions (3) High pay for success (4) Loss in case of failure (5) Separation of planning from doing and (6) Functional foremanship.

Taylor, the Father of Scientific Management, though criticised on many counts, yet stands out as a stalwart in the evolution of management thought.

## Henri Fayol (1841 - 1925)

Henri Fayol may be called the Father of Principles of Management.

Born in 1841 in France, Fayol graduated as a mining engineer. From an engineer in a large coal and steel combine, he became its Chief Executive when the undertaking was on the verge of bankruptcy. He retired making the concern financially most sound. Fayol's constant endeavour to lead the company to success has been nicely described by no less a person than Urwick as "One of the romances of French industrial history."

**Fayol highlighted the importance of management activities from the top management point of view.** Taylor worked from the bottom of the industrial hierarchy — on the operative level primarily whereas Fayol concentrated on top management and worked downwards. General management was rather the concern of Fayol and not supervision. Overall control and not details of operations was Fayol's line of management thought. In his book, **"General and Industrial Management"**, Fayol wrote : "Management plays a very important part in the government undertakings; of all undertakings, large or small, industrial, commercial, political, religious or any other."

Fayol pointed out some basic principles of administration or management. He believed in the flexibility of the principles. According to him, the light of principles, like that of light-houses, guides only those who knew the way into port.

His main principles are :

(1) Division of labour (2) Authority and Responsibility (3) Discipline (4) Unity of command (5) Unity of Direction (6) Sub-ordination of individual interest to General interest (7) Remuneration of personnel (8) Centralisation (9) Scalar chain (10) Order (11) Equity (12) Stability of tenure of personnel (13) Initiative (14) Esprit-de-corps.

To explain the principles we can say — The principle **of division of labour** is the principle of specialization. This principle is to produce more and better results.

**Authority and Responsibility** should not be conceived separately "Responsibility is a corollary of authority, it is its natural consequence and essential counterpart and wheresoever authority is exercised, responsibility arises" (Fayol).

**Discipline** is considered as "outward marks of respect". Fayol considered discipline very essential and to ensure it, he suggested, good supervisors at all levels, agreements with employees as clear and fair as possible and penalties judicially applied.

**Unity of command** — This principle emphasises that for any action whatsoever, an employee should receive order from one superior only. Dual comonand,according to Fayol, is the perpetual source of conflict.

The principle of **subordination of individual interest to general interest** stresses that the interest of one employee or group of employees should not prevail over that of the concern. He suggested firmness and good example on the part of superior, agreement as fair as possible and constant supervision to ensure good management.

As to remuneration of personnel, Fayol advocated fair ways to the satisfaction of both the employer and the employee.

Regarding **centralization**, Fayol thought that it belonged to the natural order like division of labour. Centralization is a question of proportion. It is a matter of finding the optimum degree for the particular concern.

**Scalar Chain** is the chain of superiors, ranging from the ultimate authority to the lowest ranks.

**Order,** according to Fayol, means a place of everyone and everyone in his place, the right man in the right place. He believed that the order demanded precise knowledge of the human requirements and resources of the concern and a constant balance between their requirements and resources.

**Equity** principle emphasises on "Kindliness" of the managers towards their employees. A manager should strive to instal a "sense of equity" throughout all levels of the scalar chain.

**Stability of tenure of personnel** is a big factor for the suceess of an organisation. Fayol pointed out that instability of tenure is at one and the same time cause and effect of bad running.

**Initiative** principle enjoins managers to sacrifice some "personal vanity" to permit the subordinates to keep up their zeal and initiative.

The **Esprit-de-corps** principle states that "union is strength". Fayol wanted the managers to encourage cohesiveness and *esprit-de corps* among their subordinates.

Fayol considered his list of principles not so much exhaustive and he believed that in order to have a sound management, the observance of these principles should be strictly enforced.

Fayol wrote a very important book entitled "General and Industrial Management". This book is considered to be one of the best classics of management literature. He wrote on various subjects such as education, public services, military, administration and the theory of administration in the state.

Fayol distinguished between 'General principles of management' and 'Elements of Management'. He regarded elements of management as the function of management which he divided into five parts — Planning, Organisation, Command, Co-ordination and Control.

While evaluating Fayol's work, his contribution to management thought can be stated as — (i) Management is separate skill (2) Father of Principles of management (3) Help in development of management theory (4) Systematic analysis of process of management (5) Management can and should be taught (6) Foundation of classical theory of organisation and (7) Management skills are universal.

Modern writers on management have paid considerable tributes to the work of Fayol. Fayol was a top manager and was obviously in a better position than Taylor to observe the functions of a manager. "Taylors' principles looked towards management from the bottom up while Fayol's observations were concerned with the management level from the top down" *(Haimann).*

Professor Albert Lapawsky has paid these tributes to the genius of Henri Fayol : "The twentieth century has yet to produce as balanced a combination of able practitioners and keen student of administration as Henri Fayol." Allen regards Fayol's work as "pioneering".

### Taylor vs Fayol

A comparative study of the contribution of Taylor and Fayol towards the development of management thought is quite relevant for any one interested in the evolution of management thought.

Taylor's work was primarily concerned with the operative **shop level** while Fayol's work was concerned with management at the **top level**. Taylor looked towards management from the bottom up; Fayol from the top down.

In the management world, Fayol is given considerable respect but in American literature Taylor occupies the position superior that of Fayol. The reason for such a position of Fayol in America is assigned to the late arrival of Fayol's writings to the U.S.A. and England. Many prominent thinkers on management were not familiar with the writings of Fayol and as such he could not be assessed by them.

It is also the opinion of some management

thinkers including Henry H. Albers that the ideas of Taylor were very much popular in U.S.A, "Taylorism did not produce a systematic theory of management, but it did provide the basis for great accomplishments on the production time" (Albers). H. H. Albers made it no secret to say that a vested interest in knowledge also helped keep Fayol's contribution in the background for so long. A reluctance to accept ideas that upset the existing climate of opinion is by no means confined to the management level.

There are management thinkers according to whom Taylor and Fayol had contradictions in their management thoughts. Fayol himself however, made it clear how false he found this antithesis. He openly declared in an international conference that **Taylor's work was essentially complementary to his own fielf of study.** To search for contradictions in the works of these two management giants, is a futile exercise in the sense that it does not produce anything positive for the development of management. According to Haimann, "both applied scientific methods to the problems of management."

Urwick remarked on the controversy of contradiction between Taylor and Fayol in a very apt and nice way. He said, "Fayol's capacity to see and acknowledge publicly that there was no antithesis between his and Taylor's work was an example of his intellectual integrity and generosity of spirit."

However, to conclude we can say that though management experts in the U.S.A. did not pay the expected respect to Fayol, his work has been considered as 'pioneering' by prominent management authorities. Both are big — and it is not fair to compare the 'two bigs' in a way which may be — little them in any way. Both have tremendous contributions and, to be fair, their contributions are complementary and not contradictory, though their angles of vision may be different.

## Peter F. Drucker

Born in Vienna in 1909, Drucker was educated in Austria and England. From a newspaper correspondent and an economist for international bank, he became Professor of Management in the New York University in 1950. He introduced the concept of management by objectives. According to him, performance is the ultimate test of management. It was his opinion that management can not be an exact science or a profession. To him, to create a customer is the basic purpose of a business. He was a sharp critic of the concept of scientific management and human relations approach.

His prominent books are : The Practice of Management, The End of Economic Plan, The Future of Industrial Man, Concept of the Corporation, The New Society, America's next twenty years, Landmarks of To-morrow, Managing for Results.

## Lywdall Fownes Urwick

L. F. Urwick was an English consultant and educator. He is regarded as a leading exponent of the traditional classical approach. Urwick held the opinion that rationality should take precedence over personality. In all his writings and management thoughts, there are clear impressions of the influences of Taylor, Fayol, Mooney and Reiby and others who preceded him in management thoughts.

Urwick mainly dealt with the formal structure of organisation in the formulation of his management principles. He paid particular attention to the "delegation principles". He was of the opinion that the "lack of the courage to delegate properly and of knowledge how to do it, is one of the most general causes of failure in organisation". According to Urwick, at all levels authority and responsibility must be co-terminous, co-equal and defined. He was against the use of committees for purposes of administration. He was a prolific writer on administration who covered a wide field and classfied many of the thoughts and ideas of the classic writers and contemporaries.

His important publications are : Papers on the Science of Administration, The Elements of Management, The Making of Scientific Management, A Short Survey of Industrial Management and A Golden Book on Management.

## Henry L. Gantt (1861 - 1919)

Gantt, an associate of Taylor, was born in 1861 and was educated at John Hopkins College. He qualified as a mechanical engineer and worked at Midvale Steel Co. and became assistant to Taylor. Urwick, while commenting on Gantt, said, "Gantt was adaptable and opportunist". His contribution to management thought cannot be considered insignificant. Task and Bonus Plan, Daily Balance Chart, Humanizing of the Science of Management, Importance of leadership and training of workers are some of his notable contributions to management thought. For these contributions, Urwick has called him "forerunner of modern industrial democracy" and Miller (President, American Society of Mechanical Engineers) called him "an apostle of industrial peace." These are no mean tributes paid to him by eminent personalities.

Gantt's wage incentive plan has been regarded as an improvement on Taylor's piece rate system. His task and bonus system of wage payment has been considered to be the most satisfactory among differential wage systems for reducing labour costs.

Some prominent authorities on management held the opinion that Gantt had better understanding of workers' psychology than Taylor. Gantt believed in the notion that management should be responsible for creating an environment that had favourable psychological effects on workers. He also made a substantial contribution to management planning and control. "His contribution was particularly useful in one area of Taylor's work : the improvement of production control techniques and the information techniques and the information required for decision making" *(Prof. Kaupner).* It has been observed that in industrial management, Gantt had a very understanding of the place of trade unions in an industrial society. So, he favoured co-operation rather than opposition with trade unions.

Gantt has to his credit quite a large number of publications, his earlier publications being on technical problems. From 1902 onwards his pen, so to say, had a continuous flow. Some of his major publications are : Work, Wages and Profits; Industrial Leadership and Organizing for Work.

### Frank Bunker Gilbreth (1868 - 1924)

F. B. Gilbreth, a contemporary of Taylor and Gantt, was a leading American engineer, a building contractor and a management consultant. It was in the construction industry that he first realised the huge amount of effort that got wasted. He also found that some illogical practices had been taking place. He took positive steps to eliminate them. In his work on "Gilbreth and the Measurement of Work", Michael Thickett wrote that Gilbreth became fascinated by motion study and this interest eventually became so strong that he devoted the rest of his life to this work, achieving an international reputation as a consultant and writer on the subject.

Gilbreth's contribution to management thought can be summed up as (i) Motion study (ii) Time study (iii) Discovering the 'One best way' (iv) Training of personnel and (v) Three position Plan of Promotion. But the most significant among these are Time and Motion studies. As a matter of fact, it was Gilbreth who developed 'motion study' as a primary tool of management. As regards 'time study' he was more accurate than Taylor as he used micro-chronometer and other devices. Ernest Dale wrote, "Gilbreth's one best way' was the way which involved the fewest motions performed in an accessible area and in the most comfortable position". He emphasised the importance of training workers from the very beginning.

Gilbreth developed a three-position plan of promotion. He said, each worker should be considered to occupy three positions — (i) the job he held before promotion (ii) the present position and (iii) the next higher job. He envisaged that a worker would be teaching the man below him and learning from the man above him. This, he believed, would enable the worker to qualify himself for promotion and help to provide a successor to his current job.

The main theme of Gilbreth's work was that there is a best way to do a job and this should be searched for and, when discovered, implemented. "This philosophy is sound and widely accepted by management" *(Michael Thickett).* Let us evaluate Gilbreth's work in Urwick's words, "to develop management as a social science with the human being the centre of interest, round which research and experiment revolve and towards whose development they are directed," was his most significant contribution in the field of management.

Gilbreth laid emphasis on human efforts which was his unique contribution. He devised methods for showing up wasteful and improductive movements. He also devised several systems of analysing work into distinct elements. Taylor emphasised on the external factors affecting the worker while Gilbreth looked at the worker from the stand point of social sciences. It would broaden the worker's capacity to contribute to productivity. Gilbreth considered worker-management cooper-tion very important and significant and did not approve of Taylor's practice of carrying out secret time studies on workers.

## Harrington Emerson (1853 - 1931)

Emerson, an American engineer, is well known for his principles of efficiency. He came to limelight in 1910-11 when he said that the railroads could save 'a million dollars a day' on their operating costs. He popularized scientific management. His scientific management was somewhat different from Taylor's in as much as it did not concentrate so heavily on work measurement and financial incentives. it was also less concerned with management in the shop than with the whole conduct of the business. He expounded the concepts of standard times, standard costs and preventable waste. "He was also among the first to call attention to the lessions which business management could learn from the military" *(Ernest Dab)* . He paid particular attention to the selection and training of workers.

Emerson highlighted 12 principles of efficiency : (1) a clearly defined ideal; (2) Common sense; (3) Competent counsel; (4) discipline (5) fair deal (6) reliable, immediate, adequate and permanent records; (7) despatching, (8) standards and schedules; (9) standardised conditions; (10) standardised operations; (11) Written standard practice instructions and (12) efficiency reward. These principles of efficiency, of course, were not distinct principles and they overlap to some extent.

Accord ng to Urwick, "He was a particularly original contributor to the early development of scientific management for though he was in close touch with the Taylor group, he was not part of it and his additions to the body of principles of management were independent". His work emphasised the importance of correct organisation in efforts to achieve high productivity, according to Dr. McFarland. He advocated the line and staff type of organisational structure which characterises most of our business organisations today. It was Emerson who first sounded the need of combining democratic individualism and social well being. He set forth a number of principles of efficiency and idealised the goal of eliminating waste and asserted the need for strong leadership to reconcile conflicting relationship within management.

His notable publications are — (1) Efficiency as a Basis for Operation and Wages; (2) The Twelve Principles of Efficiency (3) The Scientific selection of employees and (4) Course on Personal Efficiency.

## Mary Parker Follett (1868 - 1933)

Born in Boston in 1868 and educated at Radcliffee College , Massachusetts, U.S.A., Mary Parker Follett was recognised as a political philosopher. Her contribution to management was to apply psychological insights and findings of the social sciences to industry. She offered a new concept of the nature of management and of human relationships within industrial groups.

Her educational background of studying philosophy, history, law and political science made her to accept "a career of public service in the Boston area with the formation of a local debating society which soon became extended into a chain of social centres in the poor areas" (Gordon Wills — Mary Parker Follett and the Integration of Business Administration). In her private life she was very much sociable. "She established a deeply rooted understanding and friendship with a large number of eminent men and women on both sides of the Atlantic" (The Golden Book on Management).

Follett's management thoughts found expression in her book "Dynamic Administration". As a political scientist, Follett analysed operations of many enterprises. She was noted for her practical observations about the value of human relations for the basic principles of organisation. Her ideas about organisation were very much appreciated. "Mary Follett, it may be admitted, did not provide a formidable body of thought but the basic characteristic of her ideas are that they are simple, go deeper and are of fundamental significance and value in the solution of many industrial as well as national and international problems. Her theory virtually turns the hierarchy of administrative authority upside down." *(Albert Lapawsky)*. Urwick comments on her work thus :

It was her special merit to turn from the traditional subject of study — The state or the community as a whole — progressively to concentrate on the study of industry. In this context she not only evolved principles of human association and organisation especially in terms of industry but also convinced large number of business men of the practicality of these principles in dealing with their current problems. Her approach was to analyse the nature of the consent on which any democratic group is based by examining the psychological factor underlying it. This consent, she suggested, is not static but a continuous process generating new and living group ideas through the interpretation of individual ideas.

She felt that service should become the dominant motive in management. She wished to see multiple leadership based on integrating thinking, adpated to the evolving situation.

Metcalf and Urwick have paid tributes to her as a political and business philosopher of the first rank. Their comments ran thus :

"a truly creative, intensely vital mind which found its way to the fundamental problems first of the community and State and later of industrial organisation and administration through a keen insight into human nature and tireless devotion to the task of arriving at a practical application of the social services in government and in industry."

Her contributions to management thought are : (i) Constructive conflict (ii) The law of situation or living orders (iii) Leadership (iv) Authority and Responsibility and (v) Principles of Organisation.

As to her publications, we may mention her first publication "The Speaker of the House of Representatives." Others are "The New State and Creative Experience" and "Dynamic Administration". Her writings are a rich reward for anyone who takes them up. The simplicity of the analysis was her characteristic. "Many successful business administrators have testified to the help afforded to them in their immediate difficulties by this modest spinster lady who had never managed a business in her life" (The Goldern Book of Management).

### George Elton Mayo (1880 - 1949)

Born in Australia in 1880, Mayo studied logic and philosophy at St. Peter's College, Adelaide. He is the founder of the "human relations school".

He became eminent for his Hawthorn Experiments. These had significant impact on managment thought. Experiments were conducted in the Hawthorn plant of the Western Electric Company in Chicago. The Hawthorn studies (1927-1932) can be divided into three general phases : Test Room Studies, Interviewing Studies and Observation Studies.

**Test Room Studies** assessed the effects of single variables upon employee performance and were experimental in nature.

**Interviewing Studies** were largely concerned with improving employee attitudes and were psychological in nature.

Observation studies were carried on to understand and describe the factors influencing the informal organisation of work groups and were sociological in nature.

The above studies known as the Hawthorn studies led to certain conclusions as follows :

(1) Environmental factors are not the sole factors affecting productivity.

(2) "The worker is no mere 'economic man' motivated solely by the pay cheque" *(Dickson)*.

(3) It is the sense of security, recognition, morale and belonging that is of crucial importance in increasing productivity of the worker.

(4) There is significant impact of social informal group on the attitude of the workers towards work performance. The studies revealed that of the human factors influencing an employee's attitudes and sentiments, the most powerful are those arising from his participation in a social group.

(5) Workers respond to their **total work situation and social relations, they** are an important part of this total situation.

(6) "Comments and criticisms made by workers may often be best regarded as manifestations of other deeper or more basic dissatisfaction about their changing status or lack of recognition." *(David Ashton)*.

Other conclusions of Mayo's researches are :

(7) Work is a group activity.

(8) The social demands determine a worker's attitudes and effectiveness.

(9) Group collaboration does not occur by accident; it must be planned for and developed.

The Hawthorn studies are regarded as "a milestone and a turning point" in the history of man at work and in the path of research in industrial psychology and industrial sociology.

These experiments attempted to determine what factors largely influenced efficiency and productivity of the working groups. His contributions, though criticised as being management biased and lacking the wider social content, have been described by Urwick and Brech as important as a text-book on the practice of Management in regard to the essential human process.

Though Hawthorn studies have been considered as very commendable contribution to management thought, Mayo could not escape scathing criticisms from some distinguished thinkers on management. Their criticisms were on the following lines :

(i) Pro-management bias
(ii) Clinical bias
(iii) Omission of wider social content
(iv) Under-estimation of the importance of theory
(v) Not a scientific enquiry
(vi) Doubtful validity of conclusions
(vii) True but irrelevant conclusions
(viii) Studies are true but obvious
(ix) Conclusions cannot be carried far from the factory level
(x) Trade Unions have not been given any importance
(xi) Changes in the class and occupational structure of America had not been taken into account
(xii) "The belief in man as an end in himself has been ground under by the machine and the social science of the factory researchers is not a science of man, but a cow-sociology"
*(The Social Psychology of Industry).*

To conclude the main contributions of the Hawthrone studies are: (1) Human Relations Approach (2) Non-Economic Awards (incentives) (3) Personal counselling (4) Informal group and (5) Teaching and practice of industrial management.

The net result of the experiments carried on by Mayo was to build up constructive leadership both in the plant and in the office. Joseph L. Massie observed : "The overall impact of Hawthron experiment was to challenge the non-motivational concept of the scientific management school." The worker was no longer merely an extension of his machine but a complete human being whose social, psychological and personal needs required attention from management. The studies revealed that major productivity gains might be achieved through an improved understanding of the human factor in organisation" *(Essentials of Management).*

# PART I

# MARKETING MANAGEMENT

*"While great devices are invented in the laboratory, great products are invented in the marketing department."* **(William Daidor)**

*"There is a wide chasm between an invention and an innovation. Too many wonderful laboratory products are greated with yawns or laughs. The job of marketeers is to 'think customer' and to guide companies and non-profit organisations into developing offers that are meaningful and attractive to target customers."* **(P. Kotler)**

# CHAPTER 1

## MARKETING

In the organisation of a business unit, marketing occupies an important position, from the traditional concept of marketing as the efforts effecting transfer in ownership of goods and care for their physical distribution, marketing in its modern concept means, "............... the creation of a customer". Customer–creation is the identification of consumer needs and organising the business to meet these needs.

To know about marketing and its management stipulates the precondition of a little knowledge or understanding of the global economy. We are giving farewell to the twentieth century and stepping in the threshold of the twentyfirst century with profound changes in the economic environment of the world. In the global market, the emergence of the Far East, the development of a European Common Market, the political reforms in Eastern Europe and South Africa, the manifestation of weaknesses of state-controlled economy — all these world phenomena have impact on marketing and its management. Marketing is such a wide connotation that any event — social, political and economic in any part of the globe — has to be reckoned with while discussing marketing.

A perceptible change in the trend of marketing has set in. Fragmentation of mass markets, adoption of single channel distribution system, buying direct through catalogues, the gradual ineffectiveness of conventional advertising etc. are the features that have become the concern of the marketing management today.

Marketing management does not confine its activity to increasing the volume of sales only; rather, today's marketing management is more concerned with customer relationships based on delivering quality, service and value.

In today's competitive world, market-oriented thinking is a necessity. In the current global marketing environment, there is an abundance of goods for which customers are not many in number. These global gluts in several products, at least, have made it a trying job for the marketing management. While a few companies all over the world, today, are trying to expand the size of the market, quite a good number of companies are competing to enlarge their share of the existing market. "As a result, there are winners and losers. The losers are those who bring nothing special to the market. The winners are those who carefully analyse needs, identify opportunities and create value-laden offers for target customer groups that competitors can't match". *(P. Kolter)*

### A few definitions of Marketing

1. "Marketing — which is frequently referred to as 'distribution by businessmen' – includes all the steps or activities necessary to place tangible goods in the consumers' hands, excluding only such activities as involve a significant change in the form of the goods. In other words, it does not include those activities of manufacture and agriculture which result in the tangible goods themselves" (Marketing – Principles and Methods by Phillips and Duncan).

2. "......... a philosophy of business which states that the customers' want-satisfaction is the economic and social qualification for a firm's existence" (Fundamentals of Marketing by W. Stanton).

3. "Marketing is the business process by which products are matched with the markets and through which transfers of ownership are effected" (Cundiff and Still).

4. "......... a customer-oriented philosophy or business which focuses all corporate resources on the profitable production of customer satisfaction" (Eugene Kelley and Edward Kane).

5. "Marketing involves the design of the products acceptable to the consumers and the conduct of those activities which facilitate the transfer of ownership between sellers and buyers" (Harry L. Hansen).

6. "Marketing is a social and managerial process by which individuals and groups obtain what they need and want through creating, offering, and exchanging products of value with others" *(P.Kotler)*.

7. "Marketing is the art of creating and satisfying customers at a profit"

8. "Marketing is getting the right goods and services to the right people at the right places at the right time at the right price with the right communications and promotion" *(P. Kotler)*.

9. "Marketing is the process by which an organisation relates creatively, productively and profitably to the market place" *(P. Kotler)*.

**Production-oriented approach of the definition of marketing has now been replaced by consumer-oriented approach. It is not simply a physical process but it represents a philosophy of business. The definition given above (No. 5) is a clear indication to that direction.**

Two things are significant in marketing: (1) The matching of an article of trade with markets i.e. customer needs, wants and desires; (2) The transfer of ownership and possession at every stage in the flow of goods from the primary producer to the ultimate customer. Thus, the functions like product development, packaging, standardisation, grading, marketing research, advertising, personal selling, public relations etc. all have a bearing on the present and potential demands of the product and services and are covered by the broad term "marketing".

**In short, marketing is a process or a system of business designed to plan, price, promote and distribute want-satisfying products and services to the present and potential customers i.e., industrial users or ultimate consumers.**

## Differences between Selling & Marketing

1. Marketing precedes production; selling follows production.
2. Marketing is consumer-oriented whereas selling is production-based.
3. In marketing the consumer is the king and production is carried on to meet his needs. In selling, there is no attempt to satisfy customers, whatever is produced can be sold easily.
4. In marketing, the thrust is on the needs of the consumer; in selling, the thrust is on the immediate needs of the seller.
5. Market research, demand forecasting, planning of the product etc. precede marketing but no such activity is are necessary for selling.
6. Keeping in view long-term interests, marketing promotes respective sales and extends the market but in selling only short term interests and quick profit earning are taken into consideration.

## Importance of Marketing

Marketing, as it means today, is consumer-oriented. To serve the consumer needs after carefully and scientifically carrying on market research, the process of marketing continues. A well-conceived plan precedes marketing. Marketing is not an economic activity that can only be considered significant for a producer; but the vital role that marketing plays today in the economy of a country establishes the fact that modern economic development is to depend much on the marketing functions of industrial units. **The role of marketing as a catalyst of economic development in a developing country like ours is very much important.**

## Marketing is important, because :

1. Both agriculture and industry need marketing. In an agriculture-predominant country like India, the marketing of agricultural products occupies a vital position in the economic development of the country. Specialised marketing procedure has to be followed and here the

importance of marketing cannot be over-exaggerated. Agro-based industries depend on marketing of agricultural produces either through indigenous or organised commodity markets to develop themselves. There is, then, a very close link between agriculture and industry. Industrial products reach the agriculture population through marketing and vice versa. Marketing, thus, establishes a continuous flow of goods between the urban and rural population.

2. Marketing reaches today the remotest corner of a country. By creating customers, as marketing means today, a wide demand is created for products as a consequence of which production has to be carried-on, on a large scale. Mass production and mass distribution are the characteristics of modern economy. Marketing is the cause for making it possible.

3. Marketing benefits the society by studying customer needs, wants and desires. It is for the new concept of marketing that consumers' interest is so much looked after and their needs are properly taken care of.

4. Today's marketing is based on product planning and development to make merchandising more effective.

5. Marketing has made it possible to take an integrated view of business operations by indicating interdependence of different departments of a business organisation.

6. Marketing confers various social benefits such as employment, stability of price and, through advertising, education and culture.

7. Non-business institutions like schools, colleges, hospitals etc. are also benefited from the marketing operations. The principles and techniques of marketing can be applied with benefit in these institutions where marketing helps in propagating the causes of the institutions more effectively.

8. Marketing plays a special role in a developing country by promoting its economic growth through proper assessment of the country's requirement, better planning of products and production, better procurement of inputs and distribution of goods and services.

9. In the over-all economic development of a country, marketing has a very significant role to play. It encourages export promotion and generates an atmosphere of healthy competition in both production and distribution.

10. Marketing leads to better utilisation of social resources.

# CHAPTER 2

## MARKETING PROCESS

Marketing is a process. The process covers — (1) Marketing agencies or channels of distribution, (2) Marketing functions, (3) Flow of goods to satisfy market demand and (4) The marketing management.

Three main activities are involved in marketing. They are : Concentration, Dispersion and Equalisation. Middlemen carry on these activities and the process continues. The process starts with marketing research which aims at knowing the customer-demand through market analysis and investigation.

Marketing functions constitute the second part of the marketing process. The functions are performed in the marketing channels. These are channels of distribution and these constitute the third component of marketing process. Marketing agencies are also a component of the marketing process since the marketing management has to operate through marketing agencies.

Marketing management occupies a unique position in the process of marketing. It is the integral part of the whole process of marketing. Management has special functions to do – planning, organising, co-ordinating, controlling etc. On various problems on marketing, the management has to take decisions. So, whatever elements or activities are there in the marketing process, the entire process will stop functioning if the marketing management is not geared up to act.

### Marketing functions

In the process of marketing, marketing functions constitute one of its activities. These functions may be classified on different bases and the authorities are not unanimous as to these classifications. The list of various functions ranges from 5 to as many as 20 or 30.

In 'Marketing Principles', Pyle classifies marketing functions into two – Concentrating and Dispersing.

These two divisions of the Marketing process can be sub-divided, according to Pyle, as follows :

**Concentrating :** (a)Buying or assembling (b) Transporting (c) Storing (d) Grading (e) Financing and (f) Risk bearing.

**Dispersing :** (a) Selling (b) Transporting (c) Storing (d) Grading (e) Financing (f) Risk bearing and (g) Dividing.

In concentrating process, there is buying , whereas, in dispersing process, there is selling. Besides, in dispersing, 'dividing' gets into the process of marketing.

The more widely accepted classification of marketing functions has been given by Clark and Clark (Principles of Marketing).

Marketing functions : (a) Functions of Exchange (b) Functions of physical supply and (c) Facilitating functions.

(a) Functions of Exchange :

(i) Selling

(ii) Buying

(b) Functions of physical supply :

(i) Transportation

(ii) Storage

(c) Facilitating functions :

(i) Financing

(ii) Risk-taking

(iii) Market information

(iv) Standardisation.

We discuss the functions below :

### 1. Buying and Assembling

Buying is the first step in the marketing process. After buying raw materials, the manufacturers convert them into finished products. Wholesalers buy finished products from the manufacturers, the retailers buy from the wholesalers and ultimately consumers buy – thus the process starts functioning – marketing is on.

Assembling involves creation and maintenance of the stock of the goods purchased from one seller only. Buying from different sellers will involve not only assembling but also collecting. Thus, buying and assembling are two distinct processes.

Buying involves – determination of the needs as to the kind, quality, quantity of goods, selection of proper source of supply, carrying on negotiations with the supplier etc. Buying of goods may be by inspection, by sample and by description. All these activities involved in buying are not so simple. They require specialised knowledge and all these activities are usually carried through a centralised purchasing department.

### 2. Selling

Selling constitutes the most important function of marketing. The sellers, the consumers and the general public – all are equally involved in the good or the bad of the selling operations. Business has the ultimate object of profit-earning and, unless sales are effected, surplus cannot be created; so the prime object of a business is to sell. It is said that buying and selling constitute the critical area of a business. The importance of selling is increasing because today's mass production necessitates mass selling. Selling has different modes to operate : personal selling, sales by advertisement, sales by inspection, sales by sample and sales by description. Whatever may be the method of selling, the selling technique has now undergone a profound change and a separate department exclusively for dealing in sales is organised in every concern.

### 3. Transportation

Transportation creates place utility. The place of production is not necessarily the place of consumption. Goods have to be transported – carried from one place to another. Raw materials have to be carried, crops have to be carried, finished products have to be carried – so everywhere there is the need for transportation in the process of marketing. Marketing is inconceivable without transport facility. Mass production has enhanced the need for transportation for the collection of raw material and distribution of finished products. Transportation by facilitating warehousing also creates time utility. From the place of production to the place of storage, goods are transported.

### 4. Storage

Storage invests goods with both time and place utilities. Mass production cannot be expected to be consumed instantly on production, goods have to be stored. Waiting for the opportune moment to release the goods to the market is necessary and here is the need for storage. Storage helps in stabilising price by preventing seasonal fluctuation in prices of many agricultural commodities. It, thus, creates balance between demand and supply through time. "It is true that if transportation and communication define the length and breadth of the market area, then storage gives depth to the market. The importance of warehouses is increasing because of the necessity for storage. Private and public warehouses are operating to meet the needs of storage. The growth of warehouses in large number is a definite proof for the growing need of storage.

### 5. Financing

Financing is an ancillary of marketing but there is no doubt that the function is important. It is not conceivable how the marketing process will continue without finance. In all the activities involved in marketing, finance is required. Whether it is for production, selling or stock keeping, expenditure has to be incurred – finance will be required. Finance is needed both for fixed assets and current assets, i.e. both fixed and working capitals are necessary. For the manufacturer, fixed capital is required for his factory, plant and machinery and working capital is required for the purchase of raw materials and other current expenditure to keep the organisation going. Finance needed is procured either from the owner's own source or he can take loan for financing his business. There are various sources of finance. Commercial banks and Government financial institutions are playing a dominant role in the matter of finance besides other agencies in the public and in the private sectors. Trade credit is also an important source for the provision of working capital to the marketing enterprises.

### 6. Risk taking

Risks are inherent in any activity of marketing. Risks arise out of unforeseen circumstances; so they are not always predictable but the fact remains that risks are always there in a business, no matter what type of activity it is carrying on. Risks arise out of serious hazards such as theft, burglary, forgery etc., and out of personal disabilities such as illness, injury etc. There are risks also in transportation of goods and in the shipment of goods. Risks are also there in the decay, deterioration and accidents. A serious risk in marketing is the fluctuations in the prices of the commodities due to maladjustment between supply and demand.

So, the risks may be classified as — time risk, place risk, risk of changes in demand, risk of competition, political risk, risk of interdependence (highly specialised processes of production and distribution are inter-linked) and other risks.

Risks and uncertainty are two basic features of business. So they are, where business is. But with careful and scientific analysis of the market-conditions and through market research and also with sufficient foresight into the market forces, risks may be avoided to a large extent undoubtedly. In organised markets, such as in the commodity exchanges, hedging operations enable the speculators to guard against risks of loss.

### 7. Standardisation, grading and branding

#### Standardisation

Standardisation provides "ethical basis" for the marketing transactions. It "involves the determination of basic limits or grades, an establishment of model processes and methods of producing, handling and selling goods and services". Consumers expect a certain standard of products and, to conform to this standard, standardisation is necessary. In manufactured and industrial goods, standardisation does not pose any problem but in case of natural products such as vegetables, fruits etc. uniformity of quality is impossible and wide variations in their size and quality are found. In such cases, the principle of standardisation has to be applied in terms of grades.

#### Grading

Grading is "the process of sorting individual specimens of a given product to the standard grades or classes to which they belong". It is an important function of marketing. On the basis of certain standards, grading has to be done and the standard is the measure that is generally accepted as having fixed value. Grading may be fixed or variable. In fixed grading system, different grades are kept at some fixed levels and no changes are made from time to time. In case of variable grading system, "the weights of the grading factors may be varied to take account of changes in the general quality of the supply coming on the market".

Grading offers **advantages** such as easy selling by sample, easy marketing, and reduction of the cost of marketing. Grading helps the businessmen to use their graded goods as a good collateral security. Transportation and storage costs are also reduced due to grading since the graded goods can be easily transported. Insurance claims against the loss of graded goods can be settled more easily. Grading also helps future trading as graded goods only can be traded in future markets. Grading also provides the ethical basis in marketing.

Grading has its limitations. All goods cannot be graded and even graded goods do not always conform to the standards.

#### Branding

In today's marketing, branding is imperative. Mass production and mass selling need a brand name, trade mark or a trade name. Branding is naming a product to distinguish it from other products of similar nature. It reflects a standard of quality. A particular brand of a product of a manufacturer may be advertised in its brand name. So, advertising becomes easier. Branding also encourages improvement in the quality of the product, otherwise a particular brand of a product cannot be popular. We choose many articles of daily consumption on the basis of their brands. There are so many brands of toilet soap, detergent powder, cigarettes etc. We prefer some of these articles simply on the basis of their brands and we need not feel any difficulty in purchasing when we name the brand. Branding, actually, creates some sort of monopoly discriminating in nature. We distinguish between goods on the basis of their brands because certain brands have proved their worth and they are of great demand. Branding creates product differentiation.

Branding ensures uniform standard, enables the manufacturers to push their products in the market and eliminates middlemen in many cases from the channels of distribution. Branding also helps reduction in price of the product as the producer can maintain the resale price of the branded goods. Dealers need not be paid higher commissions for selling the popular branded goods and thus the price is reduced.

### 8. Market information

Market information, in modern marketing, is indispensable for the producers. Various information — such as the number of consumers and their location, their purchasing power, their preferences and prejudices, their motivations etc. — are very vital in the marketing of products. Data have, therefore, to be collected before actual marketing operation starts. Nothing now-a-days is done blindfolded. On the basis of the available market information, the whole plan has to be chalked up for marketing a product. Various sources are exploited for collecting market information – internal as well as external. Governments, trade associations and other relevant agencies also supply market information. Big organisations have their own market research methods for collecting information. Market intelligence is now a sure course of action before launching the actual marketing programme.

### 9. Marketing research

Marketing research is "the systematic gathering, recording and analysing of data about problems relating to the marketing of goods and services". This definition is not comprehensive. A more detailed description of Marketing research will include collection, analysis and interpretation of data for **helping marketing manager to arrive at a decision.** This is the goal of marketing research which is missing in the first definition. Marketing research includes product research, market research, sales policy research and sales promotion policy research. Marketing research is assuming importance because of the expansion of the market, time lag between production and consumption owing to mass production and mass consumption and, also, ever-changing character of the market. A complete knowledge about the market which is to be catered to must be acquired by the marketing management to be successful in the consumer-oriented market today.

### 10. Packaging

"A package is used to contain, protect and identify a product". Packaging is a very useful function of marketing because products are to be protected from deterioration and exposure during storage, transportation and use.

Packaging may make a product more attractive and may thus enhance its marketability. The package communicates product information by means of labelling. Packages are sometimes regarded as 'silent salesmen'. Package introduces customer to the rest of the members in the product line. It acts as a link between advertising and points of purchase display.

Importance of packaging is felt in more than one way. Packaging helps in building a favourable image for the firm and it is to a great extent for packaging that the sale is increased, transport cost is reduced, handling of the product is facilitated and there can be ecomonical use of the floor space.

### 11. Product planning and development

To satisfy customer needs, products should be according to specifications of the consumers. A consumer-oriented product policy has to be followed. So product planning is essential. Products should be so planned by the marketing management personnel that they can satisfy the needs of the consumers. Product planning and development is continuous on the part of the management who are with the marketing operation. To improve the quality of the products, planning is always carried on and thus in the marketing functions, product planning and development is a continuous process and not an one-time job. The changing tastes of the consumers necessitate the product quality to be improved and modified.

Besides the functions discussed here, there are functions like pricing, advertising and sales promotion which are also very important.

Proper pricing of the products is a compulsion for the producer. An improper pricing may lead to the ouster of the products from the market or heavy loss for the organisation. Whatever is produced has to be advertised either to create a new market for it or maintain the market for an old product. Efforts must be made in all conceivable ways to promote sales. There are various ways of sales promotion and the methods of sales promotion are chosen after considering various factors operating in the market.

## Product Life Cycle

A product life can be compared with a human life. The life cycle of a product is similar to that of a man. A man is born, grows, matures and then decays. So also the case with a product : a product is born, grows, attains a maturity and then enters its declining phase. The natural law of human life applies to the product-life also. What is born is sure to die. If a product is born, it is to die also — the death of a product is its declining stage. Then the product is abandoned just like the human body. When the human life ceases to exist, the body is abandoned.

Every product moves through the cycle of introduction, growth, maturity and decline. The life cycle stages of a product are described below :

**1. Introduction stage :** A product is born i.e. produced. To introduce it in the market, advertising is resorted to. Various promotional measures are adopted. This stage is very important in the life of a product. While advertising and sales promotion techniques are being followed, weaknesses may come out requiring prompt remedy. At this stage of a product, huge expenditure may have to be incurred.

**2. Growth Stage :** A product is to face competition at this stage. But even in the face of competition, efforts shall have to be made to effect more and more sales. At this stage, sales get first preference. To ensure a steady growth, there should be manufacturing and distribution efficiency. They are vital for marketing success.

**3. Maturity stage :** When a product reaches the maturity stage in its life cycle, it faces keen competition. The producer may have to compromise with falling price and increasing marketing expenditure. Gradually supply is geared up and it exceeds demand. When such a situation develops, the producer will have to stimulate demand. New markets for the product will have to be developed to prevent the decline.

**4. Decline stage :** The last stage in the life cycle of a product — the decline stage — comes when the saturation point is reached. The inevitability of the product declines. New innovations may be responsible for the decline. At this stage, sales of the product drop, competition dwindles and price becomes the weapon to combat competition. Expenses on advertising and sales promotion are reduced.

# CHAPTER 3

## MARKETING MANAGEMENT — ITS SCOPE AND NATURE

The functional area of business management which looks after marketing functions is Marketing Management. The Management is primarily responsible for the smooth flow of goods and services from the producers to the consumers. "It is the management function which organises and directs all those business activities involved in assessing and converting customer purchasing power into effective demand for a specific product or service and in moving the product or service to the final consumer or user so as to achieve the profit target or other objectives set by a Company". (U. K. Institute of Marketing). "Marketing (management) is the process of planning and executing the conception, pricing, promotion and distribution of ideas, goods and services to create exchanges that satisfy individual and organisational objectives" (American Marketing Association). The second definition considers marketing management as a process which involves analysis, planning, implementation and control of ideas, goods and services. It rests on the notion of exchange and the goal is to produce satisfaction for the parties involved. An organisation is to deal with various markets such as labour market, raw materials market, money market and customer market. Marketing management is connected with any of these markets, though historically marketing management is identified with tasks and personnel dealing with the customer market.

We mean marketing management with reference to customer market. The marketing work in the customer market is the team work of sales managers, sales people, market managers, marketing researchers, advertising managers, product managers etc. These people have their specific and well defined responsibilities and the nature of their tasks differs from one to another. The marketing manager, who is the focal point of our discussion on marketing management, is primarily concerned with the stimulation of demand for the company's products. "However, this is too limited a view of the diversity of marketing tasks performed by marketing managers. Marketing management has the task of influencing the level, timing and composition of demand in a way that will help the organization achieve its objectives. Marketing management is essentially demand management". (*P. Kotler*).

As to the **scope** of marketing management, we can say that the target market is ascertained and then an idea of a desired level of transactions at the market has to be formed. The actual demand level of the market may be of different states — weak, adequate, excessive etc. Marketing management, it is said, has to cope with **eight** different states of demand. This is done through marketing research, planning, implementation and control.

All managerial functions in the field of marketing are within the scope of marketing management. Product planning and development, market planning or marketing mix, formulation of marketing policies – all come within the purview of marketing management. Simply stated, marketing management plans, organises, directs and controls the activities of people of the marketing division of a business unit for the purpose of achieving certain objectives. The objectives are : increased sales and development of new markets. The overall objectives of a business concern, profit and growth of the business unit are achieved through the endeavours of the marketing management. In its effort to ensure the fulfilment of its objectives, the marketing management has "to evaluate continuously the effectiveness of each part of the marketing mix and introduce necessary alterations and modifications to remove discrepancies and deficiencies discovered in the actual execution of all marketing plans, policies and procedures".

Marketing management may be said to have a special characteristic that it has to deal with persons (consumers) who are outside the organisation. The personnel management deals with men within the organisation but not with the outsiders whose behaviour the marketing management has to watch keenly; particularly so in the present day consumer-oriented marketing. Considering this aspect of marketing management, we can say that this area management is more difficult than other functional areas of management.

### Importance of Marketing Management

To manage is to plan, organise, direct and control. To manage marketing is, therefore, to plan, organise, direct and control all the marketing operations of a business unit.

Marketing is a concept which is consumer-oriented. We should not confuse it with selling. When whatever is produced is sold — it is selling. But in marketing, there is the difficult task of **creating customers.** When the management is to make efforts to convert potential customers into present customers, when the management is to go through series of activities to expand market for the products of the business unit — it is marketing management.

Selling whatever is produced and creating customers – then to sell; makes a considerable difference.

In Marketing management, the area of the functional management is such that a large number of factors outside the control and jurisdiction of the business unit have to be managed.

Financial management plans for proper utilisation of the finance procured; personnel management plans for the men who work in the organisation, production management procures raw materials and concentrates on production more or less on preplanned way – the factors are not so changing but Marketing management is to deal with people who are scattered, whose tastes, fashions, moods, purchasing power etc. are constantly changing. There are many unforseeable and unpredictable factors with which the marketing management has to work.

Besides the operative side of the management which we discussed because management is, after all, a functional concept; the matter is that a business unit's ultimate goal is to make profit which, in its turn, depends on sales and turnover. So, it is on the marketing management of a business unit that the realisation of the ultimate goal of the organisation is depending.

In the changed concept of marketing and in the changing world economy acting upon the market conditions, Marketing management has been experiencing more and more complications in dealing with the marketing forces.

The importance of marketing management can well be appreciated if we take into account the fact that on the successful performance of the marketing activities the success of a business unit depends. The whole range of marketing activities – right from product planning up to the stage of finally placing the products in the hands of the consumers — is within the purview of marketing management. All these activities are themselves very difficult to perform, they have their technicalities – product planning and development, buying, selling, advertising, packing, branding, pricing – all these activities are individually like one managing the finance or the personnel of a business unit.

Marketing management is not only to be equipped with the intricacies of human beings as is required in case of personnel management, but also the management (marketing) must be endowed with the gift of foresightedness, which is imperative for success in marketing management.

The significance and importance of marketing management has been increasing steadily with the ever-increasing competition in the market coupled with the need for catering to the international market. Marketing management has become a tough activity and is now a science with ingredients of art inherent in it. "Marketing management today is a subject of growing interest in all sizes and types of organisations within and outside the business sector in all kinds of countries". ***(Kotler).***

# CHAPTER 4

## SALES ORGANISATION

In Marketing management, sales organisation forms the core function. Selling is a critical area of business and the management of this functional area is the task of the sales personnel. The sales organisation of a business has to be built up on solid foundation of judicious judgement of the top management personnel. It is no exaggeration to say that all efforts of a business enterprise will be a futile exercise unless the sales organisation is effective to promote sales.

The concept of selling is here used in a broad sense to include the marketing concept. All that is necessary to organise sales and ultimately to effect sales are considered to come under the purview of the sales organisation. It plans, co-ordinates, directs and controls the entire sales mechanism to reach the ˊ ˋles target of the business unit.

In the modern management concept, all areas of functional management of a business unit have to be coordinated in such a harmonious way that the goals and objectives of the business are achieved through concerted efforts. So, Sales management or Marketing management, so to say, cannot be expected to function in isolation of other functional areas of management to achieve its purpose.

The Sales Manager is the pivot of the sales organisation, set up to motivate the sales personnel to reach the sales target. The responsibilities and the functions of a modern Sales Manager are very wide and complicated. They cover a wide range of area — right from the idea of the product mix up to the planning of marketing mix. An eye to the market forward and an eye to the organisation behind, the Sales Manager discharges his responsibilities and performs his functions. His is forward-looking and backward-looking responsibilities. With the experiences gained in the past, he builds up his plans and programmes in the present with an eye to the future. A Sales Manager must be a man of vision as well as a man with a strong sense of pragmatic approach to solve problems confronting his sales organisation. So wide and complicated are the functions of the Sales Manager that it is well nigh impossible to give a detailed description of his functions.

### Sales Manager – Functions and Responsibilities

A Sales Manager's functions and responsibilities being too broad, extensive and exhaustive, we discuss below his principal functions and responsibilities :

1. To interpret the sales policy adopted by the top management personnel to the sales personnel. This duty of the Sales Manager actually is basic on which his other duties depend.
2. To plan, organise and control his department and its activities.
3. To maintain coordination with other functional areas of management. Cooperation between the departments is important for effective sales management.
4. To discharge the duties of a liaison officer in the sense that the Sales Manager maintains touch with the top management, propagates the management policy to his sales staff and

keeps other departments informed about what has been going on in his department because, ultimately, it is for sales — either of goods or services — that the activities of all departments are being carried on.

5. To train and supervise the sales personnel constitutes one of the main functions of the Sales Manager.
6. To see that all records of the firm's sales activities are maintained properly.
7. To prepare the sales budget for its incorporation in the main budget.
8. To ensure continuous flow of goods or services to the market, the sales manager keeps a constant watch over the stock-level and takes necessary steps to replenish stock as and when necessary.
9. To undertake territory planning after careful consideration of the effectiveness of different channels of distribution.
10. To collect and analyse the necessary market information.
11. To maintain contact with the salesmen since he is supposed to be their leader.
12. To confer with the salesmen, to give them necessary instructions and to motivate them to implement the instructions, constitute important functions of a modern sales manager.
13. To discharge his routine functions such as making tenders and quotations, handling daily correspondences, dealing with complaints and arranging for filing the papers relevant to his department.
14. To coordinate the function of his different departments, dealing with administrative matters, operational matters and public relations.

To sum up, we can say that the functions of a Sales Manager cannot be clearly distinguished from the functions of a marketing manager and thus the Sales Manager's functions overlap the functions of the marketing manager if strictly analysed. But in an organisation, it is generally found that either one Sales Manager or a marketing manager is in charge of the entire sales organisation, including marketing. So, right from the planning of the product up to the stage of placing the goods or services at the disposal of the consumer, every managerial function comes within the purview of the Sales Manager's functions and responsibilities.

To sum up, a Sales Manager's functions include : sales forecasting and planning, organising, directing, motivating and controlling the sales force and co-ordinating the work of subordinates.

# CHAPTER 5

## SALES MANAGEMENT

In the modern concept of marketing management, Sales management is clearly distinguished from marketing management. Marketing management is used in a comprehensive sense covering a wide range of activities in which is included Sales management. So, Sales management is a part of the whole – the whole denoting marketing management. To be more specific, Sales management is for the management of the sales personnel. An authentic definition given below will make the concept clear :

"Sales management is the planning, direction and control of the personal selling activities of a business unit, including recruiting, selecting, training, equipping, assigning, rating, supervising, paying and motivating as these tasks apply to the sales force". (Definitions Committee of the American Marketing Association).

### Sales Forecasting

Sales forecasting is estimating the expected sales for a specific period. It has been defined as an estimate of sales of physical units for a specified future period under a proposed marketing plan or programme and under an assumed set of economic and other forces outside the unit for which the forecast is made.

The forces behind sales forecasting may be external as well as internal. External forces imply the over-all business situation, market trends in the price level, population growth, Government policy, technological progress and such other factors on which the firm has no control. The internal force relates to the price of the product, its quality, advertising, distribution and service which are controllable.

Sales forecasting can be made by different methods or adopting different approaches.

**Statistical methods** covering — Time series, demand and correlation analysis and econometric models are used as tools of forecasting. **Market tests** is another approach to sales forecasting. **Assessment of opinion** of sales force, executives, and outside experts is found to be a very realistic approach to sales forecasting. Projection of past sales is also an indicator of future sales and thus it helps sales forecasting. In recent years, buyers' intention ascertained through face-to-face interviews is becoming fruitful in sales forecasting. It is no less important for sales forecasting to ascertain the extent of its holding in the market. Today's **market survey procedure** helps a producer to know how much is his share of the market i.e. how much of the total sales of a particular product in the market he sells. This can very will guide him to forecast for the future.

The importance of sales forecasting cannot be over-exaggerated. Some authorities put it as the foundation for planning all phases of a firm's operation. Sales forecasting helps a firm to attain many useful purposes some of which are production planning, balancing supply with demand, allocation of sales quotas and territories, the pricing of products and the preparation of budgets. It also helps in developing coordinated and goal oriented marketing programmes.

## Promotion

**The most important component of the marketing mix is promotion. Promotion is necessary after the product is made ready for sale. It is a fact that in spite of the quality of the product, it cannot be sold unless some promotional activities are adopted. Promotion is rightly called 'the spark plug' of the marketing mix. It is said that "nothing happens until somebody sells something". Here lies the importance and significance of promotion and the role that it plays in the marketing management.**

Promotion implies a process of marketing communication involving information, persuasion and influence. All means of communication with customers as well as middlemen are promotional activities. There are various media to establish such communcations such as advertising, personal selling, special sales promotion methods—sampling, composing etc.

As **ingredients** of promotion we can name – personal selling or salesmanship, advertising and publicity and sales promotion.

Personal selling is face-to-face communication; advertising is impersonal salesmanship and sales promotion — being consumer and dealer sales promotion — may take the forms of educating, informing and stimulating consumer as well as dealer interest and enthusiasm.

The main purpose of promotion is to change the location and shape of the demand curve for the product. All promotional efforts alter the demand curve by increasing the total demand for the product at every price and by altering the elasticity of demand for the product.

Thus, promotion modifies the pattern of demand for a product.

Therefore, promotional tools are : (i) Personal selling (ii) Advertising and publicity (iii) Dealers' Sales promotion and (iv) Consumers' sales promotion.

## Promotion strategies and Techniques

Promotion, to be successful, must adhere to certain strategies. Strategies, it is needless to elaborate, are all meant for ultimately increasing sales through various devices.

Promotion has, according to some authorities, four strategies known as square strategy. They are – the product, the buyer, the firm and the channel.

Product development, buyer story, firm image building and the proper selection of the channel of distribution are strategic points of attention of the Marketing/Sales manager. The channel selection, on its part, may be based on the push strategy or the pull strategy. In case of the push strategy, products are pushed to the customers through advertising and publicity. So much emphasis is given on advertising and publicity that the customers are ultimately to buy the products. In case of the pull strategy, the marketing depends on the intensive distribution system. When the products are much publicised, the retailers are compelled to store those products on account of pressure from his customers. This happens in case of popular branded goods.

In the narrow sense, sales promotion activities include stimulation to consumer purchasing and dealer effectiveness such as display shows and exhibitions, demonstrations and various non-recurring selling efforts not in the ordinary routine. Sales promotion does not include personal selling advertising and publicity. The ultimate object of sales promotion does not differ from that of personal selling or advertising, but the immediate objects of sales promotion may be to introduce new products, to attract new customers, to induce present customers to buy more, to increase sales in slack season etc. Dealer encouragement is one of the main functions of sales promotion. Various facilities are extended to dealers to stock goods in large quantity. Sales promotion measures are, as a matter of fact, devices to supplement advertising programmes. Effects are made under sales promotion policy to convert consumer awareness into a concrete buying decision.

Sales promotion measures are directed to follow certain techniques such as : (1) points of purchase displays (2) direct mail promotion (3) merchandising aids (4) premium (5) samples and free gifts (6) product demonstration (7) quiz for profit and pleasure etc.

Sales promotion may be classified into trade promotions and consumer promotions. The former concerns the wholesale and retail dealers and the latter, the consumers.

In 'Points of purchase Displays' technique, the product itself or its photograph is displayed in the windows or showrooms of the shop. These displays are so suggestive that they tell the customers about the product and its possible uses.

Direct mail promotion is effective through letters, charts, booklets, catalogues bulletins, calendars sent through mail.

Merchandising aids are aimed at free training to business buyers on such matters as stores control system and stores layout.

Premiums are in the form of sale at nominal price or distribution of a product free to induce buyers to buy some other products.

Quiz for Profits and Pleasure are contests organised for the purpose of increasing consumer awareness of a product. Rewards are given to winners. This is a modern technique adopted for sales promotion.

Sales promotion, in a broad sense, includes all those activities which are directed towards promoting sales – no matter whether it is advertising or personal selling. All marketing methods are resorted to in sales promotion. Besides the techniques and strategies discussed above, in recent years public relations methods are playing a very significant role in sales promotion. It has become a powerful tool in the hands of the Marketing management to boost up sales. Maintaining a cordial relationship and liaison between the enterprise and the consuming public goes a long way in the marketing of products. To win over the support of the customers, their complaints, grievances or prejudices are looked into and proper measures are taken to remedy customers' difficulties or the obstacles standing between the prospective customers and the marketing of products. Public are congratulated through advertising media for patronising the products of the business.

# CHAPTER 6

## FEATURES OF MARKETING IN INDIA

Marketing, in its new concept, means creation of customers. In India, the need for creating customers does not generally arise; customers are waiting for goods and services and whatever will be placed before them, they will accept. Goods and services are scarce in relation to demand. So **in India, it is not marketing – it is rather selling.**

The features of selling or, if we like to call it marketing, may be discussed as under :

1. In India there is the sellers' market in general. The sellers predominate over the market since demand for goods and services is more than supply.
2. The facilities for creation of place and time utilities are inadequate in the country. Transport facilities are not properly developed and the warehousing or storage facilities are also not satisfactory.
3. India being premodinantly an agricultural country, the marketing of agricultural commodities is an important consideration in marketing.
4. Marketing of agricultural commodities suffers from certain drawbacks such as poor storing facilities, distress selling by poor farmers, unsatisfactory transportation facilities, abundance of intermediaries, lack of scope for market information.
5. Sales promotion measures are not satisfactory.
6. Pricing of goods and services is not strictly in accordance with the latest techniques of pricing. Prices are generally high – the scientific basis of pricing not being followed.
7. Too many middlemen in the channel of distribution very often create various obstacles in the way of smooth flow of goods and services from the producers to the consumers.
8. Government regulatory measures over marketing are not so rigid since we very often find the creation of artificial scarcity of particular articles for sometime and the articles appear in the market subsequently with enhanced price. This cannot always be justified.
9. Public distribution system is very often disturbed.
10. There is dearth of properly trained salesmen in our country.
11. Because of lack of proper regulatory measures or effective implementation of the legislations, hoarding and blackmarketing feature prominently in Indian marketing scene.
12. In marketing in India, we do not have that standard of packing and grading that are noticed in the industrially developed countries.
13. Recent trend in Indian marketing is that publicity for goods and services is being propagated through various governmental media — T.V. and radio — besides advertising.
14. In the marketing of industrial goods, there is no marketing organisation and a few noted industrial houses have their own methods of marketing.

15. Marketing infrastructure not being present in India to the desirable extent, the government should feature prominently and in a more effective way in the marketing of agricultural as well as industrial goods, the absence of full-fledged active participation of our government in marketing is a feature of marketing in India.

16. In India, there is a regulated economy where the government has a big role to play in the marketing process. The marketing activities are carried on in India both by the private industrialists and the government.

17. Commercial advertising for marketing by the government is not so conspicuous in our country.

18. Goods suitable for India are not always produced by the producers of our country, rather they follow the models produced in advanced countries.

19. The philosophy of marketing concept does not flow from the top level of economic planning.

# CHAPTER 7

## MARKETING MIX

Marketing mix is the mixture of the essential ingredients of marketing in order to push up sales. It was Neil H. Borden who long ago made a list of 12 ingredients or elements to pursue in a marketing programme. The concept of 'marketing mix' by Borden included product planning, pricing, branding, channels of distribution, personal selling, advertising, promotion, packaging, display, servicing, physical handling and fact finding along with analysis.

Market mix today is the mixture of 4 P's – Product planning, Pricing, Physical distribution and Promotion.

Marketing manager is usually the mixer. The mixture offers an optimum combination of all marketing ingredients with a view to ensuring the realisation of the firm's goals such as profit return on investment, sales volume, market share and so on.

The ingredients in 'Marketing Mix' are not always mixed in the same proportion as it is in the case of medicine mixture. In the "Marketing Mix", the ingredients are composed of such activities which need adjustments and modifications to suit the purpose. Changing marketing conditions and changing environmental factors affect markets, so the "Marketing Mix" also has to be changed with all these changes.

Marketing Mix, as discussesd above, will indicate that the concept is a dynamic one. No definite formula of mixture can be laid down for all time to come for "Marketing Mix".

### Significance of "Marketing Mix"

The concept of introduction of "Marketing Mix" to the marketing programme of a business unit has some positive contributions. It aims at accomplishments of planned marketing goals. 'Marketing Mix', being dynamic in nature, adjusts to changes in internal as well as external factors relevant to the business. Marketing Mix, with product planning as one of its ingredients, serves consumer needs in a better way. Market-research being carried out, "Marketing Mix" acts as a powerful tool in sales promotion — the ultimate object of marketing management. In 'Marketing Mix', consumer behaviour, dealer attitude, competition and rivals' behaviour, legislative control and regulation of trade practices are taken into consideration which means **'Marketing Mix' is a scientific approach to the problems of marketing management.**

'Marketing Mix' imparts precision to the study of marketing and it is an effective remedy for the cure of various ills of marketing since any kind of marketing problem may very well be brought within the purview of the Mix. In such a 'Mix', a better utilisation of resources is possible. So, **'Marketing Mix' has immense social value.**

### Product Planning

The product is the starting point for all marketing activities. The task of product planning is categorised as — (1) the conception, development and launching of an altogether new product (2) the modification of an existing product and (3) the elimination of an old product. There are seven steps in the planning and development of a new product. They are : new product idea, idea screening, concept development and testing, business analysis, development programme, test marketing and commercialisation.

Product planning is a continuous process, dynamic in nature. It is not a type of planning where once the planning is done, it is done forever. There is the need for constant changes in the product-nature with the changes in the market conditions. Product planning is made to cope with this changing nature and a constant endeavour for development of the product continues.

In product planning, packaging and packing should also be considered.

**Packaging** is a necessity for the safety of the products. For storing and transport purposes, good packing is imperative to protect products against breakage, spoilage, leakage or pilferage. It has also become important now-a-days because of keen competition when the customer needs an effective means to recognise a difference and establish preference for the product ensuring its re-purchase. Packaging, branding and labelling go together and constitute an integral part of product-planning and development. It is a sales tool and the biggest advertising medium for establishing a good product image.

There is a **distinction between packing and packaging** — packing is for the protection of the articles and packaging is putting the articles in such boxes, bottles and cans as can be sold to consumers. A good package protects the **quality** of the articles, assures them correct weight and provides a means of using brand name.

Packing, simply stated, is for protecting the goods and packaging is to increase the attractiveness of the goods. They are complementary. Both of them are necessary to serve the purpose of selling in an effective way. Well packed goods with improved packaging can attract more customers for their convenience and attractiveness.

## Pricing

The **importance of pricing** in the whole marketing process need not be emphasised. Unless properly priced, a product will either be sold at a loss or will not be sold at all. The whole purpose of business will be frustrated and the existence of the business unit will be at stake. In a competitive market, pricing may scare away customers if it is fixed at an unduly high level.

There are **factors** that influence pricing decisions and these factors are both internal and external. Pricing policies, nature of the product, its physical distribution and promotional strategy and costs constitute internal factors while general economic climate, state of competition, customers' behaviour and psychology, government legislation and pressures by other groups influence as external factors in the determination of the price of a product.

But whatever may be the factors internal or/ and external in influencing the pricing of a product, the business unit must have some objectives besides profit maximisation in its view while pricing a product. **The objectives** are : (i) target return on investment (ii) stabilisation of price (iii) outselling the competitor (iv) obtaining targetted share of the market.

It is the general practice of a business unit to fix the price of its products in such a way that the expected or targetted return on investment is realised. There are products whose prices are subject to frequent fluctuations. It is desirable that prices remain constant for a considerable period; so the firm dealing in such products tries to fix the price at such a point that there can be minimum fluctuation in price and a long period price policy can be pursued. To keep out competitors from the field of marketing, as far as possible, is the objective of any business unit and this the business firm attempts by fixing prices at the most reasonable points. In a free competitive market, a constant endeavour is carried on to remain in the market or share the market and one of the factors that enables a producer to share a competitive market is the competitive price of his product.

## Pricing policies and strategies

In the Marketing Mix, price is a very important ingredient. Correct pricing is possible through pricing research and through the adoption of the test market techniques. A sound price-policy is very much needed for a producer. There are three alternatives in fixing the price of products —
(i) **Price in Line** (ii) **Market-Plus** (iii) **Market-Minus**.

**Price in Line policy** is based on the policy of fixing the price at current market rate of price. This policy is not always suitable to pursue. If a product is of such nature that its branding may create product-differentiation, then 'price-in-line' policy will not be to the benefit of the producer. In a market where branding creates least product differentiation, sellers and buyers are well-informed and there exists a free market economy, this policy is suitable.

**Market-Plus policy** of pricing means pricing above the market prices. This is profitable under free competition provided the product is unique, distinctive and commands prestige or status in the market. Market-Plus pricing policy among the price-conscious consumers can only be pursued if the product is of reputed brand and comes from a reputed manufacturer. Otherwise, this policy is likely to meet with failure. Price of a product is the consideration paid for various attributes of the product such as quality, durability, performance etc. So, only in the cases of high quality well branded products the policy of Market Plus pricing can be resorted to.

## Market-Minus Policy

The sale below the market price is Market-Minus Policy. This policy may be experimented with success only in limited cases such as in large chain stores, self-service stores and discount houses. Lower pricing can be taken as a substitute for sales promotion. If promotion expenses are less and the quality of the product is inferior, then only Market-Minus pricing policy can be followed. The large retailers such as chain stores etc. can sell at Market-Minus Price because of the products being well known for their nation-wide advertisement.

Right Pricing and Non-Price competition are also policies adopted to suit particular situations. Right pricing policy is market-based and suitable in a competitive market. Non-Price competition policy of pricing relies on methods other than price factors such as branding, packaging, liberal credit, advertising etc.

The **best** pricing policy in a competitive market is the **market-based method** of pricing. This will ensure normal profits.

## Basic pricing strategies

Pricing strategies can be broadly categorised as – cost-oriented, demand-oriented and competition oriented.

**Cost-oriented pricing strategy** is also known as cost-plus pricing. In such a strategy, price is fixed in such a way as to equal the costs of production and marketing, plus an amount to cover anticipated profit. This pricing strategy helps in linking it to profit. Since cost data are more or less certain and determinable in cost-oriented pricing, it is fair both to buyers and sellers and, if followed by the producers in general, it may help in the reduction of competition which is a social gain. Of course, in such a policy the demand factor is neglected and up-to-date cost data are not easily available which creates difficulty, particularly in case of joint products.

**Demand-oriented pricing strategy is** based on the demand situation. With the rise in demand, price is raised and with its fall, price also is lowered. Such a pricing policy takes into account the prevailing state of demand and takes its advantage. So it provides a safeguard against depressed market conditions; it is dynamic and flexible in nature. But as against these advantages, we can say that this pricing policy harms the reputation of the firm and there always remains a tendency to move with the wind – to have high profits during booms. This behaviour pattern of the producers may be resented by the consumers and then it becomes a social evil and chain reactions may start.

**Competition-oriented pricing** is fixing the price as the competitors do. The cost and the demand factors are not taken into consideration. Price is generally fixed below the price of the competitor or above. Such a price fixing policy helps the seller to keep out competition and this relieves the producer of the botheration of cost or demand calculation. But the system is devoid of any independence on the part of the producer. A lower price than the competitor may lead to the impression that the product is of inferior quality and a higher price may cause the loss of the market. Much time and energy is thus spent in ascertaining the policies of the competitor and, even after that, sellers cannot rest assured that the price fixed will continue for a long time.

As a matter of fact, no particular price strategy or policy is followed. Practical considerations predominate in the determination of pricing policy and strategy. Certain steps are followed before pricing a product when a number of factors are taken into consideration and then the best price is selected.

Apart from the above three basic strategies, there are many specific policies which are adopted in the matter of pricing to suit particular situations.

For introducing new products, two alternative policies are followed – Skim-the-Cream pricing and Penetration Pricing policies.

### Skim-the-Cream Price (High Pricing)

This is a pricing strategy followed in new concerns deliberately with a view to creating in the minds of the consumer the impression that the quality of the product is high. This enables the producer to build an image and to create prestige for his new product. The price is, however, lowered progressively as the product grows old. The manufacturers of drugs and synthetic products usually indulge in such a practice.

The arguments in favour of such a policy are :

1. Demand elasticity for the product at the initial stage being generally less, price becomes also less important in purchase decisions. In the case of new products, many customers do not care for price; this is a common psychology of the customer.
2. This policy is effective when entry of rivals is difficult, costs are uncertain and life-cycle is short.
3. Such a policy enables the seller to take the cream of the market for a certain period and then, if necessary, he may adopt the policy of lower pricing (penetration) for appeasing the price sensitive sections of the market.
4. High price can be lowered according to necessity and convenience but it is difficut to raise the low price.
5. It can keep the demand within the limit of productive capacity of the firm.
6. It has in it the element of flexibility.
7. It serves as a kind of hedge against possible mistake of the pricing.

The disadvantages of this pricing policy are that it attracts competition and if entry is easy, this policy proves risky. Again, the policy may harm the reputation of a firm and the severe consequence of such a policy may be the premature death of the product.

### Penetration Pricing (Low pricing)

This pricing policy is pursued where the product is of highly elastic demand. In case of mass production where the cost of production comes down and where there is the apprehension of rivals entering into the market and there is also dearth of high income group of people with better purchasing power, the penetration pricing policy is resorted to.

This pricing policy can be justified when the product has a long life cycle, mass market, elastic demand and the entry into the market is easier. The only difficulty that a seller may encounter is that he may have excess demand within a short period. Of course, the consumer may have the impression that the product is of inferior quality. Again, it may be difficult for the producer to recoup the initial developmental costs through this strategy.

### Resale Price Maintenance (RPM)

Resale price maintenance is a device whereby manufacturers dictate the prices below which their products will not be sold. It has been defined as "the stipulation by a supplier that his distributor (wholesaler) or retailer shall sell particular goods at prices fixed by him or for not less than those prices" (Allen). There may be collective resale price maintenance when the policy is undertaken by a group of manufacturers. In resale price maintenance policy, usually a maximum price is also fixed above which the product is not to be sold. For this, there may be a formal agreement or the manufacturer may have an informal understanding with the middleman. In any case, the ultiamte control lies with the supplier/manufacturer because he can always stop supplies to his customer.

The objects for which the policy is pursued are :

(i) To have a customary price for the product creating convenience for the consumers.

(ii) To prevent the middleman to charge any price he likes taking the advantages of the opportune moment.

(iii) To give particulars to the middlemen against the competition of other middlemen.

### Arguments in favour of resale price maintenance

(i) A healthy market condition prevails, when the retail price is fixed and uniform in whichever shop a consumer goes. This is a great convenience for a large number of customers who are against the policy of bargaining with the seller.

(ii) It prevents unhealthy price competition among the dealers.

(iii) It facilitates the entry of new firms as there is no fear of price war.

(iv) Loss leader selling is no problem under RPM. Well-advertised leading brands are used as loss leader deliberately by retailers. These brands are sold at a lower price to attract customers. This loss is more than compensated by gains due to additional sales of many other products. Loss leader, as a matter of fact, is a profit leader and it is a device of sales promotion.

(v) Absence of price competition offers protection to small volume high cost retailer.

(vi) New middlemen can take up distribution more easily.

## Arguments against RPM

(i) To the supplier or to the manufacturer its regular enforcement involves expense.

(ii) The manufacturer has to give assurance of a certain margin of profits to the middlemen.

(iii) Middlemen are encouraged to be inefficient since they are not to make any effort for changing price.

(iv) Complications arise if similar products are sold by the same retailer.

(v) The freedom of middlemen to sell at any price is restricted which many of them may not like.

(vi) Middlemen, irrespective of their efficiency, are put in a straight jacket. This leads to the loss of initiative on the part of the middlemen to pursue sales.

(vii) Consumers may not be benefitted by this scheme of uniformity. The price may be quite high.

(viii) The choice of consumers is restricted.

(ix) RPM policy, pursued widely, may result in restricting fair trade and may give rise to monopolistic conditions.

It is to be noted that, in India, RPM has been declared undesirable by the MRTP Act, 1969.

## Follow the Leader Policy of pricing

A new technique in pricing a product is to follow the leading firm's decision in pricing. A leading firm may control a market and its pricing policy, likely to be prudent, should be followed by others. The small firms cannot but do this. When undercutting of prices is harmful and overcharging is also not possible, such a 'follow the leader policy' is adopted. The adoption of such a policy of pricing makes the market free of competition. A firm promotes its sales through advertising, sales promotion and other media.

## Charging what the Traffic will bear

Professional men adopt this policy of pricing their services. Doctors, lawyers etc. charge the price of their services considering the ability of the customers. The needs and the resources of the customers are taken into account. Cost factor does not dominate the pricing policy. This policy is suitable where the product is unique in its nature. However, this pricing policy, based on the ability of customers to pay, does not find favour with the consumers in general.

## Psychological pricing

Psychological pricing is also known as odd pricing. This is pricing at odd figures, such as Rs. 19.95 or Rs. 29 etc. It is used to secure a positive buying behaviour from the customers. It is believed that the pricing works nice psychologically. Where a product is priced at Rs. 19.95 and not at Rs. 20, it may attract more customers. This pricing policy is followed by Bata Shoe Company. But we do not feel that this pricing in any way convinces the buyer that the price is attractive. It simply evokes laughter. It is not an effective pricing system.

# CHAPTER 8

## PHYSICAL DISTRIBUTION (of products)

### (Marketing Channels)

In the "Marketing Mix", physical distribution is a very important element or ingredient. The distribution of products physically takes place through channels. A **channel of distribution** in the field of marketing refers to the set of marketing institutions through which a manufacturer gains access to the target market for his products. Intra-company organisation units and extra-company agents and dealers - wholesale and retail — through which products are marketed constitute the channel of distribution. The marketing intermediaries, therefore, make up a distribution channel, also known as a marketing channel. These channels are "sets of interdependent organisations involved in the process of making a product or service available for use or consumption". *(Sten and Ansary).*

On the basis of their nature, channels may be - merchant middlemen, agents and facilitators.

On the basis of the number of intermediaries, channels may be - Zero-level, one-level, two-level and three-level.

Philip Kotler, in his 'Marketing Management', has classified the **major functions of marketing channels** as (1) Research (2) Promotion (3) Contact (4) Matching (5) Negotiation (6) Physical distribution (7) Financing and (8) Risk-taking.

The channels of distribution play a very significant role in the marketing process. Manufacturers, consumers and society at large are benefitted.

Manufacturers enjoy the benefit of reduced cost of inventory. Their turnover becomes quick and volume of sales increases. As a result of quick turnover and increased sales, the cost of physical distribution is minimised. A better relation between the manufacturers and the consumer is established which enhances the reputation of the manufacturers.

Consumers, because of the existence of the channels of distribution, can procure right products at the right time, in the right place, in the right quantity and quality at right price.

Society as a whole is benefitted in the matter of employment, stabilisation in prices and mass production.

### Choice of channels of distribution

One of the most critical decisions that the management of a company has to take is the marketing-channel decision. It is because of the fact that the channel decisions immediately affect all the other marketing decisions — the pricing decisions, sales force and advertising decisions etc. In addition, the company's channel decisions involve relatively long-term commitments to other firms.

"A distribution system ....... is a key **external** resource. Normally it takes years to build, and it is not easily changed. It ranks in importance with key **internal** resources such as manufacturing, research, engineering and field sales personnel and facilities. It represents a significant corporate commitment to large number of independent companies whose business is distribution — and to the particular markets they serve. It represents, as well, a commitment to a set of policies and practices that constitute the basic fabric on which is woven an extensive set of long term relationships". *(Corey).*

The correct choice of a suitable channel of distribution has a far-reaching effect on the performance of a manufacturing organisation. This is a very important marketing decision that calls for high degree of efficiency on the part of the marketing management. The channel of distribution correctly chosen can reduce costs, and can also prevent fluctuation in production. An appropriate channel decision influences other marketing decisions and this can improve the marketing mix. A manufacturer's interest lies in more sales at the lowest margin whereas the middlemen want to maximise their profit. These conflicting interests can be minimised through proper selection of the channel of distribution.

From the above discussion, it seems "there is a powerful inertial tendency in channel arrangements. Therefore, management must choose channels with an eye on tomorrow's likely selling environment as well as today's". *(Kotler).*

**The choice of a suitable channel is generally governed by the following factors :**

(1) The type of product (2) Market or consumers considerations (3) Size and structure of manufacturing (4) Company considerations (5) Structure of retailing (6) The customary channels (7) Selectivity of distribution and (8) The profit criterion.

The type of product refers to its perishability, seasonal availability, the servicing required, unit value and the bulk or weight of the product.

Market considerations include number of consumers, geographical location, consumer or industrial market, order size and the buying habits of the consumers.

Size and structure of manufacturing has a bearing on the choice of the channel in so far as it has a relation in the matter of access to customers. For a big manufacturer, a direct link with consumers is possible through the manufacturer's own sales force. For a small manufacturer, wholesalers and retailers may be more convenient to rely upon. With a wide range of products, a manufacturer may find it suitable to deal with the retailers directly by eliminating the wholesaler.

Company considerations mean the character of the manufacturing organisation – its reputation, financial resources, experience and the desire for control of the channel. All these have to be taken into consideration while selecting a particular mode of channel.

The structure of retailing a product has an impact on the choice of a particular channel. The number of retailers selling a particular product may influence the decision of the manufacturer in selecting the channel. If the number of retailers are large, it is better to make use of the available retail channels. Retailers may prove more convenient for the manufacturer to market his products for their services and availability which will result in higher volume of sales.

The customary channels are not generally discarded by the manufacturing organisation. The proved and established channels of distribution are always preferred to new ones.

Selectivity of distribution refers to the number of middlemen to be used. The distribution may be extensive, selective or exclusive. In extensive distribution, all distributive outlets will be utilised by the manufacturer. In selective distribution, he will select from the available outlets and, for exclusive distribution, a particular middleman is given the right or sole selling agency to sell the product.

Profit being the ultimate object, the manufacturer will take into consideration the question of profit-margin through different channels of distribution. This means that estimates of demand, revenue and costs for each channel will have to be prepared and the net gain from the comparison will be the criterion for the choice of a channel.

A manufacturer selects the channel of distribution after taking into consideration a number of factors. The **distribution policy** of the products as determined by the marketing management may be based on the following **methods** — Intensive distribution, selective distribution, exclusive distribution, consignment selling, franchise and symbolic marketing.

In the franchise method of distribution, the manufacturer grants to certain middlemen the right to sell a product in specially defined markets and also extends to them some facilities for this purpose. This is done under a contractual agreement between the parties. The middlemen — then known as franchisees or licensees — are provided with equipment, capital and management service.

**Symbolic marketing** is a recent development in the marketing process. When two or more manufacturers develop a joint marketing strategy in order to exploit new markets or new opportunities, this is symbolic marketing.

•

# CHAPTER 9

## MIDDLEMEN

Middlemen are the connecting links between the producers or manufacturers on one side and the consumers on the other. The distribution of goods produced poses a serious problem today. Because of the development of transport and the consequent expansion of the market the proximity between the manufacturer and the consumer that existed before is no more. The distance between the producer and the consumer has to be conquered, the gap has to be bridged and here lies the necessity of some agents to come forward to undertake the task of distributing the goods and services from the producer or manufacturers to the ultimate consumers. This is the task of middlemen. They operate in-between the producer/manufacturer and the consumer and this creates place utility. The emergence of the middlemen or intermediaries in-between the producer and the consumer has been necessitated by the circumstances that have led to the expansion of market and widening of separation between the manufacturer and the consuming population.

The middlemen constitute an important link in the **channels of distribution.** "The middleman is not a hired link in a chain forged by a manufacturer, but rather an independent market, the focus of a large group of customers for whom he buys". *(Philip Merey).* There are wide variations in the distribution channels among the commodities and among the producers of the same commodity. Broadly, there are five **major types of channels of distribution :**

1. Producer → consumer
2. Producer → retailer → consumer
3. Manufacturer → wholesaler → consumer (industrial)
4. Producer/Manufacturer → wholesaler → retailer → consumer
5. Producer → agent → middlemen → large scale retailers/wholesalers → retailers → consumers.

Middlemen are not all of the same categories; they do not all perform their functions on identical conditions and terms. Accordingly, we may classify middlemen — Merchant middlemen and Agent Middlemen or Functional Middlemen.

Middleman who take title of the goods while performing the marketing functions are known as the **merchant middlemen.**

Middlemen who do not take title of the goods and simply help in effecting the transfer of ownership of the goods are known as **Agent Middlemen or Functional Middlemen.**

Merchant middlemen bear the risk and perform various marketing functions. Their remuneration is not any commission but profits which they can earn through the transactions of buying and selling.

Agent or functional middlemen assist in the buying or selling of the commodities or both, but while doing so they do not acquire the ownership of the commodities. They simply act as agents of the owner of the goods and charge commission for their services either in the form of fixed amount of commission or in the form of certain percentage of the amount of goods sold. Brokers, commission agents, auctioneers, buying agents, selling agents, common carriers, banks, insurance companies – are all examples of functional middlemen.

The need for middlemen in the channel of distribution cannot be disputed. There are various types of middlemen with their style of functioning differing from one middleman to another. It will not be an exaggeration to comment that sometimes some middlemen indulge in such activities as are not desirable from the social point of view. It may also sometimes appear that in a particular circumstance, the services of middlemen could have been easily avoided. These situations naturally raise the question **whether middlemen are at all necessary.** Can the distribution system function smoothly and in a better way without some men interposing between the producer and the consumer ? We attempt to discuss the matter – its pros and cons – to arrive at a decision whether middleman are redundant or necessary in the channel of distribution. The services of middlemen have been put to test, criticised and attempts have been made and are being made to do away with the services of the middlemen. Producers or manufacturers have resorted to devices to avoid the assistance of some categories of middlemen and the government also is not indifferent to what can be done in the matter of the middlemen; wherever necessary suitable legislations are being enacted to plug the loopholes in the functioning of the intermediaries between the producer/manufacturer and the consumers. But since the elimination of the middlemen has not yet been possible, the controversy still exists as to their desirability in the distribution or marketing system.

### Advocates of the elimination of middlemen argue on the following lines :

(1) Prices of goods/services are enhanced for the commission paid to middlemen, large in number, and also for their deliberate attempt to have more profits.

(2) Middlemen earn remuneration without undertaking any risks inherent in industries.

(3) It is not unusual for the middlemen to hold/hoard stocks to take advantage of increased price of the market.

(4) Middlemen are expected to create place utility and time utility and these are the main reasons for their existence. But in many cases they are not giving proper attention to this aspect of their service.

(5) It is for the middlemen that the goods cannot move smoothly from the producer/manufacturer to the consumer. They create bottlenecks to serve their own interests.

(6) Marketing development has today reached such a stage where we can do away with the services of the middlemen and as producer we can reach the consumers directly.

The arguments against middlemen are found to be not unsubstantiated. No doubt there is truth in it but the counter-arguments in favour of the middlemen should also be considered before we give our verdict as to their continuance or elimination.

### Arguments in favour of middlemen :

(1) Marketing functions are yet not so developed to cover all the facilities to be provided by the producer or the manufacturer. The efficiency and the economy with which the middlemen render some services such as extension of credit, assumption of marketing risks, reduction of the maladjustments between production and consumption, financing of assembling and distribution of goods, performance of sale-services etc. cannot be expected from the manufacturer who is to remain completely occupied with production procedure.

(2) Middlemen relieve the manufacturers from the burden of marketing which is today a specialised job.

(3) This is an age of specialisation. If production needs specialisation, distribution too. Here comes the necessity for middlemen.

(4) Had there been no wholesalers for instance, it would have been very difficult for the consumers to have such a variety of goods.

(5) In Indian context — where agricultural marketing predominates – the need for middlemen cannot be disputed.

(6) The popular belief that with the elimination of middlemen from the channel of distribution the prices of goods will come down is not correct. Clark has rightly stated that "Much of the argument for eliminating middlemen arises from the false notion that the fewer the distinct agencies that handle a product the more quickly, efficiently and cheaply, it can be delivered to the consumers."

"Intermediaries smooth the flow of goods and services ...... This procedure is necessary in order to bridge the discrepancy between the assortment of goods and services generated by the producer and the assortment demanded by the consumer. The discrepancy results from the fact that manufacturers typically produce a large quantity of a limited variety of goods, whereas consumers usually desire only a limited quantity of a wide variety of goods" *(Stern & El-Ansary)*.

Wroe Alderson made the same point : "The goal of marketing is the matching of segments of supply and demand".

"The use of middlemen largely foils down to their superior efficiency in making goods widely available and accessible to target markets. Marketing intermediaries, through their contacts, experience, specialization and scale of operation, offer the firm more than it can usually achieve on its own. From the point of view of the economic system, the basic role of marketing intermediaries is to transform the heterogeneous supplies found in nature into assortment of goods that people want to buy" *(P. Kotler)*.

# CHAPTER 10

## THE MIDDLEMEN — WHOLESALERS AND RETAILERS

### Wholesalers

All activities in selling goods or services to those who buy for resale or business use are termed as wholesaling.

The wholesalers, as a class of middlemen, may be considered leaders in the channels of distribution. With considerable resources at their disposal and having the link between the producers and the retailers, wholesalers undoubtedly occupy a very important position in the distribution process. By warehousing huge quantity of goods and selling them to retailers, a wholesaler creates both time and place utilities – so essential in the marketing of products.

Wholesalers are not all of identical types. They can be classified as (i) manufacturer wholesalers (ii) merchant wholesalers and (iii) retailer wholesalers.

A manufacturer wholesaler is one who combines the activities of manufacturing goods along with the wholesale business.

A merchant wholesaler is a wholesaler in the popular sense of the term. He undertakes no business other than the wholesale one. He purchases goods in bulk from producers and sells them to retailers. A merchant wholesaler may be either a service wholesaler or a limited-function wholesaler. A service wholesaler carries quite complete stocks within his lines, uses salesmen to call on his customers, extends credit, makes delivery and performs other services. The limited-function wholesalers do not perform all the functions of a wholesaler. They hold limited stock only and do not extend credit for longer period.

The service wholesalers may have different types on the basis of degree of specialisation or on the basis of territory covered.

**On specialisation basis** – (a) general merchandise wholesalers, (b) general line wholesalers and (c) speciality wholesalers.

**On territory basis** — (a) national wholesaler, (b) sectional wholesaler and (c) local wholesaler.

### Functions

Before we discuss the functions of wholesalers, let us think why the manufacturers do not dispense with the services of wholesalers. Wholesalers have some definite "efficiencies" that have made them essential in the marketing channel.

Retailers and manufacturers need wholesalers for — (i) selling and promoting (2) buying and assortment building (3) bulk breaking (4) warehousing (5) transportation (6) financing (7) risk bearing (8) market information and (9) management services and counselling.

Irrespective of the types of wholesalers, they, as a class, render many useful services and discharge many functions in the process of distribution which are essential for marketing commodities.

We discuss below the functions :

(1) **Assembling** : From different manufacturers different varieties of goods are collected/purchased by wholesalers. Even in some cases goods

are imported from foreign countries. Thus, wholesalers assemble wide varieties of goods for their distribution to retailers.

(2) **Transporting :** The functions of wholesalers involve transportation of goods from different places and even from outside the country. Thus, by transporting, they create place utility. Places of production are not necessarily places of consumption. It is primarily through the wholesalers that the goods find their ultimate placement in the hands of the consumers.

(3) **Storing :** In the process of distribution, the fact is that neither the producer nor the retailer wants to store or stock goods for a long time thus blocking further production or capital but it is the wholesaler who performs this necessary function of storing and creates time utility. For various reasons goods need be stored and wholesalers do this storing fuction.

(4) **Grading :** Grading is an important function in the marketing mix. Graded goods confer conveniences to customers in the matter of selection, price quotation etc. Wholesalers undertake the task of grading.

(5) **Financing :** Nothing can be more important than providing finance to the producers to enable them to get on with their production uninterruptedly. There is usually a time lag between actual production and distribution i.e. for the money put in by the producer for production may take some time to come back to him. In the intervening period, the production can be kept on going with the money received from the wholesalers. This is the way the flow of goods continues. Therefore, the contribution of wholesalers in financing the producers/manufacturers has a very important bearing upon the whole process of marketing.

(6) **Risk bearing :** A wholesaler's function minimises the risks of the producers against price fluctuation since wholesalers order for their required quantity of goods generally far in advance. It can be interpreted in this way that wholesalers take upon themselves the risks of price fluctuation and relieve the producers of such a big business-hazard. The risk of loss due to bad debts is also inherent in the wholesaler's function.

(7) **Dispersing :** Production is more or less a localised matter but distribution is a decentralised affair. Goods produced in a particular industrial unit are distributed throughout the country and even outside the country and this dispersal function starts from the warehouse of the wholesaler. He initiates dispersal through the retailers. So, dispersing constitutes one of his functions.

Besides the general functions of wholesalers discussed above, they render services to the manufacturers and retailers .

### Services to Manufacturers

(1) A wholesaler acts as an agent of the manufacturers since he operates in-between the manufactures and the retailers and conveys the directives of the manufacturers as to any stipulation for the goods sold to retailers.

(2) Since a wholesaler is in the market, he is in a better position to know the trend in the market. He assesses the demand of the market, the quality of the goods demanded and thus he can apprise the manufacturers of the situation prevailing in the market. This is a great service to the manufacturers who, without carrying on any market research, can rely upon the wholesalers and can concentrate on production without any fear of excess or deficit output.

(3) A wholesaler is a great financial relief for the manufacturers. He buys in bulk and usually in cash which enables the manufacturer to continuously feed his production process.

(4) The function of a wholesaler obviates the need for the manufacturer to store goods for a long time. Along with production, distribution process continues. The wholesaler is always ready with money to take delivery in bulk, thus not making it essential for the manufacturer to hold stocks which means capital blocking.

(5) Manufacturers are to a great extent relieved of the disastrous effect of price fluctuation since wholesalers book their order for goods far in advance at an agreed price. Mass production, likely to be subjected to the risk of price fluctuation, is thus minimised to a considerable extent by the existence of the wholesalers.

### Services to Retailers

(1) A wholesaler is, as a matter of fact, the buying agent of the retailer. Whatever small quantity of a particular product he wants, he can take it from the wholesaler. This is no mean service. It helps the retailer in the matter of blocking much capital and also it relieves him of the botheration and cost of storing goods in large quantity.

(2) Because of the existence of the wholesalers, retailers can save much of their transportation cost for the goods they sell. Usually, goods are supplied at their door, free of cost.

(3) Financially also, the retailers are benefitted for the wholesalers. Retailers usually enjoy a period of credit. Moreover, it is usual for the retailer to pay for the goods they purchase after they are sold, at least in case of new products.

(4) It is said that wholesalers reduce retail-risk by guaranteeing the merchandise he sells and by making adjustments quickly where the retailer is dissatisfied.

(5) Wholesalers keep the retailers informed about the market trend and advise the best course they should resort to in the changed situation in the market.

## Retailers

Retailing denotes distribution and sale of goods to the ultimate consumers. The French word 'Retailler' means to 'cut again'. It may be that we use the word 'Retailer' to convey the idea that goods purchased from wholesalers are sold to the ultimate consumers in small quantity – the bulk purchased is cut again. Selling to numerous consumers in small quantities is really a service worth reckoning. To cater to the individual's needs is the function of the retailer which can be considered as a service of great significance to society.

Changes are always taking place in the business world. The functions of middlemen including retailers are also undergoing changes owing to various forces acting and reacting on one another. General economic conditions of a country have a great bearing on the process of marketing. In our developing country we notice some changes in the traditional pattern of marketing and the way of functioning of various middlemen operating between producers and ultimate consumers. The pattern of flow of goods from the producer to the consumers through wholesalers and retailers being the usual channel of distribution, is being put to different types of trials by making modifications in the channel – eliminating a particular form of middleman or adding some new type to suit the needs of the market.

## Retailers-services

(1) Customers know about the quality of a product newly released in the market.

(2) Retailers, coming face to face with the consumers, may assess their needs and can accordingly regulate supplies.

(3) Retailers also educate customers and advise them about different types of products, their values and uses.

(4) Retailers act as purchasing agents of the consumers and save them bulk purchase.

(5) Retailers are many in number, ready to serve the consumers coming to them as near as possible.

(6) Retailers exercise a considerable amount of influence over their customers in the matter of their purchase, particularly of consumption goods.

(7) Retailers are a great store-house of information as to the market trend which, when communicated to their customers, become very much valuable for their guidance.

(8) Retailer-customer relation transcends business frontiers and this helps both the retailer and the customer.

(9) Retailers, truly speaking, are friends, philosophers and guides to their established clientele.

The position of the retailer in between the consumers and the wholesalers is very significant. On the one hand, the retailer is in touch with one who knows the production position or the supply side and on the other hand the retailer is in close contact with the consumers – the actual market. So, from the retailer, information may be collected about the market and conveyed to the manufacturers by the wholesalers. To the retailers, the consumers may give out their minds which may be of much value to the producers in the matter of production. The wholesalers can also act and control their activities according to the market trend as gathered from the retailers. So, both to the manufacturer and to the wholesalers, the retailers have a great role to play in the production and marketing process.

There are different methods of retailing such as—

(i) selling through retail stores (ii) selling through mail (iii) house-to-house selling and (iv) selling through automatic vending machines.

Retail business is of various types. Mass production necessitates mass selling and the selling process followed till the other day is being found unsuitable. In the changed conditions of the market, retail trading is assuming new techniques. Retailers with enough financial strength are taking upon themselves the functions of the wholesalers; the manufacturers are also taking up retail business along with production.

In the market today, we find mobile as well as fixed shop retailers. The mobile retailers are, again, of different types – hawkers, pedlars, itinerant vendors etc. Fixed shop retailers may be small or big. Of course, still, the small scale retailers hold the key to retail business. Small stalls, general and independent stores, single-line small stores and speciality stores are all small retailers, but among them, small stalls and the general and independent stores are more prominent.

With the improvement of the general economic conditions of a country, large scale retailing developes. In our country we notice that large scale retailing is becoming popular. There are six main types of large scale retailers. They are : (1) Department stores (2) Multiple shops or chain stores (3) Mail order business houses (4) Consumers' co-operative stores (5) Super market and (6) Hire purchase trading houses.

According to P. Kotler, major retailer types are:

(1) Speciality store carrying a narrow product line with a deep assortment within that line. For example, furniture stores, sporting goods stores, book stores and florists. (2) Department store (3) Super market (4) Convenience store. For example, foodstores located near residential areas. (5) Super stores (6) Combination stores (7) Hyper market. Super stores are larger than the conventional super market. Combination stores represent a diversification of the super market store. Hyper markets are even larger than combination stores (these are in U.S.A.). (8) Discount stores selling standard merchandise at lower prices. (9) Off price retailers — when the major discount stores traded up, a new wave **off-price retailers** move in to fill the low price, high-volume gap. They are of three types — factory outlets, independents and warehouse clubs (these have relevance to the U.S.A. shops). Besides the above types of retailers, there are **catalogue show rooms** selling a broad selection of high-markup, fast moving, brand name goods at discount prices.

Before we conclude discussion on retail trading, let us examine the **trends in retailing.**

As strategies to face competition, retailers should take into account the following lines of actions — (1) new retail forms (2) shortening retail life cycles (3) non-store retailing (4) increasing inter-type competition (5) polarity of retailing (6) changing definition of one-stop shopping (7) growth of vertical marketing system (8) portfolio approach (9) growing importance of retail technology.

New retail forms are constantly emerging and posing challenge to established retail forms. These new retail forms are, of course, having short life span. In recent years, non-store retailing in the form of mail order sales is increasing. The modern retail market is characterised by increasingly intertype competitions or between different-type competitions. The intertype competition has produced retailers positioning themselves on extreme ends of the number of product lines carried. Speciality stores are becoming increasingly competitive with large department stores. Marketing channels are increasingly becoming professionally managed and programmed. When large companies extend their control over marketing channels, independent small stores are being squeezed out. A recent trend in retailing is to design and launch new store formats targetted to different life style groups. Retail technologies are becoming critically important as competitive tools. We find in metropolitan cities of our country pavement hawker stores competing with established retail shops.

# CHAPTER 11

## DEPARTMENT STORE

A department store is an example of large scale retailing. In such a store, we find a number of departments with different types of articles. It is, as a matter of fact, a number of shops dealing in various types of articles under the same roof. The management and control vests in the same personnel. It is like a miniature township, usually owned by a big company with huge capital investment. Everything, be it necessary service or goods, is available in the department store and that is why we call it complete shopping under one roof. This is also called 'one stop' shopping.

### Distinctive features

1. Decentralised buying but centralised selling
2. More sales to the same customer than less sales to numerous customers
3. Complete shopping under one roof
4. Management and control are centralised
5. Centrally located
6. Serves more affluent class of people
7. Attracts customers to the store through continuous advertising
8. Various amenities and comforts are provided to the customers
9. It caters to the needs of the class and not of the mass.

### Advantages

1. **Shopping convenience :** Since various goods and services are available under one roof, there is the shopping convenience. People are not to move from one shop to another when there is a good department store.
2. **Locational convenience :** A department store is usually located at the central place of a town or city. This facilitates customers to take advantage of such a store.
3. **Wide selection :** There is more scope for selection than an ordinary retail store.
4. **Economies of large scale operation :** It enjoys all the economies of large scale operation and reaps the benefits of a large scale organisation.
5. **Huge capital :** As it is usually in the corporate form, it can mobilise adequate capital needed for storing wide variety of goods.
6. **Automatic mutual advertising :** In such a store, one department advertises for another. A good article in one department leads the customers to other departments.
7. **Attractive layout :** A department store is generally well decorated; the layout is attractive and convenient to customers.

### Disadvantages

1. **Locality inconveinence :** To common customers, the location of a department store is inconvenient. For daily necessities, a customer cannot be expected to go all the way from his locality to the central place of the town or city.
2. **High price :** Because of high establishment expenses, the prices of articles in a department

store generally have to be fixed at a higher point.

3. **Higher risk of loss** : Huge stock in a department store may sometimes lead to risk of loss for the change of tastes and fashions of customers.
4. **Suitable in a developed country** : Huge amount of capital required for such a store may not be available in a relatively poor country. Economically weak people are not benefitted by such stores.
5. **Limited appeal** : To the weaker section of the community, a department store has a very limited appeal.
6. **Lack of personal touch** : Customer-retailer relationship in a department store is not so close as it is in a small retail store.

## Multiple shops or chain stores

The large-scale retailing through multiple shops or chain stores was devised with a view to making retailing more efficient and reducing waste in distribution.

'Multiple shops' in England are identical with 'Chain stores' in America, but, in India, some authors like to distinguish between a multiple shop and a chain store. According to them, multiple shops are the shops of the manufacturers themselves whereas chain stores are not. However, we discuss multiple shops or chain stores as of the same type.

Multiple shops usually deal in single merchandise (now a number of varieties). A large number of identical retail stores are opened throughout a city or a country; they are controlled, managed and owned by the same business unit.

### Features

(1) Sales are in cash (2) Centrlaised buying production and decentralised selling (3) Identical goods are sold in all the shops wherever they are located (4) Layout of the shops is more or less identical and customers feel no difficulty in recognising such a shop (5) Generally, one particular type of goods is sold (6) Central ownership (7) Central management and control (8) They are centrifugal in nature – try to go to customers as near as possible (9) Prices are fixed.

### Advantages

1. **Economic purchasing** : Where multiple shops are organised with goods purchased from outside producers, bulk purchases are made by experts and they can, therefore, be effected economically. Even the whole of the production of a manufacturer of a product may be purchased by the organiser of multiple shops. In that case, cost of purchases is surely to be lower.
2. **Elimination of middlemen** : This is a device to eliminate middlemen from the channel of distributors. Goods directly come to the shops from the manufacturers.
3. **Better and economic advertising** : In multiple shop system, advertising becomes less expensive because one advertisement serves the cause of all the shops located in a particular region.
4. **Economy in operating expenses** : Large scale operations and rapid turnover enable multiple shops to function more economically – operating expenses are less.
5. **Widespread risk** : Owned by one organisation, multiple shops or chain stores help in spreading business risks. Loss in one shop can be compensated by profit in another shop. Overall performance matters; individual performance may not affect the organisation.
6. **Better sale appeal** : Multiple shops cater to the needs of the consumers by going close to them. They do not ask the customers to come to them; rather they go to them. This brightens the prospects of sale with better appeal.
7. **Rapid turnover** : Because of the approach of the multiple shops at the door of the customers, they are to take least effort to custom a multiple shop.
8. **Fixed price facility** : Because of fixed price, larger number of customers who are not in favour of bargaining, prefer the fixed price shop where there is little scope for charging higher price.
9. **Better quality products** : Multiple shops generally are all nation-wide organisations owned, managed and controlled by big companies. They have expert management and can provide for latest techniques of products or resort to economic buying techniques which enable multiple shops to ensure better and uniform quality products at every shop whenever you buy.
10. **Return facility** : Multiple shops are now-a-

days giving facilities for return of the goods in exchange of other goods because of any defect found after purchase and this facility is available not only at the shop from where the goods are originally purchased but in any shop located elsewhere.

11. **Scientific storage facilities :** Because of considerable financial strength and widespread location of multiple shops, storage can be made scientifically without much loss or damage.

12. **Mutual adjustment of stocks :** Since all the multiple shops are centrally managed, the shortage of stock in one shop can easily be made good by replenishing it from other shops. The adjustments are not very difficult to make through head office accounting system.

**Disadvantages**

1. **Limited Choice :** Customers of multiple shops have limited choice. Wider selection scope is not available.
2. **Personnel problems :** Personnel problems figure prominently in multiple shops because of their multiplicity. Too many shops naturally are likely to create management problems. Recruitment and selection of personnel poses a problem in multiple shop organisation.
3. **Lack of interest of the personnel :** In a multiple shop, it is noticeable that the employees are not so keen to retain a customer. In such an organisation, employees are well organised and united under any union banner and their employment security is more or less guaranteed. Customer-service is not a matter for them to give much attention to.
4. **Inefficiency :** Because of large size, inefficiency may creep in a multiple shop organisation.
5. **Lack of proper buyer-seller relation :** In a multiple shop organisation, customers are not considered so valued. The employed personnel of the shop do not usually feel any need to develop customer-retailer relationship.
6. **Competition from other retailers :** A multiple shop is to face competition from other retailers dealing in the same type of merchandise. For various reasons, particularly for less operating expenses, they are in a better position to sell at lower price than a multiple shop.

## A comparative study of department stores and multiple shops

Department stores had their origin in economically advanced countries to cater to a particular class of people. It is basically an urban institution or organisation. Multiple shops, on the other hand, are meant for masses. They are small retail shops with some characteristics of their own. They try to go nearer to the consumers unlike department stores which try to bring consumers to them from different localities. So multiple shops are centrifugal whereas department stores are centripetal. Because of the organisational pattern of the store, a department store cannot sell at such a price as is possible for a multiple shop. Additional services for the elite class who custom a department store is one of the reasons for higher price at department stores. Both department stores and multiple shops are large scale retailing and both the types are attempts to eliminate wholesales from the channel of distribution. Direct purchases from manufacturers without going through wholesalers constitute a very important feature of both department stores and multiple shops.

In a developed economy, department stores have their utilities and are suitable. But in a country like ours, where people have less purchasing power, multiple shops are more popular.

Both the methods of marketing have their merits and demerits but one thing figures prominently, department stores have the elitist flavour whereas multiple shops are man-based. Department stores will also be popular in our country with the development of our economy but till then a multiple shop at an unknown small town of our country is much more popular and useful. Of course, a department store can supply a lot of necessaries of our life under one roof but a man who has not the ability to afford high priced commodities will have to move from one retail shop to another to collect his total necessities.

## Super Market

Originated in USA, the super market resembles a department store though there are many dissimilarities. "A super market", as defined by Phillips and Duncan "is a departmentalized retail store usually handling a variety of merchandise and in which the sale of food, much of which is on a self-service basis, plays a major role". Cundiff and Still define a supermarket as "a large retailing business unit selling mainly food and grocery items on the basis of low margin appeal, wide variety and assortments, self-service and heavy emphasis on merchandising appeal". In a super market, limited services are provided to the customers and self-service is the main feature. With all the features of a department store, a super market stands out separately on the ground that, in a super market, there is the low price appeal with much display and skilful promotion of sales. The organisational pattern of a super market is more or less on the line of a department store. Credit sales are not usually allowed. In India, there is very little development of super markets. Super markets known as 'Naya Bazars' started in India are confined to big towns only. Super bazars are being set up and a gradual increase in their number indicate that they are gaining popularity, but the appeal is very limited.

A supermarket is a department store with a definite bias for food products, fruits, vegetables, dairy products etc.

### Advantages

1. **Large turnover :** Because of the variety of choice, turnover is generally high.
2. **Low prices :** Prices are not so high as in department stores because customer-services rendered in such a market are much less, the operating expenses are much lower.
3. **Economies of large scale operation :** Super markets are quite big in size and economies of large scale operation are available.
4. **High profit :** High turnover and low costs yield better profits.
5. **Perfect freedom to the buyer :** No persuasion by salesmen, so the customers enjoy freedom of choice.

### Drawbacks

1. **Lack of personal attention :** Absence of personal attention in super markets may be considered by many customers as inconvenient.
2. **Selected commodities :** Super markets are primarily meant for food products. Other necessaries of day-to-day living are not available. So, to have them all in a particular shop, some customers prefer a department store to a super market.
3. **High investment requirement :** A super market involves huge amount of capital investment and the financial constraints act as a drawback of super markets.
4. **Lack of efficient management :** A super market needs efficient management, the lack of which stands in the way of efficient functioning of a super market.
5. **Urban orientation :** Super markets are suitable only in big cities. Even in small towns they can not survive.
6. **Large and extensive premises requirement :** It is not always possible to have large and extensive premises required for a super market. In crowded cities where they can flourish, availability of land and premises is much restricted and incur high rents.

### Mail Order House

The mail order houses establish direct link with the customers through mails. "A retail mail order house is an establishment that receives its order by mail and makes its sales (deliveries) by mail, parcel, post express, truck or freight" (Phillips & Duncan).

Standardisation, grading, branding and packaging are factors that helped the growth of mail order business. In such type of business there is no face-to-face contact between the buyer and the seller. The communication takes place through mails. So standardised, graded, branded and well packaged articles are convenient to be sent by post and price quotation is also facilitated by mentioning the standard, grade, brand etc.

In such a postal business, also described as 'mail-chain shopping', the seller maintains the up-to-date mailing list. Sometimes local agents are employed for order collection, execution, as well as collection of dues when sales is by instalments. But usually, business is done through the mail by VPP.

### Advantages

1. **Low Marketing cost :** A mail-order business is not required to employ shop assistants nor is it required to pay high rent for business premises in a busy locality.
2. **Wide scope for customers :** Mail-order customers are not localised in a particular locality or a region; they may be scattered throughout the country.
3. **Social benefit :** The mailing business helps even the customers of remotest villages when postal services are available. This is no mean social service. Moreover, this enables people living in the rural areas to improve their standard of living.
4. **Scope for development as side activity :** A department store can also start mail-order business along with its usual business. An enter-

prising manufacturer also can start mail-order business.

5. **Availability of goods on credit :** Mail-order houses in many countries have started credit sale of non-durable goods and the credit facilities are enabling men of common means to enjoy many comforts of life through mail-order business.

6. **"Sale or return" facility :** Mail-order houses also sell on 'sale or return' basis and give full guarantee regarding quality of goods.

Mail-order business is becoming more and more popular. But it has some **limitations and drawbacks** such as :

1. Unsuitable for bulk and heavy goods
2. Advertising costs are too high
3. Customers are deprived of the facility of pre-selection inspection
4. Price fluctuations may cause frequent changes of catalogues which involve constant expenditure.

## Consumers' Co-operative Stores or Retail Co-operative Societies

Consumers' co-operative stores are examples of the extension of the principles of cooperation in the field of distribution. The basic purpose is to eliminate middlemen. The economically weaker section of the society generally start co-operative retail stores not for profit motive but to render to themselves service and to get rid of the malpractices of the middlemen. It is a voluntary organisation formed on the corporate basis. Service and not profit, co-operation and not confrontation form its basic principles.

These co-operative retail stores purchase from the co-operative wholesaler stores which in their turn purchase from manufacturers direct according to agreement with the government. Government encourages co-operative organisations as they are basically social institutions set up for the upliftment of the poorer section of the society. The functioning of this type of organisation is also based on justice and equity. The power of money cannot take upper hand in a co-operative store organisation as every member with shares, irrespective of their numbers, has equal voting rights.

### Advantages

1. **Availability of goods at cheaper price :** Direct purchases by the members themselves or from wholesales' societies make it possible for the consumer stores to buy goods at cheaper price.

2. **Pure and quality goods :** Because of their own purchases, a consumers' co-operative store is likely to have pure and quality goods.

3. **Lower price :** Profit is not the motive of the co-operative stores. So, goods are sold at comparatively low price.

4. **Elimination of middlemen :** The abuses of middlemen can be done away with the establishment of consumers' co-operative stores.

5. **Patronage dividend :** It is the practice in co-operative stores to give dividend and patronage bonus as incentives for more purchases.

6. **Social and educative values :** Co-operative organisation inculcates the spirit of co-operation, justice and equity, endeavours to fight the unscrupulous middlemen and attempts to help the economically weaker section of the society. This has great social and educative values.

As to the **disadvantages,** we can say that a consumers' co-operative store type of organisation suffers from organisational inefficiency. Paucity of fund and lack of supervision may sometimes hinder the growth of the organisation. State patronage is not always up to the mark.

## Instalment selling (Hire purchase and Instalment)

High priced goods, durable and easily identifiable with stable demand and standardised specifications, are suitable for instalment selling.

Instalment selling is a device midway between cash sale system and credit sale system. This method enables a purchaser to get possession of the goods immediately after the agreement is entered into, but he is not required to make payment of the entire price at a time. The payments are made by instalments – monthly, half-yearly or annually, as the case may be. Popularly, this system is known as Instalment Retailing System.

Instalment Retailing system may be of two kinds – Hire purchase transactions and Instalment Purchase transactions. Essential points of difference between the two are :

1. Under Hire purchase system, ownership does not go to the purchaser until the last payment is made; in Instalment sale, ownership passes as soon as the contract is entered into.

2. Under H P system, the seller has the right to recover the goods, as he is legally their owner,

as well as forfeit the payment received in case the purchaser defaults in payment. In instalment sale, recovery of goods is not possible; only a suit can be filed against the purchaser for the balance credit due.

In a developing economy as ours, this instalment retailing has given opportunity to the middle class people to enjoy many luxury and necessary goods. The country, too, is being benefitted in the way that small and medium entrepreneurs are now able to start industrial units with plant and machinery purchased on H P system.

Goods are, naturally, costlier because of instalment payment facility. People are tempted to buy even beyond the capacity and this type of retailing (particularly instalment basis) puts the retailers into risk of loss (bad debts due to non-recovery).

**Vending Machine**

This is a complementary form of retailing. The coin-operated vending machines are used. Goods and services usually retailed through vending machines are : Cigarettes, soft drinks, hot beverages, candy, chocolates, platform tickets, milk, laundering, insurance policies. Vending machines are useful in case of well-known pre-sold, pre-packed brands with high turnover rate. To be suitable for vending machine, retailing goods should be of low value, small and uniform.

In a developing economy, vending machines have prospects. They suffer from certain drawbacks such as high initial and maintenance cost of the machines. Customers cannot see the goods before buying. Unwanted goods cannot be returned. Special packing is necessary to suit the machines.

**Discount Houses**

The discount houses are large retail stores. They are open to the public. Goods dealt in are well advertised and well known brands. Jewellery, appliances, sports goods, home furnishing articles are popular items for discount houses. Discount houses are specially suitable for middle income group of people – people with so many wants but having limited purchasing power. This type of retailing was developed after the Second World War, since 1950. Low margin, high turnover type operation with few services but big price cuts are the characteristics of discount houses. Operating expenses in discount houses can be reduced to 15% of sales as against 35% in department stores.

# CHAPTER 12

## PROMOTIONAL STRATEGIES AND TECHNIQUES

Promotional strategies and techniques constitute a very important aspect of marketing management. Sales have to be promoted but how — it is a big question before a producer today. Because of the consumer behaviour having undergone profound changes and with a view to making marketing consumer-oriented, promotional activities are needed to be tailored and new strategies and techniques have to be adopted. The following observation will amply demonstrate how the consumer approach needs new strategies and techniques. "People no longer buy shoes to keep their feet warm and dry. They buy them because of the way the shoes make them feel — masculine, feminine, rugged, different, sophisticated, young, glamourous, "in". Buying shoes has become an emotional experience. Our business now is selling excitement rather than shoes" *(Francis C. Rooney).*

Communication with the present and potential customers is a must for a company in modern marketing. To be cast into the role of communicator and promoter has become inevitable for every company. Through advertising agencies, sales incentive programmes and public relation, companies build up their images, establish communication to the right persons with the right words and at proper time.

In the total marketing mix, promotional strategies and techniques, undoubtedly, have a definite place but the position of promotion in the marketing mix is determined to a great extent by the life cycles of the company's products — whether highly differentiable products or simple commodities, whether they are of routine demand or have to be "sold" and some other considerations. "In theory, the total promotional budget should be established where the marginal profit from the last promotional dollar (rupee) just equals the marginal profit from the last dollar (rupee) in the best non promotional use. Implementing this principle, however, is not easy" *(P. Kotler).*

Promotion budget is distributed over the **four promotion tools — advertising, sales promotion, public relations** and **sales force.** Of course, the allocation of promotional budget varies from one company to another even within the same industry. The strategy for the companies is to continue effort to substitute one promotional tool for another as its economies become more favourable. Even one tool can be used to promote another.

The promotional mix (strategies and techniques) does not follow the same pattern in every business. The **promotional tools,** it has been observed, can be broken down as — **direct marketing,** trade shows, incentives, advertising, sales promotion, sales force management and public relations. The expenditure is generally the highest in direct marketing followed by trade shows, incentives, advertising, sales promotion, sales force management and public relations coming last in the list of the tools so far as expenditure on it is concerned. Each promotional tool — advertising, personal selling, sales promotion and publicity — has its own unique characteristics and costs. Marketeers must be well aware of the characteristics of each tool to derive the best results.

In sales promotion strategy, a wide variety of short-term incentive tools are designed to stimulate consumer markets, the trade and the organisation's own salesface. The marketeer uses tools such as samples, coupons, cash refund offers, price packs, premiums, prizes, free trials, product warranties etc. for consumer-promotion. Price-off, advertising free goods, speciality advertising items are the tools for trade promotion. To plan sales promotion, promotion objectives have to be set, tools have to be selected besides developing, pretesting and implementing the sales promotion programme and evaluating the results. Last but not the least, important promotional strategy is public relations. It has great potential for building awareness and preference in the market place, repositioning products and defending them. Public relations are carried through publication, news, events, speeches, audio-visual material, telephone information services etc.

## Personal Selling or Salesmanship

"Personal selling is an ancient art. Effective sales persons have more than instinct; they are trained in a method of analysis and customer management. Selling today is a profession that involves mastering and applying a whole set of principles". *(P. Kotler).*

Personal selling may assume different styles and all the styles may not be consistent with the marketing concept.

No sales approach works best in all circumstances.

Simply stated, salesmanship means selling techniques. But the term is now used with a sense of greater significance. To understand the meaning of salesmanship in the modern marketing context, we give a few definitions.

Salesmanship is not "an attempt to induce people to buy goods" but it is "the art of presenting an offering that the prospect appreciates the need for it and that a **naturally satisfactory sale follows**" (Carter & Whitehead).

"A face to face persuasive communication between a seller and a prospective buyer" (Daniel S. Warner).

Salesmanship is "the process whereby the seller ascertains and activates the needs or wants of the buyer and satisfies the needs or wants to the mutual continuous advantage of both the buyer and seller" (Pedeson & Wright).

Salesmanship is "the personal presentation of tangible or intangible products, including ideas of commercial significance to potential buyers" (David J. Schwartz).

"It is part of a salesman's business to create demand by demonstrating that the need does exist, although before his visit there was no consciousness of that need" (W. Major Scott).

"Salesmanship consists of winning the buyer's confidence for the seller's house and goods thereby arising a regular and permanent customer" (G. Blake).

From the definitions given above, one common feature of salesmanship emerges; that common feature is – salesmanship is an activity involving satisfaction of both the buyer and the seller.

Salesmanship contains in it the idea of persuasion. What is actually needed by a man is to be sold to him – this is salesmanship. There must be a common point of view with the prospect in regard to the desirability of some article, service or idea. As a matter of fact, salesmanship is the act of 'one human mind influencing another human mind'. A salesman actually sells his point of view but the important point to note is that the salesman must start with the point of view of the prospect and leads his mind to the point where he will accept the salesman's theory. The salesman, to be truly called a salesman, will not sell his goods or services but his ideas.

The old concept of salesmanship has, therefore, undergone changes. The art of selling is not salesmanship today; the art of knowing one's mind and influencing it is salesmanship. 'To know your mind and then to let you know my mind and then to influence or pursuade you to identify your mind with that of mine and when the two minds thus become identical, then selling of goods or services takes place. Before that, what goes on between the prospect and the salesman is the process of understanding each one's mind'.

There is a term used in the marketing world — 'aggressive salesmanship' i.e. selling by pressurizing the customer. It has been found that this approach to salesmanship does not pay in the long run. The prospect cannot be made a permanent customer. Persuasion and not pressure, understanding and not commanding, patience and not intolerance, service and not extraction - are the key-notes of modern salesmanship. Salesmanship is a matter of 'give and take'; 'give your prospect the service he needs, you will get from him the reward you expect'. On this maxim can a sound salesmanship exist and flourish.

## Importance of Salesmanship

Salesmanship, in its wider sense, is something that is going on in every sphere of our life. Today and every day, we are selling something; it is not necessary that something is an article or a service, it may be an idea or a line of thinking. The essence of salesmanship is this that the act of selling is there.

When salesmanship is so comprehensive a term, when it appears to be an integral part in our day-to-day life, its importance and significance cannot be over-exaggerated. Every man in any walk of life, be he a teacher, a political leader or a mere child, he is selling his point of view and trying to convince others to win him or them over; salesmanship is there. Such an all-embracing term is obviously very significant playing a very important role in anybody's life.

In the world of business, to be more specific, in the process of marketing or distribution of goods and services, the significance of salesmanship is all the more felt. A salesman is a friend and guide of the customer. He aids and supports the producer, too. Had there been no salesman, it would not be so easy for the prospects to know about a product. So it is the salesman, primarily, who carries to the prospects the news of the product that has recently appeared in the market, it is he who convinces him about the desirability of the product and ultiamtely, by selling his idea, converts the prospect into an actual customer. This task is very difficult and it establishes the formidable link between the producer and the ultimate customer.

A salesman awakens needs among the prospects, converts them into wants and, simultaneously, encourages the producer to produce to meet the wants created among the prospects. Thus, he renders service to both the prospects and the producers and ultimately succeeds in his endeavour to convert the prospects into present customers. By serving the producer and the consuming public, salesmen in general are rendering service to the society. By the activities of salesmen, wants for goods and services increase, production has to be geared up, resource mobilisation takes place and the whole economy of a country is benefitted through increased consumption of its people and the standard of living of the people is also raised.

In a developing country like ours, salesmanship has a special role to play. For our industrial products, we should have new outlets not only within the country but beyond the country also. This needs the knowledge of salesmanship relevant to those countries where we want to sell our products. So, salesmanship is also important in international marketing.

Salesmanship, or personal selling, to be more specific, renders the following services :

1. By pin-pointing prospect, salesmanship eliminates wastage of effort and expenditure.

2. Salesmanship enables interviews with cent per cent prospect which is not possible in advertising. A face-to-face discussion on a product is definitely a better way of converting a prospect.

3. Salesmanship is flexible; it can adjust to the reactions and objections of customers which is highly desirble in the establishment and maintenance of a continuous link between a producer and a customer.

4. Salesmanship, being personal in nature, is much more effective. It helps the producer to be constantly in touch with the customers. Customers' ways of behaviour, their tastes, their attitudes – all these can be conveyed to the producer through the salesmen and thus salesmanship helps in the better adjustment of production to meet the needs of the customers.

Salesmanship can play a very important role in the modern society if it is properly and effectively conducted. Not only a business but the whole society – the customers, the general public, the government — all may be benefitted through the services of salesmen in the field of production and distribution of goods and services.

Fabulous amounts are spent today in training salesmen. Had it not been paying, the producers would not have indulged in such enormous spending. Today's sales people are not **order takers** but they are active **order getters.**

To be **order getters,** the marketing management adopts two approaches — sales-oriented approach and a customer-oriented approach. In the first approach, sales people are imparted high-pressure selling techniques and in the latter one, they are trained in customer problem solving. Realising the importance of salesmanship, comprehensive training programme is now undertaken.

## Salesmen – their functions

In the process of marketing, there is a definite and secure place for salesmen. They are the force behind the Marketing Manager who count much in the success or failure of the Marketing Management of a business unit. Rightly it has been pointed out that 'salesmen are the men on whom, in the end, the prosperity of a company largely depends'.

The functions of salesmen are :

1. **Locating the prospects** : A saleman's first duty is to find out where a customer is. This he has to do with his special qualities that are expected of a successful salesman.
2. **Persuading the prospect** : Once the prospect is discovered, the task of persuading him starts till he is converted into a customer. This involves convincing the prospect about the quality of the product or service.
3. **Closing the sale** : After convincing the prospect about the product, the salesman proceeds to close the sale by effecting actual sales.
4. **Post sale service** : In case of some goods, post sale services may be necessary. Salesmen are to render these services. Be it a capital goods or a consumption goods, post sale services of various nature are necessary and salesmen should be always at hand of the customer to render such services. Once the goods are sold, the salesmen are often off. That is always ineffective salesmanship, which ultimately, does not pay.
5. **Providing feedback information** : It is one of the very important functions of selesmen to keep their employers informed about the reactions of the customers as to their products or services. This feedback information helps much in the maintenance of the market and also in the continuance of better relation between the seller and the buyer.

A modern salesman, truly speaking, is to render a number of services, principal as well as ancillary, to maintain the market and to expand it. Today's market is very much complicated; the psychology of the customer has to be studied thoroughly and deeply and that is only possible for the salesmen when they come face-to-face with the retailers and through them to the ultimate consumers even though to a very little amount. But this personal touch in the marketing process, which is possible because of the existence of the salesmen in the process, is of great significance. Salesmen, with their special attributes, qualities and abilities – physical, mental, social and vocational – can be expected to be of immense benefit to all – the producer, the middlemen, the consumer, the society and the country at large.

In personal selling, a number of steps have to be followed. In the first step, the need is to identify the prospects which the salesmen do through the current customers and also by cultivating other referral sources joining organisations to which prospects belong. Salesmen today have functions which were completely outside the purview of the sales force prior to Industrial Revolution. Business, as it has developed today, is not only a mass production much ahead of demand but, also, it is to operate in an environment where the prospects have to be made to be imbued with the idea of the sales person. So, the salesman sells the idea. Various techniques are resorted to reach the consumer. Salesmen, thus, have to develop leads which may be hot, warm and eventual.

In the modern complex market, many companies are assigning the salespersons pivotal roles in the marketing mix since they prove to be very effective in achieving certain marketing objectives. Marketing management of an organisation has to be sufficiently cautious when designing sales force because it entails considerable cost.

For the management, the designing of sales force is not an easy job. It calls for decisions on objectives, strategy structure, size and compensation. Objectives include prospecting, communicating, selling and securing, information gathering and allocating whereas sales force strategy involves deciding what types and mix and selling approaches are most effective. In organising the right territory size, product markets are included in structuring the sales force. The total workload and sales hours have also to be estimated by the marketing management of an organisation. Decisions on compensation include salary, commission, bonus and fringe benefits of the sales people.

Management of sales force includes recruitment and selection of sales representatives, their training, motivation, directing and evaluating. The management should periodically evaluate sales persons' performance to help their betterment. Finally, the management is to note that selling is a process involving a number of steps such as prospecting and qualifying, preapproach, approach, presentation and demonstration, handling objections, closing and follow-up. Sales force management also needs negotiation and relationship management; they are important aspects.

# CHAPTER 13

## ADVERTISING

Advertising, in its derivative sense, means turning anybody's attention to anything. But, for business purposes, it has some specific implications.

Advertising has been defined as "mass, paid communication, the ultimate purpose of which is to impart information, develop attitudes and induce actions beneficial to the advertiser".

Another definition considers advertising as "any paid form of non-personal presentation and promotion of goods, services or ideas by an identified sponsor".

An advertisement is, therefore, a paid means of communication. It is commercial in nature. An advertisement has buyers as its target in general; its sponsor is identifiable and its object is to attract attention and induce people to buy a product or service or accept an idea.

Mass production of goods needs mass distribution which necessitates advertising for mass communication. It is a potent and recognised means of sales promotion. With the minimum cost, it can reach the maximum number of prospects. It is incomprehensible for mass distribution of a product without first resorting to the technique of advertising because, without advertising, it is not possible for a vast mass of population to know the existence of a product. Advertising is, today, undoubtedly a powerful force for sales promotion because of its all-pervasiveness.

Advertising is not a new technique of marketing. It had been in the past, it exists at present and it will remain in future because of its efficacy. The methods of advertising are changing but the advertising, as such, has been continuing as before. However, ample opportunity for better advertising still exists. As a matter of fact, "advertisement as an instinct is innate in human nature". With the expansion of market and the development of international market, advertising has assumed a new dimension of importance and its indispensability is now a matter beyond any controversy.

It is to be noted that advertisement is not a mere publicity – it is something more! While publicity or propaganda for spreading certain doctrines does not take into account the cost factor, advertising must involve cost-consciousness because here the object is to maximise sales at the minimum cost.

### Advertising – a useless, wasteful exercise ?

It must be admitted that there is no complete unanimity as to the desirability of advertising, at least in certain circumstances. For example, in case of a already very popular brand of particular product.

Various arguments are placed in favour of and against advertising.

**Advertising is supported** on the grounds stated below :

1. It increases demand for a product and reduces its cost of production and thus helps in the enhancement of profit.
2. It is a cheaper method of sales promotion. The employment of salesmen in large numbers is much more expensive. So, to supplement adver-

tising, the minimum number of salesmen may be recruited.

3. Advertising, properly and effectively carried on, can reach the consumers and they enable the producer to reduce retail prices.
4. It creates goodwill for the firm which ultimately pays the producer.
5. Advertised products are generally more popular.
6. It improves the quality of the product. Most of the advertising is based on product differentiation. So, a product has to be superior for being advertised.
7. It provides employment to a large number of persons engaged in designing and writing advertisements.
8. It helps the firm to secure dealership for its products and once it is secured, it helps dealers to increase the sale of the products stored by them.
9. Advertising creates consumer awareness.
10. It plays the role of sincere public servant by communicating various information which increases the welfare of the society.

Advertising, to many of its advocates, is an accelerator of civilization. Advertising is not only a tool used in the business world but it is an effective and popular way of propagating views and news by social organisations. Thus, **advertising has a social aspect.**

Advertisi, ; that can build up the company's reputation wili help the company's sales representatives. It is one of the four major tools that a company can use to direct persuasive communications to target buyers. Although advertising is primarily a private-enterprise marketing tool, it is used in all the countries of the world including socialist countries. "Advertising is a cost-effective way to disseminate messages, whether it is to build brand preference for Coca-Cola or to motivate a developing nation's consumers to drink milk or to practice birth control".

"Advertising — the use of paid media by a seller to communicate persuasible information about its products, services or organisation — is a potent promotional tool". *(P. Kotler)*

Advertising is **opposed and criticised** as an wasteful exercise on the following grounds :

1. Advertising creates monopoly or semi-monopoly and monopoly views operate in the market.
2. It increases the prices of goods and services.
3. It induces people to purchase such goods which they may very will dispense with.
4. It drives out small business firms from the field of business.
5. Advertising causes mass production but the mass-produced products are likely to be inferior and they cannot continue in the market for a long time. Thus, ultimately, cost benefit aspect of advertising, does not hold good.
6. It is a clap-trap, since advertisement misrepresents the facts to the consumers.
7. It results in wastes of national resources. It causes frequent changes of styles, fashion and habits of the people thereby resulting in wastage of earlier products.

**In conclusion, we may say that advertising is such a tool of marketing, that depending on conditions, it may be used or abused.** Advertisement is a tool in the hands of the advertiser and we can appreciate that a particular tool can be used for a good as well as for a bad purpose. It all depends upon the person who uses it. Advertising may be harmful and socially undesirable if directed towards anti-social ends. So, whether advertising is good or bad depends on how advertising technique is utilised and for what purpose. Nothing in this world is an unmixed blessing, so it is quite possible that advertising has its demerits and harmful effects. But it must be admitted that advertising is necessary and useful to create market and to maintain it. The advertiser must be very much judicious before he uses this tool as a medium of mass communication. A new product, for example, has to be advertised for creating market and an old product has to be advertised for retention of the market. The expenses incurred for advertising are ultimately recovered through the increased total turnover. Advertising increases demand and production has to be accelerated and thus the cost of large scale production naturally comes down. Constructive advertising aimed at building up permanent market has more benefits than harmfulness.

To sum up, admitting that advertising may be harmful in a number of ways, it can be argued that the worst that we can say is that **advertising is a necessary evil.** In spite of all its harmful effects, advertisement cannot be given farewell from the marketing process. Keeping in view the benefits of the consuming people and the society at large, advertising can undoubtedly serve the society in its economic upliftment.

**"It pays to advertise"** — claim the advocates of advertising. In favour of their claim, they say advertising extends the frontier of sales, derives the benefits and economies of mass production, reduces the cost of production and the prices of products, improves the quality and makes available variety of goods and services.

**'Advertising is wasteful'** claim the opponents of advertising by pointing out that the false, deceptive as well as combative advertisements are nothing but wastage of national resources.

There is truth in the arguments of both the sides. But what cannot be ended, must be mended and cured of its evils. Legislations have been made by the government in consultation with the businessmen for regulating irresponsible and objectionable advertising. There should remain some ethical standards of advertising. The Essential Commodities and Drugs Act, the chambers of commerce, the consumers' associations are all meant for and are endeavouring for better advertising values.

## Scientific Advertising

In spite of criticisms against advertising, it has come to stay in the marketing process. Advertising is now a part and parcel of sales organisation. Advertising, as such, is not so much criticised as it is for the manner of advertising. When advertising is based on method and foresight and is not devised in the traditional trial and error method without due deliberation as to its scope and purpose, it can escape much of the criticisms levelled against it. Scientific methods of reasoning, reflection and enquiry have not been adopted in a marked way in the sphere of distribution as scientific management has been applied in production sphere.

To overcome the short-comings and the evil effects of advertising to a considerable extent, scientific approach to advertising is desirable. By scientific advertising is meant "properly-planned advertising based on a serious deliberation of all factors that have a bearing upon its success". The various unscientific methods — 'Weather Vane', 'flipped coin' emotional and authoritative — have no place in scientific advertising. Scientific methods, on the other hand, imply the clear recognition of the problem and the alternative to the solution of the problem, the collection of data in selecting a particular attractive and the weighing of these data and the application of human judgement to them in the final selection of a course of action. As a matter of fact, scientific advertising is not something that is done on a hit-or-miss method but on the basis of research. It is a fact-finding approach to the formulation and execution of an advertising programme.

It has been widely accepted that the purpose of advertising is to "interpret the want satisfying qualities of commodities and services in terms of human needs and wants". With this end in view, the advertising should then proceed towards scientific advertising. Collection of data about the prospects will have to be made first and this has to be followed by the financial planning and the selection of the media of advertising. The entire programme of advertising will continue strictly in accordance with the plans and observations made earlier. In the last phase of the programme, the performance will have to be evaluated. The plan for advertising under scientific method must have the characteristic of flexibility to allow the plan to be modified according to need.

So, in a nutshell, scientific advertising has some definite phases such as preliminary investigation, budgeting and media planning, execution of the programme and testing of results. Preliminary investigations will include market identification, product analysis and consumer research or motivation research.

## Advertising media

Advertising is a sales promotion campaign. A campaign is undertaken to achieve a goal. In the advertising campaign, the selection of appropriate media is a significant consideration. There are a number of media through which advertisement can be made. For the selection of the right medium or media, various factors have to be taken into consideration.

**The media – selection considerations are :**

(1) Nature of the product and its demand (2) The type of prospects, their location and other characteristics (3) The financial allocation for advertising (4) Competition in the market (5) Cost of the advertising media (6) Objective of advertising (whether to introduce a new product or to create demand for an existing product), (7) Assistance from the media (the amount of co-operation and assistance likely to be derived from a medium in the form of marketing research, mailing lists etc.).

**Media of advertising** may be broadly classified into four categories – (1) Mural or outdoor advertising (2) Press advertising (3) Direct mail advertising and (4) Other forms.

Under mural or outdoor advertising medium category, we have posters or hoardings, vehicular advertising, sky advertising, sandwich boards and electric light signs.

In press advertising medium, newspapers, trade journals and magazines are the vehicles.

In direct mail advertising, circular letters, sales letters, price lists, catalogues, brochures, leaflets, pamphlets, diaries, calendars are the tools.

In other forms, we may include radio, film, television, screen slides, window display, exhibitions, sample and bonus or premium etc.

## The Advertising Agency

With the growing complexities in the marketing and distribution, advertising has become a specialist job. The advertiser is a producer, say for instance: he knows how to produce but it is quite likely that he may not know the modern techniques of advertising. A specialist class, therefore, has come up in between the publisher of advertisements and the actual advertisers. This is a type of service institution composed of specialists who assist the advertisers in planning, preparing and placing advertisements. They are advertising agents who act as a mediating link between the publishers and the advertisers. They assure fuller utilisation of publishing spaces on the one hand and to rend r specialist services in respect of advertising to .he advertisers on the other. The advertising agencies have proved their utilities and we find today increasing number of advertising agencies. Advertisement media selection, advertisement copy layout, advertisement techniques require careful study of the market and here lies the need for the specialist to undertake advertising job. The advertising agencies perform these functions. They are manned by trained personnel who have acquired special qualificaiton in advertising techniques.

Advertising agencies generally perform the following functions – (1) Planning the advertising programme (2) Making the actual advertisement (3) Placing the advertisements in appropriate media (4) Conducting test campaigns, preparing sales manuals (5) Suggesting the advertiser as to the packaging, labelling and catalogues (6) Preparing the accurate advertising budgets. For these services, they charge commission. In some cases, they get commission for special services on a fee basis from the advertisement.

In recent years, a number of advertising agencies have been set up. On the recommendation of the press commission, the Advertising Council of India has been formed with constituents like the Indian Society of Advertiser, the Advertising Agencies Association of India, the Indian and Eastern News paper Society, the Indian Language Newspaper Assosiation and the Federation of Master Printers. The principal objects of the Council are : (a) To clean up what remains of unethical and anti-social practices or abuses in the advertising business, (b) To investigate and promote the use of new media suitable for adoption by all classes of advertisers for reaching the public (c) To promote joint efforts for the education and training of people in the art of advertising and (d) To promote individual or joint efforts for basic market survey, study and research in order to ensure effective advertising in the country.

Even companies with strong advertising departments use advertising agencies. It is because of the fact that specialists work in advertising agencies which are definitely more effective in sales promotion than the advertising department of a company. Moreover, agencies also bring an outside point of view to solving a company's problems, along with years of experience from working with different clients and situations. Agencies often att-ract new business through reputation or size. A recent trend is, as growth in advertising spending has slowed, many agencies have tried to keep growing by gobbling up other agencies thus creating huge agency holding companies. These new "super agencies" offer a complete list of integrated marketing and promotion services under one roof, including advertising, sales promotion, public relation, direct marketing and marketing research.

# CHAPTER 14

## PRIVATE DISTRIBUTION SYSTEM IN INDIA

In marketing management, the ultimate object is to place the products in the hands of the consumers in the most convenient way. In India, the distribution of goods is done through both public and private agencies. Ours is a mixed economy. A vast area of production is still in the private sector. Private producers are to think about distribution of their products. Of course, the Government of India rightly has put in emphasis on the distribution of essential commodities through public distribution system.

It is a matter of fact that, for various reasons, the activities of the middlemen in the channel of distribution have been subjected to criticisms. Still then, in a vast country like ours, predominantly agricultural, the distribution cannot be taken up entirely by the government. Private distribution system cannot be dispensed with.

It is needless to say that all attempts to gear up production are of no use if the products cannot be distributed properly and made available to them for whom they are meant. Distribution of commodities is a difficult and stupendous task entrusted to both public and private sectors.

In the private distribution system, goods may be supplied to the consumers in many ways. Each way is a kind of 'link-road' between the producer and the ultiamte consumer. The possible channels through which goods may reach the final consumers are many and varied. A producer and a consumer may have direct link, no doubt, but in the modern complex marketing process, there are many intermediaries between the producer and the consumers for distribution of goods.

Usually the following channels of distribution are resorted to for distribution by private producers :

1. **Producer → consumers :** Under this method of distribution, a producer comes to the consumers directly. He does not go through any middleman or agent. In agricultural products, machineries, engines etc. we find such direct selling by the manufacturers to the consumers.

2. **Producer → own shops → consumers :** Manufacturers/Industrialists open their own retail outlets and sell direct to the consumer without depending upon the middlemen.

3. **Producer → retailer → consumers :** A manufacturer may establish link with the consumers through retailer only. This is a feature of distribution system in the private sector in our country. Here the services of the wholesalers are dispensed with.

4. **Producer → wholesaler → consumer :** In this type of distribution, wholesalers act both as a link between the producers and the consumers. Retailing is also done by them. No retailer functions in between the producer and the consumers only wholesalers do.

5. **Producer → mail service → consumer :** Mail-order business is now gaining popularity. The manufacturer of a product, through adverti-

sing, establishes link with the customers. There is the mailing list. Customers can know about the products through advertisements and other methods. Goods are delivered by post.

6. **Producer → selling agents → consumers :** Producers sometimes reach the consumers through selling agents. The agents charge commission and act more or less like brokers. Commission agents, Forwarding agents, Sole agents are examples of such agency sales.

### Public distribution system in India

Public distribution system consists in distributing essential commodities through fair-price shops at government-controlled price. Public distribution system has been necessitated to maintain stable price conditions through efficient management of supplies. Various unfair trade practices of the middlemen such as creating artificial scarcity of goods with a view to earning excessive profit have called for the elimination of the middlemen from the channel of distribution of essential commodities. The demand for essential commodities is largely inelastic; so, even a marginal fall in the production and supply often leads to disproportionate increase in their prices. Ours being a predominantly agricultural country, agricultral products predominate the market and their prices are subject to large seasonal variation. Here is the need for public distribution system. Both food grains and industrial raw materials are released to the market just after the harvest when prices are generally depressed. In such a circumstance, it has been thought necessary to set up agencies by the government to buy their products to ensure a certain minimum profit to the producers. The FCI is one such institution. These goods, purchased by the government institution, are channelised through public distribution agencies to the ultimate consumers. This is to ensure supplies of essential commodities in off-season at fair price.

The constant price rise [illegible] to various reasons has made it all the more important and necessary to strengthen the public distribution system. It has now become "a stable and permanent feature of India's strategy to control prices, reduce fluctuations in prices and achieve an equitable distribution of essential consumer goods".

The public distribution system in India follows the dual pricing system.

Public agencies procure and distribute a certain proportion of the output of commodities to the vulnerable sections. The producers are allowed to sell the balance in the free market at higher prices and realise on the whole a fair price for their produce. Only the most essential goods of mass consumption are distributed through public distribution sytem. Cereals, sugar, edible oils, kerosene, controlled cloth, tea, toilet soap and washing soap, soft coke, match boxes, exercise books etc. are the commodities generally available through the public distribution system.

Both Central and State governments undertake distribution of essential commodities. FCI distributes food grain and sugar in some states. Co-operative societies also distribute sugar in some states. The STC distributes edible oils. The Department of Coal and Coal India Ltd. distribute soft coke. IOC, Hindustan Petroleum, Bharat Petroleum etc. distribute kerosene. The National Consumers' Co-operative Federation distributes controlled cloth and tea and the Coffee Board distributes coffee. At the state level, Food and Civil Supplies Departments, Civil Supplies Corporation, Essential Commodities Corporations, apex consumer co-operative federations and fair price shops undertake supplies of essential commodities.

In spite of all these arrangements, it can be said that the public distribution system is yet to render services to inaccessible areas and to the power sectors of the community. The Civil Supplies Corporations, consumers' co-operative societies and marketing societies may be utilised in this respect in more effective ways.

Improvements in the matter relating to distribution of commodities (reduction of cost of distribution, strengthening co-ordination and linkage between the consumers and marketing co-operative expansion of storage facilities etc.) have been envisaged in the Plan Programmes.

The public distribution system, in a controlled economy like ours, is expected to take upon itself more responsibilities for distribution of essential commodities to as many people as possible. India is a vast country with majority of her population living in the rural areas. These under-privileged weaker sections of the community should be well covered by the public distribution system; the basic needs of their daily life must be met by governments and, over and above, the commodities that raise the standard of living and bring some comforts to day-to-day living should also be made available to them. An effective wide-spread action oriented public distribution system is essential to enliven our developing economy. It is to be noted that the Seventh Plan strategy recognised the public distribution system as a permanent feature of the economy. In the 20-point programme for the social and economic upliftment of the various sectors of the economy, point number seventeen was to expand public distribution system through more fair price shops including mobile shops in far-flung areas and shops to cater to industrial workers, student hostels and make available to students text-books and exercise books on a priority basis and to promote a strong consumer protection movement.

A recent trend in public distribution system is to rely on selling through Panchayats. In the rural areas, agricultural needs – seeds, fertilisers etc. are being met by the public distribution system through Panchayats.

In a mixed economy like ours, both private and public distribution systems should be geared up to cater to the needs of the vast population who are repeatedly pledged for a better standard of living and welfare.

■ **In the latest economic policy of our country where liberalisation and privatisation have featured prominently, essential commodities such as Kerosene, Cooking Gas etc. are being contemplated to be distributed both through public and private agencies.**

# CHAPTER 15

## PRODUCT LIFE CYCLE (PLC)

"The product life cycle (PLC) is an important concept in marketing that provides insights into a product's competitive dynamics. At the same time, the concept can prove misleading if not carefully used." *(P. Kotler).*

The product life cycle, we have seen, has different stages like a human life. Furthermore, we shall see that the PLC portrays **distinct stages in the sales history** of a product. In the marketing strategy and profit potential, there are also distinct stages. To have better marketing plans, the marketing management is to identify the stage that a product is in.

When we talk about the life cycle of a product, we take into consideration four points — (a) Products have a limited life (b) Products pass through distinct stages (c) There are fluctuations in projects and (d) Different strategies are needed to meet the problems of the different stages of a product life.

The four stages of a product life cycle, as we have discussed at the start of this topic, portray the sales history of a typical product.

Fig. 15.1 (based on P. Kotler's Marketing Management) will give us an idea of sales and PLC.

The product life cycle concept is also applied for a product category, a product form or a brand.

**Product categories** have the longest life cycles while **branded products** tend to have short product life cycles. **Product forms** have standard product life cycles. (Cigarettes belong to product cateogo-

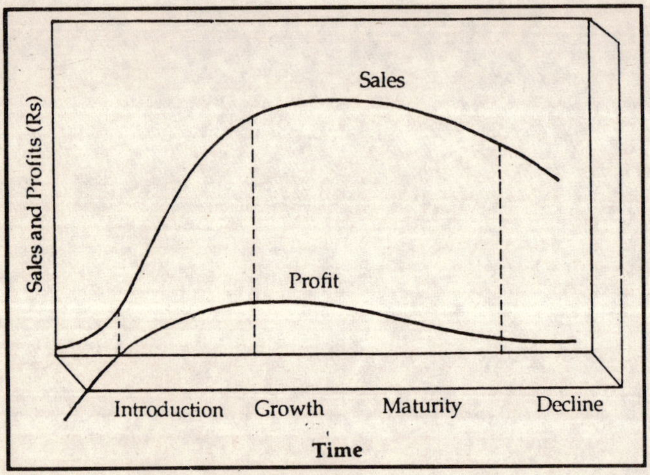


Fig. 15.1

ries, plain filter cigarettes to a product form and regular non-filter cigarettes to a brand).

In the fast changing technology, the characteristics of the life cycles of product-category and product form are changing. Usually, highly population related product-category has a long life cycle but the advent of electronic goods in the market is cutting short the life of product category. Product forms are also changing fast and thus their PLCs are becoming shorter. For instance, electric typewriters replacing the old type. Branded products have more or less three years' life expectancy but there are products in our country which have survived more than three years and are having a much longer PLCs. For example, Godrej refrigerator, Hindustan Lever products (to name, Lifebuoy soap).

There are **other shapes of the product life cycle.** Not all products exhibit an S-shaped PLC (as shown below). It has been found that there are six to seventeen different PLC patterns. The common patterns are — (a) growth-slump-maturity pattern (b) cycle-recycle pattern and (c) scalloped pattern.

A growth-slump-maturity pattern was found by researchers in case of small kitchen appliances. It was found that sales of slow cookers grew rapidly, then slid to half abruptly and thereafter stabilised or 'petrified' at that level. This 'stabilised' level came because of late adopters buying the product for the first time and early adopters replacing the product (Fig.15.2).

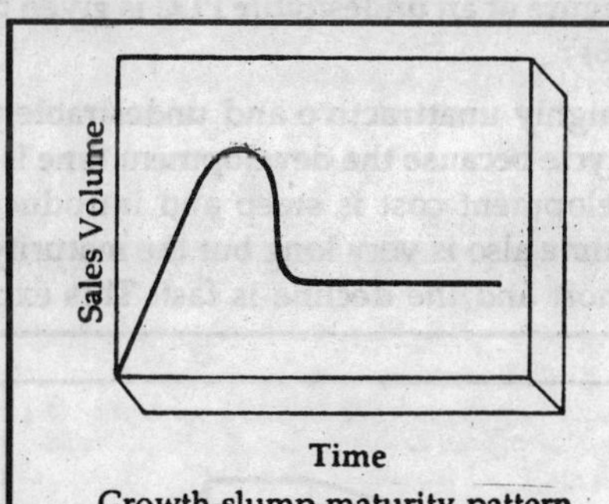


Growth-slump-maturity pattern (Sance-Kotler)

Fig. 15.2

The sales of new drugs conform to **the 'cycle-recycle' pattern.** The vigorous and aggressive campaign pushes up the sales of the new drugs and the first cycle is thus formed. Later, sales start declining and the producers once more give a push for sales which produces a second cycle usually of smaller magnitude and duration (Fig. 15.3).

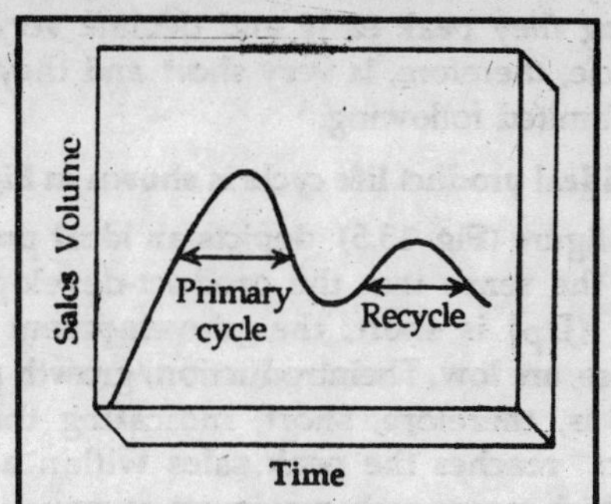


Cycle - recycle pattern (Kotler)

Fig. 15.3

When sales pass through a succession of life cycles based on the discovery of new product characteristics, uses or users, the cycle pattern is known as "scalloped". Philip Kotler cites the example of Nylon. Its sales show a scalloped pattern because of the many uses (Fig. 15.4).

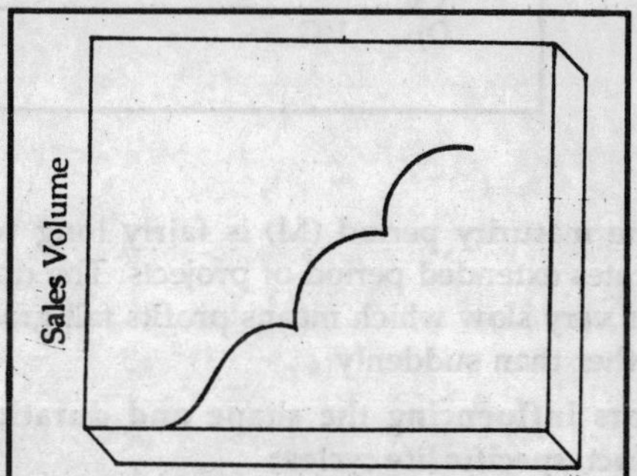


"Scalloped" pattern (Kotler)

Fig. 15.4

Product life cycles have three special categories depending upon styles, fashions and fads. Once a style is invented, it can last for generations. A style life cycle exhibits a cycle showing periods of renewed interest.

A product life cycle based on fashions passes through four stages — (a) **distinctiveness stage** — to set them apart from other consumers, some consumers take an interest in something new (b) **emulation stage** — some customers emulate the fashion leader (c) **mass-fashion stage** — extremely popular with the common people and (d) **decline stage** — consumers, abandoning the old fashion, turn towards some other fashions appearing new in the market.

Fads are fashion catching public eye quickly and they are adopted with zeal, the characteristic being they peak early and decline very fast. The cycle, therefore, is very short and they have only a limited following.

**An ideal product life cycle is shown in Fig.15.5.**

The figure (Fig. 15.5) depicts an ideal product life in the sense that the product-development period (Dp) is short; the development costs, therefore, are low. Theintroduction/growth period (I/G) is, therefore, short, indicating that the product reaches the peak sales within a short time which means early maximum revenue.

(ii) the dealers readily accept and promote the new product,

(iii) consumers have interest in the product.

The above conditions are present in the familiar consumer products. High-tech products do not fulfil these conditions.

**(c) Maturity time :** When the tastes of the consumers and product technology are fairly stable and the firm is a leading one, maturity time lasts longer.

**(d) The Decline time :** A slow change in consumers' tastes and product technology makes the decline time longer. The brand loyalty of consumers makes the decline rate slow. When the exit barriers are lower, naturally some firms will exit faster and, as a consequence, the remaining firms will meet slow rate of decline.

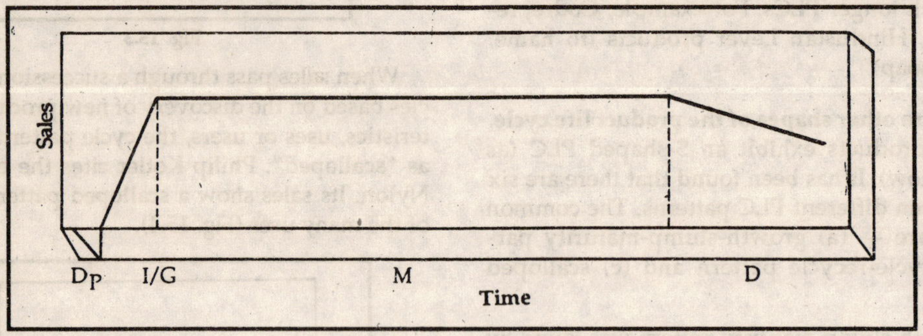


Fig. 15.5

The maturity period (M) is fairly long which indicates extended period of projects. The decline (D) is very slow which means profits fall gradually rather than suddenly.

**Factors influencing the shape and duration of product -specific life cycles :**

The factors that influence the length of each stage of PLC are : (a) development time (b) introduction and growth time (c) maturity time and (d) the decline time.

**(a) Development time :** As between high-tech products and routine products, the fomer usually take longer development time and thus become more costly than the latter ones which have normally shorter development time and thus are less costly.

**(b) Introduction and growth time :** Introduction and growth time is short when —

(i) the product does not need a new infrastructure of distribution channels, transportation, services or communication,

**The figure of an undesirable PLC is given below (Fig. 15.6) :**

It is highly unattractive and undesirable product life cycle because the development time is long; the development cost is steep and introduction/growth time also is very long but the maturity period is short and the decline is fast. This explains

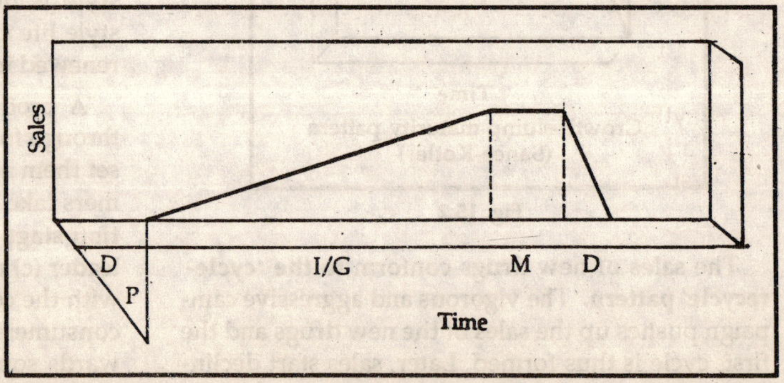


Fig. 15.6

why hightech firms consume much time and incur huge cost to develop their product. The rapid technological changes cause such a phenomenon.

## THE PRODUCT LIFE CYCLE
**(Demand/Technology Life Cycle)**

The need of the market provides the basic consideration for marketing thinking. Marketing management thinks about the product as one solution among many to meet a need. The need changes with the change of time and this changing need level is described by a **demand life-cycle curve.** There is a stage of **emergence** followed by stages of **accelerating growth, decelerating growth, maturity** and **decline.**

A need is satisfied by some technology. Each new technology is an improvement over the previous one. Each exhibits a **demand-technology life cycle** under the demand-cycle curve. Each demand-technology life cycle shows various stages. There is a succession of product form that satisfy the specific need at the time.

"Companies must decide what demand technology to invest in and when to transit to a new demand technology. Ansoff calls a demand technology a strategic business area (SBA), namely, a distinctive segment of the environment in which the firm does or may want to do business. Today's companies face many changing technologies but cannot invest in all of them. They have to bet on which demand technology will win. The pioneering firm that bets heavily on the winning technology is likely to capture leadership. Thus, firms must carefully choose the strategic business areas in which they will operate" *(P. Kotler.)*

**Rationale for the Product-Life Cycle**

The theory of the diffusion and adoption of innovations provides the underlying rationale for the product life cycle.

**Innovation** means introduction of new things — the new things may be goods, services or ideas. When anything is perceived by some one as new, it is innovation. It takes time to spread through the social system.

**'Diffusion'**, as defined by Rogers, is 'the spread of a new idea from its source of invention or creation to its ultimate users or adopters'. **Adoption** is the mental process through which an individual passes from first hearing about an innovation to final adoption. It is the decision of an individual to become a regular user of a product.

The creation of awareness and interest and their stimulation for the product and also to stimulate trial and purchase of the product is the marketing strategy for a company launching a new product. This takes time. Innovations are only a few at the introductory stage and the number of early adoptions depends on the satisfying capacity of the product. Competitors speed up the adoption process by increasing the market's awareness and by causing prices to fall. More buyers are attracted and, eventually, the growth rate decreases as the number of potential buyers approaches zero. The situation comes for the sales to become steady at the replacement-purchase rate. With the advent of new product classes, forms and brands in the market, sales decline. "Thus the product life cycle is explained by normal developments in the diffusion and adoption of new products." *(Kotler).*

In formulating marketing strategy, the product life cycle concept provides a useful framework.

## MARKETING STRATEGIES IN DIFFERENT STAGES OF PRODUCT LIFE CYCLE

**1. Marketing strategies in the Introduction stage :**

The management can pursue one of the four strategies in launching a new product. The strategies are : (a) rapid skimming strategy (b) slow skimming strategy (c) rapid penetration strategy and (d) slow penetration strategy.

On the consideration of price and promotion only, the above strategies are resorted to —

(a) **Rapid-skimming strategy :** This strategy pursues the policy of launching a new product at a **high price** and a **high promotion level.** High price brings in more gross profit and high promotion accelerates the rate of market penetration. The appropriate situations for this strategy are — the potential market is mostly **unaware** of the new product and ready to play the asking price and the firm has potential competitors for which it wants to build up brand preference.

(b) **Slow skimming strategy : High price** and **low promotion** at the launching stage result in the recovery of maximum gross profit per unit and lowering down of the marketing expenses. This combination is likely to skim a lot of profit from the market. To make the strategy effective, the market should be limited in size and **in the know of**

**the new product,** willing to pay a high price and there is no apprehension immediately of any competition.

(c) **Rapid penetration strategy :** Low price and high promotion expenses lead to the fastest market penetration and the largest market share. In a large market, unaware of the product and the buyers being price sensitive, this strategy holds good. In the market, of course, it is assumed there is strong potential competition. This strategy makes sense when the manufacturing costs permit fall with the scale of production and accumulated manufacturing experience.

(d) **Slow-penetration strategy :** Low price and low level of promotion as a result of which the product-acceptance is encouraged and the promotion expenses come down bringing more net profit. Such strategy is resorted to when the firm finds that the market demand is highly price-elastic but minimally promotion-elastic.

To make the strategy effective, the market should be large and highly aware of the product; the market price has to be sensitive and potential competition is the feature of the market.

To conclude, we can say that at the introduction stage, no firm should adopt any marketing strategy arbitrarily. The launching strategy demands utmost caution and tact since this acts as the first step in the plan for life cycle marketing.

**2. Marketing strategies in the Growth stage :**

When a firm is rapidly climbing in sales i.e. is in the growth stage, the following strategies are usually adopted :

(a) To accelerate sales further, quality of the product is improved and new features and improved stylings are added.

(b) New models and flanker products are introduced.

(c) New distribution channels and new market segments are experimented.

(d) Advertising technique is changed — from building product awareness to product conviction and purchase.

(e) Prices are lowered at the right time with a view to attracting the next layer of price-sensitive buyers.

The growth-stage strategies are actually market-expanding techniques and these strategies strengthen the firm's competitive position. From the critical point of view, the market-expansion is secured at additional cost. In the growth-stage, there is a trade off between high market share and high current profit. A considerable amount is spent today for tomorrow's larger profit expectation.

**3. Marketing strategies in the Mature stage :**

Maturity stage is very critical in the life cycle of a product. At this stage, the sales come down and it continues for a longer period. The management, actually speaking, faces a challenge. The maturity stage is more or less a must for every product in its life cycle and, therefore, most of marketing management deals with the mature product. The maturity stage has different phases — growth maturity, stable maturity and decaying maturity. The maturity phases bringing down the rate of sales create over capacity in the industry as a consequence of which intensified competition ensues.

The strategy in the mature stage is to abandon the weaker products and spend money on newer products. "Marketing managers should not ignore or passively defend aging products. A good offence is the best defence. Marketers should systematically consider strategies of market, product and marketing-mix modification". *(P. Kotler).*

**4. Marketing strategies during the Decline stage :**

The advent of decline stage is more or less a certainty for most of the product forms and brands. The decline may be due to technological advances, consumer shifts in tastes and increased domestic and foreign competition. Whatever might be the reasons for decline, the consequences that a firm faces are overcapacity, increased price cutting and project erosion. Firms may resort to devices such as cutting down the promotion budget, further reduction of price, withdrawal from smaller market segments and weaker trade channels. This is the problem of aging of the product and it should be tackled accordingly. Only sentiment will not help. As observed by Alexander R.S. in his "The Death and Burial of 'sick products'" (as article in the Journal of Marketing) , "But putting products to death or letting them die — is a drab business and often engenders much of the sadness of a final parting with old and tried friends."

Management feels that unless economy improves

or marketing strategy is changed or the product is proved there is no possibility for the sales to pick up. Unless strong reasons for retention exist, it is no good carrying a weak product.

The marketing strategies that are usually adopted to tackle aging problems are: (a) Identifying the weak products (b) Determining marketing strategies and (c) Taking the dropping decision.

Through a product-review committee, the system for **identifying weak products** is developed. The data for each product are collected and analysed by a computer programme that identifies dubious products. The number of years of sales decline, market-share trends, gross profit margin and return on investment — all these are taken into consideration. "The product-review committee examines this information and makes a recommendation for each dubious product — leave it alone, modify its marketing strategy or drop it." *(P. Kotler).*

In **determining marketing strategies,** much depends on the level of the **exit barriers** (Harrigan). "The lower the exit barriers, the easier it is for firms to leave the industry and the more tempting it is for the remaining firms to remain" *(Kotler).* According to Harrigan, there are five decline strategies — (i) increasing the firm's investment (ii) maintaining the firm's investment level until the uncertainties about the industry are resolved (iii) decreasing the firm's investment level selectively by sloughing off unprofitable customer groups, while simultaneously strengthening the firm's investment in lucrative niches, (iv) harvesting (or milking) the firm's investment to recover cash quickly and (v) divesting the business quickly by disposing of its assets as advantageously as po-ssible.

A company's relative **attractiveness and competitive strength** finally **determine what should** be the appropriate decline strategy.

While deciding **to drop a product,** a company has to take further decisions. With a strong distribution and residual goodwill of the product, the company can sell it to a smaller firm. If no buyer is available, it is to be decided whether to liquidate the brand quickly or slowly.

# CHAPTER 16

## PRICING STRATEGIES AND PROGRAMMES

Price is the only element in the marketing mix that produces revenue. Historically, prices were set by buyers and sellers negotiating with each other. Setting one price for all buyers is a relatively modern idea. Undoubtedly, for decades, price was the major determinant of buyer choice. However, non-price factors have become relatively more important in buyer-choice behaviour in recent decades. Yet, price remains one of the most important elements determining company market share and profitability.

The handling of pricing is not uniform in all companies. Top management generally set prices; in big companies pricing is handled by division and product-line managers, pricing objectives and policies, of course, are formulated by the top management.

In setting the price of a product, the company follows a six-step procedure : (1) selecting the pricing objective, (2) determining demand, (3) estimating costs, (4) analysing competitors' prices and offers, (5) selecting a pricing method and (6) selecting the final price.

In selecting the pricing objective, the company carefully establishes its marketing objectives such as survival, maximum current profit, maximum current revenue, maximum sales growth, maximum market skimming or product-quality leadership.

The company determines demand schedule that shows the probable quantity purchased per period at alternative price levels. The elasticity or inelasticity of demand is important. The price can be set at a higher level if the demand for the product is inelastic.

The estimation of costs varying at different output levels and with different levels of accumulated production experience is the third step in price setting.

In a competitive market, competitors' prices have much bearing upon the setting of price. So, the company, as a step of price setting, is to examine competitors' prices.

Selecting a pricing method, out of so many methods such as mark-up pricing, target–return pricing, perceived value pricing, going rate pricing and sealed–bid pricing, is necessary for a right selection of pricing.

Lastly the company selects its final price. The final selection is done in the most effective psychological way; various market-mix elements are coordinated after checking that it conforms to company pricing policies. The company keeps it in view that the final price is acceptable to distributors and dealers, company sales force, competitors, suppliers and government.

**Market place pricing :** The conditions prevailing in the market place have also to be taken into consideration and the pricing has to be adopted accordingly. One is **geographical pricing.** It involves the company in deciding how to price its products to customers in distant locations. Companies have evolved five different approaches to geographical pricing. They are : (1) FOB origin pricing (free-on-board), (2) Uniform delivered pricing, (3) Zone pricing, (4) Basing-point pricing and (5) Freight-absorption pricing.

In **FOB origin pricing**, the goods are placed free on board a carrier at which point the title and responsibility passes to the customer. The customer pays the freight from the factory to the destination. This pricing is considered to be the most equitable way to allocate freight charges because each customer picks up his own cost. The disadvantage is high cost to distant customers.

**Uniform delivered pricing** is the exact opposite of FOB pricing. The same price plan freight is charged to all customers regardless of their locations.

**Zone pricing** falls between FOB origin pricing and uniform delivered pricing. Two or more zones are established and the same price is charged within a zone. The more distant a zone, the more is the price charged to customers.

**Basing-point pricing** denotes designating some city as a basing point and all customers are charged the freight cost from that city to the customer location regardless of the city from which the goods are actually shipped.

**Freight-absorption pricing** is resorted to when the seller wants to do business with a particular customer or geographical area. The seller company may absorb all or part of the actual freight charges in order to get the business. This pricing is used for market penetration and also to hold on to increasingly competitive markets.

**Price discounts and allowances :** Companies now-a-days modify their basic price to reward customers. Customers who make early payments or purchase in bulk are rewarded in the form of discounts and allowances. Discounts and allowances are also allowed for off-season buying. These may be cash discounts, quantity discounts, functional discounts, seasonal discounts and allowances.

Products may be priced temporarily even below their costs or below the list price. This is known as **promotional pricing.** There are different forms of promotional pricing such as — (a) loss-leader pricing, (b) special-event pricing, (c) cash rebates, (d) low interest financing, (e) warranties and service contracts and (f) psychological discounting.

In **loss-leader** pricing, super markets and department stores drop the price on well known brands to stimulate additional store traffic. This pricing strategy is not liked by manufacturers since they apprehend that this may dilute the brand image and may be a cause for complaint of retailers who change the list price.

**Special-event pricing** relates to special prices in special seasons to attract more customers.

**Cash Rebates** is an incentive pricing strategy to encourage purchases by allowing certain cash rebates for purchases within a specified period.

Low interest financing is a technique where the company offers customers low interest facility if the price is paid within a shorter period.

**Warranties and Service contracts** is a device where the company promotes sales by adding a free warranty offer or service contract instead of charging for the warranty or service contract. This is a way of reducing the price.

**Psychological discounting** means putting an artifically high price on a product, than offering it at a discount.

**Discriminatory pricing**

In such a pricing strategy, different prices are charged to different customers. For different product forms, brand images, places and times different prices are charged. Discriminatory pricing may be effected in several forms — (i) Customer-segment pricing , (2) Product form pricing, (3) Image pricing, (4) Location pricing and (5) Time pricing.

**Product-mix pricing**

This pricing takes place when a company decides on the price zones for several products in a product line and on the pricing of optional features, captive products, byproducts and product bundles.

This price strategy is resorted to when the product is a part of a product mix. In such a case, a set of prices is thought about to maximise profits on the total product mix. Because of different degrees of competition and inter-relationship between demand and cost of various products, product mix pricing is not an easy strategy.

# CHAPTER 17

## DECIDING A MARKETING CHANNEL DESIGN

The channel-decision poses problems to manufacturers. The ideal channel, coupled with feasibility and availability, is very difficult to find out. A firm entering into the market for the first time generally does not dare venture to cater to a wider market, rather it starts operating locally, using existing middlemen.

The new firm, even when it expands its markets to new areas, usually sticks to the existing marketing channel — the existing middlemen are not eliminated. Of course, different types of marketing channels are not unusual for relatively new manufacturers but their strategy of using the middlemen is different as compared to well-established large manufacturers. Selling directly through retailers in a smaller market and through distributors in a larger market is usually the technique. In rural areas, the channel is the general goods merchants and, in the urban areas, limited-line merchants constitute the channel of distribution. The designing of a marketing channel is the result of a number of factors and a host of constraints. The environmental factors have a dominant role to play. So, designing the ideal marketing channel is a tough job requiring "analysing of customer needs, establishing channel objectives, identifying the major channel alternatives and evaluating them" *(Kotler).*

In designing the marketing channel, the marketeer must understand first the **service output levels** desired by the target customers. The lot-size, waiting time, spatial convenience, product variety and service backup constitute the five service outputs produced by channels.

The number of units that the marketing channel permits a typical customer to buy is the **lot size** and the smaller the lot size, the greater the service output level that the channel must provide.

The average time that customers of the channel have to wait for receipt of the goods is the **waiting time.** Customers generally prefer fast delivery and this requires a great service output level.

The degree to which the marketing channel makes it easy for customers to purchase the product is known as **spatial convenience.** Direct marketing enhances spatial convenience.

The assortment breadth provided by the marketing channel is the **product variety.** Greater assortment breadth is generally the preference of customers because it increases the chance of exactly meeting their demand.

The add-on services (credit, delivery, repairs etc.) provided by the channel is the **service backup.** The service backup represents the extent of service that the channel provides.

To make the channel planning effective, channel objectives must be established but there are constraints in developing the objectives. The constrains are from products, intermediaries, competition, company policies, the environment and the level of service outputs desired by the target customer. Products may be perishable, bulky, non-standardised and high unit value requiring different methods of marketing channels. Perishable products require direct marketing, bulky products require minimization of distance and handlings, nonstandardised products are sold through company's own sales representatives and high unit value products reach the consumers via the company's sales force than through middlemen.

Every middleman has his separate, individual and distinctive characteristics and while deciding the design of channels, these are to be considered with reference to products to be marketed.

The marketing channel designing does not only take into account product characteristics and middlemen characteristics; environmental company and competitors' characteristics also have much to influence the channel-choice.

In a depressive economic condition, to secure economy becomes the primary consideration of a producer and, as such, the use of shorter channels and dispensing with inessential services becomes the criterion for channel designing. When the business environment is characterised by various legal regulations and restrictions, any attempt by business enterprises to lessen competition or to create monopolistic condition in the market through the channel mechanism is objected to and prohibited by the government of the country.

A company's characteristics, such as its long-run objectives, resources, product-mix and marketing strategy, affect channel design.

Channel design is also influenced by the competititors' channels. Producers of different products resort to different strategies in channel design when there are competitors in the market. For instance, food processors want their brands to be displayed next to competitive brands; again in some industries, producers may want to avoid the competitors' channels. Door-to-door selling operation, is preferred to channel distribution in case of cosmetic products because of scarcity of space facility in retail stores affecting proper exhibition of products.

In deciding channel design, channel alternatives have to be identified after ascertaining the target market and deserved positioning. Channel alternatives signify the types of intermediaries, the number of intermediaries and terms and responsibilities of each channel participant.

As to the types of intermediaries, we can name company's sales force, manufacturers' agency, industrial distributors, and for some companies there may be different channel alternatives according to the nature of the products the company produces. A continuous search for innovative marketing channels is the usual way of marketing management of a dynamic company.

To decide on the number of middlemen to use, three strategies are generally resorted to — intensive, selective and exclusive.

In intensive distribution strategy, producers of convenience goods and common raw materials stock their products in numerous outlets to create place utility as we find in case of cigarettes.

When only certain dealers can distribute the company's products, it is exclusive distribution strategy.

In selective distribution, there is a go-between intensive and exclusive distribution methods. The strategy is to use more than one but less than all of the intermediaries who are willing to carry a particular product. Selective distribution widens market coverage with more control and less cost than intensive distribution.

## Evaluating the major channel alternatives

Identification of several channel alternatives, necessarily and quite legitimately, requires the producer to determine the best one. In order to find out the best available channel what is needed is to evaluate each alternative against **economic, control** and **adaptive criteria.**

Economic considerations are likely to predominate the selection of a particular channel from a number of alternatives. Each channel produces a different level of sales and costs. More sales and less costs will be the criteria for selection of a channel. It may be the company's own sales force or outside sales agency. But costs generally rise faster through a sales agency, because sales agents get a larger commission than company sales people.

"There is one sales level (SB) at which selling costs are the same for the two channels. The sales agency is the preferred channel for any sales volume below SB, and the company sales branch is preferred at any volume higher than SB. Not surprisingly, sales agents tend to be used by smaller firms, or by large firms in their smaller territories wherever the sales volume is too low to warrant a company sales force" *(Kotler).*

When a firm uses a sales agency the question of control arises because the sales agency is an independent business firm. A vigilant watch over the sales agents selling technique is required to be kept by the producing firm to ensure that its products are given due consideration by the agents in the dealing with the ultimate consumers.

Adopting a channel involves some duration of commitment and loss of flexibility. A contract for a few is generally entered into during which period the producer cannot change the channel. So, it must be ensured that the agency selection is economically sound and superior to any other alternative channel, at least for the time being.

A channel alternative having been chosen, individual middlemen must be selected, motivated and evaluated. The selection of able, qualified middlemen is neither easy nor inexpensive. On the whole, what we should note is that, considering the nature of business, middlemen should be selected. After selection, continuous efforts will have to be made to **motivate** the middlemen to do their best job. Finally, periodical **evaluation** of middlemen's performance will have to be carried out.

All the procedure of deciding channel design, selecting the available best channel and carrying on constant review and evaluation of the performance of middlemen do not put a stop to further action by the producer in regard to channel design. Modification becomes necessary because there cannot be any last word of any strategy. So a continuous endeavour is set a-going to improve upon the channel **design.**

### Ideal distribution systems — How to attain :

Not to speak of distribution system of products, no system in this world can be said to have attained perfection and does not need any modification. Distribution channels clearly get outmoded with the passage of time. The existing system does not fit in with the changed environment and fails to satisfy customer needs. Distribution system need be changed though the change is not so easy because of long association with the distributors.

An **eight-step process** for moving an obsolescent distribution system closer to target customers' ideal system has been outlined. The steps are :

**First step :** This calls for finding out what target customers want in the way of channel services if no constraints existed. The ascertainment of various information from customers on how to enhance their conveniences is the task involved in the first step.

**Second step :** It consists of designing alternative distribution systems to provide services desired by the target customer.

**Third step :** Evaluating the feasibility and cost of the contending ideal distribution systems.

**Fourth step :** Gathering company executives' objectives for the company's distribution system. Some executives may resist on certain principles that must be observed.

**Fifth step :** Comparing the available options given by the management's criteria on the one hand and the customers' ideal distribution system on the other.

**Sixth step :** Asking management and selected experts to confront management's key assumptions. This requires the management to know the costs of their assumption and constraints as well as the gains and risks of changing them.

**Seventh step :** This step calls for asking management to confine the gap between the existing and the ideal management system and to agree on what changes they are willing to make.

**Eighth step :** It involves preparing a plan to implement the agreed-upon changes.

(Source : Harvard Business Review — *L.W. Stern & F.D. Sturdivant* ).

# CHAPTER 18

## A MARKETING CHANNEL —ITS FUNCTIONS AND FLOWS

The marketing intermediaries constitute a **marketing channel** (distribution channel) for distributing products to the ultimate consumers. This channel overcomes the time, place and possession gaps that separate goods and services from those who would use them. A number of persons operate in the marketing channel and each of them performs key functions. The marketing channel members also participate in the marketing flows. The functions they perform and the marketing flows in which they participate can be discussed as follows :

The key functions and flows arise in the following order between any two channel members :

(1) **Information :** Information are many for the producers to know and the marketing channel supplies these information. It collects and disseminates marketing research information about potential and existing customers, competitors and forces in the marketing environment.

(2) **Promotion :** Makers of the marketing channel promote communications about the offer designed to attract customers. These are persuasive communication the development and dissemination of which is very important for the producers/ manufacturers.

(3) **Negotiation :** This is a very important step/ stage in the final settlement of a transaction. It implies the attempt to reach final agreement on price and other terms to facilitate transfer of ownership.

(4) **Ordering :** This is a backward flow or communication implying information to the manufacturer by the intending buyer.

(5) **Financing :** At the different levels of the marketing channel, funds are required to finance inventories. The members of the channel acquire and allocate such funds.

(6) **Risk taking :** The channel work involves risks and the members of the channel undertake such risks in carrying out their work.

(7) **Physical possession :** It involves storage and movement of physical products and raw materials to the final customers.

(8) **Payment :** It is one of the key functions of the members of the marketing channel to ensure that the buyers actually make payment either through banks or other financial institutions to the sellers.

(9) **Title :** It means actual transfer of ownership from one organisation or person to another. This is effected by the channel operators.

The flows listed above do not move from the same direction; of course, some of them move in both directions. The directions may be forward or backward. The forward flows or direction include physical possession, title and promotion while ordering and payment are backward flows.

Regarding these functions, the important question that arises — **who** is to perform these functions ? All the functions have three things in common — use up of scarce resources, better performance through specialisation and their suitability among channel members.

To explain, let us assume that if the manufacturer performs the function, his costs go up and, as a consequence, prices go high. If middlemen step in, they charge an amount and even then the price may be lower than the one charged by the manufacturer, if the middlemen are efficient. Consumers themselves may perform some functions to enjoy lower prices. So, it is on the relative efficiency and effectiveness depends the issue of who should perform various channel tasks.

The ultimate object of the marketing channel is to provide meaningful assortment of goods to target customers and, in order to ensure this, there may be changes in channel institutions replacing the less efficient ones and also to combine or separate economic functions.

# CHAPTER 19

## MARKETING CONTROL AND ITS STRATEGIES

Marketing is a complex process. It proceeds in accordance with plans. But, in the implementation of plans, various situations arise that need control. The marketing department has to monitor and control marketing activities continuously to realise plan objectives of marketing. Marketing control devices may be — (1) Annual plan control, (2) Profitability control, (3) Efficiency control, and (4) Strategic control.

(1) **The annual plan control** primarily rests with the top and the middle management. The purpose of control is to examine whether the planned results are being achieved. The approaches to the **annual plan control** are — (a) Sales ana-lysis (b) Market-share analysis (c) Sales-to-expense ratios, (d) Financial analysis and (e) Attitude tracking.

This control-device is, as a matter of fact, **management by objectives.** These control measures are geared up step by step — generally four steps. At the begining, monthly or quarterly goals are set. At the next step, management monitors its performance in the market place. Then comes for the management to determine the causes of serious performance deviations. Lastly, the corrective action to close the gaps between the goals and performance is taken by the management. This control model pervades all levels of the organisation. As mentioned above, managers use five tools (approaches) to check on plan performance :

(2) **Profitability control** is the prime responsibility of the marketing controller. The purpose of the control is to examine where the company is making and losing money. The approaches are profitability — (a) by product (b) by territory (c) by customer (d) by group (e) by trade channel and (f) by order size.

This control measure helps management to determine whether any products or marketing activities should be expanded, reduced or eliminated. To realise these objectives, generally three steps are taken — (a) identifying the functional expenses, (b) assigning the functional expenses to the marketing entities and (c) preparing a profit and loss statement for each marketing entity.

Profitability control endeavours to find out the actual profitability of the firm's products, territories, market segments and trade channels. Thus, the weaker marketing entities are revealed by profitability analysis.

(3) **Efficiency control** is also the responsibility of the Marketing Controller. It is the line-and-staff management. The purpose of control is to evaluate and improve the spending efficiency and impact of marketing expenditures. It is the task of increasing the efficiency of such marketing activities as personal selling, advertising, sales promotion and distribution. Managers must watch certain key ratios that indicate how efficiently these functions are being performed.

After profitability analysis, if it is found that the company is not earning satisfactory profits, more efficient ways have to be devised and inefficiencies have to be eliminated in order to improve marketing. In efficiency control, better and efficient ways of managing sales force, advertising, sales promotion and distribution in connection with products, territories or markets have to be found out.

Efficiency control, therefore, is spread over sales force, advertising, sales promotion and distribution. All the poorer performing entities have to be managed in an efficient way through efficiency control.

(4) **Strategic control** is exercised by the top management with a view to examining whether the company is pursuing its best opportunities with respect to markets, products and channels. Strategic control ensures that company objectives, strategies and systems are optimally adapted to the current and forecasted marketing environment. In the present-day competitive market, it becomes necessary for companies to undertake a critical review of their overall marketing effectiveness. Marketing is a fast changing area, so there is the need for periodical assessment of the overall approach of the company to the market place. The assessment is carried on with the help of two tools **— a marketing effectiveness rating review** and **a marketing audit.**

Marketing effectiveness may not be judged by current sales and profit performance. Even without effective marketing management, there can be more sales and larger profits for reasons outside the purview of the marketing management. So is the need for marketing effectiveness rating review device. There are five attributes of a marketing orientation, the exhibition of which shows the marketing effectiveness of a company. These attributes are : **customer philosophy, integrated marketing organisation, adequate marketing information, strategic orientation and operational efficiency.** Each of these attributes can be measured by **a marketing-effectiveness rating instrument.**

It is observed from Philip Kotler's "From Sales obsession to Marketing Effectiveness" that very few companies can achieve scores within the superior range of twentysix to thirty points. Most companies receive scores in the fair-to-good range (11 - 20 points) even not a very good range (21 - 25 points). This rating instrument enables the managers to see room for marketing improvement. The management, on the results yielded by the rating instrument, can establish a plan for correcting its major marketing weaknesses.

Marketing weaknesses revealed by the application of the marketing-effectiveness rating review call for a more thorough study known as the **marketing audit.** It is a comprehensive, systematic, independent and periodic examination of the marketing environment of a company — its objectives, strategies and activities. The marketing audit is undertaken with a view to determining marketing problem areas and recommend a corrective short-run and long-run action plan to improve the overall marketing effectiveness of the organisation.

The recent trend for marketing control has been to establish marketing controller positions to monitor marketing expenditures and develops improved financial analyses of the effect of these expenditures.

# PART II

# FINANCIAL MANAGEMENT

*"Financial Management is an applied field of business administration. Principles developed by financial managers are applied to the problems of managing money. Finance has its own theories and principles but is fundamentally concerned with applications". (J. J. Hampton)*

# CHAPTER 1

## THE CHANGING CONCEPT OF THE FINANCE FUNCTION

The function of finance in a business has undergone changes. By this we mean that the management of finance or the managerial functions as to the financial aspect of a company has changed.

Previously, the finance function was confined mainly to procurement of funds. Now no more does that concept of finance function hold good. According to S. C. Kuchhal, definition of the term "finance function" in relation to business falls into three broad groupings. One group considers the finance function as procurement of funds only. Another group considers that finance is concerned with cash only. The third group, which, according to S. C. Kuchhal, is a compromise between the two extreme definitions of the finance function, envisages finance function as procurement of funds and their effective utilisation in the business.

The concept of the finance function has, therefore, changed from mere procurement of funds to the effective use of the funds. According to the changed concept of finance, quite in conformity with the changed money market, fund utilisation is more important; no doubt funds must be procured but unless the funds procured are properly utilised, there is no effectiveness of such procurement of funds and the company does not stand to gain from such finance accommodation where the management cannot properly utilise the funds to the best interest of the company.

So, procurement and utilisation of funds both are important. There can be no utilisation without procurement but in recent years procurement of finance does not pose so much problem as its proper utilisation does. So this changed concept gives more emphasis on utilisation than procurement.

The "Traditional Approach", as Ezra Solomon says, has some basic contents :

1) It emphasises on the raising of funds.
2) It emphasises on types of securities and their markets, formation, incorporation, merger etc.
3) It emphasises on the long term problems and neglects working capital management.
4) It pays significant attention to the financing problems of non-corporate enterprises.

### The Modern Approach

It is a shift of emphasis from raising of funds to its maximum utilisation. Thus, a Finance Manager today is not only a mere fund raiser and fund custodian or a staff officer giving advice on financial matters to the line executive but he is now an independent decision-maker; a planner and controller holding a very key position in the managerial hierarchy. Van Horne, a noted author, opines that, finance has changed from primarily a descriptive study to one that encompasses vigorous analysis and normative theory; from a field that was concerned primarily with the procurement of funds to one that includes the management of assets, the allocation of capital and the valuation of the firm in the overall market".

According to the modern approach, the finance function is comprehensive. Financial management is to determine the size and technology of the firm setting the pace and direction of its growth and shaping its profitability. The Finance Manager is to make the best asset mix with the optimum financing mix. The financial management is even expected to include profit planning in its functions.

"In this sense, finance function covers financial planning, forecasting of cash receipts and disbursements, the realising of funds, use and allocation of funds and financial control. Through budgets and other devices of financial control, the financial manager attempts to bring performance closer to the targets." (S. C. Kuchhal).

**Financial Management – its scope and objectives**

The importance of finance in a business cannot be over emphasised. To manage finance is to procure and utilise finance to the greatest advantage of the business unit. It is an applied branch of general management and is the custodian of corporate funds. The financial management primarily and mainly concentrates on the planning and control of finance. Planning is the key to sound financing and control ensures the realisation of the major objectives of the finance function.

Finance function has been defined as "procurement of funds and their effective utilisation in the business". "The financial manager can hardly stop with a decision that the funds can be obtained or even with a decision that the new installation of machinery can best be financed by making a public issue of 9% cumulative preference shares. On the other hand, he has to consider whether the additional profits expected from the new installation of machinery adequately compensate for the cost and risk involved in the issue of preference shares. It may thus be noted that this approach (to finance function) entails a decision-making after analysing the alternative uses and sources of funds. The financial manager has to play a major role in planning a business concern's need for funds; raising the necessary funds, and then putting them to effective use. In this sense, finance function covers financial planning, forecasting of cash receipts and disbursements, the realising of funds, use and allocation of funds and financial control. Through budgets and other devices of financial control, the financial manager attempts to bring performance closer to the targets" (S. C. Kuchhal).

Financial Management has to take three major decisions — (i) investment decision, (ii) financing decision and (iii) dividend decision. The implementation of these decisions is the task of financial management. Analytical tools are used in the analysis, planning and control of the activities involving funds.

Financial Management can manipulate controllable variables such as sources and amount of capital, operating costs, number of employees, selling and advertising budgets, cost of research etc. It can plan for the non-controllable variables to achieve 'Return on Investment'. Non-controllable variables include national income, population, indirect sale, competition etc.

Prof. E. Solomon, in his 'The Theory of Financial Management' says that financial management is an integral part of overall management rather than merely a staff activity concerned with fund-raising operations.

"Financial Management is the operational activity of a business that is responsible for obtaining and effectively utilising the funds necessary for efficient operation" (Massie). Since finance function covers decisions not only for the acquisition of funds but also for their effective utilisation, the scope of financial management has considerably widened. Today it includes judgements about whether a company should hold, reduce or increase investment in various assets. The nature of assets, total volume of funds, the way of raising the funds are all pertinent questions which come within the scope of financial management. To deal with these matters, financial management has to take into account the growth of the company, the specific form of assets and the composition of its liabilities. So, financial management is concerned with about all aspects of business operations. But as a matter of fact, many decisions do not involve changes in the volume of funds to be used; so, strictly speaking, they are not within the scope of financial management.

"The objective of financial management is to see that adequate cash is in hand to meet required current and capital expenditures and to otherwise assist in maximizing profits" (Massie).

A workable balance between cash inflow and cash outflow must constantly be maintained. Financial Management must have its objective to have a second financial foundation for the business unit to achieve its overall objectives.

To be precise, financial management is to ensure maximisation of profits of the business unit by adhering to financial descriptions. A business has a dynamic flow of funds represented by the funds flow cycle. Financial Management has within its scope of functions to plan and control the cycle of flow of funds — inflow and outflow of funds. Profitability and liquidity of funds must be so managed and balanced by the financial management that there is the optimum fund utilisation. Financial management should, therefore, strike for the achievement of the following objectives : (i) procurement of finance on convenient terms (ii) judicious investment of funds (iii) proper tax planning (iv) propriety of financial operations (v) improvement of the market value of share (vi) balance between dividend retention and distribution (vii) overall liquidity and profitability of working capital.

**Profit Maximisation vs. Wealth Maximisation**

The objective of a company is to maximise its value to its shareholders. Often maximisation of profits is regarded as the objective of a business enterprise. But this objective is not unanimously accepted. There is a controversy as to the goals of financial decision-making — some say profit maximisation, others say wealth maximisation.

To resolve this controversy, we should have a clear idea as to the distinctions between profit and wealth. Profit is the reward for the uncertainty and risk that an entrepreneur bears. So, profit is the natural objective of an enterprise since in every business uncertainty and risk are inherent.

Wealth earning is related to capability of profit earning. It is a more comprehensive term. Profitability is the substitute for wealth.

Now let us discuss the answer to the question — **which should be the goal of financial management — profit or profitability; profits maximisation or wealth maximisation ?**

Profit and profitability can be clearly distinguished. According to Prof. Solomon, maximisation of profit in the sense of maximising wealth is an unreal motive. Profitability maximisation in the sense of using resources to yield economic values higher than the joint values of inputs is a useful goal of financial management. It is based on a different set of considerations. The operating goal of wealth maximisation based on profitability does not conflict with the other motives such as maximising sales, size, growth or market share or the survival of the management itself. Thus, the **proper goal of financial management is wealth maximisation.** Prof. Solomon has further emphasised that wealth maximisation also maximises the achievement of other motives of management. Financial decisions become meaningful and useful through maximisation of wealth. Profit maximisation is a narrow concept which cannot be the goal of financial management.

Profit maximisation is not accepted as the goal of financial management on the grounds that it relates to the problem of uncertainty and as such it is not possible to maximise what cannot be known. When expected returns are related to higher risks, a higher capitalisation rate has to be applied to opportunities that involve greater risk. "The combination of expected returns with risk variations and related capitalisation rate cannot be considered in the concept of profit maximisation". One cannot be sure as to the accuracy of the estimates of future relations, so no attempt should be made or can be made to maximise it; a certain level or rate of profit can be planned but maximisation of profit cannot be.

Thus, profit maximisation is a concept which is too narrow and the new definition of business does not suit this narrow objective. A broad objective of wealth maximisation arising at increase of profitability is nearer to the new concept of business than profit maximisation which shirks itself from the social objective of business.

To answer a question on the objective or goal of financial management, the changed concept of finance should be kept in view. "Proper utilisation of funds which can ensure maximisation of wealth is the new concept of financial management. Financial Management is an integral part of overall management and the central issue of financial policy is the rational matching of the advantage of potential uses against the cost alternative potential sources so as to achieve the broad financial goals which an enterprise sets for itself". (Solomon)

Finance today considers matters covering a wide range having cash flow implication. Finance Management evaluates resource allocation choices. Therefore, finance today is a very comprehensive term covering "size of the firm, rate of growth, asset mix, product mix, project valuation, financial analysis, financing mix, fixed vs variable costs, make or buy decisions and the like". (S C Kuchhal)

The field of finance is a subject of behavioural sciences and all market participants — management, shareholders, lenders, consumers enrich this field. Wealth maximisation is, therefore, , the real goal.

# CHAPTER 2

## FUNCTIONS OF FINANCIAL MANAGEMENT

Finance is the life-blood of any business. So, the functions of financial management are of paramount importance and merit special attention.

The function of financial management should commence with the estimation of capital requirement and the purpose of such requirement and then to find out ways and means of procuring the required amount of capital.

According to some eminent scholars, there are three inter-dependent core elements in financial management. They are : resource mobilisation, resource deployment and resource acquisition.

The functions of financial management concentrate on making decisions in three major areas — investment, financing and dividend.

### Investment decision

To create assets for their utilisation in earning income is investment. Assets are categorised into two on the basis of their yielding capacity. Assets which yield return over a period of time (usually over one year) and assets which are readily convertible into cash (usually within a year). Accordingly the investment decisions are two-fold — capital budgeting and working capital management.

Capital budgeting relates to the allocation of funds on a new asset out of the alternative courses of action or reallocation of capital where an old asset becomes non-profitable. An important aspect of capital budgeting is the determination of norm against which the benefits are to be judged. This is known as 'Cost of Capital' norm.

Working Capital Management is the management of current assets. Two considerations predominate in working capital management — one is liquidity consideration to ensure that the working capital is not less than what is required and another consideration is to see that excess capital may not be employed to bring down the profit. So, the working capital management is the "trade off between liquidity and profitability".

### Financing decision

Financing decision is a very vital function of financial management as it is closely related to the capital structure or financial leverage. The decisions as to how, when and where funds are to be acquired are financial decisions. It is the function of financial management to decide the proportion of debt capital and equity capital. In the debt capital, the risk of shareholders is less but the prospect of dividend suffers. So, return and risk are traded off in financing decision. Keeping in view the optimum capital structure with a view to ensuring maximum return to the shareholders, proportion of debt and equity capital has to be fixed. After the optimal debt equity mix, the most appropriate sources of funds are explored.

### Dividend decision

Profits of a company are distributed as dividends and/or a part of the profits is retained in the business for future provision. The dividend decision is taken after taking into consideration a host of factors — internal as well as external in nature. Relation of profits for internal financing is a big consideration for companies aspiring for expansion but the shareholders' interests must also be properly looked into. A stable dividend policy is always desirable. But the decision-making with regard to dividend is influenced by practical as well as by psychological matter. The overall economic environment of the country has much bearing on dividend decision.

Besides making decisions on investment, financing and dividend, as we discussed above, we can discuss the functions of financial management in the context of the goals of the firm. The financial managers perform tasks in several areas; they can be conveniently classified into two — one is to link the functions with the twin goals of liquidity and profitability. Each task is linked with the goal of liquidity, profitability or both. Another classification method focuses on what is being managed — assets or funds. So, the functions of the financial management have double aspects — decision-making aspects of finance and the specialised advisory role of the financial manager.

The financial management performs the task which enable it to have sufficient liquidity to carry out the firm's activities. Functions such a (a) forecasting cash flows (b) raising funds an (c) managing the flow of internal funds fall withi this category.

In seeking profits for the firm, the financi manager may provide specific input into the deci sion-making process. With respect to profitabi lity, his functions cover (i) cost control (ii) pricin (iii) forecasting profits and (iv) measuring re quired return.

In performing the functions of financial man agement, the financial manager, besides being decision-maker, acts in the role of a specialise staff officer, an expert on financial matters an money markets.

The function of financial management in manag ing assets attests to the decision-making role o the financial manager. A firm's assets must b

**A graphic overview of financial management**

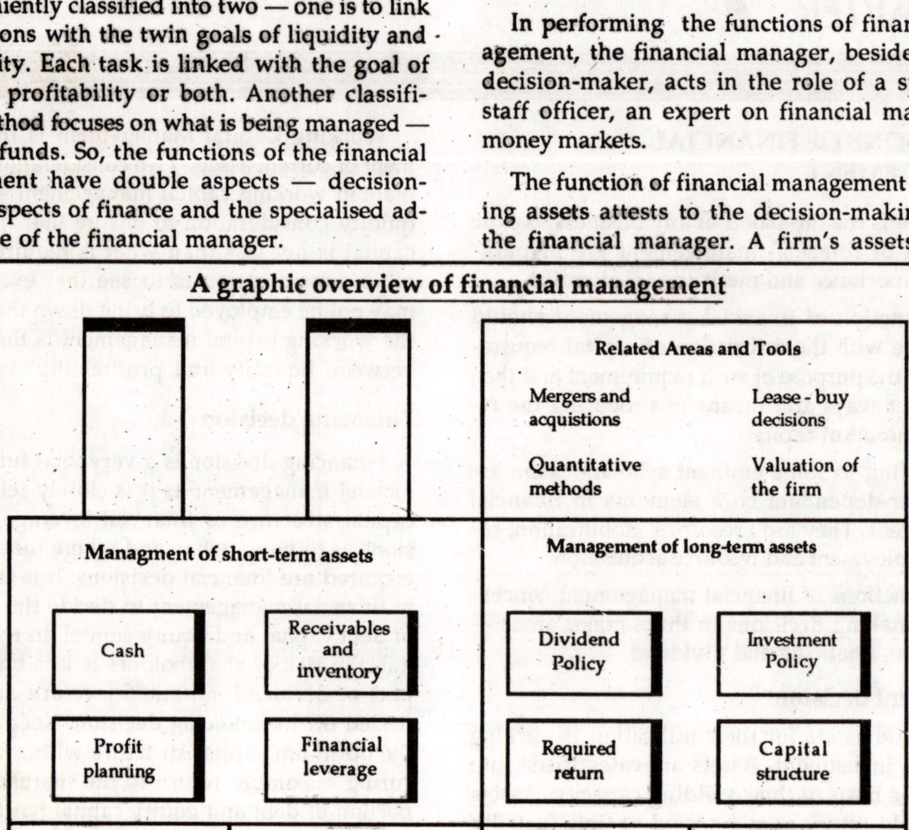


*(Based on Hampton's Financial Decision Making)*

arefully managed. In the managements of funds, e. liquid assets, the financial management acts s specialists and staff personnel.

The functions of financial management, there- re, cover decision-making and rendering special- sed service; the financial manager acting as a taff officer. "The manager is responsible for hav- ng sufficient funds for the firm to conduct its busi- ess and to pay its bills. Money must be located to inance receivables and inventories, to make ar- angements for the purchase of assets and to iden- ify sources of long term financing. Cash must be vailable to pay dividends". (*J. J. Hampton*).

The goals of the firm are achieved through goals and functions of finance. It requires planning hat covers the year's operating revenues and ex- enses and deals with leverage concepts in the irm's operations and financing. Financial man- agement is concerned with both short-term and ong-term asset management. Long term asset man- agement covers issues relating to dividend policy, nvestment policy, cost of capital and the firm's ca-pital structure. It also covers related areas such as the valuation of the firm, mergers and acquisi- ions.

## Financial Planning

Finance is the life-blood of a business. Every business, big or small, needs finance and to plan the total financial requirements of business is fi- nancial planning.

"Planning is deciding in advance what is to be done; that is, a plan is a projected course of action" (W. H. Newman). Financial planning, therefore, is to decide in advance sources of funds and their uses. In doing so, it determines the firm's goals, policies and procedures in the financial sphere. It pertains only to the function of finance.

In financial planning, the amount of capital re- quirements, the form and proportion of the securi- ties and the administration of capital of the firm are taken into consideration.

Step-wise, we can say, financial planning moves in the following manner.

**First Step** — *Determination of the firm's objec- tives* — Maximization of owner's wealth. The Fi- nance Manager lays down both long-run and short- run objectives. Only those short-term objectives that contribute to the achievement of long term ob- jectives are acceptable. The maximization of own- er's wealth means maximizing value of the firm to its shareholder – maximizing market price per share. The market value per share is a reflection of different policy decisions such as investment in fixed and current assets, financing decision or capi- tal structure decision and dividend decision. Wealth maximization takes into account present and prospective future earnings per share, the tim- ing and risk of these earnings, the dividend policy of the firm and other factors that bear on the mar- ket price of the stock. The objective of maximizing market price per share may not be the same as maximizing earnings per share. Wealth maximi- zation is an appropriate objective from sharehold- ers, management and society's view-point in so far as it represents the interests of all concerned.

**Second step** : *Formation of financial policies.* These include procurement, administration and disbursements of funds of business firms. In this step of financial planning, total capital needs, sources of funds to acquire assets, the time when they will be available and how long the require- ments for funds will continue are planned.

**Third step** : *Formation of financial procedure.* This last step in financial planning is to ensure that the policies formulated are properly trans- lated into action through detailed procedures. This is done with a view to assuring the finance manager a consistency of action.

Financial planning vitally affects the perfor- mance of a firm. So, to ensure sound financial plan- ning, the financial management must keep in view the following matters :

(i) Simplicity of the plan (ii) foresightedness (iii) scope for intensive use of funds (iv) flexibility of the plan (v) provision for contingency and (vi) liquidity element.

As discussed above, a financial planning is good and effective when it enables the firm to secure for it the best utilisation of its funds, the best return on the investment of the shareholders and these can only be ensured through proper capitalisation. Normal capitalisation based on 'Earnings Theory' is the object of a good financial planning. Over or under capitalisation is not conducive to the inter- est of the firm. Besides 'Earning Theory' in finan- cial planning, there is the 'Cost Theory' that sums up the expenses of position, establishment, fixed assets, current assets, commission, brokerage, im- provement, extension etc. The Theory, whether it is Earnings or Cost, does not matter; there must be normal capitalisation and the financial planning must see that there is proper proportion of securities in the capital structure, that is, there is proper 'Capital Gearing'.

In business management, financial planning forms the core of all other areas of management.

In many firms, the task of planning is coordinated by a department known as the corporate planning department, long-range planning department or budgeting department. This department is responsible for receiving inputs from sales, production, finance and other operating areas of the company. By coordinating the process of planning, management assures that the different departments are working to achieve the same goals and taking actions consistent with the overall objectives of the firm.

In financial planning, the firm considers the effect of different courses of action on the value of the stock. A valuable tool for analysing the future market price of the stock is the calculation of future earnings per share.

As a general rule, the firm's financial planning process involves the efforts of many operating and financial managers. Planning process continues in a definite pattern. Once plans are agreed upon by the operating units, they are usually presented to the management committee or chief operating officer of the firm for approval or modifications. The final plans become the blue print for the firm's operations.

Financial planning basically involves two major areas for analysis — external factors and inte nal factors.

The most developed portion of the firm's sho and long-term plans deals with internal factor and stresses — (a) marked demand for the produc line or service, (b) future costs and (c) sources funds.

The financial planning process confers a numbe of benefits such as (i) anticipation of problems an opportunities (ii) coordination of actions (iii) as sistance in control and (iv) providing standards o performance.

Financial planning prepares the budget and th financial planning process is very often called bud geting. Budgeting makes use of pro-forma financia statements, Balance Sheets, income statements fund-flow statements and other formal statements

Financial planning uses various analytical tools to increase the accuracy of forecasts of sales and costs. The break-even analysis and the profit volume analysis are such tools. In financial planning, break-even analysis is used to determine the level of operations at which a firm neither makes a profit nor loses money. At this level, the firm operates at zero profit level or break-even point. A modification of the break-even formula results in a tool that relates profits to sales at different operating levels. This is profit-volume analysis. The formulas for profit volume analysis use the concept of marginal analysis, because they define costs and profits using fixed and variable costs.

# CHAPTER 3

## CORPORATE PLANNING AND FINANCIAL MANAGEMENT

Corporate planning is vital for the survival of a company. Planning based on rational decisions can only ensure success for a company. Planning is nothing but sharpening the rationality and it 'deals with the futurity of present decisions in terms of setting goal, developing strategies to achieve them, translating strategies into detailed operational programmes and assuring that plans are carried out'.

The corporate management has to concentrate on a few specific goals like return on investment and sales. When a variety of goals are considered, management decisions become essential. Corporate planning proceeds through stages — determination of company's objectives, preparation of forecast and estimation of probable error, calculation of planning trap and determination of constraints and means and finally designing the strategy. While preparing the forecast, the planning needs the preparation of a profit forecast in which financial management is involved. A thorough study of the company's past performance to identify trends in the four components of profits : selling prices, variable costs, fixed costs and volume is essential. These trends are projected into the future and modified, taking into account events and trends expected to occur in the future with a significant bearing on the expected profits.

The corporate planner has to assess how much profit will satisfy the owner and the financial management is to strive for that. It has to be reconsidered from time to time whether the profit target still reflects the level of the satisfaction of shareholders. A profit forecast is prepared by the financial management. Having determined the company's profit target and forecasting the likely profits for each year, the financial management is to calculate the gap between these two figures. The financial management aims at closing the profit gaps and decides what strategies are to be followed to close the gaps.

"Capital expenditure must be integrated into the corporate plans. The economic justification for a capital expenditure requires a long-term estimate of profits which in turn involves projection of sales and costs of operation for a period of years" (S.C. Kuchhal). This needs financial planning. The financial management is involved in order to ensure profitability or wealth maximisation. Financial management, with its new connotation, has become so embracing and comprehensive that any corporate planning — in whatever sphere it may be — must consider financial implication and aspect and the extent to which financial management has to be involved. Financial plan and corporate planning are to go in close collaboration. Financial management with its wide ramifications of functions are closely identified with corporate planning. Financial planning can best be regarded as the vital organ of the comprehensive corporate planning.

### Capitalisation

There is no unanimity as to the meaning of the term 'Capitalisation'. Various authors have defined capitalisation in various ways. Some consider capitalisation as synonymous with financial planning. However, without going into the large number of interpretations given by different writers, we may classify them as **broad** and **narrow.**

Broadly speaking, capitalisation refers to the process of determining the plan or patterns of financing. It includes both the determination of the quantity of finance and the decision about the quality of financing. In the narrow sense, capitalisation is used only in its quantitative aspect and refers to the amount at which a company's business can be valued.

From all the definitions of capitalisation, one thing emerges – that **capitalisation is the sum-total of all long term securities and the surpluses not meant for distribution.** Capitalisation is, therefore, composed of the value of share, the value of surpluses and the value of bonds and debentures. Capitalisation is used only with reference to companies and it is different from capital.

## Theories of Capitalisation

**Cost theory :** (Promotion expenses + organisation expenses + cost of fixed assets + working capital + cost of getting the business well established) = Value of the Company.

The merit of the cost theory is that it helps the promoter in calculating the amount of the capital which he has to raise.

The drawbacks of the theory are : (i) It may not prove the real worth of the company (ii) It represents the value of the company momentarily as the original cost is highly static in character (iii) It fails to reflect future changes (iv) The capital equipment or the assets may have inflated values or become obsolete.

To overcome the shortcomings of 'Cost Theory' and to arrive at a correct figure of capitalisation, 'earnings approach' is used.

## Earnings Theory

This theory takes into account the various contingencies occurred and likely to occur during the life-time of business. Earnings and capital investment complement each other and are mutually dependent. The return on investment forms the basis of this theory. The amount of capitalisation is figured out from the expected volume of earnings and the prevailing rate of return. For example, if fifteen percent is the rate of return and rupees three thousand be the expected earnings of a business, the amount of capitalisation would come to rupees twenty thousand. The amount and regularity of earnings and the rate at which they should be capitalised are two important considerations in this theory. In a newly-established company, the amount and regularity of earnings cannot be easily anticipated; so cost concept is favoured. But in case of an established company, the earnings concept is more suitable as the cost concept fails as a measure of value for it.

It is practically very difficult to assess correctly and properly the requirement of capitalisation. So, what happens is, either over-capitalisation or under-capitalisation.

## Over-capitalisation

When the assets employed exceed the actual requirements of the business, it is a case of over-capitalisation and an over-capitalised firm does not earn an adequate return on the assets employed; the earnings of the firm are not enough to make its securities sell at par. "In other words, the amount of shares issued may be much in excess of actual requirements, so that the dividend rate is too low to allow the shares to sell at their par value". It means funds invested, are not properly utilised. That does not mean that there is abundance of capital.

## Causes of Over-capitalisation

A firm is over-capitalised for a variety of reasons. They are :

1) **Formation during boom period :** Inflationary condition prevailing at the time of floatation of a firm causes over-capitalisation when the boom conditions subside.
2) **Promotion with over-valued assets :** The conversion of a partnership or private company into a public limited company with their assets revalued at inflated figures leads to over-capitalisation. The inflated price does not justify the earning capacity of the company; the book value of the company being more than its real value.
3) **Excessive promotion expenses :** Over-capitalisation is very often the result of excessive promotion expenses. Payments of unduly high amount for intangible assets and non-productive assets like goodwill, copyright etc. lead to over-capitalisation.
4) **Inadequacy of capital :** In case of a company where the financial planning has flaws, additional funds may be borrowed at excessive rates of interest resulting in diminishing earning capacity. This leads to over-capitalisation; share-holders do not get extra dividends and the real value of their shares comes down.

5) **Liberal dividend policy :** The dividend policy of a company has much to do in regard to capitalisation. Without resorting to ploughing back of profits, if a company declares dividends liberally, it may result in over-capitalisation. Reserves are not created; provisions for contingencies are not made and, as a result, after a few years, the book value of shares becomes higher than their real value.

6) **Taxation policy :** The taxation policy of the Government may be responsible for over-capitalisation. Because of excessive tax burden, a company may find it difficult to make any provision for replacement and renewal of assets. This results in inefficiency of the company and as a consequence, the real value of shares, comes down.

7) **Wrong depreciation policy :** Inadequate provisions for depreciation of fixed assets may also lead to over-capitalisation. The efficiency and profit-yielding capacity of the company are reduced.

## Effects of Over-capitalisation

1) **On Corporations :** (a) The earning capacity of the company being reduced, the value of its shares diminishes (b) The credit-worthiness of the company suffers a set-back (c) Unsound depreciation policy to inflate profit may ultimately harm the company (d) Manipulation of accounts may be resorted to, to cover up the inefficiency of the management (e) Financial condition of the company may deteriorate, forcing the management to incur unweildy debt resulting in serious injury to the company.

2) **On Shareholders :** (a) The gradual decrease in the value of shares affects the shares adversely (b) Income from dividend not only decreases, it becomes uncertain (c) Speculation in shares rises affecting the interest of the shareholders (d) Share value being reduced, shares cannot be used as collateral security (e) Over-capitalisation needs reorganisation, in which case the shareholder stands to lose to a great extent.

3) **On Society :** (a) Price increase is a feature of over-capitalised company which affects society (b) An over-capitalised company, because of its difficulties, may go into liquidation which has a very adverse effect on the economic environment of the society.

4) **Creditors** of the company suffer because of liquidation which has a serious social effect.

5) **Employees** may face wage cut which has a tremendous impact on the society because of industrial unrest.

6) Over-capitalisation, with all its effects, creates **bad ethical atmosphere** in the society.

7) **Misapplication and wastage of scarce resources** of the economy is a natural consequence of over-capitalisation and this is a social wastage in the sense that the scarce resource could have been better utilised for raising the aggregate output and the natural income.

## How to correct over-capitalisation

Over-capitalisation causes much harm to the company itself, to shareholder and to the society. But some measures may be taken to correct over-capitalisation :

Firstly, attempt may be made to correct over-capitalisation by the reduction of the funded debts and thus the parity between the book value and the real value of the company may be restored.

Secondly, Debenture-holders may be persuaded to accept new debentures at a lower rate of interest.

Thirdly, if possible, redemption of preference shares may be undertaken.

Lastly, reduction of the number of shares of the company or reduction of their par value to bring their book value equal to their par value.

## Under Capitalisation

**When actual capitalisation is lower than its proper capitalisation, it is a case of under-capitalisation.** It can be understood from the earning capacity of the total long term resources. Such a company earns considerably more than the prevailing rate on the outstanding securities. It is a condition when the real value of the company is more than the book value which means the insufficiency of capital **for efficient running of the company;** it is not actually inadequacy of capital in the absolute sense.

## Causes of Under-capitalisation

Causes are many but more important among them are : (a) promotion under depression (b) conservative dividend policy (c) under-estimation of earnings and (d) efficient and sound management.

A depressive condition of the economy prevailing at the time of promoting a company enables it to earn more than expected during the period of recovery or boom. This increase in earnings becomes disproportionate to the capital employed and thus the company becomes under-capitalised.

By a conservative dividend policy and ploughing back of profits, a company may build up sufficient reserves and in course of time the reserves may assume such a proportion that the real value of the shares of the company may exceed their book value i.e. a situation of under-capitalisation develops.

It is not unlikely that the financial planning of a company may contain in it the element of under-capitalisation. An underestimation of the earnings and the capitalisation based on that may eventually lead to under-capitalisation, the earnings being more than anticipated.

An efficient management with its managerial ability may improve the performance of the company resulting in increased earning. This will lead to increasing the real value of the company more than its book value. Thus the company becomes **under capitalised.**

## Effects of Under-capitalisation

Manipulation of accounts, encouragement of competition, worsening the industrial relations and payment of higher taxes are attributed to under-capitalisation.

In an under-capitalised company, the management may be encouraged to manipulate accounts to meet their selfish ends. Inaccurate accounts may misguide the share-holders about the real state of affairs of the company and may affect their earnings. Secret reserves may be created and earnings may be understated with the consequence that with the value of shares being decreased, the management may acquire shares at lower price, thus exploiting the ill-informed share-holders.

An under-capitalised company will have higher earnings which would tempt others to promote such companies and thus competition in the industry would increase.

Industrial relations in an under-capitalised company are likely to worsen because the employees may demand higher remuneration for their services in the company which is in prosperity.

Under-capitalised companies may be required to pay higher taxes because of their excess profit.

## How to correct Under-capitalisation

To counteract the ill-effects of under-capitalisation : One remedy is to split up the shares in order to decrease the rate of earnings per share. Though it does not affect total capitalisation, it may simply result in reduction of par value of the stock. The more effective remedy lies in the capitalisation of the reserves or surplus by issuing share-dividend or bonus shares.

## Break-Even analysis

In planning the financial structure of a company, the cost-volume-profit (C-V-P) analysis is important. It helps in finding out the relationship of costs and revenues to output. The financial management can thus study the plural effect of the level of output upon income and expenses and, therefore, upon profits. This analysis is usually presented on a Break-even Chart. The stage at which the Total Sales = Total Fixed Cost + Total Variable Cost, is called Break-even Point and the Chart which shows this Break-even Point is called Break-even Chart. On a Break-even Chart, the volume is indicated on the X-axis as number of units produced and sold. The costs and revenue are indicated on the Y-axis in terms of value. The total cost (Y) at any volume (X) equals a fixed component (F) plus a variable component (V) times the number of units of volume (X) i.e. cost $Y = F + VX$.

Revenue is plotted on the assumption of constant selling price per unit. Assuming that volume can be measured as units of product and designating the unit selling price as (p), total revenue (Y) at any volume (X) equals the unit selling price (p) times the number of units of volume.

i.e. for revenue $Y = pX$, $Y = F + VX$, $Y = pX$, $pX = F + VX$.

Break-even analysis is an important tool for profit planning in the hands of management. A low break-even point is desirable to have more chances of operating the business at a profit over the years.

But the break-even analysis has its **limitations.** "Many costs and their components do not fall into neatly compartmentalised fixed or variable cost categories as they possess the characteristics of both types".

In break-even analysis, four ways of profit performance are assumed – (a) by increasing volume (b) by increasing selling price (c) by decreasing variable costs and (d) by decreasing fixed costs. This is assumed that each of the four possibilities is independent of others which is rarely the case. A break-even chart represents a short-run static relationship of costs to output but firms that are fast-growing find that break-even charts become obsolete very quickly. The relations indicated in the break-even chart do not help for all levels of operations. **Linear break-even analysis** is especially weak in what it implies about sale price. Therefore, in order to study profit possibilities under different prices, a whole series of charts is necessary, one chart for each price or a non-linear break-even analysis can be used.

However, in spite of limitations, the simplicity of the break-even charts is one of their great values.

## Capital structure

Gustenberg, in his 'Financial Organisation and Management', defines capital structure as "the make up or form or composition of capitalisation i.e, the life of securities to be issued and the relative proportion of each type of securities in the total capitalisation".

Capital structure, in simple words, refers to the permanent financing of the firm, represented by the long-term debt, preferred stock and net worth. It is the make-up of the total debt and total equity. 'Financial leverage' has to be used for the analysis of capital structure. **Financial leverage** means the ratio of total debt to total assets. **Leverge means** the employment of the asset or funds for which a company pays a fixed cost or fixed return. The cost or return may be thought of as the fulcrum, i.e. point of support of a lever. Thus, financial leverage implies the use of funds carrying 'fixed commitment charge' with the objective of increasing return to equity shareholders. When the proportion of debt is high compared to total funds employed, the company is said to be highly levered or geared.

The third major decision of the finance function is concerned with the establishment of a defensible approach to the problem of selecting an optimum combination of many kinds of financing available to the modern enterprise.

The objective of an optimal capital structure is two-fold :

(a) It maximises the value of the company (Alexandra Barges) and the wealth of its owner.

(b) It minimises the company's cost of capital thereby increasing its ability to find new wealth — creating opportunities.

The rationale of optimal capital structure points to its social value. It makes better use of society's funds of capital resources; thus the total wealth of society increases. By creating investment, optimal capital structure increases the economy's rate of investment and growth. Shareholders' wealth also is maximised.

# CHAPTER 4

## FEATURES OF SOUND CAPITAL PLAN

A sound capital plan is the *sine qua non* for the success of a company. Financial management has to make an all-out effort to ensure sound planning of capital.

A sound capital plan has the following features: (i) Flexibility (ii) Liquidity (iii) Accuracy in estimation of financial needs (iv) Pattern of capital structure (v) Optimum fund utilisation (vi) Simplicity (vii) Planning foresight and (viii) External influences.

**(I) Flexibility :** It is a feature of a sound capital plan. There should always remain the scope for changes or modification necessitated by circumstances. A sound capital plan must have elasticity to accommodate any contingency. Unforeseen events cannot be provided in the plan. So, a sound plan must have thorough flexibility to meet any contingency. Adequate funds must be kept apart to meet any unforeseen situation. In the expansion plan, there should be provision for adequate depreciation, liberal ploughing back of capital, secret reserves, conservative dividend policy and so on. Flexibility in capital plan is now all the more necessary because of the inflationary conditions. Rising costs and additional costs are very likely to affect the capital plan of a firm. So, unless the capital plan is flexible, it cannot be said to be a sound one.

**(II) Liquidity :** For efficient and smooth working of a firm, financial liquidity is a must. Share capital, reserves, long term loans represent liquidity. The financial management, while chalking out a sound capital plan, must give attention to the aspect of capital planning. A judicious compromise between profitability and liquidity must feature a sound capital plan and under no circumstances liquidity should be made the victim of profitability. Liquidity can only be ensured when there is sufficient working capital.

**(III) Accurate financial-need estimation :** Financial needs of the various components of the capital plan must be accurately assessed. Needs for finance may be for fixed assets or for current assets and there may be various capital expenditure which should be estimated correctly and precisely as far as possible to make the capital plan a sound one.

**(IV) Pattern of capital structure :** The mode of finance is a feature of sound capital plan. In a sound capital plan, there must be a clear provision as to the mode of finance. Whether a company will have only equity share capital or both equity and preference share capital must be clearly indicated in the plan. In a good capital planning, the securities are, thus, to be clearly planned in the capital structure before-hand. It may be that loan capital will have to be raised. In that case, the plan for capital must have a clear indication of that direction. In the capital structure of a company — own and loan capital – both may be provided but the plan must stipulate it earlier. So, a sound capital plan stipulates mode of finance or capital structure of the company.

**(V) Optimum fund utilisation :** A sound capital plan provides for optimum fund utilisation. It is a feature of a good capital plan to outline the measures to be taken in the management of fixed as well as working capital of the company. Maximum utilisation of fund is the technique of modern financial management and it has, therefore, become a feature of any sound capital plan to ensure optimum utilisation of funds.

(VI) **Simplicity :** It is a feature of sound capital plan. The capital plan of a company should not be made unnecessarily complicated. A simple financial structure without having so many varieties of securities is the characteristic of a good capital plan.

(VII) **Planning foresight :** Intelligent forecasting of various contingencies is a feature of sound capital plan. A good capital plan is the reflection of the financial management.

(VIII) **External influences :** In a sound capital plan, one characterstic feature is that it gives due consideration to external features such as government taxation policy, money market, business cycle etc.

## Financial Policies — Fixed Capital and Working Capital

Financial Management of a company precisely means the management of its fixed and working capital. Management, of course, includes procurement and best utilisation of the funds collected through shares, equity and preference, debentures etc.

The financial policies for fixed and working capital imply management of the corporate finance with a view to achieving the designed objectives of the organisation.

The policies with regard to fixed and working capital have a far-reaching effect on the overall performance of a company. Fixed capital for the setting up, promoting and starting the company and to put it into operation; working capital for its progress and continuance, are both indispensable. So, financial policies as to how these two types of capital can be best managed are the primary consideration of our financial manager who wants to control finance efficiently.

Fixed capital represents land, building, plant machinery, fixtures, patents etc. or other property permanently committed to the business such as the minimum working capital. The characteristic of fixed capital is that it cannot be converted into cash except through the slow accretion of depreciation allowances, without liquidation of business. So its return to the investors is slow and that through the profitable operation. Keeping in view the nature of fixed capital, financial policies should be framed. Since fixed capital cannot be recovered within a short period, fixed cost is sometimes ignored in the short period but must be recovered in the long run. Requirements of fixed capital vary from one type of company to another. In a public utility concern, say, an electricity company, fixed capital requirement is enormously a big amount. Larger the scale of operation, more is the need for fixed capital. Financial policy, therefore, will have to be formulated accordingly. So far as the financial policy of fixed capital is concerned, a proper assessment becomes a necessity to avoid unnecessary blocking of capital which is generally very expensive. But the policy must also ensure that there is no dearth of fixed capital and the company does not suffer in any way in its promotional stage in the matter of fixed assets. There should not be any interruption in the flow of business operation owing to the lack of adequate amount of fixed capital. The policy formation must ensure that, through the issue of shares, debentures and long term investments, the needs of fixed capital must be adequately met and the company will not starve for fixed capital in any way. The financial policy for fixed capital should not be to finance fixed capital requirements with short-term funds such as bank credit. In that case, the defective and imprudent financial policy may interrupt the business activities.

In formulating financial policy for fixed capital, the needs of fixed expenditure at present and the future should be properly assessed and the policy should see to it that the procurement of finance for long-term investment is made from the most suitable source, that is, at cheaper cost without any compulsion for its early redemption or repayment. A sound fixed capital policy is based on the present calculation as well as on the foresightedness about the contingencies which may entail further expenditure of fixed nature.

## Financial Policy for Working Capital

Working capital is required for keeping the company going. Current assets have to be processed for working capital. Current assets consist of raw materials, work-in-progress inventory, finished goods inventories, cash, receivables. These assets circulate in such a manner that each of them gives rise to the next one in so far as it is invented, recovered and reinvested again and again in the lifetime of the company.

The financial policy for working capital is made to avoid possible duplication. The amount of working capital is carefully determined at the time of drafting the financial plan. Various sources from where the capital has to be procured is also indicated in the plan. To avoid possible interruption in the flow of business activities, the permanent portion of working capital, together with the needs of fixed capital, must be raised from permanent sources of finance like issue of shares, debentures etc. Short term sources are explored for temporary working capital. The continuous flow of capital is the primary consideration in the financial policy for the management of working capital. The policy must also take into account the peculiarities of the particular type of business and the contingencies that may arise in future which must have to be met successfully to keep the organisation going. The financial policy cannot be a rigid one; it must be flexible to accommodate any eventuality in future.

So, prudent financial policies for fixed and working capital must be based on analysis of various factors and foresightedness must play a dominant role in the formulation of policies. Modern financial management stresses more on the proper utilisation of funds than procurement of funds and, keeping that in view, the fund procured must be properly utilised to meet fixed as well as working capital needs of the company.

## Determinants of Working Capital

The general policy of any company is to hold a small quantity of working capital since 'working cpital is a means to an end and not an end in itself'. Various considerations have to be taken into account before deciding upon the amount of working capital. The management of working capital is rather difficult because working capital is constantly affected by the criss-crossing economic currents flowing about the business. The shifting forces are always at play — the forces such as the availability of raw materials, the condition of the money market, the nature of the activities of the company and, finally, the economic health of the country.

## Factors affecting Working Capital needs

(i) Nature of business (ii) Production policies (iii) Manufacturing process (iv) Turnover of circulating capital (v) Growth and expansion of business (vi) Business cycle fluctuations (vii) Terms of purchase and sales (viii) Dividend policy (ix) Other factors.

(i) **Nature of business :** It is rather a primary factor in determining the volume of working capital. Trading concerns need more working capital but public utility have the lowest requirements for current assets because of the nature of the business. One deals in commodities, another deals in service; so the requirements for working capital vary. Industrial concerns also need large amount of working capital though the quantum of working capital may vary from one type of industry to another. Generally speaking, trading and financial firms require relatively large amounts of working capital, public utilities comparatively small amounts and the manufacturing concerns stand between these two extremes.

(ii) **Production policies :** Requirements for products of a company fluctuate seasonally in many businesses and, as such, production policies have to be adjusted accordingly. A company is able to offset the effect of seasonal fluctuations upon working capital by adjusting its production schedules. In production management, it has been the experience that to adjust production with the seasonal fluctuations is not a sound policy; certain level of production should always be maintained which involves the determination of the amount of the working capital.

(iii) **Manufacturing process :** This is another determinant of working capital. The longer the period of the manufacturing process, more is the need for working capital. It so happens that companies making heavy machinery and equipment minimise their investment in inventory or working capital by requiring advance payment from customers against their order for which the manufacturing process is continuing.

(iv) **Turnover of circulating capital :** The speed at which circulating capital turns itself over determines working capital. The turnover of circulating capital means conversion of cash into inventory of raw material and stores, inventory of raw material into inventory of finished goods, inventory of finished goods into book debts or accounts receivables and book debts into cash accounts — thus the round of circulating capital completes. In case the turnover of circulating capital is quick, less amount of working capital will not create any difficulty but the slow turnover of circulating capital needs more working capital.

(v) **Growth and expansion of business :** When a company grows in size, naturally more working capital is needed. Growth and expansion of business generally needs more commodities to be purchased or more raw materials to be purchased or more services to be rendered. In all these cases, more working capital has to be kept ready to cope with the growth and the expansion.

(vi) **Business cycle fluctuations :** Business cycle causes rise and fall in demand. During boom period, more demand is created, more production is needed and working capital requirement has to be adjusted accordingly. In depression, with the decline in demand for products or services, the need for more production does not arise; nor the present level of production has to be maintained; so the working capital need is reduced. Thus, business cycle plays an important role in determining working capital requirement.

(vii) **Terms of purchase and sale :** Terms of purchase and sale, i.e. the place of credit in regard to purchase and sale, regulates the volume of working capital. When credit in sale has to be allowed for a long period, naturally, to keep the business going, more working capital has to be maintained. In the same way, credit for short period will ensure comeback of the cash without delay which will mean the reduction of the need for working capital. In case of credit purchase also, the length of credit allowed by the creditor determines the amount of working capital to be maintained to continue purchase to keep the business going.

(viii) **Dividend policy :** To maintain a stable dividend rate, the working capital is affected. Changes in working capital bring out an adjustment of dividend policy. There is a close relationship between dividend policy and working capital and very few companies declare a dividend without giving due consideration to its effects on cash and their needs for cash. The dearth of working capital may cause skipping a cash dividend. Better working capital position enables a company to declare a better rate of dividend. So, the policy of the management as to dividend determines the requirements of working capital. Sometimes, the management has to resolve a dilemma of reducing or skipping the dividend by the adoption of stock dividend, i.e. issue of bonus shares.

Besides the factors discussed above, there are **other factors** having influence in the determination of working capital : (i) Absence of coordination in production and distribution policy of a company calls for more working capital (ii) An elaborate organisation for marketing needs more working capital (iii) To maintain big inventory of raw materials and other accessories in a country like India where transport facilities are inadequate, working capital requirement is naturally high (iv) Government policy on inputs has impact on the requirement of working capital. A company shall have to keep sufficient cash to input according to the policy of the government-specified times and (v) The hazards and contingencies in some businesses are so inherent that they have to keep cash always ready to meet the situation. So the working capital needs of those businesses are naturally more than those which have less hazards and contingencies.

# CHAPTER 5

## CAPITALISATION, CAPITAL STRUCTURE AND CAPITAL GEARING

**Capitalisation refers to the amount of securities to be issued by a company and the proportionate amounts of those securities.**

**Capital structure refers to the kinds of securities to be issued by a company.**

**Capital gearing refers to the proportion in which the various kinds of securities are to be issued by a company.**

**Therefore, capitalisation is a broader term which includes capital gearing.**

### Capital gearing

Capital gearing is the fixation of a proper ratio between two or more types of securities and the ratio which each type of security will bear to the total capitalisation.

A company can be high geared or low geared. A highly geared company is one where the proportion of **equity capital** to the total capital is **small** or where the proportion of preference shares and/or debentures because of **fixed** rate of **dividend** and/or interest is large.

A company is said to be low geared when the capital structure is just the opposite.

A low geared company will have more equity shares (bearing no fixed rate of dividend). In a highly geared company, a substantial proportion of long-term funds comes from the issue of preference shares, bonds and debentures.

To sum up –

High geared = (a) Equity capital small

(b) Preference & debenture large

Low geared = (a) Equity capital large

(b) Preference & debenture small

How to gear up capitalisation is a matter of far-reaching significance. The capital structure of a company, from the point of view of earnings, should be strongly founded on the principles of safety and economy.

Equity shares, preference shares and debentures have their distinct impacts on the earnings of a company. Equity shareholders are not guaranteed with any fixed rate of dividend or dividend at all, but in case of preference shares and debentures, fixed rate of dividend and interest, respectively, have to be paid.

So, where the earnings of a company are uncertain, the issue of equity shares is preferred provided other conditions justify such an issue. But where a company has a stable source of earning, preference shares and/or debentures may be preferred.

While planning the proportion of different kinds of securities, various factors have to be taken into consideration. But the main considerations that influence the issue of equity shares or debentures or preference shares are given above.

However, we discuss below the factors governing proper capital gearing.

## Determinants of Capital Structure/Capital gearing

### 1. Trading on the equity

Trading on the equity means taking advantage of 'stock' or ownership of a company i.e. earning additional profit through equity shares at the expense of other forms of securities. Different types of securities — equity, preference, debenture — have different nature of returns or have their relative advantages and disadvantages so far as their earnings for the company are concerned. If a company's earnings are large, it can very well pay off fixed dividend on preference shares or interest on debentures and thus it can trade on its equity. So "trading on the equity is an arrangement under which a company makes use of borrowed funds carrying a fixed rate of interest in such a way as to increase the rate of return on the equity shares". There is another advantage of trading on the equity; it saves income tax, since interest paid on debentures is a deductible expense.

### 2. Retention of Control of the Company

Capital gearing by including preference shares and debentures in the capital structure is done with a view to retaining control over the management of the company. Since preference shareholders and the debenture-holders have no voting rights, by issuing preference shares and debentures, a company does not expand its ownership and the control over management is not widely diffused.

### 3. Elasticity of Capital Structure

The consideration — for the capital structure of the company for being kept elastic to enable it to provide for expansion and raising of future capital — restrains the company management from issuing large number of debentures and preference shares as they make the capital rigid, requiring payment of fixed charges on them. Generally, at the initial stage, a company does not issue debentures and this does not create any fixed charge; rather it issues preference shares. In case of emergency or for expansion, debentures are usually issued.

### 4. Duration of fund needs

Generally, long-term funds are procured through shares and debentures and short term needs are met by bank loan or public deposits.

### 5. Nature of the business

The nature of business of a company is an important determinant of capital structure. A manufacturing company, a trading company or a public utility concern does not need the same amount and same nature of capital. Some companies are by nature capital-intensive as is the case with an electricity company.

A monopoly type company prefers bonds and debentures whereas a manufacturing company in the competitive market will rely more on the equity capital.

### 6. Market Conditions

The condition prevailing in the capital market and the money market influence capital gearing. The phase of trade cycle will have impact on the choice of securities. In times of depression, for instance, people will be interested to buy debentures having a sure return but not equity shares where income is uncertain.

### 7. Legal restrictions

In the matter of issue of securities, there are legal provisions; the company management, therefore, cannot issue any type of securities according to their will, legal provisions must be adhered to. A Banking Company can only issue equity shares.

### 8. Investors' needs and requirements

Investors want security, stability and fair return on their investments. A particular type of security may not satisfy all the conditions. So, to satisfy the needs and requirements of various types of investors, securities of various types are to be issued. For instance, to ensure the stability of income and security of principal, debentures are preferred and for higher income, preference shares are preferred. So, the capital gearing has to be so adjusted as to make it suitable to meet the needs and requirements of different types of investors.

### 9. Cost of financing

A company collects funds through securities at varying costs. So, it will see which type of security entails lowest cost in terms of interest and dividends. Also, the relationship of earnings to the price of the share will be considered at the time of capital gearing. From the cost point of view, lower interest rate will attract borrowings and higher earnings price relationship of shares will encourage issue of equity shares. The cost of issue of bonds is always lower because the investor in bonds is more interested in safety than in income. Interest paid on bonds or debentures is a deductible expense in Income tax load. So, it reduces cost of securities and the capital structure of capital gearing.

## Organisation of finance department

A big organisation like a company will have a number of areas of management — production, marketing, financial and personnel. These different areas of activities grouped and classified from the management point of view have great significance. Every area of management is a distinct activity contributing towards the main flow of activities aiming at the achievement of the overall objectives of business.

Every area of management is functional and is of staff nature. The areas of management are grouped into departments — as is the case with the finance department.

The finance department is organised usually along functional lines, whether at the central level or at the plant or branch level. There is ample scope for specialisation because of its functional nature. The department imparts special training to the personnel of the department. Executives are given a comprehensive knowledge and training in the intricacies of financial problems. The Finance Manager acts as the head of the department and he acts both as accountant/or controller and treasurer. As the departmental head, he is the custodian of corporate funds and investments. The finance department looks after the general accounting, cost accounting, budgeting with the different sections of the department taking care of company investments and wages and salary disbursements (Payroll section).

Under the Board of Directors with the Managing Director as the leader, the Finance Manager functions with the Chief Accountant, Assistant Manager and the Secretary. The Chief Accountant, as a staff person, has under him sections such as Auditing, Budgeting, General Accounts, Cost Accounts and Taxation. The Assistant Manager may have under him Credit and Collection, Payroll, Investment, Inventory, Banking and Financial Reports.

The organisation of a department, be it finance or any other department of a company, is not expected to follow a set pattern. A host of factors are to be taken into consideration before the organisation of the department. In an organisation which is finance-oriented, its finance departments will have secure special arrangements and sections to deal with the special problems that are likely to crop up in a finance company. But one thing must be made clear : a Finance Manager is a staff person. He advises the General Manager or the line executive who is ultimately to take decision. In today's emerging pattern of company management, the finance department may be headed by the Director in charge of finance. But no matter who heads the finance department, the fact remains that the department has to be organised. It is inconceivable to think of a big concern having no finance department. To organise the finance department, the principles of organisations are to be followed without doubt but the task of organisation may not entirely be the responsibility of the head of the finance department. The personnel aspect of the department may be left, and generally is left, to the Personnel Management of the Company. Finance executives are recruited, selected and trained to fit in their position — the right man for placement in the right position.

Thus, the finance department is organised more or less on the lines of other departments only with the difference that finance is a staff function and the department is so manned that the experts of finance are made available for advice and guidance of the line executives.

### Estimation of financial requirements of a firm

A firm needs finance for its setting up and for its working. The need for finance is a non-controversial matter but how much finance is required to set up and keep a firm going is a matter requiring careful planning and consideration of a number of factors. Estimation of financial requirements of a firm correctly, with as much foresightedness as possible, is very important.

To estimate the requirements of finance for a firm the following matters should be taken into consideration :

(i) Cost of fixed assets (ii) Cost of current assets (iii) Cost of promotion (iv) Cost of setting up the organisation (v) Cost of establishing the business (vi) Cost of financing and (vii) Cost of intangible assets.

**Cost of fixed assets :** Fixed assets consist of land and buildings, plant and machinery, furniture etc. These assets are essential to set up a firm/ company. To start an organisation, some expenditure, huge or small, must be blocked in the acquisition of fixed assets. Since the assets are to be tied up with the business for a long time, they are fixed, but their value is not fixed — values may depreciate or appreciate. So, these are meant for meeting the government needs of the organisation going to be set up. All firms need fixed assets but the nature of fixed assets and the volume of capital to be invested for them vary from one to another according to the nature and size of the organisation. The proprietors of the organisation are to make the assessment and compile the list for the assets to be acquired. Once the list is prepared of the fixed assets, the value can be ascertained and funds required can be found out. Prices of all the fixed assets have to be ascertained through different methods — brokers, price quotation, government sources etc. The total of all these will constitute the total costs involved in procurement of fixed assets. Now the question of raising of funds arises : it has to be done before the concern actually goes into production.

The estimation of finance requirements for fixed assets being made, the next step will be to make assessment of the working capital requirement of the funds required for current assets.

**Current assets :** Funds needed for current assets are working capital. This capital is required for the purchase of raw materials and for meeting the day-to-day expenditure of salaries, wages, rents etc. The management of working capital, i.e. to find out the amount required for current assets, is not an easy job. The factors on which current capital requirements depend are variable because of various factors. There are various uncertainties in the running of an organisation. Mass production has to be made to meet mass demand in future. During the intervening period, there may be fluctuation in the factor prices which may affect previous calculation of the current capital/working capital requirements.

The factors that generally affect the working capital requirements of a firm are the proportionate cost on raw materials, labour cost, duration of manufacturing period, volume of stock requirement, rapidity of turnover of capital, terms of credit, regional variations and cost requirements for various purposes.

The principal considerations of the financial management are the funds to be required for fixed and working capitals.

Funds required for other purposes can be estimated more easily. They are all controllable factors to a great extent. Keeping in view a happy compromise between profit maximisation and wealth maximisation, the financial management will estimate financial requirement of the firm. Paucity or abundance of funds — neither of these two is a good financial management. A correct analytical approach to the fund management will enable the financial management to be nearer the reality and the possibility of the best utilisation of funds. All controllable and uncontrollable factors have to be taken into consideration while estimating the requirements of finance of a firm. The task is a difficult one in the changing economic environment of a country as in the case with our country. Cash in-flow and cash out-flow being a common feature of financial management, the matter that must not escape the attention of the financial manager is that there should always be funds available at the disposal of the organisation to meet any emergency situation. So, all eventualities should be studied with foresightedness before the estiamtion of financial requirement of a firm.

# CHAPTER 6

## OPERATING AND FINANCIAL LEVERAGES
### (A tool of financial analysis)

'Leverage' means "meeting a fixed cost or paying a fixed return for employing resources or funds". It is the company's "ability to use fixed cost assets or funds to magnify the return to its owner". (S. C. Kuchhal)

The fixed cost or return is treated as the fulcrum of a leverage. The amount of leverage on the company's structure greatly reflects the type of risk-return trade-off it makes.

The term leverage is much akin to capital gearing. The word is derived from 'lever' which generally means a kind of handle used to operate something. In this sense, leverage is a device of applying force at a particular point to have a desired effect at another point.

There are two types of leverage in most companies — operating leverage and financial leverage. Operating leverage takes place when a company has fixed cost that must be met regardless of volume or value of sales. When fluctuations in sales revenue produce a wide fluctuation in operating profit – it is a case of operating leverage. "With fixed cost, the percentage change in operating profit accompanying a change in sales is greater than the percentage change in sales. This occurrence is known as operating leverage". (S. C. Kuchhal)

Three factors — the rupee amount of fixed cost, the variable contribution margin and the volume of sales — are responsible for operating leverage in a company. Two approaches are adopted for calculating operating leverage.

In the first approach, the degree of operating leverage can be measured at any level of output Q as:

$$L = \frac{Q(P-V)}{Q(P-V)-F}$$

Q denotes the number of units sold; P selling price per unit

V denotes variable cost per unit; F fixed cost

L denotes degree of operating leverage.

Second approach :

In terms of total rupee sales by means of break-even or cost-volume-profit analysis.

The break-even analysis shows the degree of a company's operating leverage which at any level of sales is :

$$\frac{S-VC}{S-VC-F} \quad \text{or} \quad \frac{\text{Contribution}}{\text{Operating Profit}}$$

where, Contribution = Sales – Variable cost, and Operating profit = Contribution – Fixed cost.

Precisely, operating leverage may be defined in terms of the way a given change in volume of sales affects profits and the degree of operating leverage is the percentage change in operating income that results from a percentage change in units sold.

Degree of operating leverage =

$$\frac{\text{Percentage change in operating income}}{\text{Percentage change in sales}}$$

"Both these approaches are, effectively, one and the same".

## Financial leverage

A company's ability to use fixed financial charges to magnify the effects of changes in earnings before interest and taxes on the company's earnings per share is financial leverage. It indicates the effect on earnings created by the use of fixed charge securities in the capitalisation plan.

Financial leverage involves the decision to determine the ratio of debt, both short-term and long-term, to total assets of the company. This is used to earn more or to earn less from the fixed-charged sources of funds such as debentures and preference shares than their costs. That is, the rate of return on equity capital is levered above or below the rate of return of total assets.

Financial leverage is a device to use the funds at a fixed cost in the hope of increasing return to equity shareholders.

### Changing structure of industrial finance in India

The financial instruments (methods) and the financial institutions (sources) prevail in any financial system. To maintain continuous flow of business operations, different methods and sources of finance are resorted to.

In India, there has been a rapid change in the methods and sources of finance since Independence. To appreciate the change in the industrial finance in India, an idea of the pre-independence capital-market was then characterised by — (a) Closed-circle character of industrial entrepreneurship (b) Semi-organised and narrow industrial securities market (c) Virtual absence of participation by intermediary financial institutions in the long-term financing of the industries and (d) Dependence of industries primarily on internal savings.

The above situation of the capital market indicates that financial system was not responsive to opportunities for industrial investment. The financial market was incapable of accelerating the pace of industrial development.

With the attainment of independence, the planned economy with definite emphasis on rapid industrialisation of the coutnry called for a change in the capital market. Various developments took place to reorient capital market to shake off its colonial character and to assume the responsibility of increased demand for industrial finance. So, the capital became developed. Now, it is well-diversified and broad-based in structure providing necessary finance in diverse ways ranging from direct loans, under-writing, guarantees upto rediscounting of bills. **A new pattern of corporate industrial finance has emerged owing to various developments** : (a) Now financial institutions have been set up, the IDBI being the apex term-lending institution (b) The structure and the lending policies of the existing financial institutions have been changed. Commercial banks have started term-lending, LIC is playing a dominant role in the industrial securities market and in the under-writing of new industrial issues. Investment companies too, are playing a important role; and (c) Improvements of confidence of investors by the amendments of Companies Act, 1956, and the Securities Contracts (Regulation) Act 1956.

The financial environment in India, so far as industrial finance is concerned, is now not unfavourable, though not cent per cent favourable yet owing to certain contstraints in the availability of finance. But, on the whole, the capital market has improved substantially since independence and that is reflected in the new concept of financial management. The procurement of finance does not now constitute the crucial function of financial management but the best and proper utilisation of the funds procured is the core of financial management. It is a clear indication of the fact that industrial finance in India has now become more available and the financial market has improved markedly.

# CHAPTER 7

## FINANCIAL CONTROL

The planning in any area of management is of vital importance. Financial planning is none the less important in the overall corporate planning. This planning in finance must be complemented by **Control.** Control as a function of management is to "verify whether everything occurs in conformity with the plan adopted, the instructions issued and principles established" (Henri Fayol). Its object is to point out weaknesses and errors in order to rectify them and prevent recurrence. So financial control denotes the development of financial standards of performance, and to compare the financial activities with these standards and to take corrective action so that performance may conform to those standards.

It is one of the objectives of financial planning to control the utilisation of finances so as to ensure maximum efficiency of operations and proper relations with financiers.

"The financial manager sits on the horns of a dilemma. He is charged with the responsibility of having money ready to spend for current and investment purposes and at the same time must get and keep sufficient money on hand to enable the business to achieve its profit objective. A workable balance between the cash inflow and cash outflow must be constantly maintained. This calls for continuous **Controlling**" (Massie).

To exercise financial control, certain techniques must be adopted. **Some of the techniques for financial control are :** marginal cost analysis, budgeting, performance budgeting, variance analysis. Occasionally, the financial control mechanism may be geared up to check performance and to conduct internal audit. The "return on capital employed" and the "short-term cost-volume-profit relationship" are very important components of financial centre. As a measure of control, the financial management should delegate financial authority down the line.

However, the principle of deciding the budget period is generally intended to coincide with the operating cycle of the business. The operating cycle is the period of time that separates the point of purchase of raw material and the point when debts resulting from sales of finished products are collected. Thus, it would consist of the movement of funds in a full cycle of : Cash – raw materials – work in progress – finished goods – debtors for credit sales – Cash. One year period is generally accepted as the budget period because accounts are prepared for one year. Thus comparison is facilitated between budgets and actual performance.

### Budget Committee

Budgeting is a managerial technique for financial control. To make it effective, a watch over the performance, in accordance with the budget, becomes essential. That is why a 'Budget Committee' has to be formed to derive the best results and to exercise effective budgetary control. Generally, all the Function Heads of all departments constitute the Budget Committee. The Chief Executive heads the 'Budget Committee' with its members – the Marketing Manager, Factory Manager, Financial Controller, Personnel Manager, Materials Manager and Research & Development Manager. There is generally a Budget officer who acts as the secretary of the committee. The Budget committee usually consider expenses of each budget centre, variances and statements showing variances for each department. The Budget Committee Secretary acts as a co-ordinator and is generally a man well conversant with the budgetary matters prepared to answer any query by any departmental manager.

### Budget Manual

Budgetary control is a process; it is repetitive in nature. To systemise the whole procedure, a Budget Manual is generally prepared which acts as a guide to the budget-people. This Manual contains definitions of various terms, the organisation structure, the budget centres, the chart of accounts, the composition of the Budget Committee, the procedure of the budgetary control, various formats used etc. The Budget Manual is actually the basic document, kept updated, to help exercise effective budgetary control.

### Budgetary Control

Managerial Control over financial matter comes within the purview of financial management. The various types of control techniques may be divided into two categories – Traditional and Modern. Both these techniques have financial implications and, as such, financial management is involved.

Traditional control technique of management includes budgets, standard costing, ratio analysis, break-even analysis etc.

A widely used device for managerial control is the budget. It is a statement of anticipated results expressed in numerical terms – a financial statement of the plan followed during a given period for the purpose of attaining predetermined goals. Use of budgets for controlling activities is known as budgetary control.

Budgetary control is financial control by means of budgets, "when properly used, budgetary control is one of the manager's most effective tool". (Haimann).

Budgetary control is a process of finding out what is being done and comparing actual results with the corresponding budget data in order to approve accomplishments or to remedy differences by either adjusting the budget estimates or correcting the cause of differences.

Budgetary control has been defined as "the establishment of budgets relating the responsibilities of executives to the requirements of a policy and the continuous comparison of actual with budgeted results either to secure by individual action the objective of that policy or provide a basis for its revision" (I.C.W.A., London). Budgetary control involves the use of budgets and budgetary reports throughout the period to coordinate, evaluate and control day-to-day operations in accordance with the goals specified in the budget.

Budgeting is an effective tool in the hands of the management to formulate a plan, to co-ordinate and control operations so that established policies and objectives can be achieved. Financial Management prepares the budget, places it in the hands of the top executives to clarify the programme, measure efficiency and provide definite plans to interested parties.

Budgets are of different types — fixed or variable; Revenue or Capital or Expense; Material budget, Labour budget, Cash budget, Sales budget, Production budget, Master budget (overall budget) etc.

As to its **merits**, control through budgets is very much effective. Budgeting exercises a dynamic control. A well co-ordinated and well-administered system of budgetary control contributes to the efficiency of an organisation.

Budgetary control makes for unified action and co-ordination of individual efforts. It helps management in delegating authority more freely over specified functions. It also promotes efficiency and minimises wastes.

In the words of Blocker, "budgetary control is planned to assist management in the allocation of responsibility and authority, to aid in making estimates and plans for the future, to assist in the analysis of the variations between estimated and actual result and to develop bases of measurement of standards with which to evaluate the efficiency of operations".

There are **Limitations**, no doubt. Budgets are estimates and can never be cent per cent accurate. It is simply a tool of efficient management, not a substitute for it. It so happens that the management sticks to the budget and fails to adjust when required. Budgets may be misused to find faults and restrict performance rather than improve it. It is a time-consuming process and involves expenses. Budgeting goals may lead people to supersede the enterprise goals.

Success of budgetary control depends on the motivation of people who are to install and use budgets.

Therefore, too much should not be expected of budgetary control within a short period of time. Budgeting cannot be considered as a cure to all financial maladies.

Some guide-lines should be followed to make the **budgetary control effective.**

The guidelines are :

(i) Sound organisation is essential for effective budgeting. Responsibility and authority for the preparation and administration of budgets should be clearly defined.

(ii) Actual performance must be accurately and adequately measured. Key executives must consider budgetary control a dynamic part of their way of managing.

(iii) Actual results of current events must be timely and regularly reported to help timely correction of deficiencies.

(iv) To create co-ordination and to remove differences a free and frank communication system should be developed. All managers connected with budgeting must have a part in the preparation of budgets so that they understand budgets.

(v) There must be proper indoctrination of employees in the utility and principles of budgeting. So, the human factor is very important in budgeting.

(vi) Sufficient time should be allowed to obtain desired results from budgeting and, to derive desired results, efficient forecasting and research is necessary.

(vii) There must be the scope for alternative budgets i.e. the budget should be flexible to meet the condition and needs of the particular enterprise.

(viii) It is essential to develop and make available standards by which the manager's work can be translated into needs for manpower, materials, money and other resources.

**Effectiveness of Budgetary Control**

Budgetary control is an effective controlling tool in the hands of management but this tool cannot and should not be used indiscriminately. There are situations which warrant control through budgets but situation sometimes are such that control through budget does not become effective. So, the management, particularly the financial management, must know how to use it and when to use it, otherwise the desired result will not be achieved.

It is prudent to apply the techniques of budgetary control on a limited scale at the initial stage and there it can be more forcefully and effectively applied on extensive scale if the situation so demands.

Budgetary control is a financial tool the use of which needs sufficient precaution and existence of certain conditions. Proper organisational set-up and adequate accounting system, including effective cost control measures, are pre-requisites for the success of budgetary control. It is not so unusual to find that an organisation fails to derive the results of budgetary control owing to lack of co-operation, lack of active support from top management, in-efficient supervision and administration, too much routines and details, inaccurate forecasting, lack of coordination etc.

So, budgetary control is a financial tool meant for handling by efficient management with sufficient care and tact and having a proper assessment of the overall situation prevailing in the organisation.

## Administration of Budgetary Control

To ensure effective budgetary control, financial management has to take certain definite steps and decisions. They are — (a) Budget Centre (b) Budget Period (c) Budget Committee and (d) Budget Manual.

**Budget Centre :** The decision of the management to divide the organisation into a number of budget centres is based on the consideration that more intensive budgetary control is possible in such a case. Each unit of a business is considered having separate entity and budgetary control is exercised on it. For each budget centre there is one executive responsible for the budgetary control of the unit. He is entrusted with the responsibility for performance by living within the unit. Each budget centre will plan out its activities and the budget for that centre may be fixed by management. The pooling of the budgets of all the budget centres will be the master budget for the entire company. The performance of each budget centre is judged against its budgeted amount.

**Budget Period :** The period or duration of a budget is significant. Normally, a year is the period but there is no point to stick to the one year period; the period is to be decided by the management, considering the factors that would contribute to the effectiveness of the budget.

## The Budgeting Process

Budgetary control is exercised through the budgeting process and this process involves four steps :

(a) Budget policy guidelines (b) Preparation of budgets (c) Reporting of variances and (d) Review and follow up.

### (a) Budget Policy guide-lines

A budget is based on a number of assumptions. To ensure that all managers at all levels base their estimates on exactly the same assumptions, the top management initiates the process by circulating a common set of guidelines and targets among all managers. Guidelines also lay down the fundamental targets for the progress of the business. It would be the endeavour of the functional heads of the departments to see that targets set by the top management are achieved. Guidelines, as a matter of fact, are to ensure uniformity in the matter of budgeting by different budget centres, so that the Master Budget really becomes an effective tool of financial control.

### (b) Preparation of budgets

The preparation of budget makes a manager committed to work within the budget. So the preparation of the budget must contain in it elements which are realistic in nature and which are realisable. A budget is, no doubt, an assessment and not the recording of historical event. So it needs a clear foresight about the trend of the economy and, particularly, the economic environment that may affect the functioning of the particular organisation for which the budget is being prepared. The budget of a department must be in complete harmony with those of other departments. The budgets must also be in line with the targets set. In preparing budget, the departmental managers are likely to add 'fat' to their budgets so that their performance can be proved justified. Planning for low capacity utilisation or for higher costs are instances of managers 'playing it safe'. These practices are not desirable, so it is usual for the departmental budgets to be presented to the Budget Committee. Thus, the abnormal 'safety margins' worked into the budgets are attempted to be discarded. The budgets of different departments of a company should follow the process of co-ordination with one another to make the Master Budget realistic and effective.

Budgets are prepared for sales, selling & distribution cost, production and production cost, purchase, administrative cost and capital expenditure. The cash budget is prepared after all the cost budgets are ready; the objective being to see whether the company will have sufficient cash (including bank balances) to meet all the obligations. If necessary, the management will take steps to remain within the means.

The essence of all budgets is the Master Budget. It shows the expected overall effect. The Projected Profit and Loss Account and the Projected Balance Sheet find place in the Master Budget. This budget is meant for matching with the goals already set and if it falls short of expectations, the whole process of preparation of budgets is reviewed.

### (c) Reporting of Variances

The variation between a budgeted cost and an actual cost is known as cost variance. The departmental managers should be informed occasionally the position of their departments vis-a-vis their budgets.

The cost variances which may occur may be — (i) material cost variance (ii) labour cost variance and (iii) overhead cost variance.

The variance reporting is to correct the managers. It is necessary for sound financial management and also for efficient running of the organisation with financial discipline that the Managing Director is given the oportunity to know which department, if any, is deviating from the budgets. Here lies the importance of reporting of variances in the budgetary process.

### (d) Review and Follow-up

The importance of 'Review and Follow-up' in the process of budgeting can be easily understood. It is a controlling measure. The need for reviewing and follow up of the performances of various departments by the Budget Committee occasionally affords opportunity for the management to compare the actual performance with the budget estimates. The deviations, if any, can be corrected without much delay; so it is 'necessary' that the system of 'Review and Follow-up' continues without any break. It is a step in the process of budgeting to exercise control over the performances and to signal the departmental managers as to their performance in relation to budgets.

# CHAPTER 8

## RATIO ANALYSIS

"Ratio analysis is the process of determining and interpreting numerical relationships based on financial statements. A ratio is a statistical yardstick that provides a measure of the relationship between two variables or figures" (S.C. Kuchhal).

Ratio analysis was perhaps the first financial tool developed to analyse and interpret the financial statements and is still used widely for this purpose. A financial ratio is generally taken from Profit and Loss Account or Balance Sheet.

Ratio represents relationship between numbers and, as such, a ratio can be formed by taking any two figures from the financial statements, provided the variables chosen are significantly related to each other

Some important ratios are : Structural ratios, Working Capital ratios, Profitability ratios, Miscellaneous ratios.

### Structural ratios

They indicate the relationships amongst the variables that are part of the long-term financial structure. The structural group of ratios consists of (a) funded debt to total capitalisation (b) debt to equity (c) equity to net fixed assets (d) net fixed assets to funded debt and (e) funded debt to net working capital.

**(a) Funded debt to total capitalisation**

Total capitalisation means long term debt, capital stock, reserves and surplus. The ratio of funded debt to total capitalisation is computed by dividing funded debt by total capitalisation. It can also be expressed as percentage. The management, from such ratio analysis, understands that a too heavy debt burden reduces the margin of safety for lenders, increases fixed charges upon earnings, decreases earnings available for distribution to shareholders and continued deficiency in profit may anchor the company to insolvency.

**(b) Debt to equity**

'Equity' is the sum of the share capital and Reserve and Surplus. The ratio represents the proportion of 'loan funds' to 'own funds' in the capital structure of a company. This has a bearing on several aspects like the ability to invite and absorb further loans, ability to raise further share capital, control of the operation etc.

As a thumb-rule, Debt-equity ratio of less than 1.00 is taken as acceptable. It varies from one industry to another.

$$\text{Debt-Equity ratio} = \frac{\text{Long term loans}}{\text{Share Capital + Reserve}}$$

**(c) Equity to net fixed assets**

This ratio analysis indicates the extent to which equity capital is invested in net fixed assets. If net fixed assets exceed their net worth, difficulties may arise to provide depreciation resulting in a reduction in profits. As a thumb-rule, the ratio of more than 1.00 is acceptable.

$$\text{Equity : Net fixed assets means} = \frac{\text{Net worth}}{\text{Net Fixed Assets}}$$

It can be easily understood that more the shareholders' contribution is tied up in fixed assets, the less is the amount available for investment in current assets and higher this ratio, less is the protection for creditor. Additional equity capital is needed when the net fixed assets exceed net worth.

(d) **Net fixed assets to funded debt**

It is an analysis to determine security for the lenders. For example, a ratio of 2 : 1 means that for every rupee of long-term indebtedness, there is a book value of two rupees of net fixed assets.

(e) **Funded debt to net working capital**

This means long term debt in relation to net working capital i.e. $\frac{\text{Long - term debt}}{\text{Net working capital}}$

It helps to ascertain creditor's contribution to the liquid assets of the firm. In case net working capital is less than funded debt, there may be difficulty in meeting financial obligations.

## Working Capital Ratios

The management of working capital improves by the analysis of the working capital ratios. These ratios are : (i) Current ratio (ii) Liquid ratio or Acid Test ratio (iii) Inventory turnover ratio (iv) Debtors' turnover ratio (v) Working capital turnover ratio. Variables other than those covered by the term 'working capital' are also used to gain an insight.

(i) Current ratio : $\frac{\text{Current assets}}{\text{Current liabilities}}$

The trade creditor uses this ratio to estimate the firm's ability to repay his credit. The 'acceptable' level of this ratio is more than 2.

(ii) Liquid ratio or Acid Test ratio :

$$\frac{\text{Current Assets} - \text{Inventories}}{\text{Current Liabilities} - \text{Bank Overdraft}}$$

This ratio denotes a very short-term liquidity and is, therefore, called liquid ratio. It tacitly assumes that inventories may not be realised immediately and that the bank overdraft may turn sticky. Hence it excludes these two variables. The acceptable level is more than 1.00.

(iii) Inventory Turnover Ratio: $\frac{\text{Cost of goods sold}}{\text{Inventories}}$

This ratio indicates the number of times the inventories are 'turned over' during a year. The higher this ratio, greater is the efficiency of inventory management. To show a high ratio, inventories cannot be allowed to drop down below the 'danger level' or the sale may be lost. There is another form in which this ratio can be expressed. The formula is :

$$360 \times \frac{\text{Inventories}}{\text{Cost of goods sold}}$$

In this form, the resultant figure denotes the number of days of sales. (This assumes 360 days a year)

(iv) Debtor's Turnover Ratio : $\frac{\text{Sales}}{\text{Sundry Debtors}}$

or, $360 \times \frac{\text{S. Debtors}}{\text{Sales}}$

This indicates, like the inventory turnover ratio, the number of days for which credit has been extended to the customers.

(v)Working Cap. Turnover Ratio : $\frac{\text{Sales}}{\text{Working Cap.}}$

This indicates the number of times the working capital turns itself over during a year.

## Profitability Ratios

(i) Profit to Sales and (ii) Return on Investment are found out through profitability ratio analysis. In these ratios, the numerator is always a profit figure and its relationship with some other key variable is established by the ratio.

(i) Profit to Sales

EBIT/Sales (when EBIT means Earning Before Interest and Taxes)

This ratio analysis denotes the percentage of profits earned on every rupee of sale. EBIT is taken to eliminate the impact of capital structure on profits. If there is a high proportion of debt, interest charged would be higher and vice versa. Hence EBIT is taken as it denotes the operating results.

(ii) Return on Investment (ROI)

$$\frac{\text{Pre-Tax Profit}}{\text{Share Capital + Reserves + Long term Loans}}$$

This ratio indicates the profitability per rupee of investment. In the modern large companies with so many divisions, this ratio analysis is very useful. The performance of each division in such companies is judged on the basis of its ROI. Sometimes, Net Profit is taken in place of Pre-Tax Profit while calculating return on investment.

ROI is a popular ratio in financial management and analysis. It is used in corporate planning and it is considered as integral.

A fairly integrated assessment of the business

situation is possible through close relationship between ratios. ROI is the end-product of a series of statistical measures representing the various phases of a company's operations that contribute to this ratio.

ROI is the product of earnings as a percentage of sales and the turnover of assets that produce these sales.

Thus ROI can be interpreted in the following formula :

$$\text{ROI} = \frac{\text{Earnings}}{\text{Investment}} = \frac{\text{Earnings}}{\text{Sales}} \times \frac{\text{Sales}}{\text{Cap. Employed}}$$

(not taxable assets)

**Limitations of ROI**

"ROI is a fraction with earnings as numerator and investment as denominator. Both the numerator and the denominator to the fraction are subject to a wide range of arbitrary decisions in determining the amount of earnings and investment" (S.C. Kuchhal).

ROI emphasises to generate short-term profits. As a result, costs like research, development and sales promotion are mcut down. The situation does not qualify this type of reduction of costs generally. The emphasis on improvement of ratio rather than improvement of rupee profit may deprive shareholders of maximum returns through increased rupee profits. The objective of ROI analysis being short-run, various important programmes such as training of employees may be dropped with a view to increasing the ROI ratio in the short-run.

As a measure of performance, ROI cannot be considered really much worthy. The favourable ROI analysis may not reflect the actual present performance at the organisation. Present return may be the result of the past wisdom or lack of wisdom for which the past managers and not the present incumbents are responsible.

ROI gives undue significance to capital resources vis-a-vis other inputs in profit planning.

ROI introduces conservatism and thus the climate for control is adversely affected and risk-taking is discouraged.

The effect of ROI on a decentralised company may be against public policy and against the overall interests of the company. Expansion projects may not be undertaken for apprehension of lower rate of return. On the other hand, when the profit objective is low, expansion projects which may not be viable may be undertaken.

Profit may result from fortuitous circumstances but ROI makes the Divisional Managers feel that they are to be credited for favourable ROI; this has the effect of lack of initiative on the part of the Divisional Managers to undertake any improvement scheme.

The limitations as discussed above lead us to conclude that ROI is not so precise; it creates a number of problems and requires replacement by a budgetary control system "based on establishing goals, analysing management performance and measuring it against the targeted performance through the study of management performance ratio".

**Du Pont Control Chart**

This is a system of Management Control utilising the "ratio inter-relationships to provide an important series of charts and indicators calling management's attention to desirable and undesirable trends of corporate performance". Where there are standards of performance, this chart makes it easy to judge performance changes with such a system. It isolates the elements of the final figure to appraise the individual factors affecting performance.

Du Pont control chart showing relation of factors affecting Return on Investment is developed along two tiers. The first sequence starts with turnover and the second one with earnings as a percentage of sales. An overall perspective of the financial relationships leading to the earnings rate on investment is available to the management through this chart. The final investment returns will change if changes take place in any important segment of this structure. The two-tier approach of this chart gives attention to separate forces contributing to profits. Turnover sequence helps more effective use of available capital and the profit margin sequence strengthens it through a better relationship between sales and costs and this improvement can be achieved.

The Management Achievement Chart and Profit Performance Chart have been designed after making modifications in the Du Pont Chart. These charts help in analysing the management performance as well as in establishing goals and measuring performance against them. The Management Achievement Chart has two aspects – one deals with operating management and the other financial management. So, it reflects the performance of the entire management team. Turnover of capital, margin of safety and profit/volume ratio constitute operating management performance and, for better decision-making, all these three relationships should be examined separately before the final figure is arrived at.

The financial operations ratio and the financial leverage ratio determine the financial management achievement. The financial operations ratio is calculated by dividing net profit by operating profit and the financial leverage ratio is calculated by dividing the capital employed by net worth. The financial policy of a company determines the range of this ratio. The financial executive can operate within this range to get the maximum return on the shareholders' equity by having an intelligent debt-equity mix.

The product of the financial operations ratio and the financial leverage ratio provides a good index of the performance of financial management. It is for the accounting and the finance department to see that the goals agreed upon on the management performance chart are translated into action.

# CHAPTER 9

## CORPORATE FINANCE — ITS SOURCES

A company needs two types of capital — fixed and working. Fixed capital for acquiring fixed assets and the working capital for running the business and meeting day-to-day expenses. Fixed capital is long-term capital required for a longer period and working capital for short period. The former is available from the capital market and the latter from the money market.

A company, being a large-scale business, needs a large amount of capital which may not be available from a single source. So, a number of sources are explored to procure finance for fixed capital to finance long-term projects and to meet the company's heavy initial expenses. For its working capital, various sources are also availed of, but their nature is a bit different. On the whole, we can say, that both for long term and short-term finance, a company will have to consider a number of resources taking into account a host of factors to suit the purpose for which the company is in need of finance.

The various sources of finance available for procurement of funds in India are :

(i) Issue of shares (ii) Issue of debentures (iii) Public deposits (iv) Joint stock banks (v) Indigenous bankers (vi) Ploughing back of earnings or self-financing (vii) State through various special financial institutions.

### Issue of Shares

The 'Owned Capital' of a company is divided into equal portions or units known as shares. Shares are known as "Ownership Securities" as against the "Creditorship Securities" which are represented by the debentures and bonds. Issue of shares is the most important method of raising long-term or fixed capital. Because, the share money is not to be paid back to the shareholder until the company is liquidated.

Shares are of two kinds which can be issued by a company under the Companies Act, 1956 — Equity shares and Preference shares.

**Preference shares** may be of different kinds —

(i) Convertible (ii) Non-convertible (iii) Redeemable (iv) Irredeemable (v) Participating (vi) Non-participating (vii) Cumulative (viii) Non-cumulative.

### Preference shares have some advantages

(1) They combine the security of return with the higher rate of return.

(2) They do not impose heavy burdens on the finances of the company since the rate of dividend is fixed and it is not payable if there is no profit.

(3) They are useful where debentures are not attractive to investors because of the low value of assets as collateral security.

(4) They enable the equity shareholder to get more dividend as the rate of dividend of preference shares is fixed and the shares are not participating in most cases.

(5) Promoters can retain control over the company by issuing preference shares as these shares have normally limited voting rights.

(6) The debts of the company may be converted

into preference shares at the time of the reorganisation of the company.

(7) Such shares may be given as a bonus while marketing the equity shares or debentures; thus the marketability of other shares is enhanced.

## Equity Shares

Equity shareholders occupy primary position in the company. They possess voting rights and hold control over the affairs of the company. They formulate policies to run the company and normally they earn good dividends. They actually undertake the risk of the business; where there is no profit, they get no dividend. So, it is rightly said that the equity shareholders provide 'Venture' capital to the company.

The **advantages** of equity shares :

(1) They provide a cushion of safety against temporary unfavourable developments since they do not take dividend when there is no profit.

(2) Capital is procured permanently by the issue of equity shares. They are returnable only on winding up of the company.

(3) These shares do not create any charge against the assets of the company.

However, equity shares suffer from certain **limitations** : (a) the control of the company is affected because of the undesirable interference by the equity shareholder (b) The advantages of equity on trading cannot be had if only equity shares are issued and (c) Issue of excessive number of equity shares may result in over-capitalisation.

## Issue of Debentures

A debenture may be regarded as acknowledgement of a debt by a company usually issued under common seal. The debentures are the uniform parts of a loan raised by the company.

Debentures may be of various kinds :

(i) Bearer (ii) Registered (iii) Redeemable (iv) Irredeemable (v) Unsecured or Naked (vi) Secured – with floating charge and fixed charge.

Debentures are significant as a source of corporate finance. They have some **advantages** :

(1) Without sacrificing control, the company can secure capital.

(2) Capital through debentures is available for a fixed period and the company may adjust its financial plan accordingly.

(3) Trading on equity is possible.

(4) The goodwill of the company and the prevailing capital market may be conducive for the company to issue debentures.

(5) Interest payable on debentures is usually less than the dividend payable to equity shareholders.

(6) Debenture issue is also useful where a company has a number of small debts. In such a case, a single issue of debentures proves less costly.

(7) Debenture issue is suitable for a specific class of investors who are interested in regular income without undertaking any risk.

Debentures have some **limitations** :

(1) With fluctuating earnings, debenture issue is not desirable.

(2) Debenture issue is not suitable for companies whose proportion of fixed assets to total assets is low, as, in such a case, neither its earnings will be stable nor will it be able to offer enough security.

(3) Debenture issue is not desirable when a company produces luxury goods with fluctuating demand.

(4) When further capital cannot be gainfully employed, debentures should not be issued.

Debentures were not usually popular in India because of various reasons : (a) Stamp duty on debentures is too high, so it is an expensive source of finance (b) Debentures are issued generally in high denomination for which common investors cannot afford to buy them (c) Since debenture issue means taking loan, a company loses its prestige and credit-worthiness when debentures are issued by it. (d) Capital market in India was not also favourable for debenture issue (e) Because of the presence of rival securities such as gilt-edged securities and preference shares, debentures are not so popular.

### Recent trends in debentures as a source of finance

Of late, debentures have attained popularity. Convertibility of debentures is one strong argument in favour of its recent popularity. Debentures are now being issued with attractive terms. There has also been a perceptible change in the attitude of the banks towards debenture issuing companies since companies like Standard Mills, Bombay and even the Tatas are issuing debentures. The institutional investors are also taking interest in debenture investment. To these has been added the facility of the capital market in under-writing debentures. The cost of financing debentures has been reduced on account of the fact that payment of interest on them is an item of expenditure allowed by the tax authorities. The attitude of the investors has also changed; they now prefer better security with higher yields.

### Dividend Policy

Investors in company shares naturally expect a reasonable return on their investment – more than what they can get from banks or in the money market. So, dividend distribution at reasonable rates is an accepted principle. But a company, before it distributes profit or dividend, is to think about the provision for the fixed charges such as taxes, rentals, interest payments and for additions to surplus. Certain profits are sufficient after making all allowances, the question of apportionment between dividend and surplus arises and this rests on the Board of directors. Due to legal restrictions — that dividend cannot be paid out of capital and must only be paid out of profits — it is for the Board to decide whether or not to pay dividend or the rate at which dividend will be paid. Directors, therefore, must be cautious and prudent and must take pragmatic approach in the matter of dividend. There are, of course, some fundamental rules relating to dividend policy which directors should follow in the interest of the company.

To decide upon the rate of dividend, cash or liquid asset position of the company has to be taken into consideration first. Then the prospects of business for the early future and the ability of the company to procure finance for that purpose will be the matters for considerations. Whether the additional funds to be required for any expansion or development would be collected by sale of shares or debentures and how far that also will be possible in the current money market are all matters that merit serious thinking of the Board of directors.

A consistent dividend policy may be pursued and a stable dividend rate may be maintained under all conditions of earnings. This is very important both from the point of view of the company as also from the view-point of shareholders. A uniform rate of dividend maintained every year makes the shareholders assured of a fixed return on this investment and it is not unlikely that a class of shareholders may depend upon their dividend income as a means of their living.

Regular dividend paying shares are of special value because they can be used as collateral security. The company, too, enjoys credit worthiness and its borrowing becomes easier and cheaper. Such a company will have a good market for its new issues. So it should be the policy of a good company to declare dividend every year though the rate may be low. In order to maintain a continuous dividend declaration policy, it may be necessary for the company to keep aside a portion of profits earned in the prosperous year so that uninterrupted dividend can be made available to shareholders. The best policy, however, is not to declare a very high rate of dividend even though profits permit. In this matter the conservative attitude should be followed; a minimum rate of dividend should always be maintained with reasonable rise in the years of prosperity. To be too much liberal in the matter of dividend policy may ultimately harm the interest of the company and may prove the short-sightedness of the Board of directors.

It wil not be out of context to quote here Mead who says, in order to maintain an even rate of distribution on its stock, the directors of well-balanced companies are governed by the following rules –

(a) to pay no dividends for a considerable period after the company begins operation

(b) to manage the expense accounts of the company in such a way as to reduce the fluctuations in surplus profits to the minimum and

(c) to pay out, in any one year, only a portion of profits in dividends.

Dividends not earned during a given period should not be paid out of surplus of the previous years. Again, profits should not be the only criterion for the declaration of dividend; cash position should also be taken into consideration.

The Companies Act lays down certain rules for the payment of dividends : (i) Dividends must only be paid out of profits and not out of capital (ii) Dividend must be paid in cash except where profits are capitalised with the object of issuing fully paid up "Bonus" shares (iii) Dividends can be paid after providing for depreciation (iv) Dividends can be declared after transferring to reserves of the company of such percentage of profits for the year, not exceeding 10 per cent, as may be presented (v) If authorised by its Articles, a company may declare dividends in proportion to the amount paid up on each share where a larger amount is paid up on some shares than on others

(vi) Declared dividend must be paid or the dividend warrant must be posted to the registered shareholders within 42 days of the declaration (vii) Any dividends remaining unpaid or unclaimed after the expiry of 42 days must be transferred within 7 days after the expiry of such 42 days to a special account known as "Unpaid Dividend Account" of the company (viii) Any money transferred to the unpaid dividend account which remains unpaid or unclaimed for 3 years from the date of such transfer shall be transferred to the general revenue account of the Central Government and any claim after such transfer must be preferred to the Central Government and that government will pay to the claimant (ix) Dividend shall be paid to the registered shareholder or to his order or to his banker. In case of share warrant, it is to be paid to the bearer of such share warrant (x) Dividend on shares pending registration of transfer shall be held in abeyance by transfer to the special unpaid Dividend Account, unless the transferer of such shares authorises the company to pay it to the transferee.

In spite of all that we have said, it yet remains to comment that even today there is no unanimity as to the nature of dividend : some say — it is an active decision variable, others say - it is a passive decision variable. Prominent authors like Walter, Modigliani, Miller and Lintner hold different views. Walter, Modigliani and Miller are of the view that the investor is indifferent between dividends and capital gains. Dividends are irrelevant so that the changes in the pay-out ratio do not affect shareholder's wealth in any way whatsoever. Lintner considered dividend policy to be an active decision variable. He has considered the case of target dividend pay out ratio.

Whatever may be said about dividends and their policies, dividends are paid and will be paid to shareholders. But the fact remains that dividends being rewards for investment in the best form of business organisation — the corporate form — a progressive dividend policy should be followed after taking into consideration a number of factors — internal as well as external. The company, the shareholder and the society and the nation at large — all should receive attention of the Board of directors while formulating dividend policy. The whole concept of business having been changed, the dividend policy — i.e. the policy of the return on the investment of the owner of the business — should also be considered against the vast canvas of social concept of business.

## Public deposits

Public deposits - an important and traditional source of industrial finance in India - have, of late, become very significant. This system had developed because of the imperfect banking organisation in our country. This practice of accepting deposits from the public was responsible for the development of the cotton textile industry and the tea industry of our country.

The public deposits were taken for short period from 6 months to 12 months. Of course, in some cases deposits were accepted for a term of 5 to 7 years.

With the introduction of planned economy in the sixties and the launching of Five Year Plans, availability of finance to private sector from traditional sources became scarce and costlier and, at the same time, with the savings arising to the public due to the Plans, the availability of savings waiting to be tapped at lesser cost to companies increased. In the early sixties, the corporate sector went for mobilisation of resources from the public in a major way by issue of advertisements. Raising finance by way of deposits became attractive and still continues to be attractive for two major reasons :

(a) no security need be given and (b) no prior approvals from authorities are required.

The aggregate of deposits increased from Rs.4,188 crores at the end of March 1981 to Rs.5,491.8 crores at the end of March 1982 and this trend of rise has strengthened.

(Guide to Company Deposits & Commercial Paper - K. V. Shanbhogue/K. Ganesan)

The studies made by the Reserve Bank of India reveal that there is a steady growth of public deposits. This is because of general credit stringency in the capital and money market. Public deposits are estimated to be approximately Rs. 6,000 crores. This clearly indicates the popularity of public deposits as a source of finance to companies and also how public repose confidence in companies (Of course in big and reputed companies).

Public deposits are like fixed deposits and they earn a fixed rate of return which is generally higher than bank rate of interest. These deposits, collected through prospectus, can be encashed earlier than the fixed period. The issue of public deposits is now subject to certain restrictions imposed by the government with a view to protecting the interests of depositors.

A company prefers public deposits for some advantages such as — (1) It is a good source of finance (2) The cost of deposits is lower than the rate of interest charged by the banks (3) Deposits are unsecure – they do not create any charge on the assets of the company (4) No questions are asked about their uses (5) Deposits can be had for the purposes for which government finance may not be available (6) The issue of public deposits is comparatively simple (7) Long period deposits are suitable for long-term financial plans of the company (8) They help 'trade on equity', earn higher profits and higher dividends are available for shareholders.

From the point of view of depositors, public deposits are attractive because they give them more return on their investments. Money is safe now and can be encashed earlier than the fixed period.

There are **limitations** of this method of financing. They are : (1) Financial plan cannot be prepared properly because of uncertainty of the amount to be received through public deposits (2) Public deposits are said to be 'fair weather friends', in times of need, they may not be available; hence the source cannot be relied upon so confidently (3) Generally the deposits are for short period, so no long-term projects can be undertaken with such deposits (4) This method prevents development of healthy investment market which is very much desirable for the economy of a country. (5) Sometimes the method becomes uneconomical because of high rate of interest on the deposits. (6) The deposits distort the interest rate pattern (7) They encourage non-priority sector of production (8) They defeat the restrictive credit policy of the Reserve Bank (9) Diversion of bank resources to the non-banking sector.

Public deposits are now subject to various restrictions imposed upon them by the Rules of the Central Government. (Section 58A and 58B of the Companies Amendment Act, 1974)

Companies are to declare their financial position before inviting public deposits through their prospectus. A non-banking company cannot accept more than 25 per cent of its paid-up capital and reserves by way of public deposits. No company can accept deposits repayable on demand. Companies are to file returns with detailed information of public deposits. The non-compliance of the rules or the order of the Company Law Board shall make a company liable to pay a fine of not less than Rs. 50 for everyday of non-compliance.

In spite of various restrictions, public deposits are becoming more and more popular because of various regulatory measures on bank deposits and the fact — that the bank deposits are likely to be within the knowledge of the government — may put the deposition into difficulty in regard to tax matters. According to S. C. Kuchhal, a Company Deposits Insurance Corporation can protect the depositors. But, as a matter of fact, government rules today have been so amended as to be sufficient to protect the interests of deposition. But the more important question is whether people should be made to divert their savings to public deposit scheme of their companies or be encouraged to keep their savings in nationalised banks in the greater interest of the nation.

### Administrative Control

All matters relating to deposits invited or accepted by non-financial companies are under the administrative control of the Department of Company Affairs, Ministry of Industry and Company Affairs. To decide any matter on public deposits, the Department of Company Affairs will consult the Reserve Bank of India (Rule 9). The powers and functions of the Central Government have been delegated to the Company Law Board.

Compliance with the provisions relating to deposits as per the Companies (Acceptance of Deposits) Rules, 1975 is regulated and ensured by the offices of the concerned Registrar of Companies and the Regional Director, Company Law Board, by seeking information or scrutiny of documents filed (including Accounts) and inspection under Section 209A of the Act.

### Retained earnings (Ploughing back of profits)

A portion of profits may be retained in the company to serve as a source of long, medium and short-term capital. This has become an important source of financing a company from within. It is also known as "internal financing" and "self-financing". Some companies follow a conservative policy with regard to the distribution of their earnings and save for future. They create reserves and utilise them in future for several purposes. This method of financing affects the current rate of dividend. Reserves created out of curtailment of dividend (profit) and subsequently utilised by the company in this way is also known as 'ploughing back of profits'. Not only in advanced countries, in our country too, Five Year Plans have been emphasizing the importance of this method of financing for the growth and development of industries. **This method is considered as the best method in compa-**

**ny finance.** If normal dividend payment is not affected, such retention of profits cannot be objected to by shareholders since the object of such a policy is to strengthen the company in future. So big companies with enormous profits can resort to such a practice of self-financing without any criticism and objection.

**The reasons for ploughing back of profits are**

(a) Enough profits — a portion of which can prudently be kept apart for fixed and working capital in the greater interest of the company.

(b) Retained earnings can improve efficiency of the plant and equipment, thus the cost structure can be reduced, and competition position can be strengthened. It enhances the power of the company to withstand the effects of recession.

(c) It is not unlikely that profits revealed through accounts are not correct and overstated. In such a circumstance, retention of a part of profit is a very prudent way of capital management.

**Retained earnings confer the following benefits**

(1) This is a cheaper method of meeting financial requirements

(2) It is a source of permanent finance

(3) It brings about greater financial stability

(4) It may stabilise the rate of dividend

(5) It does not cause any change in control as it does not increase equity capital

(6) Management has not to undergo legal formalities so strict as are in case of the issue of debentures or preference shares

(7) In retained earnings, there is no pledge or mortgage

(8) Shareholders stand to gain in the long run because of the increased prosperity of the company

(9) From the view-point of the nation, this is an important form of capital formation

(10) It facilitates repair and replacement of the fixed assets

(11) It causes rise in the value of shares to the interest of the shareholders

(12) It enables the company to avoid the cost of investment bankers services that would be incurred if stocks or bonds were sold to the public

(13) For small companies, since their investment financial machinery is not geared to financing small business and the funds can be raised only from local sources, the retained earnings may be the only source of funds. However, special financial institutions are now helping small companies.

**Limitations of retained earnings**

(1) It leads to monopoly due to over-investment

(2) It entails social waste because money is not made available to those who can use it to the best advantage of the community but is retained by those who have earned it.

(Prof. Pigou)

(3) There is the danger of misuse of funds

(4) The danger of over-capitalisation cannot be ruled out

(5) Changing shareholders are deprived

(6) Social waste as companies can by-pass the test of efficiency if they are to approach the open market for finance.

(7) Evasion of supertax liability by creation of unreasonable amount of savings.

To conclude, retained earnings — or ploughing back of profits as a source of finance — has undoubted merits but there is a caution to note. Excessive indulgence in such a practice of self-finance may bring with it a host of evils which will outweigh its merits.

In India, this method has passed through several tests. Till 1970, there was a declining trend in the use of this method of financing because expected dividend rates were required to be maintained by the companies. However, since 1970, the trend has reversed.

**Banking and non-banking special institutions**

The financial market consisting of capital market and money market with banking and non-banking special institutions provide short-term, medium-term and long-term finance to business firms.

Capital market deals in stocks, debentures etc. for long-term finance and money market deals in short-term financial instruments. The important participants of money market are represented by commercial banks. Commercial banks deal not only in short-term funds but also medium and long-term finance.

In the matter of providing short-term, medium

term and long-term finance to business firms, the role of capital and money market cannot be differentiated. The distinction between capital and money markets has now been almost imperceptible. So, stock exchanges, banking institutions and non-banking institutions all are providing finance on short-term, medium-term and long-term basis to industries.

"The line of demarcation between a money market and capital market is fast tending to be thinner partly due to a changed concept of liquidity and partly to the preponderance of fixed deposits in commercial banks which take an increasing part in long term investments". Similarly short-term funds are also made available by term lending institutions (development banks specially) to finance working capital needs of the business.

Role of banking and non-banking financial institutions cannot be overestimated in providing finance to business. The financial market of the economy function through financial intermediaries which in themselves constitute financial institutions and financial markets. Indian financial market functions through a number of financial intermediaries.

The institutions which have been playing a special role in industrial finance in India are : Commercial banks, National Small Industries Corporation (NSIC), Indigenous bankers, Industrial Finance Corporation of India (IFCI), State Financial Corporation, Industrial Credit & Investment Corporation of India (ICICI), The Industrial Development Bank of India (IDBI), The Unit Trust of India (UTI), Industrial Reconstruction Bank of India (IRBI) and the Export-Import Bank of India (EXIM Bank).

An analysis and study of industrial finance in India reveals that there has been a steady growth in the number of industrial units assisted in the amount of loans sanctioned and distributed. The financial institutions — banking and non-banking — — have played a very significant role in the development of the private sector industries. However, the financial assistance sanctioned by the term-lending institutions to the private-sectors of the economy declined sharply due to recessionary trends after the Third Plan. Now, the situation has changed and term-lending has picked up.

Public sector financial institutions sanction direct financial assistance to newly established companies to meet their block capital requirements. Existing companies, however, receive financial assistance for expansion of existing capacities, modernisation plans etc.

So far as the term lending is concerned, appreciable contribution has been made; small scale industries have been financed; new entrepreneurs have been benefitted and backward district industries have been given special preferences for their new projects.

The special role of IDBI deserves credit. As the apex institution, it has been playing the leading role in industrial finance since its inception. Other institutions started by the Central and State Governments with the active co-operation of RBI have also been rendering services in providing finance on short-term, mid-term and long-term basis which are no mean contribution to the strengthening of the capital structure of companies. Thus the financial constraints to industrial growth that had existed before independence have now been removed to a great extent by these banking and non-banking financial institutions. While admitting the services and the role of the banking and non-banking financial institutions in the private and the public sector, we are also to say that because of the existence of the public sector and government-owned banks, a few large industrial houses have come up and they have built industrial empires. From the passive role they had played till 1969, the public sector financial institutions have started converting their loans into equities. They are now participating in ownership and management of the industrial units. This new trend resulting from the public sector financial institutions has been playing a very significant role in so far as they have been trying to enforce the industrial houses to achieve their social objectives.

"Financial institutions have a role to play in popularising convertible debentures. These institutions can pursuade the companies to make public issues of convertible debentures so that a good market for these debentures develops and also serves as a catalyst to the growth of the conventional debenture market" (S. C. Kuchhal).

At present, with IDBI as the Apex Institution, we have well-organised capital market. There are five big public financial institutions and many other state institutions. Even during recessionary period, cheaper and liberal industrial finance is likely to be available and finance should no more be a problem for the growth and development of industries.

### Institutions of Industrial finance

State interference in the economic life of a country is the post First World War phenomenon. In our country, in 1918 the Industrial Commission had recommended for state-involvement in industrial finance. Following this recommendation, schemes of industrial financing were introduced in some provinces but unfortunately they did not succeed.

The failure of the schemes, the establishment of many 'industrial banks' and the genuine intention of the Central Government to extend financial assistance to industrial enterprises, gave birth to the Industrial Finance Corporation. It was followed by a number of specialised finance and development corporations.

Brief discussions of the institutions are given below :

### Industrial Finance Corporation (IFC)

The Industrial Finance Corporation was established in 1948 with the object of "making medium and long term credits more readily available to industrial concerns in India".

A public limited company or co-operative society incorporated and registered in India which is engaged or proposes to engage itself, in the manufacture, preservation or processing of goods, or in the shipping, mining or hotel industry or in the function of distribution of electricity or any other form of power, is eligible for financial assistance. Public sector projects are also eligible for assistance. Financial assistance from IFC is available for setting up industrial projects in certain districts in less developed states notified by the Central Government.

In different forms and on various considerations financial assistance is accorded. There is a detailed procedure for obtaining assistance. The IFC has played a vital role in industrial development through resource mobilisation of a very impressive figure.

### State Financial Corporations

There are State Financial Corporations in every state. These corporations are complementary to the Central Corporation and grant accommodation particularly to small, medium and cottage industries where the Central Corporation (IFC) does not operate much. State Financial Corporations extend financial assistance to private limited companies, partnerships and sole proprietors. The assistance is given in the form of loans. Though the latest figure of this financial assistance is not available, but an estimated amount of over Rs. 500 crores has so far been disbursed by the State Financial Corporations of different states of the Country.

The State Financial Corporations have been of great financial assistance to small scale business enterprises.

### The Industrial Credit & Investment Corporation of India (ICICI)

This Corporation was established in January 1955 by the sponsorship of the World Bank. The object was to develop mainly small and medium scale industries in the private sector.

By providing finance in the form of long or medium term loans or equity participation, the Corporation promotes new industries, helps in the expansion and modernisation of existing ones and also furnishes technical and managerial aid to increase production and employment opportunities in industries.

Large scale industrial units are specially benefitted by the services of the Corporation. It has sanctioned uptil now a substantial amount — over Rs. 1,000 crores.

### The National Industrial Development Corporation

This is a financial institution set up in 1954 in the public sector to develop those industries which are necessary to fill up gaps in the industrial structure and which require intensive capital employment. It may also set up industries which may, in their turn, lead to the growth of ancillary industries in the private sector. The Corporation has set up a Technological Consultancy Bureau to assist in the promotion of consultancy services in the country.

### National Small Industries Corporation

With the object of providing marketing service, promoting small industries and encouraging hire-purchase system of machineries, this Corporation was set up in February 1955. The activities of the Corporation are 'Promotional' and 'Commercial'.

The Corporation acts as a liaison agency between the small units and the Director General of Supplies and Disposal, Government of India. It gives credit guarantee to small business units, provides machineries on hire-purchase system to small industrial concerns. The marketing and promotional activities of the Corporation are being conducted simultaneously. Prototype production and Training Centres have been set up at Okhla, Rajkot and Howrah to produce and develope proto-type of these machines and machine tools imported from Germany and the USA. Two model industrial estates have also been set up at Okhla and Naini.

### Industrial Developmental Bank of India (IDBI)

The establishment of Industrial Development Bank of India in July, 1964 is a land-mark in the history of industrial finance in India. The entire business of Re-finance Corporation for industry was taken over by IDBI. As such, Re-finance Corporation does not function now. Developing and emerging industries are specially benefitted by its establishment. Existing financial institutions can draw funds from this Bank. The special credit of Industrial Development Bank is that it promotes key industries.

With huge amount of capital divided into Central Fund and Development Fund, the Bank is financing projects which other financial institutions do not. The Bank combines commercial, promotion and refinancing activities.

For the last 28 years the Bank has been rendering yeoman service in the field of industrial finance both as a guide to the financial institutions and as a purveyor of financial assistance. The Bank offers concessions and incentives to State Financial Corporations and banks to enable them to help industries in backward areas.

### Industrial Reconstruction Bank of India

The Industrial Reconstruction Bank of India was established as a statutory corporation in March 1985. It was set up to act as the principal credit and reconstruction agency for industrial revival. It helps in the matter of credit, equipment leasing and hire purchase. The Bank sanctions term loans for modernisation, diversification, expansion, renovation and for bridging liquidity gap as well as for providing margin money for working capital. The Bank may also purchase or underwrite issues of shares, bonds, debentures. It acts as consultant to banks and financial institutions.

### Life Insurance Corporation of India

As an investment institution, the Life Insurance Corporation occupies a very important position in the financial market. Being the largest investment institution, it provides long-term finance to industrial undertakings. It subscribes and underwrites shares, bonds and debentures of public limited companies.

The LIC follows certain principles in the matter of investment. They are : (a) Schemes must be socially useful (b) Safe securities to be selected for investment (c) Diversification of investments (d) Assistance to backward areas.

General Insurance Corporation of India and the Employees' State Insurance Corporation have been investing their fund in the securities of companies.

### The Small Industries Development Bank of India (SIDBI)

This Bank started operating from April, 1990. It acts as the apex institution to strengthen and broadbase the existing institutional arrangements to meet the requirements of industries in the tiny and small scale sector. The Bank, as the leading financial institution, co-ordinates the functions of the institutions engaged in the promotion, financing and development of industries in the small scale sector.

The SIDBI is to refinance National Industries Corporation, State Financial Corporations, State Industrial Development Corporations, State Small Industries Corporations, scheduled banks, State co-operative banks etc. and it will also purchase shares, bonds or debentures of any State Financial Corporation.

### Unit Trust of India

The Unit Trust of India was established in 1963 but started functioning from July 1964. It sells units and augments the small savings plan of the government. It then strengthens capital market by mobilising small savings and subscribing to the new issues. The overall investment objectives of the Trust are safety of capital, regular and growing income.

A Board of Trustees manages the affairs of the Trust in the public sector. The RBI, the LIC, SBI control the Board. The Board is expected to act on business principles with due regard to the interest of the unit holder.

In the investment policy, it follows the principles of safety and reasonable return.

Income tax benefit is available on Unit Trust income.

As a matter of fact, UTI acts as an intermediary institution. It pools the savings of the community and invests them in various types of securities.

The Unit Trust of India Act was amended in 1966 with a view to permitting the Trust to formulate more than one scheme as well as plans. Various schemes such as Capital Unit Scheme, 1976, Childrens' Gift Growth Fund 1986, Mutual Fund Unit Scheme, 1986 – Master shares – are some of the schemes launched by UTI.

People with moderate means find in UTI a place to invest their small savings. New schemes are being placed before the public with income tax relief and **UTI has thus been serving the cause of the economic development of the country on a massive scale.**

**Big commercial banks and Merchant Banking institutions** also render valuable services to industrial units. Commercial banks are essentially dealers in short term credit to finance current assets or circulating capital. These banks now grant medium-term loans and act as company underwriters.

Merchant Banking institutions are financial intermediaries to offer variety of services like promotion, syndication of projects, investment advice, management advisory services, acceptance credit and discount services etc.

Since 1940, individual investors are being steadily replaced by institutional investors. These institutional investors cater to medium-term and long-term needs of industries.

In conclusion, we can say that the performance of all financial institutions are, on the whole, satisfactory. These institutions provide adequate institutional set up in the capital market of the country-making it broad-based and well-organised.

## COMMERCIAL BANKS

### Commercial banks and Short-term Credit

In the money market, commercial banks occupy an important position. They deal with overwhelming proportion in supplying short-term credit. Analysis has revealed that in purely quantitative terms, commercial banks have a unique position in the institutional channels of industrial finance. More than two-thirds of their fund is made available to industries in the form of short-term credit. This is to meet the working capital needs of industry. This orthodox theory of lending is known as 'deposit banking theory' and this type of financing is 'self-liquidating assets'; the basic proposition of lending policy is to confine credit in the form of self-liquidating assets which are of short term nature.

Banks' short-term lending policy is the result of a number of factors :

**(1) Customers' deposit pattern :** Banks lend out customers' deposits. Deposits are not all of the same type. Some deposits are fixed for a definite and relatively long period but most of the deposits are savings deposits and can be withdrawn by customers as and when required by them. So, banks cannot use these funds for long period credit at the cost of sufficient liquidity essential for a commercial bank's day-to-day functioning.

**(2) Central Bank's credit policy :** The Central Bank exercises both quantitative and qualitative credit control. To make credit instruments effective, availability of liquid assets with commercial banks is necessary. For example, in open market operations, if all its assumptions are observed, immediate cost will be available and purchase or sale can be effected and desired results obtained. The Central Bank, therefore, requires commercial banks to invest in liquid assets.

**(3) Risky nature of long term investments :** Long term investments are fraught with many risks which commercial banks legitimately want to avoid. By investing on long-term basis, there is the loss of interests and the loss of security price (capital loss). The longer the period of lending the greater is the risk of changes in the rate of interest.

**(4) Project evaluation difficulties :** In granting term-loan, detailed project appraisal is very much necessary. To appraise properly, a specialised staff is needed and there is the need for the borrower to prepare the project thoroughly. Both these conditions are difficult to be fulfilled before a commercial bank is satisfied as to the advisability of lending on long-term basis; so the banks prefer shorter term lending.

So, short-term lending is safer and it is quite timely for the commercial banks to prefer this short-term lending. But the actual position is constantly undergoing changes. With the nationalisation of big commercial banks and in the context of changing economic scenario, commercial banks are changing their policy in conformity with the government policy even at the cost of liquidity principle and ignoring safety and security considerations.

### Medium term lending of Commercial banks

From deposit banking principle, the change-over to term lending is relatively new. The ever increasing demand of industries for funds to facilitate capital formation and the role of banks in the development of industries in the country have necessitated medium term lending. The reasons for term lending by banks are different in different countries. In countries like USA, the banks themselves resorted to term lending to utilise their surplus funds and in some other countries, the borrower and the government took the initiative for term lending. In a developing country like ours, industries themselves have to press for funds for a longer period and the government, to industrialise the country, initiated the policy of refinance.

In our country, the shift of the lending policy of the commercial bank has been mainly due to industrialisation as envisaged in our Plans. It started from the Second Plan period as the Plan had laid emphasis on industrial development. To meet the Plan requirements, some institutional innovation was called for. Besides institutional facilities for funds, there was desirability of expanding facilities for small and medium-sized enterprises. State Financial Corporations failed to fulfil the expectations of these enterprises for their slow-moving nature and lack of local contacts. The development of this situation necessitated the commercial banks to come forward and start term lending. In 1958, a formal scheme of term loans was started. The term loan started and continues to be a refinance type term-loan. But this scheme has had a relatively minor impact on the lending practices of commercial banks in India. Since 1963–64, the State Financial Corporations are also eligible for refinance.

## Commercial banks and long-term funds for industries

Long-term funds for industrial finance are provided by commercial banks in three different forms — (a) underwriting of securities (b) direct purchase of securities and (c) indirect supply of funds.

(a) **Underwriting of securities :** Over three decades back, Indian Central Banking Engineering Committee recommended the entry of Indian commercial banks in the underwriting of securities for strengthening the machinery engaged in the supply of long-term funds. This recommendation was also supported by the Shroff Committee which suggested the formation of a consortium or syndicate for underwriting. The Shroff Committee's idea was not accepted. But it was seen that a number of banks started underwriting of securities but they were very selective and, as such, underwriting by commercial banks did not make much headway. Generally, an underwriting bank used to act as the banker to the issue. A commercial bank undertaking underwriting business generally supplies application forms for which it earns brokerage from the issuing company and acts as a passive agent. Commercial banks usually do not have any interest in acquiring the securities which they underwrite but this is not the case with LIC and other financial institutions. Banks are not interested in holding large blocks of industrial securities and, as such, their impact on securities market is not so significant. So, underwriting of securities by commercial banks does not appeal to the companies.

(b) **Direct purchase of securities :** Commercial banks directly purchase securities of companies but, as said earlier, they are not interested in holding large blocks of securities. Data so far collected indicate that direct subscription of commercial banks to the share capital of joint stock companies in India has never been more than 1% of their deposit liabilities and 2 1/2% of their investment in securities. So, commercial banks do not play any significant role in the direct purchase of company securities.

(c) **Indirect supply of funds :** Lending against corporate securities indirectly is one of the functions of commercial banks in strengthening capital formation of companies. In the Securities Market, bank credit is available against industrial securities and according to a rough estimate of the loans and advances against corporate securities of commercial banks, the range is of 5 to 6 per cent.

From what we have discussed above, commercial banks are predominantly suppliers of short-term credit retaining the traditional role for meeting working capital requirements. However, since independence, significant changes have taken place in the economic system and political climate of the country. **The socialistic ideology has brought about a fundamental change in the attitude of the public towards banks urging upon them to fulfil the expectations of the people.** Major commercial banks have been nationalised and these banks are now serving nationally important sectors by the re-orientation in their lending policies. The 'social control over banks' is now aimed at "achieving a wider spread of bank credit, preventing the misuse, directing a large volume of credit to flow to priority sectors and making it a more effective instrument of economic development". As a matter of fact, the banking system, in spite of its efforts, could not achieve the objectives of 'social control' — one such objective being the upliftment of the weaker section of the society. As a consequence came nationalisation on July 19, 1969. The objectives of nationalisation were primarily to achieve what the 'Social Control' could not and it was expected that "the banks would endeavour to ensure that the needs of productive efforts of diverse kinds, irrespective of size and social status of the borrowers and, in particular those of farmers, small scale industries and self-employed professional groups are not in an increasing measure and to create fresh opportunities for backward areas in different parts of the country". To attain these objectives and fulfil these expectations, changes in the banking pattern and policies were called for. Besides changing methods of operation, the concept of security for loan was also changed. Special attention was given to the growth potential and developmental needs of the local areas and to forge close relations with developmental and term-financing institutions. A close watch over the banks had to be kept to ensure that big borrowers did not have more access to resources of the banks than their actual requirements for productive purposes. After nationalisation, it was also a priority task for the nationalised banks to open branches in as many areas as possible to provide banking facilities to the remote parts of the country, to the rural areas to mobilise small savings and to utilise them in the overall development of the under-developed areas and to extend various benefits to under-privileged and unemployed people of the country, particularly rural people.

To conclude, we can say that there is no unmixed blessing in this world; banking reforms cannot be an exception. Government ownership and control over the major commercial banks of the country is undoubtedly a bold step towards economic regeneration and rehabilitation of the shattered under-developed colonial economy. To realise the objectives of the planned economy, to ensure rapid industrialisation of the country, to enable the economically weaker section of the people of our country residing in villages, a comprehensive banking reform with the maximum control of government was undoubtedly the need of the hour and actually nationalisation has at least clearly demonstrated that there is the scope for banking services in the rural areas and in small towns where the branches of nationalised banks have come up, we may say, like mushroom growth. Nationalised commercial banks have been endeavouring to extend credit to priority sectors. The latest economic policy, based on unprecedented economic conditions of the country, has raised the question of privatisation of banks since a section of people think that nationalised banks have, for various reasons, failed to deliver goods to the people of the country. The future is not yet clear : the country has been passing through serious economic conditions and various remedies have been suggested and are being applied to cure the economic ills that have overtaken the country. Truly speaking, our banking system is on trial, nobody knows exactly what is going to take place in future in this integral component of any economic reconstruction of the country.

# CHAPTER 10

## INDUSTRIAL SECURITIES MARKET

The discussion on 'Financial Management' remains incomplete without highlighting the role of industrial securities market. Financial Management will find it within its scope to have close contact with the securities market to ensure not only easy flow of capital but also for its proper utilisation.

The securities market acts as an intermediary between the supplies of funds and the users of funds. The new issues market and the stock exchange are its two components.

The new issues market has institutional facility of investigation and processing proposals regarding time, pric^ ^nd magnitude of issue. The market underwrites n  w issues and distributes new securities to ultimate investors. These services of the new issues market help mobilisation of investible funds from savers to real investors. In our country, however, this market provides underwriting facilities only.

Stock Exchange is an integral segment of the securities market and its major functions are : the provision of a market for the purchase and sale of securities and the provision of capital for the purposes of industry and government. Stock exchange as a part of industrial securities market facilitates transfer of resources from savers to investors.

The new issues market and stock exchange cannot be left out of discussion while discussing financial management (of a company).

The new issues market has no geographical existence and consists essentially of institutions involved in the issue of financial securities to the investing public. The issues market does not require the issuing body and the investing public to meet. It facilitates transfer of investible funds from their owner to entrepreneur either to establish new enterprises or to expand the existing ones.

### New Issues Market

The market has no physical existence, hence the parties — the issuing body and the investing public — need not come together. It is a service-oriented market dealing in new securities facilitating the transfer of investible funds to enterprises either for their birth or for their growth. In an economy as ours, savings and real investments are not undertaken by the same individual; hence the necessity of such a market is felt all the more.

The effectiveness of the new issues market is in its ability to guide the flow of available investible funds into the most productive investment. A new issues market not only allocates funds but also directly and indirectly influences the volume of resources to be made available to industry. The market must be capable enough, to be really useful, to reach down to all potential investors.

### Methods of marketing new issues

(a) Prospectus Method (b) Offer for Sale Method (c) Placement Method (d) Right issues and (e) Issue by tender.

The choice of a particular method is dependent on consideration – such as the size of the lot and the conditions of the capital market. Random choice, therefore, cannot be a sound financial management policy.

### Issue by Prospectus (Public issue Method)

The method of new issues by prospectus has the advantages of (i) wider approach (ii) publicity on a massive scale and (iii) diffusion of ownership. Through prospectus, a company can appeal for new issues to a wider circle and on a massive scale and it also ensures shareholding by a larger section of society having a definite socio-economic impact. A large mass of people participate in the equities of a company and thus take part in the economic development of their country.

Prospectus Method is very expensive since a number of formalities have to be observed. Again, what happens usually in the Prospectus Method is that in case of over-subscription of shares, small investors may be ignored. So, large companies can suitably afford this method of issue.

### Offer for Sale Method

Under this Method, the whole lot of shares is sold to the issuing house. The issuing house issues the prospectus. Here the contact with the investing public is rather indirect; the issue-house acts as the principal and not as an agent of the company, so the company is receded to the back-ground and the issue-house becomes the direct link with the investing public. The issue-houses purchase shares from the company to offer them to the public at a slightly higher price. The difference of their purchase price and their selling price of shares is their remuneration.

This method of new issues, however, relieves a company of the botheration and risks of marketing new issues but the disadvantage that can be ascribed to such a method of selling new shares is that the favourable market trend in the price of shares is pocketed by the issuing house, the company cannot get the benefit of the higher market price of shares. This method is, therefore, suitable when market conditions are not favourable and the size of the issue is small and publicity expenses are heavy.

### Placement Method

This method refers to the sale of shares by an issuing house or a broker to their own clientele. Under this method, although a formal prospectus is not necessary to issue, the letter of placement with terms of issues can be said to constitute a prospectus. There is no need of underwriting because placement itself offers a guarantee regarding sale of issues or securities.

This method is perhaps, the cheapest. However, from investors' point of view, securities under this method are available only to a selected group of investors as there is a list with the issuing house of the investors whom only the broker approaches. Thus, the general public are deprived of shares under this method which results in the concentration of economic power in a few hands.

This method does not discriminate between smaller companies or smaller issue lots as there is a group of listed investors who will purchase through the issuing house. Capital issues in the method can be successful even if conditions in new issue market are infavourable. In the depressed condition of Indian Capital market this method is really effective.

### Rights Shares (Right issues)

Under Section 81 of the Companies Act, 1956, Indian companies are required to offer additional issues of shares to existing holders of equity shares. A right is an option to buy a security at a specified price during a designated period. In such a case, the existing equity shareholder enjoys privileged position and this offer is, therefore, known as "privileged subscription".

*Sub-section* I *to Sec.* 81 *provides* —

where at any time after the expiry of two years from the formation of a company or at any time after the expiry of one year from the allotment of shares in that company made for the first time after its formation, whichever is earlier, it is proposed to increase the subscribed capital of the company by allotment of further shares, then

(a) such (further) shares shall be offered to the persons who, at the date of the offer, are holders of the equity shares of the company, in proportion, as nearly as circumstances admit, to the capital paid-up on those shares at that date ;

(b) the offer aforesaid shall be made by notice specifying the number of shares offered and limiting a time not being less than fifteen days from the date of the offer within which the offer, if not accepted, will be deemed to have been declined;

(c) unless the Articles of the company otherwise provide, the offer aforesaid shall be deemed to include a right exercisable by the person concerned to renounce the shares offered to him or any of them in favour of any other person and the notice referred to above shall contain a statement of this right.

(d) after the expiry of the time specified in the notice or on receipt of earlier intimation from the person to whom such notice is given that he declines to accept the shares offered, the Board of Directors may dispose of them in such manner as they think most beneficial to the company.

In the financing of companies, rights play an important role but the significance of rights is not properly understood either by the issuing companies or by the shareholders.

**In formulating financial policies, the rights have significance.** The issue of 'rights' means better reception for the shares because the shareholders can thereby protect their pro-rata share in the earnings and surplus of the company. From the point of view of the company , the cost of issue of 'rights' is less than the cost of issue for public subscription. The price for rights shares is usually much below the prevailing market price. "Such a rights offering is stock-split to a certain degree and may cause the market price of the shares to fall. Stock splits also increase the number of shareholders in a company by bringing the price of a stock down to a more attractive trading level". Rights issue stimulates response from the shareholder and the investment market and the opportunities for financing become more attractive. This takes place where the market is bullish. The 'rights' may have a depressing effect on the price of the shares on the market if the issue is large in relation to the amount of equity share capital already outstanding.

The corpc ate management takes it into consideration whether the proportion of the rights to existing shares is related to the willingness and ability of shareholder to acquire additional shares. A better financial policy is, therefore, to issue less number of additional shares in relation to the already existing shares i.e. the proportion of rights to the already existing shares should be less, say 1 : 10 is better than 5 : 10. This will put less strain on an investor's wealth because the company offers them to buy 1 share for each 10 shares and not 5 shares for 10 shares. Again, the spread has to be considered. The spread between the market price and the subscription price is important in relation to the normal variations in the share price and the general market outlook. If the shares are not traded so extensively and price fluctuates widely, the management will have to set the subscription price below the market price.

General strength of the market is an important factor since it is likely to affect all shares. The earning expectation from the rights is a big consideration because the more productive the new funds, the more likely the rights offering to be successful.

There is a pre-offering pressure generally in the market where rights are likely to be issued. This has to be keenly watched. It is a common feature when rights are issued that during the subscription period itself downward pressure on the market price of outstanding shares develops. So the subscription price of the new shares should be below the current market price.

During ex-rights period, i.e. during the period when rights are offered, an investor may purchase a share on the market at the current market price or he may purchase the proper number of rights and then subscribe at the subscription price. If he takes recourse to the second method, his total cost is the price of the rights plus the subscription price. If the subscription price is not less than the ruling market price, the investors will naturally not be attracted to the new issue. So the subscription price has the problem of protecting likely market price for the security during the life of the rights.

From the above discussion it follows that **while making rights issue, the management has to keep in view certain factors such as** (a) "pricing of issue (b) price behaviour of rights (c) underwriting of rights issue (d) long range effects on market price (e) effects on earnings per share" (S C Kuchhal)

The approval of the Controller of Capital Issues has to be obtained in pricing the rights issue. Generally, the 'right' price is smaller; this is to enable the company to get the larger portion of the extra money for productive use. The price is determined taking into consideration the trend of the capital market, the trend of share price in general and of the company's shares in particular, the ruling cum-right market price and the ratio of proportion of the rights issue to the existing equity capital of the company.

In fixing the price of rights, the shareholders' satisfaction and requirement of funds by the company have to be kept in view. An established company may make rights issue at premium if it is reasonable in the context of the break-up value of the shares and profit earning capacity of the company. Success of rights issue, to a great extent, depends on the fixation of premium. Low premium means issue of higher number of shares. In case the premium is very high, the value of rights loses its worth because (M – S)/(N + 1) would not leave a significant value for R.

[The formula for determing the value of one right when the market value of a share is taken with-rights (cum-rights) is : R = (M – S)/(N + 1) when R = value of one right; M = cum-rights price; S = subscription price; N = No. of old shares entitling to purchase one new share].

[The 'ex-rights' value is determined as follows :

$$R = (P - S)/N$$

when R = value of one right; P = market value ex-rights; S = subscription price and N = Number of old shares entitling to one new share.]

## Rights vis-a-vis Small shareholders

Apparently rights have no effect on the small shareholders but in reality small shareholders suffer because of rights issue. Rights issue in large number and infrequent rights issue affect the up-switch of EPS growth trend. Small shareholders fail to take timely decision on rights issue – whether they will purchase or not. Shareholders of our country, in general, suffer from ignorance and defects because of less enlightenment and sometimes rights lapse. Shareholders are not even always financially capable of buying additional shares. Generally, after the rights issue, the share price falls and the small shareholders will then suffer if they want to sell their shares. To buy shares within a limited period of time is not always possible for the small shareholder and the pressure to find funds to exercise rights may result in forced selling on the part of the small shareholders. This has the effect of concentration of shares in a few hands. "The small shareholder may not be having the capacity to save or to borrow at a rate at which the company requires additional funds for investment. Further, the cost, time and botheration in selling rights may not leave much margin and enthusiasm for the small shareholders to exercise their rights" (S.C. Kuchhal).

## Regulatory provisions affecting rights

The issue of rights is regulated since it has perceptible consequence on the shareholders of the company which issues rights and also on the economy of a country in general. The Controller of Capital Issues acts as the Authority. The stock exchange regulations and government directives regulate rights issue. Certain conditions have been imposed on the companies issuing rights. Opportunity must be given to the shareholder to apply for additional shares. If the rights shares are not fully taken up, the balance will be distributed equally among the applicants for additional shares with reference to the shares held by them in the company at the time of the issue. Small shareholders should be given preference. If any balance is still left after making allotment against applications for additional shares, the company may dispose off those shares either at the ruling market price or at the issue price consented to, whichever is higher. Where this procedure cannot be applied for any reason, the approval of the Controller of Capital Issues must be obtained as to how to deal with these shares.

Stock exchange regulations prescribe that the rights issuing company must submit the specimen of the letter of offer to the stock exchange where the shares are listed. A formal request must be made by the company in writing for admission of the Letters of Remuneration and Coupons, if any, to official dealings on the Stock Exchange.

## Underwriting of rights issue

Because of uncertainty elements in rights the assistance of underwriters is sought by the company. Underwriters keep watch over the market, support the market, excercise the rights prior to their expiry and offer the shares publicly at a price compatible with market price. Underwriters thus help reduction of risks and afford better opportunity to the shareholder to get a price for the rights. The "second bite" technique — or 'Oversubscription privilege' as it is called — is offered by the company to increase the chances that a large part of the issue is taken by the shareholders.

## Price behaviour of rights

Rights have a definite behavioural pattern. The value of rights is high during the early period of rights and low during the late period. There is a slogan "Sell early and buy late" during the rights trading period. Therefore, in the later part of the trading period the supply of rights is increased relative to the supply in the early part and the price declines. But by analysis it has been seen that the assessment given above is not fully correct. It all depends upon the prospects of the indivdual company; the company's prospects increase the value of rights and not the rule of thumb as described above.

•

### Issue by tender

The public is invited to apply for the available securities at or above a certain minimum price and allotment is made to the highest bidder.

This is not a popular method for new issues anywhere in the world since the method is suitable where the differential is likely to be high.

**In the emerging pattern of New Issues market in India,** we see the setting up of active institutional underwriting machinery. This is a post-Independence development (between 1955 and 1964). The establishment of the Industrial Credit and Investment Corporation of India Ltd. (ICICI) in January 1955 initiated the process of underwriting facilities for new issues. To this were added the Industrial Finance Corporation of India, LCI, UTI; thus a strong organisation for new issues has been built up. Other agencies, too, are rendering no insignificant service; they are commercial banks, state governments, promoters and stock brokers.

The approach and policy standards of these different institutions and agencies in extending underwriting facilities differ. Special institutions, for example, nurse new enterprises in their formative stages by holding the securities not taken by the public. Institutional investors underwrite issues for having them in their investment portfolio. Commercial banks' role has been quite managerial. Stockbrokers underwrite on the strength of their clientele on ad hoc basis.

## Stock Exchange

Stock exchange is an organised open market where securities of joint stock companies, Government and semi-government bodies are dealt in. It is an integral segment of the securities market. The Securities Contracts (Regulation) Act, 1956 defines a stock exchange as "an association, organisation or body of individuals, whether incorporated or not, established for the purposes of assisting, regulating and controlling business in buying, selling and dealing in securities".

In the matter of corporate financial management, the role of stock exchanges cannot be overemphasised. It facilitates the transfer of existing flow of savings into the profitable channels and increases the flow of savings for the economic progress of the country. The stock exchange as a citadel of capital market and pivot of money market render very essential services to the corporate sector but for which the companies in general would have to face financial difficulties. By making provision for continuous market for securities, stock exchanges ensure liquidity, price continuity and negotiability of corporate securities.

Speculation in stock exchanges is carried on sometimes illegitimately and gambling takes place as a matter of fact. It becomes a gamblers' den instead of the economic barometer of a country. So, it is necessary to regulate stock exchanges and we have in our country some regulations in this respect. It will not be out of context to mention here the arguments put forward while the Bill to regulate stock exchanges in India was introduced. Mr. C.D. Deshmukh, the then Finance Minister, in nicely worded sentences argued in favour of a well-organised stock exchange — "The economic services which a well constituted and efficiently run securities market can render to a country with a large sector under the normal incentives and impulses of private enterprises are considerable. In the first place, it is only an organised securities market which can provide sufficient marketability and price continuity for shares so necessary for the needs of investors. Secondly, it is only such a market that can provide a reasonable measure of safety and fair dealing in the buying and selling of securities. Thirdly, through the interplay of demand for and supply of securities, a properly organised stock exchange assists in terms of their real worth.

Lastly, through such evaluation of securities, the stock exchange helps in the orderly flow of distribution of savings as between different types of competitive investments".

It has been rightly asserted that, "The task facing the stock exchanges is to devise the means to reach down to the masses, to draw the savings of the man in the street into productive investment, to create conditions in which many millions of little investors in cities, towns and villages will find it possible to make use of the facilities, which have, so far, been limited to the privileged few. This calls for far-reaching changes, institutional as well as operational".

In the corporate financial management in India today, the role of stock exchanges has assumed greater importance in view of the fact that India is engaged in accelerating the pace of her industrial development.

## Listing of Securities

Listing of securities means permission to quote shares and debentures officially on the trading floor of the stock exchange. Only listed securities can be traded through the stock exchanges. Usually, large companies get their securities listed in a stock exchange.

### Listing requirements

(1) Provisions must be made in the Memorandum and Articles

(2) Minimum public issue of capital not less than 49 p.c. of the total issued capital

(3) Open market offer by prospectus open at least for 3 days

(4) Fair and unconditional allotment — the basis of allotment to be determined in consultation with the stock exchange

(5) No dividend on advance call

(6) No forfeiture of unclaimed dividends

(7) No lien on fully paid shares

(8) Listing agreement describing the rights and obligations of the company

(9) The prescribed transfer form

(10) History of the company in brief

(11) Particulars of capital structure, dividends, statement of distribution of share capital, specimen share certificate, letter of allotment is to be provided by the company

(12) Certified copy of the consent of the Controller of Capital Issues

(13) Agreement with the underwriters, managing director etc.

(14) An undertaking regarding compliance with the provisions of the Companies Act, 1956 and Securities Contracts (Regulation) Act, 1956 as well as rules made therein.

Listed securities may be — cleared securities and non-cleared securities. Cleared securities enjoy forward trading facilities. Non-cleared securities have only cash dealings and are on the cash list.

### Advantages of listing

(1) Listed securities are easily marketable; they are more liquid

(2) They acquire high collateral value for bank loans

(3) Listing facilitates easy evaluation of real worth of securities

(4) Interest of the general public is safeguarded as there are equitable allotment, easy transfer, disclosure of prospectus, formalities etc.

(5) Tax advantages

(6) Stock exchange quotation acts as the selling point of a company in the public issue of capital by prospectus

(7) Companies having listed securities enjoy higher status and reputation.

(8) Listing creates confidence about the securities in the minds of the investing public. They can be sure that there is no fraud in the issue of shares

(9) Listing widens the market for the securities issued

### Limitations

(1) Because of speculators' interest in tested securities, there may be price fluctuation for the illegitimate speculative dealings

(2) The management of the company may carry trading on such securities to their personal advantage and at the cost of the uninformed shareholders

(3) Substantial amount of shares may be purchased by a certain group to capture management of the company

(4) Disclosure of information to stock exchange for enlisting may do harm to the company concerned. Some vital information disclosed may help the rival companies to act to the detriment of the interest of the company having listed securities.

### Short-term credit as a way of financing circulating assets

The short-term credit is one where the creditor must be paid back in the near future, possibly one year being an acceptable period and accountants generally stress one year as the dividing line between short-term and long-term credit. But according to some, this is arbitrary.

Whatever exactly the period of credit may be, one thing is certain that the credit is to be repaid within a short period and the concept of short period has not been clearly defined anywhere. This credit is generally used as a means of financing circulating assets and meeting operating expenses of the business. Borrowing from short-term sources is often an advantageous way of financing the temporary expansion of circulating assets. It is considered sound financial policy to use short-term credit to expand variable working capital because this will be converted into cash in the near future, thus providing the funds with which to pay the creditors. However, a number of companies and public utilities have borrowed from short-term sources to acquire fixed assets; then later on bonds or shares are issued and proceeds are used to repay the bank. **To use short-term credit on a temporary basis to finance the acquisition of fixed assets is not an unsound financial management,** but the move to use it to meet medium and long-term financial requirement smacks of financial imprudence.

The use of short-term credit for financing circulating assets is the usual way of utilising it but the proceeds may be used to pay off some other groups of creditors. As such, short-term credit does add to the volume of circulating assets of the enterprise. The operating business expenses are met by short-term credit. This does not result in any increase in total circulating assets.

## Reasons for using short-term credit

It is an economical method of financing circulating assets. Absence of alternate sources of funds is also a factor for using short-term credit.

The short-term credit is economical because the rate of interest is low. Since its use avoids the idleness of the funds, it becomes economical. Sometimes it so happens that no interest has to be paid on short-term loans. Since the rate of interest is lower than that on bond issue, a company can increase profits which may be made available to common stockholders.

Where the need for funds is seasonal, it becomes prudent for financial management to use short-term credit as it will cut down the interest cost to the business because the extra funds may be procured only for the period needed. Sometimes, it so happens that short-term credit may be available even without interest. Let us assume a credit transaction for one month without having any provision for discount for early payment. The debtor can very well defer payment for one month and then he can enjoy a cost-less loan.

So, lower rate of interest or no interest and avoidance of idleness of funds prompt a company or business enterprise to use short-term credit without incurring heavy interest costs.

Non-availability of alternate sources of funds sometime compels a company to resort to the use of short-term credit. Market conditions or the attitude of the management may be responsible in such a circumstance. It may be that due to the market conditions, stocks are not saleable to the public except at prices that would dilute the equity of the existing shareholder. Or it may be that if bonds were issued, they would have to carry such a high interest rate as to make them undesirable from management's point of view. These are compelling circumstances for the use of short-term credit, though cost of interest becomes high.

# CHAPTER 11

## SUPPLEMENTARY STUDIES

**Sources of Financial Information :** For the financial manager to make more informed decisions, there are various sources. It is very common for the Financial Management to secure financial information about the money market, stock market, industries and individual companies to take decisions on new financing, temporary borrowing, inventory management and capital budgeting.

Information sources can be mainly grouped as — Daily newspapers, Magazines on finance and banking, Financial Services, Company and Supplementary data.

We have daily newspapers such as The Economic Times, The Financial Express where detailed financial information necessary for the financial manager are available. These dailies publish news of stock exchanges, commodity markets, various articles pertaining to national as well as international finance. There are other daily media through which financial information affecting the decisions of the financial manager are available. Business Standard, Economic News and many other publications are now available to take us into the financial world and particularly the financial manager can find in them a valuable guide for his future course of action. Corporate news are ventilated through daily newspapers which also enable the Financial Management to assess the trend of the corporate sector. Company earnings, dividend news are all very useful for the Management to manage finance of the Company.

In the dailies, the fluctuations in the price of stocks are reflected by the opening and closing prices. Forward and spot dealings are also reported in the dailies which serve as useful information for the Financial Management.

Stock Market quotations are very significant for Financial Management. In India, there are eight recognised Stock Exchanges. For a layman, Stock Exchange quotations are not intelligible. There are many symbols and abbreviations which must be known to understand price quotations of Stock Exchanges.

Unless otherwise mentioned, the quotations refer to equity shares of a company. The previous closing prices are given in brackets after the names and the paid-up values of shares, in brackets before the names. Last closing prices appear at the end. If two or more unbracketed quotations appear at the end, the first represents the opening price of the issue which may differ from the previous closing price and the other quotations mean the fluctuations in the prices (highest and lowest) of the security with the last quotation representing the closing price of the issue.

We give below some abbreviations generally used in stock markets :

| | | |
|---|---|---|
| SOL | : | Small odd lot |
| OL | : | Odd lot |
| CT | : | Cross Transaction |
| NT | : | No trading |
| F | : | Face value |
| FP | : | Fully paid |
| SL | : | Small lot |
| Xr | : | ex (excluding right) |
| cd | : | cum (with) dividend |

Contd. from previous page

| | | |
|---|---|---|
| Con | : | Convertible |
| Defd | : | Deferred |
| r | : | redeemable |
| t | : | taxable |
| N | : | Nominal |

Stock markets being the economic barometer of a country, volume of securities traded on the floor of Stock Exchanges indicate the activities of stock exchanges. An important help in interpreting the behaviour of the stock market as a whole are various indexes and averages. The most important of these are the daily Economic Times Index of Equity Share prices, the Weekly Reserve Bank of India's Index Numbers of Security prices and the daily Financial Express's All India Equity Indedex. Financial managers very keenly watch the movements of the averages and indexes. On the basis of these movements, they can understand the bullishness (strength) or the bearishness (weakness) of the stock market in relation to plans for investing in or selling of securities. The timing of floatation of new issues is very much determined by stock exchange averages and indexes.

To Financial Management, the sources of financial information are not only for studying the financial climate of the country; the sources are also used for studying investment climate and corporate financial news of the foreign countries. The economic world today is closely knit, so a prudent and modern financial manager keeps himself abreast of the financial news all the world over.

Magazines also contribute substantially to the treasure of knowledge of the financial manager. In our country, we have magazines like Commerce, Capital, Indian Finance and Business Week which contain valuable articles and reports on Corporate finance. For sound financial planning, these magazines have a definite role to play. By enriching the financial intelligence of the Corporate managers, they help them run their corporations on sound financial line. Company Law Journal, Financial Analysis Journal, The Chartered Accountant, The Reserve Bank Bulletin, The Company Secretary's Journal — are all valuable sources of financial information.

To add to these, in our country, there are arrangements for providing financial data about individual companies and financial entities as well as summary statistics about selected industries. Investors' guide, Stock Exchange Year Book , Investors' Encyclopaedia, Investors' Year Book are some invaluable friends of the financial manager. They give information about top management personnel, objects, capital, transfer fees and closure of transfer books, working of the year, security prices, comparative financial statements of various companies worth the name. In addition, for the general interest of investors, they act as guides.

Besides the above, there are annual reports of company's manuals, the Stock Exchange Official Directory which are also very dependable sources of information for the financial manager.

# CHAPTER 12

## TOOLS OF FINANCIAL ANALYSIS AND THEIR USEFULNESS

To ensure sound Financial Management, the need for financial analysis cannot be over-emphasised. The different methods of financial analysis that are usually adopted enable the financial manager to assess the financial position and the direction which will lead him to a better Financial Management.

In the complex financial world today, a continuous study is imperative for the Financial Management, both for profit and wealth maximisation.

The different tools that are usually used by the Financial Management are : Funds Flow analysis, Ratio analysis, Cost-Volume-Profit (Break-even) analysis and analysis of operating and financial leverages.

At a certain point of time, the Balance Sheet reveals the financial status of a company. But the information that can be obtained from the study of the Balance Sheet is not sufficient for the financial manager to take necessary steps for betterment of the company financially. He needs to know the **funds flows** underlying the Balance Sheet changes. The statement of sources and uses of funds serves this end. Business operates by converting cash into non-cash assets which, after being used, come back in cash form. This is a circular flow and the funds used can be raised in a number of ways. But the selection of the particular way matters much since it has a strong impact on the soundness of financial programme of a company. An effective Financial Management can only be expected to select the right means/way and whether the Financial Management is effective or not can be judged by reviewing the record of the past as to the sources and uses of funds.

The 'Funds Flow Statement' is thus a very important tool in the hands of the Financial Management. It is a statement in the form of condensed report showing sources and uses of funds. The statement indicates how the activities of the business have been financed and how the financial resources have been utilised during the period covered by the statement. The statement, as a matter of fact, is significant as it shows the ebb and flow of funds into and out of a business. Besides, it discloses the results or the policies of the Financial Management in a more convenient form being intelligible to the common reader.

The 'Funds Flow Statement' is, therefore, "a useful tool in the financial managers" analytical kit. The funds flow statement contributes materially to the financial aspects of the answers to questions such as — (1) Why were the net current assets down though the net income was up, or vice versa ? (2) How was it possible to distribute dividends in excess of current earnings or in the presence of a net loss for the period? (3) How was the expansion in plant and equipment financed? (4) What happened to the proceeds of sale of plant and equipment ? (5) How was the retirement of debt accomplished? (6) What became of the proceeds of share issue or debenture issue ? (7) How was the increase in working capital financed ? (8) Where did the profits go ?" (S.C. Kuchhal)

The questions that find their answers in the

'Funds Flow Statement' are beyond doubt very relevant and important for any Financial Management to know to ensure better Financial Management and for better guidance to general administration of the organisation. "Though this statement cannot replace the income statement but it provides an equally significant analysis of the financial phase of business operations. This statement is also more comparable with those of other companies than are the Balance Sheets and income statements since some of the major variations in accounting procedure are eliminated in the calculation of the funds provided from operations." (S.C. Kuchhal)

In investment analysis, **'Cash flow'** is a useful concept. It is an important tool of the financial manager in judging the ability to meet debt-requirements, to maintain regular dividends and to finance replacement and expansion costs.

Before we conclude we can say that the funds flow statement has many advantages and it is a very effective weapon in the armoury of the Financial Management to fight various financial adversaries. It helps forecasting the flow of funds. It is useful to financial analysts and credit granters; it provides an insight into the financial operation of a firm and it is also useful in the evaluation of the firm's financing — what portion of the firm's growth was financed internally and what portion externally.

"An analysis of a funds statement for the future is extremely valuable to the executive in planning the intermediate and long-term financing of the firm. He is assisted in knowing the firm's total prospective needs for funds, the expected timing financing of these needs and their nature. He can thus arrange the firm's financing more effectively." (S.C. Kuchhal)

[Other tools of financial analysis — ratio analysis, break-even analysis and operating and financial leverages have been discussed elsewhere].

# CHAPTER 13

## FINANCIAL FORECASTING

Financial forecasting is a control device to fix standards of performance and evaluating the results. It is "a systematic projection of expected actions of Management in the form of financial statements, budgets etc." (S.C. Kuchhal)

Financial forecasting is a process for preparing a working plan and makes use of past records, financial ratios, funds flow behaviour and also it takes into consideration the expected economic condition in industry as well as in the firm. The technique of financial forecasting is to arrange future activities for a specified period.

The need for financial forecasting arises from the optimum utilisation of funds. This helps the management to invest un-needed cash in income-producing securities.

Financial forecasting is made by preparing pro-forma financial statements and cash budget. In addition to the preparation of the statements and cash budget, it adopts four other methods —
(1) Per cent of sales; (2) Scatter diagram or simple linear regression; (3) Curvilinear simple regression; and (4) Multiple regression.

### Per cent of Sales

In this method of financial forecasting, it is assumed that certain Balance Sheet items vary directly with sales. It means that the ratio of a given Balance Sheet item to sales remains constant. Thus, a good sales forecast can be made which is an essential foundation for forecasting financial requirements. This method of forecasting enables the finance executive to express the firm's needs in terms of the percentage of annual sales envisaged in each individual Balance Sheet.

### Scatter diagram or Simple regression method

This method is a graphic presentation of joint relations. This is based on "practical aptitude and not statistical sophistication." As compared to per cent of sales, this is a better method of financial forecasting so far as long-range forecasting is concerned.

The sales forecasting is taken as the starting point. "Based on past data of sales and inventory for different years, a line that fits the scatter of points or the line of best fit has to be drawn. This line is also known as **regression line.** Of course, all points seldom fall exactly on the regression line. The line itself may be linear or curved." In this method, it is not assumed that the line of relationship passes through the origin. It calculates the ratio between sales and the relevant Balance Sheet item at two points in time, extending a line through these two points and using the line to describe the relationship between sales and the Balance Sheet items. If more points are plotted, the accuracy of the regression is necessary. "The regression line can be fitted methodically by a technique known as the method of least squares as well as drawn in by free hand."

### Curvilinear simple regression method

This method has been necessitated for the reason that linear scatter diagram or linear regression assumes that the scope of the regression line is constant. But this is not always the case, though mostly it happens. That is why the application of curvilinear simple regression has been necessary.

## Multiple regression method

The multiple regression method is a more sophisticated approach to financial forecasting. In simple regression, sales are assumed to be a function of only one variable but here a number of variables are used. In all other approaches the assumption is that the observations fall exactly on the relationship line which seldom happens. A perfect correlation cannot be expected. In practice, the actual observations would be scattered above the regression line. If linear regression is used, the actual line of relationships might be curvilinear. Even if curvilinear regression is used, deviations still occur because inventories are determined by factors other than sales. Work stoppages at the plant of the suppliers influence inventory levels. Multiple method considers additional variables in the financial analysis to improve forecasting.

Preparation of proforma financial statements and preparation of cash budget as tools of financial forecasting are intimately related; since both are based upon the same basic information. Both are, therefore, interchangeable. Financial forecasting, according to these approaches, needs the Balance Sheet at the starting period to enable comparison at the end of the forecast period.

## Proforma financial statements

These statements are meant for displaying the effects of future circumstances. It does not need much elucidation to say that such statements are very vital as they influence the decisions for future events — future needs of firm's financial position. These projected statements are prepared on many assumptions and reasonable estimates are made of revenues, costs, profits, taxes, dividends, uses and sources of funds. In preparing such statements due consideration is given to past relationships in the form of financial ratios for projecting the future funds.

(1) *Project Income Statement*

This statement is an important step in the budgetary process and is prepared around the estimate of the **expected sales** or the forecast period. It helps the finance executive to estimate the expected revenue, costs, profits, taxes etc. For a longer period of forecasting, breakdown of the expected sales is shown monthwise. This statement considers items such as cost of goods sold, selling costs, general and administration expenses, interest, income tax and dividend payments.

This statement, however, cannot control expenses. For that purpose, a detailed breakdown of expenses becomes necessary which is actually within the purview of cost accounting.

(2) *Projected balance sheet*

The proforma income statement forms the basis of the preparation of the Balance Sheet. A projected Balance Sheet reveals the expected funds flows. To construct such a Balance Sheet, four steps are involved — (1) net investment in each of the assets is calculated, (2) selected liabilities not subject to any negotiation are shown, (3) net worth of the company is calculated after the adjustment of the projected income from the period of forecasting and (4) projected assets are compared with total source of funds (liabilities and net worth).

On the assets side of the Balance Sheet Cash, Debtors, Inventories and Fixed Assets are shown. The minimum level of cash desired at the end of the period of forecasting is usually taken. Debtors are based on Sales budget. The estimate of inventories is prepared on the basis of turnover ratios or purchase, production and selling schedules are carefully estimated on the basis of which the inventories are prepared. As to fixed assets, the estimates are based on previously planned outlays. Additions and depreciations are adjusted against fixed assets. So far as fictitious assets like goodwill or assets like prepaid expenses, patents etc. have to be projected, a simple assumption of 'no charge' is the principle.

On the liabilities side — Creditors, Loans and advances, Accrued liabilities, Provisions for taxes and dividends, Long-term debts are estimated, analysed and considered.

**Creditors** are estimated by analysing schedules of purchases. The opening balance of creditors is taken as the starting point; with it are added the expected purchases and then expected payments are deducted to find out the estimated figure of creditors.

**Loans, and advances** are usually the balancing or 'plug' figure to equalise assets and liabilities when the projected Balance Sheet is meant for ascertaining the expected amount of borrowings.

**Accrued liabilities** for wages, taxes and interest obligations are examined for analysing them. The detailed work is often avoided by making the assumption of 'no change' unless the figure is disproportionately high or low as compared to the beginning of the period.

### Provisions for taxes and dividends

From the opening balances are deducted the actual tax payments and dividend payments to find out the closing balance of the respective provisions.

**Long-term debt :** The change in debt depends on long range plans to raise or to repay long-term debts. So its projection is not so difficult.

**Net worth** is adjusted for sale of shares, redemption of shares or any other such change in future. The surplus from retained earnings is ascertained. The profit figure is obtained from the projected income statement. For allocations of profits to reserve, they are incorporated in the respective reserves.

### Cash budget

Cash budget is prepared in the form of a schedule. It is done with a view to ascertaining and locating the timing and magnitude of cash surplus and shortage. This budget is useful to the financial executive since it gives him sufficient indication as to the cash position and thus to take necessary steps in time.

Cash budget may take long-term view or it may be a budget for a short period. Whether long or short, it is a very important tool in the budgetary kit of the financial executive. This budget preparation does not follow a standardised procedure; it varies according to the nature of the firm and needs of the organisation.

## Problems in Effective Financial Forecasting

That financial forecasting is a necessity cannot be questioned. But certain problems crop up in effective financial forecasting. It is not very difficult to understand that whatever operation takes place anywhere in the company, affects cash but the fact remains that many of the areas of operation are outside the direct responsibilities of the financial executive. So, it very often becomes difficult for the financial executive to obtain necessary information from different areas of operation unless the top executive takes special care to see that such information is provided to the financial executive.

Problems of effective financial forecasting arise mainly for the reason that there are businesses where uncertainties exist to an exceedingly large extent. Violent fluctuations of price upset forecasting. In such cases, the forecasting technique should be such that it can be made as helpful as possible to enable its management to stay on top of its finances.

Where there are problems, there are solutions, but in the problems inherent in financial forecasting, solutions are not so easy to find out. A number of uncertain factors have to be foreseen to have an accurate financial forecasting which task is well-nigh impossible. Some measures and precautions may however, be taken and some guidelines may be laid down, attention to which may be given to safeguard against the upset of the financial forecasting.

### The suggested lines of action are given below

(1) Management should adopt the attitude of recognising the likely margin of errors inherent in its forecasts. It should not suffer from the false sense of accuracy to projected data based on assumptions.

(2) Different forecasts, in case of varying assumptions, should be prepared since a single forecast is a composite of estimates which is, really speaking, an approximation of what will 'really happen'. A few sets of projected financial statements and cash budgets should be prepared considering the worst and the best situation.

(3) The scope for revision of forecasts must always be left. Flexibility and not rigidity should be the principle and adjustments when and wherever necessary should be allowed to be made by the top management.

(4) To minimise the risk of forecasting, particularly in firms with high degree of unpredictability, large cash balance should be maintained.

(5) Key assumptions should be clearly stated to make them known and intelligible to the management so that, if necessary, revisions may be allowed.

(6) Through trial and error and with sufficient experience, much of the problem of forecasting can be solved.

(7) A sample financial forecast should be prepared instead of a number of detailed income statements and Balance Sheets. It is prudent not to

forecast in greater details than the uncertainties of the situation permit.

## Advantages of financial forecasting

(1) It ensures co-ordinated thinking for the optimum utilisation of funds, thus forming the basis.

(2) It is a control device for ensuring standard performance and result evaluation.

(3) Forecasting minimises emergency decisions since it anticipates the financial needs and other effects on new policies.

(4) Financial forecasting enables a company to negotiate confidently with the supplier's of funds.

(5) Last but not least, the important benefit of financial forecasting is that it is used to pre-test the financial feasibility of various programmes.

# CHAPTER 14

## METHODS OF FINANCING

A company needs finance for its various requirements. We have discussed earlier the sources of finance — issue of shares, debentures, public deposits and retained earnings.

Here we propose to study all the sources in greater details with relative merits and demerits.

The methods of financing are determined basically from the consideration of the period for which the funds are required or the funds will remain blocked. As we know, some funds are needed for fixed investment in fixed assets and some are required for carrying the business as circulating or revolving capital for investment in current assets.

Methods of raising finance are basically divided into two — owned and borrowed. Shares and internal sources provide owned capital while debentures, public deposits, loans from specialised institutions supply capital, being borrowed by a company.

**Case for India :** In India, long-term and medium-term capital are raised through issue of shares, issue of debentures, public deposits, bank loans, ploughing back of profits in case of existing companies and assistance from specialised financial institutions.

A company, to meet its regular working capital generally, resorts to such methods. But in case of seasonal or fluctuating working capital, short-term financial aid suits the situation and creditors, banks, finance companies and other sources save the purpose.

Issue of shares, debentures, public deposits and ploughing back of earnings have already been discussed. Here we attempt to throw some new light on them and give a comparative evaluation.

**Methods of corporate financing at a glance**

| Long-term | Medium-term | Short-term |
|---|---|---|
| Methods : (1) Issue of shares | (1) Issue of Pref. Shares | (1) Trade credit |
| (2) Issue of debentures | (2) Issue of debentures | (2) Bank credit |
| (3) Loans from specialised institutions | (3) Public deposits | (3) Instalment credit |
| (4) Ploughing back of earnings | (4) Bank loans (term loans) | (4) Customer advances |
| | (5) Assistance from special industrial financial institutions | |

**Shares** — As a source of corporate finance, it does not need any elucidation. It is the shareholders' money that constitutes the chief form of finance of a company and it has some merits which cannot be equalled with any other source of finance.

The share capital of the company is ideal for meeting the long-term requirements, particularly the fixed capital requirements, because it has not to be paid back to the shareholders within the life-time of the company.

Unlike the situation that had prevailed prior to 1956, a public limited company can now issue only two types of shares — Equity and Preference.

Equity Shares have merits (discussed earlier) but there are certain limitations. They are as follows:

(i) The unscrupulousness of equity shareholders may lead to manipulation of the control of the company. The equity shareholders have some rights which they may misuse and they control the company in the interest of a few members and to the detriment of the interest of others.

(ii) It is not unusual that the excessive issue of equity shares leads to over-capitalisation with all its evils.

(iii) If only equity shares are issued, the company cannot trade on equity which means the company cannot take advantage of the issue of preference shares and debentures with fixed yields lower than the dividend on equity shares.

To have an idea of the corporate finance of the industrially developed countries like the U.S.A. and Canada, we consider it relevant to discuss here a type of share issued in the U.S.A. and Canada, known as 'No-par Shares'.

## No-Par Shares

No-par shares mean shares having no face-value. In the U.S.A. and Canada the total owned capital of the company is divided into a certain number of shares. The share certificate states only the number of shares held by a particular shareholder and no face-value of the shares is mentioned. Dividends are paid at the rate of a given amount per share; not a certain percentage of the par value of each share.

These shares, as claimed, have the following advantages :

(1) The Balance Sheet of the company becomes more realistic. It does not contain imaginary amount as is the case with a company issuing shares with nominal value. In such a Balance Sheet, the capital is equal to net worth (assets-liabilities).

(2) The value of such shares being related to earnings, the real value of their holdings is known to the shareholders.

(3) In case of a no-par share company, reduction of capital does not arise since the value of the shares is automatically adjusted with the earning capacity.

(4) Further calls are not necessary because the total value of no-par shares is collected at the time of issue.

(5) Legal formalities in regard to issue of shares at a discount need not be gone through because these shares have no minimum par value.

### Disadvantages

(1) In a country like ours where investors are mostly ignorant, no-par shares may be used to deceive them. This is because of the fact that there is no standard by which fluctuations in share values can be ascertained.

(2) Creditors lose the benefit of additional security of uncalled capital.

(3) Because of the fluctuating nature of capital account, promoters may take away huge amount as remuneration.

(4) Balance Sheet of such a company is more complex and difficult to understand and, as such, investors, creditors and tax authorities are to face difficulties.

(5) Sale proceeds of shares can be more easily manipulated and dividend may be paid out of capital by the unscrupulous management.

Considering different aspects, no-par shares cannot be issued in India.

## Debentures, Equity and Preference Shares — Their evaluation (further discussion)

Debentures, as we have discussed earlier, are of different classes but all the classes have some common features and, as such, we may evaluate the desirability of debentures in general in meeting the financial needs of a company and also as investment.

Debentures carry the right of fixed rate of interest. This is a charge against profit and, as such, irrespective of the fact whether there is any profit earned or not, the interest has to be paid. Debentures are generally covered by a charge on the assets providing enough security for their redemption. So, from the point of view of the investors, there is nothing to worry about. The investors are assured of fixed return on their investment generally higher than the income on gilt-edged or government securities and also they are not exposed to any risk. As a matter of fact, the real security of the debenture-holders is the profitability of the company because, in case there is insufficient profit, interest payment to debenture-holders becomes difficult and the value of the assets of the company falls rapidly as a consequence, the security of the debentures also goes down in value.

Usually the rate of interest is lower than the rate of dividend, a company usually pays. Thus the company finds it better from the financial point of view to issue debentures in certain circumstances than the issue of shares. What is to be paid to the debenture-holders is fixed and amount is also less than what would have been paid to the shareholders, had the company issued shares. Further, a company issuing debentures can trade on equity and is thus able to pay better rates of dividend to the equity-shareholders and finally, from the point of view of the company, the desirability of issuing debentures is that it does not involve any transfer of control over the company to the persons supplying finance.

It will be relevant to mention here A. S. Dewing's axioms regarding the issue of shares and debentures (bonds).

(i) Liberal and reasonably constant future earnings of the company should be the primary consideration before the issue of bonds.

(ii) The preferred stock may be issued in case the earnings are irregular but, when averaged over a period of years, give a fair margin over preferred stock dividend.

(iii) In case earnings are irregular only equity shares should be issued.

**A comparative study of the relative features of equity and preference shares and debentures is given below**

**(1) Period of Finance**

The period of finance is long-term for equity shares but the period is both long and medium for preference shares and debentures.

**(2) Control of Management**

Equity shareholders actually have controlling power with limited power of control given to the preference shareholders. But debenture-holders, being creditors of the company, have 'no' power of control of management.

**(3) Flexibility**

From the point of view of flexibility, it can be said that it is only through re-organisation that reduction is possible for the equity shares. But preference shares can be redeemed when the purpose is fulfilled while debenture amount can be adjusted through redemption or through purchase of own debentures by a company.

**(4) Return**

Preference shares and debentures carry fixed return while equity shares have no fixed return; it is fluctuating.

**(5) Appeal to Investors**

Equity, as the name suggests, has only appeal to the adventurous investors. Less adventurous investors invest in preference shares and cautious investors invest in debentures.

**(6) Credit-worthiness of the company**

Equity shares lend increased capacity to borrow. Preference shares do not affect credit-worthiness much, either way. Debentures reduce the capacity of the company to borrow further sums.

# CHAPTER 15

## MARKETING OF SECURITIES (FURTHER DISCUSSED)

Marketing of securities (shares and debentures) constitutes one of the important and significant functions of financial management of a company. Shares and debentures being very important sources of corporate finance, their marketing naturally is a serious concern to the management. The methods and complications of marketing depend to a large extent on the prospective investors/buyers. The composition of investors — their number, character, sentiment etc. makes much difference as to the way the securities will be marketed. Individual investors naturally pose more problems than institutional investors. Today's investment market consists of mainly institutional investors; so, for the companies and many cases, it is not difficult to market securities. But in marketing securities to individual investors whose statement and character cann always be correctly predicted, underwriters help the companies in marketing securities.

**Methods,** generally resorted to, **in marketing securities** are :

1. Public issue by prospectus
2. Stock exchange placing
3. Private placing
4. Offer for sale
5. Offer to shareholders only
6. Subscription by inside coteries.

### Control of Capital Issues

It is undoubtedly necessary for a welfare state like India which is wedded to the policy of doing welfare to the people of the country and which has been pursuing planned economy to control all the vital sectors of the economy of the country. The capital market of the country cannot be left to the sweet will of the private corporate sector to do whatever they like. So, the need for control of capital issues is beyond question.

With the abolition of the policy of *laissez faire*, the Government intervention in economic affairs of a country has been the recognised policy of any Government.

In our country, even before independence, the government had introduced control over capital issue in 1943, the objective being to ensure the flow of capital investment into Government loans with a view to preventing use of resources for purposes which did not contribute to the war effort of the Government. The control was initially introduced under the Defence of India Rules. It was continued through Capital Issues (Continuance of Control) Act of 1947. This Act was meant for protecting the interest of investors against unscrupulous promoters and it was intended to remain in force only for three years. In March 1950, another Act was passed to extend the control up to March 1952. In February 1952, Capital Issues (Continuance of Control) Amendment Act was passed extending the term of the control up to March 1956 and then it was made permanent.

### The Objects of the Act

(I) To channelise investment in accordance with the plan objectives to ensure a rational and healthy growth of the corporate sector. (II) To ensure sound capital structure, (III) To ensure that offers for public subscription do not get overcrowded over any part of the year.

The Controller of Capital Issues under the Ministry of Finance (Department of Economic Affairs) administers capital issues. He is advised by An Advisory Committee in regard to the formulation of guiding principles.

The Act provides that the **consent of the Controller of Capital Issues** will be required in the following cases :

(i) While issuing a prospectus or document of publicity;

(ii) While making an issue of capital outside India;

(iii) While making an issue of capital in India;

(iv) While receiving or paying consideration for an issue of capital made or proposed to be made;

(v) While making any public offer of securities for sale;

(vi) While reviewing or postponing the date of maturity or repayment of any security maturing for payment in India.

In December, 1963, the Act exempted control of capital issues of companies making capital issues up to Rs. 25 lakhs. Under the Capital Issues Exemption Order of February 1, 1969, a company exceeding the exemption limit will have to file a statement of the proposals for capital issue at least 30 days before the date of the proposed offer of capital to the public.

Circumstances when the **consent** of the Controller of Capital Issues is **not required :**

(i) When shares are issued at par

(ii) When the debt-equity ratio does not exceed 2 : 1 and the equity-preference ratio is kept below 3 : 1. The Controller of Capital Issues permits a debt-equity ratio up to 4 : 1 in respect of capital intensive industries like cement and fertilizers.

(iii) All calls are to be fully paid-up within a period of maximum five years.

(iv) The rate of dividend and the rate of interest on debentures must not exceed the maximum limit fixed by the Controller.

(v) The shares must be offered in such a manner as to be eligible for listing on a recognised stock exchange.

The exemptions do not apply to bonus issue, out of profits.

It is found now that the consent of the Controller is not necessary in most of the fresh capital issues of shares and debentures.

# CHAPTER 16

## BANK LOAN AS A SOURCE OF CORPORATE FINANCE

Commercial banks provide finance on short-term basis mainly to trade, industry and commerce. As a source of corporate finance for short period needs, it is undoubtedly important. A company meets its working capital requirements for short period from the commercial banks. Banks grant advances, loans, cash-credits etc. and also discount bills and other commercial papers and thus they facilitate companies to have temporary as well as short-term accommodation of finance.

**Cash Credits :** This way of financing by commercial banks seems to be the most popular form of assistance. Cash credits are available against the pledge of stock of finished or semi-finished products or even raw materials by the company. Up to an agreed limit, loan is available and interest has to be paid on the amount actually withdrawn. A company, whose credit-worthiness is well established, can have cash credits without actually pledging stock; the stock may remain in the physical possession of the borrower though the banks may have legal lien on them (by hypothecation).

**Term Loans** : Cash credits may be converted into term loans. These are medium-term loans. Cash credits are 'turned over' or rolled over and thus short-term assistance becomes medium-term. However, whether a bank will resort to such practice depends on the bank's policy and the conditions in the money market. This has a very significant impact on the financial management of a company because, in case changes occur in the bank's policy or in the money market, the bank is likely to withdraw the benefit of extending the assistance.

As regards medium-term assistance from banks, there is another method. This is through a term loan for a duration of, say, 3 to 7 years. Refinancing facilities by the Re-finance Corporation made it possible for the banks to engage in term lendings to industrial concerns. The functions of the Re-finance Corporation was taken over by the Industrial Development Bank of India with effect from 1st September, 1964. The share of term loan in the advance portfolio of Commercial banks has been on increase for the last seventeen years.

Banks usually grant term loans on the consideration of the type and size of business, management, operating efficiency, general record of the borrower, financial condition, ability to repay and viability of the product.

Banks are now encouraged more to extend term loans for acquisition of fixed assets. The Reserve Bank of India has now empowered banks to grant term loans to industrial borrowers for acquisition of fixed assets without prior authorization up to the cut-off point of one crore rupees. This is independent of working capital limits available to these borrowers irrespective of whether a borrower is covered under Credit Authorization Scheme for its working capital or not. For arriving at the cut-off point, the aggregate of the balances outstanding in the existing term loans, the balances outstanding under deferred payment guarantees or acceptance limit on deferred terms should be taken into account excluding, of course, the interest portion.

### Long-term financing by banks

As regards long-term financing, commerical banks have not played any significant role so far.

Banks are more interested in commercial banking functions and a small percentage of banks investments is put into the purchase of shares and debentures of industrial companies.

## Critical evaluation

Commercial banks have thoroughly changed the criteria used for judging the borrower, his business and financial requirement. However, because of bank accommodation the borrowing companies enjoy the advantages of timely assistance, flexibility of accommodation, non-interference with management, secrecy and economy but certain disadvantages such as the burden of mortgage hypothecation, short duration of accommodation/loan and cumbersome procedures are attached to term lending.

After nationalisation of fourteen scheduled banks in 1969, a liberal attitude in lending for rapid industrialisation of the country was noticed, but, unfortunately, banks have been compelled to take a sterner attitude for the security of the loan. It must be admitted that big companies have been receiving more bank accommodation. Of course, it does not mean that smaller entrepreneurs are not getting benefit of bank loan.

In short, we can say banks play a very important role in industrial finance but institutional financing is playing more and more important role in long-term financing where banks have not been so conspicuously effective suppliers of loan.

# CHAPTER 17

## SHORT-TERM FINANCING OF A COMPANY

The variable working capital requirements of a company are mostly needed for short periods not exceeding one year, usually.

A company in need of short-term funds depends on credit facilities from suppliers and lenders. In some cases, public deposits may serve the purpose of short-term funds.

To meet short-term financial requirements, a company may depend on four principal methods of credit : (a) Trade credit, (b) Bank credit, (c) Instalment credit and (d) Customer Advances.

### Trade Credit

When manufacturers, wholesalers and jobbers, as an incident of sale, grant credit, it is known as "Trade Credit". This is required by a firm carrying on business of stock of purely seasonal goods. The usual duration of such credit is 30 to 90 days. While granting trade credit, the goodwill and the financial standing of the firm are taken into account and no security is needed. No interest as such is charged but a bit higher price is charged. This credit is on 'Open account' and a firm generally takes advantage of trade credit when credit is not available easily at cheaper rate either from banks or from any other source. Trade credit is granted provided the supplier has sound financial position and the firm has credit-worthiness. The degree of competition in the market and also the eagerness of the supplier to dispose off his stock determine the willingness of the supplier to provide trade credit.

### Bank Credit

Bank credit may be in the form of overdraft, cash credit, advances and discounting of bills. The bank may allow a firm to borrow up to a certain limit against certain amount of deposit for securing a line of credit. This credit is given against pledge, hypothecation or collateral security. In pledge, the merchandise is placed in the custody of the bank and in hypothecation, the stock remains in the possession of the borrower and an equitable charge in favour of the bank is created by the borrower. Bill of Lading, Railway Receipts, Dock warrants etc. constitute collateral securities.

Banks grant loans and advances on the personal security of the borrower and without any tangible or collateral security. More often, loans are granted against some tangible or collateral security and the security generally constitutes movable goods, shares, stocks and other negotiable instruments, documents of title to goods, Fixed Depoit receipt, landed property/real estate, life insurance policies, jewelleries or precious metals, book debts etc.

### Instalment credit

This is consumer credit granted by retailers for enabling financially weak customers to buy goods like televisions, refrigerators etc. on instalments. Hire purchase is the usual method of granting such credit.

**Customer Advances :** Sometimes a company may take advances from its customers to meet its short-term requirements of funds. It depends on the condition of the market. These advances form a part of the price and no interest is included.

# CHAPTER 18

## ROLE OF THE FINANCIAL MANAGER

While discussing the role of the financial manager today, we have to keep it in mind that a firm is to conduct its business in a rapidly changing and highly competitive environment. The ever changing market conditions call for the ability of the financial management to react quickly and correctly to the changing business environment. To ensure better management of all the aspects of a firm's operations, it becomes imperative to make extensive use of financial data and reports.

The role of the financial manager has considerably changed as compared to his counterpart of early 1980's. The financial manager had a traditional role to play — he used to keep accurate record, prepare reports on the company's status and performance and manage cash for keeping the company going. His role was confined to procuring cash. The financial manager had transcended that traditional role of preparing reports and raising external funds with the growing complexity in business and also with the enlargement of the size of business. The financial manager assumed the responsibility of dealing with the problems and decisions associated with managing the firm's assets.

Today's financial manager is less concerned with the procurement of finance and is very much involved with the total amount of capital employed by the firm, with the allocation of funds to different projects and activities and with the measurement of the results of each allocation i.e. he is more concerned with the utilisation of funds in the best possible way.

The role of the modern financial manager having been more exacting , he "needs a broad range of skills, a strong grasp of the nature and scope of the finance function and an understanding of how the firm operates in its particular market-place."

Financial managers of today also deal with developments that affect liquidity and profitability. The developments include :

(i) diversification by firms into different business, markets and product lines,

(ii) high rates of change in technology requiring expenditure on research and development,

(iii) growing inflation affecting planning and forecasting,

(iv) growth-emphasis with the need for more funds,

(v) Capital intensive environment involving risk-bearing investments calling for high financing costs,

(vi) dissemination of information through high-speed computers,

(vii) nation-wide and world-wide networks for transmitting financial and operating data.

In large organisations, financial management has not only become complicated but the role of the financial managers has become an exciting and challenging job. The 90s pose some special problems for the financial managers of big companies and financial decision-making now needs specialised skills needed to make correct decisions in a fast moving and technolgically complex corporate environment.

While discharging the role of the financial managers, the follwing problems have to be usually handled with requisite tact, skill, intelligence and foresight.

Problems are :

(i) Selection of new proposals for further capital investment.

(ii) Increase in the value of the firm's common stock — steps to be taken.

(iii) Optimum amount of working capital to support the company's operations.

(iv) Sources of long term capital — the cost of capital — the availability of such capital.

(v) Dividend declaration — its quantum.

To sum up, the role of the financial manager centres round efficient planning and control of flow of funds — inflow and outflow of funds. In order to discharge these responsibilities, the financial manager will be rigid in conforming to the plans and policies. He will keep a vigilant watch over the appropriate magnitude of funds and the prudent allocation of funds and financial resources to particular assets — fixed and current. Besides, his fund-raising activities are to be kept undisturbed for continuous flow of funds for feeding the firm with adequate and optimum finance.

The modern financial manager has a very important place in the management of a company. He has to be involved in the broad range of decision-making. As a pre-requisite for success in decision-making, the financial manager is to acquire knowledge of financial markets and financial statements. A company's future today is considerably influenced by the correct analysis of financial position of the company. The role that a modern financial manager plays in the whole complex of the corporate management assumes all the more importance when he is to use the analytical tools for measuring and forecasting the firm's activities. In the course of decision-making — short-term or long-term, the financial manager is brought into decisions on cash levels, receivables and inventory. The significance of the role of the financial manager can be realised when we feel that the decision-making of the financial manager requires planning that covers current years operating revenues and expenses and deals with concepts of leverage in the firm's operation and financing. The financial manager, in decision-making, covers issues related to dividend policy, investment policy, cost of capital and the firm's capital structure. Decisions are also made in related areas including such issues as the valuation of the firm and mergers and acquisitions.

The financial manager, today, is to do a highly specialised job and his role in the overall management of the firm is not only all-embracing but also far-reaching and significant. No area management can achieve efficiency unless its financial aspect is efficiently managed; the responsibility of the overall review of the financial position of the organisation rests with the financial management.

# CHAPTER 19

## MANAGEMENT OF WORKING CAPITAL

The administration of current assets and current liabilities is working capital management. By current assets we mean the assets convertible into cash within one year such as marketable securities, receivables, inventories besides liquid cash.

In the management of working capital, it is important to determine the appropriate levels of current assets and current liabilities which determine the level of working capital. It involves fundamental decisions on the firm's liquidity and maturity composition of its debt. A trade-off between profitability and risk influences such a decision. To be more specific, we can say that the working capital management requires the examination of the maturity composition or liquidity of the firm's assets — that is, the turnover of these assets into cash. The management is to take decisions that may affect the asset liquidity of the firm. These decisions are in regard to the management of cash and marketable securitics, credit policy and procedures, inventory management and control and the administration of fixed assets.

Working capital management proceeds with the basic assumption that the maintenance of right cash balance is of utmost importance for preventing any slow-downs. The firm must have a balance between liquidity and profitability.

**The management of working capital** should be designed to achieve **three goals :** (a) adequate liquidity (b) minimisation of risks and (c) contributing to maximising firm's value.

The need for sufficient cash to meet bills is a necessity for a firm to lead its credibility. It is considered as the most important goal for a firm to maintain adequate liquidity for the smooth conduct of day-to-day operations.

The minimisation of risks is no less important a goal for a firm since it must ensure that short-term liabilities do not become excessive compared to the current assets on hand to pay them. The matching of assets and liabilities among current accounts is a task of minimising the risk of being enable to pay bills and other obligations.

The working capital is held to maximise the present value of common stock and value of the firm. A firm should not hold idle current assets any more than it should have idle fixed assets. "The investment of excess cash, minimising of inventories, speedy collection of receivables and elimination of unnecessary and costly short-term financing — all contribute to maximising the value of the firm" (Hampton).

The **need for working capital** arises out of **four factors** — (a) sales volume (b) seasonal and cyclical factors (c) changes in technology and (d) policies of the firm.

The size and components of working capital are very much determined by the sales volume of the firm. Current assets are needed for supporting the operational activities culminating in sales. The manufacturing units usually maintain a ratio of 20 and 40 per cent (current assets/sales). In different situations, however, the levels of working capital may be different. With a steady level of sales, a fairly constant level of cash, receivables and inventory is the usual pattern of working capital management; while a firm with growing sales needs additional working capital and in case of declining sales, a reduction in permanent working capital is the prudent way of management.

Seasonal and cyclical factors affect the level of working capital. In a recession, a firm faces declining sales and the need for inventories and the level of receivables declines. While the market is characterised by high interest rates, customers pay their bills slowly and it causes an increase in receivables.

Technological developments are no less significant in the management of working capital. When production process changes, it may affect the need for and the pattern of purchase of raw materials which in its turn affects the volume of working capital.

The policies of a firm definitely have impact on the working capital management. A change in the policy affects the levels of permanent and variable working capital. For instance, if a firm changes its credit policy from net 40 to net 70, additional funds may be permanently tied up in receivables. So also, changes in production policy and safety level of cash on hand, permanent working capital may increase or decrease. If the level of cash is linked to the level of sales, variable **working capital** may be affected.

It must be noted that working capital management must centre round sound cash planning since it is the very sensitive component of working capital.

Working capital is generally classified into Net Working Capital and Gross Working Capital.

Net Working Capital means current assets minus current liabilities.

Gross Working Capital represents total current assets only and it is a concept very popular in financial management circles, though it cannot reveal the true financial position of a company which the net working capital can. The gross concept of capital is popular with companies because of separation of ownership from management. Managers are not usually interested in the ownership of current or fixed assets.

Working Capital Management is to ensure maximum productivity and profits in the employment of capital. To maintain a smooth and rapid flow of funds is of compelling necessity to enhance the efficiency of working capital or profitability of the company. In the management of working capital, it becomes a sound principle to see that sufficient cash reserve is maintained to meet all normal as well as abnormal cash needs. Cash receipts and cash outlay do never synchronise, so there is the need for maintaining cash reserves.

The amount of working capital needed, to keep the organisation on sound financial health, to maintain regular and uninterrupted cash flow, must be ascertained. A number of factors determine the amount of working capital. They are — general type of business, size of the business, terms of purchase and sales, turnover of inventories, process of manufacture, seasonal variations, banking connections, dividend policy etc. The growth and expansion of the organisation should also deserve consideration while managing working capital.

Working capital management, as we have discussed above, involves deciding upon the amount and composition of current assets and how to finance these assets. These decisions involve trade-offs between risk and profitability. It is a matter for the financial management to take note that the greater the relative proportion of liquid assets, the less the risk of running out of cash, all other things being equal; of course, the profitability will be less. The risk of cash insolvency is less when the composite maturity of schedule of securities is longer, other things being equal, and again, the profits of the company are likely to be less.

We have so far discussed working capital management in a broad sense assuming the efficient management of the various components of current assets.

Now, let us see **how to improve the efficiency of cash management** and how to invest excess funds in marketable securities. The working capital management needs to determine how much will be carried in cash out of the overall level of liquid assets and how much will be carried in marketable securities.

Cash is held for three motives — the transactions motive, the preventionary motive and the speculative motive. All these motives are quite distinct — one is for payments in the ordinary course of business; one for meeting contingencies and the third one relates to holding cash to take advantage of expected changes in security prices.

The object of cash management as a part of working capital management is to attain maximum cash availability and maximum interest inflow on any idle funds. This necessitates acceleration of collections and slowing up of disbursements.

Collections can be accelerated by various means and disbursements should be handled to give maximum transfer flexibility and the optimum ti-ming of payments.

Capital management, in the broad sense, constitutes the main objective of financial management. Fixed and working capital, with their constituents, have to be dealt with utmost care to ensure sound capital structure of a firm.

Working capital management, after consideration of several factors, leads us to comment that it is the important component of the capital structure that needs a very judicious and careful handling to have a regular cash flow to meet normal as well as abnormal situations. The effective operation and smooth going-on of a firm is more the effect of product management of working capital, which no one can dispute.

"The operation of business enterprise involves the conversion of cash into non-cash assets which, when used, are converted back in cash form. The funds used in this circuit flow can be raised in a number of ways. The selection of means to raise funds together with the associated uses has a strong bearing on the soundness of financial programme of a business firm." *(S.C. Kuchhal)*.

The funds flow statement, in the condensed report form, show how the activities of the business have been financed and how the financial resources have been used. So, this is important for the financial management to ensure sound working capital management. The funds flow statement may be prepared to analyse and study the position of net working capital.

Cash flow, though a misnomer (because it is neither cash nor flow) is a useful concept used as one of the tools of investment analysis. A related concept is that of net cash flow which means 'after-tax earnings' retained by the firm or, conversely, gross cash flow minus depreciation. It may be noted that when revenue is realised concurrently with cash receipts and expenses are recorded at time of disbursements, we have coincident flows.

A proform or projected source and uses of funds statement can be constructed to show the acquisition and employment of funds by a firm during some future period.

In this connection, depreciation can be properly included in a measure of the amount of cash flow. Though depreciation is principally an allocation of cost to operation, its financial aspect is also significant.

The funds flow statement is helpful in visualising the movement of funds that constantly take place. A build-up of working capital can be deceptive if it is obtained by reducing other liquid assets. The funds flow statement helps in detecting the sources for financing the heavy accumulation of inventory and accounts receivables.

In the management of working capital, the funds flow statement render services in more than one ways. It helps in forecasting the flow of funds. It provides an insight into the financial operations of a firm. It also helps in the evaluation of the firm's financing — what portion of the firm's growth was financed internally and what portion externally. We can judge through the statement whether the firm has expanded too fast and whether financing is strained.

Working capital management is important, complex and a number of problems associated with this management give it a separate entity. Working capital is one of the conditioning factors in the long run operations of a firm. Working capital calls for financial manoeuvering; this is to ensure effective use of funds for minimising the risk of loss to attend proper objectives.

Both internal and external financing come within the purview of the financial management. Internal financing determines the size of working capital needs in particular business situations and seeks to achieve certain long-run operating goals.

The concepts of working capital to the managements are gross and net working capitals. Gross working capital is concerned with the management of individual current assets in the day-to-day operation, while net working capital helps the management to look for permanent sources for its financing, since management is more concerned with the total current assets which constitute total funds available for operating periods than with the source from where the funds come. To say precisely, management gives attention to the total amount of current assets and their profit earning capacity so that it is higher than cost of borrowing.

The net working capital concept does not have much relevance in the corporate form of business organisation since, in this form, there is no close contact between ownership of capital and its management.

In measuring working capital balance, the financial data of balance sheet is used. Working capital balance indicates something positive but inefficient uses of working capital may exceed the sources of working capital in a particular period which may, however, be offset by efficient management in the following period. The financial manager should study the causes of changes in the balances and should take appropriate steps to correct the position. This involves the basic approach to working capital analysis. Besides measuring changes in the balances of working capital in terms of rupees, we can do so in terms of percentages by a comparative study of current assets, current liabilities and working capital over a number of years.

Various devices can be used by the management to ascertain whether working capital is being properly managed. Ratio analysis enables the management to check upon the efficiency with which working capital is being employed. In its two forms — behaviour of ratios over a certain period and comparison of ratios between similar concerns — ratio analysis may be the study of turnover of working capital over a definite period; it may be current ratio analysis or it may be current debt to tangible net worth analysis. These different ratio analysis reveal different facts to the management. The turnover of net working capital ratio measures the rate of working capital utilisation whereas the current ratio measures the relative ability of a company to pay its short term debts and current liabilities to tangible net worth ratio shows how much capital has come from short-term creditors and how much from the owners.

The working capital budget is also an important tool for the management of working capital. It measures permanent and variable working capital requirements and thus the management can be rest assured that the variable working capital requirements are duly provided for. Working capital may be fixed or variable and in arranging the finance for an enterprise, this distinction of working capital between regular and variable is important. Regular working capital is provided on a long term basis by ploughing back of profits and by the issue of shares and debentures. Variable working capital is meant for meeting temporary needs of a company and this is raised from internal operation as well as from various credit supplying agencies. Some companies, of course, prefer to raise such capital from retained earnings or from the sale or shares of from long term debt. Part of variable working capital may be obtained from trade creditors.

Working capital requirement, in general, may be reduced by favourable credit terms to customers.

Working capital requirements for short period are now being met by bank loan against hypothecation or pledge of inventory or mortgage of fixed assets.

**The planning of the sources** of working capital constitutes an important aspect of the management of working capital. Generally share-issue, net gains from operations, fixed asset sale proceeds, long-term debt, retiring of current liabilities below book value are the sources of working capital.

Operational surplus constitutes the permanent source since it relieves the firm of the external obligations. Of course, it has the limitation that it cannot usually produce much funds on short notice. All other sources are irregular and usually temporary in nature. Sale of fixed assets is also an irregular source. Proceeds from sale of shares constitute permanent source of working capital funds but this source of working capital financing widens ownership base. Returning current liabilities can be resorted to where creditors agree to accept a payment less than the face amount of debt. Returning income tax liability, of course, results in increase of net working capital. Deferred payment of taxes as a source of working capital financing is only temporary.

As a matter of fact, sales constitute the most effective source of working capital so long as costs and expenses are less than sales income.

Working capital financing sometimes assumes a new pattern — hedging in nature, i.e. defensive against possible loss. This approach to working capital financing means that, apart from current instalments on long term debt, a firm would show no current borrowings at the seasonal troughs. Each asset would be offset with a financing instrument of the same approximate maturity with a hedging approach — seasonal variations in current assets would be financed with short-term debt; permanent variations would be financed with long term funds – long term debt and/or equity. Short-term financing for long term needs is an unwise policy because even a good firm may not find it possible to meet its cash obligations for its funds having been tied up in permanent assets (both fixed and current).

In a hedging approach to financing working capital, short-term borrowings would be paid off with surplus cash. With the increase in the variable current assets of the firm, borrowings would be made on short-term basis and payments out of surplus cash generated. A firm's working capital management becomes more conservative with the increase in the percentage of funds obtained from long-term sources. Firms usually follow the policy of financing current assets by short-term credit and this is due to – flexibility, cost, and risk. In case the need for funds is seasonal or cyclical, generally a firm does not consider it prudent to resort to long-term debt; rather it prefers short-term debt for its flexibility. Again, the cost consideration in regard to the maturity decision involves the term structure of interest rates or the relationship between the maturity of debt and the interest rate on the debt. Interest rates on short-term debts, if lower, will attract the management to prefer short-term funds. Similarly, if short-term funds cost more, long-term funds would be preferred. In this connection, the risk element is also to be taken into consideration. Risky short-term debts are not preferable to less risky long-term debts.

**Types and Sources of working capital**

(1) Long term/Permanent and (2) Seasonal/ Additional.

**Permanent working capital** is required initially and regularly. Its sources are : shares, debentures, long-term loans, reserves, public deposits, private loans and sales of assets not in use.

Seasonal working capital is available from : Trade credit, Notes, Bills payable, Bank credit, Cash credit, Overdraft, Cash loan, Bank advances, Trade expenses, Public deposits, Private loans and also Finance and Discount companies.

We can show the cycle of working capital signifying assets changing in one form to another (Fig.19.1).

Let us reiterate that planning and control of working capital is a matter of sound cash planning (setting of cash policies and procedures and control over cash and credit). Cash is the most important ingredient of working capital, the efficient management of which ensures, to a considerable extent, the success of a firm.

**Conclusion**

The working capital management, we can conclude, involves two processes — forecasting for funds needed and acquisition of funds. The effective management of working capital is the primary means of achieving the firm's goal of adequate liquidity.

The working capital is of special significance because the net working capital helps measure the degree of protection that might cause a shortage of funds.

To manage working capital, quite a number of actions are needed but the following ones are noteworthy — (1) monitoring levels of Cash, Receivables and Inventory, (2) Knowing percentage of funds in current accounts and (3) Recording time spent for the management of current accounts. To ensure sound working capital management, it is necessary for the financial manager to know how much funds are tied up in each of the current asset accounts. Any deviations from expectations should be investigated. The relationship between current and fixed assets and any change in the percentage of funds in current accounts is of vital importance to a financial manager. Generally, 30 to 60 per cent of a firm's total assets are tied up in current accounts and, as such, it represents a large investment. The financial manager, to maintain overall control over the management of the finance department, has to see how much time each member of his department devotes to managing working capital. It is to be noted here that surveys disclose about one-third to two-thirds of the financial manager's time being spent in managing the working capital.

**Working or Circulating Capital Cycle**

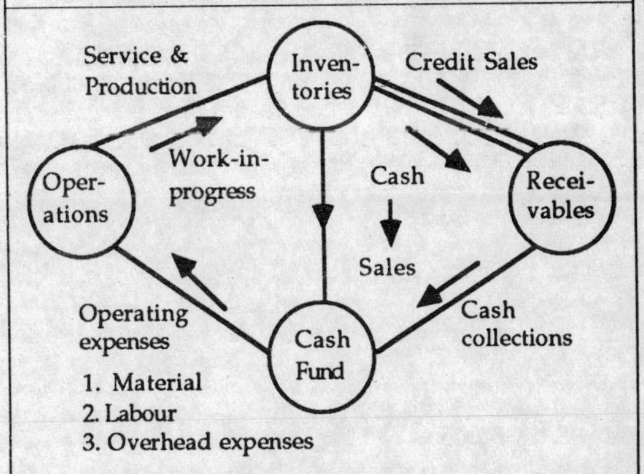


**Note :**

(1) From cash to inventories
(2) From inventories to — Cash A/c, Notes, B/R
(3) From Book debts to cash and so on

**Fig. 19.1**

The financial manager will ultimately proceed on with his work of working capital management **after ascertaining the amount of working capital needed by the firm.** He will take into consideration a number of factors such as – (a) the size of the firm (b) activities of the firm (c) availability of credit (d) attitude towards profit and (e) attitude towards risk.

To meet the liquidity needs, the working capital management must be properly geared up. The primary goal of working capital management is to avoid the risks from inadequate liquidity. One of the goals of working capital management is to earn a return for the firm. In this context, interest rate levels affect the amount of working capital. When interest is high, the firm is encouraged to reduce levels of cash, receivables and inventory. In case interest rate is low, the firm may be willing to maintain higher levels of working capital.

Maintenance of adequate liquidity, whatever the level of interest rates, is the prime consideration of the financial manager. To avoid unnecessary risks, a firm maintains sufficient funds.

# CHAPTER 20

## INTERNAL FINANCING

Dividend pay-out policy and the policy of earnings retention are the outcome of consideration which not only vary from one industry to another but among companies within a given industry and even within a company from time to time. Low dividend pay-out and high retention rates are the financial management policies of growth industries and growth companies. High profitability and rapid growth rate necessitate retention of funds for expansion and for earning higher returns.

### Dividend policy and practice

Prof. James E. Walter (The Walter Approach) is the father of a mathematical formulation in regard to dividend policy for the maximisation of the wealth of equity holders. According to this approach, over long periods, stock prices reflect the present value of expected dividends and retained earnings influence stock prices mainly through their effect on future dividends.

Dividend policy and stock prices are, therefore, closely related and Professor Walter has suggested a framework as an aid in understanding the relationship. His formula suggests the fundamental factors influencing the market value of equity shares.

Keeping in view the maximisation of the wealth position of the equity shareholders, the following formula suggests the appropriate dividend pay out :

**Walter's formula**

$$Vc = \frac{D + \frac{Ra}{Rc}(E - D)}{Rc}$$

where — Vc = theoretical market value of equity shares

Ra = Internal productivity of retained earnings

Rc = Market capitalisation rate

E = Earnings per share

D = Dividend per share

Both the dividend pay-out ratio and the relationship between the Market capitalisation rate (RC) and the internal productivity of retained earnings (Ra) are important in the **Walter Approach.** It can be understood that whenever Ra exceeds Rc, the present worth of future dividends resulting from retention of earnings is greater than the return on the earnings employed elsewhere. Where the dividend pay-out ratio is lower, the higher becomes the prospective value of the equity share. We can put it in a different way : When compared to the industry average, the profitability of a company is higher, the retention of earnings benefits the company and its shareholders. When the profitability of the retained earnings is lower than the industry average, the policy should be a higher dividend pay-out to enable shareholders to use the funds in alternate investments.

The Walter Approach is helpful in explaining dividend practices. To substantiate this observation, we can say that "a growth company is one in which profitability is likely to be very high and the internal productivity of retained funds is likely to exceed the capital productivity outside the company. Consequently, the growth company is expected to have a low dividend pay-out to maximise wealth position of its shareholders. In contrast, companies whose earning power is on the decline cannot utilise retained earnings effectively. Hence, they should have a dividend pay-out" *(S.C.Kuchhal)*.

Retained earnings in internal financing involve the cost problem. It is to be decided by a company whether it is cheaper and more profitable for its shareholders to retain corporate earnings in the business or get them in the form of cash dividend. A comparison has to be made between the cost of retaining earnings and the cost of distributing earnings. The former is an opportunity cost — the benefits that the shareholders forego by leaving the funds in the business. These benefits are not same for all the shareholders, since the funds would be taxed and used differently for consumption and for reinvestment. The measurement of benefits also presents difficulties and needs to study the economic status and investment practices of the present shareholding group and these difficulties are more in big companies where shareholders are widely scattered. In calculating the cost of retaining earnings, it is first necessary to determine the net amount of funds available for distribution without any curtailment of future operations of the company.

To maintain the capital structure of the company for future, internal funds have to be replaced with external, thus involving cost. The cost of retaining earnings entails adjustment for the taxes that the shareholders will pay on their dividend income.

We can reproduce it in the following formula :

**Cost of Retaining Earnings**

$$X = [D - C(1 - BTR)](1 - STR) \times [(1 - STR) \times R]$$

| | | |
|---|---|---|
| X | denotes | rupee cost of retaining earnings |
| D | ... | gross amount of dividend |
| C | ... | cost of replacing the funds paid as dividends |
| BTR | ... | Business Tax Rate |
| STR | ... | Shareholder Tax Rate |
| R | ... | Rate of return on investment of dividend income |

As an illustration —

Let us find out the cost of retaining Rs.1,00,000 (D) otherwise available for dividend.

It is assumed that capital replacement cost for the amount paid out as dividend works out to be 10 per cent, i.e. 10/100 × 1,00,000 = 10,000 (C).

Tax rate for company's income is 60% (BTR).

The dividends received by the shareholders are taxed at 30% (STR) on the average as also their income from reinvesting the dividends.

The shareholders could earn 15% by investing their dividends.

Using the above data —

The cost of retaining earnings will be :

$$X = [D - C(1 - BTR)](1 - STR) \times [(1 - STR) \times R]$$

$$X = \text{Rs. } [1{,}00{,}000 - 10{,}000(1 - \cdot 6)](1 - \cdot 3) \times [(1 - \cdot 3) \times \cdot 15]$$

$$= \text{Rs. } 1{,}00{,}000 - 4{,}000 \times \cdot 7 \times \cdot 105$$

$$= \text{Rs. } 7{,}056$$

The loss of income to the shareholders by retaining the earnings comes to Rs.7,056/-. Here is the need for balancing the cost of distributing the earnings. The cost of distributing the earnings is an opportunity cost which is equal to the profits that might have been earned for the shareholders by using the funds in the business. This is the rate of return earned by the business after taxes on the amount of retained earnings.

To illustrate this, we may assume three internal rates of return — 12%, 10% and 8%. In these cases, the cost of distributing earnings will be —

After tax (a) 12% $1{,}00{,}000 \times \frac{12}{100} = 12{,}000$

(b) 10% $1{,}00{,}000 \times \frac{10}{100} = 10{,}000$

(c) 8% $1{,}00{,}000 \times \frac{8}{100} = 8{,}000$

∴ Ratio of cost of retaining earnings

$$= \frac{\text{Rupee cost of retaining earnings}}{\text{Rupee cost of distributing earnings}}$$

$$(a)\ \frac{7{,}056}{12{,}000} = .588; \quad (b)\ \frac{7{,}056}{10{,}000} = .706; \quad (c)\ \frac{7{,}056}{8{,}000} = .882$$

The above ratio analysis is very meaningful. It indicates that in situation (a) and (b) the cost to the shareholders of leaving the funds in the business is less than the cost of having them distributed. So, it is profitable to leave this particular sum in the business. As the ratio rises, it becomes less profitable to retain the funds. For example, due to reduction in internal rate of return from 12% to 10%, ratio is .706 under situation (b) as compared to .588 in (a).

With the rate of return falling to 8% (situation C), the ratio increases to .882 and it is not advisable to encourage retention of earnings under such a situation.

Retention of earnings is advisable so long as the ratio of cost of retaining earnings is less than 1 (one).

## Dividend policy

The adoption of policy on dividend pay-out is a matter more concerned with the consideration of some delicate points rather than precise mathematical formulations. Theoretically, the earnings of a company should be retained so long as the return is above the company's cost of capital. This policy is to maximise the market value of the equity share over the long-run. The retention of earnings is justified up to the point where the incremental rate of return for the company just exceeds the average rate of return for the industry. But the prudent financial management demands that there should be "a balanced judgement between needs of the company for additional funds and the requirements of shareholders for regular income and capital appreciation" *(S.C. Kuchhal).*

Dividend stability is a matter which deserves serious consideration and **retained earnings** are treated only as a **residual.** This happens in recession where dividend rate is maintained in spite of the fall of earnings.

If the recession continues for a long time, the maintenance of stable dividend rate seriously injures the finances of the company. Stable dividend policy is of necessity for continuance of confidence among the shareholders in their company and also it is vitally essential for enjoying the confidence of the institutional investors such as insurance companies, investment trusts, financial companies etc.

In a nutshell we can say that a stable dividend policy is good but to continue it in all circumstances ignoring other considerations may not prove wise from the point of view of sound financial management and this policy may not serve any useful purpose. The danger inherent in the policy emphasising the importance of regularity in dividends of given size without any consideration to the role played by the investment of retained earnings is that it takes a large portion of accumulated working capital and the company loses the strength of withstanding the shock of operating losses.

**Dividend practices** follow certain policies such as — (a) distribution of a fixed rupee amount of dividend, (b) minimum rupee amount with a step-up feature, (c) fixed percentage of net profit and (d) fixed percentage of market value.

When the distribution of dividend is a fixed rupee amount, there is no connection between dividends paid and current profits earned.

Equity shareholders under such a policy are treated like preference shareholders.

The policy of dividend payment when based on the proposition that the present shareholders want a dividend income of a regular rupee amount, we call the practice with a step-up feature. Here the characteristic is that corporate profits are given more consideration. Such a practice sets the dividend low enough leaving very little scope for default but the scope for flexibility for paying higher dividends is maintained. It does commit the business to adopt the larger payments as part of the future fixed dividend. So, there is a step-up feature. Companies with fluctuating income prefer such policy of dividend pay out.

Dividend as a fixed percentage of net profit is rather mechanical and theoretically it is the most flexible dividend policy since the payments are directly related to net profits. The fixed percentage of profits is called the **pay out ratio.** Such a policy of dividend payment leaves very little scope for the management and freedom for decision-making. The implementation of such a policy of dividend opens up (before a company which is growing and profitable) the scope for building up large amount of retained earnings and its finance in the future becomes easier. As the dividend policy is related to net profit as a fixed percentage, profit stabilisation at a low level or declining profit poses a problem. The management, therefore, should adopt the policy of increasing the percentage of dividends where profits decline and decrease it as profits increase.

To pay dividends as a fixed percentage of market value has been prompted from the fact that shareholders think their dividend income as percentage returns of market price of their shares. Profits, in such a case, are not taken into consideration. This policy singles out the market as the ideal valuation mechanism, here there is no place for internal investment conditions or prospects for future financing.

### What determine dividend policy ?

Dividend policy decisions are taken on the basis of circumstances of an individual case. There are, of course, general determinants of dividend policy. They are — (a) legal restrictions (b) nature of earnings (c) reinvestment alternatives (d) dividends and cash flows (e) dividend and working capital position (f) dividend and new capital requirements (g) dividends and market value of shares (h) tax position of shares and (i) some other considerations.

**Legal restrictions** undoubtedly play a significant influence in formulating dividend policy because a frame-work is provided by legal restrictions within which dividend policy has to be framed. Of course, the legal restrictions relate to the maximum limit and not the maximum rate of dividend. Legal restrictions are justified on the ground that they prevent the management from reducing the equity capital below the amount that was originally paid-in for the protection of creditors in case of complete liquidation of the company.

**Nature of earnings** of a firm actually forms the basis for dividend pay-out. The current earnings of the firm limit the upper limit on dividends. A rational dividend policy is based on year to year assessment of earnings. Dividend policy should reflect the nature of change in earnings which may be abrupt or gradual from year to year.

**Reinvestment alternatives** should receive consideration of the management in deciding policies on dividend. There are alternative reinvestment opportunitie for the current earnings and the management should think whether it will be prudent on its part to distribute profits as dividend to shareholders or to withhold them for reinvestment in business. This policy decision is very important having its significant impact on the future of the company. The corporate management has to make a choice between dividends or the needs of the business for new capital. The practical reasons may require that retained earnings should be used as a source of funds because, as compared to other they have the advantage of being immediately available to business. Again, retained earnings do not involve immediate cash drains. "Thus, given the current level of earnings, **dividend policy is a by-product of the capital budget.**" As a matter of fact, dividend rates fluctuate in response to investment opportunities and dividend constitutes that portion of current earnings which could not be profitably reinvested. Of course, what we find does not corroborate the above observation. There is a strong preference for stability and regularity in dividend payments and the corporate management has to take it into consideration while formulating dividend policy.

**Dividends and cash flows** are very much related. When dividend is paid out, there is an outflow of cash. This necessitates the provision in the cash budget since there is the diversion of funds. Cash is needed for various purposes, so the dividend payment involving cash outflow is dependent on various considerations such as increase of the working capital, replacement of productive equipment, retirement of debt etc. It is not very difficult to comprehend that, in a company where the liquidity position is very strained, the management is to be cautious before taking decision on dividend because dividend payment is not a constructual obligation. With a high degree of liquidity position, dividend payment does not pose any problem and does not require much brain exercise for the management to take any decision.

**Working capital position and dividend** — are taken into consideration by the management for the obvious reason that cash dividends reduce current assets of a company. Keeping in view that the working capital of the company is not impaired, a projection of cash requirements should be made with a view to ensuring that funds to be used for dividend distribution are spared. To formulate a sound dividend policy, a projection of cash inflows and outflows for a longer period is desirable.

**Dividend and new capital requirements** —so far as additional fixed capital is concerned, are to be considered together. Fixed capital requirement should be projected and the available source for such capital must be kept in mind of the management before any decision on dividend policy is taken. In implementing expansion programme, circumstances may compel the management to reinvest the earnings of the company and in that case, long-term capital needs will become the chief consideration in the formulation of dividend policy.

It does not need much intelligence to understand that the market value of shares and the dividend pay-out are closely related. Shareholders are obviously interested in dividend income, a reduction of which means reduction in the investment worth of shares. The dividend policy should have effect on share value but, as a matter of fact, a host of consideration have an impact on the market price of shares. These considerations are very difficult to quantify. Moreover, because of different kinds of investors with their different objectives, the share market is greatly influenced by their emotions and rationality which are of varying proportions from time to time. Of course, some generalisations are possible on the effects of market price of shares consequent upon regular, fluctuating, high, low and variation in dividend pay-out. These are all important issues affecting both shareholders and management. Market quotations of shares are important for a company for obvious reasons because on them depends the future of a company. Dividend pay-out and market price and the prosperity of the company are all so interrelated that a master handling of this aspect of financial management is essential for the ultimate growth of the company. The trend of dividend pay out – regular or fluctuating, high, low or stable – all these are very keenly watched by investors whose effects have impact on the company in various ways than one.

There are wide variations in share holders' objectives and shareholders' groups which determine market price of shares. So, it is not only the dividend policy of the management that exercises influence of share price. There are growth companies whose dividend record shows no bright picture but the shares of the company are being quoted at more and more increased prices. This is for the probability or for possibility for the dividend rate to rise in a growth company. In management decisions, this consideration is of great significance as it has a bearing on the question of new financing. Experience shows that the precise effect of the increase in dividend on market price of shares can hardly be predicted. It is not also ethically justified for the management to manipulate the market by increasing dividend when it knows that the same rate of dividend cannot be maintained for years to come. A stable dividend policy may be preferred by shareholders and the management may adopt such a policy rather than resorting to higher dividend policy, fluctuating in nature. It can be said that the mechanism that works in the share market indicates that it is not within the control of the management of a company to manipulate share price by simply playing on dividend rate and dividend pay out.

Tax position of shareholders acts as a determining factor of dividend pay-out. A closely held company of high income group shareholders may prefer to low dividend pay-out. These shareholders are interested in taking their income in the form of capital gains rather than in dividends which are subjected to higher personal income tax rates. In a large and widely held company, however, the reverse is the case; the shareholders are interested in higher dividend pay-out. From this, it follows that "The larger the extent to which share capital in a company is owned by the shareholders in the higher income brackets, the greater the incentive to limit dividend distribution and to retain the larger part of the profits in the business" *(S.C. Kuchhal)*.

There are other factors which affect the determination of dividend policy. The dividend policy of competitive concerns, restriction on dividend policy imposed by debt contracts, the extent of management's identification with the equity shareholders, the number of influential shareholders with special investment objectives, easy access to capital markets and other forms of external financing, rate of growth in a company requiring additional funds etc. are determining factors of dividend pay-out. A single dividend policy is unlikely to satisfy all; so there is the need for a compromise of conflicting objectives. The sound dividend policy should be based on the careful consideration of the relative importance of these factors and choose a line of action which will suit the business objectives and satisfy the shareholders. The financial management considers dividend decisions as a critical area of financial management since here is the scope for the management to come into direct conflict with the shareholders and the scope of one group of shareholders being hostile to another group cannot be ruled out.

In planning the capital structure of a company, due consideration should be paid as to the potential earnings per share. An analysis should be made and that should be supplemented by examining the implication of various financial alternatives on future dividends per share (DPS). Earnings per share (EPS) should have a fair relationship with DPS. This does not necessarily imply that a fixed percentage of EPS must be maintained every year because dividend policy, as we have already mentioned, is the outcome of a number of considerations. A sound financial management policy is based on considerable caution in interpreting the significance of fixed dividend pay-out policies.

•

# CHAPTER 21

## DIVIDEND THEORIES

In the corporate management, the significance of dividend pay-out cannot be over-exaggerated. Shareholders are interested on the return of the investment in shares and the company management are also very much concerned about the attitude of the shareholders towards the company on which will depend the future prosperity of the company. Dividend pay-out and dividend policy, therefore, play a vital role in the financial management of a company.

Dividend policy affects the retention policy of a firm. There is, practically, a type of reciprocal relationship between cash dividends and retained earnings. Larger retention means smaller dividends while smaller retention is to affect higher dividend pay-out. Thus, the dividend policy and retention policy are competitive and conflicting.

Dividend pay-out in large quantum reduces the amount of retention which affects the growth and development of a company. A stable dividend policy, however, has definite advantages. So, to maintain stable dividend pay-out, retention may be affected. The management is to face such a problem and a compromise between the two in the best interest of the company is the primary consideration for a good financial management.

This problem can be discussed with reference to wealth maximisation. What we mean to say is, if the payment of dividend leads to maximise the owner's wealth, the firm may use the net profit for paying dividends among the shareholders. Contrary to this, the retention of profits is necessary for financing various investment opportunities.

Therefore, there exists a relationship between dividends and the value of the firm and this needs careful consideration before any decision on dividend is taken.

There are conflicting theories which affect the dividend decision and the valuation of a firm. According to one school of thought, the dividend decisions do not affect the valuation of a firm since the dividends are irrelevant. The other school of thought believes that the dividend decisions do affect the firm's value because the value is measured in term of market value of shares.

The view-points of the schools of thoughts are grouped into two concepts —

(i) Irrelevance concept of Dividend

(ii) Relevance concept of Dividend.

### Irrelevance concept of Dividend

The advocates of this concept are — Franco Modigliani, Morton H. Miller and E. Solomon. To them, the dividend policy of the firm is a residual decision and dividends are a passive residual. E. Solomon is the propagator of such a view. The 'Irrelevance Concept' emphasises that dividend has nothing to do with prices of shares, that is, it is irrelevant. According to the concept, investors are indifferent between dividends and capital gains. What they want is a higher return on their investment. Franco Modigliani and his colleagues who subscribe to this view argue that if the firm can hold out adequate investment opportunities before the shareholders and can assure a higher rate of return in comparison with the cost of retained earnings, the investors would be content with the firm for retaining the earnings by withholding dividend pay-out or distributing lesser amount of dividend. On the contrary, if the retention is less than the cost of retained earnings, investors would prefer to receive earnings, i.e. dividends.

It follows, therefore, that with profitable investment opportunities, a firm may retain the earnings to the satisfaction of its shareholders but, in the reverse situation, earnings should be distributed by way of dividend among the shareholders.

### Modigliani-Miller (M – M) Hypothesis

According to Modigliani-Miller, "under conditions of perfect capital market rational investors, absence of tax discrimination between dividend income and capital appreciation given the firm's investment policy, its dividend policy may have no influence on the market price of the shares." So, the dividend policy of a firm is irrelevant having no effect on the price of its shares, i.e. shareholders' wealth is not affected. The value of the firm, according to M–M, is determined by the earning power of the firm's assets or its investment policy and not the dividend decisions by splitting the earnings of retentions and dividends.

There are some **assumptions in the M-M hypothesis.** They are : (i) Existence of perfect capital market (ii) non-existence of taxes (iii) rationality in investors' behaviour (iv) non-changeability of fixed investment policy of the firm and (v) non-existence of risk and uncertainty.

### Proof of M–M Hypothesis

According to this hypothesis, the market price of a share at the beginning of a period is equal to the present value of dividend paid at the end of the period plus the market price of the share at the end of the period.

**Formula :**

$$P = \frac{1}{(I+K)} \cdot (D_1 + P_1) \quad \cdots \quad (1)$$

where P denotes prevailing market price of a share at time O.

K = cost of equity capital

$D_1$ = Dividend per share at time I

$P_1$ = Market price per share at time I

In the absence of external financing or new financing, the value of the firm (V) will simply be the number of outstanding shares, (n) times the prices of each share, (P).

By multiplying both sides of equation (1), we get :

$$V = nP = \frac{n(D_1 + P_1)}{(I+K)} \quad \cdots \quad (2)$$

If, however, the firm sells (m) number of new shares at time I at a price of $P_1$, the value of the firm (V) at time O will be :

$$V = nP = \frac{n(D_1 + P_1) + mP_1 - mP_1}{(I+K)}$$
$$= \frac{nD_1 + nP_1 + mP_1 - mP_1}{(I+K)}$$
$$= \frac{nD_1 + (n+m)P_1 - mP_1}{(I+K)} \quad (3)$$

It has been observed that the investment programme at a given period of time can be financed either from the proceeds of new issues or from the retained earnings, or from both. So, the amount of new issues will be :

$$mP_1 = I_1 - (T_1 - nD_1)$$
$$= I_1 - T + nD_1 \quad \cdots \quad (4)$$

Here, $I_1$ denotes total new investment during the period I.

and $T_1$ denotes Earnings/Profits for the period I.

The above observation indicates that total financing by the new issues is determined by the amount of investment in first period and not by retained earnings. By substituting equation (4) by equation (3), M–M reveal that the value of the firm remains unaffected by the dividend policy, i.e. $nD_1$ term cancels out as under :

$$np = \frac{nD_1 + (n+m)P_1 - mP_1}{(I+K)}$$
$$= \frac{nD_1 + (n+m)P_1 - (I_1 - T_1 + nD_1)}{(I+K)}$$
$$= \frac{nD_1 + (n_1+m)P_1 - I_1 + T_1 - nD_1}{(1+K)}$$
$$= \frac{(n+m)P_1 - I_1 + T_1}{(1+K)} \quad \cdots \quad (5)$$

Thus M–M's valuation model in equation (5) is consistent with the valuation equation (2) and (3) stated above in terms of external financing. As the value of the firm (V) can be restated as equation (5) without dividends $D_1$, it proves that dividends have no effect on the value of the firm (when the external financing is being applied).

## Criticism of M– M hypothesis

As we have seen earlier, M–M hypothesis is based on certain assumptions. Under those assumptions, the conclusion arrived at is logically sound and perfectly consistent. But the assumptions are not all well based. The existence of a perfect capital market, for instance, cannot be a reality in many countries. If the assumption themselves do not hold good in all countries and they lack in universal acceptability, the conclusion that is derived from M–M hypothesis cannot be said to be free from criticism. The lack of practical relevance in the assumptions leads to controversies. It is argued that internal and external financing are not equivalent. The shareholders/investors cannot be indifferent towards dividend and capital gains since dividend policy affects them perceptibly Thus, it is not proper to say that dividend policy is irrelevant.

The critics of M–M hypothesis highlight the following points to support them.

**(i) Tax Differential :** Non-existence of taxes is unreal. Shareholders have to pay taxes on dividend received or on capital gains. And actually tax rates are lower on capital gains. Shareholders, therefore, are likely to prefer capital gains to dividend. Moreover, capital gains tax is payable only where the shares are actually sold in the market at a profit. The cost of internal financing is cheaper than that of external financing. Thus, tax advantages lead shareholders to prefer a dividend policy with relation of earnings instead of cash dividend.

**(ii) Existence of floatation costs :** The assumption that both internal and external financing are equivalent is not tenable. It means that if dividend is paid in cash, funds have to be raised externally and there will not be any difference in shareholders' wealth whether earnings are retained or fresh shares are issued assuming no floatation cost is involved. But this is an unreal assumption; floating cost has to be incurred for issuing fresh shares but there is no such cost in the retention of earnings. As a matter of fact, the floatation cost enhances external financing and it becomes costlier than internal financing. It follows, therefore, where cost factor is properly considered, external and internal financing, i.e. fresh issue and retained earnings, cannot be equivalent.

**(iii) Existence of transaction costs :** The assumption in M-M hypothesis that dividend payment has nothing to do with shareholders' wealth is subjected to criticism. The non-availability of dividend in cash may induce a shareholder to sell his shares for current income and it involves transaction costs which fact has evaded the consideration of M-M approach. Taking the cost factor of transaction (brokerage, commission etc.) into consideration, a shareholder is quite likely to prefer dividends to capital gains.

**(iv) Diversificiation :** When shareholders desire to diversify their portfolios, they like to distribute earnings which would enable them to earn such dividends in other firms. The assumption in M-M hypothesis that discount rate should be the same – whether a firm uses internal or external financing – is not true in actual practice. Shareholders, while distributing their earnings, are inclined to have a higher value of discount rate if internal financing is resorted to and vice versa.

**(v) Uncertainty :** M–M hypothesis presumes that dividend policy of a firm is irrelevant even if the uncertainty factor is considered. According to M–M, two firms having identical investment policies, business risks and expected future earnings will have the same market price. But this view is not accepted by all. Some argue that, under conditions of uncertainty, dividends are relevant because investors want to avert risk and as such they prefer near dividends than future dividends for the reason that future dividends are discounted at a higher rate for their uncertainty. Therefore, the value of the firm is higher when dividend is paid earlier than when the firm follows a retention policy.

## Relevance Concept of Dividend

As opposed to M – M approach as to the irrelevance of dividend, there is a school of thought led by Walter, Gordon, Linter and Richardson accord ing to which dividend decision is relevant. These scholars feel that dividend policy of a firm has a direct effect on the position of a firm in a stock exchange. Since the prices of shares quoted at the stock exchange indicate the profit earning capacity of a firm, being the reflection of the firm paying high or low dividend, the relevance of dividend in determining the value of a firm has to be admitted.

"Relevance concept of dividend", as explained by Walter and Gordon, is discussed :

## Walter's Model

Prof. James E. Walter's model suggests that dividend policy and investment policy of a firm cannot be isolated; rather they are interlinked as such, choice of the former affects the value of a firm.

According to him, internal rate of returns (r) of firms and the cost of their capital or the required rate of return (k) are related. An optimum dividend policy by the relationship of r and k has got to be determined. This means a firm should retain its earnings if the return on investment exceeds the cost of capital and conversely the firm should distribute its earnings to the shareholders.

## Explanation of the Walter Model

(a) When r > k (growth firms), it implies that a firm has adequate profitable investment opportunities which enable it to earn more than what the investors expect. This is called a **growth firm.** The optimum dividend policy in the case of such a firm may be given by a $\frac{D}{P}$ ratio (Dividend pay-out ratio) of O. It means a firm should retain its entire earnings within itself and as such the market value of the shares will be maximised.

(b) When r < k (declining firms), it implies that a firm lacks in profitable investment opportunities to invest its earnings. This takes place in case of firms known as **declining firms.** In such a case, the rate of return from new investment (r) is less than the required rate of return or cost of capital (k) as a consequence of which retention is not at all profitable. The investors are satisfied if earnings are paid to them by way of dividend and they will earn a higher rate of return by investing such amounts elsewhere. The market price of shares is maximised because of the payment of entire earnings as dividends amongs the investors. There will be an optimum dividend policy when $\frac{D}{P}$ ratio is 100%.

(c) When r = k (normal firm), there is no optimum dividend policy and it does not matter whether earnings are distributed or retained because all $\frac{D}{P}$ ratios ranging from O to 100 (the market price of shares) will remain constant. This means that when the profitable investment opportunities are not available, the return from investment (r) is equal to the cost of capital (k), i.e. when r = k, the dividend policy does not affect the market price of a share.

## Assumptions in the Walter Model

(i) The external sources of funds like debt or new equity capital are not resorted to by a firm, i.e. all financing is done through retained earnings.

(ii) Internal rate of return (r) and cost of capital (k) are constant.

(iii) Key variables do not change which means beginning earnings per share E and dividend per share D, may be changed in the model in order to determine results but any given value of E and D is assumed to remain constant in determining a given value.

(iv) All earnings are either reinvested internally immediately or distributed by way of dividends.

(v) The firm has perpetual or very long life.

**Walter's formula for dividend decision**

$$P = \frac{D}{k} + \frac{r(E-D)k}{k}$$

or

$$P = \frac{D + \frac{r}{k}(E-D)}{k}$$

| | | |
|---|---|---|
| P | denotes | market price per share |
| D | denotes | dividend per share |
| E | denotes | earning per share |
| r | denotes | internal rate of return |
| and k | denotes | cost of capital or capitalisation rate |

From the above, it can well be understood that the optimal $\frac{D}{P}$ ratio is determined by varying "D" until and unless one receives the maximum market price per share.

To illustrate the above formula, let us assume —

Cost of capital (k) = 10%

Earnings per share (E) = Rs.10

Interest Rates of Return (r) = (i) 15%, (ii) 10% and (iii) 8%.

Assuming $\frac{D}{P}$ ratios are : 0; 40%; 75% and 100%. That is, dividend per share is Rs. 0, Rs.4, Rs.7.5 and Rs.10, the effect of different dividend policies for three alternatives of r will be as under :

| Where r > k | Where r = k | Where r < k |
|---|---|---|
| r = .15 | r = .10 | r = .08 |
| k = .10 | k = .10 | k = .10 |
| E = Rs.10 | E = Rs. 10 | E = Rs.10 |

**Walter - Model**

Dividend policy and the value of shares

When $r > k$

(At different levels of D the values of P will be as under :)

(a) $D = Rs.0$

$$P = \frac{0 + \frac{.15}{.10}(10-0)}{.10} = Rs.150$$

(b) $D = Rs.4$

$$P = \frac{4 + \frac{.15}{.10}(10-4)}{.10} = Rs.130$$

(c) $D = Rs.7.5$

$$P = \frac{7.5 + \frac{.15}{.10}(10-7.5)}{.10} = Rs.112.50$$

(d) $D = Rs.10$

$$P = \frac{10 + \frac{.15}{.10}(10-10)}{.10} = Rs.100$$

When $r = k$

(At different levels of D the values of P will be as under :)

(a) $D = Rs.0$

$$P = \frac{0 + \frac{.10}{.10}(10-0)}{.10} = Rs.100$$

(b) $D = Rs.4$

$$P = \frac{4 + \frac{.10}{.10}(10-4)}{.10} = Rs.100$$

(c) $D = Rs.7.5$

$$P = \frac{7.5 + \frac{.10}{.10}(10-7.5)}{.10} = Rs.100$$

(d) $D = Rs.10$

$$P = \frac{10 + \frac{.10}{.10}(10-10)}{.10} = Rs.100$$

When $r < k$

(At different levels of D the values of P will be as under :)

(a) $D = Rs.0$

$$P = \frac{0 + \frac{.08}{.10}(10-0)}{.10} = Rs.80$$

(b) $D = Rs.4$

$$P = \frac{4 + \frac{.08}{.10}(10-4)}{.10} = Rs.88$$

(c) $D = Rs.7.5$

$$P = \frac{7.5 + \frac{.08}{.10}(10-7.5)}{.10} = Rs.95$$

(d) $D = Rs.10$

$$P = \frac{10 + \frac{.08}{.10}(10-10)}{.10} = Rs.100$$

From the above model, we can draw the conclusion that according to Prof. James Walter, the optimum dividend policy depends on the relationship between the internal rate of return (r) and the cost of capital (k). Therefore, a firm should retain all earnings if r > k and it should distribute entire earnings if r < k and it will remain **indifferen** when r = k.

## Criticisms of Walter's Model

Walter's model is based on some unrealistic assumptions.

(i) The assumption that all investments are financed only by retained earnings and not by external financing is not the fact. To assume this, is to ignore the benefits of optimum capital structure.

(ii) That the internal rate of return (r) of a firm remains constant is an assumption which is divorced from reality. The rate of return generally declines with the increase in the number of investment proposals.

(iii) Walter's Model also assumes that the cost of capital (k) remains constant but in the real world situation, this assumption does not hold good. It is natural that with the change of risk pattern of a firm, there is a corresponding change in cost of capital (k). Therefore, the model ignores the effect of risk on the value of the firm.

## Gordon's Model

Gordon Myron, J. developed a theory on relevance of dividend known as Gordon's Model.

## Assumptions

(i) The firm is an all-equity firm.

(ii) The firm is of considerable longevity.

(iii) There is no corporate tax.

(iv) No external financing is available. Only retained earnings are utilised for investment programmes.

(v) Both the internal rate of return (r) and the cost of capital (k) are constant.

(vi) The retention ratio b once decided upon is constant. Thus, the growth rate g = br is also constant.

(vii) $k > br = g$.

"The market value of a share is equal to the present value of an infinite future stream of dividends" — is the proposition that Gordon Model aims at.

Therefore, Gordon Model is —

$$P_1 = \frac{E(1-b)}{k-br}$$

where, P = Price of shares;
E = Earnings per share;
b = Retention ratio/fraction of retained earnings;
k = Cost of capital;
br = g = growth rate in r;
r = Internal rate of return.

The relationship between internal rate of return (r) and the cost of capital (k) is aimed at to be established clearly in Gordon's Model. According to Gordon, dividend policy depends on the profitable investment opportunities.

## Gordon's propositions

**(a) When r > k (Growth firms)**

The value per share (P) increases, since the retention ratio (b) increases i.e. P increases with decrease in dividend pay-out ratio. A firm, in such a situation should, therefore, distribute smaller dividends and should retain higher earnings.

**(b) When r < k (declining firms)**

The value per share (P) decreases since the retention ratio (b) increases, i.e. P increases with increase in dividend pay-out ratio. It can be proved that with the increase in the value of b, the value of the shares continuously falls. If r is smaller than k (which is equal to the rate available in the market), project retention clearly becomes undesirable from the view-point of the shareholders. Each additional rupee retained reduces the amount of funds which shareholders could have invested at a higher rate elsewhere and thus it further reduces the value of the shares of the company.

**(c) When r = k (Normal firms)**

The value of the firm is not affected by dividend policy and is equal to the book value of assets, i.e. dividend policy is irrelevant. The implication is that under competitive conditions, k must be equal to r, available to investors in comparable shares in such a manner that any fund distributed as dividends, may be invested in the market at the rate which is equal to the internal rate of return of the firm. As a consequence, shareholders can neither lose nor gain by any change in the company's dividend policy and the market value of the shares remains unchanged.

We can illustrate the Gordon Model with the following data of a company —

(a) Rate of return on investment (r) :

(i) 15%; (ii) 10% and (iii) 8%.

(b) Cost of capital (k) = 10%.

(c) Earning per share (E) = Rs.10.

Let us determine the value of the shares of the company with the following assumptions :

$\frac{D}{P}$ ratio, i.e. $(1-b)$ :

(a) 100 (b) 80 (c) 70
(d) 50 (e) 35

Retention Ratio, i.e. $b = \frac{R}{E}$

(a) 0 (b) 20 (c) 30
(d) 50 (e) 65

**Dividend policy and the value of shares**
**(Gordon Model)**

| When $r > k$ (growth firm) | When $r = k$ (normal firm) | When $r < k$ (declining firm) |
|---|---|---|
| The value of P at different levels of b | The value of P at different levels of b | The value of P at different levels of b |
| (a) $b = 0 \quad \therefore\ br = 0$<br>$P = \frac{Rs.10(1-0)}{.10-0}$<br>$= \frac{Rs.10}{.10}$<br>$= Rs.100$ | (a) $b = 0 \quad \therefore\ br = 0$<br>$P = \frac{Rs.10(1-0)}{.10-0}$<br>$= \frac{Rs.10}{.10}$<br>$= Rs.100$ | (a) $b = 0 \quad \therefore\ br = 0$<br>$P = \frac{Rs.10(1-0)}{.10-0}$<br>$= \frac{Rs.10}{.10}$<br>$= Rs.100$ |
| (b) $b = .20$<br>$\therefore\ br = .20 \times .15 = .030$<br>$P = \frac{Rs.10(1-.20)}{.10-.03}$<br>$= \frac{Rs.8}{.070}$<br>$= Rs.114$ | (b) $b = .20$<br>$\therefore\ br = .20 \times .10 = .02$<br>$P = \frac{Rs.10(1-.20)}{.10-.02}$<br>$= \frac{Rs.8}{.08}$<br>$= Rs.100$ | (b) $b = .20$<br>$\therefore\ br = .20 \times .08 = .016$<br>$P = \frac{Rs.10(1-.20)}{.10-.016}$<br>$= \frac{Rs.8}{.084}$<br>$= Rs.95$ |
| (c) $b = .30$<br>$\therefore\ br = .30 \times .15 = .045$<br>$P = \frac{Rs.10(1-.30)}{.10-.045}$<br>$= \frac{Rs.7}{.055}$<br>$= Rs.127$ | (c) $b = .30$<br>$\therefore\ br = .30 \times .10 = .03$<br>$P = \frac{Rs.10(1-.30)}{.10-.03}$<br>$= \frac{Rs.7}{.07}$<br>$= Rs.100$ | (c) $b = .30$<br>$\therefore\ br = .30 \times .08 = .024$<br>$P = \frac{Rs.10(1-.30)}{.10-.024}$<br>$= \frac{Rs.7}{.076}$<br>$= Rs.92$ |
| (d) $b = .50$<br>$\therefore\ br = .50 \times .15 = .075$<br>$P = \frac{Rs.10(1-.50)}{.10-.075}$<br>$= \frac{Rs.5}{.025}$<br>$= Rs.200$ | (d) $b = .50$<br>$\therefore\ br = .50 \times .10 = .05$<br>$P = \frac{Rs.10(1-.50)}{.10-.05}$<br>$= \frac{Rs.5}{.05}$<br>$= Rs.100$ | (d) $b = .50$<br>$\therefore\ br = .50 \times .08 = .04$<br>$P = \frac{Rs.10(1-.50)}{.10-.04}$<br>$= \frac{Rs.5}{.06}$<br>$= Rs.83$ |
| (e) $b = .65$<br>$\therefore\ br = .65 \times .15 = .098$<br>$P = \frac{Rs.10(1-.65)}{.10-.098}$<br>$= \frac{Rs.3.5}{.002}$<br>$= Rs.175$ | (e) $b = .65$<br>$\therefore\ br = .65 \times .10 = .065$<br>$P = \frac{Rs.10(1-.65)}{.10-.065}$<br>$= \frac{Rs.3.5}{.035}$<br>$= Rs.100$ | (e) $b = .65$<br>$\therefore\ br = .65 \times .08 = .052$<br>$P = \frac{Rs.10(1-.65)}{.10-.052}$<br>$= \frac{Rs.3.5}{.048}$<br>$= Rs.73$ |

**Solution**

Gordon Formula for share valuation —

$$P_1 = \frac{E(1-b)}{k-br}$$

According to the formula, the value of shares of the above company for different — and retention ratios for the three alternatives of r > k, r = k and r < k is presented below :

| When r > k | When r = k | When r < k |
|---|---|---|
| r = .15<br>k = .10<br>E = Rs. 10 | r = .10<br>k = .10<br>E = Rs. 10 | r = .08<br>k = .10<br>E = Rs. 10 |

An analysis of the Table given on Gordon Model, will reveal —

(a) **When r > k** the market value of shares (P) increases with the retention ratio (b) for growth firms.

(b) **When r = k** the market value of shares is not affected in any way by dividend policy.

(c) **When r < k** the market value of shares increases with the pay-out ratio for declining firms.

**But** uncertainty has a role to play in dividend policy, according to Gordon, even when r = k. It is emphasised once again, that under Gordon Model, when **r = k,** the **dividend policy is irrelevant.**

Gordon continues "that under conditions of uncertainty, investors tend to discount distant dividends at a higher rate than they discount near dividends". This phenomenon arises out of the nature of investors — they tend to avert risks and put a premium on the return which is certain rather than on uncertain discount return; so they prefer near dividends to future dividends.' According to Krishnan John, E. (Principles of Investment), this is a **bird-in-the-hand** argument. He says "Of two stocks of identical earnings, record, prospectus, but the one paying a larger dividend than the other, the former will undoubtedly command a higher price merely because stock-holders prefer present to fututre values. Myopic vision plays a part in the price-making process. Stockholders often act upon the principle that a bird in the hand is worth two in the bushes and for this reason, they are willing to pay a premium for the stock with the higher dividend rate just as they discount the one with the lower rate."

Gordon agrees with this argument and continues that the future is, no doubt, uncertain and, as such, the more distant the future, the more uncertain it will be. So, considering dividend policy in this context of uncertainty, the cost of capital (discount rate) cannot be assumed to be constant; it increases with uncertainty. Investors are willing to pay more for the shares which pay higher current dividend rather than paying less for shares involving uncertainty. This explains why distant dividends are discounted at a higher rate than the near dividends. Of course, this is also not free from criticism. It is argued that due to low capital gains tax (particularly applicable to the investors who are in high-tax brackets), the investors may have a preference for capital gains (which is caused by high return) than the current dividends so available.

# CHAPTER 22

## MANAGERIAL CONSIDERATIONS IN DIVIDEND PAY-OUT

A host of factors have to be considered by the management before deciding upon the final dividend pay-out. Of course, these considerations must have relevance to the theory of dividend pay-out and the valuation of the firm.

The factors that deserve consideration are : (i) Fund-needs of the firm (ii) liquidity (iii) assessment of any valuation information (iv) control (v) restrictions in bond indenture or loan agreement and (vi) ability to borrow.

In dividend pay-out, first consideration to the management is the **funds needs** of the firm. Cash budgets and projected source-and-use-of-funds statements are of particular use. The cash budgets should be prepared taking into account the expected operating cash flows of the firm, expected future capital expenditures and any other thing that affects the cash position of the firm. "The key is to determine the likely cash flows and cash position of the company in the absence of a change in dividend" (J.C. Van Horne). The firm will determine if anything is left over after servicing its funds needs including profitable investment projects. The farsightedness on the part of management is of great necessity taking into account the firm's situation over a reasonable number of years to iron out fluctuations. The management should analyse the likely ability of the firm to sustain a dividend relative to the probability distributions of future cash flows and cash positions. This analysis enables the management to determine the firm's likely future residual funds.

Since dividends represent a cash outflow, dividend decisions need considerable considerations. A growing company cannot be so liquid as it needs funds for fixed assets and permanent working capital. However, some **liquidity cushion** is always a sound financial policy and the management of a company must want it for the sake of flexibility of the company and protection against uncertainty. In such a case, the management does not like to jeopardise this position for larger dividend pay-out. The liquidity of a company involves investment and financing decisions; the rate of asset expansion and the need for funds are determined by the investment decision and the financing decision is to find out the way the need will be financed.

The effect of a dividend on **valuation** is important and **information** to this effect should be collected as far as possible. Regression analysis involving similar companies may be of some use but statistical problems and the troublesome job of trying to hold all else constant make such studies difficult. So specific generalisations as to the effect of dividends on valuation cannot be easily made. Generally companies having the same growth rate follow the same dividend pay-out ratio. The management should judge the informational effect of a dividend — the expectation of the investors.

Here are the needs for security analysis and security reports. The management is to consider what information the company is conveying with its present dividend and what it would convey with a possible change in dividend.

Dividend pay-out has a direct effect on the **controlling interest** of the company. The management should, therefore, give a serious thought on this aspect of financial management. In case a company raises its dividend pay-out, it may need to raise capital at a later time through the sale of shares and this may lead to **dilution of the controlling interest.** In such a circumstance, the existing stock holder may prefer a lesser amount of dividend and financing of investment needs with retained earnings. **From the point of view of control,** therefore, the management should consider rather a lower dividend pay-out, though shareholders' wealth may not be maximised. The control-aspect of a company vis-a-vis the dividend pay-out is a matter that deserves careful consideration of the management : Control works in two ways : a low dividend pay-out may work to the advantage of the "outsider" seeking control over a company which is much sought after. The outsiders may convince the stockholder that the company is not maximising shareholders' wealth which they will do. Such companies, therefore, should resort to the policy of higher dividend pay-out.

A bond indenture or **loan agreement** may have **effect on dividend payout.** So, this should not escape the consideration of the management. The loan agreement may include a restriction on the payment of dividends to pressure the company's ability to service debt.

The restrictive clause of the loan agreement restricts the dividend pay out in terms of maximum percentage of cumulative earnings. So, the dividend policy is affected because of such a restriction. Of course, the management may sometimes intend to have such a restriction to avoid any explanation as to the lower dividend pay-out.

The ability of a firm to borrow on comparatively short notice gives the firm greater flexibility which in its turn enables it to pay a higher cash dividend. "With ready access to debt funds, management should be less concerned with the effect that a cash dividend has upon its liquidity" (Van Horne). A liquid position is, therefore, not the only way to provide for flexibility and a protection against uncertainty. The ability to borrow from a bank or a financial institution lends flexibility to a firm. When a firm is able to go to the capital markets with a bond issue, it acquires flexibility and the more a firm is established the more is its ability to have access to capital markets. Since flexibility is an important factor in determining dividend, the management is to consider it seriously before dividend pay-out.

# CHAPTER 23

## RETAINED EARNINGS (PLOUGHING BACK OF PROFITS)

Retained earnings as a source of corporate finance have been recognised since long. Companies have relied heavily on them. "Since the dividend pay-out ratio, the percentage of earnings paid to stockholders in cash, reduces the amount of earnings the firm retains, a dividend decision is a financing decision." (James C. VanHorne).

The financial management generally pursues the policy of setting aside a portion of the earnings of the company to ensure a sound dividend policy. This policy is based on the desire of the companies to grow from within gradually and **such growth effected through retained earnings is considered as the best method in company finance.** Retaining a portion of distributable profits in the form of force reserves and utilising them for further expansion is known as **ploughing-in** of profits. Its effects is to reduce "the possible dividend payment exactly by the amount put back into the business."

(S. A. Sherlekar)

Profit diversion or channelisation may be made in three different ways — taxation, ploughing back of profits and dividend payments. When substantial profits are earned; normal dividend payments and retention of sufficient funds in business do not naturally subject the management to any objection from shareholders — to the procedure of ploughing back of profits (retained earnings reinvested in the business). Should the earnings be small and the rate of dividend be lowered, shareholders object to ploughing back of profits.

Retained earnings are necessitated for fixed capital as well as for working capital for expansion and development schemes. To improve efficiency of the plant and equipment and the unreliability of account statements management is compelled to resort to the policy of ploughing back of profits or the retention of earnings. It is not unusual for a company to overstate its profits on paper whereas actually earnings are less.

However, small and medium sized companies follow the policy of ploughing back of profits because of certain practical difficulties of the money market. They cannot raise funds from sources other than local, and open market approach to raise capital is difficult for them. Banks also are not favourably disposed to financing these companies even after nationalisation. It, therefore, becomes a compelling necessity for the smaller companies to plough back their own profits in spite of rising corporate taxation.

Retained earnings (self-financing or ploughing back of profits) is not a source of corporate finance which is an unmixed blessing — there are curses. As against the advantages derived from ploughing back of profits, there are quite a number of dangers associated with this source.

**Advantages** are :

(1) A cost-free source of finance having no dilution of earnings per share. No interest has to be paid nor there is any compulsory periodic payment in the form of dividend liability.

(2) It does not bring about any change of control as there is no increase in the equity capital.

(3) The use of retained earnings does not involve management in any restriction as is the case with share or debenture issue; managerial freedom is fully maintained.

(4) It is a permanent and convenient source of finance. There is no pledge, no mortgage in the ploughing back of profits.

(5) To the management, the use of retained earnings is easier as it does away with the necessity of wasting time for planning the sale of securities, approaching the money/capital market.

(6) The ploughing back of profits or self-financing is particularly useful in a period of credit squeeze imposed by the central bank to control inflation.

(7) Retained earnings enable a company to finance working capital and further expansion.

(8) Retained earnings and dividend policy are closely related since large accumulated profits ensure stable dividend policy and thus the credit-worthiness of the company is enhanced. Procurement of working capital becomes easier from the money market and the stable dividend policy puts the company in a position where mobilisation of capital does not pose so much problem. The evils of speculation in the shares are also reduced.

(9) Self financing/ploughing back of profits contributes much to the economic development of a country by accelerating capital formation which helps growth and expansion.

But nothing in this world is an unmixed blessing; not to speak of self-financing or ploughing back of profits. Excessive resort to this practice leads to over-investment as a consequence of which monopoly vices become evident. Prof. Pigon thinks that excessive ploughing back entails social waste. The danger of misuse of funds and manipulation of share values by management are not uncommon in the excessive use of retained earnings. Over-capitalisation also takes place due to frequent issue of bonus shares. Companies resorting to the practice of ploughing back of profits naturally can by-pass the test of efficiency since they are not to approach the open market for additional capital. In such a circumstance, savings are unlikely to be channelised into the most profitable investment way and, thus, optimum utilisation of savings for investment cannot be ensured.

In spite of the fact that the economic development of the U.S.A., U.K. and many other advanced countries of the world are taking advantage of ploughing back of profits, in India there was a declining trend in retained profits till 1970. India is the highest taxed country in the world and, since 1960, we are having rising trend of taxation. Indian companies are to pay ever-growing interest charges claiming greater and greater part of gross profits. Till 1970, the management of the Indian companies had to use retained profits to maintain expected dividend rates as a consequence of which retained profits continuously declined as a source of internal finance. However, since 1970, companies have increased appreciably retained profits to be reinvested in business. In the Five Year Plans, there has been continuous emphasis on corporate savings.

To sum up, retained profits act as shock absorbers against depressions and seasonal changes in demand. The ploughing back is a policy of undoubted merit for financing the long term requirements of a business enterprise. The management, however, should follow a bold though cautious policy in regard to retained earnings on ploughing back of profits.

# CHAPTER 24

## RESERVE AND DIVIDEND POLICY

In financial management, reserves and dividends deserve very careful consideration for overall efficiency in the corporate management. Reserves for meeting contingencies and dividends for stock-holders' interest do not need much elucidation for their effects on the corporate functioning and also on the future of a company. Funds are required for both short and long-term needs of a company which may not be readily available and a company is to touch its retained profits to overcome the needs or emergencies.

A sound policy is essential by the top management in regard to dividends and reserves. Generally **the following considerations are taken into account while formulating any policy on reserves and dividends :**

(1) Maint nance of reserves (2) Existence of earned surplus (3) Cash needs of a company (4) Need for growth and expansion (5) steady and stable dividend policy (6) Government taxation policy (7) Legal restrictions on dividend distribution (8) Creditors' restrictions on the amount of dividends and (9) Need for replacement of fixed assets during rising price level.

**1. Maintenance of reserves :** The need for maintenance is beyond any controversy. The management of a big firm involves various expenses — capital and revenue, short-term and long-term, and it is quite usual that in spite of keen foresight, all future necessities of funds cannot be visualised. Unforeseen circumstances are inherent in business activities and to safeguard the firm against such eventualities, reserves are absolutely necessary.

Reserves are needed for — (a) depreciation (b) working capital (c) bad debts (d) dividend equalisation (e) expansion (f) taxation (g) debenture redemption (h) preference share redemption.

It is to be noted that after providing for above mentioned purposes, the surplus reserves are available for dividend distribution.

The Companies Act does not provide for payment of dividend out of capital profits; current profits are only available for dividend or accumulated profits may be utilised for dividend pay-out. In the absence of earned surplus, dividend payment is not permissible. Dividends are not permitted to be paid out of profits without providing for depreciation.

Expansion is life and contraction is death; for a company too, there is a constant endeavour to expand and this needs finance whether internal or external. Many companies follow orthodox dividend policy and provide for lateral ploughing back of profits into the business and these retained earnings are employed for further expansion and growth as a source of internal finance.

In the corporate management, it becomes a very essential and prudent policy for the financial management to ensure steady and stable dividend policy as it is quite natural for the stockholders of the company to be interested in the stable and good return on the share investment. Regularity of dividend depends upon stability of earnings, dividend equalisation reserves and adequate free reserves or accumulated profits. Days of prosperity for a company offer the management to lay aside funds to meet emergencies and needs during depressions.

Dividend policies have the effect of dividing the firm's after-tax profit into two categories — (a) funds to finance long-term growth and (b) funds to be distributed to shareholders.

Dividend policies, thus, affect both long-term financing and the return distributed to shareholders. Because of this, a firm may adopt two possible view-points on the decision to pay dividends; long-term financing decision and the decision to maximise wealth.

Long-term financing decision as the dividend policy views the firm's after-tax profits as a source of long-term financing. Since the declaration of cash dividends reduces funds of the firm and either restricts its growth or compels it to find out some other financing source, the firm might accept a guideline to **retain earnings** as long as either of two conditions exist — (a) sufficient profitable projects are available or (b) the capital structure needs equity funds. With either of these guidelines, cash dividends are viewed as a remainder. It is to be noted that dividends represent a distribution of earnings that cannot be profitably reinvested by the firm.

With the decision of maximising wealth, a firm recognises the influence of dividends on the market price of the common stock, higher dividends increasing stock-value and the lower dividends decreasing it. So, a firm declares sufficient dividends to fulfil the expectations of investors and shareholders. The maximisation of wealth decision generally predominates in the declaration of dividends. This approach is not accepted by all. Theoretical arguments have been developed that dividends do not affect the market price of common stock. Miller, Modigliani, Walter and few other authorities have their different views on the effect of dividend rate. So, we have no conclusive empirical evidence on whether a maximisation of wealth approach correctly deals with the dividend decision.

## Why do investors want dividends ?

Dividends are returns from the purchase of common stock. The returns may be either dividends or capital gains on the investments. But what is actually found is the preference of dividend over capital gains as return on investments. There are three major factors that account for such attitude of the investors, i.e. preference for dividends. The factors are — (a) reduction of uncertainty (b) indication of strength and (c) the need for current income.

As against capital gains, the preference for dividends can be explained thus —

(a) **Reduction of uncertainty** — Current earnings in the form of dividends are quite likely to attract the investors more than the delayed earnings in capital gains because that involves uncertainty. A current dividend represents a present-value cash inflow to the investors that cannot be lost if the firm eventually suffers any loss.

(b) **Indication of strength** — The implications in the declaration of dividends are that the firm is reasonably strong and healthy, the liquidity position of the firm is good and there is profitability of the firm. All these are aaluring for the investors.

(c) **Need for current income** —Dividend income enables investors to meet current living expenses. Investors, who are not willing to sell their shares but want to have liquid cash to tide over their current financial difficulties, are inclined to lend their support for dividends than for **capital gains.**

But dividend pay out does not always depend upon the sweet will of the management of a company. There are various **constraints** on paying dividends. We may discuss them as under—

(i) **Insufficient cash :** A firm may have sufficient income but not adequate cash to pay dividends. This is a situation which may arise for the firm's being tied up in receivables or inventory or commitments to fixed assets.

(ii) **Contractual restrictions :** In case of liquidity or profitability difficulties of a firm, it may agree as part of any contract with a creditor to restrict dividend payments. Generally, in such a case, the debt-equity ratio is agreed upon between the firm and the creditor. The firm is, thus, forced to retain earnings to increase equity and reduce the debt-equity ratio. The dividend payout may also be restricted to a certain per cent of earnings under a loan agreement. Thus, contractual restrictions may act as a restraining force to declare dividend at a higher rate.

(iii) **Legal restrictions :** The law of the land may require a firm to pay dividend from current or past income. In such countries, the firms must have sufficient retained earnings to declare dividends in the absence of which the firms are barred from declaring dividends in spite of the fact that there is enough cash available to release for dividends.

### Importance of Dividend stability

A stable dividend policy is considered by many corporate management as a right step towards consolidation of the financial position of the firms. A regular and steady declaration of dividends is a feature of the overwhelming majority of mature companies.

In defence of steady dividend pay-out, the following arguments are put forward —

**1. Perception of Stability**

A regular dividend payment creates an impression upon the investors that the company has been carrying on normal operations. A reduction in the rate of dividend immediately creates the reaction that the company is in trouble or is apprehending a future trouble. As a consequence, many investors start selling their shares and the market price of the stock comes down. So, a stable dividend policy is the way out.

**2. Preference of Investors**

There are typical shareholders who expect a steady flow of dividend and, as a matter of fact, they make commitments on the expectation of the receipt of dividend money if they do not receive which they get disappointed and go to the extent of disposing off their stock to reinvest in some other companies where a steady dividend is a greater certainty.

**3. Routinizing of Dividend Decisions**

To avoid discussions on dividend levels, a stable dividend policy is preferable. The matter of dividend payo become, a routine affair and does not entail much exercise on the part of directors. Of course, when circumstances demand a change in dividend policy, the matter must be taken up for discussion. So, a stable dividend policy helps the management in saving their valuable time to divert it to some other avenues for accomplishment of other goals of the company.

**4. Flexibility of the Extra Dividend**

A steady dividend policy enables the management to handle with flexibility a period of temporarily high earnings. An extra dividend may be declared for the quarter. Thus, a larger distribution of earnings becomes possible without raising the expectation of investors.

### How to develop dividend policies

The dividend decision is taken after taking into consideration a number of factors — internal and external, economic, social and political and also by making an assessment of the overall business environment prevailing in a country. The management generally has a number of choices before them and the financial management has to pick up the right choice to suggest the dividend policy to be declared by the Board of Directors finally.

We discuss below the several dividend policies and their suitability in different circumstances.

**1. Steady dividends at the existing level**

The decision to declare dividend at the rate as that of the previous year meets shareholders' expectations for current income and is not likely to affect market price. In case of mature firms with unused borrowing capacity, this dividend policy is suitable but otherwise this policy may result in shortages of funds when earnings have declined.

**2. Steady dividends at a lower level**

This situation arises when the firm has opportunities for investment elsewhere profitably; the funds are diverted there. The immediate effect of such a dividend policy (i.e. paying lower rate of dividend) is to alienate stockholders seeking current income. This may affect the market price of the stock. However, the management may announce that the new lower level of dividend will be maintained in the near future and there would be no further reduction of the rate. Stockholders' sentiment may also be spared from being hurt by assuring them that the low dividend would be compensated by higher dividend if the investment turns out to be profitable in near future.

**3. Steady dividends at a higher level**

This dividend policy is resorted to when the firm wants to raise the regular dividend. In the situation when the earnings of the firm have registered a stable rise and the firm does not need the excess earnings to finance growth, such a dividend policy is suitable to be adopted.

**4. Dividends fluctuating with earnings**

When a firm wants to retain funds to finance investments, the fluctuating dividend policy affords management maximum flexibility. This dividend policy fluctuating with the earnings of the firm has the disadvantage of uncertainty as a result of which the prices for the common stock of the firm become relatively low. The fluctuating dividend level reflects the fluctuating nature of the firm's earnings and this also has a dampening effect on the stock price. For all these reasons, such a dividend policy is not so desirable.

**5. Low regular dividends plus extra dividends**

For a firm with cyclical earnings and limited opportunities for growth such a dividend policy is suitable. An extra dividend may be declared in the year of good earnings and such an approach imports flexibility to a firm that might otherwise have excess funds on hand.

**6. No dividend or Dividend elimination policy**

Usually this is a policy of last resort. Such a policy is adopted either because of — (a) serious financial difficulties or (b) attractive investment opportunities. In case of serious financial difficulties, the firm is left with no other alternative but to stop payment of dividend. But, when a firm is altered by the investment opportunities for increasing its funds in future, it can appease its stockholders by properly propagating the future prospect of the company which will eventually reward the stockholders with alluring dividends.

# CHAPTER 25

## BREAK-EVEN ANALYSIS
## — A TOOL OF FINANCIAL ANALYSIS
### (Linear or straight line relationship)

The indispensability of feeding a company with finance is not a matter that needs some one to possess specialised knowledge to understand. But simply financing a business organisation does not ensure the maintenance of sound health for an organisation and the financial manager cannot rest satisfied till he feels that his company is financially managed in such a way that would hold out a promise for the viability of the organisation being based on the analysis of cost, volume and profit (Break-Even analysis).

Even in the changed concept of business, profit is the basic common feature of all business enterprises. The volume of profit and its utilisation have called for a change in the mental attitude of the entrepreneurs, but profit earning by a business organisation has not lost its relevance to any extent. The financial manager, therefore, is to devise ways and means to see that there is the continuous flow of the legitimate profit. This is essential for the survival of the organisation.

There are various tools for financial analysis that help financial management to arrive at sound decisions for the perfect financial health of the organisation.

A "Break-Even" analysis is one such tool which proves a very effective weapon in the armoury of financial management to combat any financial imprudence.

More output does not necessarily mean more profit; a harmonious relation beteween output and cost is essential for ensuring profit. This is Cost-Volume-Profit analysis or Break Even analyses or Profit-graphs.

The relationship of costs and revenues to output is a very important factor in the matter of profit. The general effect of the level of output upon income and expenses, i.e. upon profits, forms a serious concern for the financial manger. So, it is a must for any financial management to study the relationship of Cost, Volume and Profit (C-V-P).

A chart is prepared for such analysis and that chart is known as the 'Break-Even Chart.' They are also called Profit Graphs but the more popular and widely known term is Break Even Chart. (Of course, one should not think that this name implies that the objective of business is merely to break-even).

**A Break-Even Chart is, therefore, a widely known and well accepted tool for the analysis of relationship of costs and revenues to output.** The significance of the Break-Even Chart is that it helps in planning the financial structure of a compny. The financial manager while studying the breakeven analysis **is to consider "the level of the break-even point and the rapidity with which profits change in relation to output"** (S. C. Kuchhal)". The stage at which the total sales = total fixed cost + total variable cost, is called Break-Even Point. The Break-Even Chart shows this break-even point.

Let us have an example :

The fixed cost of a firm is Rs.50,000 and the variable cost is Rs.10 per production unit. The selling price is Rs.15 per unit. The Break-Even Chart will be drawn in the following manner :

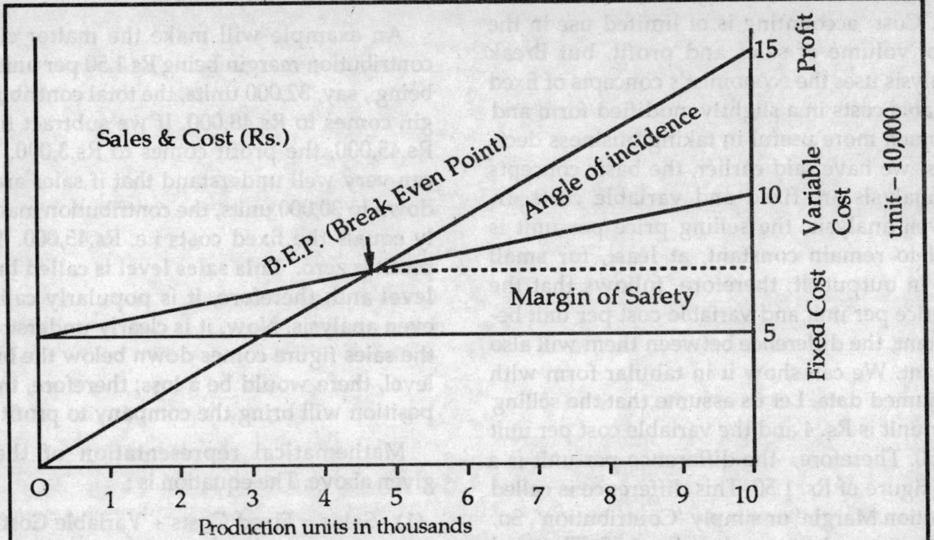


Here the Break-even point = $\frac{\text{Rs.}50{,}000}{\text{Rs. }(15-10)}$ = 10000 units

As we have already said, profit is still the most dominant driving force for any business, though social motive has been gaining predominance, but profitability deserves the primary consideration of any business organisation to exist, on which depends its responsibility-discharging capability to the society. For the financial management of any big corporation, the study of profit-trend is a continuous endeavour that can only act as a regulatory measure to avert crises of financial nature. The analysis of the relationship of costs, volume and selling prices reveals the profit-trend and the Break-Even analysis that depicts such relationship places in the hands of the management the tool that can allow reasonably accurate presentation of the effect a change in any one of the factors — costs, volume and selling prices — would have on the profit performance.

The Break-Even analysis helps the management to formulate plans. Whether the sales are to be increased, if so, which of the many products marketed should it be applied; whether increase in selling prices even though accompanied by a decrease in volume, would result in more profitable operations, whether efforts should be made to reduce costs instead of increasing volume or selling price as a step toward increased profits and if cost reduction is the answer whether pressure should be exerted to reduce variable or fixed costs, such questions and a host of other allied questions can be answered by preparing the Break-Even Chart.

The Break-Even analysis "furnishes complete picture of the profit structure which enables management to distinguish between the effect of sales volume fluctuations and the results of price or cost changes upon profits." (S.C. Kuchhel)

To permit a satisfactory level of profits, a certain level of sales volume has to be attained and, to attain that, costs have to be increased where complexities are involved. For profit forecasting, it is necessary to determine low costs change with output. This information can be presented in chart form by making distinctions between fixed and variable costs.

Fixed costs do not change with production; with the rise in output, the amount per unit declines. Variable costs, on the other hand, react proportionately with production changes. The amount per unit remains constant with output. The differentiation between fixed and variable costs is not so easy to make in many cases and the relationship between the two is also not clear-cut because of unusual circumstances.

In recent years, output and costs cannot be measured accurately during an established static period owing to technological changes and decisions are taken by executive fiat but satisfactory results may be obtained "through a statistical or engineering analysis."

It is not unlikely for us to think that traditional cost accounting can serve the purpose of Cost-Volume-Profit (C-V-P) analysis or Break-even analysis. Cost accounting is of limited use in the matter of volume of sales and profit, but Break even analysis uses the economist's concepts of fixed and variable costs in a slightly modified form and proves much more useful in taking business decisions. As we have said earlier, the basic concepts of this analysis are fixed and variable costs. In Break-even analysis, the selling price per unit is assumed to remain constant, at least, for small changes in output. It, therefore, follows that the selling price per unit and variable cost per unit being constant, the difference between them will also be constant. We can show it in tabular form with some assumed data. Let us assume that the selling price per unit is Rs. 4 and the variable cost per unit is Rs. 2.50. Therefore, the difference per unit is a constant figure of Rs. 1.50. This difference is called 'Contribution Margin' or simply 'Contribution'. So, contribution margin per unit is Rs. 1.50. The total contribution for 30,000 units is Rs. 45,000 and for 40,000 units is Rs. 60,000. This means contribution margin varies directly with sales.

| Sales (units) | 25,000 | 30,000 | 35,000 | 40,000 |
|---|---|---|---|---|
| Sales (Rs.) | 1,00,000 | 1,20,000 | 1,40,000 | 1,60,000 |
| *Less* : Variable cost | 62,500 | 75,000 | 87,500 | 1,00,000 |
| Contribution Margin | 37,500 | 45,000 | 52,500 | 60,000 |
| *Less* : Fixed Cost (assumed) | 45,000 | 45,000 | 45,000 | 45,000 |
| Profit/Loss | (–7,500) | — | (7,500) | (15,000) |

From the Table given, we get the Break-even point at 30,000 sales units where there is no gain no loss. Profit or loss is arrived at by subtracting fixed costs from contribution margin. It is to be noted that the fixed costs remain unchanged for all levels of sales and the entire increase in contribution margin with the change in sales volume is reflected in the profit figure. This explains why break-even analysis is a useful tool in the hands of the management in taking an administrative decision. The concept of 'contribution margin' emerging from the classification of costs as fixed and variable is the basis; since the contribution margin varies directly with sales. It is, therefore, possible to relate net profit to the level of sales.

An example will make the matter clear. With contribution margin being Rs.1.50 per unit and sales being , say, 32,000 units, the total contribution margin comes to Rs.48,000. If we subtract fixed costs Rs.45,000, the profit comes to Rs.3,000. Now, we can very well understand that if sales are brought down to 30,000 units, the contribution margin exactly equals the fixed costs i.e. Rs.45,000. Therefore, profit is zero. **This sales level is called break-even level** and, therefore, it is popularly called break-even analysis. Now, it is clearly understood that if the sales figure comes down below the break-even level, there would be a loss; therefore, the reverse position will bring the company to profit level.

Mathematical representation of the data is given above. The equation is :

(1) Sales = Fixed Costs + Variable Costs + Profit or adapted

(2) Sales – Variable Costs – Fixed Costs = Profit.

We can put it in the following manner :

$$S - V - F = P$$

Now, suppose n is the number of units sold; S is the selling price per unit and V is the variable cost per unit; we shall have —

$$Sn - Vn - F = P \text{ i.e. } (S - V)n - F = P$$

Since Break-even analysis (Cost-Volume-Profit) involves fixed costs, variable costs, sales, sales prices, sales-mix, **it is used as a technique for measuring the functional relationships existing among the major factors affecting profits. It also helps in determining the profit structure of a company.**

The segregation costs as fixed and variable works as the root of break-even analysis or cost-volume-profit (C–V–P) analysis. Profit forecasting and planning have been easier because of the knowledge of the break-even point and underlying functional relationships existing among costs, volume and profit. The prediction of profit at alternative sales volume is not at all difficult; so also the prediction of costs and revenues at alternative levels of output is made easier by break-even analysis. The effect of price changes on the total profits and cost changes on break-even point can easily be measured by break-even analysis.

**Nonlinear Break-Even Analysis**

Break-even analysis assumes that linear or straight line relationships exist for revenues and costs at different operating levels. But the fact is otherwise. Because in the most manufacturing and service organisations, costs rise rapidly at low levels of sales, then level-off in a range of efficient production and finally rise steeply as the firm nears full capacity. Revenues, likewise, may rise more quickly at low sales levels but then level, off as the firm offers price reductions to achieve high volume in certain markets.

**Nonlinear break-even diagram** (showing range of efficient production)

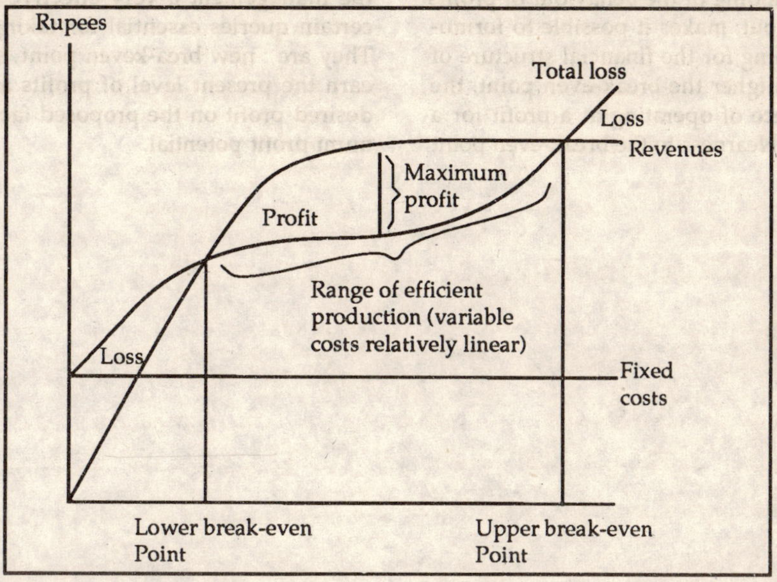


Thus, a solution to the problem can be devised through proper planning devices. The break-even analysis highlights marginal income and thus enables the management to avoid the controversial problems of locating fixed costs which remain unchanged irrespective of volume or price changes. In short-term planning, the break-even analysis "helps in determining the nature and magnitude of sales efforts and establishing volume requirements. Marginal income analysis, a by-product of break-even analysis, places emphasis on cost differentials and those, rather than total cost, are influential in deciding alternative course of action" (S. C. Kuchhal).

The diagram illustrates non — linear break-even relationships. Two break-even points are there — one point is designated for the maximum profit from operations. In linear break-even analysis, a single break-even point can be located and profits grow indefinitely once the break-even point is reached. With non-linear break-even analysis, the firm strives for an optimum output in a range of efficient production.

The non-linear analysis is theoretically superior but linear analysis is more commonly used in industrial settings. As the firms usually deal with decisions involving relatively constant unit variable costs, the linear analysis is more appropriate.

## Uses of break-even analysis

The break even analysis chart is very useful as it is very easy to understand. It is, therefore, a helpful mechanism to find out any problem connected with Cost-Volume-Profit relationships.

Following are the situations where the Break-even analysis can be conveniently used :

(1) Pricing decisions (2) Sales Mix (3) Make or Buy decisions (4) Production process decisions (5) Fi nancial structure planning (6) Sales promotion measure-taking decisions (7) Addition or deletion of product lines (8) Channels of distribution (9) Plant expansion (10) Testing the forecast.

We have seen that the management, by taking into consideration 'the contribution margin', is in a better position to arrive at the correct price decisions.

In case of production of more than one product, break-even analysis becomes complex. But, through the complex process of break-even analysis, the management may ultimately come to a decision without which the company might have to suffer. The analysis of the relative contributions of different products through the break-even device gives the management the correct direction to which product it should give more emphasis for sales.

In 'Make or Buy decision', break-even analysis becomes helpful. If the variable cost is less than the price to be paid to an outside supplier, it is better to make than to buy.

Break-even analysis, by helping management with the understanding of the behaviour of profits in relation to output, makes it possible to formulate correct planning for the financial structure of a company. The higher the break-even point, the lesser is the chance of operating at a profit for a number of years. Nearness to the break-even point stage of operation of a company is risky, because slight changes in the economic environment may, in such a case, result in losses.

The knowledge of profit structure through break-even analysis enables management to identify areas of cost increases and permits an evaluation of the forecast.

While taking a decision whether a plant is to be expanded or not, break-even analysis offers to the management a very effective tool to answer certain queries essential for taking the decision. They are : new brea-keven point, sales volume to earn the present level of profits and to earn the desired profit on the proposed facility and maximum profit potential.

# CHAPTER 26

## LEVERAGES FURTHER DISCUSSED

### Operating leverage

In the operation of a firm risks are involved which cannot be avoided. The overall business risk is inseparably related to its operating leverage which means the employment of an asset for which the firm pays a fixed cost. Operating leverage, is thus, likely to occur any time when a firm is to meet fixed costs, no matter what the volume is. In the very long run, all costs are variable, so we are concerned with short period analysis. Fixed costs are incurred on assets with the expectation of having revenues more than sufficient to cover all fixed and variable costs. Fixed costs do not vary as volume changes but variable costs directly vary with the level of output. With fixed costs, when both profits and volume change; the percentage change of profits is greater than the percentage change in volume and this is known as operating leverage. This leverage is one of the components of business risk of the firm; there are other factors responsible for business risks such as production costs, sales uncertainty or variability and operating leverage magnifies the impact of these factors on the variability of profits though it is not the source of the variability per se. Therefore, the degree of operating leverage does not represent the business risk of a firm "Because of the underlying variability of sales and costs, however, increases in operating leverage will increase the total variability of profits and hence, magnify the company's business risk" (J. C. Van Horne).

We can analyse operating leverage by studying the relationship between total costs and total revenues and one way to do that is to show it in the break-even chart. The chart will depict the relationship between profits, fixed costs, variable costs and volume, profits being operating profits before taxes. This does not include interest on debt and preferred stock dividends. In analysing operating leverage, these costs do not form part of the total fixed costs of the firm.

The break-even point is found out by the intersection of the total costs line with the total revenue line. The fixed costs that must be recovered from sales after the deduction of variable costs determine the volume necessary to break-even. At the break-even point, variable costs equal total revenue :

$$F + V(X) = P(X)$$

when F = fixed costs; V = variable costs per unit; X = Volume of output (in units) and P = price per unit.

For each additional increment of output above the break-even point there is increasing profit and when the output falls below the break-even point, there are increasing losses. The closer the volume to the break-even point, the greater the percentage change in profit in relation to a percentage change in output. The fixed costs equal variable costs at the break-even point. As total price less variable costs must equal fixed costs at the break-even point, so, too, do total variable costs.

The greater the ratio of price to variable costs per unit, the greater the absolute sensitivity of profits to volume and the greater the degree of operating leverage for all levels of output. A change in volume is not the only factor that affects projects, however, a change in selling price, in variable cost per unit or in fixed costs also affects profits.

**An increase in price lowers the break-even point; a decrease in fixed costs also lowers the break-even point and indeed that is the whole idea behind operating leverage.**

When conditions change unfavourably, i.e. a decrease in price, an increase in fixed costs and an increase in variable costs result in a higher break-even point and lower profits.

Thus, operating leverage magnifies the overall risk of the firm **but it is not the cause** of risk and increases in operating leverage increase the variability of profits.

**To sum up, operating leverage is the employment of an asset with a fixed cost in the hope that sufficient revenue will be generated to cover all fixed and variable costs.**

The use of a break-even graph for studying the operating leverage enables the financial management to analyse the relationship among profits, volume, fixed costs, variable costs and prices. These factors, if varied, the management may determine the sensitivity of profits and thus gets a better knowledge of the operating risk of the firm.

In the operating leverage, there are two approaches. In the first approach the degree of operating leverage can be measured at any level of output (the number of units sold). By the second approach, operating leverage can be determined in terms of total rupee sales by means of break-even or cost-volume-profit analysis.

Both these approaches are effectively one and the same. In the first approach Q × P (Q = number of units sold and P = selling price per unit) will give total sales and Q X V (V = variable cost per unit) will give total variable cost, i.e. the numerator will be (Sales-Variable Cost), i.e. Contribution. Similarly, the denominator will give (Contribution — Fixed cost) i.e. operating profit.

These concepts would be clear from the following illustration of the hypothetical company having :

| | | |
|---|---|---|
| Installed Capacity | ... | 2000 units |
| Capacity in operation | ... | 1600 units |
| Selling price per unit | ... | Rs. 10/- |
| Sales | ... | 1600 × 10 = 16000 (S) |
| Variable cost per unit | ... | Rs. 6/- |
| Total Variable Cost | ... | 1600 × 6 = 9600 (V) |

Contribution (S – V) ... Rs. 16000 – Rs. 9600 = Rs. 6,400

Percentage of contribution to Sales (C/S) ... 6400/16000 = .40

Fixed cost in varying situations —

(i) Rs. 600 (ii) Rs. 1500 and (iii) Rs. 1800

| | Situation (I) Rs. | Situation (II) Rs. | Situation (III) Rs. |
|---|---|---|---|
| 1. Sales | 16,000 | 16,000 | 16,000 |
| 2. Variable Cost | 9,600 | 9,600 | 9,600 |
| 3. Contribution | 6,400 | 6,400 | 6,400 |
| 4. Fixed Cost | 600 | 1,500 | 1,800 |
| 5. Operating profit | 5,800 | 4,900 | 4,600 |
| 6. Operating leverage $\left[\frac{C}{OP}\right]$ | 6,400 / 5,800 = 1.1X | 6,400 / 4,900 = 1.3 X | 6,400 / 4,600 = 1.4 X |
| 7. Break-even point $\left[\frac{F}{C/S} \text{ or } \frac{F}{.40}\right]$ | 1,500 | 3,750 | 4,500 |
| 8. Margin of Safety ratio (OP/C) | 5,800 / 6,400 = 90.5% | 4,900 / 6,400 = 76.5% | 4,600 / 6,400 = 72% |
| 9. Percentage of Sales for breakeven point (item No. 7 in relation to item No.1) | 9.5% | 24.5% | 28% |

A 10 per cent increase in the volume of sales will lead to an increase of 11 per cent in the operating profit in situation (I), 13 per cent in situation (II) and 14 per cent in situation (III). The operating leverages in all the situations are not varying much and as such a change in sales in any situation will not affect the operating profit much.

Operating leverage is a reciprocal of margin of safety ratio (Operating profit/Contribution). The margin of safety ratio in situation (I) is 90.5%, i.e. $\frac{5800}{6400}$. Under this situation the hypothetical company can afford to lose its sales up to this percentage before it reaches the break-even point. When the margin of safety ratio is less, the company will have less shock-absorbing capacity and if it is too low, the company will be in the red.

"High operating leverage, in other words, involves a very risky situation because the margin of safety is very low. On the contrary a low operating leverage gives enough cushion to the management by providing a high margin of safety against the fluctuation in sales. Break even point in a situation of high margin of safety is reached automatically at a low operational level" (S.C. Kuchhal).

### Financial Leverage

Financial leverage is nothing but capital gearing which stands for deciding the proportion which various kinds of securities should bear to total capitalisation. To secure capital most cheaply without sacrificing liquidity or solvency by adopting a judicious mix of debentures and preference shares with equity shares is the logic or rationale behind financial leverage. This is aimed at increasing and maximising income on the equity shares.

The financial leverage magnifies fluctuations in the earnings on the equity shares. By fluctuations in the earnings, we mean rise or fall in income and when magnified, there is the rapid rise or fall in income. The financial leverage brings about a compromise between liquidity and profitability functions of sound financial management.

**The financial leverage is said to be favourable** so long as marginal efficiency of capital is more than fixed liability on debentures or preference shares and there is an accelerated rate of dividends on equity shares.

When the earning of a company is much more than the rate of fixed dividends or the rate of fixed interest, the excess earnings go to the residual owners which make them earn a higher rate of return than they would have without the use of leverage.

**The leverage is said to be unfavourable** when the earnings of the owners of a company are less than the rate they pay on debentures or preference shares for securing finance from outside. In such a circumstance, the owners must make up the difference out of their share of earnings. This is a situation which enables owners to remain better-off with no leverage.

To sum up, financial leverage involves the use of funds for which the firm pays a fixed cost in the hope of increasing the return to its common stock holder. "Since increases in leverage also increase the risk of the earnings stream to common stockholder, however, we face the familiar trade off between risk and expected return. Higher expected return leads to higher stock prices, all other things being the same. Greater risk results in lower stock prices, again holding all else constant. With respect to financial leverage, the goal is to strike a happy balance between risk and expected return, maximising the market price of the firm's stock ".

— (*Van Horne*)

The degree of financial leverage at any level of operating profit is :

$$\frac{\text{Operating profit (OP or EBIT)}}{\text{EBIT – Interest (PBT)}}$$

when EBIT denotes Earnings before interest and tax and PBT denotes Profits before tax.

Financial leverage involves the use of funds at a fixed cost in the hope of increasing return to equity shareholders. Whether financial leverage is favourable or not (it is also called 'trading equity") is gudged in terms of the effect upon earnings per share to equity shareholder. The profitability of investment opportunities for which funds are used will determine whether the financial leverage is favourable or not. It will be considered favourable if the rate of return on the investment of these funds exceeds their explicit cost. This favourability consideration is in a narrow and restricted sense because no implied cost inherent in the use of debt financing is taken into account.

### Combined effect of operating and financial leverages

The operating and financial leverage combined measure their interaction on a firm. If we multiply operating and financial leverages, the degree of combined effect of these two leverages can be ascertained. A firm with a high operating leverage should not have a high financial leverage. On the other hand, a firm with a low operating leverage can fruitfully have a financial leverage, if the firm can profitably utilise its borrowed funds with ample opportunities.

"Operating and financial leverages constitute a double-edged sword. They have got tremendous acceleration or deceleration effect on EBIT and EPS (earning before interest and taxes and earnings per share). A right combination of these leverages poses a big challenge as well as an important opportunity for management" *(S.C.Kuchhal).* Leverage combination is a matter for the financial management demanding hig hdegree of prudence. The correct combination proves to be a blessing while an incorrect one may act as a curse for the organisation. Operating leverage acts as a check on financial beverage. Companies having a low operating leverage may find it advantageous to have a high dose of debt financing, but this does not prove convenient in companies which reach break-even point at a high level of their operational capacity.

Various combinations of operating and financial leverages are shown below with their effects :

| | Financial leverage | Operating leverage | Combined effect |
|---|---|---|---|
| 1. | Low | Low – | Loss of investment opportunities for expansion or diversification. This situation arises because of lack of debt financing. Low financial and operating leverages are the outcome of very cautious and conservative attitude of the management. This may lead to the loss of the opportunity for the owners to get maximum interest from their company. |
| 2. | High | High – | High leverages — both financial and operating — deserve serious consideration before their combination; since such a combination generally turns out to be risky. |
| 3. | High | Low | Low operating leverage ensures maximum profit and maximum risk when combined with high financial leverage. Because of low operating leverage, there is a built-in safety which encourages management to adopt an aggressive debt policy. |
| 4. | Low | High | Such a situation indicates that the management has taken into consideration the adverse effects of high operating leverage by adopting the policy of low financial leverage. |

**Financial management and leverages**

Leverages having direct impact upon the corporate profitability call upon the management to give serious consideration to this aspect of financial management. It is interesting to observe how the financial management is playing the game of leveraging.

It is a general tendency for the corporate management to take measures to increase return on equity investment for which they follow the policy of heavy reliance on debt, i.e. trading on their equity. The management of our traditional industries such as cotton, textile, jute and sugar corroborates this observation. The financial policy of these industries in regard to capital planning was under capitalisation. This policy of under capitalisation did not have any adverse effect so long as the market was a sellers' one. But high financial leverage policy, so long pursued, proved to be unsuitable and imprudent when the competition-market set about functioning. These big traditional companies of our country do not have only high financial leverage but also high operating leverage leading to the break-even point reaching at a very high degree of their operational capacity; thus bringing down the margin of safety to a very low point.

It is no denying the fact that stable and steady profit should deserve and actually deserves utmost consideration of the financial management. Keeping it in view, we can say that the management should endeavour to "reach break even point at a low level of the company's operational capacity though its actual operations should be far away from the break-even point. The vulnerability being very high near break-even point, a slight change in sales near break-even point results in a disproportionate change in the operating profit. This situation can be overcome considerably when actual operations are a long distance from the break even point. Suppose, the break-even point is at 80 per cent of the installed capacity of a firm, it has hardly any scope of maximising its profit as it has very little margin for increasing its production because of technical reasons; it cannot generally exceed 90 per cent or so of the installed capacity. However, if a big gap exists between the operational capacity and the installed capacity, in such cases only, there is the scope for improvement.

Both financial and operating leverages are tools of financial analysis in the hands of the financial managment but one thing should not escape our attention that the low operating leverage is actually the foundation on which stands the super-structure of financial leverage. High financial leverage brings about lop-sided capital structure if sufficient attention is not paid to operating leverage. When it is thus built-up the capital structure is characterised by high incidence of interest changes, low profits or losses and ultimately leads companies to premature end.

The management of leverages, therefore, is very much important for the financial management of a company. High or low leverages — financial and operating — are all influenced by the fiscal and environmental conditions prevailing in the economy of the country where the companies are functioning.

Corporate finance, for instance, in our country, had taken a new turn after independence. Business finance, so far as its procurement was concerned, was shy in the pre-independence days. With the attainment of independence, not only a number of financial institutions were brought into being by our government but also there came changes in the business environment and fiscal policies of the government.

In the changed financial environment characterised by easy borrowing facilities, willingness of public to release their savings to companies as deposits, the facility for bank loan — all these prompted companies to indulge in borrowing rather than procuring finance through the issue of equities. So, the financial management has changed their attitude in regard to finance-procurement. More and more reliance on debt came to dominate financial management with the debt-equity ratio rising. The facilities to borrow funds at lower than the real opportunity cost resulted in an increase of the ratio of debt to equity.

In their zeal to procure finance without allowing many more people to share in the enhanced prosperity of the company, corporate management ignore the need for analysing the operating leverage and go in for a heavy dose of debt. The prudent financial management does not permit such policy which is likely to act as a detriment to the healthy growth of the company. According to S. C. Kuchhal, "Debt is just like consumption of fat which is good for a healthy living for a healthy person. A person with high blood pressure and heart trouble has to regulate the intake of fat. Similarly there are many concerns which require an internal regulation in administering the dose of debt to themselves. Here availability of debt finance should not induce them to increase its proportion without considering their debt-absorbing and debt-repaying capacity."

# PART III

# PERSONNEL MANAGEMENT

*"Personnel Management is the planning, organising, directing and controlling of procurement, development, compensation, integration and maintenance of people for the purpose of contributing to organisation, individual and social goals".*

***(Flippo)***

# CHAPTER 1

## PERSONNEL MANAGEMENT

Personnel Management, as a distinct discipline of management, is of relatively recent origin. Being an important part of scientific management, Personnel Management has emerged in the latter part of this century. Stray attempts, however, were made earlier in the management world to look after the benefits of employees. But the essence of Personnel Management, as it means today, was lacking in all these attempts; workers were not being treated better than machines. A 'commodity approach' or, so to say, a 'factor of production' approach basically mechanical, was the concept of management, while dealing with personnel matters.

With the advent of the second half of the present century, a change of attitude towards workers was noticed. Labour as a factor of production was clearly distinguished; the feelings, sentiments, needs, desires, attitudes and interests of labour as human beings were recognised. Through decades, the management has realised that there is immense potentiality in labour and, if properly managed, they can work miracles. The spread of education among workers and consequently their acquisition of skill together with the growth of trade unions acted as forces for the management to change their attitude and thus came Personnel Management with a different outlook, with a heart compassionate and with the feelings, humane and sympathetic, for the employees. It had been a long experience for the management that to derive maximum from a worker, the maximum should be given to him. So, **Personnel Management, as it has developed today, is a pragmatic approach to management of employees : to get the best, give the best.**

The concepts of management in relation to 'the other fellow' have evolved and reached the present stage. Lawrence A. Appley, former President of the American Management Association, traced this evolution. From the feeling of savagery i.e., the other fellow is my enemy and to be destroyed, through the feelings of slavery (to be conquered), servitude (he is to serve me), welfare (to be helped), paternalism (to be looked after as a son), participation (he has to contribute), trusteeship (I am responsible for his benefit), the attitude towards fellow workers has now reached the concept of 'Statesmanship'. Management now thinks it its responsibility to help the fellow workers to develop themselves to their fullest potential. The evolution process, therefore, has been: Savagery → Slavery → Servitude → Welfare → Paternalism → Participation → Trusteeship → Statesmanship.

### Meaning of Personnel Management

Several terms are in current usage in this connection : manpower management, personnel management, labour management, employee relations and industrial relations. However, at present" industrial relations" or "employee relations" with the two major subdivisions "Personnel Management" and "labour relations" are being widely used.

Personnel Management, popularly speaking, is the task of managing the personnel of an organisation.

According to Thomas G. Spates, "Personnel administration is a code of the ways of organising and treating individuals at work, so that they will each get to greatest possible realisation of their intrinsic abilities, those attaining maximum effficiency for themselves and their group, and thereby giving to the enterprise, of which they are a part, its determining competition advantage and its optimum results."

The British Institute of Personnel Management recently has defined Personnel Management as "that part of management concerned with people at work and with their relationship within an enterprise. Its aim is to bring together and develop into an effective organisation the men and women who make up an enterprise and having regard for the well-being of the individual and of working groups to enable to make their best contribution of the success. Personnel Management is also concerned with the human and social implications of change in internal organisation and methods of working of economic and social changes in the community".

The society for Personnel Administration in U.S.A. defines: Personnel Management as the art of acquiring, developing and maintaining a competent work-force in such a manner as to accomplish with maximum efficiency and economy the functions and objectives of the organisation.

William Spriegel, along with some other authorities in the subject, defined Personnel Management as being concerned with the attaining of maximum individual development, desirable working relationship between employers and employees and employees and employees and an effective moulding of human resources as contrasted with physical resources.

From the definitions quoted above, we understand that Personnel Management aims at codifying the ways of organising employees to enable them to attain maximum efficiency and to yield maximum benefits to the organisation. It has human and social implications in so far as it is expected to bring about economic and social changes in the community. An ideal relationship between the working groups, between the employer and the employee, is an indispensable part of Personnel Management. So, Personnel Management is a concept illumined with the idea of the best labour capital relations; the management having a large fund of sympathy for the employees and the employees having a mind to give their best to the organisation. Through Personnel Management, the goals of an organisation can be achieved by improving efficiency of the employees and their productivity and also by developing their potentialities.

Personnel Management is, therefore, based on the careful handling of relationships among the individuals at work and consists in "maintaining these relations on a basis which enables all those engaged in the undertaking to make their best personal contribution to the effective working of the undertaking". (M. B. Formen – The Personnel Function of Management)

## Importance of Personnel Management

The importance of the human factor in production cannot be overemphasized. According to Peter F. Drucker : "The resources capable of enlargement can only be human resources. Man alone, of all the resources, can grow and develop, when we speak of growth and development we imply that the human being himself determines what he contributes". The physical factors of production, such as materials and machines, have their limitations : the output cannot exceed the materials used, the machine cannot exceed its capacity, but a man, with careful management, can be expected to work miracles. Here lies the importance and significance of Personnel Management. In industrial concerns, the importance of human factor is being recognised so much that good management has become synonymous with getting effective results with people. Drucker says that the function of management is to manage workers and work . (The practice of management)

Personnel Management touches all types of management; thus it constitutes the key to the managerial action and its success. In every area of management, there is the need for co-operation of workers. The bread-and-butter services of the personnel department, as referred to by Charles A. Myers; the observation on the personnel management as the nuts and bolts of an organisation and the comment of Peter Drucker that the job of a personnel officer is partly a file clerk's job, partly a house-keeping job, partly a social worker's job and partly a fire-fighting job – are all indicative of the significance of Personnel Management in the sphere of management.

On the willing and effective co-operation of workers depends the successful management of an organisation. Man, as a factor of production, has peculiarities unlike the physical factors, that he is subject to various feelings, emotions and desires and expectations. It is the Personnel Management which is to live up to these feelings and expectations of the workers and to deal with them in such a manner as to derive the maximum output from them. The management in the personnel department is to create the favourable psychological atmosphere where the workers will breathe freely as they expect. All these need an insight into the mind of the workers and, as such, Personnel Management can claim its special importance and significance.

As the days are passing on, the personnel aspect of management is attaining more and more importance. Not only because of the special nature of the human factor of production but also for the change in the management concept that the Personnel Management, today, has been playing a very vital and crucial role in all the areas of management. The consciousness of the workers as to their rights, has no doubt made the personnel department more alert but to make them understand their duties and the need for them to be more efficient, the Personnel Management of any organisation, in recent times, spares no pain.

To sum up, the Personnel Management mainly entrusted with the task of handling the unpredictable factor of production – the man – can claim to have superiority over all other management areas and, as a matter of fact, no department, no area of management, can function effectively without the active co-operation of and co-ordination with the Personnel Management.

In essence, Personnel Management is all - pervasive covering the entire gamut of management. With dynamism as one of its traits, it is continuous and is born with the organisation, moves on with the organisation and comes to an end when the organisation itself comes to an end.

# CHAPTER 2

## NATURE, AIMS AND OBJECTIVES OF PERSONNEL MANAGEMENT

**Nature :** Personnel Management deals with human beings and applies scientifically the procedures of employee selection, training, development and so on. Every man has his own way of behaving and it naturally needs careful and tactful handling to deal with them. So, it is an art to manage the human factor of production. After trials and errors, Personnel Management finds out the most suitable method of recruitment, and training of workers and placement of the right man for the right job. This calls for scientific approach of management. **Hence, Personnel Management is both an art and a science.**

Continuity, as a trait of Personnel Management, has been pointed out by George R. Terry. According to him, personnel department has to remain constantly alert and aware of human relations and their importance in everyday operation. "It cannot be turned on and off like water from a faucet". Even a day's respite in the work of the personnel department is not generally possible. So, there flows a continuity of work in personnel management.

Basically, personnel management is of staff nature. It helps line-management to detect and solve its problems. It is on the advice of personnel management that line executives take decisions. Personnel management also does line functions by directly undertaking tasks like recruitment, employee negotiation, collective bargaining etc.

In the management of an organisation, all departments and all the areas of management need the help of personnel department since every department has to deal with human beings and every area of management – production, marketing and financial – is to tackle problems connected with human resource. This is the pervasive nature of personnel management. The pervasiveness of personnel management is not continued to a particular type of organisation. No matter what the type of organisation is, persons must be there and, to deal with them, personnel department must be a necessity.

Personnel management has the attribute of dynamism. The functions of personnel department of an organisation – the development of human resources and the constructive use of manpower, the encouragement to the growth of informal organisation and the attempt to relate pay to performance – all these are clear indications of dynamism. In the dynamic world, it can be easily understood that to deal with immense potentialities of human resources, dynamism is a must. So, it is not only a feature of personnel management but a feature that imparts personnel management the credibility which matters much in the development and proper utilisation of the human factor in production.

### Aims and Objectives

Personnel Management has the ultimate object of the most effective use of the human factor of production. To achieve this objective, it has to create a very congenial environment in an organisation which enables the management to develop the human potentialities to their maximum level and thus attain the ultimate goal of the organisation.

The personnel department of an organisation continuously strives for ensuring maximum efficiency of the employees and administers justice to them by adopting various management techniques. To achieve its objectives, personnel management has to make a happy compromise between the interests of the employees and the organisation. Employee objectives of fair pay, job security, good working environment, physical safety and the organisation objectives of employee morale, team spirit, employee availability, employee loyalty, increasing output, low labour cost etc. are reconciled by personnel management through scientific management principles.

The aims and objectives of personnel management centre round the human factor – the best utilisation of human resources by their individual development and by creating the congenial atmosphere in the entire organisation for all the employees maintaining self-respecting relationship among themselves. To achieve this is not an easy task; the personnel management well-equipped with efficiency and sense of justice proceeds on with the following objectives in view :

1. Recruitment of right personnel. 2. Individual development through training. 3.Placement of right men in the right job. 4. Remuneration on just and rational basis. 5. Creation of congenial atmosphere for good inter-personal relations. 6. Provision for job satisfaction 7. Boosting up the morale of the employees. 8. Motivation. 9. Making the employees feel that they belong to the organisation. 10. Adoption of all the conceivable methods for the overall best personnel development to ensure maximum return from the employees. 11. Development of the spirit of utmost co-operation between labour and capital and between labour and labour.

To sum up, the aims and objectives of personnel management are directed towards the achievement of the optimum level of labour-capital relations as a means of deriving the best from labour with the object of ultimately reaching the goal of the organisation to the satisfaction of all – the labour, the organisation and the society.

# CHAPTER 3

## PERSONNEL MANAGEMENT — THE INDIAN SCENE

Personnel managers in India have come out with distinct entities in recent times. They echoed their superior top management personnel till recently; the policies, plans and programmes of the management – more in the capitalists' interests, would have been translated into action through the personnel management department. The whole concept of personnel management was based on the assumption that workers were unwilling to work and were devoid of any sense of responsibility. So, the top management used the personnel department as the tool to control and coerce the workers. It was the function of the personnel department to enforce the directives of the top management personnel in regard to employees. To watch whether all do's and dont's are being strictly followed by the working people was the function of the personnel manager. So his was police function but, with the enactment of various labour laws, the personnel manager became a law-man. Thanks to the growth of labour unions, that the personnel department of an organisation changed its servile attitude and became friend, philosopher and guide to the workers. The whole concept of personnel management took a turn with the adoption of various welfare measures incorporated in the labour legislations. But it is no denying the fact that at least a few entrepreneurs in India had, from the very beginning, hearts full of compassion for workers – the toiling people under them. The Indian scene, in general, was predominant with capitalists too unwilling to admit the contributions of labour as a factor of production. This attitude called for legislation to protect the legitimate rights and to recognise the contributions of workers in a productive organisation. Then came the Factories Act which conscripted a Welfare-Man into industry and put on the employer's pay roll.

The welfare officers have various responsibilities by statute and, by entrusting these responsibilities, the desired objectives have not been achieved. The personnel function being a line responsibility and a staff function, it cannot be performed by one man. So, truly speaking, the statutory provision has been a major handicap in the way of growth of the personnel function. It has been opined that "creating and spelling out a basic management function like the personnel function under a legal umbrella is patently inappropriate. Any man labelled and installed as a welfare or Personnel officer and tagged to the management would always work in a void and isolation".

In India, the recent trend has been the domination of the members of the family of the entrepreneur over the industrial concerns. Mostly these men are production-oriented and to them sound personnel management principles do not have much appeal. To this attitude of a few new business magnates in India have been added the industrial legislations which have resulted in a legalistic approach to personnel problems in our country. It is said that 'over the years, personnel executives have been spending a large percentage of their working time in conciliation and adjudication proceedings. The resulting decisions and awards satisfy neither the workmen nor the management."

In spite of all what have been said here, the personnel management functions have been facing new connotations. It is increasingly recognised by the businessmen in India that the personal aspect of production – the human resource – has immense potentialities and given proper care and due consideration, this resource can be utilised to its fullest extent. So personnel management, to-day in India, is not in a bad shape as it was a few decades back.

# CHAPTER 4

## BASIC FUNCTIONS OF PERSONNEL MANAGEMENT

The personnel department of a business organisation has to perform various functions, some of which are vital and basic for the organisation. The manning of the organisation in the most prudent way for the realisation of its goals is the essence of all the functions of personnel management. Right from man-power planning, recruitment and selection, personnel management moves on with the organisation with its functions and pursues an employee till his retirement and even still further to the point where he settles his retirement benefits or starts getting the retirement benefits. So, truly speaking, the personnel management is with an employee from his birth in the organisation till his death outside the organisation. We can quote here Edwin B. Flipps (Principles of Personnel Management P. 4, 1976) : "The personnel function is concerned with the procurement, development, compensation, integration and maintenance of the personnel of an organisation toward the accomplishment of that organisation's major goals or policies." Our National Institute of Personnel Management also indicated the personnel functions more or less on this line. Employment, Education & Training, Wages, Joint consultation, Health and safety and Employee services and Welfare – all have been considered as functions of personnel management by the National Institute of Personnel Management.

The activities of the personnel department, so to say, are spread over three areas – Recruitment, Retainment and Retirement. To these 3R's of activities, various subsidiary functions crop up and upon the successful management of all these functions depends the attainment of the goals of an organisation.

The functions of the personnel department may be classified as (a) Staff functions (b) Service functions (c) Functional activities and (d) Welfare activities.

To highlight the problems of the human resource by disseminating information to the line authorities constitutes the basic function of the personnel department. This department, as a matter of fact, acts as liaison between the workers and management. The personnel manager has to endeavour to create an atmosphere where free exchange of ideas and information between the workers and the management is possible. Through the personnel department, the top management of the organisation will keep contact even with the common workers. This department will carry on its activities to facilitate easy communication from the top to the bottom; there will not be any difficulty, because of this department, in the matter of expressing the views and feelings of the workers to the top management personnel – the line staff. Thus, the personnel department of the personnel management will discharge its **staff functions.**

As to its **service functions,** the personnel department explores the sources of recruitment, selects the best candidates and makes arrangements for their training. Merit rating, devising, suitable and satisfactory method of promotion, and maintaining of workers' discipline come within the purview of the personnel department of an organisation. It is also not a mean function of the personnel department to find out mutually satisfactory methods of wage payments with incentive elements to ensure better labour-capital relation and higher productivity. To provide for various retirement benefits and recreational facilities for the employees, at present have become very important function of the department.

To ensure better service of the organisation, the personnel department is to maintain proper records relating to employees and these activities can better be termed **functional activities** of the personnel department.

The **welfare activities** meant for the benefit of the employees such as provision for first aid, general medical services, devices for minimisation of the risks of accidents are becoming more and more important in the Welfare State.

# CHAPTER 5

## MANPOWER PLANNING — ITS NATURE AND IMPORTANCE

Manpower planning, which is a staffing function of the personnel department of an organisation, means the process of determining manpower requirements and how to meet the requirement. The significance of manpower planning cannot be over-emphasised. The development of human resources of an organisation is the aim of manpower planning and this planning concentrates on the correct estimation of future requirments of manpower in an organisation. The plans to fill up the vacancies of manpower requirements in the most suitable manner come within the purview of manpower planning.

**Manpower planning has been defined as the process of determining manpower requirements of an organisation through forecasting, developing and controlling to ensure that it has the right number of people and the right kind of people at the right places, at the right time doing work for which they are economically most useful.**

### Nature

If we analyse the definitions of some eminent authors on Management, we find that their definitions though not identical, bring out certain common characteristics of manpower planning. This is **dynamic** in nature. It provides for new factors which modify the manpower flows. Being based on long-term estimates, manpower planning is **forward-looking and future-oriented.** It is a **process** – process of determining manpower; process of forecasting, developing and controlling of manpower and the process of "determining how an organisation should form its current manpower position to its desired manpower position". Its **process is scientific,** based on facts and rational calculation.

Manpower plannning is mainly a **staff function;** it advises the line executives on the best utilisation of manpower. With 'Emphasis on the interrelationships among various personnel policies and programmes', manpower planning represents a **systems approach.**

### Importance

Manpower planning is, truly speaking, **the foundation of Personnel Management.** Various actions of this area of management are carried on in accordance with the programmes and policies of manpower planning. Manpower planning – a mental exercise – precedes the actions to be undertaken by the personnel department.

The need and importance of manpower planning arises from the fact that in an organisation, problems with the employees are many and unless they are taken up at the right time with the right knowledge of their solution, subsequently the problems may prove difficult to be solved. This necessitates in keeping the manpower-planning process always active. The most important factor in production – the human resource – is the matter of management for the personnel department and manpower-planning is its first step. In an organisation, man as a factor of production is not only very important and potential but also very difficult to handle. The quantitative and qualitative aspects of the human resource need to be carefully assessed and this is done through manpower-planning. Because of the growing complexities in the business world, the importance of manpower-planning is also increasing more and more. It goes a long way for an organisation to solve many of its problems if at the outset there is good manpower planning.

The functions of manpower-planning encompass such activities that have a far-reaching effect on the organisation. The importance of planning for manpower – i.e. to ascertain the need for personnel in future, does not need any elucidation. However mechanised an organisation may be, man in the organisation still commands the top priority for consideration. Unless there is proper manning of the organisation, the whole management exercise becomes futile.

Manpower-planning is a continuous process of work needed by the continuous change in the labour force of an organisation. For various reasons, there is a constant change in the quality and quantity of labour force (retirement, resignation, transfer etc.). There is an average annual turnover of employees which has to be taken into consideration by manpower-planning. This emphasises the significance and importance of this planning.

Manpower facilitates the expansion and modernisation by helping recruitment of skilled personnel. The lead time that an organisation needs for recruitment and selection of personnel is provided by manpower-planning of the personnel department. This is of no mean importance.

Manpower-planning has many other activities that help the organisation to function efficiently. It is this planning that makes the training of manpower more pinpointed, and thus helps executive development. By identifying areas of surplus or shortage of personnel, the manpower-planning of the personnel department saves labour-cost and assists productivity bargaining.

In an organisation where manpower-planning is effective, it has a very encouraging effect on the morale of the employees, since they understand that their management is proceeding on scientific lines.

Not to the organisation alone, but to the entire nation, manpower-planning has significance. This planning in an organisation on scientific basis provides tools to the Government of a country to use them in the formulation of economic planning. In various spheres of Government activities, manpower planning device of the personnel management has much to contribute because the correct assessment of the potentialities of working force and their other information, helps the Government in planning reforms on various spheres of its activities. For example, the employment potential of the country can be understood from the manpower-planning of different organisations.

So, to sum up, manpower-planning is important because it deals with the most complicated and unpredictable factor of production. Since this factor is of immense potentialities, it needs a careful, efficient and prudent management which manpower-planning initiates. In the unit level of an organisation, the planning of its manpower confers benefits undoubtedly but the benefits of manpower- planning have a macro aspect – the benefits go beyond the unit and help the nation in the better management of its human resources.

### Factors, steps and objectives (Manpower-planning process)

In manpower-planning, certain factors are taken into consideration and certain steps are taken to achieve certain objectives.

**Factors** that influence the management personnel in manpower-planning are – the structure of the organisation and the changes that have taken place, the conditions of the labour market and the trend of retirement, the trend in trade union movement, the technological changes calling for changed labour pattern and also changes in the job content.

With these factors under consideration, the manpower-planning proceeds following certain calculated **steps** —

(a) it analyses the plan for future expansion

(b) it estimates the quantitative and the qualitative aspects of labour

(c) it assesses the existing manpower position

(d) it formulates the plan for the best utilisation of the men of the organisation and

(e) it finalises the planning of recruitment, selection, promotion, transfer, training and development of the individual employee.

So far as the **objectives** of manpower-planning are concerned, we can say that with the ultimate object of securing the maximum utilisation of manpower, the planning promotes the development of existing personnel. The need for manpower in the future having been carefully assessed, the manpower-planning continues to achieve its objctives through ways and means necessary to meet these requirements by providing control measures.

The objectives of manpower-planning are, in a nut-shell, the equipment of the organisation with right persons in right quantity at the right time.

Before we conclude, let us reaffirm that manpower-planning precedes all other planning in the personnel department of an organisation. Through short-term and long-term planning, it maintains its process of work. Various steps are taken successively for the individual and collective development of manpower with a view to achieving the desired objectives of the organisation for higher production and higher productivity.

# CHAPTER 6

## RECRUITMENT, SELECTION AND PLACEMENT

### Recruitment

Manpower-planning determines the quantitative requirements of man and then starts the next step – recruitment. To recruit is to discover the sources of personnel and to encourage the candidates to apply for employment.

Recruitment as a step of manpower learning in personnel management is very important. On this depends, to a very great extent, the success of the organisation. To recruit the right personnel in right number at the right time, matters much in the future course of action and in the realisation of the organisation objectives.

The process of recruitment is not the same in all cases and in all the organisations. It may be simple or complicated, economical or expensive. All depend on the need and size of the organisation. In a small organisation, the matter of recruitment, naturally, is simple and not so expensive while in a big organisation, the recruitment is more or less an uphill task involving complications and huge expense. To meet the need for personnel of an organisation, either it is necessary to recruit new personnel from outside or to promote the existing employees from within, if the conditions so justify.

Recruitment is, therefore, an activity involving promotions from within as well as advertising, placing order with employment officers and visiting known sources in search of prospective employees and stimulating them to apply for jobs.

### Recruitment from within

Internal recruitment or recruitment from the organisation itself is a widely accepted policy of many organisations. The vacancy, if any, is filled up with a person already in the organisation. Specially senior positions are filled in this way and the Government usually follows this policy. This is recruitment through promotion where the seniority in service is considered.

Recruitment from within the organisation is done mainly with a view to making the employees feel that they have prospects in their organisation if they continue with their service. Internal recruitment on some accepted principle, agreed to by both the employees and the employer, relieves the management of the somewhat more long drawn process of recruitment from outside. Again, in an organisation where specialisation is a matter to consider, internal recruitment is more advantageous. But as the managers are becoming more professional, the policy of recruitment from within does not become effective. Men in the senior positions very often change organisations but men of the lower management level and other ministerial employees prefer internal recruitment and actually they demand it. From the viewpoint of the organisation, the policy of internal recruitment imparts stability to the policies and programmes of the organisation. Men already conversant with the procedure of work in the organisation, naturally, are expected to put in better service and also this policy helps bringing in the sense of belonging for the organisation among the employees.

### Recruitment from outside

Recruitment from within may not be possible or desirable or suitable for various reasons; in that case, recruitment from outside will have to be resorted to. And, as a matter of fact, because of technological and other developments and changes in the business, the companies are to recruit personnel from outside to suit the needs of the organisation. The particular right type of technical personnel may not be available within the organisation – so the search outside. The external services may be direct as well as indirect. The direct sources are – recruitment at the factory gates, recruitment on the basis of the recommendations of the existing employees, advertising in the news dailies or in relevant periodicals, journals or magazines etc. Recruitment from the colleges or universities directly also takes place; this is campus recruitment. The indirect sources include recruitment through employment exchanges, private employment agencies and contractors like jobbers, labour unions etc.

The different sources of external recruitment are explored under different circumstances to suit the needs of the organisation in the most convenient way.

We discuss certain sources of external recruitment :

**(a) Recruitment at the factory gate**

This method of recruitment is applied for filling in the vacancies of unskilled workers. From the large number of unskilled men at the gate, the requisite number on some criteria are recruited. The factory foreman or the departmental manager makes the recruitment. The need for casual workers is usually fulfilled in this manner. In our country, where a large number of people are always in search of job of any kind, this method of recruitment helps them very much and the employer also finds it suitable to recruit persons as and when he likes.

**(b) Recruitment on the basis of recommendations**

The existing employees recommend persons for employment in their organisation. This is not unusual. This has the double effect of (i) making the employees feel that the organisation belongs to them and (ii) the appointment of right person for the right job, as the existing employee who recommends knows which work will suit his man best. The policy of recruiting sons, brothers or family members of an employee is still followed in some organisation but the policy is now mostly discarded, particularly in Government offices, owing to popular agitations against such policy. Recruitment through recommendations or recruitment from the same family sometimes cause problems to the management in the form of cliques and the union circles among the close acquaintances.

**(c) Recruitment from college or university campus:**

Technical and administrative personnel are sometimes recruited from the college or the university campus. Circulars through the institution authorities are given and applications are invited. Interview is taken at the campus by a representative of the organisation intending to recruit. Selection is also made on the spot subject to their getting through the examination. This method saves time required for long drawn process of recruitment and it also has a very good effect in a country like ours where many educated young people are seeking employment. Recruitment at the campus at the technical institutions of our country is a very common method of recruitment of engineers.

**(d) Recruitment through advertisement**

This is the commonest method followed in external recruitment. Through advertisements in the dailies or in special journals, recruitments are made. Vacancies are advertised, applications are invited within a specified date, interviews are taken and appointments are made. No doubt it involves much time and wastage of money and labour. Still then this is a very common way of recruitment for commercial firms. Governments, however, are mostly to recruit through employment exchanges in our country at present to fill in general vacancies.

**(e) Recruitment through employment exchanges**

The Government has made it obligatory to recruit through employment exchanges in the Government offices. Today, employment exchanges in our country have become the main indirect source for recruitment. Employee-seekers and job-seekers get their needs registered at the employment exchanges and the exchanges act as middlemen or liaison in bringing the job-seekers to the employee-seekers. This has been done with a view to bringing some amount of equity and notice in the matter of employment. Of course, employment through employment exchanges is done for the ministerial and other lower grade staff. Management personnel or higher officials are not appointed/recruited through employment exchanges. Again, commercial firms are not to recruit through employment exchanges. So, employment exchanges have limited area of the recruitment world, still in our country today, they have been assigned to play a very important role so far as appointments to Government offices are concerned.

**(f) Recruitment through contractors or jobbers**

This is a method of external recruitment adopted in the case of factory workers. The contractors are ready with workers whom they can place at the disposal of the factory owner whenever he wants. In lieu of the service, the contractors charge commission. Jobbers are also very important persons in this area and they combine in themselves a formidable array of functions. They bring workers from villages with the promise of better wages, better amenities, comfortable employment etc. and the workers generally look to them for the protection of their rights. They put their grievances before them who try to remove them. In India, a jobber is known as Sardar, Mistry, Chowdhury, Tindal, Mukaddam, Kangany etc. His position is very important so far as workers are concerned. He actually controls them and the factory-owner has to depend on him for their performance and for better relation with them. In India, there are places where the jobbers are responsible for appointment, promotion, dismissal, leave etc. of the workers.

## Selection

Selection means choosing the best one from a number of candidates. This involves a process where there is an element of prediction. Proper selection of personnel is very important because unqualified personnel may otherwise be appointed who may prove to be 'misfit' for the jobs. In that case, it will have repercussions both on the employer and the employees. The employees will feel dissatisfied, there will be no job satisfaction, labour productivity will be very much affected; on the other hand, the employer too will suffer because of inefficiency of the workers. This is a situation that leads to higher turnover of labour which is not desirable.

Selection is a process. In this process, the interested candidates are screened out and those found qualified for the job are selected.

The process of selection turns out to be negative in the sense that more candidates are rejected than appointed. This happens because the short-comings of a candidate become more pronounced to a selector than the qualities of the candidate. In most cases, the selectors have to depend upon the subjective standards and that gives them wide discretion in selecting a candidate.

Selection is a crucial matter since it involves money to be spent for the indication and training of the candidates selected. A bad selection creates problem for the management while a good selection solves problems.

So, a manager has to be alert while selecting a candidate. It needs experience and a strong common sense to judge a person. The inability of a manager to select the right person will make his efforts and investments go waste.

## Selection procedure

There are specific steps in the selection procedure. They are : (a) Receiving and screening the application (b) Sending the application blanks (c) Testing (d) Interviewing (e) Checking references and letters of recommendation (f) Medical examination and (g) Placement.

**(a) Receiving and screening the application**

This is the first step in the selection procedure. The personnel department requisitions the number of vacancies in each department and thereafter invites applications from the candidates. The invitation may be through advertisements in the newspaper, notification at the factory gates, recommendations from existing employees and employment exchanges. Applications are properly screened and the application of the candidates not suitable for recruitment are rejected.

**(b) Sending the applications blanks**

In the second step, the list of suitable candidates is made ready and the application blanks are sent to the applicants whose names are there in the list. The form of such application blanks differs according to the nature of the job and specification required for it. The object of the form is to elicit information about the candidates and to serve that purpose in a fruitful manner the form should be printed. So, there cannot be any standard form. Slight deviation of this procedure is noticed in some firms where candidates are called for interview and before the actual interview, a form is distributed to be filled in by the candidate present. While interviewing the candidates, the interviewers give stress on the information given in the form and select the candidates on the strength of these information as well as on the performance at the interview. The application blanks may, therefore, serve as an effective preliminary screening device.

**(c) Testing**

Another step involved in the process of selection is 'testing' the candidate. That human behaviour can best be forecast by sampling it, so there is the need for testing because it creates a situation in which the applicant reacts and reactions are regarded as useful samples of his behaviour. There are different types of tests – Achievement test, Trade test, Intelligence test, Interest test, Personality test, Aptitude test etc. **Achievement test** is helpful in measuring the level of knowledge of the recruits. This is a test to know the standing of the candidate in his school, college and university. A candidate's educational background has much to do in his employment in responsible position. **Trade test** is necessary for recruitment to technical posts or posts where special knowledge is required, for example, in the case of recruitment of a typist, his typing acumen should be tested and this is trade test. In specialised jobs, therefore, it is essential that such a test is held. **Intelligence test** is aimed at the assessment of mental alertness, level of intelligence, adaptability etc. of candidates. **Interest test** is undertaken to ascertain the particular line in which the candidate has special interest or it is seen whether the candidate has interest in the matter which he will be required to handle. **Personality test** is meant for ascertaining the dominant qualities of the applicant as a whole – the combination of aptitudes, interests, temperament etc. This test helps in judging the emotional as well as physical balance in the applicant. Such an assessment, however, is subjective, complex as well as difficult. **Aptitude test** is to explore inborn tendencies. It implies determining the potential ability and capacity of the applicants.

Besides the tests mentioned above, some organisations have their own **"tailor-made"** tests to suit their individual requirements. This is suitable when a large number of new employees have to be recruited for a single job. These tests go through seven steps. Some organisations use tests which are **standardised.**

**(d) Interviewing**

Selection through personal interview is still regarded as the best device. A personal interview enables the interviewer to assess the physical as well as the mental alertness of the candidate. Interviewing, through interactions between the interviewer and the interviewee, makes it possible to know the overall personality of the candidate for the recruitment of personnel in the supervisory position, generally a board or panel is formed; a group of experts examine the candidate. Interviews are of many kinds – formal, patterned, non-directive, depth stress and group interviews, whatever be the kind, interview is the most suitable device to select the right personnel for an organisation.

While discussing interviewing as a step in the process of selection, we should not overlook the **Character analysis** method of selection. Evaluation of a candidate on the basis of his external features is character analysis. This is undoubtedly unreliable but consciously or unconsciously the interviewers are practising it. "The most persistent form of character analysis, however, involves the inference of a wide range of personal traits from physical features". The graphology or the interpretation of handwriting is still depended upon as a measure of evaluation of one's quality. Similarly, phrenology or inference from the shape of a person's skull is also resorted to. This sort of interviewing through character analysis should be discarded because human character and personality are too complex to be judged simply by external features.

**(e) Checking reference and letters of recommendation**

References and letters of recommendation are also used as a selection tool of candidates. But referees usually do not mention any drawback in their comments about a candidate nor does any letter of recommendation give unbiased judgement about a candidate. So, as a matter of fact, it is only to know the qualities of the candidate that reference is made or the letter of recommendation is wanted.

**(f) Medical examination**

Physical or medical examination is the penultimate step in the selection process. Medical check-up is undertaken and if the report goes in favour of the candidate, he is appointed. The physical and medical examinations are necessary but it is to be kept in mind that a candidate found otherwise suitable is not appointed because of adverse medical report. In that case, he should be given a job suitable to his health and physical capabilities.

### Placement

Placement is 'the assignment of employees to jobs for which they appear qualified on the basis of the selection techniques' (F. A. Draw). But before placement, employees are inducted i.e. introduced and oriented to the firm, their departments and their jobs. Simply stated, employees are given the opportunity to know their firm – its policies, procedures, organisation and the like and also their immediate superiors and colleagues.

After induction comes placement, i.e. putting the right man to the right job. Placement generally does not raise any problem for a single employee but when a group of persons are meant for a number of vacancies, the problems as to which job will suit whom arises. It needs experience on the part of the management to resolve their problem of placement.

Placement is not a short-term process only. The question of placement rises even after years of recruitment when there is any promotion or transfer. So, placement is both a short-term and long-term process. Proper placement of an employee has much bearing on the efficient working of an organisation. An employee, not temperamentally adapted to the job, cannot be expected to give the best in him. Here lies the importance of placement. An employee who finds comfort in the job in which he is employed, i.e. where he finds job satisfaction, can be said to have been rightly placed.

### Training of personnel

Training is to educate mainly by instruction, drill and discipline with a view to increasing the knowledge of the employee, so that he can develop further the abilities and potentials that are already in him. Training, today, involves both training and development.

The need for training arises to show the new employees how to do their jobs, how to make-up their deficiencies and how to develop the potentialities in them.

To make a training programme effective, certain **principles** should be adhered to. Every individual differs from another in his abilities and powers of assimiliation. So, specific needs of individuals **should be assessed.** The principles of **practical training** and motivation should be incorporated in the training programme. Trainees given opportunity for implementing their theoretical training in practice become more effficient. **Motivation** as a principle of training is needed to make the trainees more effective in their performance. For the better learning of trainees, their correct responses should be reinforced by promotions, pay increases and formal appreciation. **Reinforcement,** as a matter of principle is, therefore, accepted in training programme. It is expected that an employee should have proper mental and intellectual upliftment which is not possible without education. So, **education** is also combined with all other principles of training. Practical demonstration in training is generally preceded by theoretical briefing.

### Training methods (types)

There are various methods of training but the methods can be divided broadly into two groups. The first group (subject-matter view-point) consists of induction training, job training and promotional training. The second group (sources of training view-point) consists of on-the-job training, vestibule training, apprentice training and external or internship training.

1. **Induction training**

Induction is initial training or orientation of the employees. This training makes them familiar with the organisation and its policies. "To relate the work of the recruit to that of the total organisation" and to introduce him to his fellow workers, induction is necessary. All details of the work he will have to perform and also all details of the organisation are brought within his knowledge through induction. Service condition, various amenities available, hours of work, goods produced, techniques of productions and quality of the products – all these are made known to the new recruit during induction period. So, induction training enables a new entrant to know the background, present position of his organisation and it also creates in him interest in the organisation and fosters homely feeling through fellowship with other employees.

2. **Job training**

This training is imparted with a view to enhancing the knowledge about the job to which an employee is attached. This involves training in each process and technique of production, handling of machines and equipments, best possible use of materials eliminating wastes. Job training also covers training which enables a worker to avoid accidents and to remove bottleneck. A comprehensive job training aimed at familiarising the worker with all aspects of his job makes him efficient and improves his skill for performing the job.

**3. Promotional training**

When employees are promoted from within the organisation they need training to shoulder responsibilities of higher position. This is promotional training and many organisations provide for this training so that the promotees do not feel any difficulty in handling matters in the new positions.

**4. On-the-job training**

As the name suggests, the training is on the job itself. A new employee is put on a machine or a specific job under the guidance of a supervisor or instructor. This method of training is common for all new employees. An experienced worker works along with the new entrant and he explains to him the nature of work, the use and handling of machines and tools and how they are to be operated. The worker is expected to learn the whole process himself. This training method is not expensive and does not involve any separate or elaborate arrangement for the training of new employees. However, this method has some limitations : (a) longer time is needed for learning the whole process (b) fellow workers may not feel enthusiastic to train the new colleague (c) expert training may not be available because of the defective knowledge of the fellow workers who train the new one (d) there may be interference with the process of work and may cause a loss of time on the part of supervisors and other colleagues.

**5. Vestibule training**

Under this method, the new employee is trained in a separate training-centre within the plant itself. This type of training has been introduced with the object of avoiding the inconvenience of on-the-job training. An experienced job instructor imparts training. A natural working atmosphere is created as it prevails in the workshop where production is being carried on. Thus, the new employee is trained to learn the whole process. He thus overcomes the initial nervousness that overtakes him when he is put to learn on the job itself. Regular production of the workshops, in their method of training, is not interfered with. Emphasis is given more on instruction than work. The limitation of the training is that it is costlier.

[The word 'vestibule' refers to an entry cubicle through which one passes into rooms or an entry hall leading to a building.]

**6. Apprentice training**

This is the oldest form of training where it is intended to impart sufficient knowledge and skill of a craft to a young person with some technical background and taken as an apprentice. This enables the trainee to gain complete proficiency in the craft. Under this method, the trainees are required to gain not only actual work experience in the actual job but also to attend classroom lectures to have theoretical knowledge. Schools are set up for such training by some organisations. As a condition for employment, training is given under an agreement between the trainee and the prospective employer and the apprentices are paid some remuneration during the apprentice period. In our country, in certain specified industries, apprenticeship training has been made compulsory under the statute. The period of apprenticeship generally varies between two and three years.

This method of training combines practical experience with theoretical lessons. After a considerably long period of training, the new incumbents find it easy to adjust themselves with their work environment, nor do they feel shy in their work. A sense of loyalty is developed during the period of training and also a rapport is established between the Government and indirectly through the schemes of apprentice training as these are sponsored by Government mostly. Time factors of this method cannot be ignored. Compulsory apprenticeship schemes put additional burden on the industry so far as cost is concerned. In practice, it is found that even after training, in many cases, in the absence of agreement, trainees are not absorbed in permanent employment and sometimes it so happens that the trainee himself leaves the organisation and the training cost cannot be recovered. However, as a method of training, this method, in spite of some limitations, will continue to stay as the oldest method.

**7. External or internal training**

Mostly confined to skilled and technical personnel, this type of training is imparted in vocational schools and technical institutions. These institutions train candidates sent to them by individual enterprises. Broad-based training is given to the candidates through classroom lectures with practical class illustrations. But still they do not gain practical knowledge and experience for which they are ultimately sent to some business enterprise to gain actual work experience. To bring about a balance between theory and practice, this internship training has been introduced.

Besides the above methods of training, we find today a method of training – co-operative in nature. This training is imparted in schools, colleges and trade schools. Such a **Co-operative training** envisages that a student will spend part of his time in a practical job experience and part of his time as a student in school. His job experience is related to his academic work in the classroom. This scheme has been undertaken with the object of helping a young man to gather some experience while taking his usual academic qualification and thus he is getting a more acceptable bio-data for his employment in future. The significance of such a training scheme in a country like ours – where employment situation is very critical – cannot be over-emphasised. Special beneficiaries of such co-operative training are the co-operative companies.

**Special Course** training is provided to those who have already been trained on the job or by the vestibule method. They are deputed to outside institutions for attending special courses to improve their skill. For instance, an accounts clerk is sent to learn book-keeping. Such training obviously equips an employee with better knowledge though cost factor cannot be overlooked.

Other methods of training are : Refresher training, Learner training and supervisory training which do not need any elucidation.

## Importance and benefits of training

The discussion of different methods of training makes one convinced that training, properly imparted, can go a long way in raising the productivity of the workers. Training is for betterment; it makes a new worker good, a good worker better and a better worker best. Though limitations are there with every method of training, we can say that training, in general, is of much significance and it leads to an overall development of an organisation through individual development.

Importance of training lies in its effects on the individual as well as on the organisation as a whole.

Training **increases productivity** of labour as a consequence of which **production increases;** the firm is benefitted. Because of training, the **need for supervision is reduced.** A trained employee puts in better output; performance is well improved and the trained workers with skill in their work are in a better position to **boost up morale.**

Training gives an organisation an army of personnel who are capable of handling organisation problems with more efficiency. So, it is training that lends stability and flexibility to organisation. The development of human resource through training sets an organisation on a more solid foundation than an organisation where the personnel are not trained.

Training has to its credit of minimising accidents, damages, wastes in an organisation. This is no mean gain. Trained workers know how to secure economies and how to minimise the chances of accidents. Training also provides an organisation with persons who are readily available for appointment to higher position, thus relieving the organisation of the risks of recruiting personnel from outside.

Various benefits that are accruing from training are making it compulsory for organisations particularly big organisation to provide for training. The importance of training is now felt much more than in the previous years. It was presumed earlier that training was not necessary and the employees would be able to pick up all the necessary information about the techniques and performance of the job gradually on the basis of trial and error method. However, it has now been realised that formal training is essential and is the corner-stone of sound management. The reason for growing importance of training is the increasing complication in the process and techniques of production. In specialised job, training is a must. It may be noted that training is necessary not only for new recruits but also for existing employees. The employees with longer service may require training to obtain special skill and knowledge either to deal with the changed situation or to take up some new responsibility after being promoted. They may need frequent continuation training so that they may move through their working careers.

Training, to sum up, gives satisfaction to the employees and inculcates in them a feeling that they are being cared for which improves their morale, job satisfaction and loyalty and thus labour turnover and absenteeism are considerably reduced.

The benefits of training can be summed up as follows :

(a) The qualitative and quantitative improvements in output can be expected from the training of the employees. A trained employee with his training background can help in higher production and the quality of the products too improves.

(b) The cost of production, as a consequence of economical and better use of materials, is brought down by the trained hands.

(c) Management is relieved of too much involvement in the workshop management and can devote more time on other aspects of the organisation.

(d) In spotting out promising men and in locating mistakes in selection, training is a very good pointer. One who can quickly grasp the instructions in training can easily be singled out and thus the management is in a better position to put the right man to the right job.

## Training and Education

Training an employee and educating an employee – do they mean the same thing ?

The management authors draw a line of distinction between training and education. Education is a broader term and training is a part of it – a constituent. Education aims at all-round development of an individual while training is for the development of a particular skill of an individual. Education makes a man; training makes an employee. Education is formal in character; it is learnt in schools, colleges and universities. Training is usually confined to a work organisation and it is vocationally oriented. Education has no immediate purpose but training is for immediate utilitarian purpose. In schools, programmes for vocational training are undertaken; they are practical and job-oriented and, in industry, executive development programmes are followed which cover fundamental principles and philosophy with broader scope and should be considered as education. So, the distinction between training and education is not a practical but a theoretical exercise.

# CHAPTER 7

## SELECTION AND TRAINING IN INDIA

In India, the methods of recruitment, selection and training of the workers are not all adopted. Many Indian entrepreneurs are not willing to incur expenses on training. They are yet to realise that such expenses eventually turn out to be investments. The recruitment in many industrial enterprises is done through jobbers. They contact workers and bring them to factories and the jobbers get commission. This system suffers from several limitations.

As far back as in 1929, the Royal Commission on Labour had criticised it and recommended for the appointment of a suitable qualified officer for the purpose. The recommendation of the Royal Commission was based on the fact that the jobbers used to exploit workers in various ways. The jobbers are so cunning fellows that they always maintain a situation that does not permit the workers to come in direct contact with their employers. The situation is changing undoubtedly with the growth of organised labour unions.

Another method of recruitment followed in India is the "Budli" method. Under this method, a large number of workers are not appointed permanently. They are 'budli' workers and they serve as casual workers who are called on and called off to work in factories. They are usually kept out of employment continually for a considerable number of days as provided in the Industrial Disputes Act to prevent them from establishing their rights as permanent workers. This is done to safeguard the interests of the employer as he is not required to pay compensation to the retrenched workers.

Business concerns which are managed by personnel having progressive outlook and modern management training background do not resort to these anti-labour devices. They follow direct methods of recruitment.

Employment exchanges provide an important source of recruitment in India but they are not popular among private enterprises. Started in 1945, Employment Exchanges have achieved meagre success as liaison between prospective employers and prospective employees. The Employment Exchange (Compulsory Notification of Vacancies) Act, 1959, makes it compulsory for employers usually employing 25 or more workers to notify their vacancies to an exchange.

Training of workers in India is far from satisfactory. Proper training to unskilled workers is seldom found. On-the-job training is, however, imparted to the skilled personnel. Apprentice training is also pursued in many concerns. To the posts of the skilled persons, generally the unskilled persons with experience, skill and efficiency are promoted. The Central Training Institute for Instruction at Katni (M.P.), established in 1948, provides training to instructors. The Apprentices Act, 1961, regulates the condition of apprentices in the industries. It is provided in the Act, that it is obligatory for the employers in the specified industries to engage the requisite number of apprentices in the designated trades for undergoing training. Training standards have been prescribed by the Government in consultation with the Central Apprenticeship Council. There is the craftsmen's Training Scheme for craftmen's training. The Central Staff Training and Research Institute at Calcutta provides training to officers and staff and conducts research in training techniques. The practice of Organising Company Information Courses or Training Within Industry (T.W.I.) has found favour with some industrial concerns for supervisory training. It has four different parts —

(a) Job Relations Training (JRT), (b) Job Methods training (JMT), (c) Job Instruction Training (JIT) and (d) Job Safety Training (JST).

For managerial training, several institutions have been set up in our country. Besides, various universities have started courses for degree and diploma in management and administration. The Central Government has set up Management Institutions in Calcutta, Bangalore and Ahmedabad and Lucknow.

# CHAPTER 8

## VOCATIONAL GUIDANCE AND SELECTION

There can be no difference of opinion that for each job, the right type of man should be selected. This selection is known as **Vocational selection** — to put the right man to the right job. The necessity and significance of manning an organisation with the right types of men is beyond question. It does not only benefit an employer but also satisfies a worker to be in a job which suits him most. To ensure proper vocational selection what is needed is to guide a person as to what sort of job he should have and that is known as **Vocational guidance.** Therefore vocational guidance and vocational selection are complementary; one helps another. They are two sides of the same coin, so to say.

### Procedure for vocational guidance

***First step*** : Teachers supply information about the scholastic attainments of the candidate and parents express their opinion and feeling about their son.

***Second step*** : An analysis of the occupation suitable for candidates is undertaken with a view to finding out the factor necessary for success at these jobs.

***Third step*** : Psychological tests are undertaken — intelligence tests, aptitude tests, personality tests.

***Fourth step*** : Health and fitness reports are considered.

***Fifth step*** : All test results are considered and the job found to be most suitable for an individual is assigned to him.

In the process of vocational guidance, various factors concerning a person are taken into consideration. A young man found otherwise suitable for medical studies may not be given guidance for medical profession on consideration of his financial position. The ultimate object of vocational guidance is to settle a man in the right position in his career. Thus, vocational guidance stresses on the individual habits, temperaments, social and economic background of a candidate before its financial verdict is given for selection. Experts should take up the job of vocational guidance.

### Management Development

"An institution that cannot produce its own managers will die. From an overall point of view the ability of an institution to produce managers is more important than its ability to produce goods efficiently and cheaply." (*P. Drucker* ). This illustrates the importance of management development.

Personnel management includes the development of managerial personnel and does not confine itself only to the development of rank and file employees. To develop managerial abilities and efficiencies, what is required is training — both in course of their work and through formalised programmes from time to time.

Management development can be defined as 'the systematic process of training and development of managers'. Here the emphasis is being given to **individual** aspect — the development of individual manager. But in a broader sense, management development means "planned staffing".

As a part of Organisational Development, Management development includes procurement of new managerial personnel after assessing the number of vacancies, equipping the managers properly to be suitable for promotion and to see that the position which cannot be suitably filled by the existing managers, are manned by properly qualified new recruits.

Management development is generally used in the narrow sense of individual manager-development and in this sense, management development is more broad-based than operative training. Here a number of skills are developed such as technical skills, human skills and conceptual skills. These skills are required in all levels of management, but the emphasis of training for development varies from one level to another, from one position to another. The development training can, therefore, be classified into — (a) training of fresh graduates — the junior executives (b) training of supervisors and foremen (c) training of middle managers and (d) training of senior managers.

Management development programme propagates the philosophy that 'self-development is the best form of development'. Managers are to develop themselves; they cannot be developed — so goes the saying. This philosophy requires that each training programme should be adjusted to the needs of individual trainees and an organisational climate should be built for the self-development of managers at all levels.

For the training of managers and their development, various methods and devices are adopted, some of which are : (a) understudy (b) on the job experience (c) job rotation (d) lectures, case studies, conferences and group discussions (e) sensitivity training (f) role playing (g) business games (h) special course studies and (i) in-basket training.

A fresh appointee is generally, placed as an understudy to a senior officer to observe how the latter handles various problems. On the job experience, a manager acquires experience on the job and in job rotation training an individual is assigned one job after another in a systematic manner, moving from the easiest to the most complex. Lectures, case studies, group discussions and conferences — all are very useful methods of management development. Lectures are organised and talks are given by the experts. In case studies, actual examples are placed for study. In conferences, various managerial problems are discussed under the chairmanship of an experienced manager and solution to those problems are also discussed. Group discussions take place in small groups and thus the interaction is quicker and more intimate. In sensitivity training, the development of awareness of and sensitivity to the behavioural pattern of one's own self and of others is stressed. Role playing and business games — both are devices and training methods where attempts are made to train by stimulation. In business games, trainees are formed into a number of teams which are placed in competition with each other. Various problems relating to management are discussed and suitable solutions are found out. In role playing, each trainee is asked to play a role in the solution of a problem which involves interaction with others. Special courses are conducted by specialised institutions like management institutes. In-basket-training method also stimulates construction of a simplified version of the reality being dealt with and to so manipulate the model that it differs little from the real situation.

## Ergonomics

A new science of fitting a job or a machine to the worker is ergonomics. It studies the mental and physical capacities of people in relation to demands made upon them by their work and by the equipment they have to use to carry out their assigned work.

In ergonomics, in designing a machine, anatomical, psychological and physiological factors are given recognition. It emphasises the responsibility of management to create and maintain favourable work environment and working condition.

Anthropology, Method study, Enquiring — all are taken into consideration in Ergonomics. So the services of different specialists such as Methods analyst, Industrial engineer, Design engineer, Psychologist, Physiologist, Sociologist are sought for.

Ergonomics is applied in the design of machines, machine tools, office furniture, control panels etc.

The benefits derived from Ergonomics are — improvement in productivity, reduction in fatigue and boredom, creation of congenial working conditions, provision of safety and hygiene, reduction in accidents, assurance of job satisfaction and building up of employee morale.

# CHAPTER 9

## ROLE/PLACE OF PERSONNEL MANAGER

With the growing importance of human factor in production and the increasing complexities in the management of labour problems, the place of Personnel Manager in the management set-up of an organisation has been very important. In every organisation, a separate department known as Personnel department is being set up and to head this department an officer designated as Personnel Manager is appointed. In some organisations, a director is given the charge to look after personnel matters.

The personnel manager serves as a staff officer; he advises the line executive in the matters relating to employees. He does not execute but advises the policies ought to be followed in regard to labour, their problems and their service conditions. This is a very important role that a personnel manager plays because on his correct advice and proper understanding of the problem of the employees, will depend the future policies to be adopted by the organisation. The policies, thus adopted, may have far-reaching effects. Such is the significance of the role of the personnel manager. It is to be noted that, in the line-staff organisational pattern, it is not obligatory on the part of the line-executives to accept the advice of the staff personnel, here the personnel manager. If such a situation develops, the personnel manager can straightway ventilate his opinion to the chief executive. Of course, he has no power to take any action on his ideas or plans. He is simply to convey his expert's opinion to the line personnel and wait for the execution of his proposals. So, it has been rightly said that "the personnel manager's position requires a patient man who can gradually win the cooperation of the line organisation and establish sound personnel policies with a view to promoting harmonious human relationship".

The place or the position of the personnel manager in the entire management set-up of an organisation is, no doubt, important but the degree of importance varies from one organisation to another depending upon the nature and type of organisation.

The structure of the management organisation in a business enterprise determines the extent of responsibility of the personnel manager which in turn indicates the position and place of the personnel manager. In an enterprise, where line organisation is followed, the personnel manager will either combine his advisory functions with other functions of the line officers or the personnel department will itself act as a line department. Then it will not be purely an advisory department. The personnel manager, in such a circumstance, will not issue directives directly but he will communicate them through the chief executive only. In case the enterprise follows the functional organisational pattern, then the position of the personnel manager will be completely different. He, in such a case, will be given direct functional authority in connection with the problem related to the personnel staff.

To conclude, it may be said that the place of the personnel manager in a modern organisation is more or less important but the functional pattern of the personnel manager may vary as a result of which the degree of his importance may also vary and the fact remains that the role which a personnel manager plays in the complicated industrial relations goes a long way in solving various labour problems and in bringing about better relation between the employees and the employer.

# CHAPTER 10

## PROMOTION AND PROMOTION POLICY

Promotion refers to the placement or transfer of an employee to a higher job with more emoluments and better status. In promotion, the idea of advancement is inherent and this advancement is the assumption of greater responsibilities with greater amount of skill at his command. Promotion acts as a means of filling up vacancies in higher posts in the organisation. The vacancy in a higher position can be filled up in two ways – either by recruiting a person from outside or by raising a man already in the organisation to the higher position. Of the two courses open before the management of an organisation, experience confirms that a proved, able and known man within the organisation is better to be advanced to the higher position. So, promotion from within is preferred to recruitment from outside, in most of the cases. Of course, the circumstances may be such that the promotion from within of an existing incumbent may not be conducive to the interest of the organisation.

Promotion should not be confused with upgrading. An employee, when appointed to a job within the same occupational unit with increased pay but without any change in job grade or responsibility, is upgraded. It is promotion on a relatively smaller scale.

Promotion is a matter of careful consideration. Proper evaluation and comparison of the existing employee with the probable new employee should be made and, if the existing employee fulfills the requirements, then he should be preferred to an outsider even with some concessions to the existing employee. Promotion acts as an incentive. The scope for promotion in an organisation helps increasing productivity and maintaining discipline and morale of the employees to a great extent. It generates in them a sense of loyalty to the organisation and keeps them busy in their efforts to prove their sincerity. Thus, the policy of promotion from within is, by and large, beneficial for an organisation.

The **advantages** of the policy of promotion are derived both by the employees and the employer :

(a) It boosts the morale of the employees as they aspire to rise to higher positions.

(b) The service worker need not suffer from frustration and dissatisfaction as a result of which disputes between the employees and the employer are considerably reduced.

(c) The scope for promotion creates loyalty among the employees. They work for the concern sincerely and thus they help the organisation as well as make out a case for their promotion.

(d) Mobility of workers is restricted and continuity of service can be maintained. Frequent changes of staff causing dislocation and bottlenecks in the smooth flow of work are avoided to a great extent where the promotion scheme is prevalent.

### Promotion Policy

Promotion policy should be so conceived as to ensure benefit for the parties – the employees and the employer. There are two bases of promotion – merit and seniority. There is a long-time controversy as to which should be the basis — merit or seniority or both. Some are of the opinion that promotions should be made on the basis of merit while others say that it should be done purely on the basis of seniority. There is the third opinion that both seniority and merit should be considered.

In general, the management is in favour of promoting on the basis of merit whereas the employees and their unions prefer seniority. The reasons are not far to seek out. The management is more concerned about the quality of the service put in by an employee, so it emphasises on merit and the trade unions are more interested in the duration of their service, no matter whether the service has been efficiently put in or not. But the real problem lies elsewhere. The merit criterion that the management insists on does not, in many cases, actually means merit in the true sense of the term. It is merit plus something that gives an employee an extra advantage to be suitable for promotion whereas an employee actually putting in meritorious service is not selected for promotion because of the lack of this 'plus' element. There are other difficulties such as calculation of seniority, the judgement of efficiency etc.

Seniority means length of service. Longer service makes one senior to other. This seniority may be calculated from the time the employee's name first appeared on the pay roll; or some other criteria may be adopted. There are various methods for calculation of seniority and on the non-fulfilment of certain conditions, one may lose seniority even though the total length of service may be more. For instance, frequent absence from the pay roll may cause the loss of seniority.

**Seniority** criterion confers the following **advantages :**

(a) It is an objective basis for promotion and does not give any discretion to the superior. Thus it prevents favouritism and arbitrary action.

(b) This generates security in the service because the employees like to be in service for longer number of years to attain seniority for promotion.

(c) This policy assumes a practicable approach as it does not depend upon any controversial method of ascertaining the merit of any candidate.

(d) The cause for disputes is considerably minimised because the employees feel satisfied and their unions also prefer this system of promotions.

(e) The longer association with the organisation being rewarded by way of promotion, it develops an urge in the mind of the employee to work efficiently so that he may continue in his service for a longer period.

The **seniority**-based promotion system suffers from the following **limitations** :

(a) Since promotion is on the basis of length of service, the quality of work suffers.

(b) It affects the morale of the efficient employees who, because of their shorter period of service, cannot be promoted and are compelled to work under a promoted employee who is not efficient but only senior to him in service.

(c) Promotion becomes a matter of routine affair. The number of years put to service being the only criterion, production suffers.

(d) This promotion system only encourages employees to remain in the organisation somehow and does not motivate them to serve their organisation efficiently. So, qualitative and quantitative improvement in production cannot be expected under such a method of promotion.

Promotions on the basis of **merit** have the following **advantages** :

(a) A constant endeavour is made to prove himself efficient by putting in meritorious service.

(b) An employee becomes more and more efficient and thus helps in increased productivity and increased production.

(c) An overall improvement in the quality of service in the whole organisation is possible under this method of promotion.

(d) Quality based promotion as it is, the organisation as a whole stands to benefit and it attracts better calibred people to the organisation. Where merit is rewarded, meritorious people are naturally attracted.

The **drawbacks** of this method are :

(a) It encourages misuse of power by the supervising staff. Favouritism, nepotism, casteism etc. take the place of merit consideration and in many cases, merit is not properly rewarded.

(b) Merit, in many cases, not being recognised, this system of promotion creates frustration among really efficient employees and thus the organisation suffers.

(c) Because of misuse of power and corrupt practices of the supervising staff in the matter of judgement of merit, trade unions do not prefer this method.

(d) As the method is opposed by trade unions,

there is greater scope of conflicts between the employee and the employer under merit-based promotion system.

## Seniority vs Merit

From the above discussions, it is clear that neither of the bases of promotion is free from limitations. Now the question arises, which base would be followed. The management is inclined to place a premium on merit basis while labour unions favour seniority basis. Seniority is an objective basis for promotion and the management has no discretion to exercise in such a system of promotion. Everybody knows his position in regard to promotion and there is very little scope for dispute if the method or calculation of the length of service is well-defined. Moreover, so far as our country is concerned, the respect for age is a tradition. Thus, this base for promotion is favoured. But from the point of view of the organisation, meritorious service is a very important matter to consider because, without improvement in service, the organisation cannot achieve its goals. Simply with people having been many years in service and not being efficient, an organisation cannot increase its productivity and production.

In recent years, young men are joining the corporate sector with brilliant professional qualifications and if they are to work under old men with long experience having no specialised knowledge, naturally they get frustrated. So, divorced of merit basis, promotion demoralises the efficient staff members. As such, it is not advisable to adopt seniority as the only criterion for promotion. On the other hand, if ability is the only basis for promotion, standards of judgement are bound to vary from individual to individual. **A sound promotion policy, therefore, should be a careful blending of seniority and merit.** It should take into consideration matters such as length of service, physical fitness along with the quality of the service put in. According to Paul Pigors and Charles Myers, "Seniority should be considered but only when the qualifications of two candidates for a better job are, for practical purposes, substantially equal".

## Sound Promotion Policy

To ensure sound promotion policy, certain principles should be followed. The **essentials of sound promotion policy** are :

1) The lines of promotion should be clear-cut describing ability, education, experience and other qualifications for each job.
2) There should be little to fear from a commitment to arbitrate grievances about promotions from labour unions or aggrieved parties.
3) Promotion from within should be provided to middle management and senior management level jobs to boost up employee morale.
4) Scientific plans for rating of employees with the help of job evaluation and job rating techniques should be introduced.
5) Candidates selected for promotion should be given adequate training as a means of preparation for promotion. Re-training programmes, if necessary, for the job requirement should be arranged.
6) To enable interested employees to apply for promotion within a specified period, opening for immediate promotions may be posted to the employees in advance.
7) Probationary period should be provided to the employees to deserve confirmation.
8) Advice on promotion should come from the personnel department but the top management must consider the supervisor's recommendation.
9) Basis of selection for promotion may be seniority or merit or experience.

# CHAPTER 11

## PERFORMANCE APPRAISAL AND JOB EVALUATION

### Performance Appraisal (Merit Rating)

After the selection and placement of the employees, it is necessary to evaluate their performance. Merit rating implies systematic evaluation of the performance of the employees by some qualified persons. There are "various formal systems of appraisal or merit rating in which the individual is compared with others and ranked or rated. He is rated in the sense that he is measured or compared and classified". The need for such evaluation or appraisal arises from the fact that the human factor is the most important in the success of an enterprise. The productivity of this factor is a big determining factor of the overall performance of an organisation. Job performance of employees can be determined broadly by three factors – (a) ability (b) motivation and (c) work environment. The evaluation is done by the supervisors or senior bosses once or twice in a year.

The term 'merit rating' is now being replaced in advanced countries by the term 'personnel appraisal'. Merit rating is now considered as a part of the whole problem of personnel appraisal which has broader implications.

That the quality of the performance of different employees is necessary, is beyond question. Performance of the employee is now appraised not by merit rating only. This is supplemented by observations, records and evaluations. According to Dale Yodu, "Modern management makes some what less use of the term **rating** than was common in earlier periods, for several reasons. Most important, many managers now realize that rating is only one part or phase of a broader, continuing process of personnel appraisal."

Several methods are used for evaluating the performances and potentials of the employees such as ranking method, graphic rating scale, forced distribution method, forced choice method, critical incident method and field review method.

However, merit rating, as such, is now replaced by a new approach to performance appraisal. Management by objectives (MBO) was introduced by P. Drucker in 1954. He used the term "Management by objectives" (MBO) in his book "The Practice of Management". Drucker recognised the need of **self-set** goals. Since then it has become very popular as a method of planning, setting standards, motivating and appraising performance of employees. The better parts of the different theories of motivation such as Maslow's "Self-fulfilment need" and McGregor's Theory Y are recognised and performance appraisal is based on them. This new approach to the development of human resources accepts the concept that people prefer to be assessed according to criteria or standards which they feel as realistic and reasonable. In performance appraisal, Herzberg's motivational factor of achievement, recognition, challenging work and responsibility are taken into consideration.

The key features of performance appraisal are :

1) **Superior–subordinate Instruction :** The list of duties and areas of responsibility are jointly prepared by the superior and the subordinate

staff on the basis of mutual agreement and understanding.

2) **Superior-subordinate mutually set goals :** The subordinates set their short-term goals in consultation with their bosses. There is the mutual understanding.

3) **Superior-subordinate mutually set performance criteria :** The methods of achieving the business objectives are mutually set by the superior and his subordinates. They agree upon standards or norms for measuring and evaluating performance.

4) **Progress Evaluation :** There is the system of continual evaluation of progress to ascertain whether predetermined goals are being achieved. If necessary, the superior and subordinate, by sitting at meetings face to face, determine new goals.

5) **Superior's supportive role :** In this new approach to performance appraisal, the superior always extends supportive hands to his subordinates in realising business objectives. He acts as a friend, philosopher and guide.

The aim of performance appraisal is to emphasise on the results and not on the means or the personal traits. The superior does not act as a judge to pass his verdict on the performance of his subordinate, rather he helps him through continuous guidance to reach his goals.

Performance appraisal is more concerned with the assessment of performance and not with evaluating or rating qualities of potentials of the subordinate staff. In performance appraisal, more attention is given to work-related and career-oriented goals and primary emphasis is on self-supervision and self-regulation by the subordinates with frequent feed-back of information for effective control and communication.

Management by objective, or the new approach to performance appraisal as it is called, is a good solution to the problem of motivation. Through mutual interaction between the superior and his subordinates, it provides ample scope for employee participation in goal-setting and in planning and organising the work.

## Job Evaluation

Job Evaluation is the rating of different jobs in an organisation in objective and scientific manner to ascertain the relative worth or importance of each job.

Job Evaluation has been defined as "the process of analysis and assessment of jobs to ascertain reliably their relative worth, using the assessments as a basis for a balance wage structure".

Another definition is "Job Evaluation is the evaluation or rating of jobs to determine their position in a job hierarchy".

Job Evaluation arranges the jobs in order of importance or payment. It refers to rating of different jobs but not to the rating of the employees. Rating of employees is known as merit rating. This evaluation makes "an attempt to determine and compare the demands which the normal performance of particular job makes on normal worker, without taking account of the individual abilities or performance of the worker concerned". So, it is the evaluation of demands of each job of the organisation on the normal employees.

The **basic purpose** of such evaluation is to find out the relative importance of each job so that relative remunerations may be fixed for different jobs separately. In its absence, the management would fix the remunerations arbitrarily without taking them to the requirements of different jobs and it might have caused resentments among the employees or it would have been that the workers' unions would have forced the management to accept their dictation as to the fixation of remuneration of worker.

**Job Evaluation Vs Merit Rating**

| Job Evaluation | Merit Rating |
|---|---|
| 1. It means rating of each job indicating the relative value of jobs in terms of money. | 1. It means evaluation of the performance of each worker pointing out the relative value of employees. |
| 2. Fixation of fair base rate of wages and salaries. | 2. The efficiency of the worker performing the job is its concern. |
| 3. Scientific wage structure and wage | 3. Indication of the reward to be given for the |

| | |
|---|---|
| differentials between different jobs come within the purview of job evaluation. | performance of the employees above the base rate in the form of pay rise or promotion on the basis of merit or competence is the task of merit rating. |
| 4. Incentive wage plans evaluate or measure a worker's value regarding capacity to produce results. So, it is objective in nature. | 4. It is subjective in nature since it is a measure of worker's other qualities. |

## The Components of Job Evaluation

Job evaluation — which is an accepted tool in the hands of the personnel management for avoiding any inconsistency in job rates and for achieving uniformity in the entire wage structure — is done through certain processes. The process–elements are its components.

At the outset, job analysis to secure job date or information is necessary. For this purpose, job description and job specification are undertaken. In job description – duties, responsibilities and job conditions are described and in job specification – human qualities needed for the job are described.

In the next stage, job rating is done where job description and specification both on the basis of a pre-determined plan are studied. This study reveals a relative score or value to each job.

Then comes the question of money allocation. As per planned system or scale, a money rate of pay to each job is allotted.

While allocating money, employee–classification is undertaken. Employees are classified under right job title based upon work contents actually performed.

Thus, the components of job evaluation are : Job analysis, job description, job specification, job rating, money allocation and employee classification.

## Methods of Job Evaluations

A committee consisting of the foremen or the supervisor, the representative of the personnel department and the representative of the employees is generally formed for Job Evaluation.

Any of the following methods may be followed :

### (1) Ranking or Job-to-Job Comparison Method

This method is suitable for small organisations, though it is the oldest method of job evaluation. Under this method, a job is entirely compared with all other jobs but no details of the comparison are recorded; only the final conclusion is written. This method can be successful if the rater is fully conversant with various jobs. The rater may put the highest and the lowest job at the top and at the bottom, respectively, and then other jobs in between the two. Though simple, it lacks scientific precision and objectivity. It cannot specify why one job is rated superior to another. But it may tell the rating of different jobs.

### (2) Grading or Job Classification Method

For salaried jobs in Government and other services, this method is suitable. In this method, grades or classifications are determined beforehand, broadly taking into account the skill, responsibility, training and the like involved and then the functions corresponding to these grades are defined. Thereafter, the description for each job is prepared and matched with that of a particular grade already decided upon. On the basis of grades, various scales of remuneration are fixed and thus pay differentials on a prevailing rate basis are made possible. In case a new job is added, it would be put up in the grade with a group to which an established minimum and maximum pay rate applies. It is a qualitative method of rating the jobs and does not try to quantify the various factors of a job. A candidate is selected for appointment against a particular grade as we find in case of Government officers divided into class I, class II and class III, the clerical staff graded as lower division and upper division.

### (3) Factor Comparison Method

Under this method, comparison among different jobs is made factor by factor and not in its entirety as we find in case of ranking method. This is a quantitative method. All jobs are arranged in order of their possession of certain characteristics such as skill, effort, responsibility and working conditions. Each factor is assigned points which are totalled in the end to find out the ranking of the job. These points may then be converted into money scale. This is a method usually applied in a few basic and key jobs. Flippo has outlined the steps in this method as — (1) Select job factor (2) Select key jobs (3) Determine correct rates of key jobs (4) Rank key jobs under each factor (5) Allocate the correct rate of each key job among the job factors (6) Evaluate all other jobs in terms of these factor yard-sticks and (7) Design, adjust and operate the wage structure.

The difficulty in this method may be with regard to the weighing of the several factors equitably. The weighing may not be quite justifiable. As a matter of fact, to put it into practice is a difficult task.

**(4) Point Rating Method**

Under this method, evaluation is done on the basis of points. It is a quantitative method and is based on the assumption that "it is possible to assign points to the respective factors considered pertinent in evaluating the individual jobs and that the sum of these points will give an index of the relative significance of the jobs being rated". Whereas the ranking and grading methods measure jobs as wholesale activities, this method assesses the element that job is worth. Jobs are broken into four major factors -- skill, responsibility, effort and working conditions. Workers are paid in return for the use of these factors. Each of these factors may be subdivided into a number of minor factors such as education, experience etc. Each factor or sub-factor is classified in degrees or levels.

Each of the factors is assigned points already determined for the purpose. More weights are given for the factor which are more important; for instance 20 points may be assigned to leadership while 10 points for responsibility of machinery and equipment. In this connection, some analysts assign exact point value to each degree, while others provide a range. As a matter of fact, mathematical precision is not possible in quantifying the value of each factor. So, the range-principle appears to be better.

To establish the degree of skill complexity between jobs by using one of the four methods discussed above and then to translate those data into a pay structure with grades and rates of pay is the objective of a job evaluation study. **This involves the problems of pricing.** In the ranking method, a rate of pay has to be found for each job. In the point method, the total points for each job are added and jobs compared. A distribution of job scores is the first step and the jobs are classified into several grades. Only a few grades are desirable from the administrative point of view.

Job evaluation enabling comparison of scores helps management to ascertain the efficacy of the existing pay/wage structure; the rational pay system may be formulated on the basis of the job evaluation studies. Generally, a job evaluation committee performs this task with members from trade unions.

## Principles of Job Evaluation

Each job has certain characteristics. These characteristics create difficulty in performing the job. The purpose of job evaluation is to analyse these characteristics and thus to find out a fair and representative base rate of monetary compensation of jobs. Mathematical precision cannot be expected in formulating principles of job evaluation because it is not an exact science, but a broad set of principles can be followed. We may formulate the principles as under :

1) Job evaluation programme should contain in it the elements of over-payments at the initial stage to infuse confidence among the workers.
2) Job evaluation based on grades should aim at merit increase within labour grades and length of service.
3) Details of the job evaluation process should be made known to all the parties concerned.
4) Evaluation process, to ensure smooth functioning, should give opportunity to all interested parties to involve themselves in the process.
5) Wage rate levels should be comparable with the jobs prevailing in the organisation and in other organisations of the industry.
6) The merits of the job evaluation system introduced should be explained to all the parties concerned.
7) Since job evaluation is done by a committee with members from the workshop and management, the members so selected should be acceptable to all the parties to be affected by job evaluation method.
8) Job evaluation being an objective technique, the worth of every job should be very carefully studied by experts.
9) The size and type of organisation must be taken into consideration before a particular method of job evaluation is put to practice.

10) Job evaluation uses different forms and different terms are used. It must be a matter of principle for the management to see that the process of job evaluation will start only after the terms have been completed and explained.

11) The judgments of different rates should agree before conclusions and final appraisal of jobs.

## Importance or merits of Job Evaluation

The human resource is very vital for any organisation. Since it has immense potentialities, the efficient handling of this resource can produce unthinkable results and can crown the business organisation with success. But it is to be seen whether this resource is being properly utilised. Job evaluation is a process applied to assess the work put in by a worker.

The importance of job evaluation may be enumerated as follows :

1) It ensures rational wage and salary structure. A consistent policy can be pursued through job evaluation. So, it is a valuable technique in the hands of management.

2) Job evaluation offers advantages of job analysis process such as proper recruitment, selection, training, promotion, transfers etc.

3) Job evaluation ensures harmonious structural relationships in the organisation. This is possible because job evaluation establishes a rational and consistent wage structure.

4) The logical sequence of different steps as ensured in the job evaluation process determines the worth of jobs. It also works as a safeguard against industrial disputes.

5) It is on the basis of job evaluation that various incentive methods of wage payments can be introduced by determining the base compensation of job.

## A Comparative Study of the different methods of Job evaluation

1) **In the matter of popularity :** The point system ranks first, job grading and factor comparison enjoy more or less same popularity but simple ranking is the least popular method.

2) **In the matter of basis of comparison** : Simple ranking follows job-to-job basis. Job grading follows job-to-category basis and point system also follows this basis. But factor comparison follows the basis of simple ranking method i.e. job-to-job.

3) **In the matter of number of factors evaluated** : Job grading and simple ranking follow the same method – no factor is evaluated. In point system, an average of 11 factors is evaluated and in factor comparison not more than 7 factors are evaluated.

4) **In the matter of evaluation device used** : In simple ranking, none of the devices is used. In job grading, the single scale of job class description is the evaluation device. In the point system, multiple scales of points and factor degree definition is the device and in the factor comparison system, multiple scales of points and key job titles are the devices.

5) In the matter of similarity to other job evaluation systems, the simple ranking evaluation system, a crude form of factor comparison is applied. In job grading, crude form of point system and in point system refined job grading are methods applied. In factor comparison, refinement of simple ranking is the attribute.

6) In the matter of similarity to performance appraisal systems, the simple ranking corresponds to ranking system of appraisal whereas, in job grading, it corresponds to grading system. In point system, graphic scales and in factor comparison, man-to-man system are the ways of performance appraisal.

# CHAPTER 12

## INDUSTRIAL RELATIONS

The term "Industrial Relations" is now used in two senses. In its narrow sense, it means labour relations, but in its broader sense it includes employee relations, labour relations, public relations, customer relations etc. In this sense it covers all the relations of an industrial undertaking that it maintains with all the parties with whom it deals. Industrial relations, therefore, should be regarded as a vast complex of relationships obtaining between management and employees, union and management, union and workers and between worker and worker.

In the modern industrial society, **industrial relations constitute one of the most delicate and complex problems.** This can be attributed to the emergence of "Industrial Revolution". In the pre-industrial revolution period, the worker himself was the employer and the owner of the industrial unit, so there was practically no problem. Industrial Revolution, involving investment of huge capital, led to a complete segregation of ownership and management of industry. This resulted in the complex industrial relations.

Industrial relations, as they mean today, in countries like the U.S.A covering all parties in an organisation, call for co-operation from all persons in the organisation to improve industrial relations. Even in countries like U.K and India, where industrial relations more or less mean labour relations only, the problems are no less complicated. The capitalists as a class are becoming more and more powerful with immense wealth at their disposal and workers are weak and such a situation encourages the industrialists to exploit workers which may lead to a bitter relation between labour and capital. But the actual industrial scene is not so dismal for the workers, since they are united. Their unions are strong and sometimes militant to press their demands and get them satisfaction. **The ideal industrial relations should not be one where one party will forcefully realise its demands from the other but there should be a cordial and happy relation between labour and capital.** The areas of conflicts should carefully be avoided and the policy that prevention is better than cure should be followed.

Industrial relations today are not so peaceful. Mutual distrust between labour and capital predominates industrial relations. Though management is in a stronger position because of power and wealth, the workers are not simply passive onlookers. With the powerful weapon of strikes in their hands, they are now able to bargain with the industrialists. Employers, or the industrialists, too, are making all efforts to resist the demands of the workers. The conflicting interests have resulted in industrial friction and unrest. Such industrial unrest is reflected in the form of indiscipline, low morale, strikes, lock-outs, go-slow tactics, increased absenteeism, high labour turnover etc. Such a situation is highly undesirable. Neither the employer nor the workers and not the state benefits anything and the country, as a whole, suffers. So, state participation in the regulation of labour management relations has been constantly growing. In this context, we can very well quote Encyclopaedia Britannica where it is stated "the subject of industrial relations includes individual relations and joint consultation between employers and work people at the place of work, collective relations between employers and their organisations and trade unions and the part played by the state in regulating these relations". The ILO also holds a similar view.

**Industrial relations meaning human relations are as old as industry itself.** The nature and extent have changed with the growing complexities in the industrial world but the human relationships in industry were there, still they are and they will remain so long as industry will remain. Through ages, changes have been taking place in industrial relations with the changes in the nature of industrial management. At a time the relations between the employer and the employees were direct and simple but, with the emergence of the factory system of production, the situation has changed.

The changes that have crept into the relationships between man and man and amongst men in an industrial organisation are the natural consequences of the change in the pattern of industrial organisation, the divorce between ownership and management. Considerable distance has been created between management and labour because of modern large-scale operations. A psychological change is evident both in the employer and in the employees. Mutual trust has become a matter of past; distrust, misunderstanding and conflicts have become the order of the day in the industrial world. The employer thinks he is giving more than what is due to the worker and the worker thinks he is being deprived of his legitimate dues. In the early stage of industrialisation, since the contact between labour and capital was direct, any problem could be solved amicably before any complication could develop. But the fact remains, the problem of industrial relations was still there but solutions were not far to seek out nor was it very difficult to restore amity between the employer and the employees. So, **it is a correct statement to say that industrial relations are as old as industry itself; only the character has changed.**

With the changes in industry and industrial relations, the scope of industry has widened. All men in an organisation are parties to industrial relations and this new concept of industrial relations has thrust upon management new areas to tackle. It is absolutely necessary to win workers' cooperation. Discipline amongst workers has to be enforced. Organised labour have to be tackled with tact and prudence and finally, for an overall improvement of industrial relations, workers' participation in management have to be sought for. Therefore, industrial relations today encompass the following within its scope –

(a) Industrial unrest (b) Industrial discipline (c) Trade unionism (d) Workers' participation in management and (e) Employees motivation.

Industrial relations form the core of industrial management. It aims at maintaining and developing employee motivation as well as employee morale. Through motivation only a worker can be made to work willingly. The morale of the worker should be boosted up and this can be done by ensuring personal contentment and social satisfaction. The needs of workers must be carefully analysed because it is on the satisfaction of their personal needs that industrial relations can be improved.

The employees need have been classified into four categories – physical needs, security needs, social needs and self-expression needs. Physical needs can be fulfilled by financial rewards; they are economic in nature. Other needs are non-economic and, to fulfil them, non-economic approaches are appropriate. Morale and motivation should be used as tools to fulfil the needs of worker. Morale is concerned with personal contentment. When needs are met, the satisfaction that is derived gives immense pleasure and contentment and thus better and higher work-morale is created amongst workers. But good morale is not a good motivator of behaviour. Where wants are satisfied and morale is created, workers do not feel the urge to work more, productivity suffers. So, it is not good morale but motivation that increases productivity. Unsatisfied needs provide motivation. However, it can be said that for better industrial relations through various devices, both morale and motivation should be encouraged. The onus of improving morale and motivation is primarily on the employer since management is the dominant party. All the devices and tools at the disposal of the management should be adopted and used to improve industrial relations to fulfil the aims and objectives of the organisation as a whole.

### Importance of industrial relations

Industrial relations are human relations in industry. The importance of the human factor in an industrial organisation is beyond question. Better management of industrial relations in an industry is a *sine qua non* for the success of the industrial concern. It results in industrial peace which is essential for the countries, particularly for India, where the economy is being geared in a planned way to ameliorate the lot of the masses. Complete harmony between labour and capital may be a dream but quite a considerable amount of unrest and discontent among workers can be removed through efficient handling of industrial relations. It does not require much prudence to realise that in industry the human factor is most important; everywhere in production man is needed, no matter how sophisticated machinery have been installed. Interacting between management and workers and between worker and worker are regular features in industry and these constitute industrial relations. So, the importance of industrial relations in industry is self-evident and does not need any elucidation.

Industrial peace must be maintained at any cost to ensure better performance in industry. Industrial relations should be so maintained that it would contribute to increased productivity. Industrial relations have their impact not only on the industrial unit but also on the society. Industrial friction may inflict lasting injury on the workers. It may affect their careers. Families of workers are likely to suffer which must have repercussion on the society as a whole. Industrial unrests and conflicts foment class-hatred, embitter mutual relations, put a hurdle in the development of the society and the nation. As S. C. Kuchhal rightly put, it "the larger the range they cover and the more fundamental the commodities or services they are associated with, the more marked is their influence and damage". So, there is the impact of industrial relations not only on the economy of a country but also on its society and culture.

In a conflict between the workers and the employer, it is not the fact that only one of the parties suffer, usually the workers. A close watch will reveal that it becomes a vital concern for the community also. It has been rightly emphasised that "in the heat of the daily conflict, workers and employers are apt to forget that they are only two limbs of the body politic and that there is always a third partner, in fact, the most dominant partner, namely, the community at large, to be reckoned with". So, to ensure social justice, industrial relations play a dominant role and thus the importance of industrial relations has been gaining more and more importance. Industrial relations contribute to world peace. Peace in industry is a powerful factor for good international relations. Class struggles and class antagonisms have been responsible for bloody revolutions in the past, threatening world peace. When the entire world is striving for material well-being and when the nations of the world are moving in a planned way for industrial development; industrial relations are naturally drawing more and more attention. The recognition of the human factor in production as the supreme one puts a premium on the importance of industrial relations.

All the world over, the Government of different countries — wedded to the policy of doing welfare to the people of the country — are passing labour legislations with provisions for sufficient scope of ushering in industrial peace through various reconciliatory devices.

# CHAPTER 13

## LABOUR WELFARE

In any effort for industrial development, the question of labour figures prominently. Labour is the most important factor that has highest contribution to industrial development. But unless labour is looked after, its welfare is not considered, nothing appreciable can be expected of it. It is to be provided with the right type of work environment and basic amenities of life to ensure its physical efficiency. To increase labour efficiency, plans of labour welfare and industrial housing must be considered as important.

Workers' welfare means "such services, facilities and amenities which may be established in, or in the vicinity of, an undertaking to enable the persons employed in them to perform their work in healthy, congenial surroundings and provided with amenities conducive to good health and high morale". *(ILO – Report)*

Labour Welfare is not confined within the four walls of the workshop only. In and around the workplace lie conditions which have direct and indirect bearing on the welfare of labour. So, labour welfare includes everything that is necessary to be done for the improvement of the conditions of labour in and around the workplace. For instance, canteen and recreational facilities, sanitary and medical facilities, accommodation facilities, transport facilities from and to the workplace.

There is, however, no complete unanimity as to the meaning of labour welfare. "A series of sharply diverse opinions exist on the motive and merits of industrial welfare work" (Arthur James Todd).

In interpreting labour welfare, the Labour Investigation Committee remarked "Labour welfare activities include anything done for the intellectual, physical, moral and economic betterment of the workers whether by employers, by Government or by other agencies, over and above what was laid down by law or what was normally expected as part of the contractual benefits for which the workers might have bargained". This definition of labour welfare is comprehensive. It gives a list of various measures which are housing, medical and educational facilities, nutrition, facilities for rest and recreation, co-operative societies, day nurseries and creches, provision of sanitary accommodation, holidays with pay, social insurance measures undertaken voluntarily by employers alone or jointly with workers, provident funds, gratuities, pensions etc. All these measures are aimed at bringing about an all-round development of the workers, raising of their standard of living and make them enjoy better and lead a better life as happier citizens of the society.

The concept of welfare is related to historical, cultural and environmental conditions. So it differs from time to time and from country to country. In "The Modern Approach to Industrial Welfare" Paul Chu remarked – "Welfare services are as varied as life itself and are constantly being adapted to new circumstances. They form a fluid and developing pattern which changes as human needs change, as problems of adjustment to social environment arise or with the changes which are perpetually going on in the structure of society itself."

Certain **principles** should be adhered to while

providing welfare facilities to the workers. They are :

(a) Labour Welfare should not be considered as a substitute for low wages.

(b) Proper assessment must be made and priority must be fixed before any welfare measure is introduced.

(c) No compulsion should be made in the matter of providing labour welfare.

(d) Labour welfare schemes should involve workers.

Labour Welfare measures are intra-mural and extra-mural. Intra-mural facilities include facilities within the factory such as minimisation of industrial fatigue, health measures, safety measures, improvement in the condition of employment, recruitment, discipline, morale etc. Extra-mural facilities consist of facilities outside the factory such as measures for the general well-being of the workers like good housing, recreation, amusement, education, sports & games etc. To derive best from workers, both these types of facilities should be provided to them.

### Importance of Labour Welfare Measures

Labour Welfare measures are all meant for increasing labour productivity through all-round development of labour. By improving industrial relations, labour welfare measures contribute immensely towards creating an environment in which management with the full co-operation of workers can execute the plans and programmes of the organisation for realisation of its ultimate goals.

We can discuss the benefits of Labour Welfare measures under the following heads which will clearly indicate that these measures are very important for an industrial organisation.

1. **Improvement of industrial relations :** Labour Welfare measures are so comprehensive that they satisfy workers, if properly implemented. This satisfaction on the part of workers is a great stimulus for the industrial relations to improve. When workers are convinced that adequate measures have been taken to improve their work environment and their conditions of service, then they naturally repose confidence in the management and thus it helps maintenance of industrial peace.

2. **Creation of permanent labour force :** Well-adopted labour welfare measures restrict labour mobility. Workers generally feel reluctant to leave an organisation where their welfare is sincerely looked after. This attitude that welfare measures create helps the creation of permanent labour force which is important for an organisation to pursue plans and programmes on a continuous basis.

3. **Increase in general efficiency and income of workers :** The comprehensive welfare measures assuring workers good accommodation, proper health-care, suitable work environment make the workers contented. Their contentment is a great inducement for them to work more. They become more efficient as they are not worried about their primary needs. Since their productivity increases, they earn more; their income increases.

4. **Enhancement of the morale of workers :** Labour welfare measures act as a booster to the morale of the workers. Workers with better amenities of life shun many of their vices and offer willing co-operation to management. This is a great benefit for the organisation.

5. **Development of the sense of belonging :** Labour Welfare measures make the workers feel that they are one with the organisation. Management thinks so much for them, does so much for their welfare that they cannot isolate themselves from the organisation : they feel oneness with the organisation. This feeling that they have some stake in the organisation will help restore industrial peace. It will enhance their devotion to the job and thus the enterprise, as a whole, will be benefitted.

6. **Change in outlook of employers :** The change in the dealings of the workers consequent upon the introduction of labour welfare measures make the employers satisfied with them. Thus, there is a change in the outlook of the employers towards labour; a cordial relation is set up and the work environment improves considerably. When the employers find the workers willing to work and devote themselves to the development of the organisation, they do not even hesitate to allow them to participate in management.

7. **Improvement of the moral and mental health of workers :** Welfare measures include such measures as would prevent the workers from indulging in vices such as drinking, gambling etc. and thus their moral and mental health improves contributing overall improvement in the health of the organisation and society.

8. **Benefit to the Society :** Besides providing economic benefits to workers, labour welfare measures extend to workers various facilities that have direct bearing on their better mode of living. Because of medical benefits extended to them, the workers enjoy better health and infant mortality among the workers declines. The workers feel happier and the society as a whole is benefitted with people having better standard of living and better equipped with more purchasing power to contribute to the general welfare of the country in general and the society in particular.

## Labour Welfare – Position in India

The miserable conditions of labour are responsible for their low efficiency. The Indian workers are proverbially inefficient compared to their counterparts in the industrially developed countries. The lack of proper efficiency of labour in India is mainly due to the absence of welfare measures as are obtainable in the advanced countries.

The conditions of Indian workers were utterly deplorable. Since independence, an awakening about the welfare of workers is being noticed. The reasons are not far to seek. Ours is a developing country; rapid industrialisation of the country is of paramount importance. It has been recognised on all fronts to give due consideration to labour as a factor of production to increase industrial productivity. Workers themselves are now more united. So, an atmosphere and environment is now prevalent in India which is conducive to providing various facilities to workers. It is now an admitted fact that unless workers are given due attention and provided with all amenities, the country is sure to pay a high price for it – the pace of industrialisation has to suffer a set-back. So, the need for labour welfare is now accepted and measures are adopted by different agencies such as Governments, employers, trade unions to better off the lot of the workers through various physical amenities and legislative measures. We discuss them below :

1. **Central Government :** Ours is a welfare state wedded to the policy of doing welfare to the people of the country. For the economic rejuvenation of the country, the toiling masses must be taken care of, their lots must be improved. In this regard, the Government has an active role to play. The Government has to come forward to bring about intellectual, physical, moral and economic betterment of the workers, so that their whole-hearted and willing co-operation may be readily available for the economic upliftment of the country. In our plan objectives, workers have been accepted as an essential part of the apparatus of industrial and economic administration of the country.

The Central Government has paid its attention to improve the conditions of workers. Various enactments have been promulgated to safeguard the interests of workers, to extend to them economic benefits and social security. The Factories Act, for example, is a bold attempt to extend various facilities to factory workers – their housing facilities, economic benefits, social securities and physical safety etc. The Mines Act is another piece of legislation that aims at providing welfare to mine workers. So far as mines are concerned, Coal Mines Labour Welfare Fund has been instituted to boost the morale of coal mine workers under the Coal Mines Labour Welfare Fund Act. Similarly, Mica Mines Labour Welfare Fund and Iron Ore Mines Labour Welfare Fund have been created by specific Acts of the Central Government. Again, we find Plantation Labour Act for the welfare of plantation workers.

Besides the various Acts passed for the welfare of labour in mines, plantations and factories, the Central Government has kept its Labour Ministry alive to the conditions of workers. Measures have now been adopted to provide medical aid, legal and financial aid to workers under various schemes. To ensure industrial safety, various precautionary measures have also been enforced. Prevention of the possibility of accidents has been one of the objectives of the Government's welfare measures and actually the incidence of accident has come down. The Government of India has introduced an industrial housing scheme for the accommodation of industrial workers. Social Security legislations such as The Workmen's Compensation Act, Maternity Benefit Act and The Employees' State Insurance Act have been in force.

2. **State Governments :** The State Governments in India were more or less indifferent to labour welfare prior to independence. But now various State Governments are very alive to the conditions of labour and are up and doing for the upliftment of the lots of the workers. There are popular governments in some states where workers are adequately taken care of. Labour fronts of different political parties are now sufficiently strong to press the demands of workers to the Government and the link between the State Governments and

the labour wings of political parties is so close that various facilities are now being made available to the workers through the State Government's machinery.

3. **Employers** : Employers in India today have started realising that they should identify their interest with those of the employees. No prudent management can now ignore the interests of their workers and expect to reap the benefits of higher labour productivity. So, for their own interest, employers are being compelled to adopt welfare measures for the workers. There are only a few employers in India who have been sympathetic to labour welfare but others are extending various benefits to workers only under compulsion. Several industries such as cotton, jute, textile, engineering, sugar, cement, glass, chemical etc. have been brought under legislative measures to give facilities to the workers. Without specifying the facilities provided by different industries either under legal compulsion or under union pressure, we can say that employers in India with their professional training background are becoming more and more conscious about the workers whom they now consider the most essential tool to gear up their organisational activities. Employers who are still maintaining a negative attitude or an indifferent attitude towards workers are surely to pay for their foolishness. Days have changed. All over the world is the slogan for workers to unite. Moreover, employers who fail to understand the potentialities of the labour force, the fullest utilisation of which can bring miraculous results for the organisation, are sure to suffer.

4. **Trade Unions** : Last but not the least important agent for the welfare of workers is the 'Workers' union. Conflicts between labour and capital existed since industrialisation, they still exist and will continue to exist. The complete harmony and amity between the two opposite-interest groups cannot be achieved. Not only in India but nowhere in the world has industrial peace been ensured. Here is the role for the Trade Union to play in the matter of bargaining. Various facilities of different nature — economic, social, cultural — are made available to workers by Trade Unions.

The Indian Trade Unions have not yet been able to do much to ameliorate the lot of their members. Their participation in this sphere has been mainly through their association with the Labour Welfare Advisory Committees constituted by the Governments. It is worthwhile to mention that trade unions in the textile industry (Textile Labour Association) and the Mazdoor Sabha have made provisions for various welfare facilities to the workers. Educational and cultural upliftments through trade unions have been made possible. With the change in the attitude of the employers (many of whom are governments themselves), the nature of trade unions in India — from militancy to conciliatory — is now noticeable. Various welfare services are now made available to the workers through Trade Unions after the trade union leaders' direct discussions and deliberations with the employers across the table. However, trade unions should take some measures for the welfare of workers. They should come forward to assist the employers and the Government in formulation and administration of welfare schemes. To find out the needs of the workers and to bring them to the notice of the employers should also come under the purview of trade union activities. A modern Trade Union has to educate its members, organise for them various inexpensive programmes and to act as a watch-dog of workes' interests. Trade Unions have, as a matter of fact, a great role to play for the welfare of the workers.

## Labour Welfare — Conclusion

Labour and their welfare are very legitimate concerns for any Government of any country whether developed, undeveloped, underdeveloped or developing. No economic development of a country or the maintenance of the status quo of the economic development of any country can be conceived of without thinking about the workers of the country.

In India, the colonial economy had prevailed for about two centuries. With the attainment of Independence, the planned economy has been started, one of the objectives of which is the rapid industrialisation of the country. The National Government could not remain a passive onlooker of what had been happening in the industrial world. The human resource in industrial organisations received attention of the Government. The National Commission on Labour (1969) was formed and its recommendations were based on the findings of the committee on labour welfare. The Committee felt that the statutory welfare activities had not been properly and adequately provided, except in units managed by progressive employers. The compliance with statutory welfare provisions had also been half-hearted and inadequate. The Committee made a large number of recommendations which included, amongst others, the provision for creches, canteens, periodical medical examination, creation of the General Mines' Welfare Fund, extension of the coverage of Plantations Labour Act, extension of welfare benefits to contract labour, opening of more fair price shops for workers, setting up of consumers' cooperative societies, statutory and tripartite welfare boards etc.

The provisions in the various legislations for the welfare of the workers should be translated into action with all sincerity. The provisions in the Factories Act, for instance, must be scrupulously implemented. A National Museum of Industrial Health, Safety and Welfare is of great significance. A larger number of labour welfare centres should be set up. The Welfare Officers should have direct link with workers. Arrangements should be made to collect information on occupational diseases and steps should be taken to keep the workers free from these diseases or cure the diseases without delay. More Welfare Funds should also be set up and, finally, trade unions should play a role truly in the interest of the workers. By depriving labour of their legitimate rights and their rights to live like human beings, no state can aspire to be a Welfare State.

# CHAPTER 14

## INDUSTRIAL DISCIPLINE

Industrial discipline refers to orderly working of the employees of an industrial undertaking in accordance with established rules, regulations and conventions.

Discipline is a force that prompts an individual to observe rules, regulations and procedures to attain an objective. In the broad sense, discipline means orderliness – the opposite of confusion. In an organisation, discipline is the orderly conduct of its members.

Industrial discipline can thus be defined as "the orderly conduct of affairs by the members of an industrial organisation who adhere to its necessary regulations because they desire to co-operate harmoniously in forwarding the end which the group has in view and willingly recognise that to do this, their wishes must be brought into a reasonable union with requirements of the group in action".

Formerly, discipline meant the kind of regimentation of thought and action that obtains in the army. Discipline is definitely something which is opposite of chaos, irregularity and disorder in human behaviour and action. Mary C. Niles traces the origin of the word discipline to a root meaning "to learn". According to her, the purpose of discipline is not to punish the workers but to help them learn proper conduct.

Discipline is essential for any successful activity and, where it refers to industrial discip'ine, its essentiality gets an added value. In indust. al organisations, discipline is a must. The condition of complete peace and harmony as opposed to chaos is a very important factor for the success of an industrial unit. In an atmosphere of discipline, work environment improves, productivity of labour increases, production gears up and the organisation, as a whole, attains prosperity and achieves its objectives and goals.

Discipline may be self-imposed or enforced. In the case of self-imposed discipline, employees regulate themselves and their conduct but, in enforced discipline, regulation comes from the top. When the discipline is self-imposed, naturally there is spontaneous work on the part of the employees, no enforcement is necessary; motivation comes from within. It is a more powerful force for the workers to work more. Nevertheless, occasions arise under which managers are compelled to rely on enforced discipline for bringing in recalcitrant employees to task.

## Causes of indiscipline

Indiscipline breeds mainly amidst managerial faults and lapses. The lapses are : (a) arbitrary disciplinary measures taken by the managerial staff (b) deferring or neglecting the settlement of employee grievances (c) favouritism and nepotism in promotions and placements (d) too much bossing temperament of the management staff (e) communication gap between the management and the ordinary staff (f) lack of appropriate supervision at the operating level (g) use of 'secret police' method to collect information (h) provocation by union leaders (i) factionalism (j) personal animosity and jealousy (k) policy of 'divide and rule'.

Causes of indiscipline as we enumerate above may emerge from the employees themselves but mainly they are creations of the management. Whatever might be the cause of indicipline, the consequences sometimes become very serious. As one writer put it, "where there is no common aim between the discipliners and the disciplined, discipline becomes a mere frustration of human purpose, stunts the human pérsonality and embitters human relations, for them it is the denial of freedom to the individual".

## Maintenance of discipline

The maintenance of industrial discipline is a difficult highly complicated task and needs a very efficient handling. Varied are the ways that can be adopted but a few of them are outlined below :

1) Workers are to be consulted while framing rules and regulations.
2) Rules and regulations should be properly framed.
3) There should not be any communication gap between the management and the workers.
4) New workers should be given proper orientation.
5) Where necessary, charts, graphs and other methods should be used so that the workers may understand them.
6) Penalty for breaking rules should be used only where it is absolutely necessary.
7) Victimisation should not be the aim of punishment.
8) Favouritism, nepotism and casteism should be avoided.
9) Managerial staff should never be breakers of law which they themselves have framed for enforcing discipline.
10) Code of conduct or discipline should be framed and followed.
11) A disciplinary committee should be formed.
12) A suitable machinery should be set up to listen to the appeals made by the aggrieved party.

The ways of maintaining discipline are broadly discussed above. Where indiscipline actually takes place, some measures must be taken to enforce discipline. According to Paul Pigors and Charles A. Myres, the following steps may be taken for disciplinary action :

(a) Preliminary investigation (b) an informal, friendly talk (c) an oral warning or reprimand (d) a written or official warning and (e) a graduated series of penalties such as disciplinary lay-off, demotional downgrading or transfer and — as a last resort– discharge.

These are termed 'clinical approach'.

In India, the principles of natural justice are followed in dealing with cases of indiscipline. The accused is to be given opportunity to defend himself and, under no circumstances, a man with sense of partiality should be appointed a judge and punishment should never be disproportionate to offence. Disciplinary action is taken after domestic enquiry by the appointment of an Enquiry Officer and by framing and issuing a charge-sheet. The offender is given opportunity to submit his explanation, the enquiry notice is given, the proceedings are conducted, findings are made known and the decision is communicated to the proper authority. The authorities of the firm proceed with utmost caution before any disciplinary action is taken.

## Code of Discipline in Indian Industry

The 15th session of the Indian Labour Conference held in July, 1957, discussed the problem of discipline in industry and formulated certain principles for removing employee grievances and settling industrial disputes by mutual negotiation, conciliation and voluntary arbitration. The Code of Discipline has come into force from June, 1958.

The Code of Discipline can be described as a truce between organised labour and management.

The following principles were discussed :

1) There should be no lockout or strike without notice.
2) No unilateral action should be taken.
3) No recourse to go-slow tactics.
4) No deliberate damage to plant or property.
5) No acts of violence, intimidation, coercion or instigation.
6) Existing machinery for settlement of disputes should be utilised.
7) Awards and agreements should be speedily implemented.
8) No agreement violating cordial industrial relations should be entered into.

The above principles were accepted and incorporated in the Code of Discipline, in toto. Certain modifications were made to codify them which became a "Code of Discipline". This was ratified by the four central national labour organisations (INTUC, UTUC, AITUC, and HMS) on behalf of the workers and by the Employers' Federation of India, the All India Organisation of Industrial Employers and the All India Manufacturers' Organisation on behalf of the employers.

The Code of Discipline, however, could not prevent the major strikes in the steel plant at Jamshedpur, in dockyards at important ports, in the plantation industry in Kerala, at Calcutta Tramways, Hindustan Shipyard and Heavy Electricals at Bhopal. A seminar on the working of the Code of Discipline was held in 1965. Again, in 1967, the working of the Code of Discipline was reviewed at the meeting of the Central Implementation and Evaluation Committee and the proposal to set up a National Arbitration Promotion Board for encouraging voluntary arbitration was finalised.

# CHAPTER 15

## INDUSTRIAL DISPUTES/UNREST

Despite various efforts made and measures taken to maintain industrial peace, complete harmony in industrial relations has nowhere been achieved. The causes of industrial disputes are inherent in human psychology and can never be completely removed. So, all attempts are made to mitigate the causes of disputes. Complete absence of industrial disputes can be a theoretical concept but not a practical proposition. Disputes or unrest had always been in the industrial world, they are existing and they will continue to exist but the efforts are always on to minimise the incidence of disputes and the causes thereof, so that industries may flourish in a congenial atmosphere. As a matter of fact, industrial disputes have become the "concomitant of the present-day industrial system". Feeling of oneness between the employers and the workers is simply an ideal which is yet to be attained. In practice, neither the employers are treating the workers well nor are the workers working with zeal and co-operating with them. As a result, strikes, lockouts, go-slow tactics etc. have become the rule of the day. Industrial unrest is generally regarded as "such a degree of dissatisfaction and personal disorganisation as to cause serious deviations from normal, habitual pattern of conduct". As a consequence of industrial disputes, individuals become so disturbed and frustrated that the patterns of behaviour usually accepted and uncritically followed appear unsatisfying. Industrial unrest is not only individual but social in nature in so far as it is communicated from one individual to another. Strikes and lockouts have come to stay almost permanently in the industrial set-up of the day. "They are symptoms of industrial unrest in the same way that boils are symptoms of a disordered system" (S. H. Patterson).

### Causes of Disputes

Employee grievances give rise to industrial disputes. These grievances may be economic, social or personal in nature. However, the causes of disputes may be broadly classified into four groups – (a) wages, allowances and bonus, (b) personnel and retrenchment (c) leave and hours of work and (d) other causes. Out of these reasons, the economic reasons are most important. It is generally for better economic benefits that disputes between the employer and the employees arise. The workers feel that they are being paid less than that to which they are entitled, whereas the employer feels that he is paying more than what is legitimately due to the workers. This situation is a clear indication of mutual distrust which in spite of best efforts could not be removed, rather the incidence of mutual distrust has increased. It has been observed that the "root cause of the labour unrest can be traced directly to the failure of the Government in evolving a definite wage policy and in stabilising prices at a point which would maintain cost of living and employment at a particular level".

Another important cause as stated earlier is personnel and retrenchment. Workers go on strike due to dismissal, suspension, retrenchment and victimisation. The personnel problems involve individual and social wants of workers. The sense of insecurity among the workers leads to strikes. Due to this fact, there is "lack of an atmosphere of approval, praise and recognition". This unwanted factor of employee grievance is becoming more and more important.

The terms of employment, such as leave and hours of work, may be the cause of disputes. The workers resort to strike to get the hours of work reduced. Sometimes, disputes may arise because of not declaring holiday on some religious occasion. The refusal of leave by the employer may also lead to disputes. The workers may call for a strike to get the proper leave rules framed. The average percentage of disputes due to these reasons is not so significant.

There are several other reasons leading to disputes, no matter whether they are important or not. When the interests of the parties – the employees and the employer – are exactly opposite, there may be thousand and one reasons for disputes and it is very difficult to name them. Now-a-days, political considerations are playing significant role in industrial disputes. It happens as most of the labour leaders have political affiliations and they use their workers for political ends. There may also be reasons like police atrocities on workers, sympathy for workers' struggles elsewhere etc. These other causes are very important and about one-fourth of total disputes takes place for these 'other reasons'.

## Prevention of industrial disputes

Industrial disputes cannot be eliminated altogether. But they can be reduced. But once allowing the disputes to arise and then to take steps to settle them is not so good a management as it is to prevent the causes of disputes as far as possible before they are likely to occur. Prevention is better than cure – goes the saying. However, in practice, the preventive measures are not always successful and disputes do occur. In that case, efforts should be made to settle the disputes as early as possible so that there may be minimum loss. Employers, unions and public agencies have sought means of preventing disputes and unrest and avoiding their more spectacular expression in strikes and lockouts. The methods of preventing industrial disputes are more or less similar to the methods applied to improve industrial relations. The methods, therefore, range from simple negotiations between the employer and the workers to the compulsory progressive legislation involving the role of state.

All the world over, there are machineries operative for prevention of industrial disputes. Varied is their nature and different is their character. In different circumstances and situations different devices are adopted to prevent disputes between the employer and the workers.

In India, we have Industrial Disputes Act, 1947, for settlement and prevention of industrial disputes. Besides the method of arbitration, there are seven different authorities provided in the Act for this purpose.

They are : (1) Works Committee (2) Conciliation Officer (3) Board of Conciliation (4) Court of Enquiry (5) Labour Courts (6) Tribunals (7) National Tribunals.

The Industrial Disputes Act as amended up to 1957 provides for a three-tier machinery consisting of the Labour Courts, Industrial Tribunals and National Tribunals for adjudication of industrial disputes.

In case of public utility concerns, reference of a dispute to a tribunal is compulsory unless the notice of strike is frivolous or vexatious.

**Works Committee :** It is a bipartite body set up at the plant level. It takes steps to promote and secure good employer-employee relations and in case of differences of opinion between the two parties, to work to bring out conciliation between them. It is an advisory body. The employer constitues the Works Committee and consults the recognised union/unions in its working.

**Conciliation Officer :** The Government appoints one or more conciliation officers for mediating in and promoting the settlement of industrial disputes. The conciliation officers have statutory powers for entering into premises of establishments and for calling and inspecting documents. They are expected generally to function through suggestion and persuasion rather than compulsion and fault-finding. The conciliation officers have wide discretion.

**Board of Conciliation :** The Board is an extension of the conciliation officers' work. The Board of conciliation is usually set up as the occasion arises. It is constituted with members in equal numbers representing parties to the dispute. The Board enjoys the status of a Civil Court and can issue summons and administer oaths.

**Court of Enquiry :** A Court of Enquiry is set up at the discretion of an appropriate Government irrespective of the consent of parties to dispute. Usually, the Court of Enquiry comprises of one person. The Government can refer any one or more matters to the Court.

**Labour Court :** It is one of the adjudication authorities set up under the Industrial Disputes Act. It is a one-man court set up at the discretion of the Government. The Court is presided over by a person who has held either a judicial position in India for not less than seven years or who has been a presiding officer of a labour court constituted under any State Act for not less than five years. The functions of a Labour Court is to adjudicate as matters referred to it by the appropriate government.

## Industrial Tribunals and National Tribunals

Tribunals may be set up by the appropriate government on a temporary or permanent basis for specified disputes or for industry as a whole. The Tribunal is a one-man affair. In case of industrial disputes of national importance or in case of disputes involving more than one state, a National Tribunal is set up by the Central Government.

All the authorities provided for in the Industrial Disputes Act, 1947, are meant for constructive contribution in reducing industrial unrest and improving labour management relations in an enterprise.

Besides the above authorities, there are measures to prevent labour unrest. The measures are : "Code of discipline, collective bargaining, labour participation in management, employee oriented democratic managerial style, tripartite wage boards, speedy implementation of awards and agreements, favourable work environment, healthy and strong labour organisations with employee leaders".

# CHAPTER 16

## WORKERS' PARTICIPATION IN MANAGEMENT

### Meaning of Participation

Management consider participation as a joint consultation prior to decision-making while workers mean codetermination by the term 'participation'. Government looks at 'participation' as an association of labour with management without the final authority or responsibility in decision-making. But, generally conceived, it means a way of reducing power difference and, therefore, equality is stressed. Frankly speaking, this idea of reduction of power inequality, between management and labour through workers' participation cannot be accepted since there is the obvious difference in formal power position between the labourer and the director.

However, certain elements of participation are very much clear though the more precise conceptual properties of participation are not so clear. The elements are : the amount of verbal interaction between a supervisor and his subordinates, the extent to which a supervisor performs his role in a group-centred way and the degree to which a supervisor is active in making decisions and setting goals for his work units.

Whatever might be the interpretations of the term **participation**, the fact remains that it **means sharing, in an appropriate manner, the decision-making power with the lower ranks of the organisation.**

There are levels of participation in decision-making which range on a scale from minimum to maximum. According to an authority on labour management (V. G. Mhetras), these levels are of five types – (1) Informative participation, (2) Consultative participation, (3) Associative participation, (4) Administrative participation and (5) Decisive participation. The nomenclatures of the participations indicate their nature. "Participation has been termed as one of the most prominent constructs in group dynamics literature. Several empirical findings conducted in the laboratory and otherwise show that significant changes in human behaviour can be brought about rapidly only if the persons who are expected to change, participate in deciding what the change shall be and how it shall be made" (Monappa and Saiyadain).

As a measure to improve industrial relations, workers' participation in management is very important. It is an attempt "to extend democracy from the political to industrial plane". A socialist society remains a dream if the toiling masses are not associated with the management of an organisation where they work. This is definitely a very effective way of eliminating or reducing class-struggle. Involvement of workers in management is helpful in boosting their morale and discipline and thus improvement in production qualitatively and quantitatively can be ensured to a considerable extent. By inculcating the spirit of responsibility among the workers, their participation in management goes a long way in solving various problems arising out of mutual distrust between capital and labour; thus the industrial atmosphere improves and the environment becomes congenial for the workers and the employer to breathe in an air that encourages an industrial unit to develop its health for realisation of its objectives.

Participation of the workers in the management should be 'real' and 'effective' and not merely formal. Involvement of the workers, to be effective, must be both mental and emotional. There must be a genuine intention on the part of the management to implement the decisions arrived at after consultation with the workers. The management should not hold the reigns of controls and final decision taking powers in its own hands. In the workers' participation scheme, the role of the workers should not be conceived as that of advisers but of active participants. It does not, however, imply that all the controls should be vested in the hands of the workers. In a genuine participation, the workers are not simply asked to give consent to the proposals brought forward by the employers. The workers themselves will take initiative to bring forth creative ideas for the organisation to implement.

Workers' participation in management is still distinctly experimental even in advanced countries. Skepticism and cynicism represent a major hazard to all such plans. Neither party believes in the co-operation of the other party and, as such, the scheme is yet to attain necessary success.

Labour participation in management is a concept of "sharing of decision making power by the rank and file of an industrial organization through proper representation at all levels of management in the entire range of managerial action" (Dr. Mhetras).

In "Participative Management" by K. C. Alexander, it has been stated : "A management is participative if it gives scope to the workers to influence its decision making process on any level or sphere or if it shares with them some of its managerial prerogatives".

The planners of Indian economy feel that "for the peaceful evolution of the economic system on a democratic basis, it is essential that workers' participation in management should be accepted as a fundamental principle and an urgent need".

The concept of workers' participation is based on the principle of co-partnership in industry as opposed to master-servant relationship. Participation should mean co-functioning, playing one's part in an integrative unity, contributing all that one is capable of to the good of the organisation. It signifies workers' identification with the progress and development of business.

The practice of workers' participation differs from one country to another. However, one thing is certain that "Workers' participation is now a feasible concept and has turned into a world-wide movement", though there are different degree and levels of workers' participation.

The underlying ideas of workers' participation as understood from different definition and explanations of the concept are : (a) It is a mental and emotional involvement (b) It is a two-way psychological and social relationship and (c) It is an acceptance of responsibility by workers.

As a matter of fact, participation of workers in management rests on two foundation stones — coordination and understanding through best communication. Participation is effected through several methods such as (a) Joint consultation (b) Automanagement (c) Co-partnership (d) Workers' representation on the Board (e) Suggestion scheme (f) Multiple management (g) Democratic supervision and (h) Consultative supervision.

**Need for Participation :** Workers' participation in management was felt essential for achieving higher productivity, ensuring greater employee morale and harmonious industrial relations. The recognition of human factor in industry forms the basis of workers' participation in management. Principles of industrial psychology and the new trends in personnel management have necessitated workers' involvement in management. After satiation of their physical needs, workers crave for satisfying their social and egoistic wants and these could only be fulfilled by their association with management. Literate, educated, cultured and well-informed workers are never satisfied with the fulfilment of their lower level needs such as food, clothing and shelter; they want to be treated by their employers as responsible adults capable of assuming greater responsibilities. No management can ignore such type of labour and the need for their participation has to be admitted for better work environment. With the passage of time and because of various labour welfare measures adopted, workers today have proved their worth to participate in management. Moreover, workers now are well-organised and have enough bargaining strength with management, more or less on equal footing. The slogan for industrial democracy has strengthened the need for workers' participation in management. The management and workers now need to be considered as partners in service which necessarily emphasises the need for the participation of workers in management.

Participation of workers in management has now become indispensable and inevitable from economic, psychological and social points of view. Management is now considered as a factor of production as we consider labour as a factor of production. A harmonious inter-relationship of these factors can ensure a good organisation and here is the need for the workers to come close to management. This will not only increase the sense of responsibility of the workers but also pave the way for better overall personnel management by boosting the morale of the employees.

## Significance and benefits of participation

Workers' participation in management, if utilised meaningfully, can serve a number of purposes and it can generate a "we" feeling among workers which go a long way in achieving the desired goals of an organisation. It fosters joint responsibility and co-operation and certain specific **purposes** vital for the sound running of the organisation can be achieved through participation. **Changes** necessary for the growth and development of an organisation and which are generally objected to by workers, are generally **possible** because of workers' involvement in management. **Communication** at all levels has been easier for participation device. Industrial conflicts have been reduced and "workers' participation at the plant level can be seen as the first step to establishing democratic values in society at large" (Monappa & Saiyadain).

It is no exaggeration to say that workers' participation in management of industries is not accidental, it has come out of necessity and it will stay as a forceful device for improving industrial relations for the sake of necessity. A number of benefits accruing from workers' participation justify its significance.

Participation encourages workers to accept responsibility, makes them ego-involved and emotionally involved.

Sufficiently significant is that, contrary to the usual practice of the workers to oppose any move taken by the management, workers participating in management co-operate and encourage the acceptance of any change in the traditional pattern by the workers. This is no mean advantage on the part of the management to introduce any new idea in the organisation. Where workers participate in management, there is less resistance to the introduction of computer economy or any scheme of rationalisation.

Workers' participation in management also enriches the decisions of the management, since all decisions are taken after much deliberation with the workers.

By improving morale and team work and by using creativity of workers' participation, it plays a significant role in improving industrial relations and then it increases production and productivity.

Workers' participation in management adds dignity to workers, makes them feel one with the management, gives them confidence, encourages them to speak out – all these bring about an all-round development of the organisation.

The significance of workers' participation in management is enormous since participation in the managerial function by the workers helps solving many management problems, particularly personnel in nature. To what extent participation can go in solving various organisational problems mutually depends on the forms and nature of participation. But that the workers' participation in management is significant cannot be disputed. In almost all the countries today workers' participation in management has been accepted as a very effective and powerful tool for building up sound organisation and bridging the gap between management and labour.

Participation is significant since it improves efficiency of enterprises, develops social education and acts as a means for attaining industrial peace. It is humanitarian as it gives the workers an acceptable status within the working community and a sense of purpose in activity. Workers' participation in management is a matter of ideology that develops self-management in industry.

Participation acquires significance since it confers a number of benefits to the management, workers and the society. These benefits are : (1) enhancement of the sense of responsibility of workers' (2) change of mental attitude of workers to accept any change (3) encouragement for better decisions (4) improvement of morale and team work (5) use of the creativity of employees (6) encouragement for self expression and self advancement (7) fostering dignity to workers (8) improvement of product quality and quantity (9) reduction of workers' grievances and industrial conflicts.

So, society, business and employees are all benefitted if workers participation in management can properly be implemented.

### Workers' participation in management – Position in India

Workers' participation in management has now become inevitable and indispensable socially, psychologically and economically.

Workers — the human factor of production — cannot be kept away without having them involved in management decisions if any management really wants to attain the goals of the organisation. The economic and social changes that have taken place in different countries in recent years clearly point out that the involvement of workers is of great necessity not only to bring about an all-round development of the productive unit but also to maintain industrial peace which is so vital in increasing production and productivity. So, workers' participation is a must for an organisation wedded to the policy of furthering the betterment of both the organisation and its employees.

Economically workers have the right to share the gains of higher productivity and prosperity of the enterprise.

Psychologically, for the satisfaction of workers, they must be made to understand that they are mportant in the organisation and this can only ensure team spirit and mutual co-operation.

Socially, by participation, workers are regarded as parties of joint venture and, as such, conflicts between labour and capital can be averted to a considerable extent. In the world to-day, human resource is the most valuable resource with immense potentialities which no management can ignore. So, various forms of workers' participation in management have evolved and, though we can- not say that the optimum results have been achieved, it is no use denying the fact that bringing the workers closer to management and involving them in managerial decisions have infused in then a sense of belonging for the organisation to which they belong. This has, one must agree, salutary effect on the entire environment of the organisation.

To have an understanding with workers in the matter of decisions affecting not only workers but also the organisation as a whole, various methods of workers' involvement have been devised.

In the 'Consultative Supervision' form of participation, the supervisor meets his subordinate, when occasions so demand, just to obtain group ideas in solving operating problems.

In a 'Democrative Supervision' form of participation, decision-making responsibility is shifted to the entire group and the Manager acts as the Chairman only. He leads a decision but does not make it. This is some sort of delegation of authority and responsibility in the specific areas of managerial functions. This form of participation becomes effective when workers participating are well-equipped with necessary knowledge of the organisation.

A 'Committee System' of participation has evolved. In this system, standing committees of managers carry out studies and make recommendations to the top management. This system is also known as "Multiple management" system. The system affords ample opportunity for the management development programme as under this system, lower management, middle management and upper management – all are involved. The junior boards with middle management and lower management assume the character of advisory committees. Their unanimous recommendations are to be sent to the senior board which must approve those recommendations.

Labour-management co-operation may be achieved through works committees as provided in the Industrial Disputes Act, 1947. However, these works committees have not been successful in fostering co-operation between labour and management because of various reasons such as trade union hostility, workers' lack of interest, opposition from middle management level, general indifference by the management, incompetent workers' representatives etc.

Another tool that was used to bring about cooperation between labour and management was 'Joint Management Councils'. The councils have three sets of functions – (a) consultation on matters of general administration, (b) information through discussion and suggestion on the general economic situation of the concern, the state of the market etc. and (c) administration in respect of welfare measures, safety measures, working hours etc.

Joint Management Councils also failed to yield desired results. Big private or public enterprises did not accept JMC as a form of labour management co-operation. Besides, the spirit of co-operation was lacking, participation was not properly defined and there was no mandatory force in JMC.

Any scheme of joint consultation can succeed only if certain conditions are satisfied. In India, these conditions are missing. It can succeed here only as a supplement to collective bargaining.

There is a system of participation known as 'Suggestion Programme'. The employees submit ideas and inventions to the management for scrutiny by a special committee. This form of participation exists primarily by written communication; there is no face-to-face interaction, nor is there any joint deliberation and thinking. Hence, its scope is limited and should be supplemented by other forms of participation.

Full-fledged participation by labour in management is possible only through the involvement of labour in the Board of Directors. An employee director can represent and safeguard the labour interests and view-points. But employee representation on the board is still a matter of controversy. Of course, it must be admitted that unless and until workers are trained for assuming larger and larger responsibilities, the participation becomes a matter of decorative value. Many authorities on management believe that "the management abilities of all employees is a great untapped source of social wealth".

Workers' participation in management in the form of labour management association can also be evolved but its success depends on how the mutual wants of the management and the workers are met. Management wants to make more production at a reasonable cost and the employees want that they are given proper recognition for their labour. So, it is a matter of mutual understanding and co-operation; both parties will then have fair chance to share equaitably the fruits of prosperity. In India, such associations are not much encouraging, of course, barring a few. "Both sides often work at cross-purposes. In some cases we have occasional 'cease-fire' friendship" (Shulekar).

Prior to Independence, no serious and systematic efforts were made in India with regard to the workers' participation in management. A few progressive employers, of course, carried on their management in consultation with the workers, though formally there was no workers' participation in management. To most of the industrialists in India, the idea of workers' participation was not palatable. There came the Industrial Disputes Act, 1947, which provided for the establishment of Works Committees in all the undertakings employing 100 or more workers. The intention was "to promote measures for securing and preserving amity and good relations between the employer and workmen". The Works Committees failed to fulfil the expectations for which they were provided to be formed.

In the Second Five Year Plan, joint labour management commitees were set up. In this Plan was envisaged a more ambitious programme for securing labour participation. "A socialist society is built up not solely on monetary incentives, but on ideas of service to society and the willingness on the part of the labour to recognise such service. It is necessary in this context that the worker should be made to feel that in his own way he is helping to build a progressive state. The creation of industrial democracy, therefore, is a pre-requisite for the establishment of a socialist society" (Second Five Year Plan). A study group consisting of the representatives of the workers, the management and the Government under the chairmanship of Mr. Vishnu Sahay was sent to western countries in 1956 and its report was submitted in 1957. In this report there were concrete suggestions in the direction of Workers' participation in management. A scheme of 'Joint Management Councils' has found favour in this report.

The 15th session of the Indian Labour Conference held in New Delhi in July 1957 took up the report of the Study Group for discussion and with regard to the concept of workers' participation and adoption of the scheme, there was general agreement. It was agreed that the scheme would be implemented in certain selected industries on an experimental basis. The conference recommended the adoption of the scheme in 50 undertakings in the public as well as in the private sectors. A subcommittee was formed to work out the details of the scheme. It selected certain undertakings in both the sectors on the basis of certain criteria, such as active workers' union in the undertaking, at least 500 workers, employer's membership of one of the leading employer's organisations, affiliation of the workers' union to one of the central federations and good industrial relations of the organisation. A significant feature of the scheme was the absence of any legal sanction and tripartite agreement formed the sole basis for the introduction of the voluntary scheme.

The Third Plan envisaged a major programme of the progressive extension of the scheme of JMC's to new industries and units. It was hoped that in the course of a few years JMC's would be a normal feature of the industrial system.

Joint Management Councils and Joint Works Committees have been set up by the various industrial and commercial undertakings in India. In addition, various committees and councils had been set up at departmental and shop floor levels. On plant level, joint production committees, joint consultation councils, advisory councils etc. for facilitating consultation between labour and management on various matters connected with production and welfare of the workers have been set up.

In 1960, a second seminar on the workers' participation in management was held in New Delhi under the auspices of the Union Ministry of Labour. The general consensus of opinions was that the scheme had not been successful.

In 1963, the working of the scheme was assessed by the Ministry of Labour and Employment and a report was circulated among public enterprises suggesting measures for strengthening the joint councils. The report of the study group of the Administrative Reforms Commission was that the scheme had not made much headway for various reasons. The report suggested the setting up of joint consultative machinery. The Councils, according to the report, should function with the spirit and perspective that should characterize such institutions and if they receive the requisite support from the top management of the undertakings, the public sector will really be able to set an example in harmony and co-operation.

Since the declaration of Emergency in India in 1975 and the introduction of the 20-point economic programme, a new two-tier scheme titled workers' participation in Industry had been in operation – the shop floor or departmental level and at the plant or enterprise level.

A new scheme of Unit Councils had been introduced since 1977. In addition there are other schemes of Workers' participation –

(a) appointment of representatives of workers on the boards of management of Public Sector Undertakings; and

(b) Participation of workers in the share capital of Public Sector undertakings.

The above two schemes had been recommended to be extended to Public Limited Companies by the Sachar Committee.

It will not be out of context to mention here that some authority in labour management feels that in India a worker cannot be an equal partner with management since he is subordinated to management by the entire system. So, a dual status as an operative subordinate to the organisation is difficult to comprehend.

**The main causes of unsatisfactory progress in the attempts towards workers' involvement in management in India are:**

1) The apathetic attitude of managements.
2) Opposition of trade unions and workers themselves. When the lower level needs of the workers are satisfied, they are no more interested in achieving higher values of life. This is the peculiar nature of the workers of our country.
3) Business environment in India is not very much conducive to the growth of industrial relations which can only encourage workers' participation in management.
4) Professionalisation of management in India acts as a deterrent to the growth of workers involvement schemes.
5) Managerial personnel do not have usually that temperament and attitude which motivates workers to come closer to management and participate in the management process.
6) The schemes of workers' participation in management should be voluntary in nature and imposition of any scheme from outside cannot bear fruits.
7) Councils and committees formed to encourage labour participation are not so scientifically planned; their functions are, in most cases, overlapping and create confusion.

To sum up, it can be said that the pre-conditions for success of any labour participation scheme are not favourable in India. The spirit of participation is absent. Workers are not properly educated to understand the implications of their involvement in management nor are they conscious about the upliftment of their standard of living. Once the minimum needs are satisfied, they do not bother about the satiation of the higher needs of life. The general standard of living of the workers being low, any attempt to raise their standard of living does not appeal to them much. **Workers' participation in management is a higher philosophy of the recognition of labour on equal footing with the management. This should be appreciated; otherwise the schemes for joint actions of labour and management cannot be expected.**

In a more or less dismal picture of workers' participation in management in India, TISCO comes out as the most encouraging example where the industrial relations have been quite good. This is because of good relation between labour and management. The spirit of co-operation has always been a powerful force in maintaining close relation between labour and management in TISCO. Through various Joint Committees, TISCO's labour participation in management has been exemplary.

In the new scheme of workers' participation in management, both at shop-floor level and plant level, the Government is in favour of flexibility in the scheme so as to allow variations to suit local conditions. Shop Councils and Joint Councils have, no doubt, been set up but any scheme of workers' participation can only succeed through an effective two-way communication and exchange of information between labour and management. The Government of India has appealed to all the managements and workers and trade unions concerned to implement the schemes of workers' participation in their organisations. It is now felt that workers' participation has been a necessity for the improvement of the work environment and in general for the betterment of industrial relations. So the Government wants to make it a statutory obligation on the part of the undertakings to have schemes of workers' participation in management.

To conclude, a constant endeavour is noticed on the part of the Government to give more share of responsibility to the workers in the management of industrial concerns. Obstacles are many. The industrial background of the country and the economic and the political conditions prevailing in the country are not so conducive to the development of healthy relations between labour and capital but with sincere efforts and humane approach, workers' participation in management is likely to get more and more impetus and harmony between labour and capital may be achieved to a considerable extent in the near future.

# CHAPTER 17

## COLLECTIVE BARGAINING

Credit goes to Webbs for the concept of 'Collective bargaining' at the beginning of this century. It is called "collective" because employees form an association authorising it to act as their agents in reaching an agreement and because employers may also act as a group rather than an individual. It is described as "bargaining" in part because the method of reaching an agreement involves proposals and counter-proposals, offers and counter offers. In collective bargaining, the representatives of both the employers and workers sit together and settle matters by mutual bargaining. The agreements are not compulsorily enforceable. All depend upon mutual goodwill and trust, mainly of the employers.

As a measure for prevention of industrial disputes, it is very important and is being widely used in the western countries. It is closely associated with the growth of trade unionism. Collective bargaining as a technique is an integral part of industrial society. Workers' participation in management can be successful only as a supplement to a well-established system of collective bargaining. It is an important instrument for redressing the grievances of the employers as well as the workers. It removes class-hatred, mutual distrust and friction to a considerable extent as things are settled amicably. It educates the workers and gives them a feeling of oneness with the employers and the organisation. It helps in improving their lot without resorting to strikes. On the whole, it improves the industrial relations considerably. "A mature collective bargaining is the best child of industrial relations". Collective bargaining assumes unique importance in labour-management relations since impulse for movement in worker's participation in management must come from within and not from without or government. Labour–management relations through workers' committees or joint management councils and collective bargaining machinery are complementary and must go hand-in-hand.

Collective bargaining includes : (1) Union recognition (2) Management rights (3) Strikes and lockouts (4) Wages (5) Working conditions (6) Discipline (7) Arbitration (8) Job rights (9) Health and safety (10) Social security.

To be successful, collective bargaining should have — (1) Strong representative trade union (2) Strong and sympathetic management (3) Agreement on basic objectives (4) Mutual co-operation and trust (5) Existence of fact-finding approach and willingness to use new methods and tools for the solution of industrial problems.

Large number of companies in India have resorted to this method of labour management association. TISCO and Indian Aluminium have been using this tool with success.

The existing obstacles to collective bargaining must be removed to accord due importance to it as an effective measure for ensuring industrial peace.

# CHAPTER 18

## TRADE UNIONS

After the Industrial Revolution, there came the factory system of production which resulted in the pitiable conditions of workers. They found themselves weak and completely at the mercy of the employers. Unity became a matter of urgent necessity on the part of the workers to raise a united voice against the oppression and exploitation of the employers and to save themselves from the onslaught of the powerful employer class.

A simple definition of the trade union is it is "a continuous association of wage earners for the purpose of maintaining and improving the condition of their working lives" (Sydney & Beatrice Webb). This definition is too narrow; a trade union now encompasses various activities and is not confined to "working lives" only. "The trade union movement of to-day is not content with protecting and improving wages and conditions of labour; it concerns itself with all matters by which the workers are likely to be affected, whether as producers or consumers, whether as units of industrial man-power or as citizens" (John Price). Trade Unions play a very important role to-day in the improvement of economic, political and social conditions of the worker. S. C. Kuchhal states, "Trade Unions to-day are pluralist in character and pragmatic in method; if they are not, they are unlikely to survive the demands made upon them by so swiftly changing an environment".

The contributions of trade unions towards ameliorating the lot of the workers are now universally accepted though there is a divergence of opinion as to effects of trade unions on the incidence of strikes. However, there is no denying the fact that trade unions act not only in the interests of industry but also in the interest of the State.

The character of trade unions will be clear from the definition of Trade Union as given in the Trade Unions Act, 1926, of India. "A trade union is any combination of persons, whether temporary or permanent, primarily for the purpose of regulating the relations between workers and employers or between workers and workers and for imposing restrictive conditions on the conduct of any trade or business and includes the federation of two or more trade unions".

Sri. V.V. Giri, former President of India and an eminent trade union leader defined trade unions as "voluntary organisations of workers formed to promote and protect their interests by collective action".

### Functions

The functions of trade union can broadly be divided into two categories – protective or militant and positive or ministrant. The protective functions aim at securing certain benefits from the employer through collective bargaining, strikes, go-slow tactics or work-to-rule. 'Gheraos' may also be included in this category. The positive functions include the support given to members during strikes, temporary unemployment and some benefits such as educational facilities, recreational and other services.

The functions of trade unions are again classified into intramural and extramural. The former regulate hours of work, provision of rest houses, continuity of employment, safety, sanitation and other welfare facilities within the factory premises whereas the extramural look after the welfare of the workers in respect of their education, recreation, housing etc.

From the above discussion, it seems that the functions of trade unions are both militant and fraternal in nature.

Trade Unions secure better wages for their workers and a part of the increased prosperity of industry for their members in the form of bonus. They ensure stable employment for workers and attain better conditions for the workers. Unions train up their workers to facilitate understanding of technological advances. It is no mean function for a trade union to foster a sense of self-respect and dignity among its members. Trade unions promote national integration, influence the socio-economic policies of the community through active participation in their formulation at various levels. Thus, they instil in members a sense of responsibility towards industry and the community.

The functions of trade unions are not identical in all the countries. In advanced countries problems confronting labour are different than those of developing countries. As such, trade unions, too, are to change their functions to suit the needs of the workers of that country.

In the capitalist system, it is a truism that trade unions are friends, philosophers and guides of the workers. No system – rather, nothing – in this world is an unmixed blessing; trade unions are no exception but, on the whole, the role they play is commendable.

## Weaknesses

Trade unionism suffers from certain weaknesses in general. To be a worthy and effective institution for furtherance of the cause of labour, conditions must be favourable. A trade union can only be a friend and a guide of workers if the work environment and other conditions so warrant.

Trade Unions become weak and suffer if they fail to secure wide membership support without which sound financial position cannot be ensured. A prolonged fight against the employer may entail huge funds, the lack of which may render a trade union ineffective. As we find today, trade unions are mostly engaged in the propagation of the political ideologies of a particular political party. This sort of activity weakens a trade union as, to these trade unions, economic and industrial issues are pushed to the back-ground.

Many trade union leaders feel that militancy is the main stay of a trade union and waging a war against the employer is the function of the trade union. If this policy is pursued, a trade union is sure to be weak.

We have discussed above weaknesses of trade unions in general. We discuss below the **weaknesses of trade unions in India.**

The history of the development of trade unions in India goes back to the outbreak of the First World War. The grave economic difficulties created by the war gave birth to trade unionism. No doubt, there were sporadic labour movements prior to this formal growth of trade unions. Indian trade unions have been led by very eminent leaders of the country. Mahatma Gandhi, Lala Lajpat Rai, G. S. Deshpande. B.T. Ranadive, N.M. Joshi and many more eminent personalities of the country have contributed to the growth of trade union movement in our country.

But Indian trade unions have some weaknesses. They are :

**1. Limited membership**

Many workers do not enrol themselves as members of any trade union. Membership is mostly confined to urban area and there also it does not cover all the workers of the organisation. Even in the organised sector, membership is not satisfactory to the desirable extent. Trade unionism, it is rightly said, has only touched a fringe of the working class in India.

**2. Domination of political parties**

Political parties today dominate the trade unions in India. To achieve their narrow and selfish political motives, the real character of trade unions cannot be adhered to. Political rivalry strikes the true spirit of trade unionism and, unfortunately, the workers su-ffer.

**3. Small size of trade unions**

The size of trade unions in India is not satisfactory; it is rather small and thus it does not possess, in many organisations, the strength necessary to bargain with the employers. With limited membership and small size, they do not have the required man-power and financial strength to continue their struggle against the oppression of the employer.

**4. Lack of Unity**

The trade unions not only have limited membership and small size but also there is multiplicity of unions working in a particular industrial undertaking. This leads to division among workers; unity which is the core of trade unionism, suffers seriously.

5. **Attitude of employers**

Taking advantage of the political rivalries, small size and lack of unity of the trade unions existing in an organisation, the employers take apathetic and unbecoming attitude towards workers. They regard establishment of trade unions as "an act of treachery, disloyalty and ingratitude". Taking advantage of the ignorance, poverty, illiteracy and weakness of the worker, the employers try to disrupt the unity among them.

6. **Outside leadership**

Leadership of trade unions rests not with the worker but with the outside leaders for whom it is very difficult to feel the pangs of sufferings of the workers. Most of these leaders are professional persons like lawyers and social and political leaders who do not really feel for the workers, nor do they actually understand their problems. It does not need any elucidation to say that any one who did never suffer from any of the difficulties to which a worker is put will not appreciate the difficulty of the worker to the desirable extent. This is a serious weakness of Indian Trade Unionism.

7. **Faulty method of labour recruitment**

The method of labour recruitment that is usually followed in India weakens trade unions. Majority of the workers are recruited through intermediaries and they remain at the mercy of these intermediaries. The intermediaries themselves bargain with the employers to the detriment of the interest of the workers. The workers mostly come from villages and, being unable to adjust themselves with the new environment of the urban areas, many of them leave. So, this type of recruitment stands in the way of the growth of strong and continuous labour organisations.

8. **Lack of interests on the part of the workers**

Workers themselves do not take active interest in the activities of trade unions. This phenomenon is attributable to the migratory character of the workers, their illiteracy, poverty etc. The implication of strengthening trade unions in their interests are not intelligible to many of them; they are simply interested in earning daily wages to send them to their village-families and live contended with the meagre surplus they keep with them. Their standard of living is too low. They do not think about 'higher level' living. All these peculiar characteristics of Indian workers are obstacles to the growth of healthy unions.

9. **Inadequacy of finances**

Another weakness of the trade unions in India is the inadequacy of finances. Funds are limited because of low membership fee, many are defaulters; so when needs arise, unions cannot fight for want of funds. A continuous fight against management to bargain something needs funds since the workers may have to go on strike during which period they will have to be maintained out of the funds of the trade unions.

10. **Lack of a common goal**

Trade unions in India today suffer from the lack of a common goal. Since the workers are controlled by the labour wings of different political parties, oneness of mind among the workers cannot be expected. Workers are themselves divided, the rivalry among the trade unions is more severe than their hatred and opposition against the employer. This is a situation highly deplorable which causes a trade union to be weak.

11. **Absence of craft unions**

This is a unique feature of the trade unions in India. There is no craft-wise trade union. All workers of different crafts belong to the same trade union and this naturally stands in the way of their coming close to one another. There always remains a distance between workers specialised in different crafts. Thus, the trade unions with such members become weak.

Besides the above causes, we may mention that changing work environment, composition of labour, social and economic status of labour, change in labour management relations, change in government attitude and also change in public attitude are factors that have bearing on the strength or otherwise of trade unions in India.

The trade unions in India with leaders from outside the industrial workers are very often accused of striking deals with the employers against the interest of the workers. It is alleged that when workers, after a sustained struggle, come to a bargaining point with the employers, the leaders behave in such a manner and arrive at agreement with the employers on such terms which are not always conducive to the interests of the workers. Politics is dominating the unionism and though membership strength is now on the increase, fight with the employers for the interest of the workers is found to be lacking in sincerity and compassion for the workers. Personal ambitions of leadership and multiplicity of trade unions are two major obstacles facing Indian Trade Unionism.

In the back-ground of socio-economic and political changes, the entire attitude of trade unions should be changed. From militancy, unions should better develop fraternal aspect, they should realise that workers' interests can be best served and protected on mutual understanding and better relationship between labour and capital. In public enterprises, trade unions should have the sense of belonging for the undertakings and in private enterprises, too, a change in the attitude of many trade unions affiliated to various political parties can go a long way in solving problems of workers. Trade unions are not meant for trade unions sake only. They are for betterment of workers' lot. It is the feeling of conciliation and not of confrontation that can better solve problems of industrial relations. There are examples in the functioning of trade unions in foreign countries where we find the objectives of the unions are achieved without conflicts and problems are solved across the table.

Industrial peace is of urgent necessity now in India and Trade Unions have a big role to play. The present economic crisis in India has all the more necessitated the trade unions to come forward with national outlook to help the governments in the rehabilitation of the economy of the country. Strikes and lockouts leading to the closure of a large number of industrial units are a definite reflection on trade unions. Definitely there are problems leading to the closure of the industrial units but solutions are also there for the employers and the employees to find out with the active intervention of the government concerned. The weaknesses of trade unions in India can be removed with earnestness, sincerity, selflessness and with a better co-ordinating and understanding among all the parties involved – the workers unions, the employer and the governments.

The National Labour Commission on Labour recommended certain actions for strengthening trade unions. They are : (a) elimination of party politics (b) building up of internal leadership (c) encouragement to collective bargaining schemes (d) improvement of the system of recognition of the unions (e) extension of security to union and encouragement thereof and (f) conferment of powers to labour courts to settle labour disputes.

## Labour Welfare

Personnel management has the objective of realising organisation goals by dealing with personnel matter in such a way as would contribute to the betterment of human relations. The human factor in production is now recognised as the most important factor. On the efficiency or otherwise of this factor depends the success or failure in the performance of an organisation to a considerable extent. Efficiency of the workers cannot be increased simply by the mere wish of the employers. Workers are to be made efficient and, to make them efficient, their welfare has to be looked into. So, Labour Welfare measures constitute a very important part of the functions of personnel management.

As a measure for welfare of the workers, the basic amenities must be provided to them; the work environment has to be improved, measures must be taken to meet the basic and higher needs of workers. Physically and mentally, the workers will have to be so developed that they are capable to contribute their best to the organisation. This calls upon the employers to think about the welfare measures for the workers.

The basic needs such as food, clothing and shelter must be met to the satisfaction of the workers. Then the higher level needs for the development of mental faculties should also draw the attention of the employers. So, Labour Welfare is a comprehensive idea encompassing within it all that is necessary for the labour to live a purposeful life with all modern amenities. Labour Welfare measures are aimed at rendering such services and amenities to workers to enable them to perform their work in healthy congenial surroundings conducive to boosting their morale.

Labour Welfare, simply stated, is a concept that envisages to ensure improvement of the condition in and around the work place. Canteen facilities, recreational facilities, sanitary and medical facilities, accommodation facilities, convey ance facilities – all constitute labour welfare.

Labour Welfare, therefore, ensures —

(a) Worker's efficiency (b) morale boosting (c) reduction in labour turnover and absenteeism (d) recognition of human values and social aspect of business.

Labour Welfare activities do not take the same form in all the countries. Economic, political and social conditions are determinants of Labour Welfare measures — the nature of the measures and their extent. So they vary from one country to another. The needs of the workers of the country like ours cannot be equated with those of the workers in advanced countries. So, the approach to workers welfare will be different, the measures to be taken will also be different.

Welfare measures should be comprehensive. Workers should be provided with all amenities inside and outside the plant. In any welfare state as it is to-day all the world over, no government can remain a passive onlooker as to what has been happening in the industrial world. Happy and contented workers with high morale can only be expected to have high productivity and capacity to contribute to the growth of industries in the country.

In a country like ours, where many industrialists are reluctant to recognise the efficacy and desirability of labour welfare measures, the government has an active part to play. Enactments and legislations may be necessary to compel the unwilling industrialists to resort to worker's welfare measures.

Labour Welfare activities and labour efficiency are closely related and so low labour efficiency in India can well be ascribed to the unsatisfactory labour welfare measures. Employers, governments, trade unions and Statutory Welfare Funds are the chief agencies through which labour welfare can be ensured.

Employers have at last realised the need for Labour Welfare and the Industrial Acts have also compelled them to take some welfare measures as a matter of compulsion. So, from their side, welfare measures have improved.

So far as governments are concerned, much headway has been made since Independence. Both at the state and national levels, various legislations for the welfare of workers have come into force. The National Government, for obvious reasons, is to take active interest in the labour welfare because neglecting vast masses of working population, no popular government can expect to deliver goods to the people. By doing welfare to the workers, welfare to the people at large can be ensured and a State can then only assume the character of 'Welfare State'. Various measures adopted by governments include the institution of labour welfare funds in coal and mica mines and provident funds in many industries, the initiation of social security and industrial housing schemes, the enactment of the Factories Act, Indian Mines Act, Plantations Labour Act, Mines Welfare Cess Act etc. Many state governments have adopted labour welfare measures such as recreational facilities, educational and cultural facilities. Health Centres, Family Planning Clinics and Centres, Worker's Education Centres, Training classes in crafts for women etc. have also been set up by a number of popular state governments.

Labour Welfare activities are now not exclusively within the jurisdiction of the employers, governments and trade unions. Strictly not with a view to rendering welfare services to workers as defined in the industrial dictionary, a number of service organisations, national and international in character, have come forwared to uplift the conditions of the toiling masses. To educate them, to house them properly, to help them in medical facilities and health matters, the humanitarian institutions have been rendering no less service today in India.

In spite of all the efforts so far taken for the welfare of workers, it can be frankly admitted that there is yet enough scope and necessity for the welfare measures of the workers. Workers themselves have to press for their welfare on their unions as well as on the governments.

In India, Labour Welfare is a vast area of activities. Welfare in its comprehensive sense is very difficult for a country like ours to achieve. Problems are many to the acquisition of welfare facilities. Problems and obstacles, however difficult they are, must have to be solved and overcome, to establish industrial democracy and industrial peace. As to the problems, housing poses a serious one. To this can be added the problem of accidents which must cover any programme of welfare to workers. Statutory measures for safety of workers have been undertaken and training in safety is also being imparted. Industrial legislations should be made more comprehensive in providing measures for safety and training in safety. As to industrial housing problems, a national housing programme has been chalked out. Plantation Labour Housing Scheme, Slum Clearance Scheme, Land Acquisition and Development Schemes, Middle Income Group Housing Scheme, Rental Housing Schemes for State Government Employees, Social Housing Schemes — all are on the list of government activities. Subsidised Industrial Housing Scheme, Low Income Group Housing Schemes are additions to the Housing Schemes already undertaken by the governments, both Central and State.

The Code of Efficiency for the welfare of workers, with various suggestions for improvement of industrial relations and higher productivity and imposition of obligations on the part of the management for securing better standards of living of the workers did not receive equal attention and respect from all the labour wings of the political parties.

# CHAPTER 19

## LABOUR REMUNERATION
### (Employee Compensation)

Of all the factors that affect labour-capital relations, remuneration in the form of wages or bonus presumably figures most prominently. Majority of the industrial disputes are economic in nature and wages and bonus constitute the apple of discord between labour and management. It has, therefore, been rightly put "wages operate both on the circumference and at the centre of industrial relations". Wages, as a factor price, have the peculiarity that these have to be paid in advance of the sale of goods; the productivity measurement becomes somewhat uncertain and it gives rise to a conflict of interests between workers and employers. Wages must be fair and, in order to ensure this, certain matters must have to be taken into considerations—minimum wage, guaranteed wage, wage differentials and forms of wage payments.

There are three concepts of wages – minimum wage, fair wage and living wage.

Minimum wage is just the wage to cover bare necessities of life – food, clothing and shelter. It may provide a little for workers' efficiency – for their health and education. Minimum wage legislation is in force in most of the countries. Because of the weak bargaining power of workers, legislative action for minimum wage payment is necessary.

Fair wage means wage equal to that received by employees equal in all respects.

Living wage refers to wage concept where the wage is such as to give sufficient inducement to work. It includes components such as bare necessities, insurance schemes, children's educational expenses, recreational expenses and a certain margin for saving.

### A good wage plan should have the following characteristics

(1) Simplicity and flexibility (2) Incentive element (3) Fairness and equity (4) Adequacy in compensation (5) Facility for collective bargaining (6) Merit rating (7) Minimum wage provision (8) Money wage orientation (9) Inflation combating element (10) Grievance highlighting mechanism (11) Conformity with current rates of wages (12) Provision for fringe benefits (13) Cost control device.

A sound wage plan is essential both for the workers and the employers. Simply formulated with enough flexibility and having the element of incentiveness, a good wage system increases productivity of labour, enhances production, brings about better relation between labour and capital. Discontentment among workers is reduced to an appreciable extent, the efficient workers are duly promoted and adequately remunerated. Though a scientifically planned wage system apparently appears to be an inflated amount of wage, a careful observation discloses that ultimately it pays the employers and helps development of a more congenial atmosphere where the workers are expected to give the best in them to the organisation.

There are two fundamental methods of compensating the workers : Time Wage and Piece Wage.

Time Wage based on time spent on work is a widely used method very simple to operate. The amount of earnings is guaranteed; quality of work is likely to be improved, since a worker is not interested in the quantum of production. He is rather interested in spending the time and, if kept under proper supervision, this may help improvement of quality of the product produced slowly but carefully since he is to work under supervision. But quantity suffers; the increase in production cannot be expected to the desirable extent.

Piece wage method is based on quantum of production. "Produce more, you will get more" this is the basis of the system. A worker put under the system does not think about the quality of the product he produces but he is interested to produce as many as he can. A strict supervision may check deterioration of quality, no doubt; but, in general, it can be said that time wage system improves quality and piece wage system improves quantity.

It cannot be said straightway which system is better. It all depends on the circumstances. An enterprise more interested in production than quality will base its wage system on piece-rate whereas the enterprise interested in quality will introduce wage system based on time. Of course, the question of supervision must be kept in mind to achieve the desired objectives – whether quantity or quality.

## Incentive Wage Plans

Incentive wage systems are based on "standard" of performance for the job. The standard may be set on the basis of early experience or by time, motion or job evaluation studies. The standard is based on an average worker's capacity without putting him to undue strain. There are three broad categories of incentive schemes – Simple incentive plan, sharing incentive wage plan and Group indicative plan (Dunn & Rachel).

The **conditions favouring or disfavouring an incentive scheme** have two aspects – the external and internal environment. Incentive schemes are suitable when the product market is competitive (example – consumer goods industry) and labour costs are high, warranting a shift to the incentive system in which unit costs can be brought down with increased output. Incentive schemes can be easily introduced where trade unions are not so militant. As to the internal environment favouring or disfavouring the introduction of incentive schemes, the production cycles are to be taken into consideration. The cycles should be short and repetitive enabling high output and this should be directly related to worker effort and should also be easily translated into earnings. Variations in flow and quality of materials should be kept to the minimum.

In incentive wage payment schemes, there are **problem areas.** While money is certainly a strong motivator, single-minded pursuit of it has led to difficult problems. A U.K. researcher has revealed that, in many cases, incentive schemes have been abandoned, mainly due to the frequent disputes causing industrial unrest. It has also been observed that the quality of the product deteriorates in order to maintain higher output. Another danger of incentive plan is that employees tend to disregard safety measures or strain themselves unduly to maximise their earnings. Besides, workers resist changes of machines and production system as they are not sure of their effects on their earnings. Incentive wage receipts are considered by the workers ultimately as their legitimate minimum wage, thus there is an attempt to push up the base rate. Jealousies between workers may creep in because of differences of pay packets though arising out of the differences in their abilities and capacities. In India, it has been found that "incentive schemes have a positive impact on productivity, labour costs and industrial relations. Money has a Solutary impact on production".

A system of wage payment where both quality and quantity can be ensured may be termed an Incentive Wage Plan. It is a judicious combination of both basic systems of wage payments – Time and Piece wages.

There are three components of an incentive wage plan : (1) Establishment of standard output task or quota on which incentive earnings are based – Time & Motion Studies (2) An hourly or base or standard rate of compensation for similar jobs put on incentive – Job Evaluation Technique and (3) Incentive of Bonus or premium rate for extra output of higher efficiency.

A firm can devise its own incentive plan with wage rate using four basic elements —
(a) Unit of output (b) Time saved (c) Time worked and (d) Standard Time.

### (1) 100 per cent Time Premium Plan

Under this Plan, a worker gets 100 per cent of the bonus earned. Thus, if the hourly rate is Rs. 2, time is 8 hours, standard time per piece one hour and number of pieces completed 10, then the total earnings will be –

Total earnings = (Time × hourly rate) + (Time saved × hourly rate)

= (8 × Rs. 2) + (2 × Rs. 2) = 16 + 4 = Rs. 20.

From the point of view of budgeting, cost accounting, equity and justice, this method of wage payment is most suitable.

**(2) Rowan Plan**

Under this plan, a standard time is determined before-hand. A time wage is guaranteed and bonus is paid for the time saved.

The bonus can be computed as follows :

Bonus = (Time saved/standard time) × Time taken × Rate per hour.

A worker works on an hourly rate of Rs. 2. He has been given 10 hours to complete. He completes it in 8 hours. His bonus will be :

(2/10) × 8 × Rs 2 = Rs. 3.20.

So the worker will get altogether

Rs 16 + Rs. 3.20 = Rs. 19.20

This plan is not popular among workers as they find it difficult to understand the calculation of their earnings.

**(3) Halsey Plan**

The standard time required for a job is determined on the basis of time and motion studies or on the basis average previous times of doing jobs. One who can save time from the standard time is paid bonus. The bonus for time saved is a percentage (30 to 50 per cent) of the value of the time saved as measured by the hourly rate. Thus, the total pay of a worker is the sum of the guaranteed hourly rate time hours worked plus a predetermined percentage of the hourly rate multiplied by whatever time he has saved by working more speedily. This system is also called Halsey Weir System because the Weir System is on par with the Halsey Plan.

Halsey Plan wage and bonus calculations :

A worker's hourly rate is Rs. 2. Standard time 10 hours. Completes the task in 8 hours. Bonus is 50 per cent of the time saved.

Total earnings will be

Time × Hourly rate plus (Bonus × Time saved × hourly rate)

= 8 × Rs. 2 plus $^1/_2$ × 2 × Rs. 2 = Rs. 18/-

It is easy to introduce the method; it is also very easy to calculate earnings. Since a minimum hourly wage rate is fixed, a sense of security prevails among the workers put under this method of wage payments. Profit of saved time is divided between worker and management, thus both the parties are benefitted and the bonus rate becomes permanent. The short-comings of this method are – the unscientifically determined standard time, the question of fairness of the plan of dividing the profit of saved time between management and workers, the method of bonus calculation based on each job causes slow down on others and the decision of producing beyond standard is entirely dependent on the worker alone.

## The Bedaux or Points Plan

In this method, workers in all departments earn bonus or premium at the same rate. The foreman also shares the bonus with the worker in the ratio of 3 : 1 (75% worker, 25% foreman). A point or Bedeaux or "B" is defined as the work which a man should be able to perform in one minute. The difficulty of the job is then measured in terms of its number of B's. If the standard time for a job is 10 hours, it would be expressed as 600 'B's since the task is defined as 60 × B hours. The standard 'B's of various jobs done by a worker in a week are calculated and compared with the actual time. If the actual time exceeds the standard time, the worker gets wages for the actual time worked. Thus, wages on the time bases are guaranteed. If the standard 'B's exceed the actual time, the difference is divided by 60 to give hours saved and there 75% wages of the time saved go to the worker and the rest 25% of it to the foreman.

For example :

Standard time = 12 hours

Actual time = 10 hours

or,

Standard time = 60 × 12 = 720 B's

Actual time = 60 × 10 = 600 B's

Saving in terms of B's = (720 – 600) = 120 B's

The rate of pay is reduced to the minute basis. According to Mr. Charles E. Bedaux, the main purpose of this system is to measure human effort through time study. The Bedaux Point System, therefore, is not a wage incentive system fundamentally. This point premium plan stresses that human labour and relaxation are closely associated. Thus, basis of the Bedaux System is energy and time. This system can be useful as a basis for scientific production control, but in this system much clerical work is involved and the system is not intelligible to many workers.

### Gantt Bonus Plan

This plan guarantees the day-wage to all the workers. The standard time is fixed. No bonus is payable to a worker who shows less than 100% efficiency. The bonus may be fixed generally from 20 to 50% of the time allowed and not time saved.

Example : Standard time = 8 hours
Hourly rate = Rs. 2
Bonus as 25% of the time

If a worker can complete the job in 9 hours, he will not get any bonus as his efficiency is less than 100%, but he will be paid Rs. 18/- by way of wages at the rate of Rs. 2 per hour. But if he can complete the work in 8 hours, his efficiency is 100 per cent, he will get a bonus. He will be paid Rs. 2 by way of bonus (25% of Rs. 8) and his total earning would be Rs. 20/- .

This plan is very simple to introduce and it is intelligible to the worker. It gives enough incentive to the efficient worker and a sub-standard worker also is able to get the guaranteed wage and the efficient worker gets wages on the piece rate. This method helps improvement in the working conditions, supervision and training. The system discourages speeding up of work as, beyond the standard time fixed, the piece rate is on the diminishing scale.

This method of wage payment differentiates workers : the efficient and the inefficient workers are clearly divided. So, it creates dis-unity among workers that is injurious for the workers in general.

### Taylor's Differential Piece Rate Plan

In this system, there are two different piece-rates for two different categories of workers – standard rate for the average worker, a higher rate for the efficient worker and a lower rate for the inefficient worker. The standard output is, of course, determined after thorough investigation and analysis.

Example :

Standard task = 10 units per day

Piece rate = Rs. 2 if production is 10 units and more and Rs. 1.50 per unit if production is less than 10 units.

If a worker is able to produce 10 units, he will get at the rate of Rs. 2 and his wages would be Rs. 20 but if a worker is able to produce only 8 units, he will get at the rate of Rs. 1.50 per unit and his wages would be Rs.12 only. In case he is able to produce 15 units he will get Rs. 30/-.

This different piece rate plan devised by the Father of Scientific Management, Dr. Taylor, has the advantages of encouraging high standard of performance. It penalises the inefficient worker but encourages the efficient one. The worker endeavours to be efficient. In this system, efforts are made to standardise the work and improve the working condition and at the same time planning and supervision are carried on carefully and efficiently. The system suffers from the limitations such as it is too harsh for them who are a little less efficient. It creates disparities whereas the modern trend is towards the equalization of earnings. It is also somewhat impracticable and not acceptable to trade unions since it strikes at the very root of solidarity among the workers.

### Merrick Differential or Multiple Piece-rate Plan

This incentive plan of wage payments envisages three rates as a modification of Taylor's Differential Piece-rate method. The rates are different for the beginners, for the developing workers and for the highly skilled and efficient workers. As in the case of Taylor's wage plan, here also, a standard output through time studies is laid down. It is expected that the workers will attain that standard. No guaranteed time rate is set. Those who are able to produce up to 83% of the standard output become entitled to the first and the lowest piece rate. Workers whose output exceeds 83% of the standard but does not reach the standard are paid the second higher rate which includes an increase of 10%. Workers attaining or exceeding standard get the third – the highest piece rate which includes further 10% of the basic rate. For instance, if the basic piece rate is Re. 1 per unit, wages at this rate will be paid to those who produce below 83% of the standard task, those producing 83% will get a step-up of 10%, while others exceeding the standard task will get another increment of 10%.

In evaluating this method of incentive wage payment, we can say that this is a modification of Taylor's differential price rate method with the only exception that, in this method of wage payment, there is no sudden rise in the wages at one point and the penalty for inefficiency is lighter.

### Balance or Debt Method

This is a combination of time and piece rates. There is a minimum guaranteed weekly wage or a day rate with an alternative piece rate. If earnings at the piece rate exceed the time rate, the excess earning is credited to the worker. In the reverse case, the worker is paid his time rate but the excess paid to him over his piece rate will be debited to him and will be recovered from his extra earnings during the next week.

Such a method of wage payment should be adopted only when the piece and time rates are based on the most scientific basis on which its sucess depends. The system affords opportunity to the efficient worker to earn more and the less efficient worker is induced to achieve the standard. The worker who perennially remains below the standard stands the risk of losing his job.

### Sliding scale

To infuse the feeling of belonging for the organisation, this method of incentive wage payment contains in it elements where the workers get a share of the prosperity of the organisation. The wage rates are generally linked with the selling price of the product and they vary with the price of the product. If the price of the product rises, the wage rate also rises, and vice versa. A standard price and a standard wage rate are fixed based on a standard period, usually a year. They are periodically reviewed and the revised rates are determined. This is done on the basis of agreement between the management and labour. In this method of wage payment, therefore, are inherent the elements of co-operation, understanding and collective bargaining between capital and labour.

As to its advantages, it is pointed out that the system fosters industrial peace and a better relation between labour and capital. The feeling of dignity that is generated by such a method of wage payment and the co-operation that it brings about between the management and the workers is no mean contribution from the point of view of industrial relations which has a far-reaching effect in enhancing production and productivity. The changes in the wage rates can also be implemented with greater ease because of the co-operative attitude of the workers. Such a wage system also enables an organisation to introduce innovations without opposition by the workers as they are in a position to elicit full information of the working of the organisation through the auditor's report.

Nothing is an unmixed blessing in this world, not to speak of a method of wage payment. But what is to be considered is whether the blessings and the curses can be balanced, or curses far outweigh the blessings. In this system of wage payment, the wage rate is directly related to the price of the product — higher the price, higher is the rate of wage. So, the workers prefer higher prices of products, no matter, whether it ultimately goes against the interest of the organisation. Wage rates fluctuate with the fluctuation of price and obviously to reduce wage rates is not an easy job for the management.

With the greatest amount of tact and managerial efficiency and with the humane outlook and sympathy for the worker, this system of wage payment may do more good than harm.

### Priestman Bonus System

The productivity of workers as a whole is the basis of this system of incentive wage payment. The rise of output above the standard output will mean rise in the wage rate of all the workers in the same ratio. So, the fluctuation in output affects wage rate. Individual efficiency has nothing to do with such a system. So, it is quite likely that an efficient worker will lose initiative to work more efficiently and inefficient workers will become more inefficient since they can enjoy the benefit too of higher wage rate at the cost of others. This method of incentive wage payment, therefore, needs mental revolution on the part of workers as a whole and this needs scientific management. All workers should be so motivated as would encourage them to give the best in them and an individual worker will not isolate himself from the general initiative that can only push up output as a whole.

### Hayne's Plan

In terms of man-minutes (MANITS), the standard time of a job is fixed. Wages are paid on time basis, but if the standard time of various jobs done exceeds the actual time, a worker will be paid a share of the time saved. The saving is calculated in terms of MANITS. The resultant saving is divided by 60 to convert it into hours. By multiplying hours so calculated by the time rate, the total value of the time saved is determined. The benefit of time saved is divided : (a) if the work is standardised — 5/6ths to the worker and 1/6th to the foreman (b) in non-standardised work — half to the worker and the rest between foreman and the management in the ratio 1 : 4.

According to this plan of wage payment, standardised work means a work of repetitive nature and non-standardised work signifies work of different nature every time. The characteristic features of such a plan are : the bonus payable to the foreman is credited to a fund. In case of any fault on the part of the foreman which causes loss of time to the worker, the foreman will lose his bonus to the extent the worker has to be paid wages for idle time. MANITS, in order to be credited to the worker, must pass through inspection.

### Emerson's Efficiency Plan

To improve the efficiency of workers, Harrington Emerson devised this plan of wage payment.

The plan works as follows :

(i) Standard time for a standard task is fixed after careful study

(ii) Minimum day wage is guaranteed to all workers

(iii) Remuneration is based on the efficiency of the worker

(iv) Efficiency of a worker is determined on the basis of ratio between the standard time fixed and the actual time taken for doing a job

(v) No bonus for the worker who cannot attain $66\,^2/_3\%$ efficiency

(vi) Beyond $66^2/_3\%$ efficiency there is a gradual rise in the bonus payable to a worker.

**Illustration :** Standard Time = 10 hours. Now, if a worker performs it in 20 hours, his efficiency is 50%; if he does it in 5 hours his efficiency is 200%. Where he does it in 10 hours, he is 100% efficient. No bonus will be paid until a worker achieves $66\,^2/_3\%$; on achieving 100% efficiency, he gets a bonus at the rate of 20% of the guaranteed wage. At 120% efficiency, the bonus will be 40% and at 140%, the bonus will be 66% of the day or guaranteed wage. At $66\,^2/_3\%$ efficiency, the bonus is paid at the rate of 1 per cent of the day wage. If the standard output fixed is 100 units and the day wage is Rs. 10 and a worker produces 100 units, he will get Rs. 10 by way of guaranteed wage plus Rs. 2 (20% of Rs. 10) by way of bonus and thus his total earnings will be Rs. 12.

This plan is simple to understand and to introduce. The calculation of efficiency is simple. Sufficient incentive is given but the method itself is complicated. Bonus percentage needs to be modified under different circumstances. After a worker reaches standard efficiency, there is very little inducement for enhancement of efficiency.

### Barth Variable Sharing Plan

This plan does not guarantee any day wage. As a matter of fact, this plan is meant for the apprentices and the unskilled workers. The wages are calculated as follows :

$\sqrt{\text{(Standard hours} \times \text{Actual hours} \times \text{Rate per hour)}}$

Assumed the standard time for a particular job is 8 hours. A worker completes it in 6 hours and if the rate of wages per hour is Re. 1, the wages would be :

$\sqrt{8 \times 6 \times 1} = \text{Rs. } 6.93.$

The income of the worker would rise steeply though the rise would be at a decreasing rate.

### Group Incentive Plan

Under such a plan, incentive is provided to the whole group and not to an individual. The work is to be done on group basis. The premium is calculated for the whole group and it is distributed to the individual worker on some just basis. The premium is usually distributed on the basis of the wages earned by the individual worker.

The drawback of the plan is that both the inefficient and the efficient worker will get the same amount of premium. Of course, to overcome this drawback, the skill and efficiency of a worker may be taken into consideration.

### Profit-sharing

It is "an arrangement entered into, by which the employee receives a share, fixed in advance, of the profits". It is paid in addition to the regular wages payable to the worker. Strictly speaking, the profit sharing is not a system of wage payment at all. It is rather a form of remuneration applied "to those cases in which an employer agrees with his employees that they shall receive in partial remuneration of their labour, and in addition to their wages, a share fixed beforehand, in the profits realised by the undertaking to which the profit-sharing scheme relates". Such share is given to the worker if the total net profit exceeds certain specified amount and such payment does not form part of the total cost of production. All categories of employees are entitled to such sharing of profits.

As to the merits of such a scheme, we can say that it ensures maximum production at the lowest possible cost per unit. There is a socialistic bias in such a scheme as the workers get the fruits of their labour and profits like employers. This encourages better relationship between labour and capital. As a consequence, it helps in building up a more permanent labour force and, thus, the general atmosphere and work environment improve. Workers, under such a scheme, are better remunerated; hence their standard of living improves.

Limitations of the scheme are its failure to provide any direct incentive to the efficient worker which may cause dissatisfaction and inefficiency to efficient workers. The time-lag between their sharing of profit and the labour they put in for earning the share of profit causes disenchantment for this sharing of profit scheme. The scheme is not popular with the trade unions since they feel that the scheme stands in the way of solidarity of the worker.

In our country, the scheme has not met with success since neither the worker nor the employers favour such a scheme. The Government-appointed committee on profit-sharing submitted a report where there were 6 minutes of dissent.

## Labour Co-partnership

This is a scheme to regard labour as a co-partner. Workers will share in the profits which are accumulated and converted into shares of the firm at the market rate. Workers are given a voice in the control and management like the shareholders.

This scheme, too, is not successful. Neither the employers want the employees to have any say in management, nor is it effective on the part of the employees unless and until they become educated and experienced in the matter of management. It is only among the enlightened employees that such a scheme of workers' participation in management may be effective.

## Cost of Living Wage

The object of this method of wage payment is to relate wage to the cost of living. This has immense social significance. This was **necessary for the rising** cost of living **after World War I (1914 - 1918).** The attitude of the management for introducing such a method of wage payment is to enable a worker to maintain a uniform standard of living in order to preserve his working efficiency. But the problem arises in fixing the standard cost of living which forms the basis of such a method of wage payment. The reliable and detailed statistical information are not available. Of course, in recent years, the Ministry of Labour, Government of India, supplies the cost of living index numbers of the working class. In case of downward trend in the cost of living index, it is very difficult for the management to lower down wage rate; it would surely be resented by the workers' unions.

This system of wage payment cannot also be used as an incentive system of wage payment.

## Fringe Benefits

These benefits are supplementary compensation made in addition to wages, the object being to stimulate the interest of the workers and to make the job more attractive and conducive. They are, as a matter of fact, indirect benefits. As to their nature, we can say, they are neither mere "fringes" nor peripheral "wage trimmings" but a substantial part of the wage and salary structure. To quote Belcher, these benefits are "any wage cost not directly connected with employees productive effort, performance, service or sacrifice". Webster defines "fringe" as "an ornamental border, an edging, trimming or a margin". However, these benefits are aimed at attracting and retaining efficient and contented workforce through boosting up of their real earnings.

There are wide variations in opinions as to the benefits covered by the term "fringe benefits". We quote here Fisher and Chapman according to whom the classification of fringe benefits are — (a) premiums for time worked, (b) pay for time not worked (c) employee benefits and (d) employee activities.

In India, the government has prescribed certain minimum amenities to be provided by employers to workers. As we have said earlier that indirect benefits are tringe benefits but it is very difficult to distinguish between direct wages and indirect benefits. For instance, conducive working conditions benefit the employer directly, overtime wage paid for work done cannot be described as indirect benefit.

Cockman defines employee benefits as "those benefits supplied by an employer, to or for, the benefit of an employee which are not in the form of wages, salaries and time-related payments". According to him, benefits are basically of two types – fringe and key. Fringe benefits include status (cars, entertainment facilities, holidays, foreign travel, telephone); security (insurance, medical facilities, children's education), and work benefits (office accommodation, secretarial services, management training, company scholarships etc). Key benefits are benefits such as share schemes, profit sharing, retirement counselling and house purchase.

Fringe benefits afford better living standard to the employees and offer opportunities to the employer to have more productivity and production. So, they are relevant and useful for an organisation provided it can afford to extend fringe benefits. In term, of cost, these benefits constitute "the real total cost to the company of employing the employee" (Beath & Rands). It cannot be denied that fringe benefits are regarded as a "bonus" and, as such, they create a favourable attitude towards the particular job and company.

Example, of fringe benefits in India :

(a) **Statutory benefits** – The Employees Provident Fund Scheme, Gratuity or Pension Schemes and Employees State Insurance Scheme. (b) **Non-statutory benefits** – Payments towards Employees Provident Fund Scheme, Gratuity and Pension Fund contribution, medical facilities, canteens, uniform and recreational facilities.

Fringe benefits also cover profit and other kinds of bonus such as attendance bonus, service bonus and gratuities, loans for house purchases, leave travel concession, children's free education, fair price shops for essential commodities, loans for purchase of car.

Fringe benefits, in spite of some of these drawbacks, have come to stay. They have now become an important part of compensation plans.

So far as the corporate management is concerned, it is necessary to take several broad policy decisions regarding wages. One fundamental issue is the break-up of the compensation package. Several options are available – (a) high/low basic wage (b) high/low fringe benefit package (c) high/low retirement benefits. The management has to consider whether to pay just above or below or at par with "the going wage rate" in the area. The Bonus Act is a matter for consideration by the corporate management. "To a large extent, such issues are decided by the value system and managerial style of the corporate management and how they view wages as contributing to the organisation's mission" (Monappa and Saiyadain).

# CHAPTER 20

## PERFORMANCE APPRAISAL

Performance appraisal has a history behind it. Formally it started in China. The Imperial Rates appraised the performance of members of the official family. Thereafter, we find the appraisal introduced in the U.S.A. shortly before World War I (1914-18). It is now widely used in American companies to measure employees' performances. In India, too, this is an accepted method of checking workers' performance. The Indian companies use this tool of measurement of workers' performance for training and development, providing feedback to employees and personnel research, and in determining wages, promotions and transfers.

Performance appraisal has been defined as a systematic evaluation of personnel by supervisors or others familiar with their performance. As a matter of fact, appraisals are judgements of the characteristics, traits and performance. This is an objective way of judging the relative worth or ability of a person in performing his task. This is essential for making many administrative decisions where used in a company management. Decisions such as relating to selection training, promotion, transfer, wages, salaries etc. may be well based on performance appraisal. Also, it helps personnel research. The appraisal methods that are usually followed enable the management to judge the relative worth or ability of an employee in the performance of his task and identify the performers and non-performers of assigned tasks.

Broadly speaking, a performance appraisal is aimed at (1) identifying employees for different purposes – wages, promotions, transfers, lay-off, terminations etc, (2) determining training needs for further improvement in performance, (3) motivating employees by indicating their performance levels and (4) establishing a basis for research and reference for personnel decisions in future.

While appraising performance of an employee, a difficulty arises as to what aspects of performance have to be appraised. This can be called the problems of criterion determination. A very broad definition of criterion is "that which is to be predicted". This refers to evaluative standards which measure a person's performance, attitudes etc. When the job is clearly defined, it is not difficult to identify performance measures but in case of a broad definition of job; the identification of performance measures becomes difficult. Determining criteria for appraisal at the lower levels of an organisation does not pose so much problem as the jobs there are specific, but higher up in the hierarchy, when jobs are more complex and clear-cut, tangible standards of performance are difficult to specify.

### Performance Measures and Categories

Under three categories – personal data, production data and judgemental data — performance measures that are usually used by companies are : (1) quantity of work (2) quality of work (3) waste and breakage (4) money earned (5) job knowledge (6) job tenure (7) absenteeism (8) rate of advancement (9) sell-judgement (10) judgement by peers and (11) judgement by supervisors.

**Personal data** include personal history, number

of times of absence, number of grievances, accidents, breakages etc. These are used to differentiate between good and bad performers. However, there is little evidence to suggest that personal data can predict job performance. "The personal values of the Indian Worker militate against industrial values" (A. D. Moddie). It is remarked by noted authorities on personnel management that, unlike his western counterpart, an Indian worker is marked by excessive obedience and lack of competitiveness, deep-rooted Indian ways of life and respect for family customs and relationships. It is also said that "irrespective of social values and traditions, worker develop in their work-role a net work of relationships that is consistent with the requirements of their industrial roles" (A. K. Rice). "The Indian social environment lays more emphasis on the concepts of self loyalty and regard for authority than does the West" (Monappa & Saiyadain).

In India, most industrial workers join industries with rural background since they come from villages. Of course, the situation to-day has taken a turn. "The Indian industrial worker", as observed by B. R. Sharma, "to-day comes from an urban setting, is more educated and has a higher average income than his predecessors". Personal data as an indicator of performance appears to be extremely risky in view of its conflicting evidence.

Production data prove useful for evaluating the performance of people only in some jobs and at some levels. Though output measures are available for some jobs, production data are not the most frequently used measure of performance. Initial studies on production as a measure of performance suggest that the time period between measures can make a substantial difference to the accuracy of the data. Ghiselli and Haire (the validation of selection test in the light of dynamic character of criteria) in their "Personnel Psychology", have found the correlation between weekly time periods to be considerably higher for consecutive weeks than for weeks widely separated. So, production data can be relied upon only with reference to time when the sample of production data is taken, as well as on the time periods between measures.

Judgemental data mean self-judgement, judgement by supervisors and sometimes knowledge of the job. It is no doubt, one of the most commonly used indicators of performance but problems arise because it is based on subjective assessment either by the individual or by another individual for him.

**Performance appraisal methods** vary from one organisation to another. The following methods are usually adopted — (1) Confidential Report (2) Rating Scales (3) Ranking System (4) Paired – Comparisons Method (5) Forced Choice Method (6) Critical Incident Method (7) Cost Accounting Method and (8) Forced Distribution Method.

**The Confidential Report** method is a very old method of employee-appraisal. The confidential report of the immediate supervisor forms the basis of promotion or transfer of an employee. This report contains various aspects of the subordinate employee; the format and pattern of the report may be different in different organisations but usually every organisation has a prescribed form of the confidential report to ensure uniformity. The report depends to a great extent on the relationship between the supervisor and his subordinate where factors other than the employee's efficiency play a dominant role. Such a report cannot be very much liked by the employees.

**Rating Scales** method assesses the **degree** of certain qualities required for the job such as physical ability, reliability and dependability. The degree is usually measured on a scale which can vary from 3 point (good, average and poor) to several points.

There are three ways of presenting scales –

(a) a point scale with anchors defined, e.g. reliability.

| | 5 | 4 | 3 | 2 | 1 | |
|---|---|---|---|---|---|---|
| Excellent | | | | | | Poor |

(b) a point scale with both anchors and scale-points defined, e.g. can be relied upon :

| always | often | sometimes | seldom | never |
|---|---|---|---|---|

and (c) a point scale with the characteristics of scale (b) and a definition of the scale points – always, seldom, never etc.

It may so happen that under the Rating method two employees may have the same total rating, though on specific traits they might get different ratings.

The **Ranking system** obviates the problem of the Rating system of having similar total scores for two or more individuals. This system of appraisal is simple and more useful too when employees are small in number. Ranking can be determined either by looking at the total individual and then ranking him in relation to others. It can also be done by first identifying several relevant traits and then cumulating these trait rankings to arrive at the final employee-rankings. When the employees are roughly equal in their abilities, there may be difficulty which may be overcome by using several raters to ensure ranking on an objective rather than a random basis.

Employees apart from and between the top and bottom extremes and larger number of employees in an organisation generally pose problems in this system of appraisal.

In the **Paired-Comparison method,** the judgement is made as to who is superior between two workers. So, it is a simpler method. Usually the trait — the overall ability to perform the job — is considered. The supervisor is provided with a bunch of slips each containing a pair of names. The rater puts a tick mark against the individual whom he considers better between the two and the final ranking is determined by the number of times that individual is judged better than the others All possible pairs are evaluated. The number of times a worker is considered better than the others, yields his score. Such scores are determined for each worker and he is rank-ordered according to his score. The disadvantage that follows from this system is that, in a large number of employees, the number of permutations and combinations increases requiring more time from the evaluator. However, by creating small groups, this difficulty can be removed to a great extent.

Under the 'Forced-Choice' method, a series of groups of statements are prepared and the rater checks how effectively the statement describes each individual being evaluated. There are variations in the method. Sometimes, instead of making statements, a simple listing of traits is given. This method attempts to make performance evaluation more objective. The evaluator who does not know the score values of the statements is prevented from deliberately checking only the most favourable traits or statements of his favourite employees.

The performance appraisal through **'Critical Incident Method'** involves three steps. In the first step, a test of noteworthy on-the-job behaviour, usually of specific instances, is prepared. Secondly, scale values are assigned to them depending upon the degree of desirability for the job. Thirdly, a check list is constructed including incidents defining 'good' and 'bad' workers. Subsequently, supervisors use these lists for evaluating the worker.

The advantages of this method are : (1) Identification of the key areas in which employees are weak or strong, (2) Rating is emphasised on objective evidence rather than on subjective evaluation of traits and (3) Counselling for the supervisor becomes easier as he knows the weaknesses of his subordinates.

The **Cost Accounting Method** of performance appraisal takes into account the monetary returns yielded by an employee to his organisation. The cost involved — in the employment of a person and the return obtained from him – is related in this method.

In the **Forced Distribution Method,** the rater is forced to distribute his subordinates into performance categories – outstanding, good, poor etc. The rater distributes his subordinates on scale locations which can be top 10 per cent to bottom 10 per cent of any variation of the percentages with values in between. For large number of employees, this method is useful.

## Problems in Performance Appraisal

Performance appraisal methods are not fool-proof. There are strengths and weaknesses in every method of appraisal. Since every method involves judgements of one or other kind, there is scope for errors. These errors may be – errors of 'Central tendency' or 'Errors of leniency'. The Central tendency error is one which does not use extreme scale scorers on the judgement scale ; most of the rates are clustered in the middle. Errors of leniency occur when the rater puts most of the raters on the higher side of the scale, while the tough rater places them on the lower side of the scale.

The "halo effect" is also a problem which arises when there is a tendency to allow one trait to influence assessment on others.

Another problem arises when there is **criterion contamination** and bias because of a variety of circumstances and functions beyond the control of the rater and the ratee. These biases, according to Blum and Nylor, are :

(a) Opportunity bias, (b) Group characteristic bias (c) Knowledge of predictor bias and (d) bias in ratings.

An Opportunity bias takes place when an employee gets better facilities in his work environment as compared to another.

A Group characteristics have much to influence the overall performance. An individual's performance is greatly influenced by the group performance.

A rater's knowledge of the performance of an employee on predictors is likely to influence his appraisal ratings. One topping the selection list creates the impression that he is the best performer.

The rater's own biases and competence in rating influences the objectivity of performance appraisals. These problems of halo effect, rater's training, Central tendency errors etc. are examples of this **"contamination"**.

The methods of performance appraisal are founded on validity and reliability but case studies reveal the lack of these two vital conditions for the success of appraisal methods. Appraisal methods are, after all, substantially dependent on personal judgements which are very often influenced by various considerations having no relationship with an employee's performance.

While criticising the different methods of performance appraisal in Indian Companies, it has been observed that there is no significant relationship between evaluation vis-a-vis promotion, transfer and placement. Very often differences exist between the appraiser's face-face assessment and his report on the worker's performance. Appraisal reports are prepared mostly just at the time when they are to be submitted. Supervisors do not feel happy and comfotable in judging their subordinates. Lastly, it was found through case studies that different raters evaluate differently on the performance of the same employee.

From the discussion above, we are led to believe that appraisal methods for the evaluation of the performance of employees fail to give us cent per cent satisfaction as to the correct judgement of one's performance. So, we can say performance appral fails. The **reasons of the failure of performance appraisal** have been summarised as follows by some eminent scholars after several case studies :

1. The dual and conflicting role of both judge and helper of the supervisor.
2. Confusion due to too many objectives is very common.
3. The supervisors themselves are not very much interested in their subordinates' personal appraisal because of the apprehension of bitter relations that may develop owing to adverse reports.
4. Two appraisal programmes may take place between two long intervals.
5. There is a conflict between the skills required for daily administration and employee development.
6. Employees are generally unaware of what is expected of them because of communication gap.
7. As to the degree of excellence of the performance of an employee, there is very often difference of opinion between the supervisor and the employee.
8. Variations between ratees are less than those between raters.
9. Both to the supervisor and to the subordinate feedback on appraisal is generally unpleasant.
10. Most of the supervisors do not possess the tact and insight to communicate in a constructive way to the employees now to improve their performance.

From the observations given above, two conclusions can easily be drawn : One is that sufficient attention is not given in appraising the performance of an employee by his supervisor and the other that there is a gulf between decisions and their actual executions.

A performance appraisal entails time and money and since every method of appraisal has its shortcomings, the personnel management should ensure a sound plan involving minimum cost. The financial resources and the philosophy of the organisation must be taken into account in formulating any plan for performance appraisal.

A sound appraisal plan should be so devised and chalked out as to avoid the elements inherent in the psychology of the supervisors that are deterent to the preparation of an impartial appraisal report. Supervisors avoid playing the role of judges. They feel uneasy in criticizing their subordinates.

The militancy of trade unions also affects impartial appraisal reports. The reports should be made known to the employees and in case of unfavourable reports, employees should be informed in such a manner that their feelings are not wounded nor their ego hurt in any way. Personnel management should develop human skills to deal with such delicate matters. In view of the trend of trade unionism that has developed in our country, employees should be taken into confidence and the performance appraisal should be conducted in an atmosphere of cordial relationship between the management and the employees. A post-appraisal review committee can be formed including a few union leaders. This joint participation has a salutary effect as it establishes a two-way communication between the management and the common workers.

There are organisations where supervisors, managers and other raters meet occasionally for discussions with employees about their performance and particularly to communicate negative evaluation just to enable employees to offer their explanations, if any. This is to ensure natural justice through **appraisal interviews.** These interviews serve certain purposes :

1. They provide feed-back to the employee ensuring better performance in future.
2. The organisation itself is benefitted since it gets some idea of its working; thus its functioning can be improved.
3. In the socio-economic conditions in India, where the continuity of service of the employee is essential, appraisal interviews help the organisations to make arrangements for proper training of the employees whenever the need for it actually arises.

According to N. R. F. Maier, three appraisal interviews, each with a specific and slightly different objective, can be held for improving upon the existing performance appraisal methods. These **interview methods** are — **(a) The Tell and Sell Method (b) The Tell and Listen Method** and **(c) The Problem-solving Approach Method.**

In the **"Tell and Sell"** method, it is assumed that the evaluation has been done in fairness. The purpose of the method is to communicate the rater's evaluation to the employee as accurately as possible.

Under the **"Tell & Listen"** method, the response of the employee to his report is wanted. The rater listens to the response of the employee. Since, in this method, attempts are made to explore the feelings of the employee about the evaluation on him, there is less fear of reprisal and resistance is also very much less from the employee's side. This is a method where there is a scope for improvement of relationship between the superior and the subordinate; an atmosphere of cordiality is likely to prevail in the industrial relation.

In the **"Problem-solving"** approach method, unlike previous two methods, there is no need for communication. The employer here assumes the role of a helper rather than a judge and the thrust is upon employee development.

In this method of appraisal, there is very little effort to find fault with the employee, to point his weeknesses but attempts are made to stimulate the thinking of the employee on how to improve his performance.

## Management by Objective (MBO)

This is a concept by Peter Drucker. Performance appraisal methods, however improved they are, do not appear palatable to the employees. In the growing militancy in trade unionism and the increasing bargaining strength of the employees, performance appraisals of the employees by the supervisors are becoming increasingly difficult. But the employee-assessment cannot be done away with. Promotions, transfers, increments etc. cannot be matter of whims of the employer without having any rationale behind them. So, some sort of appraisal method must exist in order to run the organisation and to ensure better management, some measures must be resorted to reward the better worker and to warn/or to improve the worse worker.

**MBO works as follows :** It calls on the subordinate to set his short-term performance goals in consultation with his superior. Goals for the employees are clearly set. No superior appraises his subordinate; the subordinate appraises his own performance by evaluating it vis-a-vis the goals. The subordinate establishes his goals for a particular period and he himself judges his accomplishment at the end of the period against the goals. The "interview" is the assessment by the superior and subordinate together of the latter's self-appraisal. If necessary, at the instance of the superior, the goals for the next period are modified.

MBO is rather an 'analysis' and not an

'appraisal' like other methods. Since the subordinate himself assesses himself, he assumes the role of an active agent rather than a passive object. Employees in MBO are, thus, made more responsible and their importance in the set-up of the whole organisation increases. P. Drucker gives a new turn to the whole concept of performance appraisal by making the employees feel that they are sufficiently competent and able of learning more than any one else about their own needs, strengths and weaknesses. Given is the scope in MBO for the employees to explore their potentialities. Employees, it is assumed, can best determine what they can achieve and how they can achieve. Here the superior is only to help the subordinate to achieve his goals. As a matter of fact, in MBO, a superior is a friend, philosopher and guide of the subordinate and not a judge to pronounce verdict. Thus, their approach succeeds with the active co-operation of the superior and the subordinate.

The characteristics of MBO are that the employees are not to be subjected to any criticism on their personality traits, mannerisms etc. and in this approach, the accent is on performance and not on the individual's personality. There is a complete co-operation in achieving the goals by the subordinate – the superior helps his subordinate at every step in realising his goals.

As to the deficiency of MBO, it is pointed out that here the objectives are not clearly defined. However, MBO is widely used in the West but its application in India is very much limited and the outcome also is not clearly known.

The **Koontz Model** improves on the MBO approach by emphasising the process of achieving the organisation's objectives rather than the attainment of goals set by individuals. This model involves the appraisal of managers in five broad areas : planning, organising, leading, motivating and controlling and each of these consists of a series of activities and practices of management. The activities of each area of the manager's concern are elaborated.

This model, therefore, utilises the basic principles of management, as standards, for appraising managers. A check-list of evaluatory questions covers the key areas of managerial functions. These questions take into consideration the major aspects of managing fairly well. They evaluate the accepted objectives attained and analyse managerial performance. The rater is to evaluate each subordinate on a five-point scale. A manager's competence in managing the organisational environment is examined by the model.

### How to enhance the effectiveness of participation

Research has revealed that participative decision-making can be enhanced if some key parameters are taken into account. A number of broad variables have been identified.

The variables are :

1. The greater the clarity of goals, the higher the effectiveness.
2. Effectiveness varies inversely with the urgency of the decisions.
3. The degree of effectiveness varies directly with the degree with which the participation meets the motives of the participants.
4. Settlement of relatively difficult issues leads to greater effectiveness.
5. The higher the viability of the activity participative decision making, the greater the effectiveness.
6. Effectiveness varies directly with the number of administrative levels.
7. More useful information has greater effectiveness in participative decision making.

The above variables lead us to suggest that personnel management should not go the participative management way without necessary preconditions. That may pose dangerous. Workers may engage matters that are either completely unimportant or above their level of competence. Both these dangers are extremely critical.

# CHAPTER 21

## PERSONNEL FUNCTIONS IN INDIA

Since Independence, the personnel functions of management in India have been passing through changes. Various labour legislations have been enacted to improve industrial relations and help development of industries in the country in the planned way. The socio-economic changes that have been taking place in our country have a direct impact on the personnel functions. At the outset it can be said that "despite the trends in Indian industry being clear, the projection of the personnel function in India will be largely judgemental and discretionary, till these functions are conclusively demonstrated by further research" (Monappa & Saiyadain).

Despite the sincere efforts of welfare/labour officers, human problems continued in one form or another. After World War II (1939-45), technological innovations ushered in new era in the industrial sphere and complex changes in the organisational structure. Workers, as well as supervisory and managerial staff-were affected by these changes. Personnel functions expanded, new dimensions were added and the emphasis was shifted.

In recent years, growing complexities of organisation have called upon the management for the shift in emphasis from industrial engineering to concern for inter-personal and inter-group relationship.

To-day's personnel manager does not confine his activities within the shop area looking after the grievances and problems of shop floor employees only. His functions now include man-power planning, recruitment and selection, management development and training, performance appraisal, internal mobility and the welfare and working conditions of the employees of the company at all levels. These functions are professional and highly specialised and cannot be left to an administrative officer. Thus, **beginning with the concept of the paternalistic welfare officer, personnel management in India has now expanded its sphere to cover white collar workers and now executives and the board members of an organisation, too.**

In his article "Personnel directors are the new corporate Heroes", H. E. Mayer observes : "The personnel directors in organisations are the new corporate heroes in the West. Organisations are putting their personnel departments in the hands of powerful senior executives". But, in India, the situation has not reached this stage as yet though considerable significance is being attached to personnel management also.

A clear trend in India is that importance is being given to joint decision making. Whether this is for governmental legislations or trade unions or voluntary acceptance by the employers is not the question. What we notice is that, since 1958 (Seminar on Labour Management Co-operation) workers' participation in management has been on steady increase.

The Government Resolution of October, 1975 envisaged workers' participation both at the shop floor level and the level of the undertaking. It also emphasised on 'communication' within the undertaking and felt that if joint councils worked in the proper spirit, both production and productivity would improve.

The scheme, it has to be admitted, has not been well-implemented : resistance by management, multiplicity of unions, role conflict of nominated workers, lack of clear boundaries with other similar schemes, poor feedback from representatives to workers being the reasons. Recent observations, however, are optimistic. With the changing profile of the Indian workforce because of education and increasing awareness of its rights, the joint participation is getting more and more importance.

In India, where teeming millions have been suffering from the pangs of unemployment, labour supply is not a problem, at least at present. But a day may come when government measures and family planning etc. may affect labour supply; but that is yet far off to come. It is no denying the fact that quality of labour is skilled and efficient labour supply is not adequate. That is to be looked into by the personnel management of any big organisation and various methods are being resorted to for training of work force.

What is apprehended is that, in years to come, the disparity between the demand for and supply of professional managers will widen because the management graduates produced in the few management institutes in India do not usually exceed two thousand a year, mostly without work experience. A recent employment trend of the IIMs of Ahmedabad, Bangalore and Calcutta shows approximately three jobs for each graduate. In future there will be more demand, so more professionals will be required. Either more graduates will have to be supplied by the Government institutions or the organisations themselves will have to make arrangements for training in management to equip their organisations with suitable managerial personnel Of course, various public sector undertakings have started imparting management training (ONGC, Heavy Engineering etc.).

Most organisations are to-day aware of the significance of human hopes and aspirations and involve them in decision-making. Behavioural science — especially aspects related to needs, motivation, satisfaction and expectancy – is playing a significant role in promoting the new theory of management. Organisations are also recognising their social responsibilities and community relations. We can cite TISCO and TELCO to illustrate our statement.

The Declaration of Social Responsibility of Business emphasised that business should be fair and human, besides being efficient and dynamic. This will give a new outlook to the management and it can be expected that awareness of social responsibilities will increase since it has direct relevance for workers. Better working conditions and work environment will have a highly favourable impact on the workers as well as on the organisation. Personnel management in India was not so much concerned about this human aspect of production but time has come when the entire outlook have to be changed to adapt the organisations to the changed circumstances. The functions of the Personnel Manager in future will definitely be enlarged from traditional areas such as management of manpower planning, selection, recruitment, training, internal mobility and welfare. With growing personnel needs, new dimensions will be added.

# PART IV

# COMPANY MANAGEMENT

# CHAPTER 1

## NATURE OF COMPANY MANAGEMENT

Usually ownership, control and risk go together. "Bearing risk gives the right to control" — a say in management and risk should be borne by him who is the owner. So, ownership involves risk and the responsibility of risk gives the authority to control. Therefore, ownership, control and risk are generally inter-linked.

In a business organisation — sole proprietorship and partnership, ownership, control and risk are united in one and the same person — a proprietor or a partner.

But in the company form of organisation, there is a clear departure : here ownership, control and risk are not unified and there is a clear divorce or separation of management and control from ownership. The owners i.e. shareholders of a company, hold the power of management but in practice they do not manage it. Since shareholders are a heterogenous body of people, it is not possible for them to exercise the powers of controlling the affairs of the company which they legally possess; the control is held by a small group of shareholders who get themselves elected as directors and hold control over the company. **This is the nature of company management. To be precise, the company management is democratic in name but oligarchic or autocratic or feudal in practice.**

Since the shareholders reside in different places and are not acquainted with one another, they are not in a position to exercise the powers that they legally possess. The company law, therefore, authorises the shareholders to delegate their power of management to directors who are periodically elected by them. Some matters of special importance affecting the interests of all, such as alteration of the Articles and Memorandum, sale or lease of the assets and change in the capital structure need the approval of shareholders.

The numerous, unorganised and mostly disinterested shareholders are ultimately placed in the hands of a few persons who, are of course, elected by them but once elected, they wield enormous powers. The law, however, empowers a general meeting of the company to remove a director before the expiry of his term but such removals are not an easy process, for the directors, after they are elected, develop certain vested interests which frustrate such a move. Directors are not employees of the company or employed by the company, nor are they servants of the company or members of its staff. This, being the position of directors, it is not so easy for the general shareholders to exercise control over them. In practice, therefore, the management of companies exhibit some marked features of oligarchy. "In actual practice, management is the exclusive monopoly of a few business leaders. These persons constitute an 'inner ring' or a well-organised corporate group which is in a position to manipulate the working of the company to its own advantage without showing much regard for the shareholders' interests" (Y. K. Bhusan). But in law, shareholders appear to possess effective powers — as they have the right to elect directors, appoint auditors, summon meetings which are supposed to be conducted properly and matters are to be decided by voting after shareholders have been given proper opportunity to speak. It gives the impression of a perfect democracy prevailing in company management but as the matter stands in practice, **oligarchy is the feature and nature of company management.** This oligarchic nature of company management has been a natural consequence of a number of factors such as ineffective company meetings, lack of unity and organisation among shareholders, defective system of directors' election, system of proxies, closure of transfer books and corporate industrial groups.

So, **the nature of company management is oligarchic and the democratic look is 'illusory and unreal'.**

## Problems of Company Management

The problems of company management mainly arise from the fact that the nature of the management is oligarchic. A few persons manage and control the affairs of a huge number of persons — the shareholders — who are scattered and though they have common interest in the matter of their company, they are utterly disinterested and indifferent and there is very little scope for them to form a united front to ventilate their grievances jointly which create problems for the shareholders and can be considered as general problems of company management. So problems of company management emanate mainly from the problem of separation of ownership from management.

These are some problems of management common to all business enterprises. But company management has some special problems. The management entrusted to directors are just elected representatives and have not so much stake. Naturally, their interest and initiative are likely to be less. Even there are part-time directors whose interest and involvement are much less. Besides, company management, as a big organisation, is very much complicated where specialisation is very much needed in various area managements. Directors who are policy-makers cannot be expected to be always experts in all areas of management and their special problems. So, decisions which they take in regard to a particular matter may not be correct, but the management personnel are to implement the decisions taken at Board meetings. Again, because of various restrictions imposed on management by the Companies Act, the management does not feel happy and argues that the Board of the managers of the company cannot function properly because of too many constraints of law which create problems.

The emerging pattern of company management has been devised to plug various loopholes and to ensure solution of various problems confronting the management of the company.

Company management problems, therefore, relate to the oligarchic nature of management, lack of real democracy, and the ineffectiveness of the Board of Directors.

A widely owned company has to depend on a handful of directors for its management; it is unavoidable. Democracy in management cannot be expected nor is it feasible in a public company. But the problems with the Board of Directors can be solved to a great extent by various legislative measures and devices. Shareholders' various problems covering their interest have not been solved even after inserting more than 658 sections in the Companies Act. Lack of the sense of responsibility on the part of the directors cannot be ruled out. To solve shareholders' problems, Responsible Management is a dire need since shareholders 'associations, particularly in our country, are very difficult to form' and even when formed they practically are ineffective. In the emerging pattern of Company Management, a large number of companies are managed by Boards of Directors assisted by their committees. But in many companies, the Managing Director is the chief executive to implement the decisions of the Board. Management by experts has become the need of the hour to solve management problems to which direction the companies are now moving on the look out for the solution of managerial problems.

## Different Interest Groups and Company Management

In the affairs of a company, many persons or groups of persons besides the promoters and the shareholders are interested which means for any act of the company they may gain or lose.

The interested parties are: (i) Members (ii) Creditors (iii) Employees (iv) Managerial Personnel and (v) General public.

(i) **Members :** A company is formed by its members. Therefore, the first interested group is made of members. They are interested in the matter of taking part in management through participating in company meetings and directly being elected as directors and again they are interested in regard to their investment in the company, that is, monetary interest.

The members are the primary investors. As such, they are expected to be interested in more profits and distribution of higher rates of dividend. Their interest also lies in the higher profitability of their company by the creation of further income-yielding assets. The members of a company are also very much keen, quite reasonably, in keeping up the intrinsic value of their shares and in the matter of the liquidity of the shares.

(ii) **Creditors :** Creditors have stake in the company of which they are creditors, either trade creditors or non-trade creditors. Creditors are generally of four types – (a) Debenture holders (b) Depositors (c) Financial institutions and (d) Trade creditors.

Debenture holders are interested in the redemption of debentures, in the regular payment of interest in the security and in case of convertible debentures, in their convertibility into equity shares.

Depositors are interested in the regular payment of interest and the timely repayment of their deposits.

Financial institutions such as banks and specialised financial institutions are interested in getting back their advanced amounts with interests.

Trade creditors enjoy various legal protection as to their payments so that the business does not come to a standstill. But they are also very much intereste in the working of their borrower company (credit purchases) to be sure of timely payment of their dues.

(iii) **Employees :** That the employees of a company are interested in the working of the company does not need any elucidation. Their earnings, their fortune are tied up with the fortune of the company; so they are vitally interested in the company's affairs. So long as the company can continue its existence, can earn good profits, they are in the company's employment and there is the possibility for them to have better remuneration.

(iv) **Managerial personnel :** In company management, there are different levels of management, the Board being at the top. The different levels of managerial personnel have different types of interest in the affairs of the company. So, among the managerial personnel of a company different interest groups operate — directors form one group, the middle level management personnel another group and the lower level still another group. All these groups have one thing in common — they want the company to go on with its business and with the growth of prosperity of the company, it is likely that their interests will be served in a better way. Of course, in discussing the managerial personnels interest in their company, one thing must be kept in mind that there is a divorce between ownership and management in the company and this feature creates some peculiar interests among the top level executives.

(v) **General public :** In the new definition of business, the social responsibilities of business have assumed a new dimension. Public, the society have to be kept uppermost in the mind of the managers of a company because in the development of the corporate sector depends the welfare of the society – the economic upliftment of the people. So people are in general, interested in the development of companies.

## The Concept of Trusteeship in Company Management

According to Law of Trust, a trustee holds legal ownership over the trust property of which the equitable ownership lies with the **cestui que trust** i.e. the beneficiary. Directors are considered 'trustees' in relation to a company. With the changed concept of business, this trusteeship role of management has assumed a wider significance. The trusteeship of directors is not only in relation to the company to which they belong but to the whole society to which there is an implied pledge on the part of the managers of the best form of business organisation to serve. So trusteeship in the corporate management has transcended its legal definition and has assumed a new connotation.

The concept of trusteeship was introduced in the company management to make the managers conscious of their responsibilities. But "there has been a metamorphosis of the corporation"; the concept of corporation has passed through a total change. "It is no longer an organ of private capitalism. It is now considered as an embodiment of community interest". With that change, the approach to trusteeship has also changed.

In our country, the Companies Act has accepted this changed approach to trusteeship. A close analysis of the Companies Act, 1956, reveals that it has taken into consideration the Directive Principles contained in the Constitution of India. It has been provided in the Act that a company has to be managed not only in the interest of the owners of capital but also according to "sound business principles" and not harmful to the particular business or trade to which the company belongs and finally not **against public interest.** There are many regulatory measures in the Act to control the management personnel whenever the above-mentioned ideals of management are violated. The Act provides criminal liabilities for breach of trust. This can be interpreted as the new definition of trusteeship in company management. This definition is very comprehensive to widen the concept of trusteeship. The Government's concern as to the role of the managerial personnel of companies is evident from the fact that the Companies Act has kept in view really service-motivated competent trustworthy corrupt-free people to become leaders of company management. So, the Act provides so many disqualifications for a person for becoming a director of a company. A person with integrity coupled with the sense of social responsibility, appears to be a suitable person for becoming a director, according to the provisions and the spirit of the Company law. This can be interpreted as an extension of the concept of trusteeship.

It will not be out of context to mention here that the concept of trusteeship was first used in our country by Mahatma Gandhi and that concept is now being widely and respectfully recognised in corporate management. "Management by Trust" is now the motto in place of "Management by Objectives".

## The Board of Directors as Plural Executives

**A Committee** entrusted with some authority in place of individual executive is known as 'plural executive'. This is found in social as well as in business organisations. Management by committees in schools, colleges, co-operative societies, clubs etc. is quite a regular feature and in such cases an individual member of any committee is generally powerless and when he sits in the committee, he becomes powerful as a plural executive.

In case of company management, the Board of Directors exercises its power as a plural executive. But it is often found that a Board of Directors delegates executive powers to individuals. Though the plural executive is empowered to make decisions and to undertake other managerial functions such as planning, organising, staffing, directing or controlling, in company management, the Board as the plural executive is more effective in the field of planning and to some extent in controlling. In many companies, special committees are appointed in functional areas e.g. a production committee, a sales committee etc.

The responsibility of the directors of a company is collective and joint. So, the responsibility, so to say, is not of a director or directors as such but is of the Board of Directors. This responsibility is of the plural executive. The Board of Directors is a group and so an individual director, as it is, has no authority.

## The Emerging Pattern of Company Management

In the management of companies in India during the British regime, the Managing agents took the charge of management who were mostly the Britishers. It was quite natural because the concept of Company was introduced by the British rulers in India as early as in 1850 when Indian Companies Act was passed. Through this company form of organisation, the British rulers exploited the resources of India. The managing agency system, a unique system of company management, was a device to achieve this objective of the foreign rulers. The Managing agents acted in triple role of manager, financier and promoter. Indians were not given the opportunity to control the companies as far as the British could do so. But gradually, some Indian business-men entered into the field of managing agency.

The managing agents rendered yeoman-service to the development of industries in India but with the passage of time, the managing agents developed various vices and adopted all possible means to exploit the Indian companies. After independence, the system was subject to severe criticism and had to be abolished with effect from April 3, 1970. A new institution named Secretaries and Treasurers was created to replace managing agents as the predominant form of management. This new institution of Secretaries & Treasurers belied the hopes of being a proper replacement of managing agents. Their performance was far from satisfactory. This was also abolished along with the managing agency system.

Following their abolition, the following organs of management came to the fore : (i) Directors (Executive Committee), (ii) Managing Director and (iii) Manager. Of these three forms, the executive management through the Board of Directors or a Committee of the Board is becoming popular in Indian companies.

In many companies, today, the Board of Directors consists of whole-time officers of the company, the executive director rests with the Board. Actually, in this system, place of the Chief executive is assumed by a Committee comprising the top executives. The Board may assume the executive function through a standing committee generally called the executive committee. The executive committee is generally a small committee entrusted with the powers of the Company Management. It derives its authority from the Board and is accountable to the Board like an individual chief executive. The executive committee is responsible for the day-to-day affairs of the management of a company and usually consists of whole-time directors. The managerial decisions under this system are taken collectively through joint deliberations : "The system of executive management through Board or its Committee, lies in pooling together the skills and judgements of the directors". If the Board becomes truly **financial**, it can combine the advantages of individual decision-making and joint deliberations.

In the changing profile of company management, we notice that with the abolition of the managing agency system, the industrial groups started a new form of management. This is known as Consultancy and Service Company form of management. These companies, already experienced in the line of management as managing agents, render various services of administrative and secretarial nature. This type of manag nent consultants is increasing in number because t iis arrangement enables the erstwhile managing agents to continue their grip over client companies without assuming the same amount of responsibilities.

Another form of management, which has recently emerged, is the **professional management** form. Management institutes, both government and non-government, have been set up in India which have been producing management graduates. These management qualified people are taking up the responsibilities of company management. Thus the management is becoming professionalised gradually. How far it will succeed is yet to be seen. In India, company management in major cases is a family management and in such a management, professionally qualified persons are employed who advise the family group of owners and the real decisibns come from them.

## PROFESSIONALISATION IN TOP CORPORATE MANAGEMENT

With the emergence of management as a distinct discipline, there is an increasing demand for its recognition as a profession. Though judged from the criteria that make a vocation professionalised, management cannot yet be described as a profession though it has some of the characteristics of a profession.

In our discussion, we shall, however, consider management as a profession with reference to corporate management.

A company can be said to be professionally managed when the manager/management personnel are equipped with professional qualifications. This means that the persons having professional qualifications possess specialised knowledge and having training in that branch of education or discipline.

Professionalised management in companies or professionalisation in corporate management denotes the management of the company by persons who have specialised education and training in management.

The divorce of ownership from management in the large companies has made specialised knowledge and training in management. The **need** for professionalised corporate management cannot be over-emphasised. Complexities in the corporate management are increasing and there has been a new definition of 'Business'. Business is now a social institution and a company, being the best form of business organisation, is expected to serve the society in the best possible way through its business. The customer-oriented concept is a reflection of the corporate code of conduct.

Corporate management is moving at an increasing pace towards professionalisation. In our country, government and non-government management training institutes have been set up to impart professional education — management training — to young persons and company executives to equip them in a better way to tackle the corporate problems.

It will not be out of context to mention here that there is a school of opinion, according to which, Indian management has to go a long way in order to be qualified as a profession. However, some people are of the view that management should not strive towards professionalisation and there should be no statutory control over managers. According to Drucker, "Management is a practice rather than a service or profession though containing elements of both. No greater damage could be done to economy and society than to attempt to professionalise management by licensing managers or by limiting access to management to people with special academic degree."

However, in corporate management, professionalisation has become a necessity. The pattern of Company Management – the divorce between ownership and management, government's increasing regulatory measures on Company Management, growth of militant trade unions, desire of business leaders for social status and the development of scientific management are some of the factors which justify professionalisation of Corporate Management.

In a developing country like ours and with colonial history as its background, the need for professionalisation of the corporate management is all the more felt when the country is set on planned economy to ensure rapid industrialisation and economic rejuvenation. Indian industrial history during the British regime clearly demonstrates that the foreign rulers, basically traders, did never want Indians to be properly qualified and experienced to manage the affairs of big business organisations. So, with the attainment of independence, to build up a new India with strong economic foundation, the corporate sector naturally and quite legitimately drew the attention of the makers of modern independent India. All the world over there is an awakening in social consciousness in the business activities and this necessitates the most efficient management of the corporate sector with scientific outlook causing the minimum wastage of human and other resources.

Company management involves management of different areas — production, marketing, finance and personnel, besides administrative management. The Board of Directors constitutes the top management level. This Board is constituted in a way or in different ways in which we cannot expect the Board consisting of persons specialised in different areas of management to give leadership to the middle management level and down to the lower management level. Specialisation is the order of the day and it is beyond question that the top management of a company must have persons with specialisations and special education and training in different areas of management which is something not so easily available. The top management of the Board is a decision-making Body and unless the Body is equipped with adequate knowledge, one cannot expect prudent decisions from the Board or the highest Body of the company. As from the top or the Head will go directions to the departmental heads, the top management must have the requisite qualifications, acumen, efficiency, training and education to guide the lower level management.

Specialised knowledge is a must to secure efficiency in all spheres of company management. Because of growing complexities, in every area of management, new techniques are being developed which need special education. This special education is imparted in the management institutes and makes the future generation professionally qualified to undertake the responsibility of receiving the corporate management efficiently.

Professionalisation in top management signifies that there are persons in the management who are specialised in the management of different areas — marketing, finance, personnel, production and also administrative. It is needless to emphasise that these persons will be in a better position to tackle problems in the efficient running of the company. It has been recognised in India that professional corporate management is more effective and, therefore, desirable. This is evident from the fact that there is a growing demand for MBA or management trained persons and at the government level also, to run the public enterprises more efficiently, management qualified people are being preferred to people of Indian Administrative Service.

A clear swing towards professional management is noticeable in our country; this is definitely not without any rationale behind it. As the days are going on, it is being felt that corporate management is a specialised job, so for the persons who will direct the whole affairs from the top, there should be specialised knowledge.

**The emerging pattern of Company Management** is a clear emphasis on functions; as we see functional directors who take the responsibility of different areas of management — one director taking charge of marketing, another finance, yet another personnel and thus management is being done in the specialist way.

**Democratisation of Company Management**

The oligarchic nature of Company Management

has been responsible for certain evils which have retarded the healthy growth of the corporate sector. The evils such as the dictatorial attitude of the directors, financial manipulation, nepotism, favouritism and concentration of economic power in a few hands emphasise the need for democratisation of company management.

The shareholders of a company are widely scattered and there is very little scope for them to exercise direct and continuous control over the working of their company. Therefore, direct democracy is out of question. Through their elected representatives, the shareholders can only make their existence felt. So, to ensure indirect democracy and safeguard their interests, the representatives should be persons of integrity and it is for the shareholders to see that they have some effective control over the elected management. This is democratisation of company management. **Organised shareholders, directors with strong sense of integrity and legislative measures** can bring about democracy in company management to a great extent but democracy in the real sense of the term is a far cry in company management.

Shareholders are, no doubt, scattered but with determination and effort, they can form some sort of association among themselves; they can be organised to an appreciable extent. Shareholder' associations can collect proxies from the large number of disinterested shareholders and can use them for their common benefit. In India, the Company Law Board will assist the formation of such associations, as it has pledged. But to form the association and to keep it going is not an easy job. Large funds, co-operation of small shareholders and vigilant watch to frustrate any attempt by the existing company management to capture the association through backdoor, are essential conditions for the survival of shareholders' associations. In the USA, the shareholders' associations are very effective and in India, also, some amount of success is sure to be achieved if genuine attempts are made in this direction with the active co-operation of the government.

The evils of oligarchic management mainly stem from the corrupt practices of the directors. Directors who are really honest can keep the management clean and can keep the shareholders to derive the benefits of indirect democracy. So, election of proper directors is a very essential and effective step towards democratisation of company management. By introducing the system of cumulative voting by which the minority shareholders will also be able to elect their representation on the Board of Directors and by electing suitable persons as directors through the shareholders' association, democratisation of company management can be achieved to a large extent. The appointment of directors on the Board by the institutional investors in India has helped in curbing autocracy of directors. But very recently the trend in the management of companies has been undergoing so much changes that the Boards of Directors are being chained with so many legislative restrictions that the scope for their autocracy is being considerably reduced.

Besides the above measures, the government can control undemocratic practices of the management of a company through various legislature measures. We have already a number of provisions in the Companies Act and the amendments in this direction. They are —

(1) Compelling companies to submit various reports to shareholders; (2) Prohibition of issue of shares with disproportionate voting rights; (3) Proxy reform; (4) Closure of members register; (5) Provision for cumulative voting; (6) Prevention of oppression by majority; (7) Various legal actions against undesirable management personnel.

The observations of the Greene Committee on Company Law amendment appointed in England about six decades back are still quite pertinent in this connection.

"The fact is that it is neither possible nor desirable to secure in industry the sort of democracy that one may have in government. The average of shareholder or investor does not take any interest in the actual working of his company and his interest stops with the getting of dividends. There is an initimidating financial barrier in the way of carrying through a policy of direct action by shareholder (a fall in the market value of shares). Even in countries having a democratic control of industry by shareholders 'it is easier to upset a Ministry than a Board of Directors'. So long as company remains a going concern, shareholders are powerless in face of a directors' strike. Yet cases in which fraud or lesser forms of dishonesty or improper dealing occur are comparatively few."

To sum up, we can say that the democratisation of company management is possible to a great extent if there is a multipronged attack on the top management by the shareholders by the government and by the honest directors of the Boarc against unscrupulous directors. Professionalisation in company management is bringing changes which, we hope, will help in the attainment of democratic management of companies to the extent possible.

## Measures for democratisation of Company Management

The important measures that may be taken to bring about democratisation of the management of the company are : (1) role of the shareholders' association (2) election of the responsible Board of Directors and Managers and (3) legal measures.

### (1) Role of Shareholders' Association

The Shareholders of a company are scattered throughout the country. They are not acquainted with one another. At the general meeting, only a small fraction of shareholders usually meet. This non-communative feature of shareholders among themselves is a major factor contributing to the growth of share democracy in Company Organisation and Management. The shareholders' associations can perform very useful service in this direction. If any organisation can be formed by them that organisation may look to their interest in common. Such organisations should be led by competent and selfless persons interested in the cause of the large body of shareholders. This type of associations should be formed either on country or regional basis. They should try to maintain contact with the large body of shareholders, educate them about their rights, powers and duties. They should try to collect proxies from the disinterested shareholders and use them properly in the interest of the majority of the shareholders. To safeguard the interests of shareholders, the organiser of the associations should chalk out plan and act accordingly. They should play the role of opposition as in the Parliament and offer intelligent and constructive criticism.

The character of shareholders' association boils down to the voting trust of the U.S.A. The Company Law Administration is banking upon the growth and development of shareholders' association mainly for the effective and proper use of proxy votes. Such an association will obviate the necessity of individual attendance and will look after their group interests. The leader of the association will act as a watch-dog and see that the management is pursuing right policy in the interest of the member shareholders. These associations are expected to act as the processing centres for the complaints received from the shareholders and ensure that their grievances will be looked into and properly redressed. It would be proper and wise on the part of the shareholders' association to make some informal arrangement with the management of the company and discuss with them the relevant matters. The shareholders' association alone can act as a powerful agency of constant vigilance on company affairs on behalf of all members. "Self-help is the best and it is obvious there is no substitute for shareholders' vigilance. Even legislation can act as complementary supplementing shareholders' own control over company affairs. Unity constitutes real strength". (Shertekar).

To make a shareholders' association really effective, certain points should be strictly adhered to. The founder shareholders should be independent investors, not being in any way connected with company management. The men of integrity and persons who are not in the top management echelons of the companies should only hold officers in the shareholders' associations. The principle of one man, one vote for the election of office bearers of the association should be the rule of the association and under no circumstances, the associations should accept any contributions from the corporate managements. As to the functions of the association, let us reiterate that the association should function like an Advice Bureau and a processing centre for the complaints of the member shareholders. Like a watch-dog, it should watch the functioning of the management of the company. It must take special care for the minority shareholders. An association can also organise investment clubs to help investment of share savings in the shares of companies.

### (2) Election of responsible Board of Directors and Managers

The Board of Directors and Managers of a Company have a big role to play in the democratisation of the Company Management. Being the top level management personnel, the Board and Managers are greatly involved in the formulation of policies which hold the key to democracy in Company Management in reality. Directors and Managers should be men of integrity and feel responsible to the majority of the shareholders rather than satisfying their own or the minority's interests. The shareholdes' association has a big role to play in this direction. With the active cooperation of the shareholders' association, the majority of the shareholders can elect directors according to their wishes. In this direction one important step which may be taken is that the system of cumulative voting should be introduced so that the minority shareholders with less voice may also be able to elect their representative on the Board of Directors, who may safeguard their interests properly. The election of responsible Board and Managers also ensures that the management will feel doubly responsible to the shareholder – first, by managing the affairs of the company properly in the general interest of the large body of the shareholder and secondly by giving correct and adequate information to them about the affairs of the Company.

**(3) Legal measures**

In spite of various measures adopted and formation of shareholders' association, it is not possible for the shareholders to safeguard their interests properly. Therefore, legal measures are essential for the democratisation of company management. Legislative measures should be in force to regulate the power of the management, provide safeguards to the minority shareholders' interest, check undemocratic practices adopted by the Company Management. Legislative measures adopted under the Companies Act, 1956 are discussed below:

(a) Issuing shares with disproportionate voting rights is now prohibited and a company may simply issue preference and equity shares. Deferred shares which used to be issued to the founder of a company cannot be issued now, thus ensuring democratisation of company management to a great extent.

(b) The Act provides that the working results of the company should be reported to the members. Every shareholder is entitled to receive the notice of the annual general meeting 21 days in advance. Copies of Profit & Loss A/c, Balance Sheet, Auditor's Report and the Director's Report are also to be made available to the shareholders in advance so that they can ventilate their opinion at the annual general meeting.

(c) Option has been given to public companies for adopting cumulative voting with regard to the election of directors. In such a case, the appointments are made once in every three years and interim casual vacancies are filled in accordance with the provisions, **mutatis mutandis,** of Sec. 262, under the prevailing voting method – one vote for each share, directors are perpetually elected by the majority group of shareholders and the minority cannot elect even one director. The position becomes very inequitable in the case of giant companies where investments are crores of rupees.

"Complaints frequently arise that majority stockholders oppress the minority under the old-fashioned rule of voting, this oppression cannot be removed. Where, for example, five directors are to be elected, a person holding 51 shares out of 100 shares can elect his 5 candidates. To prevent this situation, the system of cumulative voting has been devised. Under this system of voting, each stockholder has as many votes as is equal to the number of voting shares he owns multiplied by the number of directors to be elected. These votes he may accumulate for one candidate or may distribute among the candidates for election in any way he sees fit.

In the example cited above, the majority stockholders would have 255 votes (51 × 5) and the minority interests would control 245 votes (49 × 5). If the majority contents itself with casting this cumulative vote for three out of five directors, it can secure their election by giving each director 85 votes. The minority may elect two directors by giving one of the directors 122 votes and another 123 votes. In this case, if the majority frittened away its strength among five directors, while the minority concentrated its strength upon four, the minority would gain control of the Board" (Notes on Americal practice – extract from Ramaya's – Guide to the Companies Act).

(d) The Companies Act provides for reforms in the matter of voting by proxy. It is now required that blank proxy forms have to be sent to the members. They should be properly informed that proxies are allowed. Moreover, the Articles of the Company, requiring the proxy forms to be deposited with the company earlier than 48 hours before the general meeting, cannot be altered.

(e) It has been provided that the register of members can be kept closed for a maximum of thirty days at a stretch and only fortyfive days during a year. Notice of the closure is also to be given through a newspaper at least seven days before the closure. However, it must be noted that a company is not bound to close its register even for a day. But if it does choose to close, the provisions of Section 154 will have to be complied with. The provision made by this section is an enabling one. There is no compulsion on the company to close its register of members but in case it chooses to do so, the failure to comply with the provisions will attract the penalty provided thereon. Company Law Board's advice as regards notice under Sec. 154 is that notices should expressly refer to the closure of the register of members. Any statement that 'transfer books are closed' is not sufficient. It is only confusing. The expression 'transfer book' does not necessarily mean the register of member. Companies that are listed on the Stock Exchange are required to give notice of the closure of transfer books to the Stock Exchange. The section applies to all companies, public and private.

(f) The Companies Act provides for the protection of the minority shareholder. They, in requisite number, can apply to the court for suitable action. They can also approach the Central Government to set the affairs of the company on proper footing. The Central Government can appoint either two persons as additional director of the company or may require fresh appointment of the director by proportional representation.

(g) To protect the interests of shareholders and to make the corporate form to attain democracy in the real sense, various provisions have been enacted in the Companies Act and in its subsequent amendments. Approval of the Central Government is necessary in several cases, such as, appointment and reappointment of certain top management personnel, changes in the constitution of the Board of Directors and increase in the remuneration beyond the fixed limit. Provisions have been made to restrict the number of companies of which the person can become director. A person cannot be director of more than 20 companies and Managing Director of more than 2 companies. The overall managerial remuneration has been fixed. The appointment of managing agents and secretaries and treasurers has been prohibited. Certain types of companies must have their accounts audited by cost auditors. The auditors, in general, have been given wider powers. They are required to disclose 'true and fair' state of affairs of the company to its members.

Indian Companies Act, 1956, as amended up to date is itself one of the greatest legislation measures for securing democratisation of Company Management.

To sum up, the Companies Act assists to promote democratic socialism. The predominance of oligarchy in company management has been severely criticised, various complaints have been raised and legislative and administrative measures on the part of the Central Government are being adopted to democratise company management as far as possible. The equity shareholder get more rights in the choice and appointment of directors. They are now in a better position to secure the removal of a director from the office. The share qualification for a director cannot be more than Rs. 5,000. The procurement of money is not now very difficult for a member to become a director. The rule of the majority is toned down to a certain extent. The minority shareholder get more rights under the new Act. Under Sec. 265, the election of the directorate of a company to the extent of not less than two-thirds may be on the principle of proportional representation (whether by the single transferable vote or by a system of cumulative voting) which would give even minority shareholders representation on the Board, for a period of three years at a time.

Equity shareholders are now in a better position to get together and forward resolutions for considerations at the general meetings. Mismanagement or oppression can be redressed really to a great extent. Sec. 247 of the Act provides for investigation of ownership of a company whose shares have been cornered or acquired to a considerable extent with a view to controlling the policy of the Company and the Management of its affairs. "Shareholders emerge under the Act as the ultimate repository of the company's powers. The Act, in short, is an instance of democratising economic institutions" (Shertekar).

**Role of Shareholders in Company Management**

In company management, shareholders have some definite role to play. The Companies Act provides certain rights to be exercised by shareholders. The company belongs to the shareholders and it is in the fitness of things that the shareholders should have a say in the management of their company. The oligarchic management of companies has made it all the more necessary for the shareholders to play very effective role in the administration and management of their companies. Matters which vitally affect shareholders' interests should not be left entirely to the discretion of the Board of Directors; the consent of the shareholders should be obtained before any decision is taken on vital issues.

Shareholders enjoy certain rights which for the sake of convenience we can discuss under two heads — individual rights and collective rights.

Shareholders enjoy certain rights individually as co-owners of a company. These rights are : – (a) Right to share profits (b) Right to share in the property and assets of the company (c) Right to vote authentic person or through proxies (d) Right to receive notices and circulars of the company (e) Right to receive notices of company meetings according to the provisions of the Act (f) Right to inspect permissible records of the company such as register of members, Minute Book of the general meetings etc. (g) Right to sell shares.

These individual rights of shareholders establish their right as the owners of the company and to play their part/role in these matters is very important to exercise control over management and administration of the company.

The collective rights of shareholders are very important because it is through collective rights that the shareholders can bring about democracy in company management. The Company law provides that the shareholders shall have the ultimate voice in the decision of important matters of the company. These rights of shareholders are managerial rights and they can only be exercised collectively as a body or through general meetings. Members enjoy some rights as per articles of the company and also in accordance with the provisions of the Companies Act through resolution passed at the shareholders' meetings. So, provisions are there in the Companies Act for the members collectively to have control over the functioning of their companies. No doubt, the Board of Directors takes decisions on policy matters but in vital matters, the approval of the shareholders must be obtained at general meetings, for example, declaration of the rate of dividend.

Some of the important collective rights of shareholders are : (1) Alteration of Memorandum and Articles of Association (special resolution), (2) Alterations (ordinary resolution), reduction and reorganisation of share capital (special resolution), (3) Adoption of annual accounts, directors' report and auditors report (ordinary resolution), (4) Election of directors and auditors (ordinary resolution), (5) Declaration of directors (ordinary resolutions), (6) Borrowing over and above company's paid-up capital and free reserves, if any (ordinary resolution), (7) Acceptance of an office of profit by a director (special resolution), (8) Reconstruction and amalgamation schemes (special resolution), (9) Issue of shares at a discount (ordinary resolution), (10) Issue of bonus shares and capitalisation of reserves (ordinary resolution), (11) Appointment of sole Selling or Buying Agents (ordinary resolution), (12) Removal of director and auditor (ordinary resolution), (13) Fixing the remuneration of directors (ordinary resolution), (14) Sanctioning remuneration to directors on the basis of percentage of profits (ordinary resolution), (15) Sale of company's property and assets (ordinary resolution).

The above powers are exercised by shareholders collectively at general meetings. The Companies Act is always in the process of amendments and various provisions are being added to increase shareholders' rights and role in the management of their company and in the democratisation of company management.

In practice, we rarely get democratisation in company management. Oligarchy still predominates in spite of various measures adopted to widen controlling powers of shareholders. A few persons – the directors – constitute an 'inner ring' or an organised small group and take all possible measures to frustrate the attempts to democratise company management. But what can be reiterated is that the situation in the matter of shareholders' role and control in company management has been leaning in favour of shareholders after various enactments and attempts are being made to widen the role of shareholders to secure real power and control over top management. More alertness coupled with more involvement on the part of the shareholders can only go a long way in striking the oligarchic structure and to build up a democratic set-up in the real sense of the term.

In spite of all efforts to give more power and rights to shareholders — the owners of the company — the separation of ownership from management and the very nature of shareholders – their indifference and lack of organisation among themselves, have made it very difficult to ensure real control of shareholders in company management. In the corporate sector, things move in a very peculiar way; the big business houses with their associates control and devise means of control over the affairs of the company through various tactful but unethical practices.

## Exercise of voting rights by shareholders at General meetings : (Sec. 182)

At general meetings every share holder may use his voting rights in his own best interests or as he thinks fit – even though such voting may be detrimental to the interests of the company. It is a firmly established rule of law that shareholders having majority voting power cannot use that power for passing any resolution in fraud of the minority shareholders or so as to discriminate between the majority and minority of the shareholders. Any resolution voted for by them should be bonafide for the benefit the company 'as a whole' meaning thereby both the company as a commercial unity and also the corporator as a general body. **The majority shareholders cannot use their votes either to defraud the company or gain for themselves or any other person an unfair advantage to the exclusion of the minority shareholders.**

A shareholder owes a duty not only to his fellow shareholders but also to the company and he should not exercise his voting right in such manner as to appropriate either the company's property or the other shareholders'.

In the case of director shareholders, as they stand in fiduciary relationship to the company, the rule is more exacting than in the case of other shareholders. Of course, the use of voting rights to pass a resolution contrary to public policy will, in all cases, be invalid, even if passed unanimously.

# CHAPTER 2

## STRUCTURE OF COMPANY MANAGEMENT

Shareholders
↓
Board of Directors
↓
Executive Committee
↓
Chief Executive → Managing Director/Manager
↓
Functional Managers
↓
(1) Purchase Manager (2) Finance Manager
(3) Production Manager (4) Marketing Manager
(5) Administrative Manager

Besides the Functional Managers, there are Heads of departments, subordinate officers and supervisory managerial groups.

Usually in a big company, there is an Executive Committee of the Board to control and supervise the Top Managerial Group and a number of Sub-Committees of the Board. These Sub-Committees may be permanent or on an ad-hoc basis. The permanent Sub-Committee, for example, Finance Committee and Ad-hoc Sub-Committee such as Allotment Committee. Management by committee is the usual feature of the management of a big company. But it has to be noted that all committees and sub-committees derive their authorities from the Board. They have no original authority; their authorities are delegated and they are to do what they are told to do. Of course, all these are subject to Board Resolution, Company's Articles and Companies Act.

The pattern of organisation may slightly differ from one company to another but the general pattern remains more or less the same. Big companies have similar nature of organisation pattern with the differences between a manufacturing and a trading company. However, we can say that the overall supervision rests with the Board and the company is managed by a large number of officials or management personnel of middle and low level under the leadership of the Managing Director. No company can employ at the same time Managing Director and Manager, either of them will have to be appointed. Earlier, the managing agents used to be the chief executives of the company but now this system has been abolished. Along with them the system of appointment of Secretaries and Treasurers has also been abolished. Therefore, only Managing Director or General Manager can be entrusted with the functions of the chief executive of the company.

### The functions of Chief Executive

The chief executive of a company has the primary responsibility to run the entire business of the company to achieve its desired goals. Various management functions such as planning, organising, co-ordinating, control etc. to ensure smooth functioning of the organisation have to be performed by him.

We can sum up the functions of the chief executive of a company as follows :

(1) To formulate various policies, plans and sub-plans within the overall policy of the company as decided upon at the Board meeting. He will see to it that the policies taken at Board meetings are translated into action.

(2) To build up proper organisational structure where he will be the central authority. From him will emanate the powers and duties of other management personnel. As the chief executive of a big organisation (a company), he is to ensure harmonious co-ordination among the different parts of the organisation.

(3) To motivate the management personnel under him to work in a team-spirit, which is to be ensured by him as the leader of the organisation of management.

(4) The chief executive, as a matter of fact, acts as a liaison between the Board and the subordinate executives. Boards occasionally meet but the members of the Board are kept abreast of every information by the chief executive. The chief executive is a man of the Board as well as a man of the subordinate executives. His is a role of co-ordination, control and motivation — a very important part to play to lead a big organisation like a company. The credit or discredit of the performance of the organisation goes to him primarily and his is not a *sine cure* position. He is the pivot of the whole organisation.

(5) The chief executive must be a man with one eye inside the organisation and the other one outside, to keep constant watch to what has been happening in the environment which will have impact on the overall performance of the organisation. He will have to keep constant touch with the Government/Governments, trade associations, trade unions which matter in the efficient running of the organisation.

## Managing Director

On and from the commencement of the Companies (Amendment) Act, 1988, every Public Company or a Private Company which is a subsidiary of a Public Company, having a paid up share capital of such firm as may be prescribed, shall have a managing or whole-time director or a manager.

### Certain persons not to be appointed managing directors

(1) An undischarged insolvent or one who has at any time been adjudged an insolvent

(2) A person who suspends or has at any time suspended payment to his creditor or makes or has at any time made, a composition with them; or

(3) One who is or has at any time been, convicted by a Court of an offence involving moral turpitude and for any other offence

(4) One who is not a citizen of India and is not resident in India

(5) One who has not attained the age of thirty years or has attained the age of sixty five years.

Appointment of the Managing Directors must be made with the approval of the Central Government unless such appointment is made in accordance with the conditions specified in Parts I and II of Schedule XIII and a return in the prescribed form is filed within ninety days from the date of such appointment.

The Board of Directors appoints the managing Director as a whole-time officer of the company and is entrusted with the detailed management of the company. A managing director is one of the members of the Board of Directors. No association of persons or any body corporate can be appointed as the Managing Director under the Companies Act 1956.

The Act defines the Managing Director as "a director who, by virtue of an agreement with the Company or of a resolution passed by the Company at the general meeting or by its Board or by virtue of its Memorandum or Articles of Association, is entrusted with substantial powers of management which would not otherwise be exercisable by him and includes a director occupying the position of a Managing Director, by whatever name called." It lays emphasis that he should have "substantial powers of management".

**Functions :** Major functions of this top managerial authority are :

(1) Within the established company goals and policy, the MD determines primary operating policies.

(2) MD organises and plans the organisation structure.

(3) In consultation with the Personnel Manager, MD plans and organises the Personnel Management.

(4) In the management of the personnel department of the company MD is directly involved in the selection, training, promotion and remuneration of the company's managerial staff in ensuring management development.

(5) As the chief executive, MD exercises overall control and supervision over purchasing and inventories.

(6) He formulates and approves budgets.

(7) To ensure sound financial position of the company MD administers finances and financial controls.

(8) Marketing plans and programmes and overall control and supervision over production are within the administrative and managerial jurisdiction of the MD.

(9) He plans and organises accelerated growth of business.

(10) As the chief executive, he maintains external relations of the company with the Government, customers, trade unions, trade associations etc.

**Term of office :** The term of office of an MD cannot exceed five years at a time but he can be reappointed for a period of another five years. On each occasion, the re-appointment or extension of his term of service can be made only in the last two years of his term.

**Number of Managing Directorship :** A person can act as a Managing Director in two companies and not more than that at the same time. In case of the second company his appointment will require the unanimous approval of the Board of Directors. The Central Government may, however, by order permit a person to be appointed as the Managing Director of more than two companies if it is satisfied that the companies should, for common management, have a common Managing Director.

**Remuneration :** Maximum limit 5 per cent of net profits for one and 10 per cent for all of them. This limit can be exceeded with the approval of the Central Government.

The Companies (Amendment) Act, 1988 provides :

Subject to the ceiling limits laid down in Sec. 198 and Section 309, remuneration by way of salary, commission or both and perquisites shall not exceed the following limits, namely :

**Salary :** Rupees, 180,000/- per annum or Rs.15,000/- per month including dearness and all other allowances calculated in the following scale :

| Where the effective Capital of the Co. is | | Monthly salary payable shall not exceed |
|---|---|---|
| (1) less than 20 lakh rupees | .......... | Rs. 6,000/- |
| (2) Rs. 20 lakhs or more but less than Rs. 50 lakhs | .......... | Rs. 7,500/- |
| (3) Rs. 50 lakhs or more but less than Rs. 1 crore | .......... | Rs. 9,000/- |
| (4) Rs. 1 crore or more but less than Rs. 3 crores | .......... | Rs. 11,000/- |
| (5) Rs. 3 crores or more but less than Rs. 5 crores | .......... | Rs. 13,000/- |
| (6) Rs. 5 crores or more | .......... | Rs. 15,000/- |

**Commission**

In case commission is also payable along with the salary, it shall not be more than one per cent of the net profits of the company, subject to a ceiling of fifty percent of the salary or Rs. 90,000/- per annum, whichever is less.

Where it is proposed to pay remuneration by way of commission only, such commission shall not exceed the following limits, namely –

| Where the effective Capital of the Co. is | | Commission payable annually shall not exceed |
|---|---|---|
| (a) less than Rs. 20 lakhs | .......... | Rs. 1,08,000/- |
| (b) Rs. 20 lakhs or more but less than Rs. 50 lakhs | .......... | Rs. 1,35,000/- |
| (c) Rs. 50 lakhs or more but less than Rs. 1 crore | .......... | Rs. 1,62,000/- |
| (d) Rs. 1 crore or more but less than Rs. 3 crores | .......... | Rs. 1,98,000/- |
| (e) Rs. 3 crores or more but less than Rs. 5 crores | .......... | Rs. 2,34,000/- |
| (f) Rs. 5 crores or more | .......... | Rs. 2,70,000/- |

"Effective Capital" means the aggregate of the paid-up share capital amount, if any, for the time being standing to the credit of share premium account, reserves and surplus, long-term loans and deposits received, if any, as reduced by the aggregate of any investments, accumulated losses and preliminary expenses, not written-off.

**Perquisites**

Perquisites may be allowed in addition to salary and/or commission or both. In the case of persons posted at Bombay, Calcutta, Delhi and Madras, perquisites shall be restricted to an amount equal to the annual salary or Rs. 1,35,000/- per annum whichever is less. In the case of persons posted at other places, perquisites shall be restricted to an amount equal to the annual salary or Rs.1,15,000/- per annum, whichever is less. Unless the context otherwise requires, perquisites are classified into three categories : 'A', 'B' and 'C', as follows :

**Category A**

This will comprise house rent allowance, medical reimbursement, club-fees, leave travel concession and personal accident insurance. These may be provided for as under :

(I) **Housing I** – The expenditure by companies on hiring unfurnished accommodation for the appointee will be subject to the following ceilings :

(a) Bombay, Calcutta, Delhi and Madras :

Sixty percent of the salary, over and above ten percent, payable by the appointee.

(b) Other places :

Fifty percent of the salary, over and above ten percent, payable by the appointee.

**Housing II** — In case the accommodation is owned by the company, ten percent of the salary of the appointee shall be deducted by the company.

**Housing III** — In case no accommodation is provided by the company, the appointee shall be entitled to house rent allowance subject to the ceilings laid down in Housing I.

**Explanation** – The expenditure incurred by companies on gas, electricity, water and furnishings shall be valued as per the Income-tax Rules, 1962. This shall, however, be subject to a ceiling of ten percent of the salary of the person proposed to be appointed.

(II) **Medical reimbursement** — Expenses incurred for the person to be appointed and the family subject to a ceiling of one month's salary in a year or three months' salary over a period of three years.

(III) **Leave Travel Concession** — For the person proposed to be appointed and his family, once in a year incurred in accordance with any rules specified by the company.

(IV) **Club-fees** — Fees of clubs subject to a maximum of two clubs. This will not include admission and life membership fees.

(V) **Personal Accident Insurance** — Premium not to exceed Rs. 1,000/- per annum.

**Explanation** — For the purposes of Category A, 'family' means the spouse, the dependant children and dependant parents of the appointee.

**Category B**

Contribution to provident fund, superannuation fund or annuity fund will not be included in the computation of the ceiling on perquisites to the extent these, either singly or put together, are not taxable under the Income Tax Act. Gratuity payable shall not exceed half a month's salary for each completed year of service, subject to a ceiling of Rs. 1,00,000/-

**Category C**

Provision of car for use on company's business and telephone at residence will not be considered as perquisites. Personal long-distance calls on telephone and use of car for private purpose shall be billed by the company to the individual appointee concerned.

The remuneration shall be subject to approval by a resolution of the shareholders in general meeting.

## Compensation for loss of office

A managing director is entitled to receive compensation for the loss of office if he ceases to hold office before the expiry of his term. But the amount of compensation is limited to the remuneration which he would have earned for the balance of his term or 3 years, whichever is shorter.

He is not entitled to compensation if —

(a) he resigns office as a result of reconstruction or amalgamation of the company with other company and he is appointed managing director or other officer in the new company.

(b) he vacates office as a result of an order by the court

(c) the company is wound up due to his negligence or default or

(d) he is guilty of fraud or breach of trust or gross negligence or mismanagement of the affairs of the company or

(e) he instigates or takes part directly or indirectly in termination of his office.

## Manager

A manager is "an individual who, subject to superintendence, control and direction of the Board of Directors, has the management of the whole or substantially the whole of the affairs of the company and includes a director or any person occupying the position of a manager by whatever name called and whether under a contract of service or not. [Sec. 2 (24)]. Only an individual can be appointed as the manager under the Companies Act. He is appointed for the general management of the company. There is no bar as to the appointment of a director as the manager of the company. No body corporate or association of persons can be appointed as the manager of the company.

The appointment, re-appointment, remuneration, terms of office and number of membership are all similar to those of a Managing Director. The specific provisions are with regard to the disqualifications of persons for the appointment as Manager.

## Disqualifications

(I) A person who is an undischarged insolvent or one who has been adjudged insolvent at any time within the preceding five years;

(II) A person who has suspended payment to his creditor or has made a composition with them;

(III) A person who has been convicted of an offence involving moral turpitude at any time within the preceding five years by a Court in India.

These disqualifications can, however, be waived by the Central Government if it deems desirable to do so.

## General Manager

In a big company, the General Manager is appointed at the head of the departmental or functional managers. He acts as a 'linking pin' between the top level management and the middle level management. Generally, a business concern appoints a General Manager. He heads the 'line' people of the organisation. There are functional managers in a business company in charge of production, perchasing and marketing. The General Manager is placed at the top of the line managers. He is, therefore, connected with technical and commercial activities unlike the Secretary of the company who is a specialist and a staff person and looks after the functions necessary to carry out the basic functions.

# CHAPTER 3

## ORGANISATION OF THE BOARD OF DIRECTORS

In all forms of company organisation the principal authority is the 'Board of Directors'. Company is a person in the eye of law but it is an artificial person. It cannot think, it cannot move, it cannot see, it cannot hear — everything on its behalf has to be done by some other persons as its agents. These persons are called Directors. They are collectively called the "Board of Directors". The shareholders delegate the power of Company Management to the directors elected by them. They act as a Board and individually they have no powers. It is, however, possible that the Board may delegate its powers to either one director or to a committee of directors. The Board of Directors is the ultimate executive authority of the company. Directors, therefore, carry on the business of the company, enter into contracts for the company and look after the property and assets of the company. As to their position, judicial pronouncements are not unanimous — some have described them as agents, some as trustees, some as managing partners and it has also been held that they stand in a fiduciary position towards the company in regard to the power conferred on them by the Articles and also the capital under their control. They are not persons in the employment of the company nor are they servants of the company or members of its staff. None of the aforesaid descriptions is exhaustive. "Directors are persons invested with strictly defined powers of management under the Articles of Association of a Corporation". (L. J. Bowen)

## CONSTITUTION OF BOARD OF DIRECTORS

**Minimum number of Directors** (Sec. 252)

(1) Every public company shall have at least three directors.

(2) Every other company shall have at least two directors.

**Only individuals to be directors** (Sec. 253)

No body corporate, association or firm shall be appointed director of a company, and only an individual shall be so appointed.

**Subscribers of Memorandum deemed to be directors** (Sec. 254)

In default of and subject to any regulations in the Articles of a company, subscribers of the Memorandum who are individuals, shall be deemed to be the directors of the company, until the directors are duly appointed in accordance with Sec. 255. The subscribers of the Memorandum or a majority of them shall determine the number and names of the first directors.

**Appointment of directors and proportion of those who are to retire by rotation** (Sec. 255).

(1) Unless the Articles provide for the retirement of all directors at every general meeting, not less than two-thirds of the total number of directors of a Public Company, or of a Private Company which is a subsidiary of a Public Company, shall — (a) be persons whose period of office is liable to termination by retirement of directors by rotation; and (b) save as otherwise expressly provided in the Companies Act, be appointed by the company in general meeting.

(2) The remaining directors in the case of any such company and the director generally in the case of a Private Company which is not a subsidiary of a Public Company, shall, in default of and subject to any regulations in the articles of the company, also be appointed by the company in general meeting.

**Ascertainment of directors retiring by rotation and filling of vacancies** (Sec. 256)

(1) At the first annual general meeting of a Public Company or a Private Company which is a subsidiary of a Public Company, held next after the date of the general meeting at which the first directors are appointed in accordance with Sec. 255 and at every subsequent annual general meeting, one-third of such directors for the time being as are liable to retire by rotation, or if their number is not three or a multiple of three, then, the number nearest to one-third, shall retire from office.

(2) The directors to retire by rotation at every annual general meeting shall be those who have been longest in office since their last appointment, but as between persons who become directors on the same day, those who are to retire shall, in default of and subject to any agreement among themselves, be determined by lot.

(3) At the annual general meeting at which a director retires as aforesaid, the company may fill up the vacancy by appointing the retiring director or some other person thereto.

(4) (a) If the place of the retiring director is not so filled up and the meeting has not expressly resolved not to fill the vacancy, the meeting shall stand adjourned till the same day next week, at the same time and place or if that day is a public holiday, till the next succeeding day which is not a public holiday, at the same time and place. (b) If at the adjourned meeting also, the place of the retiring director is not filled up and that meeting also has not expressly resolved not to fill the vacancy, the retiring director shall be deemed to have been re-appointed at the adjourned meeting, unless,

(i) at that meeting or at the previous meeting, a resolution for the re-appointment of such director has been put to the meeting and lost;

(ii) the retiring director has, by a notice in writing addressed to the Company or its Board of Directors, expressed his unwillingness to be so re-appointed;

(iii) he is not qualified or is disqualified for appointment ;

(iv) a resolution, whether special or ordinary, is required for his appointment or re-appointment in virtue of the provision of the Companies Act; or

(v) the proviso to subsection (2) of Section 263 is applicable to the case. [At a general meeting of a company, a motion shall not be made for the appointment of two or more persons as directors of the company by a single resolution, unless a resolution that it shall be so made has first been agreed to by the meeting without any vote being given against it. A resolution moved in contravention shall be void, whether or not objection was taken at the time to its being so moved; (provided that where a resolution so moved is passed, no provision for the automatic re-appointment of the director retiring by rotation in default of another appointment shall apply) Sec. 263].

**Right of persons other than retiring directors to stand for directorship**

A person who is not a retiring director shall be eligible for appointment to the office of director at any general meeting, if he or some member intending to propose him has, not less than fourteen days before the meeting, left at the office of the company a notice in writing under his hand signifying his candidature for the office of director or the intention of such member to propose him as a candidate for that office, as the case may be (Sec. 257).

**Right of Company to increase or reduce the number of directors**

A company in general meeting may, by ordinary resolution, increase or reduce the number of its directors within the limits fixed in that behalf by its Articles (Sec. 258).

Increase in number of directors require Government sanction (Sec. 259).

**Additional directors** (Sec. 260)

The Board may appoint additional directors provided that such additional directors shall hold office only up to the date of the next annual general meeting of the company. Provided further that the number of the directors and additional directors together shall not exceed the maximum strength fixed for the Board by the Articles.

**Filling of Casual Vacancies among directors** (Sec. 262)

If the office of any director appointed by the company in general meeting is vacated before his term of office will expire in the normal course, the resulting casual vacancy may, in default of and subject to any regulations in the articles of the company, be filled by the Board of Directors at a meeting of the Board. Any person so appointed shall hold office only up to the date up to which the director in whose place he is appointed would have held office if it had not been vacated as aforesaid.

Consent of candidate for directorship to be filed with the company and consent to act as director to be filed with the Registrar (Sec. 264).

**Option to company to adopt proportional representation for the appointment of director** (Sec. 265)

The Articles of a company may provide for the appointment of not less than two-thirds of the total number of the directors according to the principle of proportional representation, whether by the single transferable vote or by a system of cumulative voting or otherwise, the appointments being made once in every three years and interim casual vacancies being filled in accordance with the provisions, **mutatis mutandis** of Section 262.

**Share Qualification** (Sec. 270)

Every director is to obtain his qualification within two months after his appointment as director if he is required by the Articles of the company to hold a specified share qualification and who is not already qualified in that respect.

The nominal value of the qualification shares shall not exceed five thousand rupees, or the nominal value of one share where it exceeds five thousand rupees.

The qualification of a director shall be the holding of at least one share in the company (Sec. I)

**Disqualification of directors** (Sec. 274)

(1) A person shall not be capable of being appointed director of a company if —

  (a) he has been found to be of unsound mind by a court of competent jurisdiction and the finding is in force;

  (b) he is an undischarged insolvent;

  (c) he has applied to be adjudicated as an insolvent and his application is pending;

  (d) he has been convicted by a Court of any offence involving moral turpitude and sentenced in respect thereof to imprisonment for not less than six months and a period of five years has not elapsed from the date of expiry of the sentence;

  (e) he has not paid any call in respect of shares of the company held by him, whether alone or jointly with others and six months have elapsed from the last day fixed for the payment of the call; or

  (f) an order disqualifying him for appointment as director has been passed by a Court in pursuance of Sec. 203 and is in force, unless the leave of the Court has been obtained for his appointment in pursuance of that Section.

(2) The Central Government may, by notification in the Official Gazette, remove the disqualification incurred by any person.

(3) A Private Company which is not a subsidiary of a Public Company may, by its Articles, provide that a person shall be disqualified for appointment as a director on any grounds in addition to those specified in subsection (1) of Sec. 274.

**Restrictions on numbers of directorship** (Sec. 275)

No person shall hold office at the same time as director in more than twenty companies.

**Penalty** (Sec. 279) — Any person holding more than twenty directorship shall be punishable with fine which may extend to five thousand rupees in respect of each of those companies after the first twenty.

**Retiring age of directors has been omitted by Companies (Amendment) Act, 1965.**

**Vacation of office by director** (Sec. 283)

The office of a director shall become vacant

(a) for failure to obtain share qualification by the director,

(b) for being disqualified for reasons mentioned in Sec. 274;

(c) if he absents himself from three consecutive meetings of the Board of Directors or from all meetings of the Board for a continuous period of three months, whichever is longer, without obtaining leave of absence from the Board;

(d) if he accepts a loan or any guarantee or security for a loan from the company in contravention of Sec. 295;

(e) if he acts in contravention of Sec. 299;

(f) if he becomes disqualified by an order of Court;

(g) if he is removed in pursuance of Section 284;

(h) if having been appointed a director by virtue of his holding an office he ceases to hold such office.

A Private Company may provide, by its Articles, that the office of director shall be vacated on any grounds.

**Removal of directors** (Sec. 284)

(1) A company may, by ordinary resolution, remove a director (not being a director appointed by the Central Government) before the expiry of his period of office with some exceptions in case of a Private Company.

**Remuneration of directors** (Sec. 309)

The remuneration payable to the directors of a company shall be determined, in accordance with and subject to the provisions of Section 198 and this section, either by the articles of the company or by a resolution or, if the articles so required, by a special resolution, passed by the company in general meeting and the remuneration payable to any such director determined as aforesaid, shall be inclusive of the remuneration payable to such director for services rendered by him in any other capacity provided the services rendered are not of a professional nat. e and in the opinion of the Central Government the director possesses the requisite qualification for the practice of the profession.

A director may receive remuneration by way of a fee for each meeting of the Board, or a committee thereof, attended by him.

A director who is either in the wholetime employment of the Company or a managing director may be paid remuneration either by way of a monthly payment or at a specified percentage of the net profits of the company or partly by one way and partly by the other.

Provided that, except with the approval of the Central Government, such remuneration shall not exceed five per cent of the net profits for one such director and if there is more than one such director, ten percent for all of them together.

A director who is neither in the wholetime employment of the company nor a managing director may be paid remuneration —

either

(a) by way of a monthly, quarterly or annual payment with the approval of the Central Government;

or

(b) by way of commission if the company by special resolution authorises such payment.

Provided that the remuneration paid to such director or where there is more than one such director, to all of them together, shall not exceed —

(i) one percent of the net profits of the company, if the company has a managing or wholetime director or a manager;

(ii) three percent of the net profits of the company, in any other case.

Provided further that the company in general meeting may, with the approval of the Central Government, authorise the payment of such remuneration at a rate exceeding one percent or as the case may be, three percent of its net profits.

Any increase in remuneration requires generally sanction from the Central Government.

In addition to the remuneration payable to them, the directors may be paid all travelling, hotel and other expenses incurred by them in attending and retiring from meetings and in connection with the business.

**Appointment and term of office of alternate directors** (Sec. 313)

The Board of Directors of a company may, if so authorised by its Articles or by a resolution passed by the company in general meeting, appoint an alternate director to act for a director during his absence for a period of not less than three months from the state in which meetings of the Board are ordinarily held.

An alternate director shall not hold office for a period longer than that permissible to the original director in whose place he has been appointed and shall vacate office if and when the original director returns to the state. Any change in the term of appointment of the original director will not affect the alternate director.

No director of a company shall hold any office or place of profit. Assignment of office by a director shall be void (Sec. 312).

**Meetings of Board**

A meeting of the Board of Directors of every company shall be held **at least once in every three months** and at least four such meetings shall be held in every year. The Sachar and the Bhaba Committees recommended two months' notice.

Provided that the Central Government may, by notification in the Official Gazette, direct that the provisions of this Section (285) shall not apply in relation to any class of companies or shall apply thereto subject to such exceptions, modifications or conditions as may be specified in the notification.

**Notice of Meetings** (Sec. 286)

(1) Notice of every meeting of the Board of Directors of a company shall be given in writing to every director for the time being in India and at his usual address in India to every other director.

(2) Every officer of the company whose duty is to give notice as aforesaid and who fails to do so shall be punishable with fine which may extend to one hundred rupees.

**Quorum for Meeting** (Sec. 287)

The quorum for a meeting of the Board of Directors of a company shall be one-third of its total strength (after deducting vacant places), or two directors, whichever is higher.

[Any fraction contained in the one-third being rounded off as one.]

Where, at any time the number of 'interested directors' exceeds or is equal to two-thirds of the total strength, the number of the remaining directors, that is to say, the number of the directors who are not interested [present at the meeting being not less than two], shall be the quorum during such time.

[Interested director is one whose presence cannot count for the purpose of forming a quorum at a meeting of the Board by reason of Section 300.]

**Procedure where meeting is adjourned for want of quorum** (Sec. 288)

Unless the Articles otherwise provide, the Board meeting, that could not be held for want of quorum, shall automatically stand adjourned till the same day in the next week, at the same time and place or, if that day is a public holiday, till the next suceeding day which is not a public holiday, at the same time and place.

**Passing of resolution by Circulation** (Sec. 289)

No resolution shall be deemed to have been duly passed by the Board or by a Committee thereof by circulation, unless the resolution has been circulated in draft, together with the necessary papers, if any, to all the directors or to all the members of the Committee, then in India (not being less in number than the quorum fixed for a meeting of the Board or Committee, as the case may be) and to all other directors or members at their usual address in India and has been approved by such of the directors as are there in India or by a majority of such of them, as are entitled to vote on the resolution.

**Proceedings of Board**

The Board of Directors may meet for the despatch of business, adjourn and otherwise regulate its meetings, as it thinks fit.

A director may and the manager or secretary on the requisition of a director shall, at any time, summon a meeting of the Board.

Save as otherwise expressly provided in the Act, questions arising at any meeting of the Board shall be decided by a majority of votes.

In case of an equality of votes, the chairman of the Board, if any, shall have a second or casting vote.

The Board of Directors may elect a chairman of its meetings and determine the period for which he is to hold office.

If no such chairman is elected, or if at any meeting the chairman is not present within five minutes after the time appointed for holding the meeting, the directors present may choose one of their members to be the chairman of the meeting.

The Board may delegate any of its power to committees. A committee may elect a chairman of its meetings.

**Powers and duties of director**

The directors are the ultimate authority so far as the management and control of the company are concerned. All the property of the company is vested in their hands and they have to look into the affairs of the company. To discharge their duties, they have been given wide powers by the Act. Their power can be broadly divided as (a) Statutory powers and (b) Executive powers (exercised in connection with the management of the affair of the company).

**Statutory powers**

These powers are derived from the Companies Act, 1956. The Act has laid down the manner in which such powers are to be exercised by the Board. These powers are of three types : (a) Power which cannot be delegated. Sec. 292 of the Act provides that to make calls and to issue debentures are the power of the Board which cannot be delegated. (b) Power which can be delegated such as — to borrow money, to invest funds of the company and to advance loans. (c) There are powers which cannot be exercised by the Board without the approval of the company in its general meeting. They are : (i) to sell, lease or dispose off the undertaking of the company (ii) to remit or give time for repayment of a debt due by a director (iii) to make investment otherwise than in the trust securities (iv) to borrow money in excess of the paid-up capital and free reserves of the company (apart from the temporary loans obtained from the banks) (v) to contribute to charities etc. not related to the business or welfare of its employees exceeding Rs. 25,000 or 5% of average net profits during the three financial years immediately preceding, whichever is greater.

**Executive powers**

The Board is the chief executive. It has to exercise executive power for the efficient management of the company. The powers are :

(a) **Appointment of officer :** The Board is authorised to appoint officers such as Chairman, Secretary, Chief Accountant. The Board is empowered also to fix up their remuneration and decide their service conditions.

(b) **Formulation of main policies :** The Board formulates the broad policies of the company. It is to see that the policies are translated into action.

(c) **Recommendation about dividend :** The Board recommends rate of dividend in the general meeting. The shareholders are required to approve it but they do not have power to increase the rate of dividend recommended by the Board.

(d) **Making contracts :** The Board enters into contracts such as purchase of fixed assets, construction of buildings etc. The important contracts are generally entered into by the Board.

(e) **Issue of additional securities :** The terms, conditions, time, amount of issue of additional shares and debentures are to be decided upon by the Board to raise funds required by the company but the issue of such securities is ultimately authorised by the company in its general meeting.

(f) **Other powers :** To ensure smooth running of the company, the Board exercises some other powers. It has to decide about the organisation and charges required. The broad objectives of the company are to be laid down by it. It reviews the working from time to time. To direct and control the affairs of the company, the Board has to exercise these powers.

**Duties**

To prevent misuse of powers, various restrictions have been imposed on the powers of the directors by the Companies Act, 1956. These are restrictions as to the number of directorships, assignment of office, loans to directors, holding of office of profit, disclosure of director's interest in any contract by the company and Board's sanction for contracts. It is the duty of directors to see that these provisions of the Act are complied with.

A director has, in general, the duty to ensure protection of shareholders' rights and safeguard their interests by participating in the management of the affairs of the company efficiently. From the legal point of view, a director has to observe all the legal formalities to maintain the legality of the company itself because a company, as a body corporate, is a 'Contemplation of law'. As 'officers' of the company, the directors are subject to punishment if legal obligations are not fulfilled by them.

For their fiduciary relationship with the company, directors have the duty to act with good faith and loyalty. They have to apply care and skill in conducting the affairs of the company.

Duties of directors are both collective and individual. As the directors function collectively as a Board, most of the duties are collective. But there are specific individual duties which are as follows :

(1) Every director of a company, who is or may be interested, directly or indirectly in any contract or arrangement entered or to be entered on behalf of the company, shall **disclose his nature of interest** at a meeting of the Board (Sec. 299).

(2) Every director has the duty to disclose to the company the full particulars of his shareholdings so that the company can make record in the Register of Directors' shareholdings (Sec. 308).

(3) A director has to disclose it when he or his relative will hold any office of profit because a special resolution, in that case, is necessary (Sec. 314).

(4) It is the duty of the director to disclose in the explanatory statement appended to the agenda of

an annual general meeting if he has any interest in the special business going to be discussed at the meeting [Sec. 173 (2)].

(5) It is provided that under Sec. 221, a director, as an officer of the company, has the duty to disclose to the company as well as to the auditor, the fullest possible information required to be disclosed in the Balance Sheet and Profit & Loss Account and other attached documents.

(6) A director is under legal obligation to disclose if he has any interest in the scheme for a compromise or arrangement (Sec. 393).

**Management powers of the Board of Directors**

The powers of the directors must be exercised in a body and not individually. It means that there must be a Board meeting and Board resolution to exercise the powers granted to the directors.

The Articles of a company authorise its Board to delegate certain management powers with or without limits to the chief executives such as managing director, manager, secretary, sub-committees of the Board etc.

Some of the important managerial powers of the Board are :

(1) **Powers of Contract :** The Board has the power to negotiate and settle various contracts of the company with the third parties. These contracts include : contracts of purchase of land and property, purchase and sale of goods, purchase of plant and machinery, construction of works and buildings etc.

(2) **Declaration of dividend** : The Board decides how the annual profits will be disposed-off. It determines the rate of dividend on equity shares.

(3) **Declaration of interim dividend :** Before the declaration of final dividend at the end of the financial year, the Board can declare interim dividend.

(4) **Personnel functions :** The Board is empowered to make appointment, promotion, transfer and dismissal of chief executives of the company. These executives are — managing director or manager, company secretary, departmental managers etc. range and other middle level management personnel.

(5) **Proper management functions :** Today the Board takes upon itself management functions such as planning, organising, co-ordinating and communicating to ensure efficient functioning of the company.

The Board exercises control over the entire organisation by constant supervision and check-up, modern management needs the Board to motivate the personnel of the company to give their best. This needs the boosting up of the morale of the employees which the Board does.

Since the overall performance of a company is the responsibility of the Board, the Board, through its executives, exercises the managerial powers to ensure utmost efficiency in the conduct of the affairs of the company.

**Gradual erosion of the Board of Directors**

Law recognises the Board as the top organ of management. The Board itself does not exercise its powers. It delegates its powers to the chief executives. The Board retains the administrative control; management is delegated to the management personnel. The executive committee and other committees also perform various functions but the policy-making rests with the Board.

In recent years, the Board of Directors rely more and more on the chief executives for the management of the company. They are more in close contact with the operation of the company; so they are in a better position to carry on the day-to-day affairs of the company. The Board meets occasionally; so the full time executives actually run the show. The Board simply takes decisions and decides policies; the managerial functions are performed by the chief executives. It so happens that very often the decision-making power is also exercised by the executives, they even formulate policies. So, more and more, the powers of the Board are eroding. Peter Drucker has remarked, **"In reality the Board as conceived by the law-makers is at best a tired fiction. It is perhaps not too much to say that it has become a shadow king."**

The functions of the Board have now boiled down to confirming management functions, providing constructive advice to the executives, selecting the chief executives, reviewing the results of the current operation etc.

In theory, the Board of Directors is the chief authority but in practice, according to Drucker, **"It is an organ of review, of appraisal, of appeal. Only in crisis it becomes an organ of action."**

Company management is becoming more and more complex and it is quite likely in the reality of the circumtances that the Board cannot cope with the increasing complexities in the conduct of the management of the affairs of a company. The executives, who are more in the know of things, must control the affairs and it is undoubtedly in the best interest of a company that the chief executives perform the managerial functions including planning and controlling.

**But the present position has come to such a stage that the Board has become a mere rubber-stamp which is not desirable.**

Because of the provision of the Companies Act for the Board to meet **statutorily four times a year** as the minimum requirement, the Board has become an absentee controller. The day of controlling company matters from being outside the company is not now possible. Various problems crop up daily which need immediate solution. They cannot wait for Board decisions. Very often decisions have to be taken by the chief executives and they are ratified later at Board meetings.

**The gradual erosion of the Board of Directors is, therefore, an inevitable result of the growth of complexities in company management and the changed situation and environment in the corporate world.** Professionalised management has also eroded the power of the Board to a considerable extent. In many cases, bureaucrats control the affairs of the country, this is not desirable. The powers of the Board have been curtailed; various restrictions have been imposed by the Companies (Amendment) Acts and there has been gradual erosion of the Board. The corporate groups and big industrial houses also control the Boards and are responsible for the erosion and non-effectiveness of the Board of a company. Professionally qualified men in the Board can improve the situation and can build up the image of the Board.

The gradual erosion of the Board has made many authors comment on the Board. Some describe the Board as 'puppet', some as 'rubber-stamp', others as 'shadow king', 'tired fiction' etc. According to Drucker, "It is a mere show-case".

**In India, the Board is not so powerless.** The members of the Board generally hold majority shares. So, they retain controlling power. In India, the problem is not of erosion of the Board power but the misuse of the Board power. So, various restrictions are being imposed which are causing erosion of power of the Board. But as an authority quoted, the Board is neither a body to be kicked nor a soul to be damned. Due recognition of the Board is essential for the efficient management of the corporate sector.

**Position of Directors**

Directors are 'officers' of the company as they have legal obligations and punishments are suggested in the Act if the legal obligations are not fulfilled by them. The Act makes provisions for removal, disqualification and penal action against directors if the business of a company is not conducted on sound business principles and is conducted in any manner harmful to the trade or industry to which the company belongs or in a manner which is against public interest. The Act, therefore, requires commercial, moral as well as social obligation of director. Since there is no contractual relationship among directors, one director is not liable for any default of any other individual director, unless there is a charge of abetment.

By implication, the directors have fiduciary relationship with the company as the **legal position of directors is partly that of agents and partly that of trustees.** They have to apply care and skill in conducting the business of their company.

Justice L. Bowen commented in the case Imperial Hydropathic Hotel Co., Blackpool V Hampson, **"Directors are described sometimes as agents, sometimes as trustees and sometimes as managing partners."**

**As agents :** That directors are agents is their first characteristic. A company is an artificial person and it functions through human agents — the directors. However, directors being agents are not personally liable for their acts unless they contravene the provisions of the Act as specifically mentioned in it. It is said that the principle of agency operates as **alter ego.** It is quite distinct from the principle of agency. The acts and intention of its agents are the acts and intention of the body corporate. Even a company can be held liable for the malice contended by its directors. Directors are **not agents of the members** of the company. The position of directors as agents is superior to that of ordinary agents and thus they are more than agents. An ordinary agent derives his authority from his principal but the directors as agents derive their authority not only from their principal, i.e. the company, by virtue of its Article but they also derive their authority from the Act itself. Such authority cannot be overridden.

**As trustees**

Directors are trustees of the company's money and property. They safeguard them and use them for and on behalf of the company. According to

Law of Trust, a trustee holds legal ownership over the trust property of which the equitable ownership lies with the **cestui que trust,** i.e. the beneficiery. From this viewpoint **directors are not full-fledged trustees.** A trustee can make contracts in respect of the trust property in **his own name** but the directors cannot do so. They can make such contracts under the common seal of the company. The company is the legal owner. In the Companies Act, the duties and rights of a trust are not defined as they are defined in the Law of Trust. In fact, the position of directors is of fiduciary nature with power delegated on them by the members. The directors, as trustees in limited sense, shall act in good faith. The directors do not hold any fiduciary relationship with individual members of the company. The directors are not trustees of a debt due to a company or for the company's creditors. The directors are, as such, **quasi-trustees.**

**Managing partners**

In a company the management is in the hands of 'plural executives'. So, the directors are managing partners (the term 'partner' not used in the sense of the Partnership Act). Even though substantial powers may be entrusted upon a director or to an outsider, such a person has to act under the 'superintendence, control and direction ' of the Board of Directors. Therefore, unlike in a partnership firm, no power can be delegated on a single director as a managing partner. The principle of **delegatus non protest delegare,** i.e., power once delegated cannot be further delegated, is applicable to company management.

The Board may revoke any time the power it has delegated to a committee or an individual director.

From the discussions above, it is clear that directors are neither agents, nor trustees nor managing partners in the popular and legal sense of the terms. But they have in them the elements of agency, trusteeship and partnership. But none of these terms can describe directors in their totality. Directors are, after all, shareholders, proprietors and principals in respect of the company.

So, the position of director is a combination of **agency, trusteeship and elements of partnership and not an agent or a trustee or a managing partner in its real sense.**

# CHAPTER 4

## ADMINISTRATION OF COMPANIES IN INDIA

In the administration of companies in India, there is a 4-tier hierarchy of authorities — (1) The Union Ministry of Industry (2) The Company Law Board (3) The Regional Directors and (4) The Registrar of Companies.

There is an Advisory Committee to advise the Central Government and the Company Law Board on such matters referred to them. The Committee has no statutory power of its own nor the Central Government or the Company Law Board has any statutory obligation to the Committee to seek its advice.

The Union Ministry of Industry is at the top of company administration. There is a separate Department for Company Affairs.

### The Company Law Board

As soon as may be after the commencement of the Companies (Amendment) Act, 1988, the Central Government shall, by notification in the Official Gazette, constitute a Board to be called the Board of Company Law Administration.

The Company Law Board shall exercise and discharge such powers and functions as may be conferred on it, by or under the Companies Act or any other law, and shall also exercise and discharge such other power and functions of the Central Government as may be conferred on it by the Central Government by notification in the Official Gazette.

The Company Law Board shall consist of such number of members not exceeding nine, as the Central Government deems fit, to be appointed by that Government by notification in the Official Gazette. The members of the Board shall possess such qualifications and experience as may be prescribed. One of the members shall be appointed by the Central Government to be the Chairman of the Company Law Board. No act done by the Company Law Board shall be called in question on the ground only of any defect in the constitution of or the existence of any vacancy in, the Company Law Board.

The Board may, by order in writing from one or more Benches from among its members and authorise each such Bench to exercise and discharge such of the Boards powers and functions as may be specified in the order; and every order made or act done by a Bench in exercise of such powers or discharge of such functions shall be deemed to be the order or act, as the case may be, of the Board.

Every Bench shall have powers which are vested in a Court while trying a suit in respect of the following matters, namely :

(a) discovery and inspection of documents or other material objects producible as evidence;

(b) enforcing the attendance of witnesses and requiring the deposit of their expenses;

(c) compelling the production of documents or other material objects producible as evidence and impounding the same;

(d) examining witnesses on oath;

(e) granting adjournments;

(f) reception of evidence on affidavits.

Every Bench shall be deemed to be a Civil Court and every proceeding before the Bench shall be deemed to be a judicial proceeding.

The Company Law Board shall, in the exercise of its powers and the discharge of its functions, be guided by the principles of natural justice and shall act in its discretion. The Company Law Board shall have power to regulate its own procedure.

Any person aggrieved by any decision or order of the Company Law Board may file an appeal to the High Court.

## The Regional Directorates

There are four regional directorates at Bombay, Calcutta, Madras and Delhi, consisting of a Regional Director, a Company Accountant and a Company Law Solicitor in each region.

The required directorates maintain close contacts with the State Governments and direct, supervise and co-ordinate the activities of the Registrars of companies. The regional directorates act as liasion offices between the state concerned and the Central Government. They guide and explain the Companies Act and watch the progress of enquiries and investigations into the company affairs by the Inspector. In their wider scope of activities, the Regional Directorates constantly keep themselves in touch with the important developments in commerce and industry in the states and the trends of Company Management. To enforce Company Law and to take any corrective measures whenever and wherever necessary are the functions of the Regional Directorates.

## Registrar of Companies

Sec. 2 (40) defines Registrar as "a Registrar, or an Additional, a Joint, a Deputy or an Assistant Registrar, having the duty of registering companies under the Companies Act".

The Registrar of Companies of a state has his office generally in its capital city. He is regarded as an officer of the Central Government. A company, for being incorporated, needs his Certificate of Incorporation. During the existence of a company, returns, documents, copies of resolutions etc. have to be regularly filed by the company with the Registrar under statutory obligations. In the winding up of a company, the Registrar has to be kept constantly informed. So, from its birth till its death, the Registrar is an inseparable guide or controller of a company; he is the symbol for the Act itself.

There are four types of functions of a Registrar. They are : (a) Receiving all kinds of documents (b) Allowing members to inspect the documents (c) Ensuring submission of documents in proper form and within time with prescribed fees and (d) Scrutinising the documents and returns.

As to his powers, he can inspect the books of account of any company, demand additional information from a company, make petition to the Court for winding up of a company and if a company makes any default in matter of filing documents or returns or accounts or notice, he may serve a notice to the company to make good the default.

### Regulatory measures as to Company Management

Companies, as the principal form of business organisation, have always been within the close watch of the Government of any country. Legal formalities, right from inception to the day of winding up of a company are many; rigid and rigorous in many cases. Widely diffused ownership with centralised control by a few lies at the root of various problems and malpractices in company management. With comprehensive legislative measures even today, various lapses in company management could not be removed. Loopholes and undesirable activities of the Management are still awaiting measures for their plugging and suitable control. Government in any country has been constantly amending Companies Act to make the corporate form of organisation more responsive to the obligation to the shareholders and to the society. "Company law in every country is virtually a saga of restrictions on the activities of those who direct and manage the affairs of companies". So large is the number of restrictions that it is well-nigh impossible to give a detailed account of these restrictions. However, we give below the important restrictions as to company management in our country.

### Direct restrictions on Company Management

The Companies Act provides some direct steps for controlling company management. They are administered through (a) the Registrar (b) the Central Government and (c) the Court.

The Registrar is empowered to ask for some additional information from the company other than the usual returns and reports. In case of any doubts, he may refer the matter to the Central Government for necessary action.

The Central Government is armed with a large number of powers to regulate company management. They are :

(1) The Government may ask for special audit of a company's accounts for such period or periods as wanted by the Government if the Government thinks that the company is managed not on sound business policy or against public interest (Sec. 233 A).

(2) The Central Government prescribes limits, in consultation with the Reserve Bank of India, up to which, the manner in which and the conditions subject to which deposits may be invited or accepted by a company either from the public or from its members [58A (1)].

(3) The Government can direct that the conditions contained in the memorandum of association of a company, regarding an option attached to debentures issued or loans raised by it, shall stand altered and the nominal share capital of such company shall stand increased by an amount equal to the amount of the value of the shares into which such debentures or loans or part thereof has been converted by any public financial institution [94 A(2)].

(4) The Central Government has the power to appoint a person as a public trustee to discharge the functions and to exercise the rights and powers as such trustee (153 A).

(5) Where default is made in calling an annual general meeting in accordance with Section 166, the Central Government calls such a meeting [167 (1)].

(6) The Government has the power to appoint one or more inspectors to investigate and report as to whether the provisions of Sec. 197 – C have been complied with relating to beneficial ownership of shares in certain cases (187 – D).

(7) The Government requires any class of companies engaged in production, governing, manufacturing or mining activities, to include particulars relating to utilisation of material or labour or to other items of cost as may be prescribed in the books of accounts [209 (1) (d)].

(8) The Central Government is empowered to authorise an officer of Government to inspect the books of account and other books and paper of every company, without giving any previous notice to the company or any office thereof [309 A(I)].

(9) The Government has the power to prescribe rate of interest and period for which such interest is to be paid out of capital in certain cases [208 (5)/(6)].

(10) Where at an annual general meeting, no auditors are appointed or re-appointed, the Government is empowered to appoint a person to fill the vacancy [224 (3)].

(11) The Central Government after directing special audit of a company, can direct any person specified in the order to furnish to the special auditor within such time as may be specified therein such information or additional information as may be required by special auditor in connection with the special audit [233 A (5)].

(12) On receipt of the report of the special auditor, the Government has the power to take such action on the report as the Government may consider necessary [233 A (6)].

(13) In relation to any company required under Section 209 (1) (d) to include in its books of account the particulars referred to therein, the Government can direct that all audit of cost accounts shall be conducted in such a manner as may be specified in the order, by an auditor who shall be a Cost Accountant. Also, the Government can direct cost audit by Chartered Accountants.

(14) The Government may call for such further information or explanation as may be necessary on the scrutiny of the report of the cost auditor. Also, necessary action may be taken by the Government.

(15) The Government may direct the company whose cost accounts have been audited under Section 233 B, to circulate to its members, along with the notice of the annual general meeting to be held for the first time after the submission of such report, the whole or such portion of the said report, as may be specified.

(16) The Central Government may appoint one or more competent persons as inspectors to investigate the affairs of any company and to report thereon in such a manner as it may direct (Sec. 235). It may also appoint inspectors in certain specified cases (Sec. 237).

(17) The Government can bring in the name of a company or body corporate whose affairs have been investigated, proceedings for recovery of damages or for recovery of any property [244 (1)].

(18) The Government has the power to impose specified restrictions upon shares and debentures and prohibit transfer of shares or debentures in certain cases for a period, not exceeding three years, as may be specified in the order [250 (1)].

(19) The Government requires a company to furnish such information regarding the terms and conditions of the appointment of the sole selling agents as it considers necessary and has the power to regulate the terms and conditions under which the appointment of sole selling agents is made and the Government also has the right and power to declare that any of the selling agents would be the sole selling agents for a particular area. It may restrict appointment of sole-selling agents in respect of certain categories of goods.

(20) The Government can remove from office any managerial personnel on the basis of the decisions of the High Court.

(21) With a view to preventing oppression or mismanagement, the Central Government can appoint such number of persons to hold office as director for such period, not exceeding three years on any one occasion, as it may think fit; or can direct the company to amend its articles in the manner provided in Section 265, where the company has not availed itself of the option given to it under that Section and can make fresh appointment of director in pursuance of the articles as so amended within such time as may be specified [408 (1)].

(22) Where any person is appointed by Government to hold office as director or additional director of a company in pursuance of Section 408 (1) or (2), it can issue such directions to the company as it may consider necessary or appropriate in regard to its affairs and to require such persons as director or additional director to report to it from time to time with regard to the affairs of the company [408 (6) (7)].

(23) The Central Government is empowered to prevent change in Board of Directors likely to affect a company prejudicially [409 (1)].

(24) The Government can direct local investigation to be made of the books and vouchers of the liquidator.

(25) In the event of winding up continuing for more than one year, the Government can permit the liquidator to call general meeting after such time beyond the statutory period as it may allow.

(26) The Government has the power to direct companies to furnish such information or statistics with regard to their constitution or working within such time as may be specified and direct an enquiry to be made for finding out whether or not the information or statistics supplied to it is correct and complete [615 (1) (5)].

(27) It is in the power of the Central Government to authorise a person to make a complaint in writing in regard to offences against the Act committed by any company or officer thereof [621 (1)].

(28) The Government accords approval etc. subject to conditions and also prescribes fees payable on applications [637 A (1)].

(29) The Central Government fixes remuneration of the managerial personnel within the limits specified in the Act at such amount or percentage of profits of the company as it may deem fit under specified conditions [637 AA].

(30) The Government can alter any of the regulations, rules, tables, forms and other provision's contained in any of the Schedules to the Act, except Schedules XI and XII.

(31) It has power to make rules for all or any of the matters which by the Act are to be, or may be prescribed by it, and generally to carry out the purposes of the Act [642 (1)].

(32) In case of a company which has no profits or its profits are inadequate, the Central Government has to approve payment of remuneration to its managerial personnel such sum not exceeding fifty thousand rupees per annum as it considers reasonable.

(33) The Central Government is to approve initial appointment or employment of a firm or body corporate to or in any office or place of profit for a period not exceeding ten years.

(34) The approval of the Central Government is required for a term providing for an option attached to debentures or loans raised by the company, before the issue of debentures or the raising of the loans [81 (3)].

(35) The Central Government shall direct that debentures issued to or loans obtained from, the Government by a company or any part thereof

be converted into shares in the company on such terms and conditions as may appear to it to be reasonable in the circumstances of a case, even if the terms of issue of such debentures or the terms of such loans do not include a term providing for an option for such conversion [81 (4)].

(36) The Central Government has to approve the issue of share warrants by a Public Company Limited by shares to bearer.

(37) The Government's permission has to be taken for payment of unpaid or unclaimed dividend.

(38) The Government approval must be obtained before removing an auditor from office before the expiry of his term.

(39) To increase the number of its directors beyond the maximum number permitted to it by its articles, Government's approval is obligatory. [Where the permissible maximum number is twelve or less than twelve, it may not be necessary to secure the approval].

(40) The Central Government is to approve payment of remuneration to a director who is either in the whole-time employment of the company or a managing director and such remuneration does not exceed five percent of net profits for one such director and, if there is more than one such director, ten percent for all of them together.

(41) Approval of the Government is also required to increase remuneration in certain cases, and in the terms of any re-appointment or appointment of a managing or whole time director which purport to increase remuneration than what he was receiving before such reappointment or appointment.

There are still many other provisions in the Act which empower the Central Government to regulate company management.

A company cannot change its name without complying with the directions of the Central Government.

**For making untrue statements in the prospectus, provision has been made for punishment. So, by regulatory measure, promoters are prevented from making untrue statements in the prospectus or a statement in lieu of prospectus.**

In the matters of minimum subscription, allotment procedure listing of securities on a stock exchange, there are restrictive measures to prevent mushroom growth of companies.

Commencement of business by a Company is subject to fulfilment of certain conditions, so restrictions are imposed there also.

**The Court,** on receiving complaint from required number of members or from the Central Government, may order for the regulation of the company's conduct in future. The Court may also order for (a) the purchase of the shares or interests of any members by other members or by the company (leading to reduction of capital), (b) termination or modification of any agreement with managing director or manager or any director (c) setting aside any transfer, delivery, execution of any act, payment etc. by the company and (d) any other just and equitable provision. For settlement of disputes among members to save the company from liquidation, for reconstruction or amalgamation, the Court is empowered to make orders and take necessary measures.

**The Central Government and the Court have been empowered to take measures to safeguard the interest of the minority members and also to see** that the company carries on its business in its own interest and in the interest of the business as a whole keeping in view the interest of the public at large.

**Important regulatory measures** can be discussed under the following heads : (1) Allotment and transfer of shares (2) Shares with disproportionate voting rights (3) Loan by companies (4) Investment by companies (5) Holding of remunerative position (6) Disclosure of interest by a director (7) Unlimited liability of directors (8) Unwanted persons in management (9) Direct controlling measures (discussed above) (10) Making of Rules (11) Penal measures (12) Other measures.

In the matter of allotment of shares, a chronological record of the application for shares has to be made so that allotment can be made correctly on priority basis. Some rigid restrictions have been introduced by the amendment of 1974 to check transfer of shares to the hands of a group.

Shares with disproportionate voting rights cannot be issued with the exception of preference shares, of course.

A Public Company, in order to give loan to other companies under the same management and the total loan exceeding 10% of the leading company, is to be backed by the special resolution of the members.

Company investment is now very much regulated; the scheme must be sanctioned by the Central Government if the total investment exceeds 10% of the subscribed capital of the company where investment is made or the amount exceeds 30% of the investing company's subscribed capital or exceeds 20% when all the companies where investment is made, belong to the same group. This is a restriction which prevents, to a great extent, concentration of economic powers through inter-company investment.

The holding of remunerative positions in certain cases needs special resolution of the members.

Directors' interest in any contract with the company shall have to be disclosed.

The liability of directors in a limited liability-company may be made unlimited by mentioning the fact in the Memorandum or by altering the liability clause of the Memorandum subsequently.

Qualifications for being in the management have been prescribed by categorically defining the disqualifications.

There are various penal measures for any breach of the provision of the Act and the Central Government can make rules in connection with the functioning of a company. There are Acts having bearing on the Companies Act to regulate a company's affairs such as Capital Issue (Central) Act, Monopolies Restrictive and Trade Practices Act etc. The Supreme Court can also make rules.

There are other measures such as the creation of the Company Law Board for regulating company affairs and it is entrusted with the power of a Court.

The very form of company organisation with its ownership separated from its management has given rise to the necessity of providing in the Companies Act a large number of regulatory measures to safeguard the interests of the owners (shareholders) and also to ensure that the best business form — the company form — fulfills the expectations of the society by acting in the interest of the country at large.

The various legislative measures aimed at controlling the affairs of companies are so comprehensive and all-embracing that they leave no room for doubt as to the objects of the legislative provisions. The shareholders, the persons dealing with companies, the companies themselves as separate entities, the management, the employees in general and, last but not the least, the country where the companies are born — all of them have been kept in view while framing the rules, regulations and provisions relating to the organisation and management of companies.

The birth of companies is regulated, the growth is carefully watched with an eye to the interests of various groups, the functioning is rigorously controlled and finally it is also seen that the company born does not meet a tragic end to the detriment of the interest of the society.

With a view to achieving the objectives of this best form of business organisation, therefore, there is a constant endeavour to amend the law to plug any loop-hole and to make the organisation more purposeful. But in spite of efforts, it must be admitted, such a big form of business organisation cannot be freed from all the flaws. The clash of interests of various groups and the basic nature of human beings will play their part. So, as and where needed, amendments have to be made in the Companies Act and in other allied legislations to regulate company management.

## Oppression by majority-members and its remedies

Though oppression has not been defined categorically in the Companies Act, it means that a majority group of members taking advantage of their position corner the minority group and exert their supremacy. When oppression actually takes place in terms of judgements in various cases, provisions are there in the Companies Act for relief. According to Section 397, any member of a company who complains that the affairs of the company are being conducted in a manner prejudicial to public interest or in a manner oppressive to any member or members may apply to the Court for an order. If on the basis of the application, the Court is of the opinion that the complaint is right and the winding-up of the company should be the just and equitable consequence but that shall be unfair to the members, the Court may make order to bring an end to the complaints. It is desirable that the management of a company must consider the impact of its policies on the society.

The **Court** is empowered to make the following orders for relief against oppression — (i) the regulation of the conduct of the affairs of the company (ii) the purchase of the shares or interests of any member by the other members or by the company (iii) in case of a purchase of shares by the company as aforesaid, the consequent reduction of its share capital (iv) termination, setting aside or modification of any agreement between the company and the managing director, any other director or the manager, upon such terms and conditions as the Court thinks fit (v) setting aside of any transfer, delivery of goods, payment, execution or other act relating to property made within 3 months before the application and the transaction would be deemed as a fraudulent preference in insolving proceeding (vi) termination, setting aside or modification of any agreement with any other person provided notice is given to him and the modification, if any, is done with his consent. (vii) Any other matter which the Court thinks just and equitable.

If necessary, the Court may appoint an administrator or special officer. The Court may order for an enquiry before making order for relief. The Court may make any interim order before making the final order. Any order of the Court may effect alteration of the memorandum or articles of the company.

It is provided in the Act that if any officer or member of a company in respect of which an application has been made falsifies, destroys or omits to keep proper accounts or does any fraudulent act with an intention of deceiving or defrauding any person, the Court may declare that such person would be personally liable to compensate the person concerned, also liable to compensate the company. If the Court makes an order of termination, setting aside or modification of any agreement with any person, such person shall not be utilised to any claims against the company for damages or for compensation for loss of office or in any other respect; no managing or other director or manager whose agreement has been terminted or set aside shall be re-appointed within 5 years of time without the leave of the Court. Any person who acts as managing or other director or manager of the company and commits violation shall be punishable with imprisonment for a term up to one year or with fine which may go up to Rs. 5,000 or with both.

**Powers of the Central Government** may be exercised either on its own or on receiving application or even apprehending some undesirable situation to come.

The Central Government may appoint such number of persons as may be necessary to effectively safeguard the interest of the company or its shareholders or the public interest, to hold office as directors for such period not exceeding 3 years on any occasion or, in lieu of making such appointment, direct the company to introduce proportional representation on the Board and to make fresh appointment of directors within such period as specified as the directors. Until new directors are appointed, the Central Government may appoint such number of additional directors as it thinks fit. The Central Government may take over an undertaking under the Industries (Development & Regulation) Act, 1951.

**Summary**

A company is a democratic organisation and everything is done there by the support of the majority. But, as a matter of fact, majority in a company does not necessarily mean majority of the members. So, manipulation by a few is practised for personal gains at the cost of the company and of a large number of innocent members. In this context, necessity arises for some regulatory measures for keeping the democratic character of a company.

Measures taken are :

(i) Allotment and transfer of shares are controlled by making provision for receiving subscriptions and making allotments when a company is formed. There are rigorous formalities for allotment.

(ii) Shares with disproportionate voting rights cannot be issued.

(iii) Loan by companies is possible only by speedal resolution of members. Approval of the Central Government is also necessary in certain cases.

(iv) Investment by companies is not possible without passing a resolution at a Board meeting. The whole scheme must be sanctioned by a resolution at a general meeting and approved by the Central Government.

(v) Holding of remunerative position must be sanctioned by members by a special resolution. Permission of the Central Government is also necessary.

(vi) Disclosure of interests by a director at the Board meeting is a regulatory provision.

(vii) Unlimited liability of directors is provided in the Act by mentioning the fact in the Memorandum or by altering the liability clause of the Memorandum subsequently.

(viii) Unwanted persons in management is prevented by providing disqualification of a person willing to be a director.

(ix) Direct controlling measures through the Registrar, the Central Government and the Court.

(x) The Central Government reserves the right to make rules in connection with the functioning of a company.

(xi) Penal measures for violation of the provisions of the Companies Act are meant for controlling and regulating management personnel.

(xii) Other measures such as the formation of the Company Law Board for regulating company affairs.

**To conclude, in India, the regulatory measures have immense significance because majority of the members are not adequately educated and conscious.**

# CHAPTER 5

## POWER OF CENTRAL GOVERNMENT TO REMOVE MANAGERIAL PERSONNEL FROM OFFICE ON THE RECOMMENDATION OF HIGH COURT

Where in the opinion of the Central Government there are circumstances suggesting —

(a) that any person concerned in the conduct and management of the affairs of a company is or has been in connection therewith guilty of fraud, misfeasance, persistent negligence or default in carrying out his obligations and functions under the law, or breach of trust ; or

(b) that the business of a company is not or has not been conducted and managed by such person in accordance with sound business principles or prudent commercial practices ; or

(c) that a company is or has been conducted and managed by such person in a manner which is likely to cause, or has caused, serious injury or damage to the interest of the trade, industry of business to which such company pertains ; or

(d) that the business of a company is or has been conducted and managed by such person with intent to defraud its creditors, members or any other persons or otherwise for a fraudulent or unlawful purpose or in a manner prejudicial to public interest.

The Central Government may state a case against the person aforesaid and refer the same to the High Court with a request that the High Court may inquire into the case and as to whether or not such person is a fit and proper person to hold the office of a director or any other office connected with the conduct and management of any company.

When during the pendency of a case before the High Court it appears necessary to the High Court so to do in the interest of the members or creditors of the company or in the public interest, the High Court may, on the application of the Central Government or on its own motion, by an order –

(a) direct that the respondent shall not discharge any of the duties of his office until further orders of the High Court and

(b) appoint a suitable person in place of the respondent to discharge the duties of the office held by the respondent subject to such terms and conditions as the High Court may specify in the order.

The Central Government may remove from office any director or any other person concerned in the conduct and management of the affairs, of a company, against whom there is a decision of the High Court. In such a case, that person shall not hold the office of a director or any other office connected with the conduct and management of the affairs of any company during a period of five years from the date of the order of removal.

"The main points in regard to this consideration are that provision is being introduced in law to deal swiftly and effectively with management of companies where the behaviour of the officers has been found to be not proper. Such persons, even if they have committed such anti-social acts in respect of one company only under their management, will be debarred from being employed by other companies." (Lok Sabha Debates, dated 28th November, 1963)

## Power of Central Government (Oppression and Mismanagement)

Secs. 408 and 409 provide for powers of Central Government to prevent oppression and mismanagement and to prevent change in Board of Directors likely to affect company prejudicially.

The Central Government may appoint persons as directors to effectively safeguard the interests of the company or its shareholders or the public interest for such period not exceeding three years on any one occasion. On the application of not less than one hundred members of the company or of the member of the company holding not less than one-tenth of the total voting power therein, the Central Government is empowered to make appointment or appointments in order to prevent the affairs of the company being conducted either in a manner which is oppressive to any member of the company or in a manner which is prejudicial to the interests of the company. Until new directors are appointed in pursuance of the order of the Central Government, the persons appointed shall hold office as additional directors of the company. A person so appointed as a director or as an additional director, shall not be required to hold any qualification shares nor his period of office shall be liable to determination by retirement of directors by rotation ; but any such director or additional director may be removed by the Central Government from his office at any time and the person may be appointed by the government in his place to hold office.

No change in the Board of Directors made after a person is appointed or directed to hold office as a director or additional director shall have effect unless confirmed by the Central Government.

Where any person is appointed by the Central Government to hold office as director or additional director of a company, the Central Government may issue such directions to the company as it may consider necessary or appropriate in regard to its affairs.

The Central Government may require the person appointed to report to the Central Government from time to time with regard to the affairs of the company.

The Joint Committee's opinion, "the Central Government should be vested with power to prevent mis-management or oppression by nominating one or two members of the company to hold office as director for a period not exceeding three years". By one of the amendments, it is intended to provide that the director nominated by the Government need not be a member of the company.

Under Sec. 409 of the Companies Act, the Central Government is empowered to prevent change in Board of Directors likely to affect company prejudicially. If as a result of a change which has taken place or is likely to take place in the ownership of any shares held in the company, a change in the Board of Directors is likely to take place which (if allowed) would affect prejudicially the affairs of the company, the Central Government, on being satisfied may prevent such change to take place.

The primary purpose of this provision is to check the activities of raiders and speculators to gain control of Public Companies having substantial reserves and good profits with a view to superseding the management or compelling the management to purchase their shares at extortionate prices in order to retain control.

"The power of the Central Government under Sec. 409 is very wide. It may by order direct that no resolution passed after the date of the complaint (by the managing director or any other director or the manager) and no action taken to effect the change, e.g., registration of transfer of any shares shall have effect. The object is to prevent a company being made subsidiary of another by change in the Board of Directors to prejudice the affairs of the Company" (A. Ramaiya's – Guide to the Companies Act).

# CHAPTER 6

## COMPANIES ACT AND COMPANY AS A FORM OF ORGANISATION

Company as a legal form of business organisation evolved first in Rome wherefrom the concept of corporation came to Great Britain. It was first introduced as Chartered Company with the charter received from the King or the Queen of England, the East India Company being one example of such a company. The Companies Act was first enacted in England in 1845 and in India in 1850 as the Societies Registration Act. In 1857 it was amended with limited liability facility. Of course, even before that, in India we had joint stock company business. In 1913, Companies Act was amended in India. Private and Public Companies were created with distinctions between them.

On the recommendation of the Bhaba Committee, Indian Companies Act was rewritten and introduced on 1st April, 1956. **The Companies Act contains fourteen schedules and 658 sections and is the biggest legislation in the commercial field.** Since 1956, there have been amendments after amendments to the Act. The amendments of 1960 under the recommendations of the Shastri Committee, 1963 under the recommendations of Viran Bose Commission, 1969 under the recommendation of the Patel Committee and the amendment of 1974 are very significant. In 1977, the Government appointed a high powered Expert Committee under the Chairmanship of Justice Rajender Sachar for a review of the company legislation. The amendment of 1978 on the recommendations of the Sachar Committee deserves special mention.

"Indian Companies Act" was enacted by the British to serve their own interests and, as such, Indians did not derive the benefits of this novel form of business organisation during the British regime in India. So there could not be any healthy growth of Public Companies in the real sense. The Bhaba Committee was appointed to consider and to report with special reference to the following points :

"(a) the formation of companies and the day-today conduct of their business;

(b) the powers of the management vis-a-vis shareholders and the relations between them;

(c) the safeguards required against abuse of such company practices as the interlocking of directorates, voting control by majority interests in company ownership and management etc. which may be prejudicial to the public interest;

(d) the measures necessary to promote efficient and economic management of companies."

In spite of the legislation being so elaborate, many loop-holes have subsequently come to light and, to plug them, amendments have been necessary in the greater interest of the people and the country at large. It is obvious that in line with the changed objectives of business and the recognition of social responsibilities by companies, the Companies Act will go through amendments whenever and wherever it is necessary to serve social purpose.

**Company as a legal form of business organisation** has evolved last after the evolution of Soleproprietorship and Partnership organisations. It was primiarily with a view to removing the shortcomings of the existing forms of business organisations and to derive more benefits from the organisational point of view that the corporate form of organisation was conceived. Whatever may be the legal definition of a company, it is nothing but the name of a group of persons doing some business together. Of course, the most useful definition has been given by Lord Lindlay in his famous book — 'A Treatise on the Law of Companies'. According to him, "By a company is meant an association of many persons who contribute money or money's worth to a common stock and employ it in some trade or business, and who share the profit and loss (as the case may be) arising therefrom. The common stock so contributed is denoted in money and is the capital of the company. The persons who contribute it or to whom it belongs are members. The proportion of capital to which each member is entitled is his share."

The Companies Act provides elaborate provisions for the formation of a company including requisition or incorporation, which is the primary part of formation. Once the registration or incorporation is complete, the Registrar of Companies issues a Certificate of incorporation and once the certificate is issued, the **company becomes a body corporate** (Sec 34). So **a company means a registered body and a body corporate.**

**As a body corporate, a company has the following features/characteristics :**

(1) **Registration** — It is a pre-requisite for a company to come into being.

(2) **Formation** — After registration, a company has to go through certain formalities to be formed and to be eligible for commencing business.

(3) **Association of Members** — A company is an association of members who may have disproportionate shares in it.

(4) **Separate legal entity** — A company has a legal entity of its own distinct from its members. It can hold property, can sue and can be sued in its own name.

(5) **Artificial person** — A company is a person in the eye of law, though it is not a person of flesh and blood. It is an artificial person.

(6) **Perpetual succession** — As a body corporate, a company has perpetual succession. It continues to exist unless it is wound up according to the procedure provided in the Act. The existence of a company is not affected by the death, insolvency, retirement etc. of any member.

(7) **Company has a capital** — A company must have capital to carry on its business; the amount of capital depending on the nature and size of the company. Capital comes from different sources. The members generally take limited liability from the company and up to that extent each member is a debtor to the company.

(8) **Common seal** — Since a company is an artificial person, it cannot sign and do anything. It must have a common seal in the form of rubber stamp bearing the name of the company which will be fixed on all documents where signature of the company as a person is necessary. The human agents are necessary to do the job and the directors are such human agents.

(9) **Agency** — As stated above, a company being an artificial person is managed by some human agents called directors. Every company must have a Board of Directors who shall function subject to the provisions of the Act.

(10) **Contractual relationships** — The concept of company is based on contractual relationship. A company must have some minimum number of members. There is contractual relationship between the company and its members. This contractual relationship also exists between a company and its directors, creditors, suppliers, customers, employees etc.

(11) **Centrally administered** — The Companies in India are administered by the Central Government and the Companies Act is applicable everywhere in India.

(12) **Types** — There are various types of companies as the Act provides different kinds of classification.

# CHAPTER 7

## COMPANY PROMOTION

Gerstenberg defines promotion as "the discovery of business opportunities and subsequent organisation of funds, property and managerial ability into a business concern for the purpose of making profits from the newly floated enterprise".

"The term is not one of land but familiar to the business world. It points to a person who form a company and gets it going. It indicates 'a person who originates the scheme for the formation of the company, has the Memorandum and Articles prepared, executed and registered and finds the first directors, settles the terms of the preliminary contracts and prospectus (if any) and makes arrangement for advertising and circulating the prospectus and placing the capital, is emphatically a promoter in the fullest sense'. He controls the formation and future of the company and it is this control which lies at the root of the fiduciary relation of the promoter to the company.

In our country, promoters are usually the persons who, in forming the company, secure for themselves the management of the company in forming or persons who convert their own private business into a limited company, public or private, and secure for themselves more or less a secure position and/or controlling interest in the Company's Management" (A. Ramaiya).

A promoter is one who conceives the idea of forming a company. He studies the prospects of a business critically, chalks out a tentative scheme of organisation, brings together the requisite men, materials, machines, money and managerial ability and floats the enterprise. He acts as a pioneer, creator and leading spirit in the formation of the company. A promoter may be an individual, firm, syndicate, association or even a company.

### General functions of promoters

A company promoter considers — (1) the location and size of the business after taking into account the availability of raw materials, power, labour supply, transport and banking faci- lities (2) planning of building, factories, plant, machinery etc. (3) nature and type of managerial control (4) preparation of financial plan (5) legal formalities for licences, foreign exchange etc. (6) negotiation of company contracts (7) adver- tisement, publicity etc. by prospectus or otherwise.

### Steps in Company promotion

Company promotion may conveniently be divided under four heads — (i) discovery (ii) investigation (iii) assembling and (iv) financing.

(i) **Discovery :** It is the development of a feasible idea involving a preliminary analysis and inspection of the proposed idea to ascertain whether the business would be viable or not. This step in promotion also takes into consideration the risks involved in the proposition and the amount of capital to be needed. So, discovery does not mean mere finding a business opportunity.

(ii) **Investigation** : At this stage of promotion a detailed and intensive research is undertaken to ascertain the soundness of the proposition; investigation is made to reveal the probable cost of production, the estimated selling price of the goods or service and the expected amount of profit. Market research is undertaken to assess the demand for the products or the services to be rendered and to see whether the calculations on the basis of which the promoter is proceeding will prove correct or will be upset by any contingencies. Investigations are aimed for being satisfied as to whether he should go ahead with the project or not.

(iii) **Assembling** : A detailed plan of the organisation is prepared and the promoter arranges for assembling men, materials, money and managerial ability by making contracts. While chalking out the plan, the promoter estimates the total capital requirements — fixed and working — and also the development capital to ensure sound financial planning. Simultaneouly with this, the steps are taken for the registration of the company and some funds are released for acquisition of some essential assets to have an early start of the project.

(iv) **Financing** : At the last step, the promoter procures finance through public participation. Prospectus is issued and the public is invited to subscribe or other methods of raising finance are resorted to. Underwriters and financial institutions are consulted for capital gearing and with the actual marketing of securities, the promotional stage comes to an end.

(v) **Plan-presentation** : Professional promoters usually have arrangement with companies and to business magnates and industrialists, they sell the concrete plans. In such a case, the promoter has no further duty ; the execution of the plan is left to the Company Management.

## Status of a promoter

A promoter stands in a fiduciary position with the company which he promotes. But he is neither an agent nor a trustee to the future company. The reason is obvious, there cannot be an agent of a person not in existence, nor there can be a trustee for a non-existent beneficiary. Even then, the principles of agency and trusteeship are returned to the care of a promoter. A promoter, even though he may act only as agent or trustee, is personally liable where the contract is made on behalf of an intended company.

## Duties of promoters

Promoters have some duties the violation of which make them liable for punishment. The duties are :

(i) To prepare and submit documents — Memorandum, Articles and Prospectus.

(ii) To see that all property and assets are taken over by the proposed company at reasonable prices and on justifiable terms.

(iii) **To disclose** to the company or to the independent Board of Directors after the company has been formed **secret profits**, if any, enjoyed by them as vendors.

## Liabilities of promoters

A promoter may be made liable in a suit by an aggrieved shareholder or debenture holder for damages for deceit, besides being liable for compensation. A promoter, even though he may only act as agent or trustee, is personally liable for the contract on behalf of the company. A promoter is liable to pay compensation for mis- statements in prospectus, for non-disclosure of any matter in the prospectus and for non-compliance of the provisions under Sec. 56. There is a liability of the promoter under the general law enforceable by suit for recovery of damages on the ground of fraud etc. For untrue statements in the prospectus, a promoter has criminal liability.

## Rights of promoters

Since promoters have duties, it implies that they have rights too. Rights are :

(i) They are entitled to take assistance of the experts in preparing the documents.

(ii) They can enter into preliminary or pre-incorporation contracts on behalf of the proposed company.

(iii) They may claim reasonable remuneration for their services.

## Company promotion in India

The industrial history of India is the history of company promotion by managing agents during the British regime. Directors and partners of old firms did also promote business enterprises. In India, we do not have generally any professional or specialised agencies for promotion of companies. The National Industrial Development Corporation was started in 1954 as a specialist promoting institution. It prepared project reports for a number of industrial units.

In company promotion in India, promoters usually follow the standard stages. But, if necessary, they also undertake the task of incorporation and formation, underwriting of shares, substantial share contribution and above all, direct charge of routine management of business.

Promoters in India, therefore, perform various functions in the formational stage of a company. They act as manager and controller of new companies. A controlling interest in the affairs of the company is generally retained by the Indian promoters. Promoters are generally the first directors of a company.

# CHAPTER 8

## SOCIAL RESPONSIBILITIES OF A COMPANY

The Company Organisation is the best and the most important form of business organisation. The big business enterprises are usually in this form. So, the management of a company calls for an outlook which is compatible with social outlook Social respsonsibilities of business can now be considered as the ultimate objectives of business in the changed concept of business. No doubt, a business is an economic unit and it must justify its existence on its economic performance but that is now considered as a means and not an end — the end is social service.

In the words of P. F. Drucker :

"The business enterprise must be so managed as to make the public good the private good of the enterprise".

The concept of trusteeship has been gaining ground and a business enterprise is a trust of the community and as such it must discharge its obligations towards the various sections of the society.

A company, popularly considered as a democratic organisation owned by a large number of shareholders scattered all over the country and even outside the country, has undoubtedly its **obligations towards its shareholders.** The company must provide a fair return on capital to shareholders. The shareholders, being owners, have the rights to be kept informed about their company affairs and, as such, it is the responsibility of the company to supply them regular, accurate and full information about the working of their company.

A big form of organisation as it is, a company has a large number of **employees** who constitute an important segment of society. The company should provide them with meaningful work. All possible endeavour should be made to ensure better living of the workers. It should be the aim of the management to see that their economic rights are fully protected, their collective rights are not affected and their social rights and other benefits as member of society are encouraged and safeguarded through the benevolent attitude of their employers — the Company Management.

**Consumers** and the company are closely related and it does not require any elucidation. One cannot go without the other. They are interdependent. Therefore, goods and services provided by a company must be of such standard and quality which will be above any criticism. At fair price, better goods and services suitable and proper for the society should be provided. No illegal and restrictive trade practices should be adopted to the detriment of the interest of the consumer. In short, in the whole form of business, a company should always hold the ethical standards at the highest level possible and under no circumstances sheer lust for profit should predominate. Here lies the social responsibilities of the company.

The company and the **community** are inseparable. So the company should behave like a good citizen — honest and scrupulous. Obedience to law, regular payment of taxes and discharge of other obligations — monetary and social as imposed by conscience and the Government of the country — should be the way of conduct of a good management of a company.

Besides the responsibilities of a company towards different segments of society as discussed above, it must be noted that to build up an image of the company, it has a co-ordinative function. To help establish a relation among different sections of society, a company should maintain a good public relations department; the company will maintain a 'liaison'.

In our country, we know the Tatas have very effective public relations organ of the organisation which maintains public relations in all its modern aspects. The results have been obvious — the image of the Tatas definitely beam brighter. This image building through the discharge of social responsibilities is a new technique in business management and the professional management of the companies today gives attention to this. Thus goodwill is created, more business is done, the company prospers and the objectives, both social and economic, are achieved.

So, social responsibilities of a company need be discharged not only in the interest of the society but also in the interest of the company itself. Business is not an one-way traffic. 'Give and take' should be the policy and it is now an accepted truth that business cannot survive without discharging its social responsibilities. Even a sole proprietorship concern is to admit it, not to speak of a big concern like a company which has interaction with various sections of the society.

Company Management should be based on 'Scientific Management' principles, as far as possible, to establish the claim of the corporate form of organisation as the 'best form' and to pursue the changed concept of business as a social institution.

"Social responsibilities of business are now an accepted concept. All companies, public or private must work in public interest. The objective includes not only a reasonable return on capital but also a concern for the interest of the consumers, the interest of labour and an overall interest of the nation" (The Sachar Committee).

In explaining the concept of social responsibility of corporations, D. L. Majumdar indicated the important implications as follows :

(1) the responsibility of management for ensuring the continued **efficient management** of the company.

(2) **the responsibility to employees** for better wages, better standards of living, opportunities for improvement and participation at appropriate levels in management.

(3) the **accountability** of management to **consumers.**

(4) the **responsibility** of management for the physical health and well-being of the **locality.**

(5) the **responsibility** of management to the **community** at large.

# CHAPTER 9

## LEVELS AND HIERARCHY IN COMPANY MANAGEMENT

The Companies Act provides for **hierarchy** in Company Management. Within a legal framework, a company is managed by a triad of human agents having a hierarchy. The triad consists of :

(1) Members in general meeting

(2) The Board of Directors

(3) The executives like the managing director, wholetime or executive director, the manager, the secretary and others.

Theoretically, the Board of Directors, on being appointed by the members, shall carry out the day-to-day business with the help of executives on whom powers are partly and even substantially delegated. The powers of the Board are categorised by the Act. The members exercise their overall control in general meetings and particularly in the annual general meetings where stock-taking is made of the performance of the Board in the outgoing year. The general meetings are called by the directors but the members may requisition meetings or get the meetings called and held on the directors of the Central Government or the Company Law Board or the Court.

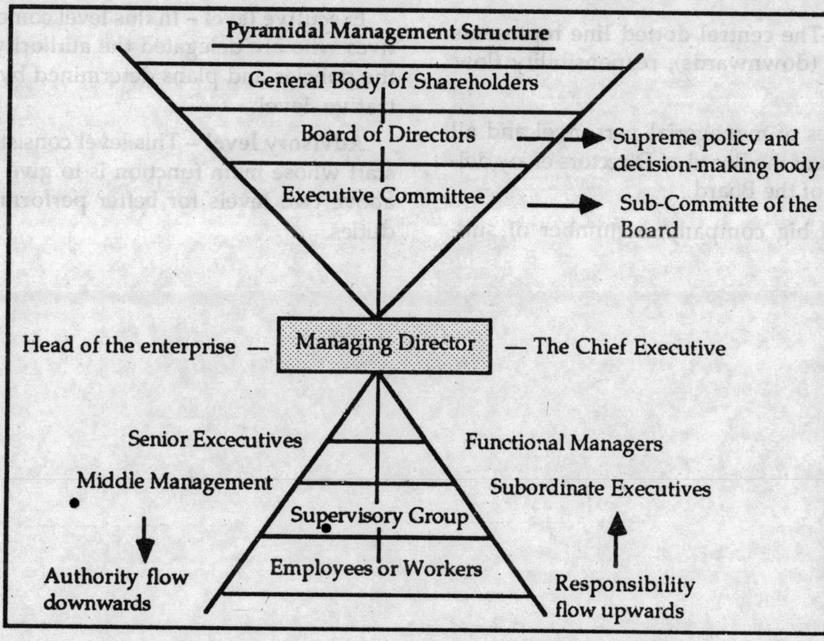

The members have exclusive powers in respect of taking any decision on any change in the very constitution of the company or putting the company into liquidation voluntarily.

Justice Ray remarked in the case Murarka Paint and Varnish Works V. Mohanlal Murarka, "The directors and the shareholders in general meeting are the primary organs of the company between whom the company's powers are divided. The general meeting retains ultimate control, but only through its powers to amend the Articles, to take away powers from the directors and to remove the directors and to substitute others to the taste of the shareholders."

Generally a big company is managed by an Executive Committee or Working Committee of the Board to Control and supervise the Top Managerial Group (The Managing Director with secretary, Head of departments, Chief Accountant, Treasurer, Auditors).

Junior Executives constitute Middle Management Group. They have supervisory and controlling functions and work under departmental managers.

In the structure of company management each Functional Manager is in charge of a particular functional area of business management viz, Production, Marketing, Finance, Purchase and Administration.

[Notes : (1) The central dotted line represents authority flow (downwards), responsibility flow (upwards).]

All categories of managerial personnel and all sub-committees of the Board of Directors enjoy delegated powers of the Board.

In case of a big company, a number of sub-committees of the Boards have to be formed such as Finance sub-committee, Allotment sub-committee.

Management by committees is a common arrangement in the management of big companies.

To sum up, the fundamental authority in the management of a company vests with the owners, i.e. shareholders. The owners elect their representatives on the Board of Directors and the directors act as agents of the company and the general body of shareholders. The management of a company is essentially representative in character and all residual powers are enjoyed by the directors. Under the supreme control and supervision of directors, there is a select body of business executives. This executive and administrative arm of the Board of Directors may be — (1) an executive committee or working committee of the Board of Directors or such sub-committees of the governing board either standing or ad-hoc committees, (2) One or more whole-time managerial directors or general managers and (3) Heads of departments.

On the basis of functions performed in a company there are three levels in management – administrative, executive and advisory levels.

**Administrative level** – This level consists of directors who formulate policies, lay down directives and objectives of the company. **They are responsible for overall results.**

**Executive level** – In this level come those executives who are delegated the authority to carry out the policies and plans determined by the administrative level.

**Advisory level** – This level consists of specialist staff whose main function is to give advice to the above two levels for better performance of their duties.

# CHAPTER 10

## MEETINGS, RESOLUTIONS AND OFFICE

Company Management studies cannot be complete without discussing broad outlines of company meetings and resolutions, company office organisation and its management.

The Management of the company is carried on and controlled through meetings. It is through meetings that the shareholders of the company get opportunities to elect the management and "sit in judgement over the working of the company at the meetings of the company. The Board of Directors can also act as a team only if it meets properly and passes resolutions embodying its decisions. The meetings and resolutions form the most important part of the process of the management in the case of companies" (Y. K. Bhusan).

Company meetings are :

(i) Board meetings and meetings of the Board Committees.

(ii) General meetings (meetings of members).

(iii) Creditors' and Debentureholders' meetings.

It is no exaggeration to say that all these meetings are concerns of the management of the company. The holding of these meetings and the resolutions passed in those meetings have bearing on the management of the company.

The Board of Directors manages the affairs of the company. So, it is needless to say that the Board meetings, where policy decisions as to the running of the company are taken, vitally affect the management of the company and the middle and the lower-level management personnel are to translate the decisions taken at Board meetings into action. In Company Management, authorities, plans and policies percolate through Board meetings which constitute, therefore, an important consideration for management.

The importance of the meetings of members or general meetings in Company Management is obvious. The ultimate authority in Company Management vests in shareholders and in the Companies Act there are provisions which specify that without the consent of the shareholders at general meetings certain matters cannot be decided. So, the, Company Management takes special care and gives considerable significance to general meetings. The statutory meetings, Annual General Meeting and Extra-Ordinary General meetings — each has its special significance and the resolution adopted have much to do with the Management of the company.

### Company Office

In Company Management, the company office is used as a very important tool. With the Company Secretary as the organiser, manager and controller of the administrative office, the management of the company is supplied with all kinds of information necessary for formulation of policies and programmes. Communication, which is an important medium of co-ordination, the essence of management organisation, is the core function of an office. Within the organisation and with the outside, the office through correspondences maintains liaison which is so vital for efficient management. A good and efficient office is, therefore, a very important contributory to an efficient Company Management. It is for the office to ensure the proper communication of the decisions taken at the management level.

"The office is truly the nerve centre of management activity constantly co-ordinating and controlling the activities of the organisation. It is an important aid to management or rather a tool in the hands of management to frame and work its policies."

In modern times, an office is looked upon more as a function than a mere place in the premises of the company; it is a separate basic operational activity of the business enterprise.

A modern office of a company is not meant for merely handling its records and correspondences but is concerned with the organisation, co-ordination, standardisation and supervision of paper handling activities. Factory records, personnel records, records of Board of Directors, sales records, financial records etc. are all maintained by office and these are all essential for the management to consult in order to form future policies and to manage the affairs of the company in the day-to-day running of the organisation.

An office, thus, maintaining records through filing and indexing and installing the latest labour saving equipments, provides the management an effective weapon to fight various adversaries arising out of present-day complexities in the business world.

# CHAPTER 11

## COMMENTS ON COMPANY MANAGEMENT

**1. 'Majority must prevail' is the principle of Company Management.**

Company is considered a democratic form of business organisation. In democracy, majority opinion or decisions prevail. In the management of companies, therefore, it is expected that majority principle must prevail. In the company's management structure, the Board of Directors has a unique position but in many matters Boards can only recommend, the majority shareholders' decision will be binding. Annual accounts, declaration of dividend, election of directors, appointment of auditors and their remuneration are all matters to be passed at the annual general meeting by the majority shareholders. In some cases, the quantum of majority is also fixed by the Companies Act, as we find, two-thirds majority are required in changing the name of the company, the registered office of the company, the objects of the company as mentioned in the memorandum, capital of the company etc. So, the principle of majority rule prevails.

There are case laws justifying this principle of Company Management in India and abroad (Foss V Harbottle, Raja Mundry Electric Supply Corporation V Nageshwara Rao).

But this principle of company management is not intended to arm the majority shareholders to attack the minorities. Even the intention of any act of the majority is to jeopardise the interests of the minority, then this principle will not be applied. Majority shareholders cannot approve any illegal action of the company nor can they defraud minority shareholders. Majority shareholders have no legal right to approve such activities which might injure the rights of any individual member. Mismanagement of the company's affairs and oppression against minority shareholders cannot be approved by the majority shareholders.

So, 'majority must prevail' is no doubt, the principle of company management but it does not necessarily mean that the majority are at liberty to do whatever they like. Majority principle is followed only to strengthen democracy in company management and not to weaken it.

**2. "Company management is democratic in form but not in content".**

In a widely owned company, owners are many in number, their elected representatives administer the organisation; the majority rule is followed. These all are indications of the existence of democracy in the company management. The company form of organisation can well be compared with a democratic country like ours. The country belongs to millions of people but as it is not feasible for all these people to participate in the governance of the country, the representatives are elected and the Government is formed; truly speaking a few persons rule over the country being accountable through Parliament to the people, the owner of the country. This is indirect democracy. So, also the case with a widely owned company where the owners/shareholders cannot personally participate in the management of their organisation — the Company. Directors are elected from among the shareholders and these handful of persons managed the affairs of the company. Ultimate authority lies with the shareholders – the owners. This is what we see in theory. But in practice and in reality what we find is that once a director, always a director. The provision for retirement of a director is there, but there is also the provision for his re-election; provision for retirement by rotation is also there. In the company organisation, a few persons may hold a large number of shares by virtue of which they will have larger number of votes which will enable them to elect persons of their choice as directors. Naturally, directors, when elected, will try to safeguard their interests by whose votes they are occupying the position of director. A careful look at the composition of the Board of Directors of even a widely owned company will make it clear that a few persons from a particular family are directors of the Board, though it is a Public Company. So, theoretically a company is a democratic form of organisation but, as a matter of fact, the essentials of democracy — by the people, for the people and of the people — are lost in the actual management of a company. Rule by a few, separation of management from ownership, the indirect democracy — all these frustrate the very essence of 'democracy' and company democracy remains in form only.

3. **"Shareholders' democracy has signally failed in India" or "Democracy is a myth in Company Management".**

Democracy is a political concept where vigilance is a condition. In company management, in India particularly, what we notice is — that the shareholders are very much indifferent and they are only interested in their dividends. It is the general idea that democracy in a company is in form only and not in content. But it is all the more a fact in case of Indian companies. Indian shareholders are proverbially non-interested as to what have been happening in their company management. Company is such an organisation where because of divorce between ownership and management, there is enough scope for indirect democracy to suffer a set-back unless the shareholders are vigilant. But shareholders in India are 'sleeping masters.' Taking advantage of the callousness of shareholders and the absence of any effective shareholders' association, the Board of Directors can indulge in all sorts of malpractices which are possible because of the loopholes in the Companies Act.

It is no exaggeration to say that shareholders' democracy has signally failed in India. Unlike USA, in India we have no strong shareholders' association, nor the shareholders here are otherwise qualified generally to understand the functioning of a company. Thus, they cannot enjoy democracy to the extent they could because of these inherent difficulties in our country. But there is now a clear trend of extending more democracy to shareholders through various restrictions on the Board's activities, by professionalisation of management and by making various provisions in the Companies Act to widen the controlling power of shareholders in the management of their company. Certain provisions such as closure of share transfer book much ahead of Annual General Meeting, issue of bonus shares to employee shareholders etc. help in the frustration of the democracy of shareholders. If the Government makes appropriate amendments and shareholders become conscious of their rights, their democracy can be maintained to a great extent, otherwise it will remain a myth.

4. **"Company Management in India is a glaring example of economic oligarchy".**

'Oligarchy' is a political concept used first by Aristotle. It means governance by a few. 'Economic oligarchy' refers to the rule by a few in the economic sphere. Comapny Management is an example of oligarchy all the world over but in India the oligarchy is much more pronounced and glaring. A few business families control the majority of comapnies in India; here in India, the economic oligarchy is not only in the hands of a few directors of the Board of a company but it is actually in a few families. So in India it is so glaring. It is a plain truth in India that the Tatas, the Birlas, the Goenkas and a few other business families are identified with Company Management, as we say Tata Company, Birla Company, Goenka Company, Dalmia Company etc. This is so conspicuous in the Company Management in India because of the lower economic standard of the people of the country in general. For the promoters of a company, financial soundness is necessary and that explains why a few business families are in the corporate sector with their full strength and dominance. The oligarchic management of a company here in India actually means economic oligarchy not by the directors as such but by the business families. It will not be possible to eliminate economic oligarchy altogether from Company Management but with more rigorous provisions in the Companies Act and amendments of loop-holes together with the alertness and enlightenment of the shareholders, much of the economic oligarchy can be removed and can be brought to a tolerable limit. It has become the pressing need that the shareholders should be united and they should give up their passive attitude and should urge upon the Government to plug the loop-holes of the Companies Act and to enact other legislations if necessary, to curb economic oligarchy. Democratisation of Company Management which is under way will, no doubt, go a long way to control the ramification of the economic oligarchy but, after all, it is shareholders, vigilance, alertness, willingness, involvement, unification and enlightenment that can counteract the evils of economic oligarchy.

**5. "Board of Directors of a Company is an organ of review, of appraisal and of appeal. Only in crisis, it becomes an organ of action". Drucker**

or

**"In reality the Board as conceived by the lawmakers is at best a tired fiction. It is perhaps not too much to say that it has become shadowking." Drucker**

In law, the Board of Directors is the top organ of management. It is meant for governing the organisation. But, in actual practice, the Board delegates most of its managerial powers to the Chief executives. The Board of Directors occasionally meet and as such it is not possible to have first-hand information about the company nor is it possible for the Board to carry on the managerial functions of the company in its day-to-day conduct of the business. The chief executive — the Managing Director/Manager as the case may be, along with his management team manage the affairs of the company and, if necessary, take on-the-spot decisions. Though strictly it is not within the jurisdiction of his managerial power, the Managing Director is very often to take policy decisions and implement them by the management personnel under him. Of course, he has to get many of his decisions ratified later on by the Board of Directors of which he is a member.

The Board of Directors, therefore, confirms management decisions, provides constructive suggestion, selects Chief Executives and reviews the results of the functioning of the management personnel. The Board actually oversees what has been going on in the management of the company. The concept of the Board function has undergone changes. So the above comments are by no less a person than Peter Drucker, the management expert. According to Drucker, the pattern of function of the Board has changed but it does not mean that the Board has nothing to do; it has lost all its relevance. The ultimate responsibility rests with the Board. It acts as the "Supreme Court" in regard to organisational problems and it keeps its finger on the pulse of the company. The Board now reviews the work of the chief executives, appraises their functions and performances and hears appeals in the matter of management. This is the ordinary way of the functioning of the Board but when crisis crops up, the Board itself tackles it and takes action.

**6. "If a Company does anything ultra vires the directors but intra vires the Company, the act is not void."**

There is the doctrine of ultra vires applicable to the memorandum in the context how far a company can do any act which is not permitted by the memorandum.

Another doctrine known as **the doctrine of indoor management** is applicable to the Articles of a company.

The doctrine of ultra vires is applied to the Objects Clause in the Memorandum of a company. The objects clause specifies the purpose for which a company is being formed and it limits the powers of the company beyond which a company cannot act. If the company does anything beyond that limit, it is ultra vires act and it is void. But a company can do an act which, though not expressly mentioned in the Objects Clause, is incidental and consequential to the objects. The doctrine of ultra vires entails that if a company does an act **Ultra-Vires**, the company is beyond the parameter of the Objects Clause, such an act is void and cannot be ratified subsequently even if all members agree. (Ashbury Raillwy Carriage & Iron Co. Ltd. Vs Richie).

The doctrine of indoor management states that if a company does anything ultra vires the directors but intra vires the company, that act is not void and can be subsequently ratified by the members at a general meeting. The company is managed by directors and their powers are given in the Act and also specified in the Articles. If the directors do something which is beyond their authority i.e. not within the specified powers given in the Articles, then subsequently that act can be ratified by the members at a general meeting. So the act cannot be considered as void. If the act is not satisfied, the directors may be held personally liable to the company. Since Articles (as well as Memorandum) of a company together with all returns and submitted resolutions are public exhibits, there is a condition of constructive notice and so a third party cannot complain against directors for their ultra vires acts. (Royal British Bank Vs. Targuand). The doctrine of 'indoor management' cannot, however, be applied to an act which itself is unlawful.

**7. "What the Company can do, its Board of Directors can do."**

A company can do what it is empowered to do by its Memorandum of Association. But, as a matter of fact, a company can do nothing. It is an abstraction in law. It has no physical existence. Law has animated it but it has no brain to think, no ears to hear, no eyes to see, no hands to work. Some human agency is required for a company to function. Sec. 291 (1) of the Companies Act, 1956, provides, "the Board of Directors of a company shall be entitled to exercise all such powers and to do all such acts and things, as the company is authorised to exercise and do".

Memorandum of Association determines the scope of activity of the company and the extent of its powers. A company cannot act beyond this scope and anything done outside the scope shall be ultra vires and void. So also the case with the Board of Directors. The Board is to act within the scope set by the Memorandum. Actually the Board acts on behalf of the company and it can bend the company if the Board's act is intra vires the Memorandum. When the Board acts in the name of the company and in the best interest of the company with reasonab! skill and care within the powers confirmed by the Memorandum, a company is bound by the act of its Board. Even if acts are done in excess of the authority of the Board, but are capable of ratification, they can be ratified by the company in general meeting. That a director and his company are very much same in the eyes of law, can be seen in Sec. 229 of the Indian Contract Act where it is provided that a notice to a director in the course of a company's business amounts to a notice to the company. Actually directors stand in a fiduciary relation with the company. They exercise some powers in trust on behalf of the company. So, it is rightly said that what the company can do, its Board of Directors also can do.

**8. "The Board is an organ of management only under the law, the real music is played by the executives."**

The company is a person in the eye of law. It is a legal person; an artificial person with no organ of a living being to function. So, it has to function through human agencies. In law, the Board has been given the top authority to manage the affairs of the company but it is provided that the Board can meet occasionally to manage a company. So, it is easily conceivable that a big organisation like a company cannot be managed by casually present persons, i.e. directors. There must be some persons in the management who will have active participation in management in the day-to-day affairs of the company.

The separation of management from ownership in the company form of organisation has necessitated to entrust the management to a handful of persons known as Directors. At best, the Board of Directors can formulate policies but to implement those policies, quite a large number of persons are required. In recent years, the trend has been to have functional directors but under them there are many executives who are there to execute the plans and programmes of the company. So, theoretically, the Board is at the helm of affairs but in reality the day-to-day functions, even some policy decisions, are performed and taken by the executives. In the day-to-day management of a company, various problems arise that need immediate solution and prompt decision. The executives are to take decisions and get them ratified by the Board later on. In reality, in many companies till the other day, the Board was mere ornamental with eminent persons on the Board. Even today, the Chief Executive appointed by the Board — the Managing Director —plays the role of conductor and the music is actually played by the executives.

**9. "In Indian conditions, the social responsibilities of corporate business are more in theory than in practice".**

The concept of trusteeship is now recognised in corporate management. Responsibilities to different segments of society are recognised. Under the Companies Act, a company has to be managed not only in the interest of the owners of capital but also according to "sound business principles" and not harmful to the particular trade to which the company belongs and finally not against public interest. It must be admitted that a company is, after all, an economic unit and its purpose is to do business. But in the changed concept of business, "profit cannot be the sole objective of business than eating is the sole object of living". So, theoretically, a company is meant for social service and the profit it will earn will be for its survival and since it is business, it will create surplus.

In reality, we find in India that profit maximisation becomes the ultimate object of a company. Throwing all the ethics of social responsibilities into winds, the companies in general, in India, indulge in such practices which subordinate social responsibilities to private gains. In India, consumerism has not so developed, consumers are disorganised and, generally do not form themselves into associations. The social environment and the political environment are not conclusive to raising a united protest against unscrupulousness of the corporate sector. The corporate management are yet to recognise and appreciate fully the implications of social responsibilities. Goods are being adulterated, services of inferior standard are being rendered and various restrictive and unfair trade practices are being resorted to by the corporate sector. Had the situation been really detrimental to the interest of the society, various acts like Essential Commodities Act would not have been enacted. Even in spite of various restrictions imposed on the corporate management and various legislative provisions to safeguard the interests of shareholders, the management do not seem to be keen to comply with them and are not alive to their responsibilities to society. It is not uncommon in our country for the companies taking advantage of certain political situation and thus raising prices of their products unduly when the Government is compelled to intervene.

It is no use denying the fact that there has been a marked change in the outlook of the company management and social objectives are getting attention but, in Indian conditions, it can rightly be said that the concept of social responsibilities is more in theory than in practice. We are yet to wait to find the materialisation of social responsibilities in the corporate sector in the real sense of the concept. Even today, we know many companies do not feel it their social obligations to pay Government dues in time; taxes are evaded.

Professionalisation by company management may help realisation of the social objectives since the professionally qualified management know it quite well that it is of supreme importance for a company to build up its image to do better business. But the policy of 'give and take' must not be lost sight of.

**10. "Board of Directors are the brains and the only brains of the company which is the body and the company can and does act only through them".**

The concept of company is a contemplation of law. Law recognises it as a person and as such company is an Artificial Person. As soon as a company is registered, it becomes a legal entity. But law cannot animate a company; it has no flesh and blood. It cannot be treated as a citizen of the country and it has no voting right in general election. A company cannot be treated as a 'resident' under the tenancy legislation but it has a domicile and residence i.e, the state in which it is registered. It cannot act like a human being; it cannot see, cannot hear, nor can it talk. Since it has separate legal entity it is to do its job. It can sue and can be sued. It must have, therefore, human agents to do its job. Here comes the need and indispensibility of the Board of Directors. This Board acts as its brain and makes it function through various human agents. In Bata v. Standard Land Company, the judgment was "Board of Directors are the brains and the only brains of the company which is the body and the company can and does act only through them." The Board of Directors of a company is the supreme policy-making body; it formulates policies, thinks and plans how the company will run and the actual implementation of their plans and policies is left to the middle and lower level managerial personnel. A company being mute, blind, disabled, the Board performs the thinking function and the actions are carried on by the managerial staff.

The artificial personality of a company and the need for human agents for a company to carry on its business has also been said by Lord Marshall, the former Chief Justice of the U.S.A. According to him : "A Company is an artificial person, invisible, intangible, existing only in contemplation of law".

In conclusion, we can say that the directors are the brain of a company, they think and plan and leave the plans to be worked out by the functional personnel. So, all the persons working in a company animate it. It becomes a reality; it can function.

**11. "A company is an abstraction in law".**

A company is an abstraction in law which implies that it is only in the contemplation of law. There is no real physical existence of a company; it is a concept. Even its existence is recognised only after it is registered. So, it is a creation of law unlike sole-proprietorship or partnership which can come into being without legal recognition. It is only the Companies Act that can create a company and nothing else can give birth to a company. After it is registered, it has to be formed. Various formalities have to be observed before a Public Company gets the certificate to commence business. So, it is law and law at every step that makes a company to stay, to move and to grow. Since a company is born, it is subject to death but that is also possible through elaborate legal procedure. So from birth till death, law nourishes and controls a company; it is a child of law, so to say. Rightly therefore, it is said, that "a company is an abstraction in law".

**12. The corporate veil is a device to conceal the misdeeds of its members.**

The word 'veil' means a concealing curtain. A company has such a veil — the critics say. A company is a corporation aggregate formed by a group of persons and having a separate legal entity of its own. This concept of legal entity makes it possible for a company to distinguish itself from its members and then the members fade out and outwardly their presence cannot be felt. The company looks like a veil or a clock or a curtain which hides the members. It is said that the curtain is opaque and not transparent so that through that veil, the members cannot be seen.

In fact, it is not desirable that the veil shall be lifted or pierced or cracked under normal circumstances but an occasion may arise when the lifting becomes necessary or even automatic.

It is not uncommon that taking advantage of the corporate veil, members indulge in misdeeds as we find in the case of deceiving creditors. Taxes are sometimes evaded behind the corporate veil. So, the corporate veil may be used to avoid legal obligations of a company and this may be utilised to shield the misdeeds of its members. As a matter of fact, one Mr. Dinshaw did so. He had an enormous income from dividend and interest and to evade these, he floated private companies and transferred his income as investments to these companies he had floated. The companies, in their turn, showed the income from investments as loan to Mr. Dinshaw. It is needless to say that these loans were always absolutely fake and Mr. Dinshaw never paid them back. This was made just to avoid tax payment.

However, there are definitely occasions when the corporate veil is necessary in the interest of the public. But the Act has made provisions to lift the veil deliberately when there is reason to believe that some people are using the company as a tool for personal gains and even by unscrupulous methods and shielding personal liability behind the veil of the company.

There are various cases where the Court has found it justified to lift the corporate veil and pay regard to the economic realities behind the legal facade. This has taken place on the following grounds :

(i) when the company belongs to an enemy country (ii) prevention of fraud (iii) evasion of tax and (iv) exploitation of the Act.

# SELECTED QUESTIONS
## (Chapterwise)

## ❑ INTRODUCTION

Chapter — 1 : (1) "Management is to get things done through others", — Do you agree with the definition?

(2) "Management is a process" — Explain

(3) "Management is both an art and a science" — Discuss

(4) "Management is the development of people not the direction of things." Amply this statement, bringing out clearly the nature and scope of management.

(5) Write short notes on :
(a) Universality of Management (b) Management as a Profession.

Chapter — 2 : (1) "When land, labour, capital and organisation are available, there is no need for management". Discuss the statement pointing out the significance of Management in business.

Chapter — 3 : (1) Discuss the important schools of Management thought and conclude the discussion with your comment.

Chapter — 4 : (1) Define 'Scientific Management'. Discuss Taylor's contribution to the development of management.

(2) "In its essence scientific management involves a complete mental revolution on the part of both workmen and management. And without this mental revolution on both sides scientific management does not exist." — Elucidate.

Chapter — 5 : (1) What is the behavioural approach to management? Describe the essential characteristics of this approach.

(2) Describe in brief, the contribution of the behaviourists to the Management thought.

(3) Analyse the behavioural aspect of Management.

Chapter — 6 : (1) Write in brief about the prominent philosophers of management thought.

(2) Discuss Fayol's contribution to management thought.

(3) Compare Fayol with Taylor. Do you think Fayol's theory is superior to that of Taylor ?

## ❑ PART —•I : MARKETING MANAGEMENT

Chapter — 1 : (1) Define Marketing. Why is marketing considered to be the most important of all types of business activities ? Give arguments in support.

(2) Distinguish between selling and marketing.

Chapter — 2 : (1) What do you mean by marketing process ?
(2) Discuss the marketing functions in brief.
(3) What is meant by 'a product-life cycle' ? What are its different stages ?
(4) Explain the importance of packaging.

Chapter — 3 : (1) What is Marketing Management ? Discuss its scope and nature.
(2) Discuss the importance of marketing management.
(3) Discuss the salient features of marketing management.

Chapter — 4 : (1) Give an idea of Sales Organisation.
(2) Discuss the functions and responsibilities of a Sales Manager.

Chapter — 5 : (1) What is Sales Management ? Discuss Sales forecasting.
(2) What is promotion in marketing ? Discuss its strategies and techniques.

Chapter — 6 : (1) Discuss the features of Marketing in India.

Chapter — 7 : (1) What do you mean by 'Marketing Mix'. What is its significance ?
(2) Discuss the process of marketing activities.
(3) "The importance of pricing in the whole marketing process need not be emphasised" — Elucidate the statement.
(4) Discuss pricing policies and strategies.
(5) What do you mean by Marketing-Minus Policy ?
(6) Write notes on : (a) Skim-the-Cream Price (b) Penetration pricing (c) Resale Price Maintenance (RPM) (d) Follow the Leader Policy of Pricing (e) Changing what the traffic will bear (f) Psychological princing.
(7) Give arguments in favour of and against Resale Price Maintenance.

Chapter — 8 : (1) What are the factors that guide the choice of a suitable channel of distribution (of products) ?

Chapter — 9 : (1) Who are middlemen ? Give arguments for and against middlemen.

Chapter — 10 : (1) Discuss the functions of wholesalers.
(2) Discuss the functions of retailers.

Chapter — 11 : (1) Discuss the features, advantages and disadvantages of departmental stores.
(2) Discuss the features, advantages and disadvantages of multiple shops.
(3) Make a comparative study of department stores and multiple shops.
(4) What is a Super Market ? What are its advantages and drawbacks ?
(5) Discuss Mail Order business with its advantages and limitations.
(6) Write notes on : (a) Consumers' Cooperative Stores, (b) Instalment selling, (c) Vending Machine and (d) Discount Houses.

Chapter — 12 : (1) What is salesmanship ? Discuss its importance and functions of salesmen.

Chapter — 13 : (1) "Advertising is a useless, wasteful exercise" — Discuss.
(2) What is Scientific advertising ? Discuss.
(3) What are the usual advertising media ? What are the factors you will take into consideration while selecting a particular medium of advertising ?
(4) Write a note on Advertising Agency.

Chapter — 14 : (1) Discuss the private distribution system in India.
(2) "The public distribution system in India is yet to be geared up". Discuss.

Chapter — 15 : (1) Discuss Product Life Cycle with diagrams.

(2) What are the factors influencing the shape and duration of product-specific life cycles ? Discuss.

(3) Write a note on the Product Life Cycle with reference to Demand Life Cycle curve.

(4) What is the rationale for the product life cycle ?

(5) Discuss the marketing strategies in different stages of product life cycle.

Chapter — 16 : Write in detail the pricing strategies and programmes.

Chapter — 17 : (1) How would you decide a marketing channel design ?

(2) Discuss the procedure of evaluating the major channel alternatives.

(3) Discuss the way you can attain the ideal distribution systems.

Chapter — 18 : Discuss the functions and flows of a marketing channel.

Chapter — 19 : Discuss the strategies of marketing control.

## ❑ PART — II : FINANCIAL MANAGEMENT

Chapter — 1 : (1) What is the changing concept of the finance function ?

(2) Discuss the scope and objectives of financial management.

(3) 'Profit maximisation and wealth maximisation' — Do they mean the same thing ? Discuss.

Chapter — 2 : (1) Discuss the functions of financial management.

(2) What are the successive steps in financial planning ? Discuss them.

Chapter — 3 : (1) Point out the importance of financial management in corporate planning.

(2) What do you mean by capitalisation ? Discuss the theories of capitalisation.

(3) What are the causes of over-capitalisation and what are its effects ?

(4) What do you mean by under-capitalisation? What are its causes and effects?

(5) Discuss how under-capitalisation can be corrected.

(6) (a) What is meant by capital structure ? (b) What is the objective of optimal capital structure ?

Chapter — 4 : (1) What are the features of a Sound Capital Plan ?

(2) Discuss the financial policies in regard to fixed and working capital.

(3) What are the determinants of working capital ?

Chapter — 5 : (1) What is capital gearing ? Discuss the considerations affecting capital gearing in a growing corporate undertaking.

(2) Dicusss the determinants of capital structure.

(3) How is the finance department organised ?

(4) How can you estimate the financial requirements of a firm ?

Chapter — 6 : (1) What do you mean by operating and financial leverages ?

(2) Explain — (a) operating leverage and (b) financial leverage.

(3) Write a note on the changing structure of industrial finance in India.

Chapter — 7 : (1) What do you mean by financial control ? What are its techniques ?

(2) What is Budgetary Control ? Discuss the guidelines for budgetary control.

(3) How is budgetary control administered ?

Chapter — 8 : (1) What is Ratio analysis ? Explain. What are its limitations ?

(2) Discuss some important ratios.

(3) Write a note on Working Capital ratios.

(4) What do you mean by Profitability ratios ?

(5) "The higher the rate of return on investment, the better the corporate management." Is this statement true for all companies ? Explain.

(6) Write a note on Return on Investment (ROI) with its limitations.

(7) What is meant by Du-Pont Control Chart ?

Chapter — 9 : (1) What are the sources of corporate finance ? Discuss in brief.

(2) Evaluate Equity shares, Preference shares and Debentures as sources of Corporate finance.

(3) Discuss the recent trends in debentures as a source of finance.

(4) Discuss the Dividend Policy that should be followed by a good financial management of a company.

(5) Evaluate Public Deposits as a source of Corporate finance with reference to India.

(6) Write a note on the Administrative Control of Public Deposits.

(7) Discuss the reasons behind ploughing back of profits and the occasions when such a course is resorted to in financing a company.

(8) What are the benefits and limitations of retained earnings (ploughing back of profits) ?

(9) Name the important institutions in India providing industrial finance and discuss them in brief.

(10) Assess the role of commercial banks in providing short-term and long-term funds to industries.

Chapter — 10 : (1) Discuss the relevance of Industrial Securities Market and New Issues Market to the financial management of a company.

(2) Discuss the methods of marketing new issues.

(3) What do you mean by Rights Shares ?

(4) Discuss the significance of Right issues in formulating financial policies.

(5) Discuss Rights issue vis-a-vis small shareholders.

(6) What are the regulatory provisions affecting rights ?

(7) Discuss underwriting of rights issue and price behaviour of rights.

(8) Discuss the significance of Stock Exchange to financial management of a company.

(9) What do you mean by listing of securities? What are the listing requirements ?

(10) Discuss the advantages and limitations of listing of securities.

(11) Assess short-term credit as a way of financing circulating assets.

(12) What are the reasons for using short-term credit as a method of financing circulating assets ?

Chapter — 11 : (1) (a) What are the sources of financial information ? Discuss these with reference to India ? (b) What is their significance to financial management ?

Chapter — 12 : (1) What are the tools of financial analysis ? Discuss their usefulness.

Chapter — 13 : (1) What do you mean by financial forecasting ? What are the methods adopted for their forecasting ?

(2) Write notes on : (a) Scatter diagram/Simple regression method. (b) Curvilinear Simple regression method. (c) Multiple regression method.

(3) What do you mean by Proforma financial statements ? How are they prepared ?

(4) What are the problems in effective financial forecasting ?

(5) Discuss the advantages of financial forecasting.

Chapter — 14 : (1) Review the methods of corporate financing in India.

(2) What do you mean by No-par shares ? What are their advantages and disadvantages ?

Chapter — 15 : (1) Write a note on 'Control of Capital Issues.'

(2) Discuss the important provisions of the Capital Issues (continuance of central) Act, 1952.

(3) When is the consent of the Controller of Capital Issues not required ?

Chapter — 16 : (1) Evaluate a bank as a source of corporate finance.

(2) Write notes on : (a) Term loans (b) Cash credits.

Chapter — 17 : (1) Discuss the short-term financing of a company.

Chapter — 18 : Discuss the role of the financial manager.

Chapter — 19 : (1) What are the types and sources of working capital ? Discuss with the diagram of the working capital cycle.

(2) Discuss, in detail, the management of Working Capital.

Chapter — 20 : (1) What do you mean by internal financing ? What are the factors that determine dividend policy ?

(2) Discuss dividend policy and practices.

(3) Write a note on Walter's formula on dividend policy.

Chapter — 21 : (1) Discuss, in brief, the dividend theories.

(2) Explain Modigliani – Miller (M – M) hypothesis.

(3) What are the criticisms levelled against Modigliani – Miller hypothesis ?

(4) Explain Walter's model. What are its assumptions ?

(5) Discuss Walter's formula for dividend decision.

(6) Write a note on the criticism of Walter's model.

(7) What is Gorden's model ? What are its assumptions ?

(8) Explain Gorden's model on Dividend policy and the value of shares by illustration.

Chapter — 22 : Discuss Managerial considerations in dividend payout.

Chapter — 23 : What do you mean by 'Retained earnings' ? Discuss its relevance and advantages in financial management.

Chapter — 24 : (1) How can you co-relates reserves and dividend policy ? Why do investors want dividend ?

(2) Discuss the importance of dividend stability.

(3) Discuss the question of stability of dividend policy under different circumstances.

Chapter — 25 : (1) Discuss Break-even analysis (linear or straight-line relationship) with diagram.

(2) Discuss non-linear Break-even analysis with diagram.

(3) What are the uses of Break-even analysis ?

(4) Discuss, with illustration, operating leverage.

(5) Write a note on Financial leverage.

(6) "In breakeven approach one only has to worry about variable costs whereas the fixed costs take care of themselves.

(7) Discuss the combined effect of operating and financial leverages.

(8) How are leverages important to Financial Management ?

(9) "Operating and financial leverages constitute a double-edged sword." Explain.

## ❑ PART — III : PERSONNEL MANAGEMENT

Chapter — 1 : (1) What is personnel management ? Discuss its importance.

Chapter — 2 : (1) Discuss the nature, aims and objectives of personnel management.

Chapter — 3 : (1) Discuss personnel management as found in India.

Chapter — 4 : (1) Enumerate the basic functions of personnel management.

Chapter — 5 : (1) What do you mean by man-power planning ? Discuss its importance.

(2) Discuss the process of man-power planning — its factors, steps and objectives.

Chapter — 6 : (1) Discuss recruitment, selection and placement as functions of personnel management.

(2) What are the different forms of training that are usually given to the employees ?

(3) Evaluate the importance of training of employees.

(4) 'Training and educating an employee'. — Do they mean the same thing ?

Chapter — 7 : (1) Discuss the methods of selection and training of workers in India.

Chapter — 8 : (1) What do you mean by vocational guidance ? Discuss the procedure of vocational guidance.

(2) What is 'Management development' ? What is its importance ?

(3) Write a note on Ergonomics.

Chapter — 9 : (1) Discuss the role of Personnel Manager.

Chapter — 10 : (1) What should be the sound promotion policy ?

(2) 'Seniority or merit' — What should be criterion for promotion ?

Chapter — 11 : (1) What do you mean by merit rating ? What are its key features ?
(2) What is job evaluation and how is it done ?
(3) Discuss the principles involved in job evaluation. What is its importance ?
(4) Make a comparative study of the different methods of job evaluation.

Chapter — 12 : (1) Explain the term 'Industrial relations'. What is its significance in personnel management ?

Chapter — 13 : (1) 'Labour welfare is a matter of serious concern to personnel management' — Discuss.
(2) Discuss the importance of labour welfare measures with reference to India.

Chapter — 14 : (1) Explain the term 'Industrial Discipline'. What are the causes of industrial indiscipline ?
(2) How can you maintain industrial discipline as the Personnel Manager ?
(3) Discuss the code of discipline in Indian industry.

Chapter — 15 : (1) What do you mean by industrial disputes ? What are their causes and how can they be prevented ?

Chapter — 16 : (1) Explain workers' participation in management. Discuss its significance.
(2) Discuss workers' participation in management with reference to India.

Chapter — 17 : (1) What is meant by Collective bargaining ? Explain and assess its importance.

Chapter — 18 : (1) Discuss the functions of trade union.
(2) Discuss the weaknesses of trade union in India.
(3) Write a note on 'Labour Welfare'.

Chapter — 19 : (1) What are the characteristics of a good wage plan ?
(2) Discuss Rowan and Halsey plan.
(3) Discuss some important bonus plans.
(4) Write notes on: (a) Taylor's Differential Piece Rate (b) Emerson's Efficiency Plan (c) Co-partnership.
(5) Evaluate profit sharing as a form of labour remuneration.

Chapter — 20 : (1) What do you mean by performance appraisal ? Discuss performance measures and categories.
(2) What are the different performance appraisal methods ? Discuss.
(3) Discuss the problems in performance appraisal.
(4) What do you mean by Management by Objectives (MBO) ? Discuss.

Chapter — 21 : Discuss the personnel functions in India.

## ❑ PART — IV : COMPANY MANAGEMENT

Chapter — 1 : (1) Discuss the nature of company management.
(2) What are the problems in company management.
(3) What are the different interest groups in company management ?
(4) Discuss the concept of trusteeship in company management.
(5) Write a note on the Board of Directors as Plural Executives.
(6) Discuss the emerging pattern of company management in India.

(7) 'Professionalisation in the top corporate management is the need of the hour' — Discuss.

(8) Justify democratisation of company management.

(9) Discuss the role of shareholders in company management.

Chapter — 2 : (1) Give an idea about the structure of company management.

(2) Discuss the features of the chief executive of a company.

(3) Who is a Managing Director ? What are his functions ?

(4) Discuss the term of office, number of managing directorship, remuneration, commission to the Managing Director.

(5) Write a note on the perquisites provided in the Companies Act for the managerial personnel.

(6) Give short notes on : (a) Manager and (b) General Manager.

Chapter — 3 : (1) How is the Board of Director of a company organised and constituted ?

(2) What are the provisions in the Companies Act as to the ascertainment of directors retiring by rotation and filling of vacancies ?

(3) What are the provisions for filling of casual vacancies among directors ?

(4) When is a person disqualified for being a director ?

(5) When is a director compelled to vacate his office ? How can a director be removed ?

(6) Write a note on the remuneration of directors.

(7) How is an alternate director appointed and what is the term of his office ?

(8) Write on :

(a) the meetings of the Board (b) notice of Board meetings (c) quorum for the meeting and (d) the procedure where the meeting is adjourned for want of quorum.

(9) When can a resolution be passed by circulation ?

(10) Discuss the powers and duties of directors.

(11) Do you agree that the power of the Board is gradually eroding ?

(12) Discuss the position of directors or "Directors are agents, trustees and managing partners" Discuss.

Chapter — 4 : (1) How are companies administered in India ?

(2) Who is the Registrar of companies ? What are his functions and powers ?

(3) What are the direct restrictions on company management in India ? Write in brief.

(4) What provisions have been made in the Companies Act to safeguard minority shareholders' rights ?

Chapter — 5 : (1) Discuss the power of the Central Government to remove managerial personnel from office on the recommendation of a High Court.

(2) Discuss the power of the Central Government to prevent oppression and mismanagement of the Board of Directors of a company.

Chapter — 6 : (1) Evaluate company as a form of business organisation.

(2) What are the characteristics of a company as a body corporate ?

Chapter — 7 : (1) What do you mean by promotion of a company? What are the steps involved in promotion ?

(2) Discuss the status, duties and rights of a promoter.

Chapter — 8 : (1) Discuss social responsibilites of a Company.

Chapter — 9 : (1) Discuss the levels and hierarchy in company management.

Chapter — 10 : (1) Discuss the relevance of meetings, resolutions and company office to company management.

Chapter — 11 : Prepare all the comments.

# CALCUTTA UNIVERSITY

## BUSINESS MANAGEMENT
## 1993

*Answer one question from each group*

### *Group A*

1. "Management is a process" — Discuss 6
2. Analyse the behavioural aspect of Management 6

### *Group B*

3. (a) Discuss briefly the importance of Marketing 6
   (b) Discuss the salient features of Marketing Management 16

4. (a) Explain the importance of packaging 6
   (b) Discuss the nature and importance of Public Distribution system 16

### *Group C*

5. (a) What is meant by Financial Management ? 8
   (b) Describe the main features of a sound capital structure of a business enterprise. What factors should be taken into consideration in case of capital gearing ? 16

6. (a) Discuss the importance and nature of financial control 8
   (b) Examine the different methods of providing loans and advances to business undertakings by commercial banks. 16

### *Group D*

7. (a) What is the importance of training of workers and employees ? 8
   (b) What factors would you take into account for the purpose of job-evaluation of a large industrial undertaking and why ? Discuss any two methods of job-evaluation. 16

8. (a) Briefly discuss the need for industrial discipline. 8
   (b) Examine the pros and cons of participation of workers' representatives in the management of a business firm. 16

### *Group E*

9. (a) Mention any four of the different problems of company management. 8
   (b) Discuss the main features of company management. 16

10. (a) Mention the different forms of chief executive in company management. 8
    (b) Describe the nature of organization of the Board of Directors of a company. 16

# GLOSSARY

## Important Management Terms

### ADMINISTRATIVE MANAGEMENT (Introductory Chapter)

*Accountability* — This is a very common and popular term in management literature. It means a subordinate's obligation to render an account or report of his activities to his superior. "To be accountable is to be answerable for one's conduct in respect to obligation fulfilled or unfulfilled."

*Administration* — In practice, management and administration are synonymous. The term administration is used in government sector while management is a common term in business. However, administration is defined as the total of planning, organising, coordinating, motivating, controlling and operating work. Administration is that part of management which is concerned with the installation and carrying out of the procedures by which the programme is laid down and communicated and the progress of activities is regulated and checked against plans. According to this view, administration involves execution of policies formulated by management.

*Authority* — It is the right to give orders and the power to exact obedience. In the context of management principles, the term 'Authority' has a special connotation. Henry Fayol, in enunciating his principles of management, listed 'authority and responsibility as one of the principles'. Authority is conceived in management as a part of responsibility. It is a relationship between two individuals, one 'superior' and the other subordinate. Authority is thus an interpersonal relationship on the basis of the acceptance theory of authority.

*Behavioural Approach* — This is in relation to management thought. This approach to management began with the famous Hawthorne Experiments. The experiments were designed to find out the factors which have a real impact on labour productivity and performance. This approach views management as a complex interaction of human beings in groups in a given situation. It recognises the informal social group having a powerful impact on employees' attitudes and sentiments. The Hawthorne studies led to the recognition that an organisation is a social system and the human factor is the most important element within it.

*Centralisation* — Centralisation refers to the location of decision-making authority in an organisation. When authority is concentrated largely at higher levels of management and majority of decisions are made at a level higher than the point of action, there is centralisation. When a manager delegates little of his authority, it is centralisation. It is "the systematic and consistent reservation of authority at central points in an organisation". A majority of decisions having to do with the work being performed are not made by those doing the work but at a point higher in the organisation. Absolute centralisation is impossible as it means no organisation but one-man operation. Everything that goes to reduce the subordinate's role is centralisation.

*Comparative School of Management Thought* — It is a school of management thought which seeks to develop generalisations from a study of management systems in diverse cultures. It studies and analyses management as a process and a philosophy in all managerial situations. This school of management thought believes that a comparative study will provide an insight into the problems of large scale enterprises and develop a rationale for the organisation and management to minimize ineffectuality and maximise effectiveness. Further, the Comparative School of Management thought believes in providing a veritable source of information for adapting managerial techniques of one country in another setting. An insight into the types of problems which may be common to many countries fostering increased internationally pooled efforts to solve these problems and also an opportunity to study the major aspects of the governing forces of economic growth are also the benefits likely to accrue from the comparative school of management thought.

*Co-ordination* — Coordination is the essence of management organisation. It deals with "the task of blending efforts in order to ensure successful attainment of an objective." It is a "process whereby an executive develops an orderly pattern of group effort among his subordinates and secures unity of action in the pursuit of common purposes." Coordination is an orderly synchronization of efforts to provide the proper amount, timing and directing of execution resulting in harmonious and unified actions to a stated objective. L. Urwick said that "the purpose of organisation itself is coordination." Coordination has assumed added significance on account of growing complexity of business and specilisation.

*Control* — It is a technique by which the executive measures the actual performance and guides it towards the achievement of pre-determined goals. It is basically aimed at stimulating action. Control can be defined as a process of making sure that performance takes place in conformity with plans. "The modern concept of control envisages a system that not only provides a historical record of what has happened to the business as a whole but pinpoints the reasons why it has happened and provides data that enable the chief executive to take corrective steps" (Earnest Dale). As characteristics of control, we can say, it is a manager's function and it is forward looking and is exercised at all levels.

*Committee Management* — Modern management is very much in favour of forming committees for management of the organisation. "Formation of committees has become a usual and common feature in modern organisation. Though they are regarded as the most ubiquitous and controversial devices of organisation, yet they are playing an important role in modern business" (Koontz and O'Donnell). At committee meetings, there is a pooling of ideas which is extremely valuable in itself. They all allow members the right of participation which is a contribution to good human relations. Committees bring together members of management so that they can communicate, deliberate and come to decisions about matters. "The fundamental purposes of committee utilisation are to obtain group opinion and careful group consideration of facts assembled by staff, executive or administrative management, to interchange ideas, concepts and points of view of members in selected groups and to formulate a joint decision based on sound judgment of organised facts" : (Glover). Committee management is considered one of the most efficient problem-solving techniques in management. Committees are regarded as of great value as a means of coordinating the efforts of the departments which are represented. Spriegel, a noted management authority, thinks that the committee recognises the human factors, fosters the spirit of cooperation, implants the new ideas of organisation and its fundamentals in the minds of all members of the organisation and gives every one the contacts necessary to perform his tasks properly.

*Decentralisation* — "Decentralisation is the systematic and consistent delegation of authority to the levels where the work is performed" (Allen). It refers to the physical location of facilities as well as to the degree to which decision making authority and responsibility are dispersed throughout an organisation. Decentralisation of authority, however, means "a situation in which ultimate authority to command and ultimate responsibility for results is localized as far down in the organisation as efficient management of the organisation permits" (McFarland). Centralisation and decentralisation are counterforces that shape and reshape an organisation. When authority is delegated throughout the organisation, so that decisions are made largely near the point of action, it is decentralisation. It relieves top executives from operating details; it promotes initiative and responsibility and improves the motivation and morale of subordinates. Stability and continuity of the organisation along with growth and diversification through democratic management are contributions of decentralisation. Needless to say, it is not free from defects; it makes coordination difficult and it pushes up the administrative costs.

*Delegation* — It is a means of assigning work to others and giving them due authority to do the same. It enables a manager to put the organisational plan in action. According to McFarland, "Delegation is the primary formal mechanism by which the network of authority relationship is established". Some authorities describe delegation as a process whereby a superior divides his total work assignment between himself and subordinate managers or operative personnel in order to achieve both operative and management specialisation. Delegation is also defined as consisting of granting authority or the right to decision-making in certain defined areas and charging the subordinate with responsibility for carrying through an assigned task. In modern management, delegation of authority is of crucial importance for effective and efficient functioning of the organisation. "The importance of delegation also stems from the fact that lack of courage to delegate properly and lack of knowledge how to do it has been one of the most general causes of failure in organisation" (Urwick).

*The Decision Theory School of Management Thought* — This school of management thought emphasises on the rational approach to decision-making. Management is looked upon as a process of decision- making. The contention of this school is that decision-making is the central function and real heart of management. The principal contribution of this school to the management process is in those problem areas where parameter relationships are quantifiable and clear and where parameters can be either directly measured or reliably estimated.

*The Empirical School of Management Thought* — This school of thought believes that by analysing the experience of successful managers or the mistakes of poor managers, it is possible to learn how to apply the most effective management techniques. It is believed that by analysing a large number of cases, it is possible to have general insights into the nature of management challenges, problems, errors and opportunities. The pitfall of this approach is that very few management situations report themselves in practically the same manner. Koontz commented that management is not a science based on precedent and situations in the future exactly comparable to the past are exceedingly unlikely to occur.

*Esprit de corps* — This is one of the principles of management propounded by Henry Fayol. It means "Union is Strength." The management of an organisation should keep it in mind that harmony and proper understanding among personnel is maintained to ensure efficient management of the organisation. To achieve this objective of management, the observance of the principle of "unity of command" is a necessity and avoidance of the policy of "divide and rule" should be considered as a precondition to the establishment of congenial environment in the organisation. The principle of "Esprit de corps" emphasises the need for complete elimination of misunderstanding and a vigilant watch over the situation in the organisation to avoid personal politics, difference of opinion etc. which might vibrate the work environment of the enterprise.

*Hawthorne Experiments* — The behavioural approach to management began with the famous Hawthorne Experiments. George Elton Mayo and his team of researchers from the Harvard Business School conducted these experiments at the Hawthorne Works of Western Electric Company in Chicago (1927-1932). The experiments were aimed at finding out the factors having a real impact on labour productivity and performance. There were different phases of these experiments — The Test Room Studies, Interviewing Studies and Observational Studies. These studies revealed that physical and environmental factors do not materially influence workers' performance and attitude to work. The studies led to the recognition that an organisation is a social system and the human factor is the most important element within it. Management is viewed as a complex interaction of human beings in groups in a given situation.

*Levels of Management* — The term Level of Management refers to a line of demarcation between various management positions in the organisation. The managerial levels have no fixed number; they vary from one organisation to another according to the size and nature of the organisation. It is quite natural that, in an organisation, there is a chain of command or scalar chain ranging from the ultimate authority to the lowest ranks. Various executives at different levels of authority are linked in a managerial hierarchy. The managerial hierarchy consists of several levels of management. Levels of management are broadly divided into — (i) Top management (ii) Intermediate/upper middle management (iii) Middle management and (iv) Supervisory or operating management.

*Motivation* — Motivation is the work a manager performs to inspire, encourage and impel people to take required action. It is the art of stimulating people towards purposive behaviour. In other words, "motivation refers to the way in which urges, drives, desires, aspirations, strivings or needs direct, control or explain the behaviour of human beings." More explicitly, it is concerned with "how behaviour gets started, is energised, is sustained, is directed, is stopped and what kind of subjective reaction is presented in the organisation while all this is going on". In the words of Brech, in motivation "the task is to fuse the varied individual human capabilities and powers of the many people employed into a smoothly working team with high morale and high productivity." A sound system of motivation is desirable for higher efficiency, better image, better human relations and also for low turnover and absenteeism. A manager, to function effectively and efficiently, must motivate his subordinates and that is why motivation is called the motor of the management process.

*M.B.O.* — Management By Objectives is a concept which is said to have been evolved by Peter F. Drucker during the fifties. It is one of the most dynamic approaches that have been developed to improve organisational efficiency and managerial effectiveness. The heart of MBO is that the supervisor and subordinates jointly decide goals to be reached and the manner of reaching them and conduct a joint and systematic review of the progress made. In India, the philosophy of MBO was introduced by multinational corporations during the late sixties. In recent years, MBO has gained considerable popularity because of dynamic environment, growing importance of the individual in organisations, emerging techno structure, need for result oriented performance appraisal, increasing attention on long range planning and executive development etc. In general, MBO consists of involving managers and subordinates in defining areas of responsibility in terms of the results expected. The other names of MBO are : (i) Management by Results (ii) Accountability Management (iii) Goals Management (iv) Performance Results and Individual Developments Evaluation (PRIDE).

"MBO is a result-centred, non-specialist, operational managerial process for the effective utilisation of the material, physical and human resources of the organisation; by integrating the individual with the organisation and the organisation with the environment" (S.K. Chakraborty).

MBO has many advantages but it is no panacea for management ills. It has to be admitted, however, that MBO has a great potential for making organisations and management effective in a changing world.

*Motion Study* — It is a mechanism of scientific management. It involves minute observation of the movements involved in performing a job. Its purpose is to eliminate wasteful motions so as to find out the one best way of doing the job. It is considered as one of the corner-stones of scientific management.

*Scalar Chain* — It is one of the fourteen principles of management propounded by Fayol. He says that there should be a clear line of authority ranging from top to bottom. The chain is the hierarchy of authority. Management orders and communications should pass through the proper channels of authority along the scalar chain. The chain of command should be short-circuited only when it is essential to do so to make the communication fast and effective.

*Systems Approach* — It is an approach to management thought. This approach looks upon management as a system of cultural interrelationships. Thus, it attempts to integrate these cultural interrelationships into a system. It views an organisation as an open adaptive system that interacts with its environment. The systems scientists empahsise the organisation theory and the need to adapt organisation to the changes in society. They are concerned with a rational approach to decision-making and regard management as simply a process of decision-making. This school of thought is probably the most comprehensive and also the most realistic. Representatives of this school rightly point to the influence of technical and technologi l factors on the social organisation.

*The Test Room Studies* — It is one of the phases of the Hawthorne Experiments in the Behavioral Approach to Management thought. The Test Room studies were designed to determine the effect of changes in working conditions such as working hours, lighting, temperature, humidity, rest pauses, piecework, etc. on employee efficiency. These studies revealed that output increased irrespective of a deterioration in working conditions due to a favourable change in the workers attitude towards their work and their work team. The attitude of the management and morale of the workers is more important than physical environment.

*Unity of Command* — This is one of the principles of organisation. This principle emphasises that each person should be accountable to a single superior. Thus, no one in the organisation should have more than one boss. It clarifies authority-responsibility relationship. It is a system of structure and function.

*Universality of Management* — "The principles of management are universal. They are applicable to any kind of enterprise wherever there is the coordinated effort of human beings. The type of enterprise is not significant." The principles of universality of management functions imply that all managers, regardless of the level at which they work, perform essentially the same task. The universal applicability of management principles is based on the theory that the organic functions of management are deemed to be the same at all levels of management and in all organisations. "The universality of management concept is not restricted to certain nations or societies of the world. Execution of the organic function of the management varies from culture to culture but the functions themselves and the principles they involve are constant" (Megginson). The credit of popularising the universality aspect of management goes to F. W. Taylor who said, "The fundamental principles of scientific management are applicable to all kinds of human activities, from our simplest individual acts to the work of our great corporations." However, it was left to Henry Fayol to fully propound and sell the universality thesis of management and C. L. Urwick to convince people of this concept.

## MARKETING MANAGEMENT

### MARKET :

*Marketing* — It is a comprehensive term embracing within it all economic activities and all resources necessary to maintain the flow of goods and services from producer to consumer. Marketing is a distribution process having four components — marketing management, marketing channels, marketing functions and market demand. Marketing is customer oriented. In short, marketing is designed to plan, price, promote and distribute want-satisfying products and services to the present and potential customers.

*Marketing Process* — Marketing is a process and this process covers – (i) marketing agencies or channels of distribution, (ii) marketing functions, (iii) flow of goods and (iv) the marketing management. This process starts with marketing research to know customer demand. Marketing functions constitute the second part of the marketing process. While performing these marketing functions, channels of distribution become the third component of marketing process. Marketing management, the fourth component, operates through marketing agencies for distribution of goods in the market. Marketing management constitutes the integral part of the marketing process.

*Sales Forecasting* — In modern marketing management, the significance of sales forecasting has enhanced considerably. A guess for the future sales trend is, undoubtedly, imperative and precondition for a business to succeed. To define sales forecast, one can simply say that it "is an estimate of sales, in monetary or physical units, for a specified future period under a proposed business plan or programme and under an assumed set of economic and other environmental forces (planning premises) outside the business organisation for which the forecast or estimate is made." Sales forecast is the starting point in customer-oriented business planning. All relevant functions - some controllable, some partially controllable, some uncontrollable environmental functions are taken into consideration while making a sales forecast. "Rational decision in any area of business without sales forecasts are impossible" (Sherlekar).

*Sales Promotion* — The marketing activities excluding personal selling, advertising and publicity are promotional activities. They include activities which stimulate consumer purchasing and dealer enthusiasm and effectiveness. Sales promotion is considered as a plus ingredient in the marketing mix. Experts are of the opinion that it is a vital bridge or a connecting link removing the gap between personal selling and advertising — the two vital wings of promotion. We can classify sales promotion into consumer sales promotion and Dealer Sales Promotion.

*Marketing Mix* — It is the mixer of all marketing ingredients. The mixer is prepared by the marketing manager to offer an optimum combination of all the ingredients/elements to ensure realisation of company pools such as profit, return on investment, sales volume, market share and so on. The ingredients which constitute marketing mix can be broadly grouped under four heads — product planning, pricing, physical distribution and promotion. Marketing mix have some important uses such as the facility of precisely studying the market by providing a good problem-solving tool. Various marketing problems can be solved through marketing mix. Further marketing mix, by proper blending of policies and strategies, brings about better utilisation of resources. It is to be noted that there are external forces governing a marketing mix. These forces are : consumer behaviour, dealer attitude, competition and rivals' behaviour, legislative control etc. The mix must be dynamic to adapt itself with the changed marketing environment.

*Product life Cycle* — Similar to the human life cycle, a product is born, grows, matures and declines. These different stages are : Introduction stage, Growth stage, Maturity stage and Decline stage. Every product passes through these stages. At the Introduction stage, a product is introduced in the market. During the Growth stage, the product grows in the face of competition. At the Maturity stage, keen competition has to be faced through additional advertising and sales promotion. At the final stage, that is, at the Decline stage, the saturation point is reached, sales drop severely and the product goes out of the market because of innovation.

*Marketing Strategies* — Marketing is a complex process. To implement the process, marketing control is necessary and special strategies have to be adopted. The strategic devices are exercised through various control measures such as — annual plan control, profitability centre, efficiency control and strategic control. Marketing strategy ensures that company objectives, strategies and systems are optimally adapted to the current and forecasted marketing environment. Marketing strategies are fast changing requiring periodical assessment to cope with the changed situation. There are different strategies to suit the situation such as — rapid skimming strategy, slow skimming strategy, rapid and slow penetration strategies.

**PRICING :**

*Charging what the traffic will bear* — Two principles are followed in pricing — the cost of service principle and the value of service principle. The value of service principle is also termed as *charging what the traffic will bear.* This is, as a matter of fact, the policy of fixing fare rate by the railways. This principle of pricing is based on demand, so it is demand pricing policy. Professionals also fix up their fees considering the paying capacity and the nature of demand by their customers for their services. It has in it the element of justice. For instance, we have in India different rates for electricity consumption — domestic and industrial.

*F.O.B.* — This is a pricing strategy. The goods are placed free on board a carrier at which point the title and responsibility passes to the customer. The customer pays the freight from the factory to the destination.

*Zone pricing* — This falls between F.O.B. origin pricing and uniform delivered pricing (opposite of FOB pricing). Two or more zones are established and the same price is charged within a zone. The more distant a zone, the more is the price charged to customers.

*Basing point pricing* — It denotes designating some city as a basing point and all customers are charged the freight cost from that city to the customer location regardless of the city from which the goods are actually shipped.

*Freight-absorption pricing* — This pricing strategy is resorted to when the seller wants to do business with a particular customer or geographical area. The seller company may absorb all or part of the actual freight charges in order to get the business. This pricing is used for market penetration and also to hold on to increasingly competitive market.

*Loss-Leade pricing* — This is a technique of pricing when the price of well-known brands are dropped to stimulate additional store traffic.

*Psychological pricing* — Such a pricing strategy is based on the belief that a buyer is mentally prepared to pay a little less than the rounded figure; say Rs.12.90 instead of Rs.13. Bata Shoe Co. follows this policy of pricing. This is nothing but creating an illusion of a bargain. An element of motivation can also be ascribed to such a pricing policy.

*Resale Price Maintenance (R.P.M.)* — It is a marketing policy which is alternatively known as fair trading. It envisages agreement between the manufacturer and dealers under which all traders are bound to sell the branded goods at a certain fixed retail price and not below that price on any pretext. The objects of RPM are : to establish a customary price for a product, to prevent the reseller from charging an exhorbitant price and to give protection to the reseller against the competition of other middlemen. RPM practice, however, kills competition and the consumers cannot have benefits of price competition. As RPM is on the basis of highest low volume retailers, it amounts to premium on inefficiency. This practice also prevents distributors to sell their private brands at lower prices. RPM is now considered as unfair trade practice even in India. MRTP Act, 1969, gave protection to Indian consumers against RPM.

*Market-Plus & Market-Minus* — The sale above the market price is called Market-Plus pricing. This is possible only when the product is a distinctive one, unique and has prestige or status in the market.

The sale below the market price is Market-Minus pricing policy. This pricing policy is profitable in large chain stores, self service stores and discount houses. Large retailers can sell nationally advertised brands below the suggested retail prices, list prices or fixed resale prices by the manufacturers.

*Penetration pricing* — This pricing strategy refers to low pricing with a view to capturing the market. As a result of this pricing, it is expected that the seller will have a larger share of the market and thus profitability will increase. The long term object of such pricing will be an increase in production as a consequence of increased demand which eventually will lead to reduction in cost of production by securing economies of large scale production. This pricing strategy has the effect of lowering the price still further because of increasing demand and increased production. Of course, it may be difficult to recoup the initial developmental costs and in such a pricing strategy customers may doubt the quality of the product because of lower and lower price. Again, it may be difficult for the producer to raise the price when it becomes necessary.

*Skim-the-Cream Price strategy* — This price strategy refers to setting the price high in order to take away the cream of the market in initial stages. Then the price is lowered progressively with the product growing old. Synthetic products are priced under this policy of pricing strategy.

*Follow the Leader Policy of pricing* — There are business enterprises who act as leaders of the market for setting the price by others. The policy they pursue in fixing the price is followed by others and this is known as "Follow the leader policy of pricing".

*Discount Houses* — In the list of various types of retailers, the latest addition is the 'discount house'. The discount houses are large retail stores. They generally deal in well-known brands of hard goods such as appliances, sports goods, jewellery etc. They deliberately and consistently sell their goods below the advertised list prices. In a low margin high turn-over type operation with very few services but big price cuts, discount houses have prospects.

*Itinerant Retailers* — These retailers include hawkers, pedlars, street vendors, stall owners in fairs and exhibitions. The characteristics of such retailers are that they have no fixed locality; more or less they are mobile retailers dealing in limited stocks with minimum establishment expenses. Generally, perishable articles such as vegetables, fruits, milk, eggs, bread etc. are suitable for itinerant retailing.

*Scientific Advertising* — It is properly planned advertising based on a serious deliberation of all factors that have a bearing upon its success. Advertising, when scientifically and logically conducted, can be called scientific advertising. The logical reasoning and scientific principles are involved in an advertising where there is the clear recognition of the problem to be solved and the alternative to the solution of the problem is also envisaged. The scientific advertising is based on the data collected in selecting the right medium or media. It is no exaggeration to say that in today's competitive market, advertising compaigns must follow the principle of science and the traditional method of advertising will be of little use.

*Marketing Channels* — Marketing channels denote routes or passages of marketing the products. In the field of marketing, channels refer to the set of marketing institutions through which an organisation gains access to the target market for its products. According to the American Marketing Association, a channel of distribution or marketing channel is the structure of intra company organisation units and extra company agents and dealers, wholesale and retail through which a commodity, product or service is marketed.

*Advertising Campaign* — An advertising campaign is a coordinated series of promotional efforts built to reach the pre-determined goal of marketing the products of an organisation. The campaign consists of message, appeal, copy and media of advertising. Campaign strategies are of considerable significance in modern marketing.

## FINANCIAL MANAGEMENT

*Finance (the new concept)* — The new concept of finance is that its function envisages procurement of funds and their effective utilisation in the business. In this concept the financial manager has to consider whether the additional profits expected from the new investments adequately compensate for the cost and risk involved in raising the finance.

*Profit maximisation and Wealth maximisation* — In formulating goals of financial decision-making the controversy arises whether the financial manager will aim at profit maximisation or wealth maximisation. Profit maximisation relates to the problem of uncertainty as the future cannot be predicted with certainty. There is the problem of balancing between expected return and risk. Again, the decision maker may not have enough confidence in the estimates of future returns. Finally, we can say that profit maximisation as the goal of financial decision-making suffers from the narrow outlook that it disregards the interests of the government, workers and other persons who are no less important in running a company.

Wealth maximisation meaning thereby profitability maximisation is a useful goal, according to Prof. Solomon. By using resources to yield economic values higher than the joint values of inputs, more useful purpose can be served. Financial management should, therefore, strive for wealth maximisation rather than profit maximisation.

*Components of financial decision-making* — There are three components — Investment decisions, financing decisions and dividend decisions. Through the medium of the cost of capital to attain the objective of financial management (wealth maximisation), these three components interact among themselves.

*Capitalisation* — Capitalisation is the valuation of capital. It includes the capital stock and debt. Capitalisation covers both own and loan capital. There are three ingredients of capitalisation — the value of all kinds of shares, the value of bonds outstanding and the value of surpluses — capital or earned surpluses not meant for distribution. Capitalisation today means capital structure or financial plan and has quantitative as well as qualitative connotations.

*Over Capitalisation* — It signifies a situation when a company regularly fails to earn the prevailing rate of return on its outstanding securities.

*Under Capitalisation* — When a company's actual capitalisation is lower than its proper capital as warranted by its earning capacity, it is said to be under capitalised.

*Capital Budgeting* — It is the planning of capital expenditure. Since the decisions regarding capital expenditure are sufficiently significant for success or failure of an organisation, capital budgeting is an important function of the financial management. Purchase of capital assets deserves very careful consideration as it is not so easy to dispose off the capital assets at the sweet will of the management. Capital budgeting necessitates control over capital expenditure and a very prudent planning should precede capital budgeting.

*Capital Gearing* — It denotes the proportion which various kinds of securities should bear to total capitalisation. Capital gearing is, as a matter of fact, the ascertainment of the proper ratio between the various types of securities, particularly the ratio between the ownership resources and borrowed resources. In this connection, *high geared and low geared* capital structures are conceived. A highly geared capital *structure* is one when there is a substantial part of capitalisation in the form of fixed income securities, i.e. preference shares, loans and debentures. On the other hand, when ownership capital constitutes greater part of capitalisation, it is said to be low geared.

*Break-even analysis (Cost-Volume-Profit analysis) (C-V-P)* — Break-even analysis, Cost-volume-profit analysis and profit graphs are interchangeable words. The analysis is to find out the relationship of costs and revenues to output. The object of such an analysis is to enable the management to study the general effect of the level of output upon income and expenses, that is, on profits. A break-even chart is utilised to present such analysis. The significance of such an analysis lies in planning the financial structure of a company. The analysis is directly concerned with the effect on profit of changes in : (i) fixed costs, (ii) variable costs, (iii) sales quantities, (iv) sales prices and (v) sales mix. It is a technique used for measuring the functional relationships between the major factors affecting profits and for determining the profit structure of an enterprise. While the management is to take decisions in pricing, in buying or manufacturing, in production process, in selecting channels of distribution, in devising ways of sales promotion, in adding or deleting product lines or in choosing sales mix, the break-even analysis serves a very useful purpose.

*Break-even Point* — The point where the total revenue (i.e. total sales) is equal to total cost is the break-even point. The chart which shows the breakeven point is known as the *Break-even Chart.*

*Funds-flow Analysis* — By funds, we commonly mean working capital or net current assets. The broader meaning of funds is 'all financial resources' — including assets or financial resources which do not affect or flow through the working capital accounts. It is imperative for the financial executive to know the funds flows underlying the balance sheet changes of the company. The preparation of a statement for analysis is needed. The sources and uses of funds can then be analysed. "The operation of business enterprise involves the conversion of cash into non-cash assets which when used are recovered back in cash form. The funds used in this circuit flow can be raised in a number of ways" (S.C.Kuchhal). The selection of means to raise funds and their uses have a profound impact on the effectiveness of the financial management. A condensed report known as the 'funds flow statement' is prepared to know how the activities of the business have been financed and how the financial resources have been used during the period covered by the statement. The funds flow statement is used widely by financial analysts, credit granting institutions and financial managers. "Funds flow statement (meant for analysis) is a useful tool in the financial manager's analytical kit."

*Cash-flow Analysis* — One of the tools of investment analysis is the cash flow analysis. The expression 'Cash flow' is usually an equivalent of "funds provided by operations" in the typical funds statement. In funds analysis, cash flow means net income after adding back expense items which currently do not use funds, such as depreciation. It is very interesting to note that the term 'Cash flow' is a misnomer. It is neither cash nor flow. The concept of cash flow is used as a major factor in judging the ability to meet debt-retirement requirements to maintain regular dividends and to finance replacement and expansion costs.

The related concept is that of net cash flow which means after-tax earnings retained by the company.

*Discounted Cash Flow* — A project involves outlay of fund at one point but revenue from sales flows over the whole life of the project. Entrepreneurs or the shareholders, who invest their present fund, do it in the expectation that they will get a better yield in future. This expectation is the basis of investment motive which generates economic activities in the economy. This concept is based on a theory which is called Time Value of Money. When we are moving forward from present value to future value, we go on adding interest to the principal every year at a given rate but when we are moving backward from future value to present value we *discount* the future value at the same rate. A project appraiser is more interested in discounting future values i.e. cash flows of a project to decide on its viability.

As Present Value (PV) is just the inverse of Future Value (FV), we can adopt an inverse approach and discount the future sum back to its present value. The discounted value is nothing but the inverse of the future value.

*Ratio analysis* — The process of determining and interpreting numerical relationships based on financial statements is the "Ratio analysis". Being a statistical yardstick, a ratio provides a measure of the relationship between two variables/figures. Ratio analyses are important for Management to measure costs, efficiency, liquidity and profitability. Three groups of persons — owners/investors, creditors and financial executives —are interested in the analyses of financial statements and the significance of ratios varies for these three groups. Investors in shares are primarily interested in per share ratios like earnings per share, book value per share, market price per share, dividend per share etc. Creditors are interested in the ability of a borrowing enterprise. For the financial executives, the ratio analysis is helpful to study the situation of competing companies over a period of years. Ratios are classified under the groups — (a) Structural (b) Liquidity (c) Profitability (d) Turnover and (e) Miscellaneous.

**PROFITABILITY GROUP OF RATIO ANALYSIS :**

*Operating ratio* — Total operating expenses divided by net sales = operating ratio. This ratio is found out with a view to measuring operating efficiency of an organisation.

*Coverage of interest payment ratio* — Interest charges on long-term borrowings and dividend on preference shares into the company's earnings before interest and taxes (EBIT) for the period have a significant ratio-importance. We can put this as :

$$\frac{\text{EBIT (Earnings before interest and taxes)}}{\text{Interest}}$$

The numerator indicates the extent of earnings available for the payment of interest.

*Return on Investment (ROI)* — This relationship is examined under two heads : EBIT/Capital Employed and Net Profit to Net Worth. The size of operating profits and the capital employed — the ratio between these two is examined. It provides a good indication of the profitability of the capital employed in the firm.

For determining return on the investment of the equity holder in a company, the relationship between the net profits and the net worth is more meaningful. "ROI has been found as the end-product of a series of statistical measures representing the various phases of a company's operations that contribute to this ratio" (Kuchhal).

ROI suffers from certain limitations; to overcome them a budgetary control system is resorted to.

*Inventory turnover (Turnover group of ratio analysis)* — Inventory turnover ratio can be found out in two ways :

(i) $\frac{\text{Sales}}{\text{Ending Inventory}}$ (ii) $\frac{\text{Cost of goods sold}}{\text{Average inventory}}$

The inventory turnover is a valuable measure of selling efficiency and inventory quality.

*Pay out Ratio : (Miscellaneous group of ratio analysis)* — When dividend per share is divided by the earnings per share, the pay out ratio is ascertained. The rate of earnings per share is the best single meausre of profitability. This rate also indicates the dividend protection available to equity shares which is particularly significant in a growth situation.

The pay out ratio is considered as a test of management efficiency.

*Cash Break-even Analysis* — Some of the firm's fixed costs are non-cash outlays; for this reason, the cash breakeven analysis is prepared. It indicates a picture of the flow of funds from operations but fails to represent fully the cash flows for which a cash budget has to be prepared.

*Leverages* — They describe a firm's ability to use fixed cost assets on funds to magnify the return to its owners. In other words, leverage is "to meet a fixed cost or paying a fixed return for employing resources or funds."

*Operating Leverage* — When fluctuations in sales revenue produce a wide fluctuation in operating profit, the operating leverage takes place. It occurs when a firm has fixed cost that must be met regardless of volume or value of sales. Three factors combine to give rise to operating leverage, they are : the rupee amount of fixed cost, the variable contribution margin and the volume of sales.

*Financial Leverage* — It is the firm's ability to use fixed financial changes to magnify the effects of changes in EBIT on the firm's EPS (earnings per share). By financial leverage, the management can assess the effect on earnings created by the use of fixed charge securities in the capitalisation plan. The degree of financial leverage at any level of operating profit is :

$$\frac{\text{Operating profit (OP or EBIT)}}{\text{EBIT} - \text{Interest (P B T)}}$$

PBT = Profits before tax

*Debt-equity Ratio* — It is the ratio between the external equities and internal equities, that is, between borrowed capital and owned capital. This ratio indicates the solvency of a company. The norm of such ratio is 2 : 1. The higher the ratio the greater will be the risk to the creditors; a lower ratio, on the other hand, is indicative of higher margin of safety to the creditors.

*EPS* — Earning per share. This is calculated by dividing the net profit (after tax and dividends of pref. shares) available to the shareholders by the number of equity shares. This ratio does not recognise the effect of increase in equity capital as a result of retention of earnings. So, profitability measurement by this ratio should be very cautiously considered.

*The Walter Approcah (Dividend Policy)* — Prof. James E. Walter has given a mathematical formula to suggest that the financial management can use dividend policy to maximise the wealth position of equity holders. His theory states that, "Over long periods, stock prices reflect the present value of expected dividends and retained earnings stock prices through their effect on future dividends." This approach is helpful in explaining dividend practices. It suggests the importance of both the dividend payout ratio and the relationship between the market capitalisation rate and the internal productivity of retained earnings .

*Present Value (PV) method : (Capital Budgeting)* — This is also known as Discounted Benefit Cost Ratio method. It takes account of all income whenever received. This method is based on the basic rule that an investment proposal should be accepted if the present value of its cash inflows, discounted at a specified rate of return, equals or exceeds the amount of the investment required.

$$\text{Formula: } PV = \frac{1}{(1+K)^n}$$

when K is the discount rate.

*Net Present Value (NPV)* — This method of capital budgeting accepts all independent projects whose NPV is greater than zero and ranks mutually exclusive projects by their net present values, selecting the project with the higher net present value. In case the management wants to maximise the value of the firm, the correct decision will be to select the project with the higher NPV. The usefulness of NPV lies in evaluating capital investment proposals.

*Capital Rationing* — This situation arises when a firm operates within a fixed budget. It restricts investments to the funds available from depreciation accruals plus retained earnings (cash throw-off) generated by internal operations.

*Critical Path Method (CPM) and PERT* — While planning a project, these techniques for capital expenditure are adopted. In estimating completion time and establishing control over time schedule, these new techniques have proved effective. In these techniques, "the basic principle is the development of a net work of project tasks for turning the critical path which identifies these events most crucial to completing the project in time" (Kuchhal). The benefit derived from these new techniques is mainly the improvement of the project schedule as areas of excess slack or no slack can be balanced and tasks can be rearranged for the plan most advantageous to its overall purpose. Both CPM and PERT are meant for time planning.

*Trading on the Equity* — 'Trading on the equity' means taking advantage of ownership. Equity which means ownership or interest in the assets of a company. This interest may be in the form of the funds invested by equity shareholder and by retained earnings, reinvested in the business. According to Gastenbug, when a person or corporation uses loan capital as well as owned capital in the regular conduct of the business, he or it is said to be trading on the equity. There are certain limitations of trading on the equity and the financial management has to secure judicious compromise between liquidity and profitability while planning for a sound and a balanced capital structure.

*Internal Rate of Return ( IRR ) — Capital Budgeting* — In the present value method of capital budgeting, the required earnings rate is selected in advance. An alternative to this method is called the 'time-adjusted return', 'discounted cash flow (DCF) rate of return, internal rate of return' or 'marginal efficiency of capital' rate.

The IRR is the rate which brings the sum of the future cash flows to the same level as the original investment. In other words, the internal rate of return is the rate of discount which equates the present value of the net benefits with the cost of the project.

*Payback period* — This is an approach to capital budgeting. Payback period represents the length of time required for the stream of cash proceeds produced by the investment to be equal to the original outlay.

$$\text{Formula : Pay back period} = \frac{\text{Original investment}}{\text{Annual Cash flow}}$$

This method of capital budgeting occupies an important place in any discussion of investment criteria because of its wide usage. It reflects the liquidity of a project and thereby the risk of recovering investment.

## PERSONNEL MANAGEMENT

*Ergonomics* — This is comparatively a new term in management. Two Greek words — *Ergo* and *Nomos* — have been combined. Ergo means work and nomos implies rule or norm. Ergonomics, therefore, is tantamount to fitting the job to the worker. It has been defined by the British Standards Institution as "the relation between man, and his occupation, equipment and environment and particularly the application of anatomical, physiological and psychological knowledge to problems arising therefrom." Ergonomics involves a multi disciplinary approach and the team of ergonomics in an organisation consists of a designer, an engineer, an anatomist, a physiologist, a psychologist and a social scientist. The benefits derived are : reduction of fatigue and monotony, better physical safety, improvement of work environment and also of morale and productivity.

*Job Evaluation* — It is a process of analysis and assessment of jobs to ascertain reliably their relative worth, using the assessments as a basis for a balanced wage structure. We may call it 'rating of jobs to determine their position in a job hierarchy'. The significance of job evaluation is that it forms the basis on which the basic wage of a job is determined. The process includes — job analysis, job description and job specification.

Usually four methods are adopted for job evaluation. They are : job ranking, grading, point-rating and factor comparison.

*Performance Appraisal* — It is a systematic evaluation of personnel by supervisors or others familiar with their performance. This is an objective way of judging the relative worth or ability of a person in performing his task. In administrative decision-making, performance appraisal has a very significant role to play.

*Manpower Planning* — "It is the process of determining manpower requirements and the means for meeting those requirements in order to carry out the integrated plan of the organisation" (Coleman). This process includes forecasting, developing and controlling. The object of manpower planning is to determine how an organisation should move from its current manpower position to its desired manpower position. To derive the maximum long-range benefit, the management carries on manpower planning and determines the right number and the right kinds of people at the right places and at the right time.

*Motivation of Employees* — It is a process in personnel management to arouse the desire or need. "A motive is a particular need or desire — a psychological force within our mind — setting us in motion to fulfil our need or desire which is aroused" (Sherlekar).

The Motivation-Hygiene (M-H) theory of F. Heizbug considers human nature having two separate elements — the animal part and human part. According to this theory, the items that determine job content are considered motivational factors which include achievement, recognition, the work itself, responsibility and advancement. The elements influencing the job context are company policy and administration, technical supervision, salary, inter-personal relations, working conditions and benefits and services. The effectiveness of motivation depends on the ability of the personnel manager to co-ordinate the various influences that lead to motivation. "Motivation involves will to work, to contribute and to cooperate with interest and zeal in any joint effort. It is causing an activity to occur in order to achieve desired results" (Sherlekar).

*Merit Rating* — This is the systematic evaluation of any given worker so far as his assignment is concerned. Merit rating indicates the relative value of the employee. In job evaluation, we evaluate a job whereas in merit-rating we evaluate the performance of each worker pointing out the relative value of employees. Merit rating appreciates the performance of an employee on the job.

*Collective Bargaining* — It refers to the relations between trade unions and the management. Since chosen representatives of labour and management act as bargaining agents, it is called collective bargaining. Its success depends on the relation between labour and capital. Deliberations, persuasions, arguments take place in the collective bargaining process.

*Workers' participation in management* — It is conceived as industrial democracy. Industry is a social institution and as such the workers of an industrial enterprise have interest no less insignificant than those of the management and the community at large. The concept of workers' participation in management is a democratic principle of management of industry. The decision-making power of the organisation at all appropriate levels of management is shared by the ranks of the enterprise. This new outlook to management is based on the principle of co-partnership in industry. Coordination and understanding form the foundation stones of participation concept. This co-functioning signifies workers' identification with the progress of the organisation. The underlying ideas of workers' participation in management are : mental and emotional involvement, two-way psychological and social relationship and acceptance of responsibility. It is needless to emphasise that, in today's changed business environment, participation of workers in management is indispensable and a must.

*Industrial Discipline* — The Indian Labour Conference, 1957, codified certain principles for ensuring discipline in indstry which is considered essential for industrial peace, harmony between labour and capital and overall improvement of industrial environment. The principles that should be adhered to are : no lock out or strike without notice, no unilateral decision in any matter pertaining to both labour and capital, no recourse to go-slow tactics, no deliberate damage to plant, no act of violence, coercion or instigation, the utilisation of the existing machinery for settlement of disputes, speedy implementation of awards and agreements and finally no agreement vitiating labour-capital relations to be encouraged.

*Work Environment* — It refers to the conditions of work in the factory. The personnel management has to be concerned with this problem. It is easy to understand that the environment in which workers are required to work should be congenial as to induce them to feel the urge to work. To ensure high morale and high production and productivity, the need for favourable work environment cannot be over-exaggerated. The factors, both physical and mental, must be given due consideration to the well being of physical as well as mental conditions. The lay-out of the factory should be so planned as to avoid pollution and to create conditions conducive to high productivity. Mental and social environment plays no insignificant role in boosting the morale of the worker. Work environment also includes the length of the working hours, working week and proper rest pauses and the personnel management should pay adequate attention to this aspect of workers' fatigue.

*Vestibule Training* — While thinking about training and development of workers, the personnel management is to resort to various methods of training. One such training method is 'Vestibule Training' method. In big organisations, the need for training is all the more felt and the facilities for on-the-job training are far less than the requirement. This situation calls for the setting up of a kind of vestibule school for the training of workers. The word 'vestibule' means an entry cubicle through which one passes into rooms or an entry hall leading to a building. In a vestibule school training, the trainees are used to be trained in a surrounding which resembles the actual work environment. The characteristic feature of such training is that more emphasis is given on instruction than on work. A special instructor from the personnel department generally takes the responsibility of training and no line-supervisor is engaged for this job. The benefit of such a training method is that it is speciality-oriented which results in proper handling of machines. However, we cannot claim this method of workers' training free from defects.

## COMPANY MANAGEMENT

*Artificial Personality* — A company is a person in the eye of law but this person has no flesh and blood. It is a legal personality; so not a real person but an artificial person recognised by law to confer it certain rights. As a form of business organisation, the corporate form, because of this legal personality, enjoys certain privileges which are denied to other forms. Because of this personality, it is considered a distinct being separate from its shareholders. Company law gives company animation but, inanimate as it is, as a matter of fact, it is an artificial person. This artificial personality is a distinctive feature of the corporate form of organisation.

*Body Corporate* — A company means a registered body and a body corporate. The term 'Body corporate' means an artificial person, a creation of law. The Companies Act, 1956, recognises a company as a body corporate. The 'body corporate' has these characteristics — (1) Creation of law (2) separate legal entity (3) perputal succession (4) common seal. A body corporate must have some objects for its functions. The

Companies Act states that "from the date of incorporation mentioned in the certificate of incorporation, such of the subscribers of the memorandum and other persons as from time to time be members of the company, shall be a *body corporation". A company is a corporation aggregate.*

*Corporate Veil* — A veil is a concealing curtain. A company is a corporation aggregate formed by a group of persons. It has a separate legal entity. By this concept, the members of a company fade out and outwardly their presence cannot be felt. The company looks like a veil or a curtain which hides the members. It is said that the curtain is opaque and not transparent and the members cannot be seen through the veil.

*Lifting the Corporate Veil* is not desirable as this will defeat the very purpose of the veil, that is the incorporation of the company. Occasions, however, occur when the lifting of the corporate veil becomes necessary or even automatic. There may be a situation when the veil is automatically lifted and the situation may so warrant that it becomes desirable to lift it (discussed in greater detail elsewhere).

*Doctrine of ultra vires* — This is applicable to the objects clause in the memorandum of a company. This clause limits the powers of the company beyond which a company cannot act. If the company does any thing beyond that limit, it is an ultra vires act and it is void. This doctrine entails that if a company does an act ultra vires the company i.e. beyond the parameter of the objects clause, such an act is void and cannot be ratified subsequently even if all the members agree.

*Doctrine of indoor management* — If a company does anything ultra vires the directors but intra vires the company, that act is not void and can be subsequently ratified by the members at a general meeting. The powers of the directors who manage the company are given in the Act and also specified in the Articles. If, in any case, they act beyond their authority, that act can be ratified by the members at a general meeting in which the articles may stand as altered. The doctrine of indoor management is substantiated by the famous case — *Royal British Bank vs. Turquand.* The directors borrowerd money without approval by the company by the issue of bonds. It was held that the issue of bonds was not invalid. This was case of indoor management. The doctrine cannot be applied to an act which itself is unlawful.

*Hierarchy in company management* — Within a legal framework, a company is managed by a triad of human agents having a hierarchy. The triad consists of — (1) Members in general meeting (2) The Board of Directors and (3) The executives like the Managing Director, whole-time or executive directors, the manager and others.

*Plural Executives* — In company management, there is the legal compulsion of having plural executives. This indicates that company management is democratic in character. The management of a company is entrusted to the Board of Directors and an individual director has no power. He is powerful when he is at the Board meeting and acts as one of the plural executives. Of course, a director may exercise powers, provided some substantial powers are delegated, but the powers must be exercised under the superintendence, direction and control of the Board of Directors.

*Concept of Trusteeship in Company Management* — Trusteeship is a legal concept. A man (say a minor) may have property but he is debarred from managing it because of his legal incapacity, he cannot enter into contractual relationship. In such a case, trustrees are appointed according to the Trust Act who manage the property of the beneficiaries, i.e. actual owners. In case of a company, the directors are partially trustees. This concept of trusteeship in company management is used in a broader sense.

*Oligarchy in Company Management* — Oligarchy is government by the few; a form of government in which the power is confined to a few persons or families (Oxford Dictionary). With reference to company management, it is not very difficult to understand that a company cannot be managed by all the owners (shareholders); so the management is entrusted to a few known as directors. This is in line with the administration of a democratic country where the elected few administer the country. Management by a handful of persons known as directors and elected at the general meeting of a company closely resembles the administration of a democratic country. This oligarchic management of a company, whose owners are scattered and are not generally formed into an effective association, leaves much scope for the directors to indulge in malpractices to the detriment of the interest of the shareholders. To prevent this and to safeguard the interest of shareholders against other oligarchic management, various provisions have been enacted in the Companies Act.

*Erosion of Directors* — That the Board of Directors manages a company is a commonsense knowledge. But in most of the large companies, it has, in effect, been deposed and its place taken by executive management. This is really what is meant by 'gradual erosion' of directors. The powers of the directors are gradually withering away and the vacuum is being filled up by trained executives.

*Democratisation of Company Management* — Oligarchy is the usual feature of a company management, though it is undesirable. It may be considered as a necessary evil. But attempts are being made to overcome the evils of the oligarchic management. Adoption of professional management is a positive step towards democratisation of the corporate management. It is believed that with the spread of education, the elements of democracy in company management will be ingrained. Shareholders will be more conscious and aware of their interests as well as think about the interest of the country as a whole.

*Right Shares* — A right is an option to buy a security at a specified price during a designated period. The Companies Act, 1956, provides that the Indian companies are required to offer additional issue of shares to existing holders of equity shares. This offer is known as *"privileged subscription"*. This is legally known as "pre-emptive" right. A very significant role is played by Rights in financing a company. Rights may be issued at par or premium. A number of procedures are involved in connection with rights offering. The timing aspect is of major significance in case of rights issues as the rights typically are exercised during a relatively short period. The Controller of Capital Issues takes decisions on application for rights issue in concurrence with the company. When a listed company makes a rights issue, it has to comply with the stock exchange formalities. From the point of view of financial management, rights issues have significance. "By offering rights to existing shareholders a company increases the likelihood of a favourable reception for the shares as they can thereby protect their pro-rata share in the earnings and surplus of the company. It should be noted that successive rights issue can significantly affect the upswitch of EPS growth trend" (Kuchhal).

*Rights Debentures* — In September, 1978, the Government of India announced guidelines for the issue of rights debentures by public limited companies for working capital requirements and for reducing the dependence on fixed deposits from the public and loans from shareholders.

*Term Lending* — Before nationalisation of banks, term financing was a domain almost exclusively reserved for term lending institutions. Banks restricted themselves to short-term financing. But, after nationalisation, the banks gradually entered into the field of term lending. The share of term loans in the advance portfolio of commercial banks has increased substantially. Although term loan portfolio of banks is on the increase, it is unfortunate that sufficient expertise is yet to develop in banks to handle term loan proposals. Proposal for term loan may come either for installation of new project or for expansion of existing capacity. The confidence of the lending institution in repayment prospects of a loan is largely conditioned by its opinion of the borrowing unit's management. Where the technical competence, administrative ability, integrity and resourcefulness of the management are well established, the loan application gets the most favourable consideration.